ISBN: 9781290903998

Published by:
HardPress Publishing
8345 NW 66TH ST #2561
MIAMI FL 33166-2626

Email: info@hardpress.net
Web: http://www.hardpress.net

PREFACE.

THE first idea of this History was conceived many years ago, at a time when ancient Hellas was known to the English public chiefly through the pages of Mitford; and my purpose in writing it was to rectify the erroneous statements as to matter of fact which that history contained, as well as to present the general phænomena of the Grecian world under what I thought a juster and more comprehensive point of view. My leisure however was not at that time equal to the execution of any large literary undertaking; nor is it until within the last three or four years that I have been able to devote to the work that continuous and exclusive labour, without which, though much may be done to illustrate detached points, no entire or complicated subject can ever be set forth in a manner worthy to meet the public eye.

Meanwhile the state of the English literary world, in reference to ancient Hellas, has been materially changed in more ways than one. If my early friend Dr. Thirlwall's History of Greece had appeared a few years sooner, I should probably never have conceived the design of the present work at all; I should certainly not have been prompted to the task by any deficiencies such as those which I felt and regretted in Mitford. The comparison of the two authors affords indeed a striking proof of the progress of sound and enlarged views respecting the ancient world during the present generation. Having studied of course the same evidences as Dr. Thirlwall, I am better enabled than others to bear testimony to the learning, the sagacity, and the candour which pervade his excellent work; and it is the more incumbent on me to give expression to this sentiment, since the particular points on which I shall have occasion to advert to it will unavoidably be points of dissent oftener than of coincidence.

The liberal spirit of criticism, in which Dr. Thirlwall stands so much distinguished from Mitford, is his own : there are other features of superiority which belong to him conjointly with his age. For during the generation since Mitford's work, philological studies have been prosecuted in Germany with remarkable success : the stock of facts and documents, comparatively scanty, handed down from the ancient world, has been combined, and illustrated in a thousand different ways : and if our witnesses cannot be multiplied, we at least have numerous interpreters to catch, repeat, amplify and explain their broken and half-inaudible depositions. Some of the best writers in this department— Boeckh, Niebuhr, O. Müller—have been translated into our language ; so that the English public has been enabled to form some idea of the new lights thrown upon many subjects of antiquity by the inestimable aid of German erudition. The poets, historians, orators and philosophers of Greece have thus been all rendered both more intelligible and more instructive than they were to a student in the last century ; and the general picture of the Grecian world may now be conceived with a degree of fidelity, which, considering our imperfect materials, it is curious to contemplate.

It is that general picture which an historian of Greece is required first to embody in his own mind, and next to lay out before his readers ;—a picture not merely such as to delight the imagination by brilliancy of colouring and depth of sentiment, but also suggestive and improving to the reason. Not omitting the points of resemblance as well as of contrast with the better-known forms of modern society, he will especially study to exhibit the spontaneous movement of Grecian intellect, sometimes aided but never borrowed from without, and lighting up a small portion of a world otherwise clouded and stationary. He will develop the action of that social system, which, while ensuring to the mass of freemen a degree of protection elsewhere unknown, acted as a stimulus to the creative impulses of genius, and left the superior minds sufficiently unshackled to soar above religious and political routine, to overshoot their own age, and to become the teachers of posterity.

To set forth the history of a people by whom the first spark was set to the dormant intellectual capacities of our nature— Hellenic phænomena as illustrative of the Hellenic mind and character—is the task which I propose to myself in the present work ; not without a painful consciousness how much the deed falls short of the will, and a yet more painful conviction, that full success is rendered impossible by an obstacle which no human ability can now remedy—the insufficiency of original evidence. For in spite of the valuable expositions of so many able commentators, our stock of information respecting the ancient world still remains lamentably inadequate to the demands of an enlightened curiosity. We possess only what has drifted ashore from the wreck of a stranded vessel ; and though this includes some of the most precious articles amongst its once-abundant cargo, yet if any man will cast his eyes over the citations in Diogenes Laertius, Athenæus or Plutarch, or the list of names in Vossius de Historicis Græcis, he will see with grief and surprise how much larger is the proportion which, through the enslavement of the Greeks themselves, the decline of the Roman Empire, the change of religion, and the irruption of barbarian conquerors, has been irrecoverably submerged. We are thus reduced to judge of the whole Hellenic world, eminently multiform as it was, from a few compositions ; excellent indeed in themselves, but bearing too exclusively the stamp of Athens. Of Thucydidês and Aristotle indeed, both as inquirers into matter of fact and as free from narrow local feeling, it is impossible to speak too highly ; but unfortunately that work of the latter which would have given us the most copious information regarding Grecian political life—his collection and comparison of 150 distinct town-constitutions—has not been preserved ; while the brevity of Thucydidês often gives us but a single word where a sentence would not have been too much, and sentences which we should be glad to see expanded into paragraphs.

Such insufficiency of original and trustworthy materials, as compared with those resources which are thought hardly sufficient for the historian of any modern kingdom, is neither to be concealed nor extenuated, however much we may lament it. I advert to the point here on more grounds than one. For it not only limits the amount of information which an historian of Greece can give to his readers—compelling him to leave much of his picture an absolute blank,—but it also greatly spoils the execution of the remainder. The question of credibility is perpetually obtruding itself, and requiring a decision, which, whether favourable or unfavourable, always introduces more or less of controversy; and gives to those outlines, which the interest of the picture requires to be straight and vigorous, a faint and faltering character. Expressions of qualified and hesitating affirmation are repeated until the reader is sickened; while the writer himself, to whom this restraint is more painful still, is frequently tempted to break loose from the unseen spell by which a conscientious criticism binds him down—to screw up the possible and probable into certainty, to suppress counterbalancing considerations, and to substitute a pleasing romance in place of half-known and perplexing realities. Desiring in the present work to set forth all which can be ascertained, together with such conjectures and inferences as can be reasonably deduced from it, but nothing more—I notice at the outset that faulty state of the original evidence which renders discussions of credibility, and hesitation in the language of the judge, unavoidable. Such discussions, though the reader may be assured that they will become less frequent as we advance into times better known, are tiresome enough even with the comparatively late period which I adopt as the historical beginning; much more intolerable would they have proved had I thought it my duty to start from the primitive terminus of Deukaliôn or Inachus, or from the unburied Pelasgi and Leleges, and to subject the heroic ages to a similar scrutiny. I really know nothing so disheartening or unrequited as the elaborate balancing of what is called evidence—the comparison of infinitesimal probabilities and conjectures all uncertified—in regard to these shadowy times and persons.

The law respecting sufficiency of evidence ought to be the same for ancient times as for modern; and the reader will find in this

history an application to the former, of criteria analogous to those
which have been long recognised in the latter. Approaching,
though with a certain measure of indulgence, to this standard, I
begin the real history of Greece with the first recorded Olympiad,
or 776 B.C. To such as are accustomed to the habits once universal, and still not uncommon, in investigating the ancient world, I
may appear to be striking off one thousand years from the scroll
of history : but to those whose canon of evidence is derived from
Mr. Hallam, M. Sismondi, or any other eminent historian of
modern events, I am well-assured that I shall appear lax and
credulous rather than exigent or sceptical. For the truth is,
that historical records, properly so called, do not begin until long
after this date ; nor will any man, who candidly considers the
extreme paucity of attested facts for two centuries after 776 B.C.,
be astonished to learn that the state of Greece in 900, 1000, 1100,
1200, 1300, 1400 B.C., &c.—or any earlier century which it may
please chronologists to include in their computed genealogies—
cannot be described to him upon anything like decent evidence.
I shall hope, when I come to the lives of Sokrates and Plato, to
illustrate one of the most valuable of their principles—that
conscious and confessed ignorance is a better state of mind, than
the fancy, without the reality, of knowledge. Meanwhile I
begin by making that confession in reference to the real world
of Greece anterior to the Olympiads ; meaning the disclaimer to
apply to anything like a general history,—not to exclude rigorously
every individual event.

The times which I thus set apart from the region of history
are discernible only through a different atmosphere—that of epic
poetry and legend. To confound together these disparate matters
is, in my judgment, essentially unphilosophical. I describe the
earlier times by themselves, as conceived by the faith and feeling
of the first Greeks, and known only through their legends—
without presuming to measure how much or how little of historical matter these legends may contain. If the reader blame
me for not assisting him to determine this—if he ask me why I
do not undraw the curtain and disclose the picture—I reply in
the words of the painter Zeuxis, when the same question was

addressed to him on exhibiting his master-piece of imitative art
—" The curtain *is* the picture ". What we now read as poetry
and legend was once accredited history, and the only genuine
history which the first Greeks could conceive or relish of their
past time : the curtain conceals nothing behind, and cannot by
any ingenuity be withdrawn. I undertake only to show it as it
stands—not to efface, still less to re-paint it.

Three-fourths of the two volumes now presented to the public
are destined to elucidate this age of historical faith, as distinguished from the later age of historical reason : to exhibit its
basis in the human mind—an omnipresent religious and personal
interpretation of nature ; to illustrate it by comparison with the
like mental habit in early modern Europe ; to show its immense
abundance and variety of narrative matter, with little care for
consistency between one story and another : lastly, to set forth
the causes which overgrew and partially supplanted the old
epical sentiment, and introduced, in the room of literal faith, a
variety of compromises and interpretations.

The legendary age of the Greeks receives its principal charm
and dignity from the Homeric poems : to these, therefore, and
to the other poems included in the ancient epic, an entire chapter
is devoted, the length of which must be justified by the names of
the Iliad and Odyssey. I have thought it my duty to take some
notice of the Wolfian controversy as it now stands in Germany,
and have even hazarded some speculations respecting the structure
of the Iliad. The society and manners of the heroic age, considered as known in a general way from Homer's descriptions
and allusions, are also described and criticised.

I next pass to the historical age, beginning at 776 B.C.; pre-
fixing some remarks upon the geographical features of Greece.
I try to make out, amidst obscure and scanty indications, what
the state of Greece was at this period ; and I indulge some cautious
conjectures, founded upon the earliest verifiable facts, respecting
the steps immediately antecdent by which that condition was
brought about. In the present volumes I have only been able
to include the history of Sparta and the Peloponnesian Dorians,
down to the age of Peisistratus and Crœsus. I had hoped to have

comprised in them the entire history of Greece down to this last-mentioned period, but I find the space insufficient.

The history of Greece falls most naturally into six compartments, of which the first may be looked at as a period of preparation for the five following, which exhaust the free life of collective Hellas.

I. Period from 776 B.C. to 560 B.C., the accession of Peisistratus at Athens and of Crœsus in Lydia.

II. From the accession of Peisistratus and Crœsus to the repulse of Xerxes from Greece.

III. From the repulse of Xerxes to the close of the Peloponnesian war and overthrow of Athens.

IV. From the close of the Peloponnesian war to the battle of Leuktra.

V. From the battle of Leuktra to that of Chæroneia.

VI. From the battle of Chæroneia to the end of the generation of Alexander.

The five periods from Peisistratus down to the death of Alexander and of his generation, present the acts of an historical drama capable of being recounted in perspicuous succession, and connected by a sensible thread of unity. I shall interweave in their proper places the important but outlying adventures of the Sicilian and Italian Greeks—introducing such occasional notices of Grecian political constitutions, philosophy, poetry, and oratory, as are requisite to exhibit the many-sided activity of this people during their short but brilliant career.

After the generation of Alexander, the political action of Greece becomes cramped and degraded—no longer interesting to the reader, or operative on the destinies of the future world. We may indeed name one or two incidents, especially the revolutions of Agis and Kleomenês at Sparta, which are both instructive and affecting ; but as a whole, the period between 300 B.C. and the absorption of Greece by the Romans is of no interest in itself, and is only so far of value as it helps us to understand the preceding centuries. The dignity and value of the Greeks from that time forward belong to them only as individual philosophers, preceptors, astronomers and mathematicians, literary men and

critics, medical practitioners, &c. In all these respective capacities, especially in the great schools of philosophical speculation,
they still constitute the light of the Roman world ; though as
communities they have lost their own orbit, and have become
satellites of more powerful neighbours.

I propose to bring down the history of the Grecian communities
to the year 300 B.C., or the close of the generation which takes
its name from Alexander the Great, and I hope to accomplish
this in eight volumes altogether. For the next two or three
volumes I have already large preparations made, and I shall
publish my third (perhaps my fourth) in the course of the ensuing
winter.

There are great disadvantages in the publication of one portion
of a history apart from the remainder ; for neither the earlier
nor the later phænomena can be fully comprehended without the
light which each mutually casts upon the other. But the practice
has become habitual, and is indeed more than justified by the
well-known inadmissibility of "long hopes" into the short span
of human life. Yet I cannot but fear that my first two volumes
will suffer in the estimation of many readers by coming out alone
—and that men who value the Greeks for their philosophy, their
politics, and their oratory, may treat the early legends as not
worth attention. And it must be confessed that the sentimental
attributes of the Greek mind—its religious and poetical vein—
here appear in disproportionate relief, as compared with its more
vigorous and masculine capacities—with those powers of acting,
organising, judging, and speculating, which will be revealed in the
forthcoming volumes. I venture however to forewarn the reader
that there will occur numerous circumstances in the after political
life of the Greeks which he will not comprehend unless he be
initiated into the course of their legendary associations. He will
not understand the frantic terror of the Athenian public during
the Peloponnesian war, on the occasion of the mutilation of the
statues called Hermæ, unless he enters into the way in which
they connected their stability and security with the domiciliation
of the gods in the soil ; nor will he adequately appreciate the
habit of the Spartan king on military expeditions,—when he

offered his daily public sacrifices on behalf of his army and his country,—"always to perform this morning service immediately before sunrise, in order that he might be beforehand in obtaining the favour of the gods,"[1] if he be not familiar with the Homeric conception of Zeus going to rest at night and awaking to rise at early dawn from the side of the "white-armed Hêrê". The occasion will indeed often occur for remarking how these legends illustrate and vivify the political phænomena of the succeeding times, and I have only now to urge the necessity of considering them as the beginning of a series,—not as an entire work.

[1] Xenophon, Repub. Lacedæmon., cap. xiii. 3. Ἀεὶ δὲ, ὅταν θύηται, ἄρχεται μὲν τούτου τοῦ ἔργου ἔτι κνεφαῖος, προλαμβάνειν βουλόμενος τὴν τοῦ θεοῦ εὔνοιαν.

London, March 5, 1846.

PREFACE

In preparing a Second Edition of the two First Volumes of my History, I have profited by the remarks and corrections of various critics, contained in Reviews both English and Foreign. I have suppressed, or rectified, some positions which had been pointed out as erroneous, or as advanced upon inadequate evidence. I have strengthened my argument in some cases where it appeared to have been imperfectly understood—adding some new notes, partly for the purpose of enlarged illustration, partly to defend certain opinions which had been called in question. The greater number of these alterations have been made in Chapters XVI. and XXI. of Part I.—and in Chapter VI. of Part II.

I trust that these three Chapters, more full of speculation, and therefore more open to criticism than any of the others, will thus appear in a more complete and satisfactory form. But I must at the same time add that they remain for the most part unchanged in substance, and that I have seen no sufficient reason to modify my main conclusions even respecting the structure of the Iliad, controverted though they have been by some of my most esteemed critics.

In regard to the character and peculiarity of Grecian legend, as broadly distinguished throughout these volumes from Grecian history, I desire to notice two valuable publications with which I have only become acquainted since the date of my first edition. One of these is a short Essay on Primæval History, by John Kenrick, M.A. (London, 1846, published just at the same time as these volumes), which illustrates with much acute reflection the

general features of legend, not only in Greece but throughout the
ancient world—see especially pages 65, 84, 92, *et seq.*   The other
work is Rambles and Recollections of an Indian Official, by
Colonel Sleeman—first made known to me through an excellent
notice of my History in the Edinburgh Review for October, 1846.
The description given by Colonel Sleeman, of the state of mind
now actually prevalent among the native population of Hindostan,
presents a vivid comparison, helping the modern reader to understand and appreciate the legendary æra of Greece.   I have
embodied in the notes of this Second Edition two or three passages
from Colonel Sleeman's instructive work : but the whole of it
richly deserves perusal.

Having now finished six volumes of this History, without
attaining a lower point than the peace of Nikias in the tenth
year of the Peloponnesian war, I find myself compelled to
retract the expectation held out in the preface to my First
Edition, that the entire work might be completed in eight
volumes.   Experience proves to me how impossible it is to
measure beforehand the space which historical subjects will
require.   All I can now promise is, that the remainder of the
work shall be executed with as much regard to brevity as is
consistent with the paramount duty of rendering it fit for public
acceptance.

G. G.

London, April 3, 1849.

NAMES OF GODS, GODDESSES, AND HEROES.

FOLLOWING the example of Dr. Thirlwall and other excellent scholars, I call the Greek deities by their real Greek names, and not by the Latin equivalents used among the Romans. For the assistance of those readers to whom the Greek names may be less familiar I here annex a table of the one and the other.

Greek.	*Latin.*
Zeus,	Jupiter.
Poseidôn,	Neptune.
Arês,	Mars.
Dionysus,	Bacchus.
Hermês,	Mercury.
Hêlios,	Sol.
Hêphæstus,	Vulcan.
Hadês,	Pluto.
Hêrê,	Juno.
Athênê,	Minerva.
Artemis,	Diana.
Aphroditê,	Venus.
Eôs,	Aurora.
Hestia,	Vesta.
Lêtô,	Latona.
Dêmêtêr,	Ceres.
Hêraklês,	Hercules.
Asklêpius.	Æsculapius.

A few words are here necessary respecting the orthography of Greek names adopted in the above table and generally throughout this history. I have approximated as nearly as I dared to the Greek letters in preference to the Latin; and on this point I venture upon an innovation which I should have little doubt of vindicating before the reason of any candid English student. For the ordinary practice of substituting, in a Greek name, the English C in place of the Greek K is indeed so obviously incorrect, that it admits of no rational justification. Our own K precisely and in every point coincides with the Greek K: we have thus the means of reproducing the Greek name to the eye as well as to the ear, yet we gratuitously take the wrong letter in preference to the right. And the precedent of the Latins is here against us rather than in our favour, for their C really coincided in sound with the Greek K, whereas our C entirely departs from it, and becomes an S, before e, i, $æ$, $œ$, and y. Though our C has so far deviated in sound from the Latin C, yet there is some warrant for our continuing to use it in writing Latin names—because we thus reproduce the name to the eye, though not to the ear. But this is not the case when we employ our C to designate the Greek K, for we depart here not less from the visible than from the audible original; while we mar the unrivalled euphony of the Greek language by that multiplied sibilation which constitutes the least inviting feature in our own. Among German philologists the K is now universally employed in writing Greek names, and I have adopted it pretty largely in this work, making exceptions for such names as the English reader has been so accustomed to hear with the C, that they may be considered as being almost Anglicised. I have farther marked the long e and the long o (η, ω) by a circumflex (Hêrê) when they occur in the last syllable or in the penultimate of a name.

CONTENTS OF VOLUME I.

PART I.—LEGENDARY GREECE.

CHAPTER I.

LEGENDS RESPECTING THE GODS.

b

CHAPTER I.—*continued.*

CHAPTER II.

LEGENDS RELATING TO HEROES AND MEN.

CHAPTER III.

LEGEND OF THE IAPETIDS.

CHAPTER IV.

HEROIC LEGENDS—GENEALOGY OF ARGOS.

CHAPTER V.

DEUKALIÔN, HELLÊN, AND SONS OF HELLÊN.

CHAPTER VI.

THE ÆOLIDS, OR SONS AND DAUGHTERS OF ÆOLUS.

CHAPTER VI.—*continued.*

CHAPTER IX.

ARCADIAN GENEALOGY.

CHAPTER X.

ÆAKUS AND HIS DESCENDANTS—ÆGINA, SALAMIS, AND PHTHIA.

CHAPTER XI.

ATTIC LEGENDS AND GENEALOGIES.

CHAPTER XII.

Krétan Legends—Minôs and his Family.

CHAPTER XIII.

Argonautic Expedition.

CHAPTER XIV.

Legends of Thêbes.

CHAPTER XIV.—*continued.*

SIEGES OF THÊBES.

CHAPTER XV.

LEGEND OF TROY.

CHAPTER XV.—*continued*

CHAPTER XVI.

GRECIAN MYTHES, AS UNDERSTOOD, FELT, AND INTERPRETED BY THE GREEKS THEMSELVES.

CHAPTER XVI.—continued.

ð*

CHAPTER XVI.—*continued.*

CHAPTER XVII

THE GRECIAN MYTHICAL VEIN COMPARED WITH THAT OF MODERN
EUROPE.

CHAPTER XVIII.

CLOSING EVENTS OF LEGENDARY GREECE.—PERIOD OF INTERMEDIATE
DARKNESS, BEFORE THE DAWN OF HISTORICAL GREECE.

CHAPTER XVIII.—*continued.*

CHAPTER XIX.

APPLICATION OF CHRONOLOGY TO GRECIAN LEGEND.

CHAPTER XIX.—*continued*

HISTORY OF GREECE.

PART I.
LEGENDARY GREECE.

CHAPTER I.
LEGENDS RESPECTING THE GODS.

THE mythical world of the Greeks opens with the gods, anterior as well as superior to man : it gradually descends, first to heroes, and next to the human race. Along with the gods are found various monstrous natures, ultra-human and extra-human, who cannot with propriety be called gods, but who partake with gods and men in the attributes of volition, conscious agency, and susceptibility of pleasure and pain,—such as the Harpies, the Gorgons, the Grææ, the Sirens, Scylla and Charybdis, Echidna, Sphinx, Chimæra, Chrysaôr, Pegasus, the Cyclôpes, the Centaurs, &c. The first acts of what may be termed the great mythical cycle describe the proceedings of these gigantic agents—the crash and collision of certain terrific and overboiling forces, which are ultimately reduced to obedience, or chained up, or extinguished, under the more orderly government of Zeus, who supplants his less capable predecessors, and acquires presidence and supremacy over gods and men—subject however to certain social restraints from the chief gods and goddesses around him, as well as to the custom of occasionally convoking and consulting the divine agora.

Opening of the mythical world.

1—1

I recount these events briefly, but literally, treating them
simply as mythes springing from the same creative
imagination, addressing themselves to analogous tastes
and feelings, and depending upon the same authority,
as the legends of Thebes and Troy.   It is the inspired voice of
the Muse which reveals and authenticates both, and from which
Homer and Hesiod alike derive their knowledge—the one, of the
heroic, the other, of the divine, foretime.   I maintain, moreover,
fully, the character of these great divine agents as Persons,
which is the light in which they presented themselves to the
Homeric or Hesiodic audience.   Uranos, Nyx, Hypnos and Oneiros
(Heaven, Night, Sleep and Dream), are Persons, just as much as
Zeus and Apollo.   To resolve them into mere allegories is unsafe and unprofitable : we then depart
from the point of view of the original hearers, without acquiring any consistent or philosophical point of view of our
own.[1]   For although some of the attributes and actions ascribed
to these persons are often explicable by allegory, the whole series
and system of them never are so : the theorist who adopts this
course of explanation finds that, after one or two simple and
obvious steps, the path is no longer open, and he is forced to
clear a way for himself by gratuitous refinements and conjectures.
The allegorical persons and attributes are always found mingled
with other persons and attributes not allegorical ; but the two
classes cannot be severed without breaking up the whole march
of the mythical events, nor can any explanation which drives us
to such a necessity be considered as admissible.   To suppose
indeed that these legends could be all traced by means of
allegory into a coherent body of physical doctrine, would be
inconsistent with all reasonable presumptions respecting the age
or society in which they arose.   Where the allegorical mark is
clearly set upon any particular character, or attribute, or event,
to that extent we may recognise it ; but we can rarely venture to
divine further, still less to alter the legends themselves on the
faith of any such surmises.   The theogony of the Greeks contains
some cosmogonic ideas ; but it cannot be considered as a system

How the mythes are to be told.

Allegory rarely admissible.

---

[1] It is sufficient, here, to state this position briefly : more will be said re-specting the allegorizing interpretation in a future chapter.

of cosmogony, or translated into a string of elementary, plane-
tary, or physical changes.

In the order of legendary chronology, Zeus comes after Kronos
and Uranos ; but in the order of Grecian conception,
Zeus is the prominent person, and Kronos and   Zeus—fore-
                                               most in
Uranos are inferior and introductory precursors, set   Grecian
                                               conception.
up in order to be overthrown and to serve as mementos of the prowess of their conqueror. To Homer and
Hesiod, as well as to the Greeks universally, Zeus is the great
and predominant god, "the father of gods and men," whose
power none of the other gods can hope to resist, or even deliberately think of questioning. All the other gods have their
specific potency and peculiar sphere of action and duty, with
which Zeus does not usually interfere : but it is he who maintains the lineaments of a providential superintendence, as well
over the phænomena of Olympus as over those of earth. Zeus
and his brothers, Poseidôn and Hadês, have made a division of
power : he has reserved the æther and the atmosphere to himself—Poseidôn has obtained the sea—and Hadês the under-world
or infernal regions ; while earth, and the events which pass upon
earth, are common to all of them, together with free access to
Olympus.[1]

Zeus, then, with his brethren and colleagues, constitute the
present gods, whom Homer and Hesiod recognise as   The gods—
in full dignity and efficiency. The inmates of this   how con-
                                                      ceived :
divine world are conceived upon the model, but not   human type
upon the scale, of the human. They are actuated   enlarged.
by the full play and variety of those appetites, sympathies,
passions and affections, which divide the soul of man ; invested
with a far larger and indeterminate measure of power, and an
exemption as well from death as (with some rare exceptions)
from suffering and infirmity. The rich and diverse types thus
conceived, full of energetic movement and contrast, each in his
own province, and soaring confessedly above the limits of ex-

[1] See Iliad, viii. 405, 463 ; xv. 20, 130,
185. Hesiod. Theog. 885.
   This unquestioned supremacy is the
general representation of Zeus : at the
same time the conspiracy of Hêrê,
Poseidôn, and Athênê against him,
suppressed by the unexpected appari-
tion of Briareus as his ally, is among
the exceptions. (Iliad, i. 400.) Zeus
is at one time vanquished by Titan,
but rescued by Hermês. (Apollodôr.
i. 6, 3.)

perience, were of all themes the most suitable for adventure and narrative, and operated with irresistible force upon the Grecian fancy. All nature was then conceived as moving and working through a number of personal agents, amongst whom the gods of Olympus were the most conspicuous ; the reverential belief in Zeus and Apollo being only one branch of this omnipresent personifying faith. The attributes of all these agents had a tendency to expand themselves into illustrative legends—especially those of the gods, who were constantly invoked in the public worship. Out of the same mental source sprang both the divine and heroic mythes—the former being often the more extravagant and abnormous in their incidents, in proportion as the general type of the gods was more vast and awful than that of the heroes.

As the gods have houses and wives like men, so the present Past history dynasty of gods must have a past to repose upon;[1] of the gods and the curious and imaginative Greek, whenever he fitted on to does not find a recorded past ready to his hand, is present conception. uneasy until he has created one. Thus the Hesiodic theogony explains, with a certain degree of system and coherence, first the antecedent circumstances under which Zeus acquired the divine empire, next the number of his colleagues and descendants.

First in order of time (we are told by Hesiod) came Chaos ; next Gæa, the broad, firm, and flat Earth, with deep and dark Tartarus at her base. Erôs (Love), the subduer of gods as well as men, came immediately afterwards. [2]

From Chaos sprung Erebos and Nyx ; from these latter Æthêr and Hêmera. Gæa also gave birth to Uranos, equal in breadth to herself, in order to serve both as an overarching vault to her, and as a residence for the immortal gods ; she further produced the mountains, habitations of the divine nymphs, and Pontus, the barren and billowy sea.

Then Gæa intermarried with Uranos, and from this union Gæa and came a numerous offspring—twelve Titans and Titan- Uranos. ides, three Cyclôpes, and three Hekatoncheires or

---

[1] Arist. Polit. i. 1. ὥσπερ δὲ καὶ τὰ εἴδη ἑαυτοῖς ἀφομοιοῦσιν ἄνθρωποι, οὕτως καὶ τοὺς βίους, τῶν θεῶν.

[2] Hesiod, Theog. 116. Apollodôrus begins with Uranos and Gæa (i. 1); he does not recognise Erôs, Nyx, or Erebos.

beings with a hundred hands each. The Titans were Oceanus, Kœos, Krios, Hyperiôn, Iapetos, and Kronos : the Titanides, Theia, Rhea, Themis, Mnêmosynê, Phœbê, and Têthys. The Cyclôpes were Brontês, Steropês, and Argês,—formidable persons, equally distinguished for strength and for manual craft, so that they made the thunder which afterwards formed the irresistible artillery of Zeus.[1] The Hekatoncheires were Kottos. Briareus, and Gygês, of prodigious bodily force.

Uranos contemplated this powerful brood with fear and horror ; as fast as any of them were born, he concealed them in cavities of the earth, and would not permit them to come out. Gæa could find no room for them, and groaned under the pressure : she produced iron, made a sickle, and implored her sons to avenge both her and themselves against the oppressive treatment of their father. But none of them, except Kronos, had courage to undertake the deed : he, the youngest and the most daring, was armed with the sickle and placed in suitable ambush by the contrivance of Gæa. Presently night arrived, and Uranos descended to the embraces of Gæa : Kronos then emerged from his concealment, cut off the genitals of his father, and cast the bleeding member behind him far away into the sea.[2] Much of the blood was spilt upon the earth, and Gæa in consequence gave birth to the irresistible Erinnys, the vast and muscular Gigantes, and the Melian nymphs. Out of the genitals themselves, as they swam and foamed upon the sea, emerged the goddess Aphroditê, deriving her name from the foam out of which she had sprung. She first landed at Kythêra, and then went to Cyprus : the island felt her benign influence, and the green herb started up under her soft and delicate tread. Erôs immediately joined her, and partook with her the function of suggesting and directing the amorous impulses both of gods and men.[3]

Uranos being thus dethroned and disabled, Kronos and the

Uranos disabled.

---

[1] Hesiod, Theog. 140, 156. Apollod. ut sup.

[2] Hesiod, Theog. 160, 182. Apollod. i. 1, 4.

[3] Hesiod, Theog. 192. This legend respecting the birth of Aphroditê seems to have been derived partly from her name (ἀφρὸς, *foam*), partly from the surname Urania, Ἀφροδίτη Οὐρανία, under which she was so very extensively worshipped, especially both in Cyprus and Kythêra, seemingly originated in both islands by the Phœnicians. Herodot. i. 105. Compare the instructive section in Boeckh's Metrologie, c. iv. § 4.

Titans acquired their liberty and became predominant: the Cyclôpes and the Hekatoncheires had been cast by Uranos into Tartarus, and were still allowed to remain there.

Each of the Titans had a numerous offspring: Oceanus, especi-
Kronos and ally, marrying his sister Têthys, begat three thousand
the Titans. daughters, the Oceanic nymphs, and as many sons:
the rivers and springs passed for his offspring.   Hyperiôn and his sister Theia had for their children Hêlios, Selênê, and Eôs; Kœos with Phœbê begat Lêtô and Asteria : the children of Krios were Astræos, Pallas, and Persês,—from Astræos and Eôs sprang the winds Zephyrus, Boreas, and Notus.   Iapetos marrying the Oceanic nymph Klymenê, counted as his progeny the celebrated Promêtheus, Epimêtheus, Menœtius, and Atlas.   But the offspring of Kronos were the most powerful and transcendent of all.   He married his sister Rhea, and had by her three daughters—Hestia, Dêmêtêr, and Hêrê—and three sons, Hadês, Poseidôn, and Zeus, the latter at once the youngest and the greatest.

But Kronos foreboded to himself destruction from one of his own children, and accordingly, as soon as any of them were born, he immediately swallowed them and retained them in his own
Kronos belly.   In this manner had the five first been treated,
over-
reached. and Rhea was on the point of being delivered of Zeus.
Birth and Grieved and indignant at the loss of her children, she
safety of
Zeus and his applied for counsel to her father and mother, Uranos
brethren. and Gæa, who aided her to conceal the birth of Zeus.
They conveyed her by night to Lyktus in Crête, hid the new-born child in a woody cavern on Mount Ida, and gave to Kronos, in place of it, a stone wrapped in swaddling clothes, which he greedily swallowed, believing it to be his child.   Thus was the safety of Zeus ensured.[1]   As he grew up his vast powers fully developed themselves : at the suggestion of Gæa, he induced Kronos by stratagem to vomit up, first the stone which had been given to him,—
next the five children whom he had previously devoured.   Hestia, Dêmêtêr, Hêrê, Poseidôn and Hadês were thus allowed to grow up along with Zeus ; and the stone to which the latter owed his preservation was placed near the temple of Delphi, where it ever

---

[1] Hesiod, Theog. 452, 487. Apollod. i. 1, 6.

afterwards stood, as a conspicuous and venerable memorial to the religious Greek.[1]

We have not yet exhausted the catalogue of beings generated during this early period, anterior to the birth of Zeus. Other deities. Nyx, alone and without any partner, gave birth to a numerous progeny : Thanatos, Hypnos and Oneiros ; Mômus and Oïzys (Grief); Klôthô, Lachesis, and Atropos, the three Fates ; the retributive and equalizing Nemesis ; Apatê and Philotês (Deceit and amorous Propensity), Geras (Old Age) and Eris (Contention). From Eris proceeded an abundant offspring, all mischievous and maleficent : Ponos (Suffering), Lêthê, Limos (Famine), Phonos and Machê (Slaughter and Battle), Dysnomia and Atê (Lawlessness and reckless Impulse), and Horkos, the ever-watchful sanctioner of oaths, as well as the inexorable punisher of voluntary perjury.[2]

Gæa, too, intermarrying with Pontus, gave birth to Nereus, the just and righteous old man of the sea ; to Thaumas, Phorkys and Kêtô. From Nereus, and Doris daughter of Oceanus, proceeded the fifty Nereids or Sea-nymphs. Thaumas also married Elektra daughter of Oceanus, and had by her Iris and the two Harpies, Aellô and Okypetê,—winged and swift as the winds. From Phorkys and Kêtô sprung the Dragon of the Hesperides, and the monstrous Grææ, and Gorgons : the blood of Medusa, one of the Gorgons, when killed by Perseus, produced Chrysaôr, and the horse Pegasus ; Chrysaôr and Kallirhoê gave birth to Geryôn as well as to Echidna,—a creature half-nymph and half-serpent, unlike both to gods and to men. Other monsters arose from the union of Echidna with Typhaôn,—Orthros, the two-headed dog of Geryôn ; Cerberus, the dog of Hadês with fifty heads, and the Lernæan Hydra. From the latter proceeded the Chimæra, the Sphinx of Thêbes, and the Nemean lion.[3]

A powerful and important progeny, also, was that of Styx, daughter of Oceanus, by Pallas ; she had Zêlos and Nikê (Imperiousness and Victory), and Kratos and Bia (Strength and Force). The hearty and early co-operation of Styx and her four

[1] Hesiod, Theog. 498—

Τὸν μὲν Ζεὺς στήριξε κατὰ χθονὸς εὐρυοδείης
Πυθοῖ ἐν ἠγαθέῃ, γυάλοις ὑπὸ Παρνήσοιο,

Σῆμ' ἔμεν ἐξοπίσω, θαῦμα θνητοῖσι βροτοῖσι.

[2] Hesiod, Theog. 212—232.
[3] Hesiod, Theog. 240—320. Apollodôr. i. 2, 6, 7.

sons with Zeus was one of the main causes which enabled him to achieve his victory over the Titans.

Zeus had grown up not less distinguished for mental capacity than for bodily force. He and his brothers now deter-

Ambitious schemes of Zeus. mined to wrest the power from the hands of Kronos and the Titans, and a long and desperate struggle commenced, in which all the gods and all the goddesses took part. Zeus convoked them to Olympus, and promised to all who would aid him against Kronos, that their functions and privileges should remain undisturbed. The first who responded to the call, came with her four sons, and embraced his cause, was Styx. Zeus took them all four as his constant attendants, and conferred upon Styx the majestic distinction of being the Horkos, or oath-sanctioner of the Gods,—what Horkos was to men, Styx was to the Gods.[1]

Still further to strengthen himself, Zeus released the other Uranids who had been imprisoned in Tartarus by

Victory of Zeus and his brethren over Kronos and the Titans. their father,—the Cyclôpes and the Centimanes,—and prevailed upon them to take part with him against the Titans. The former supplied him with thunder and lightning, and the latter brought into the fight their boundless muscular strength.[2] Ten full years did the combat continue ; Zeus and the Kronids occupying Olympus, and the Titans being established on the more southerly mountain-chain of Othrys. All nature was convulsed, and the distant Oceanus, though he took no part in the struggle, felt the boiling, the noise, and the shock, not less than Gæa and Pontus. The thunder of Zeus, combined with the crags and mountains torn up and hurled by the Centimanes, at length prevailed, and the Titans were defeated and thrust down into Tartarus. ·Iapetos, Kronos, and the remaining Titans (Oceanus excepted) were imprisoned perpetually and irrevocably, in that subterranean dungeon, a wall of brass being built around them by Poseidôn, and the three Centimanes being planted as guards.

Of the two sons of Iapetos, Menœtius was made to share this prison, while Atlas was condemned to stand for ever at the

---

[1] Hesiod, Theog. 385—403.   [2] Hesiod, Theog. 140, 624, 657. Apollodôr. i. 2, 4.

extreme west, and to bear upon his shoulders the solid vault of heaven.[1]

Thus were the Titans subdued, and the Kronids with Zeus at their head placed in possession of power.   They were not, however, yet quite secure ; for Gæa, intermarry- Typhôeus. ing with Tartarus, gave birth to a new and still more formidable monster called Typhôeus, of such tremendous properties and promise, that, had he been allowed to grow into full development, nothing could have prevented him from vanquishing all rivals and becoming supreme.   But Zeus foresaw the danger, smote him at once with a thunderbolt from Olympus, and burnt him up : he was cast along with the rest into Tartarus, and no further enemy remained to question the sovereignty of the Kronids.[2]

With Zeus begins a new dynasty and a different order of beings. Zeus, Poseidôn and Hadês agree upon the distribution Dynasty of before noticed of functions and localities : Zeus retain- Zeus. ing the Æthêr and the atmosphere, together with the general presiding function : Poseidôn obtaining the sea, and administering subterranean forces generally : and Hadês ruling the under-world, or region in which the half-animated shadows of departed men reside.

It has been already stated, that in Zeus, his brothers and his sisters, and his and their divine progeny, we find the *present* Gods ; that is, those, for the most part, whom the Homeric and Hesiodic Greeks recognised and worshipped.   The His wives of Zeus were numerous as well as his offspring. offspring. First he married Mêtis, the wisest and most sagacious of the goddesses ; but Gæa and Uranos forewarned him that if he permitted himself to have children by her, they would be stronger than himself and dethrone him.   Accordingly, when Mêtis was on the point of being delivered of Athênê, he swallowed her up,

---

[1] The battle with the Titans, Hesiod, Theog. 627—735.   Hesiod mentions nothing about the Gigantes and the Gigantomachia : Apollodôrus, on the other hand, gives this latter in some detail, but despatches the Titans in a few words (i. 2, 4 ; i. 6, 1).   The Gigantes seem to be only a second edition of the Titans,—a sort of duplication to which the legendary poets were often inclined.

[2] Hesiod, Theog. 820—869.   Apollod. i. 6, 3.   He makes Typhôn very nearly victorious over Zeus.   Typhôeus, according to Hesiod, is father of the irregular, violent, and mischievous winds: Notus, Boreas, Argestês, and Zephyrus are of divine origin (870).

and her wisdom and sagacity thus became permanently identified with his own being.[1] His head was subsequently cut open, in order to make way for the exit and birth of the goddess Athênê.[2] By Themis, Zeus begat the Hôræ; by Eurynomê, the three Charites or Graces: by Mnêmosynê, the Muses; by Lêtô (Latona), Apollo and Artemis; and by Dêmêtêr, Persephonê. Last of all he took for his wife Hêrê, who maintained permanently the dignity of queen of the Gods; by her he had Hêbê, Arês, and Eileithyia. Hermês also was born to him by Maia, the daughter of Atlas; Hêphæstos was born to Hêrê, according to some accounts by Zeus; according to others, by her own unaided generative force.[3] He was born lame, and Hêrê was ashamed of him; she wished to secrete him away, but he made his escape into the sea, and found shelter under the maternal care of the Nereids Thetis and Eurynomê.[4]

Our enumeration of the divine race, under the presidency of Zeus, will thus give us,[5]—

General distribution of the divine race.   1. The twelve great gods and goddesses of Olympus, —Zeus, Poseidôn, Apollo, Arês, Hêphæstos, Hermês, Hêrê, Athênê, Artemis, Aphroditê, Hestia, Dêmêtêr.

2. An indefinite number of other deities, not included among the Olympic, seemingly because the number *twelve* was complete without them, but some of them not inferior in power and dignity to many of the twelve:—Hadês, Hêlios, Hekatê, Dionysos, Lêtô, Diônê, Persephonê, Selênê, Themis, Eôs, Harmonia, the Charites, the Muses, the Eileithyiæ, the Mœræ, the Oceanids and the Nereids, Proteus, Eidothea, the Nymphs, Leukothea, Phorkys, Æolus, Nemesis, &c.

3. Deities who perform special services to the greater gods:— Iris, Hêbê, the Hôræ, &c.

4. Deities whose personality is more faintly and unsteadily conceived:—Atê, the Litæ, Eris, Thanatos, Hypnos, Kratos, Bia, Ossa, &c.[6] The same name is here employed sometimes to designate the person, sometimes the attribute or event not personi-

1 Hesiod, Theog. 885—900.
2 Apollod. i. 3, 6.
3 Hesiod, Theog. 900—944.
4 Homer, Iliad, xviii. 397

5 See Burckhardt, Homer. und Hesiod. Mythologie, sect. 102. (Leipz. 1844.)
6 Λιμὸς—*Hunger*—is a person, in Hesiod, Opp. Di. 299.

fied,—an unconscious transition of ideas, which, when consciously performed, is called Allegory.

5. Monsters, offspring of the Gods :—the Harpies, the Gorgons, the Græœ, Pegasus, Chrysaôr, Echidna, Chimæra, the Dragon of the Hesperides, Cerberus, Orthros, Geryôn, the Lernæan Hydra, the Nemean lion, Scylla and Charybdis, the Centaurs, the Sphinx, Xanthos and Balios the immortal horses, &c.

From the gods we slide down insensibly, first to heroes, and then to men; but before we proceed to this new mixture, it is necessary to say a few words on the theogony gene-rally. I have given it briefly as it stands in the Hesiodic Theogonia, because that poem—in spite of great incoherence and confusion, arising seemingly from diversity of authorship as well as diversity of age—presents an ancient and genuine attempt to cast the divine foretime into a systematic sequence. Homer and Hesiod were the grand authorities in the pagan world respecting theogony. But in the Iliad and Odyssey nothing is found except passing allusions and implications; and even in the Hymns (which were commonly believed in antiquity to be the productions of the same author as the Iliad and the Odyssey) there are only isolated, unconnected narratives. Accordingly men habitually took their information respecting their theogonic antiquities from the Hesiodic poem, where it was ready laid out before them; and the legends con-secrated in that work acquired both an extent of circulation and a firm hold on the national faith, such as independent legends could seldom or never rival. Moreover the scrupulous and sceptical pagans, as well as the open assailants of paganism in later times, derived their subjects of attack from the same source; so that it has been absolutely necessary to recount in their naked simplicity the Hesiodic stories, in order to know what it was that Plato deprecated and Xenophanês denounced. The strange proceedings ascribed to Uranos, Kronos, and Zeus have been more frequently alluded to in the way of ridicule or condemna-tion than any other portion of the mythical world.

But though the Hesiodic theogony passed as orthodox among the later pagans,[1] because it stood before them as the only

Hesiodic theogony— its autho-rity.

---

[1] See Göttling, Præfat. ad Hesiod. p. 23.

system anciently set forth and easily accessible, it was evidently
not the only system received at the date of the poem
itself.   Homer knows nothing of Uranos, in the sense
of an arch-God anterior to Kronos.   Uranos and Gæa,
like Oceanus, Têthys and Nyx, are with him great
and venerable Gods, but neither the one nor the other present
the character of predecessors of Kronos and Zeus.[1]   The Cyclôpes,
whom Hesiod ranks as sons of Uranos and fabricators of thunder,
are in Homer neither one nor the other: they are not noticed in the
Iliad at all, and in the Odyssey they are gross gigantic shepherds
and cannibals, having nothing in common with the Hesiodic
Cyclôpes except the one round central eye.[2]   Of the three Centimanes enumerated by Hesiod, Briareus only is mentioned in
Homer, and, to all appearance, not as the son of Uranos, but as
the son of Poseidôn; not as aiding Zeus in his combat against the
Titans, but as rescuing him at a critical moment from a conspiracy formed against him by Hêrê, Poseidôn, and Athênê.[3]
Not only is the Hesiodic Uranos (with the Uranids) omitted in
Homer, but the relations between Zeus and Kronos are also
presented in a very different light.   No mention is made of
Kronos swallowing his young children : on the contrary, Zeus is
the eldest of the three brothers, instead of the youngest, and the
children of Kronos live with him and Rhea: there the stolen
intercourse between Zeus and Hêrê first takes place without the
knowledge of their parents.[4]   When Zeus puts Kronos down
into Tartarus, Rhea consigns her daughter Hêrê to the care of
Oceanus: no notice do we find of any terrific battle with the
Titans as accompanying that event.   Kronos, Iapetos, and the
remaining Titans are down in Tartarus, in the lowest depths
under the earth, far removed from the genial rays of Hêlios;
but they are still powerful and venerable, and Hypnos makes
Hêrê swear an oath in their name, as the most inviolable that he
can think of.[5]

Points of difference between Homer and Hesiod.

---

[1] Iliad, xiv. 249 ; xix. 259. Odyss. v. 184. Oceanus and Têthys seem to be presented in the Iliad as the primitive Father and Mother of the Gods :—

'Ωκεανόν τε θεῶν γένεσιν, καὶ μητέρα
Τηθύν.   (xiv. 201.)

[2] Odyss. ix. 87.

[3] Iliad, i. 401.

[4] Iliad, xiv. 203—295 ; xv. 204.

[5] Iliad, vii. 482; xiv. 274—279.   In the Hesiodic Opp. et Di., Kronos is represented as ruling in the Islands of the Blest in the neighbourhood of Oceanus (v. 168).

In Homer, then, we find nothing beyond the simple fact that Zeus thrust his father Kronos, together with the remaining Titans, into Tartarus ; an event to which he Homeric
Zeus. affords us a tolerable parallel in certain occurrences even under the presidency of Zeus himself. For the other gods make more than one rebellious attempt against Zeus, and are only put down, partly by his unparalleled strength, partly by the presence of his ally the Centimane Briareus. Kronos, like Laërtes or Pêleus, has become old, and has been supplanted by a force vastly superior to his own. The Homeric epic treats Zeus as present, and like all the interesting heroic characters, a father must be assigned to him : that father has once been the chief of the Titans, but has been superseded and put down into Tartarus along with the latter, so soon as Zeus and the superior breed of the Olympic gods acquired their full development.

That antithesis between Zeus and Kronos—between the Olympic gods and the Titans—which Homer has Amplified
theogony of
Zeus. thus briefly brought to view, Hesiod has amplified into a theogony, with many things new and some things contradictory to his predecessor ; while Eumêlus or Arktinus in the poem called Titanomachia (now lost) also adopted it as their special subject.[1] As Stasinus, Arktinus, Leschês and others enlarged the Legend of Troy by composing poems relating to a supposed time anterior to the commencement, or subsequent to the termination of the Iliad,—as other poets recounted adventures of Odysseus subsequent to his landing in Ithaka,—so Hesiod enlarged and systematised, at the same time that he corrupted, the skeleton theogony which we find briefly indicated in Homer. There is violence and rudeness in the Homeric gods, but the great genius of Grecian Epic is no way accountable for the stories of Uranos and Kronos,—the standing reproach against pagan legendary narrative.

[1] See the few fragments of the Titanomachia, in Düntzer, Epic. Græc. Fragm. p. 2 ; and Heyne, ad Apollodôr. i. 2. Perhaps there was more than one poem on the subject, though it seems that Athenæus had only read one (viii. p. 277).

In the Titanomachia, the generations anterior to Zeus were still further lengthened by making Uranos son of Æthêr (Fr. 4 Düntzer). Ægæon was also represented as son of Pontos and Gæa, and as having fought in the ranks of the Titans : in the Iliad he (the same who is called Briareus) is the fast ally of Zeus.

A *Titanographia* was ascribed to Musæus (Schol. Apollon. Rhod. iii. 1178 ; compare Lactant. de Fals. Rel. i. 21).

How far these stories are the invention of Hesiod himself is impossible to determine.[1]   They bring us down to a cast of fancy more coarse and indelicate than the Homeric, and more nearly resembling some of the Holy Chapters (ἱεροὶ λόγοι) of the more recent mysteries, such (for example) as the tale of Dionysos

[1] That the Hesiodic Theogony is referable to an age considerably later than the Homeric poems, appears now to be the generally admitted opinion ; and the reasons for believing so are, in my opinion, satisfactory.   Whether the Theogony is composed by the same author as the Works and Days is a disputed point.   The Bœotian literati in the days of Pausanias decidedly denied the identity, and ascribed to their Hesiod only the Works and Days: Pausanias himself concurs with them (ix. 31. 4 ; ix. 35. 1), and Völcker (Mythologie des Japetisch. Geschlechts, p. 14) maintains the same opinion, as well as Göttling (Præf. ad Hesiod. xxi.) : K. O. Müller (History of Grecian Literature, ch. 8. § 4) thinks that there is not sufficient evidence to form a decisive opinion.

Under the name of Hesiod (in that vague language which is usual in antiquity respecting authorship, but which modern critics have not much mended by speaking of the Hesiodic school, sect, or family) passed many different poems, belonging to three classes quite distinct from each other, but all disparate from the Homeric epic :—1. The poems of legend cast into historical and genealogical series, such as the Eoiai, the Catalogue of Women, &c. 2. The poems of a didactic or ethical tendency, such as the Works and Days, the Precepts of Cheirôn, the Art of Augural Prophecy, &c. 3. Separate and short mythical compositions, such as the Shield of Hêraklês, the marriage of Keyx (which, however, was of disputed authenticity, Athenæ. ii. p. 49), the Epithalamium of Pêleus and Thetis, &c.   (See Marktscheffel, Præfat. ad Fragment. Hesiod. p. 89.)

The Theogony belongs chiefly to the first of these classes, but it has also a dash of the second in the legend of Promêtheus, &c. ; moreover in the portion which respects Hekatê, it has both a mystic character and a distinct bearing upon present life and customs, which we may also trace in the allusions to Krête and Delphi. There seems reason to place it in the same age with the Works and Days, perhaps in the

half century preceding 700 B.C., and little, if at all, anterior to Archilochus. The poem is evidently conceived upon one scheme, yet the parts are so disorderly and incoherent, that it is difficult to say how much is interpolation. Hermann has well dissected the exordium: see the preface to Gaisford's Hesiod (Poetæ Minor. p. 63).

K. O. Müller tells us (ut sup. p. 90): " The Titans, according to the notions of Hesiod, represent a system of things in which elementary beings, natural powers, and notions of order and regularity are united to form a whole.   The Cyclôpes denote the transient disturbances of this order of nature by storms, and the Hekatoncheires, or hundred-handed Giants, signify the fearful power of the greater revolutions of nature." The poem affords little presumption that any such ideas were present to the mind of its author, as, I think, will be seen if we read 140—155, 630—745.

The Titans, the Cyclôpes, and the Hekatoncheires, can no more be construed into physical phænomena than Chrysaôr, Pegasus, Echidna, the Grææ, or the Gorgons. Zeus, like Hêraklês, or Jasôn, or Perseus, if his adventures are to be described, must have enemies, worthy of himself and his vast type, and whom it is some credit for him to overthrow.   Those who contend with him or assist him must be conceived on a scale fit to be drawn on the same imposing canvas : the dwarfish proportions of man will not satisfy the sentiment of the poet or his audience respecting the grandeur and glory of the gods.   To obtain creations of adequate sublimity for such an object, the poet may occasionally borrow analogies from the striking accidents of physical nature, and when such an allusion manifests itself clearly, the critic does well to point it out.   But it seems to me a mistake to treat these approximations to physical phænomena as forming the *main scheme* of the poet,— to look for them everywhere, and to presume them where there is little or no indication.

Zagreus.   There is evidence in the Theogony itself that the
author was acquainted with local legends current both at Krête
and at Delphi ; for he mentions both the mountain-cave in Krête
wherein the new-born Zeus was hidden, and the stone near the
Delphian temple—the identical stone which Kronos had swallowed—"placed by Zeus himself as a sign and wonder to mortal
men". Both these two monuments, which the poet ex-   Hesiodic
pressly refers to, and had probably seen, imply a whole   mythes
train of accessory and explanatory local legends—cur-   Krête and
rent probably among the priests of Krête and Delphi,   Delphi.
between which places, in ancient times, there was an intimate
religious connexion.   And we may trace further in the poem—
that which would be the natural feeling of Krêtan worshippers
of Zeus—an effort to make out that Zeus was justified in his
aggression on Kronos, by the conduct of Kronos himself both
towards his father and towards his children : the treatment of
Kronos by Zeus appears in Hesiod as the retribution foretold
and threatened by the mutilated Uranos against the son who had
outraged him.   In fact, the relations of Uranos and Gæa are in
almost all their particulars a mere copy and duplication of those
between Kronos and Rhea, differing only in the mode whereby
the final catastrophe is brought about.   Now castration was a
practice thoroughly abhorrent both to the feelings and to the
customs of Greece ;[1] but it was seen with melancholy frequency
in the domestic life as well as in the religious worship of Phrygia
and other parts of Asia ; and it even became the special qualifica-
tion of a priest of the Great Mother Cybelê,[2] as well as of the
Ephesian Artemis.   The employment of the sickle ascribed to
Kronos seems to be the product of an imagination familiar with
the Asiatic worship and legends, which were connected with and

---

[1] The strongest evidences of this feeling are exhibited in Herodotus, iii. 48 ;
viii. 105.   See an example of this mutilation inflicted upon a youth named
Adamas by the Thracian king Kotys,
in Aristot. Polit. v. 8, 12, and the tale
about the Corinthian Periander, Herod.
iii. 48.
   It is an instance of the habit, so
frequent among the Attic tragedians,
of ascribing Asiatic or Phrygian manners to the Trojans, when Sophocles
in his lost play Troilus (ap. Jul. Poll.
x. 165), introduced one of the characters
of his drama as having been castrated
by order of Hecuba, Σκαλμῇ γὰρ ὄρχεις
βασιλὶς ἐκτέμνουσ' ἐμούς,—probably the
Παιδαγωγός or guardian and companion
of the youthful Troilus.   See Welcker,
Griechisch. Tragöd. vol. i. p. 125.

   [2] Herodot. vii. 105, εὐνοῦχοι. Lucian, De Deâ Syriâ, c. 50. Strabo, xiv.
pp. 640—641.

partially resembled the Krêtan.[1] And this deduction becomes the more probable when we connect it with the first genesis of iron, which Hesiod mentions to have been produced for the express purpose of fabricating the fatal sickle ; for metallurgy finds a place in the early legends both of the Trojan and of the Krêtan Ida, and the three Idæan Dactyls, the legendary inventors of it, are assigned sometimes to one and sometimes to the other.[2]

As Hesiod had extended the Homeric series of gods by pre-fixing the dynasty of Uranos to that of Kronos, so the Orphic theogony lengthened it still further.[3] First came Chronos, or
Orphic theogony. Time, as a person, after him Æthêr and Chaos, out of whom Chronos produced the vast mundane egg. Hence emerged in process of time the first-born god Phanês, o. Mêtis, or Hêrikapæos, a person of double sex, who first generated the Kosmos, or mundane system, and who carried within him the seed of the gods. He gave birth to Nyx, by whom he begat Uranos and Gæa ; as well as to Hêlios and Selênê.[4]

From Uranos and Gæa sprang the three Mœræ, or Fates, the three Centimanes, and the three Cyclôpes : these latter were cast by Uranos into Tartarus, under the foreboding that they would rob him of his dominion. In revenge for this maltreatment of her sons, Gæa produced of herself the fourteen Titans, seven male and seven female : the former were Kœos, Krios, Phorkys,

[1] Diodôr. v. 64. Strabo, x. p. 469. Hoeck, in his learned work Krêta (vol. i. books 1 and 2), has collected all the information attainable respecting the early influences of Phrygia and Asia Minor upon Krête : nothing seems ascertainable except the general fact ; all the particular evidences are lamentably vague.

The worship of the Diktæan Zeus seems to have originally belonged to the Eteokrêtes, who were not Hellens, and were more akin to the Asiatic population than to the Hellenic. Strabo, x. p. 478. Hoeck, Krêta, vol. i. p. 139.

[2] Hesiod, Theogon. 161—

Αἶψα δὲ ποιήσασα γένος πολιοῦ ἀδά-
μαντος,
Τεῦξε μέγα δρέπανον, &c.

See the extract from the old poem *Phorônis* ap. Schol. Apoll. Rhod. 1129 ; and Strabo, x. p. 472.

[3] See the scanty fragments of the Orphic Theogony in Hermann's edition of the Orphica, pp. 448, 504, which it is difficult to understand and piece together, even with the aid of Lobeck's elaborate examination (Aglaophamus, p. 470, &c.). The passages are chiefly preserved by Proclus and the later Platonists, who seem to entangle them almost inextricably with their own philosophical ideas.

The first few lines of the Orphic Argonautica contain a brief summary of the chief points of the Theogony.

[4] See Lobeck, Aglaoph. p. 472—476, 490—500, Μῆτιν σπέρμα φέροντα θεῶν κλυτὸν Ἡρικεπαῖον ; again, Θῆλυς καὶ γενέτωρ κρατερὸς θεὸς Ἡρικέπαιος. Compare Lactant. iv. 8, 4 ; Suidas, v. Φάνης : Athenagoras, xx. 296 ; Diodôr. i. 27.

This egg figures, as might be expected, in the cosmogony set forth by the Birds, Aristophan. Av. 695. Nyx gives birth to an egg, out of which steps the golden Erôs ; from Erôs and Chaos spring the race of birds.

Kronos, Oceanus, Hyperiôn, and Iapetos ; the latter were Themis, Têthys, Mnêmosynê, Theia, Diônê, Phœbê, and Rhea.[1] They received the name of Titans because they avenged upon Uranos the expulsion of their elder brothers. Six of the Titans, headed by Kronos, the most powerful of them all, conspiring against Uranos, castrated and dethroned him : Oceanus alone stood aloof and took no part in the aggression. Kronos assumed the government, and fixed his seat on Olympus ; while Oceanus remained apart, master of his own divine stream.[2] The reign of Kronos was a period of tranquillity and happiness, as well as of extraordinary longevity and vigour.

Kronos and Rhea gave birth to Zeus and his brothers and sisters. The concealment and escape of the infant Zeus, and the swallowing of the stone by Kronos, are given in the Orphic Theogony substantially in the same manner as by Hesiod, only in a style less simple and more mysticised. Zeus is concealed in the cave of Nyx, the seat of Phanês Zeus and Phanês. himself, along with Eidê and Adrasteia, who nurse and preserve him, while the armed dance and sonorous instruments of the Kurêtês prevent his infant cries from reaching the ears of Kronos. When grown up, he lays a snare for his father, intoxicates him with honey, and, having surprised him in the depth of sleep, enchains and castrates him.[3] Thus exalted to the supreme mastery, he swallowed and absorbed into himself Mêtis, or Phanês, with all the pre-existing elements of things, and then generated all things anew out of his own being and comformably to his own divine ideas.[4] So scanty are the remains of this system,

---

[1] Lobeck, Ag. p. 504. Athenagor. xv. p. 64.

[2] Lobeck, Ag. p. 507. Plato, Timæus, p. 41. In the Διονύσου τρόφοι of Æschylus, the old attendants of the god Dionysos were said to have been cut up and boiled in a caldron, and rendered again young, by Medeia. Pherecydês and Simonidês said that Jasôn himself had been so dealt with. Schol. Aristoph. Equit. 1321.

[3] Lobeck, p. 514. Porphyry, de Antro Nympharum, c. 16, φησὶ γὰρ παρ' Ὀρφεῖ ἡ Νὺξ, τῷ Διΐ ὑποτιθεμένη τὸν διὰ τοῦ μέλιτος δόλον,

Εὗτ' ἂν δή μιν ἴδηαι ὑπὸ δρυσὶν ὑψικόμοισι

Ἐργοισιν μεθύοντα μελισσάων ἐριβόμβων,
Αὐτίκά μιν δῆσον.

Ὁ καὶ πάσχει ὁ Κρόνος καὶ δεθεὶς ἐκτέμνεται, ὡς Οὐρανός.
Compare Timæus ap. Schol. Apoll. Rhod. iv. 983.

[4] The Cataposis of Phanês by Zeus is one of the most memorable points of the Orphic Theogony. Lobeck, p. 519 ; also Fragm. vi. p. 456 of Hermann's Orphica.

From this absorption and subsequent reproduction of all things by Zeus, flowed the magnificent string of Orphic predicates about him,—

that we find it difficult to trace individually the gods and god-desses sprung from Zeus beyond Apollo, Dionysos, and Persephonê—the latter being confounded with Artemis and Hekatê.

But there is one new personage begotten by Zeus, who stands pre-eminently marked in the Orphic Theogony, and whose adventures constitute one of its peculiar features.

Zagreus. Zagreus, "the horned child," is the son of Zeus by his own daughter Persephonê : he is the favourite of his father, a child of magnificent promise, and predestined, if he grow up, to succeed to supreme dominion, as well as to the handling of the thunderbolt.   He is seated, whilst an infant, on the throne beside Zeus, guarded by Apollo and the Kurêtês.   But the jealous Hêrê intercepts his career, and incites the Titans against him, who, having first smeared their faces with plaster, approach him on the throne, tempt his childish fancy with playthings, and kill him with a sword while he is contemplating his face in a mirror.   They then cut up his body and boil it in a caldron, leaving only the heart, which is picked up by Athênê and carried to Zeus, who in his wrath strikes down the Titans with thunder into Tartarus ; whilst Apollo is directed to collect the remains of Zagreus and bury them at the foot of Mount Parnassus.   The heart is given to Semelê, and Zagreus is born again from her under the form of Dionysos.[1]

Ζεὺς ἀρχὴ, Ζεὺς μέσσα, Διὸς δ' ἐκ
πάντα τέτυκται,

an allusion to which is traceable even in Plato, de Legg. iv. p. 715. Plutarch, de Defectu Oracul. T. ix. p. 379, c. 48. Diodôrus (i. 11) is the most ancient writer remaining to us who mentions the name of Phanês, in a line cited as proceeding from Orpheus ; wherein, however, Phanês is identified with Dionysos.   Compare Macrobius, Satur-nal. i. 18.

[1] About the tale of Zagreus, see Lo-beck, p. 552, seq.   Nonnus in his Diony-siaca has given many details about it :—

Ζαγρέα γειναμένη κέροεν βρέφος, &c. (vi. 264).

Clemens Alexandrin.   Admonit. ad Gent. p. 11, 12, Sylb.   The story was treated both by Kallimachus and by Euphoriôn, Etymolog. Magn. v. Ζαγ-ρεύς, Schol. Lycophr. 208.   In the old epic poem Alkmæônis or Epigoni,

Zagreus is a surname of Hadês.   See Fragm. 4, p. 7, ed. Düntzer.   Respect-ing the Orphic Theogony generally, Brandis (Handbuch der Geschichte der Griechisch-Römischen Philosophie, c. xvii., xviii.), K. O. Müller (Prolegg. Mythol. pp. 379—396), and Zoega (Ab-handlungen, v. pp. 211—263) may be consulted with much advantage.   Bran-dis regards this Theogony as consider-ably older than the first Ionic philosophy, which is a higher antiquity than ap-pears probable : some of the ideas which it contains, such, for example, as that of the Orphic egg, indicate a departure from the string of purely personal generations which both Homer and Hesiod exclusively recount, and a resort to something like physical ana-logies.   On the whole, we cannot rea-sonably claim for it more than half a century above the age of Onomakritus. The Theogony of Pherekydês of Syros seems to have borne some analogy to

Such is the tissue of violent fancies comprehended under the title of the Orphic Theogony, and read as such, it appears, by Plato, Isokratês, and Aristotle.   It will be seen that it is based upon the Hesiodic Theogony, but, according to the general expansive tendency of Grecian legend, much new matter is added : Zeus has in Homer one predecessor, in Hesiod two, and in Orpheus four.

The Hesiodic Theogony, though later in date than the Iliad and Odyssey, was coeval with the earliest period of what may be called Grecian history, and certainly of an age earlier than 700 B.C.   It appears to have been widely circulated in Greece, and being at once ancient and short, the general public consulted it as their principal source of information respecting divine antiquity.   The Orphic Theogony belongs to a later date, and contains the Hesiodic ideas and persons, enlarged and mystically disguised.   Its vein of invention was less popular, adapted more to the contemplation of a sect specially prepared than to the taste of a casual audience. And it appears accordingly to have obtained currency chiefly among purely speculative men.[1]   Among the majority of these latter, however, it acquired greater veneration, and above all was

Comparison of Hesiod and Orpheus.

---

the Orphic. See Diogen. Laërt. i. 119, Sturz. Fragm. Pherekyd. § 5—6, Brandis, Handbuch, *ut sup.* c. xxii.   Pherekydês partially deviated from the mythical track or personal successions set forth by Hesiod.   ἐπεὶ οἵ γε μεμιγμένοι αὐτῶν καὶ τῷ μὴ μυθικῶς ἅπαντα λέγειν, οἷον Φερεκύδης καὶ ἕτεροί τινες, &c. (Aristot. Metaphys. N. p. 301, ed. Brandis.) Porphyrius, de Antro Nymphar. c. 31, καὶ τοῦ Συρίου Φερεκύδου μυχοὺς καὶ βόθρους καὶ ἄντρα καὶ θύρας καὶ πύλας λέγοντος, καὶ διὰ τούτων αἰνιττομένου τὰς τῶν ψυχῶν γενέσεις καὶ ἀπογενέσεις, &c. Eudêmus the Peripatetic, pupil of Aristotle, had drawn up an account of the Orphic Theogony as well as of the doctrines of Pherekydês, Akusilaus, and others, which was still in the hands of the Platonists of the fourth century, though it is now lost. The extracts which we find seem all to countenance the belief that the Hesiodic Theogony formed the basis upon which they worked. See about Akusilaus, Plato, Sympos. p. 178; Clem. Alex. Strom. p. 629.

[1] The Orphic Theogony is never cited

in the ample Scholia on Homer, though Hesiod is often alluded to. (See Lobeck, Aglaoph. p. 540.) Nor can it have been present to the minds of Xenophanês and Herakleitus, as representing any widely diffused Grecian belief : the former, who so severely condemned Homer and Hesiod, would have found Orpheus much more deserving of his censure : and the latter could hardly have omitted Orpheus from his memorable denunciation :—Πολυμαθίη νόον οὐ διδάσκει· Ἡσίοδον γὰρ ἂν ἐδίδαξε καὶ Πυθαγόρην, αὗτις δὲ Ξενοφάνεά τε καὶ Ἑκαταῖον. Diog. Laër. ix. 1. Isokratês treats Orpheus as the most censurable of all the poets. See Busiris, p. 229 ; ii. p. 300, Bekk.   The Theogony of Orpheus, as conceived by Apollonius Rhodius (i. 504) in the third century, B.C., and by Nigidius in the first century, B.C. (Servius ad Virgil. Eclog. iv. 10), seems to have been on a more contracted scale than that which is given in the text. But neither of them notice the tale of Zagreus, which we know to be as old as Onomakritus.

supposed to be of greater antiquity than the Hesiodic. The belief in its superior antiquity (disallowed by Herodotus, and seemingly also by Aristotle),[1] as well as the respect for its contents, increased during the Alexandrine age and through the declining centuries of paganism, reaching its maximum among the New-Platonists of the third and fourth century after Christ. Both the Christian assailants, as well as the defenders of paganism, treated it as the most ancient and venerable summary of the Grecian faith. Orpheus is celebrated by Pindar as the harper and companion of the Argonautic maritime heroes : Orpheus and Musæus, as well as Pamphos and Olên, the great supposed authors of theogonic, mystical, oracular, and prophetic verses and hymns, were generally considered by literary Greeks as older than either Hesiod or Homer.[2] And such was also the common opinion oı modern scholars until a period comparatively recent. But it has now been shown, on sufficient ground, that the compositions which passed under these names emanate for the most part from poets of the Alexandrine age, and subsequent to the Christian æra ; and that even the earliest among them, which served as the stock on which the latter additions were engrafted, belong to a period far more recent than Hesiod : probably to the century preceding Onomakritus (B.C. 610-510). It seems, however, certain that both Orpheus and Musæus were names of established reputation at the time when Onomakritus flourished ; and it is distinctly stated by Pausanias that the latter was himself the author of the most remarkable and characteristic mythe of the

---

[1] This opinion of Herodotus is implied in the remarkable passage about Homer and Hesiod, ii. 53, though he never once names Orpheus—only alluding once to "Orphic ceremonies," ii. 81. He speaks more than once of the prophecies of Musæus. Aristotle denied the past existence and reality of Orpheus. See Cicero de Nat. Deor. i. 38.

[2] Pindar, Pyth. iv. 177. Plato seems to consider Orpheus as more ancient than Homer. Compare Theætét. p. 179 ; Cratylus, p. 402 ; De Republ. ii. p. 364. The order in which Aristophanês (and Hippias of Elis, ap. Clem. Alex. Str. vi. p. 624) mentions them indicates the same view, Ranæ, 1030. It is un-

necessary to cite the later chronologers, among whom the belief in the antiquity of Orpheus was universal ; he was commonly described as son of the Muse Calliopê. Androtiôn seems to have denied that he was a Thracian, regarding the Thracians as incurably stupid and illiterate. Androtiôn, Fragm. 36, ed. Didot. Ephorus treated him as having been a pupil of the Idæan Dactyls of Phrygia (see Diodôr. v. 64), and as having learnt from them his τελετάς and μυστήρια, which he was the first to introduce into Greece. The earliest mention which we find of Orpheus, is that of the poet Ibycus (about B.C. 530), ὀνομάκλυτον Ὀρφῆν. Ibyci Fragm. 9, p. 341, ed. Schneidewin.

Orphic Theogony—the discerption of Zagreus by the Titans, and his resurrection as Dionysos.[1]

The names of Orpheus and Musæus (as well as that of Pythagoras,[2] looking at one side of his character) represent facts of importance in the history of the Grecian mind —the gradual influx of Thracian, Phrygian, and Egyptian religious ceremonies and feelings, and the increasing diffusion of special mysteries,[3] schemes for religious purification, and orgies (I venture to anglicise the Greek word, which contains in its original meaning no implication of the ideas of excess to which it was afterwards diverted), in honour of some particular god,—distinct both from the public solemnities and from the gentile solemnities of primitive Greece,—celebrated apart from the citizens generally, and approachable only through a certain course of preparation and initiation—sometimes even forbidden to be talked of in the presence of the uninitiated under the severest threats of divine judgment. Occasionally such voluntary combinations assumed the form of permanent brotherhoods, bound together by periodical solemnities as well as by vows of an ascetic character. Thus the Orphic life (as it was called), or regulation of the Orphic brotherhood, among other injunctions, partly arbitrary and partly abstinent, forbade animal food universally, and, on certain occasions, the use of woollen

Influence of foreign religions upon Greece.

---

[1] Pausan. viii. 37, 3. Τιτᾶνας δὲ πρῶτον ἐς ποίησιν ἐσήγαγεν Ὅμηρος. θεοὺς εἶναι σφᾶς ὑπὸ τῷ καλουμένῳ Ταρτάρῳ· καί ἐστιν ἐν Ἥρας ὅρκῳ τὰ ἔπη· παρὰ δὲ Ὁμήρου Ὀνομάκριτος, παραλαβὼν τῶν Τιτάνων τὸ ὄνομα, Διονύσῳ τε συνέθηκεν ὄργια, καὶ εἶναι τοὺς Τιτᾶνας τῷ Διονύσῳ τῶν παθημάτων ἐποίησεν αὐτουργούς. Both the date, the character, and the function of Onomakritus are distinctly marked by Herodotus, vii. 6.

[2] Herodotus believed in the derivation both of the Orphic and Pythagorean regulations from Egypt—ὁμολογέουσι δὲ ταῦτα τοῖσι Ὀρφικοῖσι καλεομένοισι καὶ Βακχικοῖσι, ἐοῦσι δὲ Αἰγυπτίοισι (ii. 81). He knows the names of those Greeks who have borrowed from Egypt the doctrine of the metempsychosis, but he will not mention them (ii. 123): he can hardly allude to any one but the Pythagoreans, many of whom he probably knew in Italy. See the curious extract from Xenophanês respecting the doctrine of Pythagoras, Diogen.

Laërt. viii. 37 : and the quotation from the Silli of Timôn, Πυθαγόραν δὲ γόητος ἀποκλίναντ᾽ ἐπὶ δόξαν, &c. Compare Porphyr. in Vit. Pyth. c. 41.

[3] Aristophan. Ran. 1030—

Ὀρφεὺς μὲν γὰρ τελετάς θ᾽ ἡμῖν κατέδειξε,
   φόνων τ᾽ ἀπέχεσθαι·
Μουσαῖος τ᾽, ἐξακέσεις τε νόσων καὶ χρησμούς. Ἡσίοδος δὲ,
Γῆς ἐργασίας, καρπῶν ὥρας, ἀρότους· ὁ δὲ θεῖος Ὅμηρος
Ἀπὸ τοῦ τίμην καὶ κλέος ἔσχεν, πλὴν τοῦθ᾽, ὅτι χρήστ᾽ ἐδίδασκεν,
Ἀρετὰς, τάξεις, ὁπλίσεις ἀνδρῶν, &c.

The same general contrast is to be found in Plato, Protagoras, p. 316; the opinion of Pausanias, ix. 30, 4. The poems of Musæus seem to have borne considerable analogy to the Melampodia ascribed to Hesiod (see Clemen. Alex. Str. vi. p. 628); and healing charms are ascribed to Orpheus as well as to Musæus. See Eurip. Alcestis, 986.

clothing.[1]   The great religious and political fraternity of the Pythagoreans, which acted so powerfully on the condition of the Italian cities, was one of the many manifestations of this general tendency, which stands in striking contrast with the simple, open-hearted, and demonstrative worship of the Homeric Greeks.

Festivals at seed-time and harvest—at the vintage and at the opening of the new wine—were doubtless coeval with the earliest habits of the Greeks ; the latter being a period of unusual joviality.

Especially in regard to the worship of Dêmêtêr and Dionysos.

Yet in the Homeric poems, Dionysos and Dêmêtêr, the patrons of the vineyard and the cornfield, are seldom mentioned, and decidedly occupy little place in the imagination of the poet as compared with the other gods : nor are they of any conspicuous importance even in the Hesiodic Theogony.   But during the interval between Hesiod and Onomakritus, the revolution in the religious mind of Greece was such as to place both these deities in the front rank.   According to the Orphic doctrine, Zagreus, son of Persephonê, is destined to be the successor of Zeus ; and although the violence of the Titans intercepts this lot, yet even when he rises again from his discerption under the name of Dionysos, he is the colleague and co-equal of his divine father.

This remarkable change, occurring as it did during the sixth and a part of the seventh century before the Christian æra, may be traced to the influence of communication with Egypt (which only became fully open to the Greeks about B.C. 660), as well as with Thrace, Phrygia, and Lydia.   From hence new religious ideas and feelings were introduced, which chiefly attached themselves to the characters of Dionysos and Dêmêtêr.   The Greeks identified these two deities with the great Egyptian Osiris and Isis, so that what was borrowed from the Egyptian worship of the two latter naturally fell to their equivalents in the Grecian system.[2] Moreover the worship of Dionysos (under what name cannot be certainly made out) was indigenous in Thrace,[3] as that of the

---

[1] Herod. ii. 81 ; Euripid. Hippol. 957, and the curious fragment of the lost Κρῆτες of Euripides.   'Ορφικοὶ βίοι, Plato, Legg. vii. 782.

[2] Herodot. ii. 42, 59, 144.

[3] Herodot. v. 7, vii. 111 ; Euripid. Hecub. 1249, and Rhêsus, 969, and the Prologue to the Bacchæ : Strabo, x. p.

470 ; Schol. ad Aristophan. Aves, 874 ; Eustath. ad Dionys. Perieg. 1069 ; Harpokrat. v. Σάβοι ; Photius, Εὐοῖ Σαβοῖ. The "Lydiaca" of C. Th. Menke (Berlin, 1843), traces the early connexion between the religion of Dionysos and that of Cybelê, c. 6, 7.   Hoeck's Krêta (vol. i. p. 128—134) is instructive respecting the Phrygian religion.

Great Mother was in Phrygia and in Lydia—together with those
violent ecstasies and manifestations of temporary frenzy, and
that clashing of noisy instruments which we find afterwards cha-
racterizing it in Greece.   The great masters of the pipe—as well
as the dithyramb,[1] and indeed the whole musical system appropriated to the worship of Dionysos, which contrasted so pointedly
with the quiet solemnity of the Pæan addressed to Apollo—were
all originally Phrygian.

From all these various countries, novelties, unknown to the
Homeric men, found their way into the Grecian worship : and
there is one amongst them which deserves to be specially
noticed, because it marks the generation of the new class of ideas
in their theology.   Homer mentions many persons guilty of private or involuntary homicide, and compelled either to go into
exile or to make pecuniary satisfaction ; but he never once describes any of them to have either received or required
purification for the crime.[2]   Now in the times subsequent to Homer, purification for homicide comes to
be considered as indispensable : the guilty person is regarded as unfit for the society of man or the worship of the gods
until he has received it, and special ceremonies are prescribed whereby it is to be administered.   Herodotus tells us that the ceremony
of purification was the same among the Lydians and among the
Greeks :[3] we know that it formed no part of the early religion of

Purifi-
cation for
homicide
unknown
to Homer.

---

[1] Aristotle, Polit. viii. 7, 9.   Πᾶσα
γὰρ Βάκχεια καὶ πᾶσα ἡ τοιαύτη κίνησις
μάλιστα τῶν ὀργάνων ἐστὶν ἐν τοῖς αὐ-
λοῖς· τῶν δ' ἁρμονίων ἐν τοῖς Φρυγιστὶ
μέλεσι λαμβάνει ταῦτα τὸ πρέπον, οἶον ὁ
διθύραμβος δοκεῖ ὁμολογουμένως εἶναι
Φρύγιον.   Eurip. Bacch. 58.—

Αἴρεσθε τἀπιχώρι' ἐν πόλει Φρυγῶν
Τύμπανα, 'Ρέας τε μητρὸς ἐμὰ θ' εὑρή-
    ματα, &c.

Plutarch, Ei in Delph. c. 9 ; Philochor.
Fr. 21, ed. Didot, p. 389.   The complete
and intimate manner in which Euripidês identifies the Bacchic rites of
Dionysos with the Phrygian ceremonies
in honour of the Great Mother is very
remarkable.   The fine description given
by Lucretius (ii. 600—640) of the Phrygian worship is much enfeebled by his
unsatisfactory allegorizing.

[2] Schol. ad Iliad. xi. 690—οὐ διὰ τὰ
καθάρσια Ἰφίτου πορθεῖται ἡ Πύλος, ἐπεί

τοι Ὀδυσσεὺς μείζων Νέστορος, καὶ παρ'
Ὁμήρῳ οὐκ οἴδαμεν φονέα καθαιρόμενον,
ἀλλ' ἀντιτίνοντα ἢ φυγαδευόμενον.   The
examples are numerous, and are found
both in the Iliad and the Odyssey.
Iliad. ii. 665 (Tlêpolemos) ; xiii. 697
(Medôn) ; xiii. 574 (Epeigeus) ; xxiii. 99
(Patroklos) ; Odyss. xv. 224 (Theoklymenos) ; xiv. 380 (an Ætolian).   Nor
does the interesting mythe respecting
the functions of Atê and the Litæ harmonise with the subsequent doctrine
about the necessity of purification.
(Iliad, ix. 498.)

[3] Herodot. i. 35—ἔστι δὲ παραπλησίη
ἡ κάθαρσις τοῖσι Λυδοῖσι καὶ τοῖσι Ἑλ-
λησι.   One remarkable proof, amongst
many, of the deep hold which this idea
took of the greatest minds in Greece,
that serious mischief would fall upon
the community if family quarrels or
homicide remained without religious
expiation, is to be found in the objec-

the latter, and we may perhaps reasonably suspect that they borrowed it from the former. The oldest instance known to us of expiation for homicide was contained in the epic poem of the Milesian Arktinus,[1] wherein Achillês is purified by Odysseus for the murder of Thersitês : several others occurred in the later or Hesiodic epic—Hêraklês, Pêleus, Bellerophôn, Alkmæôn, Amphiktyôn, Pœmander, Triopas—from whence they probably passed through the hands of the logographers to Apollodôrus, Diodôrus, and others.[2] The purification of the murderer was originally operated, not by the hands of any priest or specially sanctified man, but by those of a chief or king, who goes through the appropriate ceremonies in the manner recounted by Herodotus in his pathetic narrative respecting Crœsus and Adrastus.

The idea of a special taint of crime, and of the necessity as well as the sufficiency of prescribed religious ceremonies as a means of removing it, appears thus to have got footing in Grecian practice subsequent to the time of Homer. The peculiar rites or orgies, composed or put together by Onomakritus, Methapus,[3] and other men of more than the ordinary piety, were founded upon a similar mode of thinking, and adapted to the same mental exigencies. They were voluntarily religious manifestations, superinduced upon the old public sacrifices of the king or chiefs on behalf of the whole society, and of the father on his own family hearth. They marked out the details of divine service proper to appease or gratify the god to whom they were addressed, and to procure for the believers who went through them his blessings and protection here or hereafter—the exact performance of the divine service in all its specialty was held necessary, and thus the priests or

New and peculiar religious rites.

tions which Aristotle urges against the community of women proposed in the Platonic Republic. It could not be known what individuals stood in the relation of father, son, or brother : if, therefore, wrong or murder of kindred should take place, the appropriate religious atonements (αἱ νομιζόμεναι λύσεις) could not be applied and the crime would go unexpiated. (Aristot. Polit. ii. 1, 14. Compare Thucyd i. 125—128.)

[1] See tho Fragm. of the Æthiopis of Arktinus, in Däntzer's Collection, p. 16.

[2] The references for this are collected in Lobeck's Aglaophamos. Epimetr. ii. ad Orphica, p. 968.

[3] Pausanias (iv. 1, 5)—μετεκόσμησε γὰρ καὶ Μέθαπος τῆς τελετῆς (the Eleusinian Orgies, carried by Kaukon from Eleusis into Messênia), ἔστιν ἅ. Ὁ δὲ Μέθαπος γένος μὲν ἦν Ἀθηναῖος, τελετῆς τε καὶ ὀργίων παντοίων συνθέτης. Again, viii. 37, 8, Onomakritus Διονύσῳ συνέθηκεν ὄργια, &c. This is another expression designating the same idea as the Rhêsus of Euripidês, 944—

Μυστηρίων τε τῶν ἀποῤῥήτων φάνας
Ἔδειξεν Ὀρφεύς.

Hierophants, who alone were familiar with the ritual, acquired a commanding position.[1] Generally speaking, these peculiar orgies obtained their admission and their influence at periods of distress, disease, public calamity, and danger, or religious terror and despondency, which appear to have been but too frequent in their occurrence.

The minds of men were prone to the belief that what they were suffering arose from the displeasure of some of the gods, and as they found that the ordinary sacrifices and worship were insufficient for their protection, so they grasped at new suggestions proposed to them with the view of regaining the divine favour.[2] Such suggestions were more usually copied, either in whole or in part, from the religious rites of some foreign locality, or from some other portion of the Hellenic world ; and in this manner many new sects or voluntary religious fraternities, promising to relieve the troubled conscience and to reconcile the sick or suffering with the offended gods, acquired permanent establishment as well as considerable influence. They were generally under the superintendence of hereditary families of priests, who imparted the rites of confirmation and purification to communicants generally ; no one who went through the prescribed ceremonies being excluded. In many cases such ceremonies fell into the hands of jugglers, who volunteered their services to wealthy men, and degraded their profession as well by obtrusive venality as by extravagant promises.[3] Sometimes the price was lowered to

Circulated by voluntary teachers and promising special blessings.

---

[1] Tĕlinĕs, the ancestor of the Syracusan despot Gelô, acquired great political power as possessing τὰ ἱρὰ τῶν χθονίων θεῶν (Herodot. vii. 153); he and his family became hereditary Hierophants of these ceremonies. How Tĕlinĕs acquired the ἱρά, Herodotus cannot say—ὅθεν δὲ αὐτὰ ἔλαβε, ἢ αὐτὸς ἐκτήσατο, τοῦτο οὐκ ἔχω εἶπαι. Probably there was a traditional legend, not inferior in sanctity to that of Eleusis, tracing them to the gift of Dĕmĕtĕr herself.

[2] See Josephus cont. Apiôn. ii. c. 85 ; Hesych. Θεοὶ ξένιοι ; Strabo, x. p. 471 ; Plutarch, Περὶ Δεισιδαιμον. c. iii. p. 166 ; c. vii. p. 167.

[3] Plato, Republ. ii. p. 364 ; Demosthen. de Coronâ, c. 79, p. 313. The δεισιδαίμων of Theophrastus cannot be

comfortable without receiving the Orphic communion monthly from the Orpheotelestæ (Theophr. Char. xvi.). Compare Plutarch, Περὶ τοῦ μὴ χρᾶν ἔμμετρα, &c., c. 25, p. 400. The comic writer Phrynichus indicates the existence of these rites of religious excitement, at Athens, during the Peloponnesian war. See the short fragment of his Κρόνος, ap. Schol. Aristoph. Aves, 989—

Ἀνὴρ χορεύει, καὶ τὰ τοῦ θεοῦ καλῶς ·

Βούλει Διοπείθη μεταδράμω καὶ τύμπανα ;

Diopeithĕs was a χρησμολόγος, or collector and deliverer of prophecies, which he sung (or rather, perhaps, recited) with solemnity and emphasis,

bring them within reach of the poor and even of slaves. But the wide diffusion and the number of voluntary communicants of these solemnities prove how much they fell in with the feeling of the time, and how much respect they enjoyed—a respect which the more conspicuous establishments, such as Eleusis and Samothrace, maintained for several centuries. And the visit of the Kretan Epimenidês to Athens—in the time of Solôn, at a season of the most serious disquietude and dread of having offended the gods— illustrates the tranquillizing effect of new orgies [1] and rites of absolution, when enjoined by a man standing high in the favour of the gods, and reputed to be the son of a nymph. The supposed Erythræan Sibyl, and the earliest collection of Sibylline prophecies, [2] afterwards so much multiplied and interpolated, and referred (according to Grecian custom) to an age even earlier than Homer, appear to belong to a date not long posterior to Epimenidês. Other oracular verses, such as those of Bakis, were treasured up in Athens and other cities: the sixth century before the Christian æra was fertile in these kinds of religious manifestations.

Epimenidês, Sibylla, Bakis.

Amongst the special rites and orgies of the character just described, those which enjoyed the greatest Pan-Hellenic reputation were attached to the Idæan Zeus in Krête, to Dêmêtêr at Eleusis, to the Kabeiri in Samothrace, and to Dionysos at Delphi and Thebes. [3] That they were all to a great degree analogous is shown by the way in

Principal mysteries of Greece.

---

in public. ὥστε ποιοῦντες χρησμοὺς αὐτοὶ Διδόασ᾽ ᾄδειν Διοπείθει τῷ παρα-μαινομένῳ. (Ameipsias ap. Schol. Aristophan. *ut sup.*, which illustrates Thucyd. ii. 21.)

[1] Plutarch, Solôn, c. 12; Diogen. Laërt. i. 110.

[2] See Klausen, "Æneas und die Penaten": his chapter on the connexion between the Grecian and Roman Sibylline collections is among the most ingenious of his learned book. Book ii. pp. 210—240: see Steph. Byz. v. Γέργις.

To the same age belong the χρησμοί and καθαρμοί of Abaris and his marvellous journey through the air upon an arrow (Herodot. iv. 36).

Epimenidês also composed καθαρμοί in epic verse; his Κουρήτων and Κορυ-

βάντων γένεσις, and his four thousand verses respecting Minôs and Rhadamanthys, if they had been preserved, would let us fully into the ideas of a religious mystic of that age respecting the antiquities of Greece. (Strabo, x. p. 474; Diogen. Laërt. i. 10.) Among the poems ascribed to Hesiod were comprised not only the Melampodia, but also ἔπη μαντικά and ἐξηγήσεις ἐπὶ τέρασιν. Pausan. ix. 31, 4.

[3] Among other illustrations of this general resemblance, may be counted an epitaph of Kallimachus upon an aged priestess, who passed from the service of Dêmêtêr to that of the Kabeiri, then to that of Cybelê, having the superintendence of many young women. Kallimachus, Epigram. 42, p. 308, ed. Ernest.

which they unconsciously run together and become confused in
the minds of various authors. The ancient inquirers themselves
were unable to distinguish one from the other, and we must be
content to submit to the like ignorance. But we see enough to
satisfy us of the general fact, that during the century and a half
which elapsed between the opening of Egypt to the Greeks and
the commencement of their struggle with the Persian kings, the
old religion was largely adulterated by importations from Egypt,
Asia Minor,[1] and Thrace. The rites grew to be more furious and
ecstatic, exhibiting the utmost excitement, bodily as
well as mental: the legends became at once more
coarse, more tragical, and less pathetic. The manifestations of this frenzy were strongest among the
women, whose religious susceptibilities were often found extremely unmanageable,[2] and who had everywhere congregative
occasional ceremonies of their own, apart from the men—indeed,
in the case of the colonists, especially of the Asiatic colonists, the
women had been originally women of the country, and as such
retained to a great degree their non-Hellenic manners and
feelings.[3] The god Dionysos,[4] whom the legends described as

*Ecstatic
rites intro-
duced from
Asia 700-
500 B.C.*

---

[1] Plutarch (Defect. Oracul. c. 10, p.
415) treats these countries as the original seat of the worship of Dæmons
(wholly or partially bad, and intermediate between gods and men), and
their religious ceremonies as of a corresponding character: the Greeks were
borrowers from them, according to
him, both of the doctrine and of the
ceremonies.

[2] Strabo, vii. p. 297. Ἅπαντες γὰρ τῆς
δεισιδαιμονίας ἀρχηγοὺς οἴονται τὰς γυ-
ναῖκας· αὖται δὲ καὶ τοὺς ἄνδρας προκα-
λοῦνται ἐς τὰς ἐπὶ πλέον θεραπείας τῶν
θεῶν, καὶ ἑορτὰς, καὶ ποτνιασμούς.
Plato (De Legg. x. pp. 909, 910) takes
great pains to restrain this tendency
on the part of sick or suffering persons,
especially women, to introduce new
sacred rites into his city.

[3] Herodot. i. 146. The wives of the
Ionic original settlers at Miletos were
Karian women, whose husbands they
slew.

The violences of the Karian worship
are attested by what Herodotus says
of the Karian residents in Egypt, at
the festival of Isis at Busiris. The
Egyptians at this festival manifested
their feeling by beating themselves,

the Karians by cutting their faces with
knives (ii. 61). The Καρικὴ μοῦσα became proverbial for funeral wailings
(Plato, Legg. vii. p. 800): the unmeasured effusions and demonstrations of
sorrow for the departed, sometimes
accompanied with cutting and mutilation self-inflicted by the mourner, was
a distinguishing feature in Asiatics
and Egyptians as compared with
Greeks. Plutarch, Consolat. ad Apollon. c. 22, p. 123. Mournful feeling was,
in fact, a sort of desecration of the
genuine and primitive Grecian festival,
which was a season of cheerful harmony and social enjoyment, wherein
the god was believed to sympathise
(εὐφροσύνη). See Xenophanês ap. Aristot. Rhetor. ii. 25; Xenophan. Fragm.
1. ed. Schneidewin; Theognis, 776;
Plutarch, De Superstit. p. 169. The
unfavourable comments of Dionysius
of Halikarnassus, in so far as they
refer to the festivals of Greece, apply
to the foreign corruptions, not to the
native character, of Grecian worship.

[4] The Lydian Hêraklês was conceived
and worshipped as a man in female
attire: this idea occurs often in the
Asiatic religions. Menke, Lydiaca, c.·

clothed in feminine attire, and leading a troop of frenzied
women, inspired a temporary ecstasy. · Those who resisted the inspiration, being disposed to disobey his
will, were punished either by particular judgments or
by mental terrors; while those who gave full loose to the feeling,
in the appropriate season and with the received solemnities, satisfied his exigencies, and believed themselves to have procured
immunity from such disquietudes for the future.[1] Crowds of
women, clothed with fawn-skins, and bearing the sanctified
thyrsus, flocked to the solitudes of Parnassus, or Kithærôn, or
Taygetus, during the consecrated triennial period, passed the
night there with torches, and abandoned themselves to demonstrations of frantic excitement, with dancing and clamorous
invocation of the god. They were said to tear animals limb
from limb, to devour the raw flesh, and to cut themselves
without feeling the wound.[2] The men yielded to a similar
impulse by noisy revels in the streets, sounding the cymbals and
tambourine, and carrying the image of the god in procession.[3] It
deserves to be remarked that the Athenian women never practised these periodical mountain excursions, so common among the
rest of the Greeks : they had their feminine solemnities of the
Thesmophoria,[4] mournful in their character and accompanied

(marginal note beside paragraph): Connected with the worship of Dionysos.

8, p. 22. Διόνυσος ἄῤῥην καὶ θῆλυς.
Aristid. Or. iv. 28; Æschyl. Fragm.
Edoni, ap. Aristoph. Thesmoph. 135.
Ποδαπὸς ὁ γύννις; τίς πάτρα; τίς ἡ
στολή;
[1] Melampos cures the women (whom
Dionysos has struck mad for their
resistance to his rites), παραλαβὼν τοὺς
δυνατωτάτους τῶν νεανίων μετ' ἀλαλαγ-
μοῦ καί τινος ἐνθέου χορείας. Apollodôr.
ii. 2, 7. Compare Eurip. Bacch. 861.
Plato (Legg. vii. p. 790) gives a similar theory of the healing effect of the
Korybantic rites, which cured vague
and inexplicable terrors of the mind
by means of dancing and music con-
joined with religious ceremonies—αἱ τὰ
τῶν Κορυβάντων ἰάματα τελοῦσαι (the
practitioners were women), αἱ τῶν ἐκ-
φρόνων Βακχείων ἰάσεις—ἡ τῶν ἔξωθεν
κρατεῖ κίνησις προσφερομένη τὴν ἐντὸς
φοβερὰν οὖσαν καὶ μανικὴν κίνησιν—
ὀρχουμένους δὲ καὶ αὐλουμένους μετὰ
θεῶν, οἷς ἂν καλλιερήσαντες ἕκαστοι
θύωσιν, κατειργάσατο ἀντὶ μανικῶν ἡμῖν
διαθέσεων ἕξεις ἔμφρονας ἔχειν.

[2] Described in the Bacchæ of Euripidês (140, 735, 1135, &c.). Ovid, Trist.
iv. i. 41. "Utque suum Bacchis non
sentit saucia vulnus, Cum furit Edonis
exululata jugis." In a fragment of the
poet Alkman, a Lydian by birth, the
Bacchanal nymphs are represented as
milking the lioness, and making cheese
of the milk, during their mountain
excursions and festivals. (Alkman,
Fragm. 14, Schn. Compare Aristid.
Orat. iv. p. 29.) Clemens Alexand.
Admonit. ad Gent. p. 9, Sylb.; Lucian,
Dionysos, c. 3, T. iii. p. 77, Hemsterh.
[3] See the tale of Skylês in Herod. iv.
79, and Athenæus, x. p. 445. Herodotus mentions that the Scythians abhorred the Bacchic ceremonies, accounting the frenzy which belonged to
them to be disgraceful and monstrous.
[4] Plutarch, De Isid. et Osir. c. 69, p.
378; Schol. ad Aristoph. Thesmoph.
There were, however, Bacchic ceremonies practised to a certain extent
by the Athenian women. (Aristoph.
Lysist. 388.)

with fasting, and their separate congregations at the temples of Aphroditê, but without any extreme or unseemly demonstrations. The state festival of the Dionysia, in the city of Athens, was celebrated with dramatic entertainments, and the once rich harvest of Athenian tragedy and comedy was thrown up under its auspices. The ceremonies of the Kurêtes in Krête, originally armed dances in honour of the Idæan Zeus, seem also to have borrowed from Asia so much of fury, of self-infliction, and of mysticism, that they became at last inextricably confounded with the Phrygian Korybantes, or worshippers of the Great Mother; though it appears that Grecian reserve always stopped short of the irreparable self-mutilation of Atys.

The influence of the Thracian religion upon that of the Greeks cannot be traced in detail, but the ceremonies contained in it were of a violent and fierce character, like the Phrygian, and acted upon Hellas in the same general direction as the latter. And the like may be said of the Egyptian religion, which was in this case the more operative, inasmuch as all the intellectual Greeks were naturally attracted to go and visit the wonders on the banks of the Nile: the powerful effect produced upon them is attested by many evidences, but especially by the interesting narrative of Herodotus. Now the Egyptian ceremonies were at once more licentious, and more profuse in the outpouring both of joy and sorrow than the Greek;[1] but a still greater difference sprang from the extraordinary power, separate mode of life, minute observances, and elaborate organisation of the priesthood. The ceremonies of Egypt were multitudinous, but the legends concerning them were framed by the priest, and, as a general rule, seemingly, known to the priests alone: at least they were not intended to be publicly talked of, even by pious men. They were "holy stories," which it was sacrilege publicly to mention, and which from this very prohibition only took firmer hold of the minds of the Greek visitors who heard them. And thus the element of secrecy and mystic silence—foreign to Homer, and only faintly glanced at in Hesiod—if it was not originally de-

[Marginal note: Thracian and Egyptian influence upon Greece.]

---

[1] "Ægyptiaca numina fere plangoribus gaudent, Græca plerumque choreis, barbara autem strepitu cymbalistarum et tympanistarum et choraularum." (Apuleius, De Genio Socratis, v. ii. p. 149, Oudend.)

rived from Egypt, at least received from thence its greatest
Encourage- stimulus and diffusion. The character of the legends
ment to themselves was naturally affected by this change
mystic
legends. from publicity to secrecy : the secrets when revealed
would be such as to justify by their own tenor the interdict on
public divulgation: instead of being adapted, like the Homeric
mythe, to the universal sympathies and hearty interest of a
crowd of hearers, they would derive their impressiveness from
the tragical, mournful, extravagant, or terror-striking character of
the incidents.[1] Such a tendency, which appears explicable and
probable even on general grounds, was in this particular case
rendered still more certain by the coarse taste of the Egyptian
priests. That any recondite doctrine, religious or philosophical,
was attached to the mysteries or contained in the holy stories,
has never been shown, and is improbable, though the affirmative
has been asserted by learned men.

Herodotus seems to have believed that the worship and ceremonies of Dionysos generally were derived by the
Melampus Greeks from Egypt, brought over by Kadmus, and
the earliest
name as taught by him to Melampus. And the latter appears
teacher of in the Hesiodic Catalogue as having cured the daugh-
the Diony-
siac rites. ters of Prœtus of the mental distemper, with which
they had been smitten by Dionysos for rejecting his ritual. He
cured them by introducing the Bacchic dance and fanatical
excitement: this mythical incident is the most ancient mention
of the Dionysiac solemnities presented in the same character as
they bear in Euripidês. It is the general tendency of Herodotus
to apply the theory of derivation from Egypt far too extensively
to Grecian institutions: the orgies of Dionysos were not originally borrowed from thence, though they may have been much
modified by connexion with Egypt as well as with Asia. The
remarkable mythe composed by Onomakritus respecting the dis-
memberment of Zagreus was founded upon an Egyptian tale very
similar respecting the body of Osiris, who was supposed to be

---

[1] The legend of Dionysos and Pro-
symnos, as it stands in Clemens, could
never have found place in an epic poem
(Admonit. ad Gent. p. 22 Sylb.). Compare page 11 of the same work, where,
however, he so confounds together
Phrygian, Bacchic, and Eleusinian
mysteries, that one cannot distinguish
them apart.
  The author called Demetrius Phalê-
reus says about the legends belonging
to these ceremonies—Διὸ καὶ τὰ μυστή-

identical with Dionysos.[1] Nor was it unsuitable to the reckless
fury of the Bacchanals during their state of temporary excitement, which found a still more awful expression in the mythe of
Pentheus,—torn in pieces by his own mother Agavê at the head
of her companions in the ceremony, as an intruder upon the
feminine rites, as well as a scoffer at the God.[2] A passage in the
Iliad (the authenticity of which has been contested, but even as
an interpolation it must be old)[3] also recounts how Lykurgus was
struck blind by Zeus, for having chased away with a whip " the
nurses of the mad Dionysos," and for having frightened the god
himself into the sea to take refuge in the arms of Thetis: while
the fact that Dionysos is so frequently represented in his mythes
as encountering opposition and punishing the refractory, seems
to indicate that his worship under its ecstatic form was a late
phænomenon, and introduced not without difficulty. The mythical Thracian Orpheus was attached as Eponymos
to a new sect, who seem to have celebrated the
ceremonies of Dionysos with peculiar care, minute-
ness, and fervour, besides observing various rules
in respect to food and clothing. It was the opinion of Herodotus
that these rules, as well as the Pythagorean, were borrowed from
Egypt. But whether this be the fact or not, the Orphic brotherhood is itself both an evidence, and a cause, of the increased
importance of the worship of Dionysos, which indeed is attested
by the great dramatic poets of Athens.

Orphic sect,
a variety of
the Dio-
nysiac
mystics.

The Homeric Hymns present to us, however, the religious ideas
and legends of the Greeks at an earlier period, when
the enthusiastic and mystic tendencies had not yet
acquired their full development. Though not referable
to the same age or to the same author as either the
Iliad or the Odyssey, they do to a certain extent con-

Contrast of
the mys-
teries
with the
Homeric
Hymns.

ρια λέγεται ἐν ἀλληγορίαις πρὸς ἔκ-
πληξιν καὶ φρίκην, ὥσπερ ἐν
σκότῳ καὶ νυκτί. (De Interpretatione,
c. 101.)
  [1] See the curious treatise of Plutarch, De Isid. et Osirid. c. 11—14, p.
355, and his elaborate attempt to allegorise the legend. He seems to have
conceived that the Thracian Orpheus
had first introduced into Greece the
mysteries both of Dèmètèr and Dionysos, copying them from those of Isis
and Osiris in Egypt. See Fragm. 84,

from one of his lost works, tom. v. p.
891, ed. Wyttenb.
  [2] Æschylus had dramatised the
story of Pentheus as well as that of
Lykurgus: one of his tetralogies was
the Lykurgeia (Dindorf, Æsch. Fragm.
115). A short allusion to the story of
Pentheus appears in Eumenid. 25.
Compare Sophokl. Antigon. 985, and
the Scholia.
  [3] Iliad, vi. 130. See the remarks of
Mr. Payne Knight ad loc.

tinue the same stream of feeling, and the same mythical tone and
colouring, as these poems—manifesting but little evidence of
Egyptian, Asiatic, or Thracian adulterations. The difference is
striking between the god Dionysos as he appears in the Homeric
hymn and in the Bacchæ of Euripidês. The hymnographer
describes him as standing on the sea-shore, in the guise of a beautiful and richly-clothed youth, when Tyrrhenian pirates suddenly
approach : they seize and bind him and drag him on board their
vessel. But the bonds which they employ burst spontaneously,
and leave the god free. The steersman, perceiving this with
affright, points out to his companions that they have
unwittingly laid hands on a god,—perhaps Zeus
himself, or Apollo, or Poseidôn. He conjures them to desist, and
to replace Dionysos respectfully on the shore, lest in his wrath he
should visit the ship with wind and hurricane : but the crew
deride his scruples, and Dionysos is carried prisoner out to sea
with the ship under full sail. Miraculous circumstances soon
attest both his presence and his power. Sweet-scented wine is
seen to flow spontaneously about the ship, the sail and mast appear
adorned with vine and ivy-leaves, and the oar-pegs with garlands.
The terrified crew now too late entreat the helmsman to steer his
course for the shore, and crowd round him for protection on the
poop. But their destruction is at hand : Dionysos assumes the
form of a lion—a bear is seen standing near him—this bear rushes
with a loud roar upon the captain, while the crew leap overboard
in their agony of fright, and are changed into dolphins. There
remains none but the discreet and pious steersman, to whom
Dionysos addresses words of affectionate encouragement, revealing
his name, parentage, and dignity.[1]

Hymn to
Dionysos.

---

[1] See Homer, Hymn 5, Διόνυσος ἢ
Λῆσται.—The satirical drama of Euripidês, the Cyclôps, extends and alters
this old legend. Dionysos is carried
away by the Tyrrhenian pirates, and
Silênus at the head of the Bacchanals
goes everywhere in search of him (Eur.
Cyc. 112). The pirates are instigated
against him by the hatred of Hêrê,
which appears frequently as a cause
of mischief to Dionysos (Bacchæ, 286).
Hêrê in her anger had driven him mad
when a child, and he had wandered in
this state over Egypt and Syria ; at

length he came to Cybela in Phrygia,
was purified (καθαρθείς) by Rhea, and
received from her female attire (Apollodôr. iii. 5, 1, with Heyne's note).
This seems to have been the legend
adopted to explain the old verse of the
Iliad, as well as the maddening attributes of the god generally.
  There was a standing antipathy between the priestesses and the religious
establishments of Hêrê and Dionysos
(Plutarch, Περὶ τῶν ἐν Πλαταίαις
Δαιδάλων, c. 2, tom. v. p. 755, ed.
Wytt. Plutarch ridicules the legen-

This hymn, perhaps produced at the Naxian festival of Dionysos, and earlier than the time when the dithyrambic chorus became the established mode of singing the praise and glory of that god, is conceived in a spirit totally different from that of the Bacchic Teletæ, or special rites which the Bacchæ of Euripidês so abundantly extol— rites introduced from Asia by Dionysos himself at the head of a thiasus or troop of enthusiastic women—inflaming with temporary frenzy the minds of the women of Thebes—not communicable except to those who approach as pious worshippers—and followed by the most tragical results to all those who fight against the god.[1] The Bacchic Teletæ, and the Bacchic feminine frenzy, were importations from abroad, as Euripidês represents them, engrafted upon the joviality of the primitive Greek Dionysia ; they were borrowed, in all probability, from more than one source, and introduced through more than one channel, the Orphic life or brotherhood being one of the varieties.   Strabo ascribes to this latter a Thracian original, considering Orpheus, Musæus, and Eumolpus as having been all Thracians.[2]   It is curious to observe how, in the Bacchæ of Euripidês, the two distinct and even conflicting ideas of Dionysos come alternately forward ; sometimes the old Grecian idea of the jolly and exhilarating god of wine— but more frequently the recent and important idea of the terrific and irresistible god who unseats the reason, and whose *œstrus* can only be appeased by a willing though temporary obedience.   In the fanatical impulse which inspired the votaries of the Asiatic Rhea or Cybelê, or of the Thracian Kotys, there was nothing of spontaneous joy ; it was a sacred madness, during which the soul appeared to be surrendered to a stimulus from without, and accompanied by preternatural strength and temporary sense of power[3]—altogether distinct from the unrestrained hilarity of the

Marginal notes: Alteration of the primitive Grecian idea of Dionysos.

Asiatic frenzy grafted on the joviality of the Grecian Dionysia.

dary reason commonly assigned for this, and provides a symbolical explanation which he thinks very satisfactory.

[1] Eurip. Bacch. 325, 464, &c.
[2] Strabo, x. p. 471.   Compare Aristid. Or. iv. p. 28.
[3] In the lost *Xantriæ* of Æschylus, in which seems to have been included the tale of Pentheus, the goddess Λύσσα was introduced, stimulating the Bacchæ, and creating in them spasmodic excitement from head to foot: ἐκ ποδῶν δ' ἄνω Ὑπέρχεται σπαραγμὸς εἰς ἄκρον κάρα, &c. (Fragm. 155, Dindorf.) His tragedy called *Edoni* also gave a terrific representation of the Bacchanals and their fury, exaggerated

original Dionysia, as we see them in the rural demes of Attica, or in the gay city of Tarentum. There was indeed a side on which the two bore some analogy, inasmuch as, according to the religious point of view of the Greeks, even the spontaneous joy of the vintage-feast was conferred by the favour and enlivened by the companionship of Dionysos. It was upon this analogy that the framers of the Bacchic orgies proceeded ; but they did not the less disfigure the genuine character of the old Grecian Dionysia.

Dionysos is in the conception of Pindar the Paredros or companion in worship of Dêmêtêr.[1] The worship and religious estimate of the latter has by that time undergone as great a change as that of the former, if we take our comparison with the brief description of Homer and Hesiod: she has acquired [2] much of the awful and soul-disturbing attributes of the Phrygian Cybelê. In Homer, Dêmêtêr is the goddess of the corn-field, who becomes attached to the mortal man Jasiôn ; an unhappy passion, since Zeus, jealous of the connexion between goddesses and men, puts him to death. In the Hesiodic Theogony, Dêmêtêr is the mother of Persephonê by Zeus, who permits Hadês to carry off the latter

by the maddening music : Πίμπλησι μέλος, Μανίας ἐπαγωγὸν ὁμοκλάν (Fr. 54).

Such also is the reigning sentiment throughout the greater part of the Bacchæ of Euripidês: it is brought out still more impressively in the mournful Atys of Catullus :—

"Dea magna, Dea Cybele, Dindymi Dea, Domina,
Procul a meâ tuus sit furor omnis, hera, domo :
Alios age incitatos : alios age rabidos !"

We have only to compare this fearful influence with the description of Dikæopolis and his exuberant joviality in the festival of the rural Dionysia (Aristoph. Acharn. 1051 seq. ; see also Plato, Legg. i. p. 637), to see how completely the foreign innovations recoloured the old Grecian Dionysos— Διόνυσος πολυγηθής, who appears also in the scene of Dionysos and Ariadnê in the Symposion of Xenophôn, c. 9. The simplicity of the ancient Dionysiac processions is dwelt upon by Plutarch, De Cupidine Divitiarum, p. 527 ; and the original dithyramb addressed by Archilochus to Dionysos is an effusion of drunken hilarity (Archiloch. Frag 69, Schneid.).

[1] Pindar, Isthm. vi. 3. χαλκοκρότου πάρεδρον Δημήτερος,—the epithet marks the approximation of Dêmêtêr to the Mother of the Gods. ἢ κροτάλων τυπάνων τ' ἰαχῆ, σύν τε βρόμος αὐλῶν Εὔαδεν (Homer. Hymn. xiii.) ;—the Mother of the Gods was worshipped by Pindar himself along with Pan ; she had in his time her temple and ceremonies at Thêbes (Pyth. iii. 78 ; Fragm. Dithyr. 5, and the Scholia ad l.) as well as, probably, at Athens (Pansan. i. 3, 3).

Dionysos and Dêmêtêr are also brought together in the chorus of Sophoklês, Antigonê, 1072, μέδεις δὲ παγκοίνοις Ἐλευσινίας Δηοῦς ἐν κόλποις ; and in Kallimachus, Hymn. Cerer. 70. Bacchus or Dionysos are in the Attic tragedians constantly confounded with the Dêmêtrian Iacchos, originally so different,—a personification of the mystic word shouted by the Eleusinian communicants. See Strabo, x. p. 468.

[2] Euripidês in his Chorus in the Helena (1320 seq.) assigns to Dêmêtêr all the attributes of Rhea, and blends the two completely into one,

as his wife ; moreover Dêmêtêr has, besides, by Jasiôn, a son
called Plutos, born in Krête.   Even from Homer to Hesiod, the
legend of Dêmêtêr has been expanded and her dignity exalted ;
according to the usual tendency of Greek legend, the expansion
goes on still further.   Through Jasiôn, Dêmêtêr becomes connected
with the mysteries of Samothrace, through Persephonê, with
those of Eleusis.   The former connexion it is difficult to follow
out in detail, but the latter is explained and traced to its origin
in the Homeric Hymn to Dêmêtêr.

Though we find different statements respecting the date as well
as the origin of the Eleusinian mysteries, yet the   Eleusinian
popular belief of the Athenians, and the story which   mysteries.
found favour at Eleusis, ascribed them to the presence and dicta-
tion of the goddess Dêmêtêr herself ; just as the Bacchic rites are,
according to the Bacchæ of Euripidês, first communicated and
enforced on the Greeks by the personal visit of Dionysos to
Thêbes, the metropolis of the Bacchic ceremonies.[1]   In the
Eleusinian legend, preserved by the author of the   Homeric
Homeric Hymn, she comes voluntarily and identifies   Hymn to
herself with Eleusis ; her past abode in Krête being   Dêmêtêr.
briefly indicated.[2]   Her visit to Eleusis is connected with the
deep sorrow caused by the loss of her daughter Persephonê, who
had been seized by Hadês, while gathering flowers in a meadow
along with the Oceanic Nymphs, and carried off to become his
wife in the under-world.   In vain did the reluctant Persephonê
shriek and invoke the aid of her father Zeus : he had consented
to give her to Hadês, and her cries were heard only by Hekatê
and Hêlios.   Dêmêtêr was inconsolable at the disappearance of
her daughter, but knew not where to look for her : she wandered
for nine days and nights with torches in search of the lost maiden
without success.   At length Hêlios, the "spy of gods and men,"
revealed to her, in reply to her urgent prayer, the rape of Persephonê, and the permission given to Hadês by Zeus.   Dêmêtêr
was smitten with anger and despair: she renounced Zeus and the
society of Olympus, abstained from nectar and ambrosia, and
wandered on earth in grief and fasting until her form could no

[1] Sophokl. Antigon. Βακχᾶν μητρό-
πολιν Θήβαν.
[2] Homer, Hymn. Cerer. 123.   The

Hymn to Dêmêtêr has been translated,
accompanied with valuable illustrative
notes, by J. H. Voss (Heidelb. 1826).

longer be known. In this condition she came to Eleusis, then
governed by the prince Keleos. Sitting down by a well at the
wayside in the guise of an old woman, she was found by the
daughters of Keleos, who came thither with their pails of brass
for water. In reply to their questions, she told them that she
had been brought by pirates from Krête to Thorikos, and had
made her escape ; she then solicited from them succour and
employment as a servant or as a nurse. The damsels prevailed
upon their mother Metaneira to receive her, and to entrust her
with the nursing of the young Dêmophoôn, their late-born
brother, the only son of Keleos. Dêmêtêr was received into the
house of Metaneira, her dignified form still borne down by grief :
she sat long silent, and could not be induced either to smile or to
taste food, until the maid-servant Iambê, by jests and playfulness, succeeded in amusing and rendering her cheerful. She
would not taste wine, but requested a peculiar mixture of barley-
meal with water and the herb mint.[1]

The child Dêmophoôn, nursed by Dêmêtêr, throve and grew
up like a god, to the delight and astonishment of his parents : she
gave him no food, but anointed him daily with ambrosia, and
plunged him at night in the fire like a torch, where he remained
unburnt. She would have rendered him immortal had she not
been prevented by the indiscreet curiosity and alarm of Metaneira,
who secretly looked in at night, and shrieked with horror at the
sight of her child in the fire.[2] The indignant goddess, setting
the infant on the ground, now revealed her true character to
Metaneira : her wan and aged look disappeared, and she stood
confest in the genuine majesty of her divine shape, diffusing a
dazzling brightness, which illuminated the whole house. "Foolish
mother," she said, "thy want of faith has robbed thy son of immortal life. I am the exalted Dêmêtêr, the charm and comfort
both of gods and men : I was preparing for thy son exemption
from death and old age ; now it cannot be but he must taste of
both. Yet shall he be ever honoured, since he has sat upon my
knee, and slept in my arms. Let the people of Eleusis erect for
me a temple and altar on yonder hill above the fountain : I will

[1] Homer, Hymn. Cerer. 202—210.
[2] This story was also told with reference to the Egyptian goddess Isis in
her wanderings. See Plutarch, De
Isid. et Osirid. c. 16, p. 357.

myself prescribe to them the orgies which they must religiously perform in order to propitiate my favour."[1]

The terrified Metaneira was incapable even of lifting up her child from the ground : her daughters entered at her cries, and began to embrace and tend their infant brother, but he sorrowed and could not be pacified for the loss of his divine nurse. All night they strove to appease the goddess.[2]

Strictly executing the injunctions of Dêmêtêr, Keleos convoked the people of Eleusis, and erected the temple on the spot which she had pointed out. It was speedily completed, and Dêmêtêr took up her abode in it, apart from the remaining gods, still pining with grief for the loss of her daughter, and withholding her beneficent aid from mortals. And thus she remained a whole year—a desperate and terrible year : [3] in vain did the oxen draw the plough, and in vain was the barley-seed cast into the furrow—Dêmêtêr suffered it not to emerge from the earth The human race would have been starved, and the gods would have been deprived of their honours and sacrifice, had not Zeus found means to conciliate her. But this was a hard task ; for Dêmêtêr resisted the entreaties of Iris and of all the other goddesses and gods whom Zeus successively sent to her. She would be satisfied with nothing less than the recovery of her daughter. At length Zeus sent Hermês to Hadês, to bring Persephonê away : Persephonê joyfully obeyed, but Hadês prevailed upon her before she departed to swallow a grain of pomegranate, which rendered it impossible for her to remain the whole year away from him.[4]

With transport did Dêmêtêr receive back her lost daughter, and the faithful Hekatê sympathised in the delight felt by both at the reunion.[5] It was now an easier undertaking to reconcile

Temple of Eleusis, built by order of Dêmêtêr for her residence.

---

[1] Homer, Hymn. Cerer. 274—

'Οργια δ' αὐτὴ ἐγὼν ὑποθήσομαι, ὡς ἄν ἔπειτα
Εὐαγέως ἔρδοντες ἐμὸν νόον ἰλάσκησθε.

The same story is told in regard to the infant Achilles. His mother Thetis was taking similar measures to render him immortal, when his father Peleus interfered and prevented the consummation. Thetis immediately left him

in great wrath. (Apollon. Rhod. iv. 866.)

[2] Homer, Hymn. 290—

τοῦ δ' οὐ μειλίσσετο θυμὸς,
Χειρότεραι γὰρ δή μιν ἔχον τρόφοι ἠδὲ τιθῆναι.

[3] Homer. H. Cer. 305.

Αἰνότατον δ' ἐνιαυτὸν ἐπὶ χθόνα που λυβότειραν
Ποίησ' ἀνθρώποις, ἰδὲ κύντατον.

[4] Hymn, v. 375.

[5] Hymn, v. 413.

her with the gods. Her mother Rhea, sent down expressly by Zeus, descended from Olympus on the fertile Rharian plain, then smitten with barrenness like the rest of the earth : she succeeded in appeasing the indignation of Dêmêtêr, who consented again to put forth her relieving hand. The buried seed came up in abundance, and the earth was covered with fruit and flowers. She would have wished to retain Persephonê constantly with her ; but this was impossible, and she was obliged to consent that her daughter should go down for one-third of each year to the house of Hadês, departing from her every spring at the time when the seed is sown. She then revisited Olympus, again to dwell with the gods ; but before her departure she communicated to the daughters of Keleos, and to Keleos himself, together with Triptolemus, Dioklês, and Eumolpus, the divine service and the solemnities which she required to be observed in her honour.[1] And thus began the venerable mysteries of Eleusis, at her special command : the lesser mysteries, celebrated in February, in honour of Persephonê ; the greater, in August, to the honour of Dêmêtêr herself. Both are jointly patronesses of the holy city and temple.

Dêmêtêr prescribes the mystic ritual of Eleusis.

Such is a brief sketch of the temple legend of Eleusis, set forth at length in the Homeric Hymn to Dêmêtêr. It is interesting not less as a picture of the Mater Dolorosa (in the mouth of an Athenian, Dêmêtêr and Persephonê were always The Mother and Daughter, by excellence), first an agonised sufferer, and then finally glorified—the weal and woe of man being dependent upon her kindly feeling,—than as an illustration of the nature and growth of Grecian legend generally. Though we now read this Hymn as pleasing poetry, to the Eleusinians, for whom it was composed, it was genuine and sacred history. They believed in the visit of Dêmêtêr to Eleusis, and in the Mysteries as a revelation from her, as implicitly as they believed in her existence and power as a goddess.

Homeric Hymn a sacred Eleusinian record.

The Eleusinian psalmist shares this belief in common with his countrymen, and embodies it in a continuous narrative,

---

[1] Hymn, v. 475—

'Η δὲ κίουσα θεμιστοπόλοις βασιλεῦσι
Δεῖξεν, Τριπτολέμῳ τε, Διοκλεῖ τε
πληξίππῳ,

Εὐμόλπου τε βίη, Κελέῳ θ' ἡγήτορι
λαῶν,
Δρησμοσύνην ἱερῶν· καὶ ἐπέφραδεν
ὄργια παισὶν
Πρεσβυτέρῃς Κελέοιο, &c.

in which the great goddesses of the place, as well as the great
heroic families, figure in inseparable conjunction.   Keleos is the
son of the Eponymous hero Eleusis, and his daughters, with the
old epic simplicity, carry their basons to the well for water.
Eumolpus, Triptolemus, Dioklês, heroic ancestors of the privileged families who continued throughout the historical times of
Athens to fulfil their special hereditary functions in the Eleusinian solemnities, are among the immediate recipients of inspiration from the goddess : but chiefly does she favour Metaneira
and her infant son Dêmophoôn, for the latter of whom her greatest
boon is destined, and intercepted only by the weak
faith of the mother.   Moreover every incident in the Explanatory of the
Hymn has a local colouring and a special reference. details of
The well overshadowed by an olive-tree near which divine service.
Dêmêtêr had rested, the stream Kallichoros and the
temple-hill, were familiar and interesting places in the eyes of
every Eleusinian ; the peculiar posset prepared from barley-meal
with mint was always tasted by the Mysts (or communicants)
after a prescribed fast, as an article in the ceremony,—while it
was also the custom, at a particular spot in the processional
march, to permit the free interchange of personal jokes and taunts
upon individuals for the general amusement.   And these two
customs are connected in the Hymn with the incidents, that
Dêmêtêr herself had chosen the posset as the first interruption of
her long and melancholy fast, and that her sorrowful thoughts
had been partially diverted by the coarse playfulness of the ser-
vant-maid Iambê.   In the enlarged representation of the Eleusinian ceremonies, which became established after the incorporation of Eleusis with Athens, the part of Iambê herself was enacted
by a woman, or man in woman's attire, of suitable wit and imagination, who was posted on the bridge over the Kephissos, and
addressed to the passers-by in the procession,[1] especially the great
men of Athens, saucy jeers probably not less piercing than those
of Aristophanês on the stage.   The torch-bearing Hekatê received
a portion of the worship in the nocturnal ceremonies of the

[1] Aristophanês, Vesp. 1363. Hesych.
v. Γεφυρίς. Suidas, v. Γεφυρίζων. Compare, about the details of the ceremony,
Clemens Alexandr. Admon. ad Gent.
p. 13. A similar licence of unrestrained-
jocularity appears in the rites of Dêmêtêr in Sicily (Diodor. v. 4 ; see also
Pausan. vii. 27, 4), and in the worship
of Damia and Auxesia at Ægina (Herodot. v. 83).

Eleusinia : this too is traced in the Hymn to her kind and affectionate sympathy with the great goddesses. •

Though all these incidents were sincerely believed by the Eleusinians as a true history of the past, and as having been the real initiatory cause of their own solemnities, it is not the less certain that they are simply mythes or legends, and not to be treated as history either actual or exaggerated. They do not take their start from realities of the past, but from realities of the present combined with retrospective feeling and fancy, which fills up the blank of the aforetime in a manner at once plausible and impressive. What proportion of fact there may be in the legend, or whether there be any at all, it is impossible to ascertain and useless to inquire ; for the story did not acquire belief from its approximation to real fact, but from its perfect harmony with

Importance of the mysteries to the town of Eleusis. Eleusinian faith and feeling, and from the absence of any standard of historical credibility. The little town of Eleusis derived all its importance from the solemnity of the Dêmêtria, and the Hymn which we have been considering (probably at least as old as 600 B.C.) represents the town as it stood before its absorption into the larger unity of Athens, which seems to have produced an alteration of its legends and an increase of dignity in its great festival. In the faith of an Eleusinian, the religious as well as the patriotic antiquities of his native town were connected with this capital

Stronghold of the legend upon Eleusinian feelings. solemnity. The divine legend of the sufferings of Dêmêtêr and her visit to Eleusis was to him that which the heroic legend of Adrastus and the siege of Thebes was to a Sikyonian, or that of Erechtheus and Athênê to an Athenian—grouping together in the same scene and story the goddess and the heroic fathers of the town. If our information were fuller, we should probably find abundance of other legends respecting the Dêmêtria : the Gephyræi of Athens, to whom be-

Different legends respecting Dêmêtêr elsewhere. longed the celebrated Harmodios and Aristogeitôn, and who possessed special Orgies of Dêmêtêr the Sorrowful, to which no man foreign to their Gens was ever admitted,[1] would doubtless have told stories not only different but contradictory ; and even in other Eleusinian

---

[1] Herodot. v 61.

mythes we discover Eumolpus as king of Eleusis, son of Poseidôn, and a Thracian, completely different from the character which he bears in the Hymn before us.[1] Neither discrepancies nor want of evidence, in reference to alleged antiquities, shocked the faith of a non-historical public. What they wanted was a picture of the past, impressive to their feelings and plausible to their imagination : and it is important to the reader to remember, while he reads either the divine legends which we are now illustrating, or the heroic legends to which we shall soon approach, that he is dealing with a past which never was present,—a region essentially mythical, neither approachable by the critic nor measurable by the chronologer.

The tale respecting the visit of Dêmêtêr, which was told by the ancient Gens, called the Phytalids,[2] in reference to another temple of Dêmêtêr between Athens and Eleusis, and also by the Megarians in reference to a Dêmêtrion near their city, acquired under the auspices of Athens still further extension. Expansion of the legends. The goddess was reported to have first communicated to Triptolemus at Eleusis the art of sowing corn, which by his intervention was disseminated all over the earth. And thus the Athenians took credit to themselves for having been the medium of communication from the gods to man of all the inestimable blessings of agriculture which they affirmed to have been first exhibited on the fertile Rharian plain near Eleusis. Such pretensions are not to be found in the old Homeric hymn. The festival of the Thesmophoria, celebrated in honour of Dêmêtêr Thesmophoros at Athens, was altogether different from the Eleusinia, in this material respect, as well as others, that all males were excluded and women only were allowed to partake in it: the surname Thesmophoros gave occasion to new legends in which the goddess was glorified as the first authoress of laws and legal sanctions to mankind.[3] This festival for women apart and alone

---

[1] Pausan. i. 38, 3 ; Apollodôr. iii. 15, 4. Heyne in his Note admits several persons named Eumolpus. Compare Isokratês, Panegyr. p. 55. Philochorus the Attic antiquary could not have received the legend of the Eleusinian Hymn, from the different account which he gave respecting the rape of Persephonê (Philoch. Fragm. 46, ed. Didot), and also respecting Keleos (Fr. 28, ibid.).

[2] Phytalus, the Eponym or godfather of this gens, had received Dêmêtêr as a guest in his house, when she first presented mankind with the fruit of the fig-tree. (Pausan. i. 37, 2.)

[3] Kallimach. Hymn. Cerer. 19. Sophoklês, Triptolemos, Fragm. 1. Cicero Legg. ii. 14, and the note of Servius ad Virgil. Æn. iv. 58.

was also celebrated at Thebes, at Paros, at Ephesus, and in many other parts of Greece.[1]

Altogether, Dêmêtêr and Dionysos, as the Grecian counterparts of the Eygptian Isis and Osiris, seem to have been the great recipients of the new sacred rites borrowed from Eygpt, before the worship of Isis in her own name was introduced into Greece : their solemnities became more frequently recluse and mysterious than those of the other deities. The importance of Dêmêtêr to the collective nationality of Greece may be gathered from the fact that her temple was erected at Thermopylæ, the spot where the Amphiktyonic assemblies were held, close to the temple of the Eponymous hero Amphiktyôn himself, and under the surname of the Amphiktyonic Dêmêtêr.[2]

Hellenic importance of Dêmêtêr.

We now pass to another and not less important celestial personage—Apollo.

Legends of Apollo.

The legends of Dêlos and Delphi, embodied in the Homeric Hymn to Apollo, indicate, if not a greater dignity, at least a more widely diffused worship of that god than even of Dêmêtêr. The Hymn is, in point of fact, an aggregate of two separate compositions, one emanating from an Ionic bard at Dêlos, the other from Delphi. The first details the birth, the second the mature divine efficiency, of Apollo ; but both alike present the unaffected charm as well as the characteristic peculiarities of Grecian mythical narrative. The hymnographer sings, and his hearers accept in perfect good faith, a history of the past ; but it is a past, imagined partly as an introductory explanation to the present, partly as the means of glorifying the god. The island of Dêlos was the accredited birthplace of Apollo, and is also the place in which he chiefly delights, where the great and brilliant Ionic festival is periodically convened in his honour. Yet it is a rock narrow, barren, and uninviting : how came so glorious a privilege to be awarded to it ? This the poet takes upon himself to explain. Lêtô, pregnant with Apollo and persecuted by the jealous Hêrê, could find no spot wherein to give birth to her offspring. In vain did she

Delian Apollo.

---

[1] Xen. Hell. v. 2, 29. Herodot. vi. 16, 134. ἔρκος Θεσμοφόρου Δήμητρος   —τὰ ἐς ἔρσενα γόνον ἄρρητα ἱερά. [2] Herodot. vii. 200.

address herself to numerous places in Greece, the Asiatic coast, and the intermediate islands ; all were terrified at the wrath of Hêrê, and refused to harbour her.   As a last resort, she approached the rejected and repulsive island of Dêlos, and promised that if shelter were granted to her in her forlorn condition, the island should become the chosen resort of Apollo as well as the site of his temple with its rich accompanying solemnities.[1]   Dêlos joyfully consented, but not without many apprehensions that the potent Apollo would despise her unworthiness, and not without exacting a formal oath from Lêtô,—who was then admitted to the desired protection, and duly accomplished her long and painful labour.   Though Diônê, Rhea, Themis, and Amphitritê came to soothe and succour her, yet Hêrê kept away the goddess presiding over childbirth, Eileithyia, and thus cruelly prolonged her pangs. At length Eileithyia came, and Apollo was born.   Hardly had Apollo tasted, from the hands of Themis, the immortal food, nectar and ambrosia, when he burst at once his infant bands, and displayed himself in full divine form and strength, claiming his characteristic attributes of the bow and the harp, and his privileged function of announcing beforehand to mankind the designs of Zeus.   The promise made by Lêtô to Dêlos was faithfully performed : amidst the numberless other temples and groves which men provided for him, he ever preferred that island as his permanent residence, and there the Ionians with their wives and children, and all their " bravery," congregated periodically from their different cities to glorify him.   Dance and song and athletic contests adorned the solemnity, while the countless ships, wealth, and grace of the multitudinous Ionians had the air of an assembly of gods.   The Delian maidens, servants of Apollo, sang hymns to the glory of the god, as well as of Artemis and Lêtô, intermingled with adventures of foregone men and women, to the delight of the listening crowd.   The blind itinerant bard of Chios (composer of the Homeric hymn, and confounded in antiquity with the author of the Iliad), having found honour and acceptance at this festival, commends himself, in a touching fare-

---

[1] According to another legend, Lêtô was said to have been conveyed from the Hyperboreans to Dêlos in twelve days, in the form of a she-wolf, to escape the jealous eye of Hêrê.   In connexion with this legend, it was affirmed that the she-wolves always brought forth their young only during these twelve days in the year (Aristot. Hist. Animal. vii. 35).

well strain, to the remembrance and sympathy of the Delian maidens.[1]

But Dêlos was not an oracular spot : Apollo did not manifest Pythian Apollo. himself there as revealer of the futurities of Zeus. A place must be found where this beneficent function, without which mankind would perish under the innumerable doubts and perplexities of life, may be exercised and rendered available. Apollo himself descends from Olympus to make choice of a suitable site : the hymnographer knows a thousand other adventures of the god which he might sing, but he prefers this memorable incident, the charter and patent of consecration for the Delphian temple. Many different places did Apollo inspect : he surveyed the country of the Magnêtes and the Perrhæbians, came to Iôlkos, and passed over from thence to Eubœa and the plain of Lelanton. But even this fertile spot did not please him : he crossed the Euripus to Bœotia, passed by Teumêssus and Mykalêssus, and the then inaccessible and unoccupied forest on which the city of Thebes afterwards stood. He next proceeded to Onchêstos, but the grove of Poseidôn was already established there ; next across the Kêphissus to Okalea, Haliartus, and the agreeable plain and much-frequented fountain of Delphusa, or Tilphusa. Pleased with the place, Apollo prepared to establish his oracle there, but Tilphusa was proud of the beauty of her own site, and did not choose that her glory should be eclipsed by that of the god.[2] She alarmed him with the apprehension that the chariots which contended in her plain, and the horses and mules which watered at her fountain, would disturb the solemnity of his oracle ; and she thus induced him to proceed onward to the southern side of Parnassus, overhanging the harbour of Krissa. Here he established his oracle, in the mountainous site not frequented by chariots and horses, and near to a fountain, which however was guarded by a vast and terrific serpent, once the nurse of the monster Typhaôn. This serpent Apollo slew with an arrow, and suffered its body to rot in the sun : hence the name of the place, Pythô,[3] and the surname of the Pythian Apollo. The plan of his temple being marked out, it was built by Trophônios and Agamêdês, aided by a crowd of forward auxiliaries from the

---

[1] Hom. Hymn. Apoll. i. 179.
[2] Hom. Hymn. Apoll. 262.

[3] Hom. Hymn. 363 : πύθεσθαι, to rot.

neighbourhood. He now discovered with indignation, however, that Tilphusa had cheated him, and went back with swift step to resent it. "Thou shalt not thus," he said, "succeed in thy fraud and retain thy beautiful water : the glory of the place shall be mine, and not thine alone." Thus saying, he tumbled down a crag upon the fountain, and obstructed her limpid current ; establishing an altar for himself in a grove hard by near another spring, where men still worship him as Apollo Tilphusios, because of his severe vengeance upon the once beautiful Tilphusa.[1]

Apollo next stood in need of chosen ministers to take care of his temple and sacrifice, and to pronounce his responses at Pythô. Descrying a ship, "containing many and good men," bound on traffic from the Minoian Knossus in Krête, to Pylus in Peloponnêsus, he resolved to make use of the ship and her crew for his purpose. Assuming the shape of a vast dolphin, he splashed about and shook the vessel so as to strike the mariners with terror, while he sent a strong wind, which impelled her along the coast of Peloponnêsus into the Corinthian Gulf, and finally to the harbour of Krissa, where she ran aground. The affrighted crew did not dare to disembark : but Apollo was seen standing on the shore in the guise of a vigorous youth, and inquired who they were and what was their business. The leader of the Krêtans recounted in reply their miraculous and compulsory voyage, when Apollo revealed himself as the author and contriver of it, announcing to them the honourable function and the dignified post to which he destined them.[2] They followed him by his orders to the Rocky Pythô on Parnassus, singing the solemn Io-Paian such as it is sung in Krête, while the god himself marched at their head, with his fine form and lofty step, playing on the harp. He showed them the temple and site of the oracle, and directed them to worship him as Apollo Delphinios, because they had first seen him in the shape of a dolphin. "But how," they inquired, "are we to live in a spot where there is neither corn, nor vine, nor pasturage?" "Ye silly mortals," answered the god, "who look only for toil and privation, know that an easier lot is yours. Ye shall live by the cattle which crowds of pious visitors will bring to the temple:

Foundation legend of the Delphian oracle.

---

[1] Hom. Hymn. Apoll. 381.   [2] Hom. Hymn. Apoll. 475, seq.

ye shall need only the knife to be constantly ready for sacrifice.[1]
Your duty will be to guard my temple, and to officiate as ministers
at my feasts : but if ye be guilty of wrong or insolence, either by
word or deed, ye shall become the slaves of other men, and shall
remain so for ever. Take heed of the word and the warning."

Such are the legends of Dêlos and Delphi, according to the
Homeric Hymn to Apollo. The specific functions of
the god, and the chief localities of his worship, together with the surnames attached to them, are thus
historically explained, being connected with his past
acts and adventures. Though these are to us only
interesting poetry, yet to those who heard them sung they
possessed all the requisites of history, and were fully believed as
such ; not because they were partially founded in reality, but
because they ran in complete harmony with the feelings ; and, so
long as that condition was fulfilled, it was not the fashion of the
time to canvass truth or falsehood. The narrative is purely
personal, without any discernible symbolised doctrine or allegory,
to serve as a supposed ulterior purpose : the particular deeds
ascribed to Apollo grow out of the general preconceptions as to
his attributes, combined with the present realities of his worship. It is neither history nor allegory, but simple mythe or
legend.

They served the purpose of his-torical explana-tion.

The worship of Apollo is among the most ancient, capital,
and strongly marked facts of the Grecian world, and
widely diffused over every branch of the race. It is
older than the Iliad or Odyssey, in the latter of which
both Pythô and Dêlos are noted, though Dêlos is not named in
the former. But the ancient Apollo is different in more respects
than one from the Apollo of later times. He is in a peculiar
manner the god of the Trojans, unfriendly to the Greeks, and
especially to Achilles ; he has, moreover, only two primary
attributes, his bow and his prophetic powers, without any distinct
connexion either with the harp, or with medicine, or with the
sun, all which in later times he came to comprehend. He
becomes not only, as Apollo Karneius, the chief god of the Doric

Extended worship of Apollo.

[1] Homer. Hymn. Apoll. 535—

Δεξιτέρῃ μάλ᾽ ἕκαστος ἔχων ἐν χειρὶ
μάχαιραν

Σφάζειν αἰεὶ μῆλα· τὰ δ᾽ ἄφθονα πάντα
    πάρεστ αι,
Ὅσσα ἐμοίγ᾽ ἀγάγωσι περίκλυτα φῦλ᾽
    ἀνθρώπων.

race, but also (under the surname of Patrôus) the great protecting
divinity of the gentile tie among the Ionians : [1] he is moreover
the guide and stimulus to Grecian colonization, scarcely any
colony being ever sent out without encouragement and direction
from the oracle at Delphi : Apollo Archêgetês is one of his great
surnames.[2] His temple lends sanctity to the meetings of the
Amphiktyonic assembly, and he is always in filial subordination
and harmony with his father Zeus : Delphi and Olympia are
never found in conflict.　 In the Iliad, the warm and earnest
patrons of the Greeks are Hêrê, Athênê, and Poseidôn : here too
Zeus and Apollo are seen in harmony, for Zeus is decidedly well-
inclined to the Trojans, and reluctantly sacrifices them to the
importunity of the two great goddesses.[3] The worship of the
Sminthian Apollo, in various parts of the Troad and the neighbouring territory, dates before the earliest periods of Æolic
colonization : [4] hence the zealous patronage of Troy ascribed to
him in the Iliad.　 Altogether, however, the distribution and
partialities of the gods in that poem are different from what they
become in later times,—a difference which our means of information do not enable us satisfactorily to explain.　 Besides the
Delphian temple, Apollo had numerous temples throughout
Greece, and oracles at Abæ in Phôkis, on the Mount Ptôon, and
at Tegyra in Bœotia, where he was said to have been born,[5] at
Branchidæ near Milêtus, at Klarus in Asia Minor, and at Patara
in Lykia.　 He was not the only oracular god : Zeus at Dodona
and at Olympia gave responses also : the gods or heroes Trophônius, Amphiaraus, Amphilochus, Mopsus, &c., each at his own
sanctuary and in his own prescribed manner, rendered the same
service.

　　The two legends of Delphi and Dêlos, above noticed, form of
course a very insignificant fraction of the narratives which

---

[1] Harpokration, v. 'Απόλλων πατρῷος
and 'Ερκεῖος Ζεύς. Apollo Delphinios
also belongs to the Ionic Greeks generally. Strabo, iv. 179.
　[2] Thucydid.　vi.　3 ;　Kallimach.
Hymn. Apoll. 56—

　　Φοῖβος γὰρ ἀεὶ πολίεσσι φιληδεῖ
　　Κτιζομέναις, αὐτὸς δὲ θεμείλια Φοῖβος
　　ὑφαίνει.

[3] Iliad, iv. 30—46.
[4] Iliad, i. 38, 451 ; Stephan. Byz.

'Ιλιον, Τένεδος. See also Klausen,
Æneas und die Penaten, b. i. p. 69.
The worship of Apollo Sminthios and
the festival of the Sminthia at Alexandria Troas lasted down to the time
of Menander the rhetor, at the close of
the third century after Christ.
　[5] Plutarch. Defect. Oracul. c. 5, p.
412 ; c. 8, p. 414 ; Steph. Byz. v. Τεγύρα.
The Temple of the Ptôan Apollo had
acquired celebrity before the days of
the poet Asius. Pausan. ix. 23, 3.

once existed respecting the great and venerated Apollo. They
Multifa-   serve only as specimens, and as very early speci-
rious local   mens,[1] to illustrate what these divine mythes were, and
legends re-
specting   what was the turn of Grecian faith and imagination.
Apollo.   The constantly recurring festivals of the gods caused
an incessant demand for new mythes respecting them, or at least
for varieties and reproductions of the old mythes. Even during
the third century of the Christian æra, in the time of the rhêtôr
Menander, when the old forms of paganism were waning and
when the stock of mythes in existence was extremely abundant,
we see this demand in great force ; but it was incomparably more
operative in those earlier times when the creative vein of the
Grecian mind yet retained its pristine and unfaded richness.
Each god had many different surnames, temples, groves, and
solemnities ; with each of which was connected more or less of
mythical narrative, originally hatched in the prolific and spontaneous fancy of a believing neighbourhood, to be afterwards
expanded, adorned, and diffused by the song of the poet. The
Festivals   earliest subject of competition[2] at the great Pythian
and Agones.   festival was the singing of a hymn in honour of Apollo :
other *agones* were subsequently added, but the ode or hymn constituted the fundamental attribute of the solemnity : the Pythia
at Sikyon and elsewhere were probably framed on a similar footing.
So too at the ancient and celebrated Charitêsia, or festival of the
Charites, at Orchomenos, the rivalry of the poets in their various
modes of composition both began and continued as the predominant feature :[3] and the inestimable treasures yet remaining to us

---

[1] The legend which Euphorus followed about the establishment of the
Delphian temple was something radically different from the Homeric Hymn
(Ephori Fragm. 70, ed. Didot) ; his
narrative went far to politicise and
rationalise the story. The progeny of
Apollo was very numerous, and of the
most diverse attributes : he was father
of the Korybantes (Pherekydês, Fragm.
6, ed. Didot), as well as of Asklêpios
and Aristæus (Schol. Apollon. Rhod.
ii. 500 ; Apollodôr. iii. 10, 3).

[2] Strabo, ix. p. 421. Menander the
Rhetor (ap. Walz. Coll. Rhett. t. ix. p.
136) gives an elaborate classification of
hymns to the gods, distinguishing them
into nine classes —κλητικοὶ, ἀποπεμπτι-

κοὶ, φυσικοὶ, μυθικοὶ, γενεαλογικοὶ, πεπ-
λασμένοι, εὐκτικοὶ, ἀπευκτικοὶ, μικτοί :—
the second class had reference to the
temporary absence or departure of a
god to some distant place, which were
often admitted in the ancient religion.
Sappho and Alkman in their *kletic*
hymns invoked the gods from many
different places,—τὴν μὲν γὰρ Ἄρτεμιν
ἐκ μυρίων μὲν ὀρέων, μυρίων δὲ πόλεων,
ἔτι δὲ ποτάμων, ἀνακαλεῖ,—also Aphroditê and Apollo, &c. All these songs
were full of adventures and details respecting the gods,—in other words, of
legendary matter.

[3] Pindar, Olymp. xiv. ; Boeckh,
Staatshaushaltung der Athener, Appendix, § xx. p. 357.

of Attic tragedy and comedy, are gleanings from the once numerous dramas exhibited at the solemnity of the Dionysia.   The
Ephesians gave considerable rewards for the best hymns in honour
of Artemis, to be sung at her temple.[1]   And the early lyric poets
of Greece, though their works have not descended to us, devoted
their genius largely to similar productions, as may be seen by the
titles and fragments yet remaining.

Both the Christian and the Mahomedan religions have begun
during the historical age, have been propagated from one common centre, and have been erected upon the ruins of a different
pre-existing faith.   With none of these particulars did Grecian
paganism correspond.   It took rise in an age of imagination and feeling simply, without the restraints, as   *State of
mind and*
well as without the aid, of writing or records, of   *circumstances out*
history or philosophy.   It was, as a general rule, the   *of which*
spontaneous product of many separate tribes and locali-   *Grecian
mythes*
ties, imitation and propagation operating as subor-   *arose.*
dinate causes ; it was moreover a primordial faith, as far as our
means of information enable us to discover.

These considerations explain to us two facts in the history of
the early pagan mind.   First, the divine mythes, the matter of
their religion, constituted also the matter of their earliest history ;
next, these mythes harmonised with each other only in their
general types, but differed incurably in respect of particular incidents.   The poet who sang a new adventure of Apollo, the trace
of which he might have heard in some remote locality, would
take care that it should be agreeable to the general conceptions
which his hearers entertained respecting the god.   He would not
ascribe the cestus or amorous influences to Athênê, nor armed
interference and the ægis to Aphroditê ; but, provided he maintained this general keeping, he might indulge his fancy without
restraint in the particular events of the story.[2]   The feelings and

---

[1] Alexander Ætolus, apud Macro-
bium, Saturn. v. 22.

[2] The birth of Apollo and Artemis
from Zeus and Lêtô is among the
oldest and most generally admitted
facts in the Grecian divine legends.
Yet Æschylus did not scruple to describe Artemis publicly as daughter of
Dêmêtêr (Herodot. ii. 156; Pausan.
viii. 37, 3). Herodotus thinks that he

copied this innovation from the
Egyptians, who affirmed that Apollo
and Artemis were the sons of Dionysos
and Isis.

The number and discrepancies of the
mythes respecting each god are attested by the fruitless attempts of
learned Greeks to escape the necessity of rejecting any of them by multiplying homonymous personages,—

faith of his hearers went along with him, and there were no critical scruples to hold them back : to scrutinize the alleged proceedings of the gods was repulsive, and to disbelieve them impious. And thus these divine mythes, though they had their root simply in religious feelings, and though they presented great discrepancies of fact, served nevertheless as primitive matter of history to an early Greek : they were the only narratives, at once publicly accredited and interesting, which he possessed. To them were aggregated the heroic mythes (to which we shall proceed presently),—indeed the two are inseparably blended, gods, heroes, and men almost always appearing in the same picture,—analogous both in their structure and their genesis, and differing chiefly in the circumstance that they sprang from the type of a hero instead of from that of a god.

We are not to be astonished if we find Aphroditê, in the
Iliad, born from Zeus and Dionê, and, in the Theo-
Discrepan-
cies in the   gony of Hesiod, generated from the foam on the sea
legends
little   after the mutilation of Uranos; nor if in the Odyssey
noticed.   she appears as the wife of Hêphæstos, while in the
Theogony the latter is married to Aglaia, and Aphroditê is described as mother of three children by Arês.[1] The Homeric hymn to Aphroditê details the legend of Aphroditê and Anchisês, which is presupposed in the Iliad as the parentage of Æneas: but the author of the hymn, probably sung at one of the festivals of· Aphroditê in Cyprus, represents the goddess as ashamed of her passion for a mortal, and as enjoining Anchisês under severe
menaces not to reveal who the mother of Æneas was,[2]
Aphroditê.   while in the Iliad she has no scruple in publicly owning him, and he passes everywhere as her acknowledged son. Aphroditê is described in the hymn as herself cold and unimpressible, but ever active and irresistible in inspiring amorous feelings to gods, to men, and to animals. Three goddesses are recorded as memorable exceptions to her universal empire,— Athênê, Artemis, and Hestia or Vesta. Aphroditê was one of the most important of all the goddesses in the mythical world:

three persons named Zeus ; five named Athênê; six named Apollo, &c. (Cicero, de Natur. Deor. iii. 21; Clemens Alexand. Admon. ad Gent. p. 17.)

[1] Hesiod. Theogon. 188, 934, 945 ; Homer, Iliad, v. 371 ; Ödyss. viii. 268.

[2] Homer, Hymn. Vener. 248, 286 · Homer, Iliad, v. 320, 386.

for the number of interesting, pathetic, and tragical adventures deducible from misplaced or unhappy passion was of course very great; and in most of these cases the intervention of Aphroditê was usually prefixed, with some legend to explain why she manifested herself. Her range of action grows wider in the latter epic and lyric and tragic poets than in Homer.[1]

Athênê, the man-goddess,[2] born from the head of Zeus, without a mother and without feminine sympathies, is the antithesis partly of Aphroditê, partly of the effeminate or womanised God Dionysos—the latter is an importation from Asia, but Athênê is a Greek conception—the type of composed, majestic, and unrelenting force. It appears however as if this goddess had been conceived in a different manner in different parts of Greece. For we find ascribed to her, in some of the legends, attributes of industry and home-keeping; she is represented as the companion of Hêphæstos, patronising handicraft, and expert at the loom and the spindle: the Athenian potters worshipped her along with Promêtheus. Such traits of character do not square with the formidable ægis and the massive and crushing spear which Homer and most of the mythes assign to her. There probably were at first at least two different types of Athênê, and their coalescence has partially obliterated the less marked of the two.[3]   Athênê is the constant and watchful

Athênê.

[1] A large proportion of the Hesiodic epic related to the exploits and adventures of the heroic women,—the Catalogue of Women and the Eoiai embodied a string of such narratives. Hesiod and Stesichorus explained the conduct of Helen and Klytæmnestra by the anger of Aphroditê, caused by the neglect of their father Tyndareus to sacrifice to her (Hesiod, Fragm. 59, ed. Düntzer; Stesichor. Fragm. 9, ed. Schneidewin): the irresistible ascendancy of Aphroditê is set forth in the Hippolytus of Euripidês not less forcibly than that of Dionysos in the Bacchæ. The character of Daphnis the herdsman, well-known from the first Idyll of Theocritus, and illustrating the destroying force of Aphroditê, appears to have been first introduced into Greek poetry by Stesichorus (see Klausen, Æneas und die Penaten, vol. i. pp. 526—529: compare Welcker, Kleine Schriften, part i. p. 189). Compare a striking piece among the Frag-

menta Incerta of Sophoklês (Fr. 63, Brunck) and Euripid. Troad. 946, 995, 1048. Even in the Opp. et Di. of Hesiod, Aphroditê is conceived rather as a disturbing and injurious influence (v. 65).
  Adonis owes his renown to the Alexandrine poets and their contemporary sovereigns (see Bion's Idyll and the Adoniazusæ of Theocritus). The favourites of Aphroditê, even as counted up by the diligence of Clemens Alexandrinus, are however very few in number. (Admonitio ad Gent. p. 12, Sylb.)
  [2] Ἀνδροθέα δῶρον . . . Ἀθάνᾳ Simmias Rhodius; Πέλεκυς, ap. Hephæstion. c. 9. p. 54, Gaisford.
  [3] Apollodôr. ap. Schol. ad Sophokl. Œdip. Col. 57; Pausan. i. 24, 3; ix. 26, 3: Diodôr. v. 78; Plato, Legg. ix. p. 920. In the Opp. et Di. of Hesiod, the carpenter is the servant of Athênê (429): see also Phereklos the τέκτων in the Iliad, v. 61: compare viii

protectress of Hêraklês: she is also locally identified with the
soil and people of Athens, even in the Iliad: Erechtheus, the
Athenian, is born of the earth, but Athênê brings him up,
nourishes him, and lodges him in her own temple, where the
Athenians annually worship him with sacrifice and solemnities.[1]
It was altogether impossible to make Erechtheus son of Athênê—
the type of the goddess forbade it ; but the Athenian mythe-
creators, though they found this barrier impassable, strove to
approach to it as near as they could, and the description which
they give of the birth of Erichthonios, at once un-Homeric and
unseemly, presents something like the phantom of maternity.[2]

The huntress Artemis, in Arcadia and in Greece proper,
generally exhibits a well-defined type with which the
legends respecting her are tolerably consistent. But
the Ephesian as well as the Tauric Artemis partakes more of the
Asiatic character, and has borrowed the attributes of the Lydian
Great Mother as well as an indigenous Tauric Virgin :[3] this
Ephesian Artemis passed to the colonies of Phokæa and Milêtus.[4]
The Homeric Artemis shares with her brother Apollo in the
dexterous use of the far-striking bow, and sudden death is described
by the poet as inflicted by her gentle arrow. Jealousy of the
gods at the withholding of honours and sacrifices, or at the
presumption of mortals in contending with them,—a point of
character so frequently recurring in the types of the Grecian
gods,—manifests itself in the legends of Artemis. The memorable Kalydônian boar is sent by her as a visitation upon Œneus,
because he had omitted to sacrifice to her, while he did honour to
other gods.[5] The Arcadian heroine Atalanta is however a re-

Artemis.

385 ; Odyss. viii. 493 ; and the Homeric
Hymn to Aphroditê, v. 12. The learned
article of O. Müller (in the Encyclo-
pædia of Ersch and Gruber, since re-
published among his Kleine Deutsche
Schriften, p. 134 *seq.*), *Pallas Athênê,*
brings together all that can be known
about this goddess.

[1] Iliad, ii. 546 ; viii. 362.

[2] Apollodôr. iii. 4, 6. Compare the
vague language of Plato, Kritias, c. iv.,
and Ovid, Metamorph. ii. 757.

[3] Herodot. iv. 103 ; Strabo, xii. p.
534 ; xiii. p. 650. About the Ephesian
Artemis, see Guhl, Ephesiaca (Berlin,
1843), p. 79, *seq.* ; Aristoph. Nub. 590 ;
Autokratês in Tympanistis apud Ælian.

Hist. Animal. xii. 9 ; and Spanheim ad
Callimach. Hymn. Dian. 36. The dances
in honour of Artemis sometimes appear
to have approached to the frenzied
style of Bacchanal movement. See the
words of Timotheus ap. Plutarch. de
Audiend. Poet. p. 22, c. 4, and περὶ
Δεισιδ. c. 10, p. 170, also Aristoph.
Lysist. 1314. They seem to have been
often celebrated in the solitudes of the
mountains, which were the favourite
resort of Artemis (Kallimach. Hymn.
Dian. 19), and these ὀρειβάσιαι were
always causes predisposing to fanatical
excitement.

[4] Strabo, iv. p. 179.

[5] Iliad, ix. 529.

production of Artemis, with little or no difference, and the goddess is sometimes confounded even with her attendant nymphs.

The mighty Poseidôn, the earth-shaker and the ruler of the sea, is second only to Zeus in power, but has no share in those imperial and superintending capacities which the Father of Gods and men exhibits. He numbers a numerous heroic progeny, usually men of great corporeal strength, and many of them belonging to the Æolic race. The great Neleid family of Pylus trace their origin up to him; and he is also the father of Polyphêmus the Cyclôps, whose well-earned suffering he cruelly revenges upon Odysseus. His Dêlos is the island of Kalaureia,[1] wherein there was held an old local Amphiktyony, for the purpose of rendering to him joint honour and sacrifice. The isthmus of Corinth, Helikê in Achaia, and Onchêstos in Bœotia, are also residences which he much affects, and where he is solemnly worshipped. But the abode which he originally and specially selected for himself was the Acropolis of Athens, where by a blow of his trident he produced a well of water in the rock: Athênê came afterwards and claimed the spot for herself, planting in token of possession the olive-tree which stood in the sacred grove of Pandrosos: and the decision either of the autochthonous Cecrops, or of Erechtheus, awarded to her the preference, much to the displeasure of Poseidôn. Either on this account, or on account of the death of his son Eumolpus, slain in assisting the Eleusinians against Erechtheus, the Attic mythes ascribed to Poseidôn great enmity against the Erechtheid family, which he is asserted to have ultimately overthrown: Theseus, whose glorious reign and deeds succeeded to that family, is said to have been really his son.[2] In several other places,—in Ægina, Argos and Naxos,—Poseidôn had disputed the privileges of patron-god with Zeus, Hêrê and Dionysos: he was worsted in all, but bore his defeat patiently.[3] Poseidôn endured a long slavery, in common with Apollo, gods as they were,[4] under Laomedôn, king of Troy,

Poseidôn.

---

[1] Strabo, viii. p. 374. According to the old poem called Eumolpia, ascribed to Musæus, the oracle of Delphi originally belonged to Poseidôn and Gæa, jointly: from Gæa it passed to Themis, and from her to Apollo, to whom Poseidôn also made over his share as a compensation for the surrender of Kalaureia to him. (Pausan. x. 5, 8.)

[2] Apollodôr. iii. 14, 1; iii. 15, 8, 5.
[3] Plutarch, Sympos. viii. 6, p. 741.
[4] Iliad, ii. 716, 766; Euripid. Alkestis, 2. See Panyasis, Fragm. 12, p. 24, ed. Düntzer.

at the command and condemnation of Zeus: the two gods rebuilt the walls of the city, which had been destroyed by Hêraklês. When their time was expired, the insolent Laomedôn withheld from them the stipulated reward, and even accompanied its refusal with appalling threats; and the subsequent animosity of the god against Troy was greatly determined by the sentiment of this injustice.[1]

Such periods of servitude, inflicted upon individual gods, are among the most remarkable of all the incidents in the divine legends. We find Apollo on another occasion condemned to serve Admêtus, king of Pheræ, as a punishment for having

Stories of
temporary
servitude
imposed on
gods. killed the Cyclôpes, and Hêraklês also is sold as a slave to Omphalê. Even the fierce Arês, overpowered and imprisoned for a long time by the two Alôids,[2] is ultimately liberated only by extraneous aid. Such narratives attest the discursive range of Grecian fancy in reference to the gods, as well as the perfect commingling of things and persons, divine and human, in their conceptions of the past. The god who serves is for the time degraded: but the supreme god who commands the servitude is in the like proportion exalted, whilst the idea of some sort of order and government among these superhuman beings was never lost sight of. Nevertheless the mythes respecting the servitude of the gods became obnoxious afterwards, along with many others, to severe criticism on the part of philosophers.

The proud, jealous, and bitter Hêrê,—the goddess of the once-

Hêrê. wealthy Mykênæ, the *fax et focus* of the Trojan war, and the ever-present protectress of Jasôn in the Argonautic expedition,[3]—occupies an indispensable station in the mythical world. As the daughter of Kronos and wife of Zeus, she fills a throne from whence he cannot dislodge her, and which gives her a right perpetually to grumble and to thwart him.[4] Her unmeasured jealousy of the female favourites of Zeus, and her antipathy against his sons, especially against Hêraklês, has been the suggesting cause of innumerable mythes : the general type of her character stands here clearly marked, as furnishing both stimulus and guide to the mythopœic fancy. The "Sacred

---

[1] Iliad, vii. 452; xxi. 459.
[2] Iliad, v. 886.
[3] Iliad, iv. 51; Odyss. xii. 72.
[4] Iliad, i. 544 : iv. 29—38 : viii. 408,

Wedding," or marriage of Zeus and Hêrê, was familiar to epithalamic poets long before it became a theme for the spiritualizing ingenuity of critics.

Hêphæstos is the son of Hêrê without a father, and stands in her in the same relation as Athênê to Zeus : her pride and want of sympathy are manifested by her casting him out at once in consequence of his deformity.[1]   He is the god of fire—especially of fire in its practical applications to handicraft—and is indispensable as the right-hand and instrument of the gods.   His skill and his deformity appear alternately as the source of mythical stories : wherever exquisite and effective fabrication is intended to be designated, Hêphæstos is announced as the maker, although in this function the type of his charaoter is reproduced in Dædalos.   In the Attic legends he appears intimately united both with Promêtheus and with Athênê, in conjunction with whom he was worshipped at Kolônus near Athens.   Lêmnos was the favourite residence of Hêphæstos ; and if we possessed more knowledge of this island and its town Hêphæstias, we should doubtless find abundant legends detailing his adventures and interventions.

Hêphæstos.

The chaste, still, and home-keeping Hestia, goddess of the family hearth, is far less fruitful in mythical narratives, in spite of her very superior dignity, than the knavish, smooth-tongued, keen and acquisitive Hermês.   His function of messenger of the gods brings him perpetually on the stage, and affords ample scope for portraying the features of his character.   The Homeric hymn to Hermês describes the scene and circumstances of his birth, and the almost instantaneous manifestation, even in infancy, of his peculiar attributes.   It explains the friendly footing on which he stood with Apollo,—the interchange of gifts and functions between them,—and lastly, the inviolate security of all the wealth and offerings in the Delphian temple, exposed as they were to thieves without any visible protection.   Such was the innate cleverness and talent of Hermês, that on the day he was born he invented the lyre, stringing the seven chords on the shell of a tortoise [2]—

Hestia.
Hermês.

---

[1] Iliad, xviii. 306.

[2] Homer, Hymn. Mercur. 18—

'Ηῷος γεγονὼς, μέσῳ ἤματι ἐγκιθάριζεν,
'Εσπέριος βοῦς κλέψεν ἑκηβόλου 'Απόλλωνος, &c.

and also stole the cattle of Apollo in Pieria, dragging them backwards to his cave in Arcadia, so that their track could not be detected.   To the remonstrances of his mother Maia, who points out to him the danger of offending Apollo, Hermês replies, that he aspires to rival the dignity and functions of Apollo among the immortals, and that if his father Zeus refuses to grant them to him, he will employ his powers of thieving in breaking open the sanctuary at Delphi, and in carrying away the gold and the vestments, the precious tripods and vessels.[1]   Presently Apollo discovers the loss of his cattle, and after some trouble finds his way to the Kyllênian cavern, where he sees Hermês asleep in his cradle.   The child denies the theft with effrontery, and even treats the surmise as a ridiculous impossibility : he persists in such denial even before Zeus, who however detects him at once, and compels him to reveal the place where the cattle are concealed.   But the lyre was as yet unknown to Apollo, who has heard nothing except the voice of the Muses and the sound of the pipe.   So powerfully is he fascinated by hearing the tones of the lyre from Hermês, and so eager to become possessed of it, that he is willing at once to pardon the past theft, and even to conciliate besides the friendship of Hermês.[2]   Accordingly a bargain is struck between the two gods and sanctioned by Zeus.   Hermês surrenders to Apollo the lyre, inventing for his own use the syrinx or panspipe, and receiving from Apollo in exchange the golden rod of wealth, with empire over flocks and herds as well as over horses and oxen and the wild animals of the woods.   He presses to obtain the gift of prophecy, but Apollo is under a special vow not to impart that privilege to any god whatever.   He instructs Hermês however how to draw information, to a certain extent, from the Mœræ or Fates themselves ; and assigns to him, over and above, the function of messenger of the gods to Hadês.

Hermês inventor of the lyre.

Bargain between Hermês and Apollo.

Although Apollo has acquired the lyre, the particular object of his wishes, he is still under apprehension that Hermês will steal it away from him again, together with his bow, and he exacts a formal oath by Styx as security.   Hermês promises solemnly that

[1] Homer, Hymn. Merc. 178—

Εἶμι γὰρ ἐς Πυθῶνα, μέγαν δόμον ἀντιτορήσων,

Ἔνθεν ἅλις τρίποδας περικαλλέας ἠδὲ
λέβητας
Πορθήσω καὶ χρυσόν, &c.
[2] Homer, Hymn. Merc. 442—454.

he will steal none of the acquisitions, nor ever invade the sanctuary of Apollo ; while the latter on his part pledges himself to recognise Hermês as his chosen friend and companion, amongst all the other sons of Zeus, human or divine.[1]

So came to pass, under the sanction of Zeus, the marked favour shown by Apollo to Hermês. But Hermês (concludes the hymnographer, with frankness unusual in speaking of a god) "does very little good : he avails himself of the darkness of night to cheat without measure the tribes of mortal men."[2]

Here the general types of Hermês and Apollo, coupled with the present fact that no thief ever approached the rich and seemingly accessible treasures of Delphi, engender a string of expository incidents; cast into a quasi-historical form, and detailing how it happened that Hermês had bound himself by especial convention to respect the Delphian temple. The types of Apollo seem to have been different in different times and parts of Greece : in some places he was worshipped as Apollo Nomios,[3] or the patron of pasture and cattle; and this attribute, which elsewhere passed over to his son Aristæus, is by our hymnographer voluntarily surrendered to Hermês, combined with the golden rod of fruitfulness. On the other hand, the lyre did not originally belong to the Far-striking King, nor is he at all an inventor : the hymn explains both its first invention and how it came into his possession. And the value of the incidents is thus partly expository, partly illustrative, as expanding in detail the general preconceived character of the Kyllênian god.

Expository value of the Hymn.

To Zeus more amours are ascribed than to any of the other gods,—probably because the Grecian kings and chieftains were especially anxious to trace their lineage to the highest and most glorious of all,—each of these amours

Zeus.

[1] Homer, Hymn. Merc. 507—521—

καὶ ὁ μὲν Ἑρμῆς
Λητοΐδην ἐφίλησε διαμπερὲς, ὡς ἔτι καὶ νῦν, &c.
*   *   *   *   *
Καὶ τότε Μαιάδος υἱὸς ὑποσχόμενος κατένευσε
Μή ποτ' ἀποκλέψειν, ὅσ' Ἐκηβόλος ἐκτεάτισται,
Μηδέ ποτ' ἐμπελάσειν πυκινῷ δόμῳ·
αὐτὰρ Ἀπόλλων

Λητοΐδης κατένευσεν ἐπ' ἀρθμῷ καὶ φιλότητι
Μή τινα φίλτερον ἄλλον ἐν ἀθανάτοισιν ἔσεσθαι
Μήτε θεὸν, μήτ' ἄνδρα, Διὸς γόνον, &c.

[2] Homer, Hymn. Merc. 577—

Παῦρα μὲν οὖν ὀνίνησι, τὸ δ' ἄκριτον ἠπεροπεύει
Νύκτα δι' ὀρφναίην φῦλα θνητῶν ἀνθρώπων.

[3] Kallimach. Hymn. Apoll. 47.

having its representative progeny on earth.[1] Such subjects were
among the most promising and agreeable for the interest of
mythical narrative, and Zeus as a lover thus became the father of
a great many legends, branching out into innumerable inter-
ferences, for which his sons, all of them distinguished individuals,
and many of them persecuted by Hêrê, furnished the occasion.
But besides this, the commanding functions of the Supreme God,
judicial and administrative, extending both over gods and men,
was a potent stimulus to the mythopœic activity. Zeus has to
watch over his own dignity,—the first of all considerations with
a god : moreover as Horkios, Xenios, Ktêsios, Meilichios (a small
proportion of his thousand surnames), he guaranteed oaths and
punished perjurers, he enforced the observance of hospitality, he
guarded the family hoard and the crop realized for the year, and
he granted expiation to the repentant criminal.[2] All these
different functions created a demand for mythes, as the means of
translating a dim, but serious presentiment into distinct form,
both self-explaining and communicable to others. In enforcing
the sanctity of the oath or of the tie of hospitality, the most
powerful of all arguments would be a collection of legends
respecting the judgments of Zeus, Horkios, or Xenios ; the more
impressive and terrific such legends were, the greater would be
their interest, and the less would any one dare to disbelieve them.
They constituted the natural outpourings of a strong and common
sentiment, probably without any deliberate ethical intention : the
preconceptions of the divine agency, expanded into legend, form
a product analogous to the idea of the divine features and
symmetry embodied in the bronze or the marble statue.

But it was not alone the general type and attributes of the
gods which contributed to put in action the mythopœic propensities. The rites and solemnities forming the worship of each

Mythes
arising out
of the re-
ligious
ceremonies.

god, as well as the details of his temple and its locality,
were a fertile source of mythes, respecting his exploits
and sufferings, which to the people who heard them
served the purpose of past history. The exegetes, or
local guide and interpreter, belonging to each temple, preserved
and recounted to curious strangers these traditional narratives,

---

[1] Kallimach. Hymn. Jov. 79. 'Εκ δὲ
Διὸς βασιλῆες, &c.

[2] See Herodot. i. 44. Xenoph. Anabas. vii. 8. 4. Plutarch, Thêseus, c. 12.

which lent a certain dignity even to the minutiæ of divine service. Out of a stock of materials thus ample, the poets extracted individual collections, such as the "Causes" (Αἴτια) of Kallimachus, now lost, and such as the Fasti of Ovid are for the Roman religious antiquities.[1]

It was the practice to offer to the gods in sacrifice the bones of the victim only, enclosed in fat: how did this practice arise? The author of the Hesiodic Theogony has a story which explains it: Promêtheus tricked Zeus into an imprudent choice, at the period when the gods and mortal men first came to an arrangement about privileges and duties (in Me-kônê). Promêtheus, the tutelary representative of man, divided a large steer into two portions: on the one side he placed the flesh and guts, folded up in the omentum and covered over with the skin; on the other, he put the bones enveloped in fat. He then invited Zeus to determine which of the two portions the gods would prefer to receive from mankind. Zeus "with both hands" decided for and took the white fat, but was highly incensed on finding that he had got nothing at the bottom except the bones.[2] Nevertheless the choice of the gods was now irrevocably made: they were not entitled to any portion of the sacrificed animal beyond the bones and the white fat; and the standing practice is thus plausibly explained.[3] I

Small part of the animal sacrificed.

Promêtheus had out-witted Zeus.

[1] Ovid, Fasti, iv. 211, about the festivals of Apollo:—

    "Priscique imitamina facti
Æra Deæ comites raucaque terga movent".

And Lactantius, v. 19, 15. "Ipsos ritus ex rebus gestis (deorum) vel ex casibus vel etiam ex mortibus natos:" to the same purpose Augustin. De Civ. D. vii. 18; Diodôr. iii. 56. Plutarch's Quæstiones Græcæ et Romaicæ are full of similar tales, professing to account for existing customs, many of them religious and liturgic. See Lobeck, Orphica, p. 675.

[2] Hesiod, Theog. 550:—

Φῆ ῥα δολοφρονέων· Ζεὺς δ' ἄφθιτα μήδεα
   εἰδώς
Γνῶ ῥ' οὐδ' ἠγνοίησε δόλον· κακὰ δ'
   ὄσσετο θυμῷ
Θνητοῖς ἀνθρώποισι, τὰ καὶ τελέεσθαι
   ἔμελλεν.
Χερσὶ δ' ὅγ' ἀμφοτέρῃσιν ἀνείλετο λευκὸν
   ἄλειφαρ·

Χώσατο δὲ φρένας, ἀμφὶ χόλος δέ μιν
   ἵκετο θυμὸν,
'Ὡς ἴδεν ὀστέα λευκὰ βοὸς δολίῃ ἐπὶ
   τέχνῃ.

In the second line of this citation, the poet tells us that Zeus saw through the trick, and was imposed upon by his own consent, foreknowing that after all, the mischievous consequences of the proceeding would be visited on man. But the last lines, and indeed the whole drift of the legend, imply the contrary of this: Zeus was really taken in, and was in consequence very angry. It is curious to observe how the religious feelings of the poet drive him to save in words the prescience of Zeus, though in doing so he contradicts and nullifies the whole point of the story.

[3] Hesiod. Theog. 557—

'Εκ τοῦ δ' ἀθανάτοισιν ἐπὶ χθονὶ φῦλ'
   ἀνθρώπων
Καίουσ' ὀστέα λευκὰ θυηέντων ἐπὶ βωμῶν,

select this as one amongst a thousand instances to illustrate the genesis of legend out of religious practices. In the belief of the people, the event narrated in the legend was the real producing cause of the practice : but when we come to apply a sound criticism, we are compelled to treat the event as existing only in its narrative legend, and the legend itself as having been in the greater number of cases engendered by the practice,—thus reversing the supposed order of production.

In dealing with Grecian mythes generally, it is convenient to
Gods, He-   distribute them into such as belong to the Gods and
roes, and   such as belong to the Heroes, according as the one or
Men, appear   the other are the prominent personages. The former
together in
the mythes.   class manifest, more palpably than the latter, their real
origin as growing out of the faith and the feelings, without any necessary basis, either of matter of fact or allegory : moreover, they elucidate more directly the religion of the Greeks, so important an item in their character as a people. But in point of fact, most of the mythes present to us Gods, Heroes, and Men, in juxtaposition one with the other. And the richness of Grecian mythical literature arises from the infinite diversity of combinations thus opened out ; first by the three class-types, God, Hero, and Man ; next by the strict keeping with which each separate class and character is handled. We shall now follow downward the stream of mythical time, which begins with the Gods, to the Heroic legends, or those which principally concern the Heroes and Heroines ; for the latter were to the full as important in legend as the former.

CHAPTER II.

LEGENDS RELATING TO HEROES AND MEN.

The Hesiodic theogony gives no account of anything like a creation of man, nor does it seem that such an idea was much entertained in the legendary vein of Grecian imagination ; which commonly carried back the present men by successive generations to some primitive ancestor, himself sprung from the soil, or from a neighbouring river, or mountain, or from a god, a nymph, &c. But the poet of the Hesiodic " Works and Days " has given us a narrative conceived in a very different spirit respecting the origin of the human race, more in harmony with the sober and melancholy ethical tone which reigns through that poem.[1]

Races of men as they appear in the Hesiodic "Works and Days".

First (he tells us) the Olympic gods made the golden race,— good, perfect, and happy men, who lived from the spontaneous abundance of the earth, in ease and tranquillity, like the gods themselves : they suffered neither disease nor old-age, and their death was like a gentle sleep. After death they became, by the award of Zeus, guardian terrestrial dæmons, who watch unseen over the proceedings of mankind—with the regal privilege of dispensing to them wealth, and taking account of good and bad deeds.[2]

The Golden.

---

[1] Hesiod, as cited in the Etymologicon Magnum (probably the Hesiodic Catalogue of Women, as Marktscheffel considers it, placing it Fragm. 133), gives the parentage of a certain *Brotos*, who must probably be intended as the first of men : Βρότος, ὡς μὲν Εὐήμερος ὁ Μεσσήνιος, ἀπὸ Βρότου τινὸς αὐτόχθονος· ὁ δὲ Ἡσίοδος, ἀπὸ Βρότου τοῦ Αἰθέρος καὶ Ἡμέρας.

[2] Opp. Di. 120.—

Αὐτὰρ ἐπειδὴ τοῦτο γένος κατὰ γαῖα κάλυψε,
Τοὶ μὲν δαίμονές εἰσι Διὸς μεγάλου διὰ βουλὰς
Ἐσθλοὶ, ἐπιχθόνιοι, φύλακες θνητῶν ἀνθρώπων·
Οἵ ῥα φυλάσσουσίν τε δίκας καὶ σχέτλια ἔργα,
Ἠέρα ἑσσάμενοι, πάντη φοιτῶντες ἐπ' αἶαν
Πλουτόδοται· καὶ τοῦτο γέρας βασιλήϊον ἔσχον.

Next, the gods made the silver race,—unlike and greatly inferior, both in mind and body, to the golden. The
men of this race were reckless and mischievous
towards each other, and disdainful to the immortal gods, to
whom they refused to offer either worship or sacrifice. Zeus in
his wrath buried them in the earth ; but there they still enjoy a
secondary honour, as the Blest of the under-world.[1]

The Silver.

Thirdly, Zeus made the brazen race, quite different from the
silver. They were made of hard ash-wood, pugnacious
and terrible : they were of immense strength and ada-
mantine soul, neither raising nor touching bread. Their arms,
their houses, and their implements were all of brass : there was
then no iron. This race, eternally fighting, perished by each
other's hands, died out, and descended without name or privilege
to Hadês.[2]

The Brazen.

Next, Zeus made a fourth race, far juster and better than the
last preceding. These were the Heroes or demigods,
who fought at the sieges of Troy and Thêbes. But
this splendid stock also became extinct : some perished in war,
others were removed by Zeus to a happier state in the islands of
the Blest. There they dwell in peace and comfort, under the
government of Kronos, reaping thrice in the year the spontaneous produce of the earth.[3]

The Heroic.

The fifth race, which succeeds to the Heroes, is of iron : it is
the race to which the poet himself belongs, and bitterly
does he regret it. He finds his contemporaries mischievous, dishonest, unjust, ungrateful, given to perjury, careless
both of the ties of consanguinity and of the behests of the gods :
Nemesis and Ædôs (Ethical Self-reproach) have left earth and
gone back to Olympus. How keenly does he wish that his lot
had been cast either earlier or later ![4] This iron race is doomed

The Iron.

---

[1] Opp. Di. 140.—
Αὐτὰρ ἐπεὶ καὶ τοῦτο γένος κατὰ γαῖα
κάλυψε,
Τοὶ μὲν ὑποχθόνιοι μάκαρες θνητοὶ καλέονται
Δεύτεροι, ἀλλ᾽ ἔμπης τιμὴ καὶ τοῖσιν
ὀπηδεῖ.
[2] The ash was the wood out of which
spear-handles were made (Iliad, xvi.
124): the Νύμφαι Μέλιαι are born along
with the Gigantes and the Erinnyes
(Theogon. 187).—"gensque virûm trun-

cis et duro robore nata" (Virgil, Æneid,
viii. 315),—hearts of oak.
[3] Opp. Di. 157.—
'Ανδρῶν Ἡρώων θεῖον γένος, οἳ καλέονται
'Ημίθεοι προτέρῃ γενέῃ κατ᾽ ἀπείρονα
γαῖαν.
[4] Opp. Di. 173.—
Μήκετ᾽ ἔπειτ᾽ ὤφειλον ἐγὼ πέμπτοισι
μετεῖναι
'Ανδράσιν, ἀλλ᾽ ἢ πρόσθε θανεῖν, ἢ ἔπειτα
γενέσθαι.
Νῦν γὰρ δὴ γένος ἐστὶ σιδήρεον. . . .

to continual guilt, care, and suffering, with a small infusion of good ; but the time will come when Zeus will put an end to it. The poet does not venture to predict what sort of race will succeed.

Such is the series of distinct races of men, which Hesiod, or the author of the " Works and Days," enumerates as having existed down to his own time. I give it as it stands, without placing much confidence in the various explanations which critics have offered. It stands out in more than one respect from the general tone and sentiment of Grecian legend : moreover, the sequence of races is neither natural nor homogeneous,—the heroic race not having any metallic denomination, and not occupying any legitimate place in immediate succession to the brazen. Nor is the conception of the dæmons in harmony either with Homer or with the Hesiodic theogony. In Homer, there is scarcely any distinction between gods and dæmons : farther, the gods are stated to go about and visit the cities of men in various disguises for the purpose of inspecting good and evil proceedings.[1] But in the poem now before us, the distinction between gods and dæmons is generic. The latter are invisible tenants of earth, remnants of the once happy golden race whom the Olympic gods first made : the remnants of the second or silver race are not dæmons, nor are they tenants of earth, but they still enjoy an honourable posthumous existence as the Blest of the under-world. Nevertheless the Hesiodic dæmons are in no way authors or abettors of evil : on the contrary, they form the unseen police of the gods, for the purpose of repressing wicked behaviour in the world.

Different both from the Theogony and from Homer.

We may trace, I think, in this quintuple succession of earthly races, set forth by the author of the " Works and Days," the confluence of two veins of sentiment, not consistent one with the other, yet both co-existing in the author's mind. The drift of his poem is thoroughly didactic and ethical. Though deeply penetrated with the injustice and suffering which darken the face of human life, he nevertheless strives to maintain both in himself and in others, a conviction that on the whole the just and laborious man will come off well,[2] and he

Explanation of this difference.

---

[1] Odyss. xvii. 486.
[2] There are some lines in which he appears to believe that, under the present wicked and treacherous rulers,

enforces in considerable detail the lessons of practical prudence and virtue. This ethical sentiment, which dictates his appreciation of the present, also guides his imagination as to the past. It is pleasing to him to bridge over the chasm between the

Ethical vein of sentiment. gods and degenerate man, by the supposition of previous races,—the first altogether pure, the second worse than the first, and the third still worse than the second ; and to show further how the first race passed by gentle death-sleep into glorious immortality ; how the second race was sufficiently wicked to drive Zeus to bury them in the underworld, yet still leaving them a certain measure of honour ; while the third was so desperately violent as to perish by its own animosities, without either name or honour of any kind. The conception of the golden race passing after death into good guardian dæmons, which some suppose to have been derived from a comparison with oriental angels, presents itself to the poet partly as approximating this race to the gods, partly as a means of constituting a triple gradation of post-obituary existence, proportioned to the character of each race whilst alive. The denominations of gold and silver, given to the two first races, justify themselves, like those given by Simonidês of Amorgos and by Phokylidês to the different characters of women, derived from the dog, the bee, the mare, the ass, and other animals ; and the epithet of brazen is specially explained by reference to the material which the pugnacious third race so plentifully employed for their arms and other implements.

So far we trace intelligibly enough the moralising vein : we **Intersected by the mythical.** find the revolutions of the past so arranged as to serve partly as an ethical lesson, partly as a suitable preface to the present.[1] But fourth in the list comes "the

---

it is not the interest of any man to be just (Opp. Di. 270) :—

Νῦν δὴ ἐγὼ μήτ' αὐτὸς ἐν ἀνθρώποισι δίκαιος
Εἴην, μήτ' ἐμὸς υἱός· ἐπεὶ κακόν ἐστι δίκαιον
Ἔμμεναι, εἰ μείζω γε δίκην ἀδικώτερος ἕξει·
Ἀλλὰ τόδ' οὔπω ἔολπα τελεῖν Δία τερπικέραυνον.

On the whole, however, his conviction is to the contrary.

Plutarch rejects the above four lines, seemingly on no other ground than because he thought them immoral and unworthy of Hesiod (see Proclus ad loc.). But they fall in perfectly with the temper of the poem ; and the rule of Plutarch is inadmissible, in determining the critical question of what is genuine or spurious.
[1] Aratus (Phænomen. 107) gives only three successive races,—the golden, silver, and brazen : Ovid superadds to these the iron race (Metamorph. i. 89—

divine race of Heroes"; and here a new vein of thought is opened
by the poet. The symmetry of his ethical past is broken up, in
order to make way for these cherished beings of the national faith.
For though the author of the "Works and Days" was himself of
a didactic cast of thought, like Phokylidês, or Solôn, or Theognis,
yet he had present to his feelings, in common with his countrymen, the picture of Grecian foretime, as it was set forth in the
current mythes, and still more in Homer and those other epical
productions which were then the only existing literature and history. It was impossible for him to exclude, from his sketch
of the past, either the great persons or the glorious exploits which
these poems ennobled ; and even if he himself could have consented to such an exclusion, the sketch would have become repulsive to his hearers. But the chiefs who figured before Thêbes
and Troy could not be well identified either with the golden,
the silver, or the brazen race : moreover, it was essential that they
should be placed in immediate contiguity with the present race,
because their descendants, real or supposed, were the most prominent and conspicuous of existing men. Hence the poet is
obliged to assign to them the fourth place in the series, and to
interrupt the descending ethical movement in order to interpolate
them between the brazen and the iron race, with neither of which
they present any analogy. The iron race, to which the poet himself unhappily belongs, is the legitimate successor, not of the
heroic, but of the brazen. Instead of the fierce and self-annihi-
lating pugnacity which characterises the latter, the iron race
manifests an aggregate of smaller and meaner vices and mischiefs.
It will not perish by suicidal extinction—but it is growing worse
and worse, and is gradually losing its vigour, so that Zeus will
not vouchsafe to preserve much longer such a race upon the
earth.

I conceive that the series of races imagined by the poet of the
"Works and Days" is the product of two distinct and incon-

144); neither of them notice the heroic
race.

The observations both of Buttmann
(Mythos der ältesten Menschengesch-
lechter, t. ii. p. 12 of the Mythologus)
and of Völcker (Mythologie des Jape-
tischen Geschlechts, § 6, pp. 250—279)
on this series of distinct races are ingenious and may be read with profit.

Both recognise the disparate character
of the fourth link in the series, and
each accounts for it in a different manner. My own view comes nearer to
that of Völcker, with some considerable differences; amongst which one
is, that he rejects the verses respecting
the dæmons, which seem to me capital
parts of the whole scheme.

grucus veins of imagination,—the didactic or ethical blending

The "Works and Days," earliest didactic poem.

with the primitive mythical or epical. His poem is remarkable as the most ancient didactic production of the Greeks, and as one of the first symptoms of a new tone of sentiment finding its way into their literature, never afterwards to become extinct. The tendency of the "Works and Days" is antiheroic : far from seeking to inspire admiration for adventurous enterprise, the author inculcates the strictest justice, the most unremitting labour and frugality, and a sober, not to say anxious, estimate of all the minute specialties of the future. Prudence and probity are his means,—practical comfort and happiness his end. But he deeply feels, and keenly exposes, the manifold wickedness and shortcomings of his contemporaries, in reference to this capital standard. He turns with displeasure from the present men, not because they are too feeble to hurl either the spear of Achilles or some vast boundary-stone, but because they are rapacious, knavish, and unprincipled.

The dæmons first introduced into the religious atmosphere of

First intro- duction of dæmons.

the Grecian world by the author of the "Works and Days"—as generically different from the gods, but essentially good, and forming the intermediate agents and police between gods and men,—are deserving of attention. They are the seed of a doctrine which afterwards underwent many changes, and became of great importance, first as one of the constituent elements of pagan faith, then as one of the helps to its subversion. It will be recollected that the buried remnants of the half-wicked silver race, though they are not recognised as dæmons, are still considered as having a substantive existence, a name, and dignity, in the under-world. The step was easy, to treat them as dæmons also, but as dæmons of a defective and malignant character: this step was made by Empedoclês and Xenocratês, and to a certain extent countenanced by Plato.[1] There

Changes in the idea of dæmons.

came thus to be admitted among the pagan philosophers dæmons both good and bad, in every degree: and these dæmons were found available as a means of explaining many phænomena for which it was not convenient to admit the agency of the gods. They served to relieve the gods

---

[1] See this subject further mentioned—*infra*, chap. xvi.

from the odium of physical and moral evils, as well as from the necessity of constantly meddling in small affairs. The objectionable ceremonies of the pagan religion were defended upon the ground that in no other way could the exigencies of such malignant beings be appeased. The dæmons were most frequently noticed as causes of evil, and thus the name came insensibly to convey with it a bad sense,—the idea of an evil being as contrasted with the goodness of a god. So it was found by the Christian writers when they commenced their controversy with paganism. One branch of their argument led them to identify the pagan gods with dæmons in the evil sense, and the insensible change in the received meaning of the word lent them a specious _Employed_ assistance. For they could easily show, that not only _in attacks on the_ in Homer, but in the general language of early pagans, _pagan faith_ all the gods generally were spoken of as dæmons—and therefore, verbally speaking, Clemens and Tatian seemed to affirm nothing more against Zeus or Apollo than was involved in the language of paganism itself. Yet the audience of Homer or Sophoklês would have strenuously repudiated the proposition, if it had been put to them in the sense which the word *dæmon* bore in the age and among the circle of these Christian writers.

In the imagination of the author of the "Works and Days," the dæmons occupy an important place, and are re- _Functions_ garded as being of serious practical efficiency. When _of the Hesiodic_ he is remonstrating with the rulers around him upon _dæmons._ their gross injustice and corruption, he reminds them of the vast number of these immortal servants of Zeus who are perpetually on guard amidst mankind, and through whom the visitations of the gods will descend even upon the most potent evil-doers.[1] His supposition that the dæmons were not gods, but departed men of the golden race, allowed him to multiply their number indefinitely, without too much cheapening the divine dignity.

As this poet, enslaved by the current legends, has introduced the heroic race into a series to which they do not legitimately belong—so he has under the same influence inserted in another part of his poem the mythe of Pandôra and Promêtheus,[2] as a means of explaining the primary diffusion, and actual abundance,

---

[1] Opp. Di. 252. Τρὶς γὰρ μύριοί εἰσιν ἐπὶ χθονὶ πουλυβοτείρῃ, &c.   [2] Opp. Di. 50—105.

of evil among mankind. Yet this mythe can in no way consist
with his quintuple scale of distinct races, and is in fact a totally
distinct theory to explain the same problem,—the transition of
mankind from a supposed state of antecedent happiness to one of
present toil and suffering. Such an inconsistency is not a sufficient reason for questioning the genuineness of either passage;
for the two stories, though one contradicts the other, both

Personal
feeling
which
pervades·
the "Works
and Days".

harmonise with that central purpose which governs
the author's mind,—a querulous and didactic appreciation of the present. That such was his purpose appears not only from the whole tenor of his poem, but
also from the remarkable fact that his own personality,
his own adventures and kindred, and his own sufferings figure in
it conspicuously. And this introduction of self imparts to it a
peculiar interest. The father of Hesiod came over from the
Æolic Kymê, with the view of bettering his condition, and
settled at Askra in Bœotia, at the foot of Mount Helicon. After
his death his two sons divided the family inheritance: but Hesiod
bitterly complains that his brother Persês cheated and went to
law with him, and obtained through corrupt judges an unjust
decision. He farther reproaches his brother with a preference
for the suits and unprofitable bustle of the agora, at a time when
he ought to be labouring for his subsistence in the field. Askra
indeed was a miserable place, repulsive both in summer and
winter. Hesiod had never crossed the sea, except once from
Aulis to Eubœa, whither he went to attend the funeral-games of
Amphidamas, the chief of Chalkis: he sung a hymn, and gained
as prize a tripod, which he consecrated to the muses in Helicon.[1]

These particulars, scanty as they are, possess a peculiar value,
as the earliest authentic memorandum respecting the doing or
suffering of any actual Greek person. There is no external
testimony at all worthy of trust respecting the age of the "Works
and Days": Herodotus treats Hesiod and Homer as belonging
to the same age, four hundred years before his own time; and

Probable
age of the
poem.

there are other statements besides, some placing Hesiod
at an earlier date than Homer, some at a later. Looking at the internal evidences, we may observe that the
pervading sentiment, tone, and purpose of the poem is widely

[1] Opp. Di. 630—650. 27—45.

different from that of the Iliad and Odyssey, and analogous to what we read respecting the compositions of Archilochus and the Amorgian Simonidês. The author of the "Works and Days" is indeed a preacher and not a satirist: but with this distinction, we find in him the same predominance of the present and the positive, the same disposition to turn the muse into an exponent of his own personal wrongs, the same employment of Æsopic fable by way of illustration, and the same unfavourable estimate of the female sex,[1] all of which may be traced in the two poets above-mentioned, placing both of them in contrast with the Homeric epic. Such an internal analogy, in the absence of good testimony, is the best guide which we can follow in determining the date of the "Works and Days," which we should accordingly place shortly after the year 700 B.C. The style of the poem might indeed afford a proof that the ancient and uniform hexameter, though well adapted to continuous legendary narrative or to solemn hymns, was somewhat monotonous when called upon either to serve a polemical purpose or to impress a striking moral lesson. When poets, then the only existing composers, first began to apply their thoughts to the cut and thrust of actual life, aggressive or didactic, the verse would be seen to require a new, livelier, and smarter metre; and out of this want grew the elegiac and the iambic verse, both seemingly contemporaneous, and both intended to supplant the primitive hexameter for the short effusions then coming into vogue.

[1] Compare the fable (αἶνος) in the "Works and Days," v. 200, with those in Archilochus, Fr. xxxviii. and xxxix., Gaisford, respecting the fox and the ape; and the legend of Pandôra (v. 95 and v. 705) with the fragment of Simonidês of Amorgos respecting women (Fr. viii. ed. Welcker, v. 95—115); also Phokylidês ap. Stobæum, Florileg. lxxi.

Isokratês assimilates the character of the "Works and Days" to that of Theognis and Phokylidês (ad Nicocl. Or. ii. p. 2ɔ).

CHAPTER III.

LEGEND OF THE IAPETIDS.

THE sons of the Titan god Iapetus, as described in the Hesiodic theogony, are Atlas, Menœtius, Promêtheus, and Epimêtheus.[1] Of these, Atlas alone is mentioned by Homer in the Odyssey, and even he not as the son of Iapetus: the latter himself is named in the Iliad as existing in Tartarus along with Kronos. The Homeric Atlas "knows the depths of the whole sea, and keeps by himself those tall pillars which hold the heaven apart from the earth ".[2]

As the Homeric theogony generally appears much expanded in
Iapetids in   Hesiod, so also does the family of Iapetus, with their
Hesiod.   varied adventures. Atlas is here described, not as the
keeper of the intermediate pillars between heaven and earth, but as himself condemned by Zeus to support the heaven on his head and hands;[3] while the fierce Menœtius is pushed down to Erebus as a punishment for his ungovernable insolence. But the remaining two brothers, Promêtheus and Epimêtheus, are among the most interesting creations of Grecian legend, and distinguished in more than one respect from all the remainder.

First, the main battle between Zeus and the Titan gods is a
Promêtheus   contest of force purely and simply—mountains are
and Epi-   hurled and thunder is launched, and the victory re-
mêtheus.   mains to the strongest. But the competition between

---

[1] Hesiod. Theog. 510.
[2] Hom. Odyss. I. 52.—

Ἄτλαντος θυγάτηρ ὀλοόφρονος, ὅστε θαλάσσης
Πάσης βένθεα οἶδεν, ἔχει δέ τε κίονας
αὐτὸς
Μακρὰς, αἳ γαῖάν τε καὶ οὐρανὸν ἀμφὶς
ἔχουσιν.

[3] Hesiod. Theog. 516—

Ἄτλας δ' οὐρανὸν εὐρὺν ἔχει κρατερῆς
ὑπ' ἀνάγκης
Ἑστηὼς, κεφαλῇ τε καὶ ἀκαμάτοισι
χέρεσσι.

Hesiod stretches far beyond the simplicity of the Homeric conception.

Zeus and Promêtheus is one of craft and stratagem : the victory does indeed remain to the former, but the honours of the fight belong to the latter. Secondly, Promêtheus and Epimêtheus (the fore-thinker and the after-thinker [1]) are characters stamped at the same mint, and by the same effort, the express contrast and antithesis of each other. Thirdly, mankind are here expressly brought forward, not indeed as active partners in the struggle, but as the grand and capital subjects interested,—as gainers or sufferers by the result. Promêtheus appears in the exalted character of champion of the human race, even against the formidable superiority of Zeus.

In the primitive or Hesiodic legend, Promêtheus is not the creator or moulder of man; it is only the later additions which invest him with this character.[2] The race are supposed as existing, and Promêtheus, a member of the dispossessed body of Titan gods, comes forward as their representative and defender. The advantageous bargain which he made with Zeus on their behalf, in respect to the partition of the sacrificial animals, has been recounted in a preceding chapter. Zeus felt that he had been outwitted, and was exceeding wroth. In his displeasure he withheld from mankind the inestimable comfort of fire, so that the race would have perished, had not Promêtheus stolen fire, in defiance of the Supreme Ruler, and brought it to men in the hollow stem of the plant called giant-fennel.[3]

Counter-manœuvring of Promêtheus and Zeus.

Zeus was now doubly indignant, and determined to play off a still more ruinous stratagem. Hêphæstos, by his direction, moulded the form of a beautiful virgin ; Athênê dressed her, Aphroditê and the Charites bestowed upon her both ornament and fascination, while Hermês infused into her the mind of a dog, a deceitful spirit, and treacherous words.[4] The messenger

---

[1] Pindar extends the family of Epimêtheus and gives him a daughter, Πρόφασις (Pyth. v. 25), *Excuse*, the offspring of After-thought.

[2] Apollodôr. i. 7, 1. Nor is he such either in Æschylus, or in the Platonic fable (Protag. c. 30), though this version became at last the most popular. Some hardened lumps of clay, remnants of that which had been employed by Promêtheus in moulding man, were shown to Pausanias at Panopeus in Phokis (Paus. x. 4, 3).

The first Epigram of Erinna (Anthol. i. p. 58, ed. Brunck) seems to allude to Promêtheus as moulder of man. The expression of Aristophanês (Aves, 689) —πλάσματα πηλοῦ—does not necessarily refer to Promêtheus.

[3] Hesiod. Theog. 566 ; Opp. Di. 52.

[4] Theog. 580 ; Opp. Di. 50—85.

of the gods conducted this "fascinating mischief" to mankind, at a time when Prometheus was not present. Now Epimetheus had received from his brother peremptory injunctions not to accept

Pandôra. from the hands of Zeus any present whatever ; but the beauty of Pandôra (so the newly-formed female was called) was not to be resisted. She was received and admitted among men, and from that moment their comfort and tranquillity was exchanged for suffering of every kind.[1] The evils to which mankind are liable had been before enclosed in a cask in their own keeping; Pandôra in her malice removed the lid of the cask, and out flew these thousand evils and calamities, to exercise for ever their destroying force. Hope alone remained imprisoned, and therefore without efficacy, as before—the inviolable lid being replaced before she could escape. Before this incident (says the legend) men had lived without disease or suffering; but now both earth and sea are full of mischiefs. Maladies of every description stalk abroad by day as well as by night,[2] without any hope for man of relief to come.

The Theogony gives the legend here recounted, with some

Pandôra in the Theogony. variations—leaving out the part of Epimetheus altogether, as well as the cask of evils. Pandôra is the ruin of man, simply as the mother and representative of the female sex.[3] And the variations are thus useful, as they enable us to distinguish the essential from the accessory circumstances of the story.

---

[1] Opp. Di. 81—90.

[2] Opp. Di. 93. Pandôra does not bring with her the cask, as the common version of this story would have us suppose : the cask exists fast closed in the custody of Epimetheus, or of man himself, and Pandôra commits the fatal treachery of removing the lid. The case is analogous to that of the closed bag of unfavourable winds which Æolus gives into the hands of Odysseus, and which the guilty companions of the latter force open, to the entire ruin of his hopes (Odyss. x. 19—50). The idea of the two casks on the threshold of Zeus, lying ready for dispensation—one full of evils, the other of benefits—is Homeric (Iliad, xxiv. 527) :—

Δοίοι γάρ τε πίθοι κατακείαται ἐν Διὸς οὔδει, &c.

Plutarch assimilates to this the πίθος

opened by Pandôra, Consolat. ad Apollon. c. 7, p. 105. The explanation here given of the Hesiodic passage relating to Hope is drawn from an able article in the Wiener Jahrbücher, vol. 109 (1845), p. 220, by Ritter; a review of Schömann's translation of the Prometheus of Æschylus. The diseases and evils are inoperative so long as they remain shut up in the cask ; the same mischief-making influence which lets them out to their calamitous work, takes care that Hope shall still continue a powerless prisoner in the inside.

[3] Theog. 590.—

Ἐκ τῆς γὰρ γένος ἐστὶ γυναικῶν θηλυτεράων,

Τῆς γὰρ ὀλοΐόν ἐστι γένος · καὶ φῦλα γυναικῶν

Πῆμα μέγα θνητοῖσι μετ' ἀνδράσι ναιετάουσι, &c.

" Thus (says the poet, at the conclusion of his narrative) it is not possible to escape from the purposes of Zeus."[1] His mythe, connecting the calamitous condition of man with the malevolence of the supreme god, shows, first, by what cause such an unfriendly feeling was raised ; next, by what instrumentality its deadly results were brought about. The human race are not indeed the creation, but the protected flock of Promêtheus, one of the elder or dispossessed Titan gods. When Zeus acquires supremacy, mankind along with the rest become subject to him, and are to make the best bargain they can, respecting worship and service to be yielded. By the stratagem of their advocate Promêtheus, Zeus is cheated into such a partition of the victims as is eminently unprofitable to him ; whereby his wrath is so provoked, that he tries to subtract from man the use of fire. Here, however, his scheme is frustrated by the theft of Promêtheus : but his second attempt is more successful, and he in his turn cheats the unthinking Epimêtheus into the acceptance of a present (in spite of the peremptory interdict of Promêtheus) by which the whole of man's happiness is wrecked. This legend grows out of two feelings; partly as to the relations of the gods with man, partly as to the relation of the female sex with the male. The present gods are unkind towards man, but the old gods, with whom man's lot was originally cast, were much kinder—and the ablest among them stands forward as the indefatigable protector of the race. Nevertheless, the mere excess of his craft proves the ultimate ruin of the cause which he espouses. He cheats Zeus out of a fair share of the sacrificial victim, so as both to provoke and justify a retaliation which he cannot be always at hand to ward off ; the retaliation is, in his absence, consummated by a snare laid for Epimêtheus and voluntarily accepted. And thus, though Hesiod ascribes the calamitous condition of man to the malevolence of Zeus, his piety suggests two exculpatory pleas for the latter; mankind have been the first to defraud Zeus of his legitimate share of the sacrifice—and they have moreover been consenting parties to their own ruin. Such are the feelings, as to the relation between the gods and man, which have been

General feeling of the poet.

Man wretched, but Zeus not to blame.

---

[1] Opp. Di. 105.—Οὕτως οὔτι πῆ ἐστι Διὸς νόον ἐξαλέασθαι.

one of the generating elements of this legend.   The other element,

Mischiefs arising from women.   a conviction of the vast mischief arising to man from women, whom yet they cannot dispense with, is frequently and strongly set forth in several of the Greek poets—by Simonidês of Amorgos and Phokylidês, not less than by Euripidês.

But the miseries arising from woman, however great they might be, did not reach Promêtheus himself.   For him, the rash champion who had ventured "to compete in sagacity"[1] with Zeus, a different punishment was in store.   Bound by heavy chains to a pillar, he remained fast imprisoned for several

Punishment of Promêtheus.   generations : every day did an eagle prey upon his liver, and every night did the liver grow afresh for the next day's suffering.   At length Zeus, eager to enhance the glory of his favourite son, Hêraklês, permitted the latter to kill the eagle and rescue the captive.[2]

Such is the Promêthean mythe as it stands in the Hesiodic poems ; its earliest form, as far as we can trace.   Upon it was founded the sublime tragedy of Æschylus, "The Enchained Promêtheus," together with at least one more tragedy, now lost, by the same author.[3]   Æschylus has made several important alterations ; describing the human race, not as having once enjoyed and subsequently lost a state of tranquillity and enjoyment, but as originally feeble and wretched.   He suppresses both the first trick played off by Promêtheus upon Zeus respecting the partition of the victim—and the final formation and sending of Pandôra—which are the two most marked portions of the Hesi-

The Promêtheus of Æschylus.   odic story ; while on the other hand he brings out prominently and enlarges upon the theft of fire,[4] which in Hesiod is but slightly touched.   If he has thus relinquished the antique simplicity of the story, he has rendered more than ample compensation by imparting to it a grandeur of *idéal*, a large reach of thought combined with appeals to our

---

[1] Theog. 534. Οὕνεκ' ἐρίζετο βουλὰς ὑπερμενέϊ Κρονίωνι.
[2] Theog. 521—532.
[3] Of the tragedy called Προμηθεὺς Λυόμενος some few fragments yet remain : Προμηθεὺς Πύρφορος was a satyric drama, according to Dindorf : Welcker recognises a third tragedy, Προμηθεὺς Πύρφορος, and a satyric drama, Προμηθεὺς Πυρκαεύς (Die Griechischen Tragödien, vol. 1, p. 30). The story of Promêtheus had also been handled by Sappho in one of her lost songs (Servius ad Virgil. Eclog. vi. 42).
[4] Apollodôrus too mentions only the theft of fire (i. 7, 1).

earnest and admiring sympathy, and a pregnancy of suggestion
in regard to the relations between the gods and man, which soar
far above the Hesiodic level, and which render his tragedy the
most impressive, though not the most artistically composed, of
all Grecian dramatic productions.   Promêtheus there appears not
only as the heroic champion and sufferer in the cause and for the
protection of the human race, but also as the gifted teacher of all
the arts, helps, and ornaments of life, amongst which fire is only
one : [1] all this against the will and in defiance of the purpose of
Zeus, who, on acquiring his empire, wished to destroy the human
race and to beget some new breed.[2]   Moreover, new relations
between Promêtheus and Zeus are superadded by Æschylus.   At
the commencement of the struggle between Zeus and the Titan
gods, Promêtheus had vainly attempted to prevail upon the latter
to conduct it with prudence ; but when he found that they
obstinately declined all wise counsel, and that their ruin was inevitable, he abandoned their cause and joined Zeus.   To him and
to his advice Zeus owed the victory ; yet the monstrous ingrati-
tude and tyranny of the latter is now manifested by nailing him
to a rock, for no other crime than because he frustrated the purpose of extinguishing the human race, and furnished to them the
means of living with tolerable comfort.[3]   The new ruler Zeus,
insolent with his victory over the old gods, tramples down all
right, and sets at naught sympathy and obligation, as well
towards gods as towards man.   Yet the prophetic Promêtheus,
in the midst of intense suffering, is consoled by the foreknowledge
that the time will come when Zeus must again send for him,
release him, and invoke his aid, as the sole means of averting from
nimself dangers otherwise insurmountable.   The security and
means of continuance for mankind have now been placed beyond
the reach of Zeus—whom Promêtheus proudly defies, glorying in
his generous and successful championship,[4] despite the terrible
price which he is doomed to pay for it.

As the Æschylean Promêtheus, though retaining the old linea-

---

[1] Æsch. Prom. 442—506.—

Πᾶσαι τέχναι βροτοῖσιν ἐκ Προμη-
θέως.

[2] Æsch. Prom. 231.—

Βροτῶν δὲ τῶν ταλαιπώρων λόγον

Οὐκ ἔσχεν οὐδέν᾽, ἀλλ᾽ ἀϊστώσας
γένος
Τὸ πᾶν, ἔχρῃζεν ἄλλο φιτῦσαι νέον
[3] Æsch. Prom. 198—222. 123.—
διὰ τὴν λίαν φιλότητα βροτῶν.
[4] Æsch. Prom. 169—770.

ments, has acquired a new colouring, soul, and character, so he
has also become identified with a special locality.
Locality in which Promêtheus was confined. In Hesiod there is no indication of the place in which he is imprisoned ; but Æschylus places it in Scythia,[1] and the general belief of the Greeks supposed it to be on Mount Caucasus. So long and so firmly did this belief continue, that the Roman general Pompey, when in command of an army in Kolchis, made with his companion, the literary Greek Theophanês, a special march to view the spot in Caucasus where Promêtheus had been transfixed.[2]

---

[1] Prometh. 2. See also the Fragments of the Promêtheus Solutus, 177-179, ed. Dindorf, where Caucasus is specially named; but v. 719 of the Promêtheus Vinctus seems to imply that Mount Caucasus is a place different from that to which the suffering prisoner is chained.

[2] Appian, Bell. Mithridat. c. 103.

CHAPTER IV.

HEROIC LEGENDS.—GENEALOGY OF ARGOS.

HAVING briefly enumerated the gods of Greece, with their chief attributes as described in legend, we come to those genealogies which connected them with historical men.

In the retrospective faith of a Greek, the ideas of worship and ancestry coalesced. Every association of men, large or small, in whom there existed a feeling of present union, traced back that union to some common initial progenitor; that progenitor being either the common god whom they worshipped, or some semi-divine person closely allied to him. What the feelings of the community require is, a continuous pedigree to connect them with this respected source of existence, beyond which they do not think of looking back. A series of names, placed in filiation or fraternity, together with a certain number of family or personal adventures ascribed to some of the individuals among them, constitute the ante-historical past through which the Greek looks back to his gods. The names of this genealogy are, to a great degree, gentile or local names familiar to the people,—rivers, mountains, springs, lakes, villages, demes, &c.,—embodied as persons, and introduced as acting or suffering. They are moreover called kings or chiefs, but the existence of a body of subjects surrounding them is tacitly implied rather than distinctly set forth; for their own personal exploits or family proceedings constitute for the most part the whole matter of narrative. And thus the genealogy was made to satisfy at once the appetite of the Greeks for romantic adventure, and their demand for an unbroken line of filiation between themselves and the gods. The eponymous personage, from whom the community derive their name, is sometimes the begotten son of the local god,

Structure and purposes of Grecian genealogies.

To connect the Grecian community with their common god.

sometimes an indigenous man sprung from the earth, which is indeed itself divinized.

It will be seen from the mere description of these genealogies that they included elements human and historical, as well as elements divine and extra-historical. And if we could determine the time at which any genealogy was first framed, we should be able to assure ourselves that the men then represented as

Lower members of the genealogy historical— higher members non- historical. present, together with their fathers and grandfathers, were real persons of flesh and blood. But this is a point which can seldom be ascertained; moreover, even if it could be ascertained, we must at once set it aside, if we wish to look at the genealogy in the point of

view of the Grecks. For to them, not only all the members were alike real, but the gods and heroes at the commencement were in a

The non- historical portion equally be- lieved, and most valued, by the Greeks. certain sense the most real; at least, they were the most esteemed and indispensable of all. The value of the genealogy consisted, not in its length, but in its continuity; not (according to the feeling of modern aristocracy) in the power of setting out a prolonged series of human fathers and grandfathers, but in the

sense of ancestral union with the primitive god. And the length of the series is traceable rather to humility, inasmuch as the same person who was gratified with the belief that he was descended from a god in the fifteenth generation, would have accounted it criminal insolence to affirm that a god was his father or grand- father. In presenting to the reader those genealogies which constitute the supposed primitive history of Hellas, I make no pretence to distinguish names real and historical from fictitious creations; partly because I have no evidence upon which to draw the line, and partly because by attempting it I should altogether depart from the genuine Grecian point of view.

Nor is it possible to do more than exhibit a certain selection of

Number of such gene- alogies— pervading every fraction of Greeks. such as were most current and interesting; for the total number of them which found place in Grecian faith exceeds computation. As a general rule, every deme, every gens, every aggregate of men accustomed to combined action, religious or political, had its own.

The small and unimportant demes into which Attica was divided had each its ancestral god and heroes, just as much as the great

Athens herself. Even among the villages of Phokis, which Pausanias will hardly permit himself to call towns, deductions of legendary antiquity were not wanting. And it is important to bear in mind, when we are reading the legendary genealogies of Argos, or Sparta, or Thêbes, that these are merely samples amidst an extensive class, all perfectly analogous, and all exhibiting the religious and patriotic retrospect of some fraction of the Hellenic world. They are no more matter of historical tradition than any of the thousand other legendary genealogies which men delighted to recall to memory at the periodical festivals of their gens, their deme, or their village.

With these few prefatory remarks, I proceed to notice the most conspicuous of the Grecian heroic pedigrees, and first, that of Argos.

The earliest name in Argeian antiquity is that of Inachus, the son of Oceanus and Têthys, who gave his name to the river flowing under the walls of the town. According to the chronological computations of those who regarded the mythical genealogies as substantive history, and who allotted a given number of years to each generation, the reign of Inachus was placed 1986 B.C., or about 1100 years prior to the commencement of the recorded Olympiads.[1] Argeian genealogy —Inachus.

The sons of Inachus were Phorôneus and Ægialeus; both of whom however were sometimes represented as autochthonous or indigenous men, the one in the territory of Argos, the other in that of Sikyôn. Ægialeus gave his name to the north-western region of the Peloponnêsus, on the southern coast of the Corinthian Gulf.[2] The name of Phorôneus was of great celebrity in the Argeian mythical genealogies, and furnished both the title and the subject of the ancient poem called Phorônis, in which he is styled "the father of mortal men".[3] He is said to have imparted to mankind, who had before him lived altogether isolated, the first notion and habits of social existence, and even Phorôneus.

---

[1] Apollodôr. ii. 1. Mr. Fynes Clinton does not admit the historical reality of Inachus; but he places Phorôneus seventeen generations, or 570 years prior to the Trojan war, 978 years earlier than the first recorded Olympiad. See Fasti Hellenici, vol. iii. c. i. p. 19.

[2] Pausan. ii. 5, 4.

[3] See Düntzer, Fragm. Epic. Græc. p. 57. The Argeian author Akusilaus, treated Phorôneus as the first of men, Fragm. 14. Didot. ap. Clem. Alex. Stromat. i. p. 321. Φορωνῆες, a synonym for Argeians: Theocrit. Idyll. xxv. 200.

the first knowledge of fire : his dominion extended over the whole Peloponnêsus. His tomb at Argos, and seemingly also the place, called the Phorônic city, in which he formed the first settlement of mankind, were still shown in the days of Pausanias.[1] The offspring of Phorôneus, by the nymph Teledikê, were Apis and Niobê. Apis, a harsh ruler, was put to death by Thelxiôn and Telchin, having given to Peloponnêsus the name of Apia : he was succeeded by Argos, the son of his sister Niobê by the god Zeus. From this sovereign Peloponnêsus was denominated Argos. By his wife Evadnê, daughter of Strymôn,[2] he had four sons, Ekbasus, Peiras, Epidaurus, and Kriasus. Ekbasus was succeeded by his son Agênôr, and he again by his son Argos Panoptês,

Argos Panoptês.

—a very powerful prince, who is said to have had eyes distributed over all his body, and to have liberated Peloponnêsus from several monsters and wild animals which infested it :[3] Akusilaus and Æschylus make this Argos an earthborn person, while Pherekydês reports him as son of Arestôr. Iasus was the son of Argos Panoptês by Ismênê, daughter of Asôpus. According to the authors whom Apollodôrus and Pausanias prefer, the celebrated Iô was his daughter : but the Hesiodic epic (as well as Akusilaus) represented her as daughter of

Iô.

Peiras, while Æschylus and Kastor the chronologist affirmed the primitive king Inachus to have·been her father.[4] A favourite theme, as well for the ancient genealogical poets as for the Attic tragedians, were the adventures of Iô ; of whom, while priestess of Hêrê, at the ancient and renowned Hêræon between Mykênæ and Tiryns, Zeus became amorous. When Hêrê discovered the intrigue and taxed him with it, he denied the charge, and metamorphosed Iô into a white cow. Hêrê, requiring that the cow should be surrendered to her, placed her under the keeping of Argos Panoptês ; but this guardian was slain by Hermês, at the command of Zeus ; and Hêrê then drove the cow Iô away

---

[1] Apollodôr. ii. 1, 1 ; Pausan. ii. 15, 5 ; 19, 5 ; 20, 3.

[2] Apollod. l. c. The mention of Strymôn seems connected with Æschylus, Suppl. 255.

[3] Akusil. Fragm. 17, ed. Didot ; Æsch. Prometh. 568 ; Pherekyd. Fragm. 22, ed. Didot ; Hesiod. Ægimias, Fr. 2, p. 56, ed. Düntzer : among the varieties of the story, one

was that Argos was changed into a peacock (Schol. Aristoph. Aves, 102). Macrobius (i. 19) considers Argos as an allegorical expression of the starry heaven, an idea which Panofka also upholds in one of the recent Abhandlungen of the Berlin Academy, 1837, p. 121 seq.

[4] Apollod. ii. 1, 1 ; Pausan. ii. 16, 1 ; Æsch. Prom. v. 590—663.

from her native land by means of the incessant stinging of a gad-
fly, which compelled her to wander without repose or sustenance
over an immeasurable extent of foreign regions. The wandering
Iô gave her name to the Ionian Gulf, traversed Epirus and
Illyria, passed the chain of Mount Hæmus and the lofty summits
of Caucasus, and swam across the Thracian or Cimmerian
Bosporus (which also from her derived its appellation) into Asia.
She then went through Scythia, Cimmeria, and many Asiatic
regions, until she arrived in Egypt, where Zeus at length bestowed
upon her rest, restored her to her original form, and enabled her
to give birth to his black son Epaphos.[1]

Such is a general sketch of the adventures which the ancient
poets, epic, lyric, and tragic, and the logographers after them,
connect with the name of the Argeian Iô—one of the numerous
tales which the fancy of the Greeks deduced from the amorous
dispositions of Zeus and the jealousy of Hêrê. That the scene
should be laid in the Argeian territory appears natural, when we
recollect that both Argos and Mykênæ were under the special
guardianship of Hêrê, and that the Hêræon near Mykênæ was
one of the oldest and most celebrated temples in which she was
worshipped. It is useful to compare this amusing fiction with
the representation reported to us by Herodotus, and derived by
him as well from Phœnician as from Persian antiquarians, of the
circumstances which occasioned the transit of Iô from
Argos to Egypt,—an event recognised by all of them
as historical matter of fact. According to the Persians,
a Phœnician vessel had arrived at the port near Argos,
freighted with goods intended for sale to the inhabitants of the country. After the vessel had remained a few days,

Romance of Iô histori-cised by Persians and Phœnicians.

---

[1] Æschyl. Prom. v. 790—850; Apollod. ii. 1. Æschylus in the Supplices
gives a different version of the wanderings of Iô from that which appears in
the Promêtheus : in the former drama
he carries her through Phrygia, Mysia,
Lydia, Pamphylia, and Kilikia into
Egypt (Supplic. 544—566): nothing is
there said about Promêtheus, or Caucasus, or Scythia, &c.

The track set forth in the Supplices
is thus geographically intelligible: that
in the Promêtheus (though the most
noticed of the two) defies all comprehension, even as a consistent fiction ;

nor has the erudition of the commentators been successful in clearing it up.
See Schütz, Excurs. iv. ad Prometh.
Vinct. pp. 144—149 ; Welcker, Æschy-
lische Trilogie, pp. 127—146, and especially Völcker, Mythische Geographie
der Griechen und Römer, part i. pp.
3—13.

The Greek inhabitants at Tarsus in
Kilikia traced their origin to Argos :
their story was, that Triptolemus had
been sent forth from that town in quest
of the wandering Iô, that he had followed her to Tyre, and then renounced
the search in despair. He and his com-

and disposed of most of her cargo, several Argeian women, and among them Iô the king's daughter, coming on board to purchase, were seized and carried off by the crew, who sold Iô in Egypt.[1] The Phœnician antiquarians, however, while they admitted the circumstance that Iô had left her own country in one of their vessels, gave a different colour to the whole by affirming that she emigrated voluntarily, having been engaged in an amour with the captain of the vessel, and fearing that her parents might come to the knowledge of her pregnancy. Both Persians and Phœnicians described the abduction of Iô as the first of a series of similar acts between Greeks and Asiatics, committed each in revenge for the preceding. First came the rape of Eurôpê from Phœnicia by Grecian adventurers,—perhaps, as Herodotus supposed, by Krêtans: next, the abduction of Mêdeia from Kolchis by Jasôn, which occasioned the retaliatory act of Paris, when he stole away Helena from Menelaos. Up to this point the seizures of women by Greeks from Asiatics, and by Asiatics from Greeks, had been equivalent both in number and in wrong. But the Greeks now thought fit to equip a vast conjoint expedition to recover Helen, in the course of which they took and sacked Troy. The invasions of Greece by Darius and Xerxes were intended, according to the Persian antiquarians, as a long-delayed retribution for the injury inflicted on the Asiatics by Agamemnôn and his followers.[2]

panions then settled partly at Tarsus, partly at Antioch (Strabo, xiv. 673; xv. 750). This is the story of Kadmos and Eurôpê inverted, as happens so often with the Grecian mythes.

Homer calls Hermês Ἀργειφόντης; but this epithet hardly affords sufficient proof that he was acquainted with the mythe of Iô, as Völcker supposes: it cannot be traced higher than Hesiod. According to some authors, whom Cicero copies, it was on account of the murder of Argos that Hermês was obliged to leave Greece and go into Egypt: then it was that he taught the Egyptians laws and letters (De Natur. Deor. iii. 22).

[1] The story in Parthênius (Narrat. 1) is built upon this version of Iô's adventures.

[2] Herodot. i. 1—6. Pausanias (ii. 15, 1) will not undertake to determine whether the account given by Hero-dotus, or that of the old legend, respecting the cause which carried Iô from Argos to Egypt, is the true one: Ephorus (ap. Schol. Apoll. Rhod. ii. 168) repeats the abduction of Iô to Egypt by the Phœnicians, subjoining a strange account of the etymology of the name Bosporus. The remarks of Plutarch on the narrative of Herodotus are curious: he adduces as one proof of the κακοήθεια (bad feeling) of Herodotus, that the latter inserts so discreditable a narrative respecting Iô, daughter of Inachus, "whom all Greeks believe to have been divinized by foreigners, to have given names to seas and straits, and to be the source of the most illustrious regal families". He also blames Herodotus for rejecting Epaphos, Iô, Iasus, and Argos, as highest members of the Perseid genealogy. He calls Herodotus φιλοβάρβαρος (Plutarch, De Malign. Herodoti, c. xi. xii. xiv. pp. 856, 857).

The account thus given of the adventures of Iô, when contrasted with the genuine legend, is interesting, as it tends to illustrate the phænomenon which early Grecian history is constantly presenting to us,—the way in which the epical furniture of an unknown past is recast and newly coloured so as to meet those changes which take place in the retrospective *Legendary* feelings of the present. The religious and poetical *abductions* character of the whole legend disappears: nothing *of heroines* remains except the names of persons and places, and *adapted to the feelings* the voyage from Argos to Egypt: we have in exchange *prevalent during* a sober, quasi-historical narrative, the value of which *the Persian* consists in its bearing on the grand contemporary conflicts *war.* between Persia and Greece, which filled the imagination of Herodotus and his readers.

To proceed with the genealogy of the kings of Argos, Iasus was succeeded by Krotôpus, son of his brother Agênôr; Krotôpus by Sthenelas, and he again by Gelanôr.[1] In the reign of the latter, Danaos came with his fifty daughters from Egypt to Argos; and here we find another of those romantic adventures which so agreeably decorate the barrenness of the *Danaos* mythical genealogies. Danaos and Ægyptos were two *and the* brothers descending from Epaphos, son of Iô: Ægyptos *Danaïdes.* had fifty sons, who were eager to marry the fifty daughters of Danaos, in spite of the strongest repugnance of the latter. To escape such a necessity, Danaos placed his fifty daughters on board of a penteconter (or vessel with fifty oars) and sought refuge at Argos; touching in his voyage at the island of Rhodes, where he erected a statue of Athênê at Lindos, which was long exhibited as a memorial of his passage. Ægyptos and his sons

---

[1] It would be an unprofitable fatigue to enumerate the multiplied and irreconcileable discrepancies in regard to every step of this old Argeian genealogy. Whoever desires to see them brought together may consult Schubart, Quæstiones in Antiquitatem Heroicam, Marburg, 1832, capp. 1 and 2.

The remarks which Schubart makes (p. 35) upon Petit-Radel's Chronological Tables will be assented to by those who follow the unceasing string of contradictions, without any sufficient reason to believe that any one of them is more worthy of trust than the remainder,

which he has cited:—" Videant alii, quomodo genealogias heroicas, et chronologiæ rationes, in concordiam redigant. Ipse abstineo, probe persuasus, stemmata vera, historiæ fide comprobata, in systema chronologiæ redigi posse : at ore per sæcula tradita, a poetis reficta, sæpe mutata, prout fabula postulare videbatur, ab historiarum deinde conditoribus restituta, scilicet, brevi, qualia prostant stemmata — chronologiæ secundum annos distributæ vincula semper recusatura esse."

followed them to Argos, and still pressed their suit, to which Danaos found himself compelled to assent; but on the wedding night he furnished each of his daughters with a dagger, and enjoined them to murder their husbands during the hour of sleep. His orders were obeyed by all, with the single exception of Hypermnêstra, who preserved her husband Lynkeus, incurring displeasure and punishment from her father. He afterwards, however, pardoned her; and when, by the voluntary abdication of Gelanôr, he became king of Argos, Lynkeus was recognised as his son-in-law, and ultimately succeeded him. The remaining daughters, having been purified by Athênê and Hermês, were given in marriage to the victors in a gymnic contest publicly proclaimed. From Danaos was derived the name of Danai, applied to the inhabitants of the Argeian territory,[1] and to the Homeric Greeks generally.

From the legend of the Danaïdes we pass to two barren names of kings, Lynkeus and his son Abas. The two sons of Abas were Akrisios and Prœtos, who, after much dissension, divided between them the Argeian territory; Akrisios ruling at Argos, and Prœtos at Tiryns. The families of both formed the theme of romantic stories. To pass over for the present the legend of Bellerophôn, and the unrequited passion which the wife of Prœtos conceived for him, we are told that the daughters of Prœtos, beautiful, and solicited in marriage by suitors from all Greece, were smitten with leprosy and driven mad, wandering in unseemly guise throughout Peloponnêsus. The visitation had overtaken them, according to Hesiod, because they refused to take part in the Bacchic rites; according to Pherekydês and the Argeian Akusilaus,[2] because they had treated scornfully the wooden statue and simple equipments of Hêrê: the religious character of the old legend here displays itself in a remarkable manner. Unable to cure his daughters, Prœtos invoked the aid

Akrisios and Prœtos.

---

[1] Apollod. ii. 1. The Supplices of Æschylus is the commencing drama of a trilogy on this subject of the Danaïdes,— Ἱκετίδες, Αἰγύπτιοι, Δαναΐδες. Welcker, Griechisch. Tragödien, vol. i. p. 48 : the two latter are lost. The old epic poem called Danaïs or Danaïdes, which is mentioned in the Tabula Iliaca as containing 5000 verses, has perished and is, unfortunately, very little al-

luded to : see Düntzer, Epic. Fragm. p. 3 ; Welcker, Der Episch. Kyklus, p. 35.
[2] Apollod. l. c. : Pherekyd. ap. Schol. Hom. Odyss. xv. 225 : Hesiod, Fragm. Marktsch. Fr. 36, 37, 38. These Fragments belong to the Hesiodic Catalogue of Women : Apollodôrus seems to refer to some other of the numerous Hesiodic poems. Diodôrus (iv. 68) assigns the anger of Dionysos as the cause.

of the renowned Pylian prophet and leech, Melampus son of Amythaôn, who undertook to remove the malady on condition of being rewarded with the third part of the kingdom. Prœtos indignantly refused these conditions : but the state of his daughters becoming aggravated and intolerable, he was compelled again to apply to Melampus ; who, on the second request, raised his demands still higher, and required another third of the kingdom for his brother Bias. These terms being acceded to, he performed his part of the covenant. He appeased the wrath of Hêrê by prayer and sacrifice ; or, according to another account, he approached the deranged women at the head of a troop of young men, with shouting and ecstatic dance,—the ceremonies appropriate to the Bacchic worship of Dionysos,—and in this manner effected their cure. Melampus, a name celebrated in many different Grecian mythes, is the legendary founder and progenitor of a great and long-continued family of prophets. He and his brother Bias became kings of separate portions of the Argeian territory : he is recognised as ruler there even in the Odyssey, and the prophet Theoklymenos, his grandson, is protected and carried to Ithaka by Telemachus.[1] Herodotus also alludes to the cure of the women, and to the double kingdom of Melampus and Bias in the Argeian land : recognising Melampus as the first person who introduced to the knowledge of the Greeks the name and worship of Dionysos, with its appropriate sacrifices and phallic processions. Here again he historicises various features of the old legend in a manner not unworthy of notice.[2]

The Prœtides cured of frenzy by Melampus.

But Danaê, the daughter of Akrisios, with her son Perseus, acquired still greater celebrity than her cousins the Prœtides. An oracle had apprised Akrisios that his daughter would give birth to a son by whose hand he would himself be slain. To guard against this danger, he imprisoned Danaê in a chamber of brass under ground. But the god Zeus had become amorous of her, and found means to descend

Akrisios, Danaê, and Zeus.

---

[1] Odyss. xv. 240—256.
[2] Herod. ix. 34 ; ii. 49 : compare Pausan. ii. 18, 4. Instead of the Prœtides, or daughters of Prœtos, it is the Argeian women generally whom he represents Melampus as having cured, and the Argeians generally who send to Pylus to invoke his aid : the heroic personality which pervades the primitive story has disappeared.

Kallimachus notices the Prœtid virgins as the parties suffering from madness, but he treats Artemis as the healing influence (Hymn. ad Dianam. 235).

through the roof in the form of a shower of gold : the consequence of his visits was the birth of Perseus.   When Akrisios discovered that his daughter had given existence to a son, he enclosed both the mother and the child in a coffer, which he cast into the sea.[1] The coffer was carried to the isle of Seriphos, where Diktys, brother of the king Polydektês, fished it up, and rescued both Danâê and Perseus.   The exploits of Perseus, when he grew up, against the three Phorkydes or daughters of Phorkys, and the three Gorgons, are among the most marvellous and imaginative in all Grecian legend : they bear a stamp almost Oriental.   I shall not here repeat the details of those unparalleled hazards which the special favour of Athênê enabled him to overcome, and which ended in his bringing back from Libya the terrific head of the Gorgon Medusa, endued with the property of turning every one who looked upon it into stone.   In his return he rescued Andromeda, daughter of Kêpheus, who had been exposed to be devoured by a sea-monster, and brought her back as his wife.   Akrisios trembled to see him after this victorious expedition, and retired into Thessaly to avoid him ; but Perseus followed him thither, and having succeeded in calming his apprehensions, became competitor in a gymnic contest where his grandfather was among the spectators. By an incautious swing of his quoit, he unintentionally struck Akrisios, and caused his death : the predictions of the oracle were thus at last fulfilled.   Stung with remorse at the catastrophe, and unwilling to return to Argos, which had been the principality of Akrisios, Perseus made an exchange with Megapenthês, son of Prœtos king of Tiryns.   Megapenthês became king of Argos, and Perseus of Tiryns : moreover the latter founded, within ten miles of Argos, the far-famed city of Mykênæ.   The massive walls of this city, like those of Tiryns, of which a large portion yet remains, were built for him by the Lykian Cyclôpes.[2]

We here reach the commencement of the Perseid dynasty of Mykênæ.   It should be noticed, however, that there were among the ancient legends contradictory accounts of the foundation of this city.   Both the Odyssey and the great Eoiai enumerated,

Perseus and the Gorgons.

---

[1] The beautiful fragment of Simonidês (Fragm. vii. ed. Gaisford, Poet. Min.), describing Danâê and the child thus exposed, is familiar to every classical reader.

[2] Paus. ii. 16, 4 ; ii. 16, 5. Apollod. ii. 2. Pherekyd. Fragm. 26, Dind.

among the heroines, Mykênê, the Eponyma of the city; the former poem classifying her with Tyrô and Alkmênê, the latter describing her as the daughter of Inachus and wife of Arestôr. And Akusilaus mentioned an Eponymous Mykêneus, the son of Spartôn and grandson of Phorôneus.[1]

Foundation of Mykênæ —commencement of Perseid dynasty.

The prophetic family of Melampus maintained itself in one of the three parts of the divided Argeian kingdom for five generations, down to Amphiaraos and his sons Alkmæôn and Amphilochos. The dynasty of his brother Bias, and that of Megapenthês, son of Prœtos, continued each for four generations : a list of barren names fills up the interval.[2] The Perseids of Mykênæ boasted a descent long and glorious, heroic as well as historical, continuing down to the last kings of Sparta.[3] The issue of Perseus was numerous : his son Alkæos was father of Alkmênê;[4] a third, Sthenelos, father of Eurysthenes.

After the death of Perseus, Alkæos and Amphitryôn dwelt at Tiryns. The latter became engaged in a quarrel with Elektryôn respecting cattle, and in a fit of passion killed him;[5] moreover the piratical Taphians from the west coast of Akarnania invaded the country, and slew the sons of Alektryôn, so that Alkmênê alone was left of that family.

Amphitryôn, Alkmênê, Sthenelos.

She was engaged to wed Amphitryôn ; but she bound him by oath not to consummate the marriage until he had avenged upon the Têleboæ the death of her brothers. Amphitryôn, compelled to flee the country as the murderer of his uncle, took refuge in Thêbes, whither Alkmênê accompanied him : Sthenelos was left

---

[1] Odyss. ii. 120. Hesiod. Fragment. 154. Marktscheff.—Akusil. Fragm. 16. Pausan. ii. 16, 4. Hekatæus derived the name of the town from the μύκης of the sword of Perseus (Fragm. 360, Dind.). The Schol. ad Eurip. Orest. 1247, mentions Mykêneus as son of Spartôn, but grandson of Phêgeus the brother of Phorôneus.

[2] Pausan. ii. 18, 4.

[3] Herodot. vi. 53.

[4] In the Hesiodic Shield of Hêraklês, Alkmênê is distinctly mentioned as daughter of Elektryôn : the genealogical poet, Asios, called her the daughter of Amphiaraos and Eriphyle (Asii Fragm. 4, ed. Markt. p. 412). The date of Asios cannot be precisely fixed ;

but he may be probably assigned to an epoch between the 30th and 40th Olympiad.

Asios must have adopted a totally different legend respecting the birth of Hêraklês and the circumstances preceding it, among which the deaths of her father and brothers are highly influential. Nor could he have accepted the received chronology of the sieges of Thêbes and Troy.

[5] So runs the old legend in the Hesiodic Shield of Hêraklês (12—82). Apollodôrus (or Pherekydês, whom he follows) softens it down, and represents the death of Elektryôn as accidentally caused by Amphitryôn. (Apollod. ii. 4, 6. Pherekydês, Fragm. 27, Dind.)

in possession of Tiryns. The Kadmeians of Thêbes, together with the Lokrians and Phokians, supplied Amphitryôn with troops, which he conducted against the Têleboæ and the Taphians:[1] yet he could not have subdued them without the aid of Komæthô, daughter of the Taphian king Pterelaus, who conceived a passion for him, and cut off from her father's head the golden lock to which Poseidôn had attached the gift of immortality.[2] Having conquered and expelled his enemies, Amphitryôn returned to Thêbes, impatient to consummate his marriage: but Zeus on the wedding-night assumed his form and visited Alkmênê before him: he had determined to produce from her a son superior to all his prior offspring,—"a specimen of invincible force both to gods and men".[3] At the proper time Alkmênê was delivered of twin sons: Hêraklês, the offspring of Zeus, —the inferior and unhonoured Iphiklês, offspring of Amphitryôn.[4]

Zeus and Alkmênê.

When Alkmênê was on the point of being delivered at Thêbes, Zeus publicly boasted among the assembled gods, at the instigation of the mischief-making Atê, that there was on that day about to be born on earth, from his breed, a son who should rule over all his neighbours. Hêrê treated this as an empty boast, calling upon him to bind himself by an irremissible oath that the prediction should be realized. Zeus incautiously pledged his solemn word; upon which Hêrê darted swiftly down from Olympus to the Achaic Argos, where the wife of Sthenelos (son of Perseus, and therefore grandson of Zeus) was already seven months gone with child. By the aid of the Eileithyiæ, the special goddesses of parturition, she caused Eurystheus, the son of Sthenelos, to be born before his time on that very day, while she retarded the delivery of Alkmênê. Then returning to Olympus, she announced the fact to Zeus: "The good man Eurystheus, son of the Perseid Sthenelos, is this day born of thy loins: the sceptre of the Argeians worthily belongs to him". Zeus was thunderstruck at the consummation which he had improvidently bound himself to accomplish. He seized Atê his evil counsellor by the

Birth of Hêraklês.

---

[1] Hesiod. Scut. Herc. 24. Theocrit. Idyll. xxiv. 4. Teleboas, the Eponymous of these marauding people, was son of Poseidôn (Anaximander, ap. Athen. xi. p. 498).
[2] Apollod. ii. 4, 7. Compare the fable of Nisus at Megara, *infra*, chap. xii.
[3] Hesiod. Scut. Herc. 29. ὄφρα θεοῖσιν Ἀνδράσι τ' ἀλφηστῇσιν ἀρῆς ἀλκτῆρα φυτεύσῃ.
[4] Hesiod. Sc. H. 50—56.

hair, and hurled her for ever away from Olympus : but he had no
power to avert the ascendency of Eurystheus and the servitude of
Hêraklês. "Many a pang did he suffer when he saw his favourite
son going through his degrading toil in the tasks imposed upon
him by Eurystheus."[1]

The legend, of unquestionable antiquity, here transcribed
from the Iliad, is one of the most pregnant and charac-   Homeric
teristic in the Grecian mythology.   It explains, ac-   legend of
cording to the religious ideas familiar to the old epic   its exposi-
poets, both the distinguishing attributes and the end-   tory value.
less toils and endurances of Hêraklês,—the most renowned and
most ubiquitous of all the semi-divine personages worshipped by
the Hellênes,—a being of irresistible force, and especially beloved
by Zeus, yet condemned constantly to labour for others and to
obey the commands of a worthless and cowardly persecutor.   His
recompense is reserved to the close of his career, when his afflicting trials are brought to a close : he is then admitted to the godhead and receives in marriage Hêbê.[2]   The twelve labours, as they
are called, too notorious to be here detailed, form a very small
fraction of the exploits of this mighty being, which filled the Hêrakleian epics of the ancient poets.   He is found not only in most
parts of Hellas, but throughout all the regions then known
to the Greeks, from Gadês to the river Thermôdôn in the Euxine
and to Scythia, overcoming all difficulties and vanquishing all
opponents. Distinguished families are everywhere to be traced
who bear his patronymic, and glory in the belief that they are his
descendants.   Among Achæans, Kadmeians, and Dôrians, Hêraklês is venerated: the latter especially treat him as their principal
hero,—the Patron Hero-God of the race: the Hêrakleids form
among all Dôrians a privileged gens, in which at Sparta the
special lineage of the two kings was included.

His character lends itself to mythes countless in number, as
well as disparate in their character.   The irresistible force remains constant, but it is sometimes applied with reckless violence

---

[1] Homer, Iliad. xix. 90-133; also
viii. 361.—

Τὴν αἰεὶ στενάχεσχ', ὅθ' ἑὸν φίλον υἱὸν
    ὁρῷτο
Ἔργον ἀεικὲς ἔχοντα, ὑπ' Εὐρυσθῆος
    ἀέθλων.

[2] Hesiod, Theogon. 951, τελέσας στο-
νόεντας ἀέθλους. Hom. Odyss. xi. 620 ;
Hesiod. Eœæ, Fragm. 24, Düntzer, p.
36, πονηρότατον καὶ ἄριστον.

against friends as well as enemies, sometimes devoted to the relief of the oppressed. The comic writers often brought him out as a coarse and stupid glutton, while the Keian philosopher Prodikos, without at all distorting the type, extracted from it the simple, impressive, and imperishable apologue still known as the choice of Hercules.

After the death and apotheosis of Hêraklês, his son Hyllos and his other children were expelled and persecuted by Eurystheus; the fear of whose vengeance deterred both the Trachinian king Kêyx and the Thebans from harbouring them. The Athenians alone were generous enough to brave the risk of offering them shelter. Eurystheus invaded Attica, but perished in the attempt by the hand of Hyllos, or by that of Iolaos, the old companion and nephew of Hêraklês.[1] The chivalrous courage which the Athenians had on this occasion displayed on behalf of oppressed innocence was a favourite theme for subsequent eulogy by Attic poets and orators.

The Hêra-kleids ex-pelled.

All the sons of Eurystheus lost their lives in the battle along with him, so that the Perseid family was now represented only by the Hêrakleids, who collected an army and endeavoured to recover the possessions from which they had been expelled. The united forces of Iônians, Achæans, and Arcadians, then inhabiting Peloponnêsus, met the invaders at the isthmus, when Hyllos, the eldest of the sons of Hêraklês, proposed that the contest should be determined by a single combat between himself and any champion of the opposing army. It was agreed that if Hyllos were victorious, the Hêrakleids should be restored to their possessions—if he were vanquished, that they should forego all claim for the space of a hundred years, or fifty years, or three generations,—for in the specification of the time accounts differ. Echemos, the hero of Tegea in Arcadia, accepted the challenge, and Hyllos was slain in the encounter; in consequence of which the Hêrakleids retired, and resided along with the Dôrians under the protection of Ægimios, son of Dôrus.[2] As soon as the stipulated period of truce had expired, they renewed their attempt upon Peloponnêsus, conjointly with the Dôrians, and with complete success: the great Dôrian establishments of

[1] Apoll. ii. 8, 1 ; Hecatæ. ap. Longin. c. 27 ; Diodôr. iv. 57.   [2] Herodot. ix. 26 ; Diodôr. iv. 58.

Argos, Sparta, and Messênia were the result. The details of this victorious invasion will be hereafter recounted.

Sikyôn, Phlios, Epidauros, and Trœzen[1] all boasted of respected eponyms and a genealogy of dignified length, not exempt from the usual discrepancies—but all just as much entitled to a place on the tablet of history as the more renowned Æolids or Hêrakleids. I omit them here because I wish to impress upon the reader's mind the salient features and character of the legendary world,—not to load his memory with a full list of legendary names.

Their recovery of Peloponnêsus and establishment in Argos, Sparta, and Messênia.

[1] Pausan. ii. 5, 5; 12, 5; 26, 3. His statements indicate how much the predominance of a powerful neighbour like Argos tended to alter the genealogies of these inferior towns.

CHAPTER V.

DEUKALIÔN, HELLÊN, AND SONS OF HELLÊN.

In the Hesiodic theogony, as well as in the "Works and Days," the legend of Promêtheus and Epimêtheus presents an import religious, ethical, and social, and in this sense it is carried forward by Æschylus ; but to neither of the characters is any genealogical function assigned. The Hesiodic Catalogue of Women brought both of them into the stream of Grecian legendary lineage, representing Deukaliôn as the son of Promêtheus and Pandôra, and seemingly his wife Pyrrha as daughter of Epimêtheus.[1]

Deukaliôn is important in Grecian mythical narrative under two points of view. First, he is the person specially saved at the time of the general deluge : next, he is the father of Hellên, the great eponym of the Hellenic race : at least this was the more current story, though there were other statements which made Hellên the son of Zeus.

Deukaliôn, son of Promêtheus.

The name of Deukaliôn is originally connected with the Lokrian towns of Kynos and Opus, and with the race of the Leleges, but he appears finally as settled in Thessaly, and ruling in the portion of that country called Phthiôtis.[2] According to what seems to have been the old legendary account, it is the

---

[1] Schol. ad Apollôn. Rhod. iii. 1085. Other accounts of the genealogy of Deukaliôn are given in the Schol. ad Homer. Odyss. x. 2, on the authority both of Hesiod and Akusilaus.

[2] Hesiodic Catalog. Fragm. xi ; Gaisf. lxx. Düntzer—

'Ήτοι γὰρ Λοκρὸς Λελέγων ἡγήσατο λαῶν,
Τούς ῥά ποτε Κρονίδης Ζεὺς ἄφθιτα μήδεα εἰδὼς,

Λεκτοὺς ἐκ γαίης λάας πόρε Δευκαλίωνι.

The reputed lineage of Deukaliôn continued in Phthia down to the time of Dikæarchus, if we may judge from the old Phthiot Pherekratês, whom he introduced in one of his dialogues as a disputant, and whom he expressly announced as a descendant of Deukaliôn (Cicero, Tuscul. Disp. i. 10).

deluge which transferred him from the one to the other; but according to another statement, framed in more historicising times, he conducted a body of Kurêtes and Leleges into Thessaly, and expelled the prior Pelasgian occupants.[1]

The enormous iniquity with which earth was contaminated—as Apollodôrus says, by the then existing brazen race, or as others say, by the fifty monstrous sons of Lykaôn—provoked Zeus to send a general deluge.[2] An unremitting and terrible rain laid the whole of Greece under water, except the highest mountain tops, whereon a few stragglers found refuge. Deukaliôn was saved in a chest or ark, which he had been forewarned by his father Promêtheus to construct. After floating for nine days on the water, he at length landed on the summit of Mount Parnassus. Zeus having sent Hermês to him, promising to grant whatever he asked, he prayed that men and companions might be sent to him in his solitude: accordingly Zeus directed both him and Pyrrha to cast stones over their heads: those cast by Pyrrha became women, those by Deukaliôn men. And thus the "stony race of men" (if we may be allowed to translate an etymology which the Greek language presents exactly, and which has not been disdained by Hesiod, by Pindar, by Epicharmus, and by Virgil) came to tenant the soil of Greece.[3] Deuka-

(margin notes:) Phthiôtis: his permanent seat.

General deluge.—Salvation of Deukaliôn and Pyrrha.

---

[1] The latter account is given by Dionys. Halic. i. 17 : the former seems to have been given by Hellanikus, who affirmed that the ark after the deluge stopped upon Mount Othrys, and not upon Mount Parnassus (Schol. Pind. *ut sup.*), the former being suitable for a settlement in Thessaly.

Pyrrha is the eponymous heroine of Pyrrhæa or Pyrrha, the ancient name of a portion of Thessaly (Rhianus, Fragm. 18, p. 71, ed. Düntzer).

Hellanikus had written a work, now lost, entitled Δευκαλιώνεια : all the fragments of it which are cited have reference to places in Thessaly, Lokris, and Phokis. See Preller, ad Hellanicum, p. 12 (Dörpt. 1840). Probably Hellanikus is the main source of the important position occupied by Deukaliôn in Grecian legend. Thrasybulus and Akestodôrus represented Deukaliôn as having founded the oracle of Dôdôna, immediately after the deluge (Etym. Mag. v. Δωδωναῖος).

[2] Apollodôrus connects this deluge with the wickedness of the brazen race in Hesiod, according to the practice, general with the logographers, of stringing together a sequence out of legends totally unconnected with each other (i. 7, 2).

[3] Hesiod, Fragm. 135, ed. Markts. ap. Strabo. vii. p. 332, where the word λᾶας, proposed by Heyne as the reading of the unintelligible text, appears to me preferable to any of the other suggestions. Pindar, Olymp. ix. 47. 'Ατερ δ' Εὐνᾶς ὁμόδαμον Κρησάσθαν λίθινον γόνον· Λαοὶ δ' ὠνόμασθεν. Virgil, Georgic. i. 63. "Unde homines nati, durum genus." Epicharmus ap. Schol. Pindar. Olymp. ix. 56, Hygin. f. 153. Philochorus retained the etymology, though he gave a totally different fable, nowise connected with Deukaliôn, to account for it : a curious proof how pleasing it was to the fancy of the Greeks (see Schol. ad Pind. l. c. 68).

liôn on landing from the ark sacrificed a grateful offering to Zeus
Phyxios, or the god of escape; he also erected altars in Thessaly
to the twelve great gods of Olympus.[1]

The reality of this deluge was firmly believed throughout the
historical ages of Greece ; the chronologers, reckoning up by
genealogies, assigned the exact date of it, and placed it at the
same time as the conflagration of the world by the rashness of
Phaëthôn, during the reign of Krotôpos, king of Argos, the
seventh from Inachus.[2]   The meteorological work of Aristotle
admits and reasons upon this deluge as an unquestionable fact,
though he alters the locality by placing it west of Mount Pindus,
near Dôdôna and the river Achclôus.[3]   He at the same time
treats it as a physical phænomenon, the result of periodical cycles
in the atmosphere,—thus departing from the religious character
of the old legend, which described it as a judgment inflicted by
Zeus upon a wicked race.   Statements founded upon this event
were in circulation throughout Greece even to a very late date.

Belief in
this deluge
throughout
Greece.

The Megarians affirmed that Megaros, their hero, son
of Zeus by a local nymph, had found safety from the
waters on the lofty summit of their mountain Geraneia,
which had not been completely submerged.   And in
the magnificent temple of the Olympian Zeus at Athens a cavity
in the earth was shown, through which it was affirmed that the
waters of the deluge had retired.   Even in the time of Pausanias,
the priest poured into this cavity holy offerings of meal and
honey.[4]   In this, as in other parts of Greece, the idea of the
Deukalionian deluge was blended with the religious impressions
of the people, and commemorated by their sacred ceremonies.

<hr/>

[1] Apollod. i. 7, 2. Hellanic. Fr. 15,
Did.   Hellanikus affirmed that the ark
rested on Mount Othrys, not on Mount
Parnassus (Fr. 16. Did.) ; Servius (ad
Virg. Eclog. vi. 41) placed it on Mount
Athôs ; Hyginus (f. 153), on Mount
Ætna.

[2] Tatian adv. Græc. c. 60, adopted
both by Clemens and Eusebius. The
Parian marble placed this deluge in
the reign of Kranaos at Athens, 752
years before the first recorded Olympiad, and 1528 years before the Christian æra ; Apollodôrus also places it in
the reign of Kranaos, and in that of
Nyctimus in Arcadia (iii. 8, 2 ; 14, 5).
The deluge and the *ekpyrosis* or con-

flagration are connected together also
in Servius ad Virgil. Bucol. vi. 41 : he
refines both of them into a "muta-
tionem temporum".

[3] Aristot. Meteorol. i. 14.   Justin
rationalises the fable by telling us that
Deukaliôn was king of Thessaly, who
provided shelter and protection to the
fugitives from the deluge (ii. 6, 11).

[4] Pausan. i. 18, 7 ; 40, 1. According
to the Parian marble (s. 5), Deukaliôn
had come to Athens after the deluge,
and had there himself founded the
temple of the Olympian Zeus. The
etymology and allegorization of the
names of Deukaliôn and Pyrrha, given
by Völcker in his ingenious Mythologie

The offspring of Deukaliôn and Pyrrha were two sons, Hellên and Amphiktyon, and a daughter, Prôtogeneia, whose son by Zeus was Aëthlius : it was however maintained by many that ·Hellên was the son of Zeus and not of Deukaliôn.   Hellên had by a nymph three sons, Dôrus, Xuthus, and Æolus.   He gave to those who had been before called Greeks[1] the name of Hellênes, and partitioned his territory among his three children.   Æolus reigned in Thessaly ; Xuthus received Peloponnêsus, and had by Kreüsa as his sons Achæus and Iôn ; while Dôrus occupied the country lying opposite to the Peloponnêsus, on the northern side of the Corinthian Gulf.   These three gave to the inhabitants of their respective countries the names of Æolians, Achæans and Iônians, and Dôrians.[2]

Hellên and Amphik-tyôn.

Such is the genealogy as we find it in Apollodôrus.   In so far as the names and filiation are concerned, many points in it are given differently, or implicitly contradicted, by Euripidês and other writers.   Though as literal and personal history it deserves no notice, its import is both intelligible and comprehensive.   It expounds and symbolises the first fraternal aggregation of Hellênic men, together with their territorial distribution and the institutions which they collectively venerated.

Sons of Hellên : Dôrus, Xuthus, Æolus.

There were two great holding-points in common for every section of Greeks.   One was the Amphiktyonic assembly, which met half-yearly, alternately at Delphi and at Thermopylæ ; originally and chiefly for common religious purposes, but indirectly and occasionally embracing political and social objects along with them.   The other was the public festivals or games, of which the Olympic came first in importance ; next the Pythian, Nemean, and Isthmian,—institutions which combined religious solemnities with recreative effusion and hearty sympathies, in a manner so imposing and so unparalleled.   Amphiktyôn represents

Amphiktyonic assembly.—Common solemnities and games.

---

des Iapetischen Geschlechts (Giessen, 1824), p. 343, appears to me not at all convincing.

[1] Such is the statement of Apollodôrus (i. 7, 3) ; but I cannot bring myself to believe that the name (Γραῖκοί) Greeks is at all old in the legend, or that the passage of Hesiod, in which Græcus and Latinus purport to be mentioned, is genuine.

See Hesiod, Theogon. 1013, and Catalog. Fragm. xxix. ed. Göttling : with the note of Göttling ; also Wachsmuth, Hellen. Alterth. i. 1, p. 311, and Bernhardy, Griech. Literat. vol. i. p. 167.

[2] Apollod. i. 7, 4.

the first of these institutions, and Aëthlius the second. As the Amphiktyonic assembly was always especially connected with Thermopylæ and Thessaly, Amphiktyôn is made the son of the Thessalian Deukaliôn ; but as the Olympic festival was nowise locally connected with Deukaliôn, Aëthlius is represented as having Zeus for his father, and as touching Deukaliôn only through the maternal line. It will be seen presently that the only matter predicated respecting Aëthlius is, that he settled in the territory of Elis, and begat Endymiôn : this brings him into local contact with the Olympic games, and his function is then ended.

Having thus got Hellas as an aggregate with its main cementing forces, we march on to its sub-division into parts, through Æolus, Dôrus, and Xuthus, the three sons of Hellên,[1] a distribution which is far from being exhaustive : nevertheless, the genealogists whom Apollodôrus follows recognise no more than three sons.

Division of Hellas: Æolians, Dôrians, Iônians.

The genealogy is essentially post-Homeric ; for Homer knows Hellas and the Hellênes only in connexion with a portion of Achaia Phthiôtis. But as it is recognised in the Hesiodic Catalogue [2]—composed probably within the first century after the commencement of recorded Olympiads, or before 676 B.C.—the peculiarities of it, dating from so early a period, deserve much attention. We may remark, first, that it seems to exhibit to us Dôrus and Æolus as the only pure and genuine offspring of Hellên. For their brother Xuthus is not enrolled as an eponymus ; he neither founds nor names any people ; it is only his sons Achæus and Iôn, after his blood has been mingled with that of the Erechtheid Kreüsa, who become eponyms and founders, each of his own separate people. Next, as to the territorial dis-

---

[1] How literally and implicitly even the ablest Greeks believed in eponymous persons, such as Hellên and Iôn, as the real progenitors of the races called after him, may be seen by this, that Aristotle gives this common descent as the definition of γένος (Metaphysic. iv. p. 118, Brandis) :—

Γένος λέγεται, τὸ μὲν . . . τὸ δὲ, ἀφ' οὗ ἂν ὧσι πρώτου κινήσαντος εἰς τὸ εἶναι. Οὕτω γὰρ λέγονται οἱ μὲν, Ἕλληνες τὸ γένος, οἱ δὲ, Ἴωνες· τῷ, οἱ μὲν ἀπὸ Ἕλληνος, οἱ δὲ ἀπὸ Ἴωνος, εἶναι πρώτου γεννήσαντος.

[2] Hesiod, Fragm. 8. p. 278, ed. Marktsch.—

Ἕλληνος δ' ἐγένοντο θεμιστόπολοι βασιλῆες
Δῶρός τε, Ξοῦθός τε, καὶ Αἴολος ἱππιοχάρμης.
Αἰολίδαι δ' ἐγένοντο θεμιστόπολοι βασιλῆες
Κρηθεὺς ἠδ' Ἀθάμας καὶ Σίσυφος αἰολομήτης
Σαλμωνεύς τ' ἄδικος καὶ ὑπέρθυμος Περιήρης.

tribution, Xuthus receives Peloponnêsus from his father, and unites himself with Attica (which the author of this genealogy seems to have conceived as originally unconnected with Hellên) by his marriage with the daughter of the indigenous hero Erechtheus. The issue of this marriage, Achæus and Iôn, present to us the population of Peloponnêsus and Attica conjointly as related among themselves by the tie of brotherhood, but as one degree more distant both from Dôrians and Æolians. Æolus reigns over the regions about Thessaly, and calls the people in those parts Æolians ; while Dôrus occupies "the country over against Peloponnêsus on the opposite side of the Corinthian Gulf," and calls the inhabitants after himself Dôrians.[1] It is at once evident that this designation is in no way applicable to the confined district between Parnassus and Œta, which alone is known by the name of Dôris, and its inhabitants by that of Dôrians, in the historical ages.   In the view of the author of this genealogy, the Dôrians are the original occupants of Large the large range of territory north of the Corinthian extent of Gulf, comprising Ætôlia, Phôkis, and the territory of plied in this the Ozolian Lokrians.   And this farther harmonises genealogy. with the other legend noticed by Apollodôrus, when he states that Ætôlus, son of Endymiôn, having been forced to expatriate from Peloponnêsus, crossed into the Kurêtid territory,[2] and was there hospitably received by Dôrus, Laodokus, and Polypœtes, sons of Apollo and Phthia. He slew his hosts, acquired the territory, and gave to it the name of Ætôlia ; his son Pleurôn married Xanthippê, daughter of Dôrus ; while his other son, Kalydôn, marries Æolia, daughter of Amythaôn. Here again we have the name of Dôrus, or the Dôrians, connected with the tract subsequently termed Ætôlia. That Dôrus should in one place be

---

[1] Apoll. i. 7, 3. Ἕλληνος δὲ καὶ Νύμφης Ὀρσηΐδος (?), Δῶρος, Ξοῦθος, Αἴολος. Αὐτὸς μὲν οὖν ἀφ' αὑτοῦ τοὺς καλουμένους Γραϊκοὺς προσηγόρευσεν Ἕλληνας, τοῖς δὲ παισὶν ἐμέρισε τὴν χώραν. Καὶ Ξοῦθος μὲν λαβὼν τὴν Πελοπόννησον, ἐκ Κρεούσης τῆς Ἐρεχθέως Ἀχαιὸν ἐγέννησε καὶ Ἴωνα, ἀφ' ὧν Ἀχαιοὶ καὶ Ἴωνες καλοῦνται. Δῶρος δὲ, τὴν πέραν χώραν Πελοποννήσου λαβὼν, τοὺς κατοίκους ἀφ' ἑαυτοῦ Δωριεῖς ἐκάλεσεν. Αἴολος δὲ, βασιλεύων τῶν περὶ Θετταλίαν τόπων, τοὺς ἐνοικοῦντας Αἰολεῖς προσηγόρευσεν.

Strabo (viii. p. 383) and Conôn (Nar. 27), who evidently copy from the same source, represent Dôrus as going to settle in the territory properly known as Dôris.

[2] Apollod. i. 7, 6. Αἰτωλὸς . . . φυγὼν εἰς τὴν Κουρητίδα χώραν, κτείνας τοὺς ὑποδεξαμένους Φθίας καὶ Ἀπόλλωνος υἱοὺς, Δῶρον καὶ Λαόδοκον καὶ Πολυποίτην, ἀφ' ἑαυτοῦ τὴν χώραν Αἰτωλίαν ἐκάλεσεν. Again, i. 8, 1. Πλευρὼν (son of Ætôlus) γήμας Ξανθίππην τὴν Δώρου, παῖδα ἐγέννησεν Ἀγήνορα.

called the son of Apollo and Phthia, and in another place the son
of Hellên by a nymph, will surprise no one accustomed to the
fluctuating personal nomenclature of these old legends : moreover
the name of Phthia is easy to reconcile with that of Hellên, as
both are identified with the same portion of Thessaly, even from
the days of the Iliad.

This story, that the Dôrians were at one time the occupants,
or the chief occupants, of the range of territory between the river
Achelôus and the northern shore of the Corinthian gulf, is at
least more suitable to the facts attested by historical evidence than
the legends given in Herodotus, who represents the Dôrians as
originally in the Phthiôtid ; then as passing under Dôrus, the son
of Hellên, into the Histiæôtid, under the mountains of Ossa and
Olympus ; next, as driven by the Kadmeians into the regions of
Pindus; from thence passing into the Dryopid territory, on Mount
Œta; lastly, from thence into Peloponnêsus.[1] The received story
was, that the great Dôrian establishments in Peloponnêsus were
formed by invasion from the north, and that the invaders crossed
the gulf from Naupaktus,—a statement which, however disputable
with respect to Argos, seems highly probable in regard both to
Sparta and Messênia.   That the name of Dôrians comprehended
far more than the inhabitants of the insignificant tetrapolis of
Dôris Proper must be assumed, if we believe that they conquered
Sparta and Messênia : both the magnitude of the conquest itself

This form
of the
legend
harmonises
with the
great esta-
blishments
of the
historical
Dôrians.

and the passage of a large portion of them from Naupaktus, harmonise with the legend as given by Apollodôrus, in which the Dôrians are represented as the
principal inhabitants of the northern shore of the gulf.
The statements which we find in Herodotus, respecting the early migrations of the Dôrians, have been
considered as possessing greater historical value than
those of the fabulist Apollodôrus.   But both are equally matter of
legend, while the brief indications of the latter seem to be most in
harmony with the facts which we afterwards find attested by history.

It has already been mentioned that the genealogy which makes
Æolus, Xuthus, and Dôrus sons of Hellên, is as old as the Hesiodic
Catalogue ; probably also that which makes Hellên son of Deu-
kaliôn.   Aëthlius also is an Hesiodic personage : whether Am-

[1] Herod. i. 56.

phiktyôn be so or not, we have no proof.[1] They could not have
been introduced into the legendary genealogy until after the
Olympic games and the Amphiktyonic council had acquired an
established and extensive reverence throughout Greece.

Respecting Dôrus the son of Hellên, we find neither legends nor
legendary genealogy ; respecting Xuthus, very little beyond the
tale of Kreüsa and Iôn, which has its place more naturally among
the Attic fables. Achæus, however, who is here represented as
the son of Xuthus, appears in other stories with very different
parentage and accompaniments. According to the statement
which we find in Dionysius of Halikarnassus, Achæus, Phthius,
and Pelasgus are sons of Poseidôn and Larissa. They migrate
from Peloponnêsus into Thessaly, and distribute the Thessalian
territory between them, giving their names to its principal divi-
sions : their descendants in the sixth generation were driven out
of that country by the invasion of Deukaliôn at the head of the
Kurêtes and the Leleges.[2] This was the story of
those who wanted to provide an eponymus for the
Achæans in the southern districts of Thessaly : Pausanias accomplishes the same object by different means,
representing Achæus the son of Xuthus as having
gone back to Thessaly and occupied the portion of it to which his
father was entitled.   Then, by way of explaining how it was that
there were Achæans at Sparta and at Argos, he tells us that
Archander and Architelês the sons of Achæus, came back from
Thessaly to Peloponnêsus, and married two daughters of Danaus :
they acquired great influence at Argos and Sparta, and gave to
the people the name of Achæans after their father Achæus.[3]

*Achæus—
purpose
which his
name
serves in
the legend.*

[1] Schol. Apollon. Rhod. iv. 57. Τὸν
δὲ Ἐνδυμίωνα Ἡσίοδος μὲν Ἀεθλίου τοῦ
Διὸς καὶ Καλύκης παῖδα λέγει . . .
Καὶ Πείρανδρος δὲ τὰ αὐτά φησι, καὶ
Ἀκουσίλαος, καὶ Φερεκύδης, καὶ Νίκαν-
δρος ἐν δευτέρῳ Αἰτωλικῶν, καὶ Θεόπομπος ἐν Ἐποποιίαις.
Respecting the parentage of Hellên,
the references to Hesiod are very confused. Compare Schol. Homer. Odyss.
x. 2, and Schol. Apollon. Rhod. iii. 1086.
See also Hellanic. Frag. 10. Didot.
Apollodôrus and Pherekydês before
him (Fragm. 51. Didot), called Protogeneia daughter of Deukaliôn ; Pindar
(Olymp. ix. 64) designated her as
daughter of Opus. One of the strata-

gems mentioned by the Scholiast to
get rid of this genealogical discrepancy
was the supposition that Deukaliôn
had two names (διώνυμος) ; that he was
also named Opus. (Schol. Pind. Olymp.
ix. 85.)
That the Deukalidæ or posterity of
Deukaliôn reigned in Thessaly, was
mentioned both by Hesiod and Hekatæus, ap. Schol. Apollon. Rhod. iv. 265.
[2] Dionys. H. A. R. i. 17.
[3] Pausan. vii. 1, 1—3. Herodotus also
mentions (ii. 97) Archander, son of
Phthius and grandson of Achæus, who
married the daughter of Danaus.
Larcher (Essai sur la Chronologie d'Hérodote, ch. x. p. 321) tells us that this

Euripidês also deviates very materially from the Hesiodic genealogy in respect to the eponymous persons. In the drama called Iôn, he describes Iôn as son of Kreüsa by Apollo, but adopted by Xuthus : according to him, the real sons of Xuthus and Kreüsa are Dôrus and Achæus,[1]—eponyms of the Dôrians and Achæans in the interior of Peloponnêsus. And it is a still

Genealogical diversities.

more capital point of difference that he omits Hellên altogether—making Xuthus an Achæan by race, the son of Æolus, who is the son of Zeus.[2] This is the more remarkable, as in the fragments of two other dramas of Euripidês, the Melanippê and the Æolus, we find Hellên mentioned both as father of Æolus and son of Zeus.[3] To the general public even of the most instructed city of Greece, fluctuations and discrepancies in these mythical genealogies seem to have been neither surprising nor offensive.

cannot be the Danaus who came from Egypt, the father of the fifty daughters, who must have lived two centuries earlier, as may be proved by chronological arguments : this must be another Danaus, according to him.

Strabo seems to give a different story respecting the Achæans in Peloponnêsus : he says that they were the original population of the peninsula, that they came in from Phthia with Pelops, and inhabited Laconia, which was from them called Argos Achaicum, and that on the conquest of the Dôrians, they moved into Achaia properly

so called, expelling the Ionians therefrom (Strabo, viii. p. 365). This narrative is, I presume, borrowed from Ephorus.

[1] Eurip. Ion, 1590.

[2] Eurip. Ion, 64.

[3] See the Fragments of these two plays in Matthiae's edition ; compare Welcker, Griechisch. Tragöd. v. ii. p. 842. If we may judge from the Fragments of the Latin Melanippê of Ennius (see Fragm. 2, ed. Bothe), Hellên was introduced as one of the characters of the piece.

CHAPTER VI.

THE ÆOLIDS, OR SONS AND DAUGHTERS OF ÆOLUS.

If two of the sons of Hellên, Dôrus and Xuthus, present to us families comparatively unnoticed in mythical narrative, the third son, Æolus, richly makes up for the deficiency. From him we pass to his seven sons and five daughters, amidst a great abundance of heroic and poetical incident.

In dealing, however, with these extensive mythical families, it is necessary to observe, that the legendary world of Greece, in the manner in which it is presented to us, appears invested with a degree of symmetry and coherence which did not originally belong to it. For the old ballads and stories which were sung or recounted at the multiplied festivals of Greece, each on its own special theme, have been lost: the religious narratives, which the Exêgêtês of every temple had present to his memory, explanatory of the peculiar religious ceremonies and local customs in his own town or deme, had passed away. All these primitive elements, originally distinct and unconnected, are removed out of our sight, and we possess only an aggregate result, formed by many confluent streams of fable, and connected together by the agency of subsequent poets and logographers. Even the earliest agents in this work of connecting and systematising—the Hesiodic poets— have been hardly at all preserved. Our information respecting Grecian mythology is derived chiefly from the prose logographers who followed them, and in whose works, since a continuous narrative was above all things essential to them, the fabulous personages are woven into still more comprehensive pedigrees, and the original isolation of the legends still better disguised. Hekatæus, Pherekydês, Hellanikus, and Akusilaus lived at a

Legends of Greece, originally isolated, afterwards thrown into series.

time when the idea of Hellas as one great whole, composed of fraternal sections, was deeply rooted in the mind of every Greek, and when the hypothesis of a few great families, branching out widely from one common stem was more popular and acceptable than that of a distinct indigenous origin in each of the separate districts. These logographers, indeed, have themselves been lost; but Apollodôrus and the various scholiasts, our great immediate sources of information respecting Grecian mythology, chiefly borrowed from them: so that the legendary world of Greece is in fact known to us through them, combined with the dramatic and Alexandrine poets, their Latin imitators, and the still later class of scholiasts—except indeed such occasional glimpses as we obtain from the Iliad and the Odyssey, and the remaining Hesiodic fragments, which exhibit but too frequently a hopeless diversity when confronted with the narratives of the logographers.

Though Æolus (as has been already stated) is himself called the son of Hellên along with Dôrus and Xuthus, yet the legends concerning the Æolids, far from being dependent upon this genealogy, are not all even coherent with it: moreover the name of Æolus in the legend is older than that of Hellên, inasmuch as it occurs both in the Iliad and Odyssey.[1] Odysseus sees in the under-world the beautiful Tyrô, daughter of Salmôneus, and wife of Krêtheus, son of Æolus.

Æolus.

Æolus is represented as having reigned in Thessaly: his seven sons were Krêtheus, Sisyphus, Athamas, Salmôneus, Deiôn, Magnês, and Periêrês: his five daughters, Canacê, Alcyonê, Peisidikê, Calycê, and Perimêdê. The fables of this race seem to be distinguished by a constant introduction of the god Poseidôn, as well as by an unusual prevalence of haughty and presumptuous attributes among the Æolid heroes, leading them to affront the gods by pretences of equality, and sometimes even by defiance. The worship of Poseidôn must probably have been diffused and pre-eminent among a people with whom those legends originated.

His seven sons and five daughters.

[1] Iliad, vi. 154. Σίσυφος Αἰολίδης, &c. Again, Odyss. xi. 234.—

'Ενθ' ἤτοι πρώτην Τυρὼ ἴδον εὐπα-τέρειαν,

'Η φάτο Σαλμωνῆος ἀμύμονος ἔκγονος εἶναι,
Φῆ δὲ Κρηθῆος γυνὴ ἔμμεναι Αἰο-λίδαο.

SECTION I.—SONS OF ÆOLUS.

Salmôneus is not described in the Odyssey as son of Æolus, but he is so denominated both in the Hesiodic Catalogue and by the subsequent logographers.   His daughter Tyrô became enamoured of the river Enipeus, the most beautiful of all streams that traverse the earth; she frequented the banks assiduously, and there the god Poseidôn found means to indulge his passion for her, assuming the character of the river-god himself.   The fruit of this alliance

1 First Æolid line—Salmôneus, Tyrô.

were the twin brothers, Pelias and Nêleus : Tyrô afterwards was given in marriage to her uncle Krêtheus, another son of Æolus, by whom she had Æsôn, Pherês, and Amythaôn—all names of celebrity in the heroic legends.[1]   The adventures of Tyrô formed the subject of an affecting drama of Sophoklês, now lost.   Her father had married a second wife, named Sidêrô, whose cruel counsels induced him to punish and torture his daughter on account of her intercourse with Poseidôn.   She was shorn of her magnificent hair, beaten and ill-used in various ways, and confined in a loathsome dungeon.   Unable to take care of her two children, she had been compelled to expose them immediately on their birth in a little boat on the river Enipeus; they were preserved by the kindness of a herdsman, and when grown up to manhood, rescued their mother, and revenged her wrongs by putting to death the iron-hearted Sidêrô.[2]   This pathetic tale respecting the long imprisonment of Tyrô is substituted by Sophoklês in place of the Homeric legend, which represented her to have become the wife of Krêtheus, and mother of a numerous offspring.[3]

Her father, the unjust Salmôneus, exhibited in his conduct the most insolent impiety towards the gods.   He assumed the name

---

[1] Homer, Odyss. xi. 234—257 ; xv. 226.

[2] Diodôrus, iv. 68.   Sophoklês, Fragm. 1. Τυρώ. Σαφῶς Σιδηρὼ καὶ φέρουσα τοὔνομα.   The genius of Sophoklês is occasionally seduced by this play upon the etymology of a name, even in the most impressive scenes of his tragedies.   See Ajax, 425.   Compare Hellanik. Fragm. p. 9, ed. Preller. There was a first and second edition of the Tyrô—τῆς δευτέρας Τυροῦς.   Schol.

ad Aristoph. Av. 276.   See the few fragments of the lost drama in Dindorf's Collection, p. 53.   The plot was in many respects analogous to the Antiopê of Euripidês.

[3] A third story, different both from Homer and from Sophoklês, respecting Tyrô, is found in Hyginus (Fab. lx.): it is of a tragical cast, and borrowed, like so many other tales in that collection, from one of the lost Greek dramas.

and title even of Zeus, and caused to be offered to himself the sacrifices destined for that god: he also imitated the thunder and lightning, by driving about with brazen caldrons attached to his chariot, and casting lighted torches towards heaven. Such wickedness finally drew upon him the wrath of Zeus, who smote him with a thunderbolt, and effaced from the earth the city which he had founded, with all its inhabitants.[1]

Pelias and Nêleus, "both stout vassals of the great Zeus," became engaged in dissension respecting the kingdom of Iôlkos in Thessaly. Pelias got possession of it, and dwelt there in plenty and prosperity; but he had offended the goddess Hêrê by killing Sidêrô upon her altar, and the effects of her wrath were manifested in his relations with his nephew Jasôn.[2]

Pelias and Nêleus.

Nêleus quitted Thessaly, went into Peloponnêsus, and there founded the kingdom of Pylos. He purchased, by immense marriage presents, the privilege of wedding the beautiful Chlôris, daughter of Amphiôn, king of Orchomenos, by whom he had twelve sons and but one daughter[3]—the fair and captivating Pêrô, whom suitors from all the neighbourhood courted in marriage. But Nêleus, "the haughtiest of living men,"[4] refused to entertain the pretensions of any of them : he would grant his daughter only to that man who should bring to him the oxen of Iphiklos, from Phylakê in Thessaly. These precious animals were carefully guarded, as well by herdsmen as by a dog whom neither man nor animal could approach. Nevertheless, Bias, the son of Amythaôn, nephew of Nêleus, being desperately enamoured of Pêrô, prevailed upon his brother Melampus to undertake for his sake the perilous adventure in spite of the prophetic knowledge

---

[1] Apollod. i. 9, 7. Σαλμωνεύς τ' ἄδικος καὶ ὑπέρθυμος Περιήρης. Hesiod, Fragm. Catal. 8. Marktscheffel.

Where the city of Salmôneus was situated, the ancient investigators were not agreed ; whether in the Pisatid, or in Elis, or in Thessaly (see Strabo, viii. p. 356). Euripidês in his Æolus placed him on the banks of the Alpheius (Eurip. Fragm. Æol. 1). A village and fountain in the Pisatid bore the name of Salmônê ; but the mention of the river Enipeus seems to mark Thessaly as the original seat of the legend. But the *naïveté* of the tale preserved by Apollodôrus (Virgil in the Æneid, vi.

586, has retouched it) marks its ancient date : the final circumstance of that tale was, that the city and its inhabitants were annihilated.

Ephorus makes Salmôneus king of the Épeians and of the Pisatæ (Fragm. 15, ed. Didot).

The lost drama of Sophoklês, called Σαλμωνεύς, was a δρᾶμα σατυρικόν. See Dindorf's Fragm. 483.

[2] Hom. Od. xi. 280. Apollod. i. 9, 9. κρατέρω θεράποντε Διός, &c.

[3] Diodôr. iv. 68.

[4] Νηλέα τε μεγάθυμον, ἀγανότατον ζωόντων (Hom. Odyss. xv. 229).

of the latter, which forewarned him that though he would ultimately succeed, the prize must be purchased by severe captivity and suffering. Melampus, in attempting to steal the oxen, was seized and put in prison ; from whence nothing but his prophetic powers rescued him. Being acquainted with the language of worms, he heard these animals communicating to each other, in the roof over his head, that the beams were nearly eaten through and about to fall in. He communicated this intelligence to his guards, and demanded to be conveyed to another place of confinement, announcing that the roof would presently fall in and bury them. The prediction was fulfilled, and Phylakos, father of Iphiklos, full of wonder at this specimen of prophetic power, immediately caused him to be released. He further consulted him respecting the condition of his son Iphiklos, who was childless ; and promised him the possession of the oxen on condition of his suggesting the means whereby offspring might be ensured. A vulture having communicated to Melampus the requisite information, Podarkês, the son of Iphiklos, was born shortly afterwards. In this manner Melampus obtained possession of the oxen, and conveyed them to Pylos, ensuring to his brother Bias the hand of Pêrô.[1] How this great legendary character, by miraculously healing the deranged daughters of Proetos, procured both for himself and for Bias dominion in Argos, has been recounted in a preceding chapter.

Pêrô, Bias, and Melampus.

Of the twelve sons of Nêleus, one at least, Periklymenos,—besides the ever memorable Nestôr,—was distinguished for his exploits as well as for his miraculous gifts. Poseidôn, the divine father of the race, had bestowed upon him the privilege of changing his form at pleasure into that of any bird, beast, reptile, or insect.[2] He had occasion for all these resources, and he employed them for a time with success in

Periklymenos.

---

[1] Hom. Od. xi. 278, xv. 234. Apollod. i. 9, 12. The basis of this curious romance is in the Odyssey, amplified by subsequent poets. There are points, however, in the old Homeric legend, as it is briefly sketched in the fifteenth book of the Odyssey, which seem to have been subsequently left out or varied. Nêleus seized the property of Melampus during his absence: the latter, returning with the oxen from Phylakê, revenges himself upon Nêleus for the injury. Odyss. xv. 233.

[2] Hesiod, Catalog. ap. Schol. Apollôn. Rhod. i. 156 ; Ovid, Metam. xii. p. 556 ; Eustath. ad Odyss. xi. p. 284. Poseidôn carefully protects Antilochus, son of Nestôr, in the Iliad, xiii. 554—563.

defending his family against the terrible indignation of Hêraklês, who, provoked by the refusal of Nêleus to perform for him the ceremony of purification after his murder of Iphitus, attacked the Nêleids at Pylos.   Periklymenos by his extraordinary powers prolonged the resistance, but the hour of his fate was at length brought upon him by the intervention of Athênê, who pointed him out to Hêraklês while he was perched as a bee upon the hero's chariot.   He was killed, and Hêraklês became completely victorious, overpowering Poseidôn, Hêrê, Arês, and Hadês, and even wounding the three latter, who assisted in the defence. Eleven of the sons of Nêleus perished by his hand, while Nestôr, then a youth, was preserved only by his accidental absence at Gerêna, away from his father's residence.[1]

The proud house of the Nêleids was now reduced to Nestôr ; but Nestôr singly sufficed to sustain its eminence. Nestôr and his exploits. He appears not only as the defender and avenger of Pylos against the insolence and rapacity of his Epeian neighbours at Elis, but also as aiding the Lapithæ in their terrible combat against the Centaurs, and as companion of Thêseus, Peirithöus, and the other great legendary heroes who preceded the Trojan war.   In extreme old age his once marvellous power of handling his weapons has indeed passed away, but his activity remains unimpaired, and his sagacity as well as his influence in counsel is greater than ever.   He not only assembles the various Grecian chiefs for the armament against Troy, perambulating the districts of Hellas along with Odysseus, but takes a vigorous part in the siege itself, and is of pre-eminent service to Agamemnôn.   And after the conclusion of the siege, he is one of the few Grecian

---

[1] Hesiod, Catalog. ap. Schol. Ven. ad Iliad. ii. 336 : and Steph. Byz. v. Γερηνία; Homer, Il. v. 392 ; xi. 693 ; Apollodôr. ii. 7, 3 ; Hesiod, Scut. Herc. 360 ; Pindar, Ol. ix. 32.

According to the Homeric legend, Nêleus himself was not killed by Hêraklês : subsequent poets or logographers, whom Apollodôrus follows, seem to have thought it an injustice, that the offence given by Nêleus himself should have been avenged upon his sons and not upon himself ; they therefore altered the legend upon this point, and rejected the passage in the Iliad as spurious (see Schol. Ven. ad Iliad. xi. 682).

The refusal of purification by Nêleus to Hêraklês is a genuine legendary cause : the commentators, who were disposed to spread a coating of history over these transactions, introduced another cause,—Nêleus, as king of Pylos, had aided the Orchomenians in their war against Hêraklês and the Thêbans (see Schol. Ven. ad Iliad. xi. 689).

The neighbourhood of Pylos was distinguished for its ancient worship both of Poseidôn and of Hadês : there were abundant local legends respecting them (see Strabo, xiii. pp. 344, 345).

princes who returns to his original dominions. He is found, in a strenuous and honoured old age, in the midst of his children and subjects,—sitting with the sceptre of authority on the stone bench before his house at Pylos,—offering sacrifice to Poseidôn, as his father Nêleus had done before him,—and mourning only over the death of his favourite son Antilochus, who had fallen along with so many brave companions in arms in the Trojan war.[1]

After Nestôr the line of the Nêleids numbers undistinguished names,—Bôrus, Penthilus, and Andropompus,—three successive generations down to Melanthus, who on the invasion of Peloponnêsus by the Herakleids, quitted Pylos and retired to Athens, where he became king, in a manner which I shall hereafter recount. His son Kodrus was the last Athenian king; and Nêleus, one of the sons of Kodrus, is mentioned as the principal conductor of what is called the Ionic emigration from Athens to Asia Minor.[2]

Nêleids down to Kodrus.

It is certain that during the historical age, not merely the princely family of the Kodrids in Milêtus, Ephesus, and other Ionic cities, but some of the greatest families even in Athens itself, traced their heroic lineage through the Nêleids up to Poseidôn ; and the legends respecting Nestôr and Periklymenos would find especial favour amidst Greeks with such feelings and belief. The Kodrids at Ephesus, and probably some other Ionic towns, long retained the title and honorary precedence of kings, even after they had lost the substantial power belonging to the office. They stood in the same relation, embodying both religious worship and supposed ancestry, to the Nêleids and Poseidôn, as the chiefs of the Æolic colonies to Agamemnôn and Orestês. The Athenian despot Peisistratus was named after the son of Nestôr in the Odyssey ; and we may safely presume that the heroic worship of the Nêleids was as carefully cherished at the Ionic Milêtus as at the Italian Metapontum.[3]

Having pursued the line of Salmôneus and Nêleus to the end

---

[1] About Nestôr. Iliad, i. 260—275 ; ii. 370 ; xi. 670—770 ; Odyss. iii. 5, 110, 409.

[2] Hellanik. Fragm. 10, ed. Didot ; Pausan. vii. 2, 3 ; Herodot. v. 65 ; Strabo, xiv. p. 633. Hellanikus, in giving the genealogy from Nêleus to Melanthus, traces it through Periklymenos and not through Nestôr ; the words of Herodotus imply that *he* must have included Nestôr.

[3] Herodot. v. 67 ; Strabo, vi. p. 264 ; Mimnermus, Fragm. 9, Schneidewin.

of its legendary career, we may now turn back to that of another
son of Æolus, Krêtheus,—a line hardly less celebrated
Second
Æolid line   in respect of the heroic names which it presents.
—Krêtheus.   Alkêstis, the most beautiful of the daughters of Pelias,[1]
was promised by her father in marriage to the man who could
bring him a lion and a boar tamed to the yoke and drawing together.   Admêtus, son of Pherês, the eponymus of Pheræ in
Thessaly, and thus grandson of Krêtheus, was enabled by the aid
of Apollo to fulfil this condition, and to win her ;[2] for Apollo
happened at that time to be in his service as a slave (condemned
to this penalty by Zeus for having put to death the Cyclôpes),
in which capacity he tended the herds and horses with such success, as to equip Eumêlus (the son of Admêtus) to the Trojan war
with the finest horses in the Grecian army.   Though menial
duties were imposed upon him, even to the drudgery of grinding
in the mill,[3] he yet carried away with him a grateful and friendly
sentiment towards his mortal master, whom he interfered to
rescue from the wrath of the goddess Artemis, when she was
indignant at the omission of her name in his wedding sacrifices.

Admêtus   Admêtus was about to perish by a premature death,
and   when Apollo, by earnest solicitation to the Fates, ob-
Alkêstis.   tained for him the privilege that his life should be
prolonged, if he could find any person to die a voluntary death
in his place.   His father and his mother both refused to make
this sacrifice for him, but the devoted attachment of his wife
Alkêstis disposed her to embrace with cheerfulness the condition

---

[1] Iliad. ii. 715.
[2] Apollodôr. i. 9, 15 ; Eustath. ad
Iliad. ii. 711.
[3] Euripid. Alkêst. init. Welcker,
Griechische Tragöd. (p. 344) on the lost
play of Sophoklês called Admêtus or
Alkêstis ; Hom. Iliad. ii. 766 ; Hygin.
Fab. 50—51 (Sophoklês, Fr. Inc. 730 ;
Dind. ap. Plutarch. Defect. Orac. p.
417). This tale of the temporary servitude of particular gods, by order of
Zeus as a punishment for misbehaviour,
recurs not unfrequently among the
incidents of the mythical world. The
poet Panyasis (ap. Clem. Alexand.
Adm. ad Gent. p. 23)—

Τλῆ μὲν Δημήτηρ, τλῆ δὲ κλυτὸς Ἀμφι-
    γυήεις,
Τλῆ δὲ Ποσειδάων, τλῆ δ' ἀργυρότοξος
    Ἀπόλλων

Ἀνδρὶ παρὰ θνητῷ θητεύσεμεν εἰς
    ἐνιαυτόν·
Τλῆ δὲ καὶ ὀβριμόθυμος Ἄρης ὑπὸ πατ-
    ρὸς ἀνάγκης.

The old legend followed out the
fundamental idea with remarkable
consistency : Laômedôn, as the temporary master of Poseidôn and Apollo,
threatens to bind them hand and foot,
to sell them in the distant islands, and
to cut off the ears of both when they
come to ask for their stipulated wages
(Iliad, xxi. 455). It was a new turn
given to the story by the Alexandrine
poets, when they introduced the motive
of love, and made the servitude voluntary on the part of Apollo (Kallimachus, Hymn. Apoll. 49 ; Tibullus,
Eleg. ii. 3, 11—30).

of dying to preserve her husband. She had already perished, when Hêraklês, the ancient guest and friend of Admêtus, arrived during the first hour of lamentation ; his strength and daring enabled him to rescue the deceased Alkêstis even from the grasp of Thanatos (Death), and to restore her alive to her disconsolate husband.[1]

The son of Pelias, Akastus, had received and sheltered Pêleus when obliged to fly his country in consequence of the involuntary murder of Eurytiôn. Krêthêis, the wife of Aka-   Pêleus and stus, becoming enamoured of Pêleus, made to him   the wife of advances which he repudiated. Exasperated at his   Akastus. refusal, and determined to procure his destruction, she persuaded her husband that Pêleus had attempted her chastity : upon which Akastus conducted Pêleus out upon a hunting excursion among the woody regions of Mount Pêlion, contrived to steal from him the sword fabricated and given by Hêphæstos, and then left him, alone and unarmed, to perish by the hands of the Centaurs or by the wild beasts. By the friendly aid of the Centaur Cheirôn, however, Pêleus was preserved, and his sword restored to him : returning to the city, he avenged himself by putting to death both Akastus and his perfidious wife.[2]

But amongst all the legends with which the name of Pelias is connected, by far the most memorable is that of Jasôn and the Argonautic expedition. Jasôn was son of Æsôn, grandson of Krêtheus, and thus great-grandson of Æolus. Pelias, having consulted the oracle respecting the security of his dominion at Iôlkos, had received in answer a warning to beware of the man who should appear before him with only one sandal. He was celebrating a festival in honour of Poseidôn, when it so happened that Jasôn appeared before him with one of his feet unsandaled : he had lost one sandal in wading through the swollen current of the river Anauros. Pelias immediately understood that this was the enemy against whom the oracle had forewarned him. As a

---

[1] Eurip. Alkêstis, Arg. ; Apollod. i. 9, 15. To bring this beautiful legend more into the colour of history, a new version of it was subsequently framed : Hêraklês was eminently skilled in medicine, and saved the life of Alkêstis when she was about to perish from a desperate malady (Plutarch, Amator. 17, vol. iv. p. 53, Wytt.).

[2] The legend of Akastus and Pêleus was given in great detail in the Catalogue of Hesiod (Catalog. Fragm. 20—21. Marktscheff.); Schol. Pindar. Nem. iv. 95; Schol. Apoll. Rhod. i. 224 ; Apollod. iii. 13, 2.

means of averting the danger, he imposed upon Jasôn the despe-
Pelias and   rate task of bringing back to Iôlkos the Golden Fleece,
Jasôn.   —the fleece of that ram which had carried Phryxos
from Achaia to Kolchis, and which Phryxos had dedicated in the
latter country as an offering to the god Arês.   The result of this
injunction was the memorable expedition—of the ship Argô and
her crew called the Argonauts, composed of the bravest and
noblest youths of Greece—which cannot be conveniently included among the legends of the Æolids, and is reserved for a
separate chapter.

The voyage of the Argô was long protracted, and Pelias, per-
Jasôn and   suaded that neither the ship nor her crew would ever
Mêdea.   return, put to death both the father and mother of
Jasôn, together with their infant son.   Æsôn, the father, being
permitted to choose the manner of his own death, drank bull's
blood while performing a sacrifice to the gods.   At length, however, Jasôn did return, bringing with him not only the golden
fleece, but also Mêdea, daughter of Æêtês, king of Kolchis, as his
wife,—a woman distinguished for magical skill and cunning, by
whose assistance alone the Argonauts had succeeded in their project.   Though determined to avenge himself upon Pelias, Jasôn
knew that he could only succeed by stratagem.   He remained
with his companions a short distance from Iôlkos, while Mêdea,
feigning herself a fugitive from his ill-usage, entered the town
alone, and procured access to the daughters of Pelias.   By exhibitions of her magical powers she soon obtained unqualified
ascendancy over their minds.   For example, she selected from
the flocks of Pelias a ram in the extremity of old age, cut him up
and boiled him in a caldron with herbs, and brought him out in
the shape of a young and vigorous lamb :[1] the daughters of Pelias
were made to believe that their old father could in like manner
be restored to youth.   In this persuasion they cut him up with
their own hands and cast his limbs into the caldron, trusting that
Mêdea would produce upon him the same magical effect.   Mêdea
pretended that an invocation to the moon was a necessary part of

the ceremony : she went up to the top of the house as if to pronounce it, and there lighting the fire-signal concerted with the
Argonauts, Jasôn and his companions burst in and possessed
themselves of the town. Satisfied with having thus revenged
himself, Jasôn yielded the principality of Iôlkos to Akastus, son
of Pelias, and retired with Mêdea to Corinth. Thus did the goddess Hêrê gratify her ancient wrath against Pelias : she had constantly watched over Jasôn, and had carried the " all-notorious "
Argô through its innumerable perils, in order that Jasôn might
bring home Mêdea to accomplish the ruin of his uncle.[1] The
misguided daughters of Pelias departed as voluntary exiles to
Arcadia : Akastus his son celebrated splendid funeral games in
honour of his deceased father.[2]

---

[1] The kindness of Hêrê towards Jasôn seems to be older in the legend than her displeasure against Pelias ; at least it is specially noticed in the Odyssey, as the great cause of the escape of the ship Argô: Ἀλλ' Ἥρη παρέπεμψεν, ἐπεὶ φίλος ἦεν Ἰήσων (xii. 70). In the Hesiodic Theogony Pelias stands to Jasôn in the same relation as Eurystheus to Hêraklês,—a severe taskmaster as well as a wicked and insolent man, — ὑβριστὴς Πελίης καὶ ἀτάσθαλος, ὀβριμόεργος (Theog. 995). Apollônius Rhodius keeps the wrath of Hêrê against Pelias in the foreground, i. 14 ; ii. 1134; iv. 242; see also Hygin. f. 13.

There is great diversity in the stories given of the proximate circumstances connected with the death of Pelias : Eurip. Mêd. 491; Apollodôr. i. 9, 27 ; Diodôr. iv. 50—52 ; Ovid, Metam. vii. 162, 203, 297, 347 ; Pausan. viii. 11, 2 ; Schol. ad Lycoph. 175.

In the legend of Akastus and Pêleus, as recounted above, Akastus was made to perish by the hand of Pêleus. I do not take upon me to reconcile these contradictions.

Pausanias mentions that he could not find in any of the poets, so far as he had read, the names of the daugh-ters of Pêleus, and that the painter Mikôn had given to them names (ὀνό-ματα δ' αὐταῖς ποιητὴς μὲν ἔθετο οὐδείς, ὅσα γ' ἐπελεξάμεθα ἡμεῖς, &c., Pausan. viii. 11. 1). Yet their names are given in the authors whom Diodôrus copied ; and Alkêstis, at any rate, was most memorable. Mikôn gave the names Asteropeia and Antinoê, altogether

different from those in Diodôrus. Both Diodôrus and Hyginus exonerate Al-kêstis from all share in the death of her father (Hygin. f. 24).

The old poem called the Νόστοι (see Argum. ad Eurip. Mêd., and Schol. Aristophan. Equit. 1321) recounted, that Mêdea had boiled in a caldron the old Æsôn, father of Jasôn, with herbs and incantations, and that she had brought him out young and strong. Ovid copies this (Metam. vii. 162—203). It is singular that Pherekydês and Simonidês said that she performed this process upon Jasôn himself (Schol. Aristoph. l. c.). Diogenes (ap. Stobœ. Florileg. t. xxix. 92) rationalises the story, and converts Mêdea from an enchantress into an improving and re-generating preceptress. The death of Æsôn, as described in the text, is given from Diodôrus and Apollodôrus. Mêdea seems to have been worshipped as a goddess in other places besides Corinth (see Athenagor. Legat. pro Christ. 12 ; Macrobius, i. 12, p. 247, Gronov.).

[2] These funeral games in honour of Pelias were among the most renowned of the mythical incidents : they were celebrated in a special poem by Stêsi-chorus, and represented on the chest of Kypselus at Olympia. Kastôr, Meleager, Amphiaraos, Jasôn, Pêleus, Mopsos, &c., contended in them (Pau-san. v. 17, 4 ; Stesichori Fragm. 1. p. 54, ed. Klewe ; Athên. iv. 172). How familiar the details of them were to the mind of a literary Greek is in-directly attested by Plutarch, Sympos. v. 2, vol. iii. p. 762, Wytt.

Jasôn and Mêdea retired from Iôlkos to Corinth where they
Mêdea at Corinth. resided ten years : their children were—Medeius, whom the Centaur Cheirôn educated in the regions of Mount Pêlion,[1]—and Mermerus and Pherês, born at Corinth. After they had resided there ten years in prosperity, Jasôn set his affections on Glaukê, daughter of Kreôn[2] king of Corinth ; and as her father was willing to give her to him in marriage, he determined to repudiate Mêdea, who received orders forthwith to leave Corinth. Stung with this insult and bent upon revenge, Mêdea prepared a poisoned robe, and sent it as a marriage present to Glaukê: it was unthinkingly accepted and put on, and the body of the unfortunate bride was burnt up and consumed. Kreôn, her father, who tried to tear from her the burning garment, shared her fate and perished. The exulting Mêdea escaped by means of a chariot with winged serpents furnished to her by her grandfather Hêlios : she placed herself under the protection of Ægeus at Athens, by whom she had a son named Mêdus. She left her young children in the sacred enclosure of the Akræan Hêrê, relying on the protection of the altar to ensure their safety ; but the Corinthians were so exasperated against her for the murder of Kreôn and Glaukê, that they dragged the children away from the altar and put them to death. The miserable Jasôn perished by a fragment of his own ship Argô, which fell upon him while he was asleep under it,[3] being hauled on shore, according to the habitual practice of the ancients.

[1] Hesiod, Theogon. 998.

[2] According to the Schol. ad Eurip. Mêd. 20, Jasôn marries the daughter of Hippotês the son of Kreôn, who is the son of Lykæthos. Lykæthos, after the departure of Bellerophôn from Corinth, reigned twenty-seven years ; then Kreôn reigned thirty-five years ; then came Hippotês.

[3] Apollodôr. i. 9, 27 ; Diodôr. iv. 54. The Mêdea of Euripidês, which has fortunately been preserved to us, is too well known to need express reference. He makes Mêdea the destroyer of her own children, and borrows from this circumstance the most pathetic touches of his exquisite drama. Parmeniskos accused him of having been bribed by the Corinthians to give this turn to the legend; and we may regard the accusation as a proof that the older and more current tale imputed the murder of

the children to the Corinthians (Schol. Eurip. Med. 275, where Didymos gives the story out of the old poem of Kreophylos). See also Ælian, V. H. v. 21, Pausan. ii. 3, 6.

The most significant fact in respect to the fable is, that the Corinthians celebrated periodically a propitiatory sacrifice to Hêrê Akræa and to Mermerus and Pherês, as an atonement for the sin of having violated the sanctuary of the altar. The legend grew out of this religious ceremony, and was so arranged as to explain and account for it (see Eurip. Mêd. 1376, with the Schol. Diodôr. iv. 55).

Mermerus and Pherês were the names given to the children of Mêdea and Jasôn in the old Naupaktian Verses ; in which, however, the legend must have been recounted quite differently, since they said that Jasôn and

The first establishment at Ephyrê, or Corinth, had been founded by Sisyphus, another of the sons of Æolus, brother of Salmôneus and Krêtheus.[1] The Æolid Sisyphus was distinguished as an unexampled master of cunning and deceit. He blocked up the road along the isthmus, and killed the strangers who came along it by rolling down upon them great stones from the mountains above. He was more than a match even for the arch thief Autolykus, the son of Hermês, who derived from his father the gift of changing the colour and shape of stolen goods, so that they could no longer be recognised: Sisyphus, by marking his sheep under the foot, detected Autolykus when he stole them, and obliged him to restore the plunder. His penetration discovered the amour of Zeus with the nymph Ægina, daughter of the river-god Asôpus. Zeus had carried her off to the island of Œnônê (which subsequently bore the name of Ægina); upon which Asôpus, eager to recover her, inquired of Sisyphus whither she was gone; the latter told him what had happened, on condition that he should provide a spring of water on the summit of the Acro-Corinthus. Zeus, indignant with Sisyphus for this revelation, inflicted upon him in Hadês the punishment of perpetually heaving up a hill a great and heavy stone, which, so soon as it attained the summit, rolled back again, in spite of all his efforts, with irresistible force into the plain.[2]

Third Æolid line —Sisyphus.

Mêdea had gone from Iôlkos, not to Corinth, but to Corcyra; and that Mermerus had perished in hunting on the opposite continent of Epirus. Kinæthôn again, another ancient genealogical poet, called the children of Mêdea and Jasôn Eriôpis and Mêdos (Pausan. ii. 3, 7). Diodôrus gives them different names (iv. 34). Hesiod in the Theogony speaks only of Medeius as the son of Jasôn.

Mêdea does not appear either in the Iliad or Odyssey: in the former we find Agamêdê, daughter of Augeas, "who knows all the poisons (or medicines) which the earth nourishes" (Iliad. xi. 740); in the latter we have Circê, sister of Æêtês father of Mêdea, and living in the Ææan island (Odyss. x. 70). Circê is daughter of the god Hélios, as Mêdea is his grand-daughter, —she is herself a goddess. She is in many points the parallel of Mêdea:

she forewarns and preserves Odysseus throughout his dangers, as Mêdea aids Jasôn: according to the Hesiodic story she has two children by Odysseus, Agrius and Latinus (Theogon. 1001).

Odysseus goes to Ephyrê to Ilos the son of Mermerus, to procure poison for his arrows: Eustathius treats this Mermerus as the son of Mêdea (see Odyss. i. 270, an. Eust.). As Ephyrê is the legendary name of Corinth, we may presume this to be a thread of the same mythical tissue.

[1] See Euripid. Æol. — Fragm. 1, Dindorf; Dikæarch. Vit. Græc. p. 22.

[2] Respecting Sisyphus, see Apollodôr. i. 9, 3; iii. 12, 6. Pausan. ii. 5, 1, Schol. ad Iliad. i. 180. Another legend about the amour of Sisyphus with Tyrô is in Hygin. fab. 60, and about the manner in which he overreached even Hadês (Pherekydês ap. Schol. Iliad. vi. 153). The stone rolled by Sisyphus

In the application of the Æolid genealogy to Corinth, Sisyphus, the son of Æolus, appears as the first name: but the old Corinthian poet Eumêlus either found or framed an heroic genealogy for his native city, independent both of Æolus and Sisyphus. According to this genealogy, Ephyrê, daughter of Oceanus and Têthys, was the primitive tenant of the Corinthian territory, Asôpus of the Sikyônian: both were assigned to the god Hêlios, in adjusting a dispute between him and Poseidôn, by Briareus. Hêlios divided the territory between his two sons Æêtês and Alôeus: to the former he assigned Corinth, to the latter Sikyôn. Æêtês, obeying the admonition of an oracle, emigrated to Kolchis, leaving his territory under the rule of Bunos, the son of Hermês, with the stipulation that it should be restored whenever either he or any of his descendants returned. After the death of Bunos, both Corinth and Sikyôn were possessed by Epôpeus, son of Alôeus, a wicked man. His son Marathôn left him in disgust, and retired into Attica, but returned after his death and succeeded to his territory, which he in turn divided between his two sons, Corinthos and Sikyôn, from whom the names of the two districts were first derived. Corinthos died without issue, and the Corinthians then invited Mêdea from Iôlkos as the representative of Æêtês: she, with her husband Jasôn, thus obtained the sovereignty of Corinth.[1] This legend of Eumêlus, one of the earliest of the genealogical poets, so different from the story adopted by Neophrôn or Euripidês, was followed certainly by Simonidês, and seemingly by Theopompus.[2] The incidents in it are imagined and arranged with a view to the

Corinthian genealogy of Eumêlus.

---

in the under-world appears in Odyss. xi. 592. The name of Sisyphus was given during the historical age to men of craft and stratagem, such as Derkyllidês (Xenoph. Hellenic. iii. 1, 8). He passed for the real father of Odysseus, though Heyne (ad Apollodôr. i. 9, 3) treats this as another Sisyphus, whereby he destroys the suitableness of the predicate as regards Odysseus. The duplication and triplication of synonymous personages is an ordinary resource for the purpose of reducing the legends into a seeming chronological sequence.

Even in the days of Eumêlus a religious mystery was observed respecting the tombs of Sisyphus and Nêleus,—the latter had also died at Corinth,—no one could say where they were buried (Pausan. ii. 2, 2).

Sisyphus even overreached Persephonê, and made his escape from the under-world (Theognis, 702).

[1] Pausan. ii. 1, 1; 3, 10. Schol. ad Pindar. Ol. xiii. 74. Schol. Lycoph. 174—1024. Schol. Ap. Rh. iv. 1212.

[2] Simonid. ap. Schol. ad Eurip. Mêd. 10—20: Theopompus, Fragm. 340, Didot; though Welcker (Der Episch. Cycl. p. 29) thinks this does not belong to the historian Theopompus. Epimenidês also followed the story of Eumêlus in making Æêtês a Corinthian (Schol. ad Apoll. Rhod. iii. 242).

supremacy of Mêdea; the emigration of Æêtês and the conditions under which he transferred his sceptre, being so laid out as to confer upon Mêdea an hereditary title to the throne. The Corinthians paid to Mêdea and to her children solemn worship, either divine, or heroic, in conjunction with Hêrê Akræa,[1] and this was sufficient to give to Mêdea a prominent place in the genealogy composed by a Corinthian poet, accustomed to blend together gods, heroes, and men in the antiquities of his native city. According to the legend of Eumêlus, Jasôn became (through Mêdea) king of Corinth; but she concealed the children of their marriage in the temple of Hêrê, trusting that the goddess would render them immortal. Jasôn, discovering her proceedings, left her, and retired in disgust to Iôlkos; Mêdea also, being disappointed in her scheme, quitted the place, leaving the throne in the hands of Sisyphus, to whom, according to the story of Theopompus, she had become attached.[2] Other legends recounted that Zeus had contracted a passion for Mêdea, but that she had rejected his suit from fear of the displeasure of Hêrê; who, as a recompense for such fidelity, rendered her children immortal:[3] moreover, Mêdea had erected, by special command of Hêrê, the celebrated temple of Aphroditê at Corinth. The tenor of these fables manifests their connexion with the temple of Hêrê: and we may consider the legend of Mêdea as having been originally quite independent of that of Sisyphus, but fitted on to it, in seeming chronological sequence, so as to satisfy the feelings of those Æolids of Corinth who passed for his descendants.

Coalescence of different legends about Mêdea and Sisyphus.

Sisyphus had for his sons Glaukos and Ornytiôn. From Glaukos sprang Bellerophôn, whose romantic adventures commence with the Iliad, and are further expanded by subsequent poets: according to some accounts, he was really the son of Poseidôn, the prominent deity of the Æolid family.[4] The youth

---

[1] Περὶ δὲ τῆς εἰς Κόρινθον μετοικήσεως, Ἴππυς ἐκτίθεται καὶ Ἑλλάνικος· ὅτι δὲ βεβασίλευκε τῆς Κορίνθου ἡ Μήδεια, Εὔμηλος ἱστορεῖ καὶ Σιμωνίδης· ὅτι δὲ καὶ ἀθάνατος ἦν ἡ Μήδεια, Μουσαῖος ἐν τῷ περὶ Ἰσθμίων ἱστορεῖ, ἅμα καὶ περὶ τῶν τῆς Ἀκραίας Ἥρας ἑορτῶν ἐκτιθεὶς (Schol. Eurip. Mêd. 10). Compare also v. 1376, of the play itself, with the Scholia and Pausan. ii. 3, 6. Both Alkman and

Hesiod represented Mêdea as a goddess (Athenagoras, Legatio pro Christianis, p. 54, ed. Oxon.).
[2] Pausan. ii. 3, 10; Schol. Pindar. Olymp. xiii. 74.
[3] Schol. Pindar. Olymp. xiii. 32—74; Plutarch, De Herodot. Malign. p. 871.
[4] Pindar, Olymp. xiii. 98, and Schol. ad 1; Schol. ad Iliad. vi. 155; this seems to be the sense of Iliad. vi. 191.

and beauty of Bellerophôn rendered him the object of a strong
passion on the part of Anteia, wife of Prœtos, king of
Argos. Finding her advances rejected, she contracted
a violent hatred towards him, and endeavoured, by false accusations, to prevail upon her husband to kill him. Prœtos refused
to commit the deed under his own roof, but despatched him to
his son-in-law, the king of Lykia in Asia Minor, putting into his
hands a folded tablet full of destructive symbols. Conformably
to these suggestions, the most perilous undertakings were imposed upon Bellerophôn. He was directed to attack the monster
Chimæra and to conquer the warlike Solymi as well as the
Amazons: as he returned victorious from these enterprises, an
ambuscade was laid for him by the bravest Lykian warriors, all
of whom he slew. At length the Lykian king recognised him
"as the genuine son of a god," and gave him his daughter in
marriage together with half of his kingdom. The grand-children
of Bellerophôn, Glaukos and Sarpêdôn,—the latter a son of his
daughter Laodameia by Zeus,—combat as allies of Troy against
the host of Agamemnôn.[1]

*Bellero-
phôn.*

We now pass from Sisyphus and the Corinthian fables to
another son of Æolus, Athamas, whose family history
is not less replete with mournful and tragical incidents, abundantly diversified by the poets. Athamas,
we are told, was king of Orchomenos; his wife Nephelê was a
goddess, and he had by her two children, Phryxus and Hellê.
After a certain time he neglected Nephelê, and took to himself as
a new wife Inô, the daughter of Kadmus, by whom he had two
sons, Learchus and Melikertês. Inô, looking upon Phryxus with
the hatred of a stepmother, laid a snare for his life. She persuaded the women to roast the seed-wheat, which, when sown in
this condition, yielded no crop, so that famine overspread the
land. Athamas, sending to Delphi to implore counsel and a

*Fourth
Æolid line
—Athamas.*

The lost drama called *Iobatês* of
Sophoklês, and the two by Euripidês
called *Sthenebœa* and *Bellerophôn*,
handled the adventures of this hero.
See the collection of the few fragments
remaining in Dindorf, Fragm. Sophoc.
280; Fragm. Eurip. p. 87—108; and
Hygin. fab. 67.
Welcker (Griechische Tragöd. il. p.
777—800) has ingeniously put together
all that can be divined respecting the
two plays of Euripidês.
Völcker seeks to make out that
Bellerophôn is identical with Poseidôn
Hippios,—a separate personification of
one of the attributes of the god Poseidôn. For this conjecture he gives
some plausible grounds (Mythologie
des Japetisch. Geschlechts, p. 129 *seq.*).
[1] Iliad, vi. 155—210.

remedy, received for answer, through the machinations of Inô with the oracle, that the barrenness of the fields could not be alleviated except by offering Phryxus as a sacrifice to Zeus. The distress of the people compelled him to execute this injunction, and Phryxus was led as a victim to the altar. But the power of his mother Nephelê snatched him from destruction, and procured for him from Hermês a ram with a fleece of gold, Phryxus upon which he and his sister Hellê mounted and and Hellê. were carried across the sea. The ram took the direction of the Euxine sea and Kolchis: when they were crossing the Hellespont, Hellê fell off into the narrow strait, which took its name from that incident. Upon this, the ram, who was endued with speech, consoled the terrified Phryxus, and ultimately carried him safe to Kolchis: Æêtês, king of Kolchis, son of the god Hêlios, and brother of Circê, received Phryxus kindly, and gave him his daughter Chalkiopê in marriage. Phryxus sacrificed the ram to Zeus Phyxios, suspending the golden fleece in the sacred grove of Arês.

Athamas—according to some both Athamas and Inô—were afterwards driven mad by the anger of the goddess Hêrê; insomuch that the father shot his own son Learchus, and would also have put to death his other son Melikertês, if Inô Inô and had not snatched him away. She fled with the boy Palæmôn.— across the Megarian territory and Mount Geraneia, to games. the rock Moluris, overhanging the Sarônic Gulf: Athamas pursued her, and in order to escape him she leaped into the sea. She became a sea-goddess under the title of Leukothea; while the body of Melikertês was cast ashore on the neighbouring terri- tory of Schœnus, and buried by his uncle Sisyphus, who was directed by the Nereïds to pay to him heroic honours under the name of Palæmôn. The Isthmian games, one of the great periodical festivals of Greece, were celebrated in honour of the god Poseidôn, in conjunction with Palæmôn as a hero. Athamas abandoned his territory, and became the first settler of a neigh- bouring region called from him Athamantia, or the Athamantian plain.[1]

---

[1] Eurip. Méd. 1250, with the Scholia, according to which story Inô killed both her children :—

Ἰνὼ μανεῖσαν ἐκ θεῶν, ὅθ᾽ ἡ Διὸς Δάμαρ νιν ἐξέπεμψε δωμάτων ἄλῃ. Compare Valckenaer, Diatribe in Eurip.;

The legend of Athamas connects itself with some sanguinary re-
Local root   ligious rites and very peculiar family customs, which
of the   prevailed at Alos, in Achaia Phthiôtis, down to a
legend of
Athamas.   time[1] later than the historian Herodotus, and of which
some remnant existed at Orchomenos even in the days of Plutarch. Athamas was worshipped at Alos as a hero, having both
a chapel and a consecrated grove, attached to the temple of Zeus
Laphystios. On the family of which· he was the heroic progenitor, a special curse and disability stood affixed. The eldest of
the race was forbidden to enter the prytaneion or government-
house : if he was found within the doors of the building, the
other citizens laid hold of him on his going out, surrounded
him with garlands, and led him in solemn procession to be
sacrificed as a victim at the altar of Zeus Laphystios. The
prohibition carried with it an exclusion from all the public
meetings and ceremonies, political as well as religious, and from
the sacred fire of the state : many of the individuals marked
out had therefore been bold enough to transgress it. Some
had been seized on quitting the building and actually sacri-

Apollodôr. i. 9, 1—2 : Schol. ad Pindar.
Argum. ad Isthm. p. 180. The many
varieties of the fable of Athamas and
his family may be seen in Hygin. fab.
1—5 ; Philostephanus ap. Schol. Iliad.
vii. 86 : it was a favourite subject with
the tragedians, and was handled by
Æschylus, Sophoklês, and Euripidês
in more than one drama (see Welcker,
Griechische Tragöd. vol. i. p. 312—332;
vol. ii. p. 612). Heyne says that the
proper reading of the name is *Phrixus*,
not *Phryxus*, — incorrectly, I think :
Φρύξος connects the name both with
the story of roasting the wheat (φρύγειν),
and also with the country Φρυγία, of
which it was pretended that Phryxus
was the Eponymus. Inô, or Leukothea,
was worshipped as a heroine at Megara
as well as at Corinth (Pausan. i. 42, 3):
the celebrity of the Isthmian games
carried her worship, as well as that of
Palæmôn, throughout most parts of
Greece (Cicero, De Nat. Deor. iii. 16).
She is the only personage of this family
noticed either in the Iliad or Odyssey :
in the latter poem she is a sea-goddess,
who has once been a mortal, daughter
of Kadmus ; she saves Odysseus from
imminent danger at sea by presenting
to him her κρήδεμνον (Odyss. v. 433;
see the refinements of Aristidês, Orat.

iii. p. 27). The voyage of Phryxus and
Hellê to Kolchis was related in the
Hesiodic Eoiai : we find the names of
the children of Phryxus by the daughter
of Æêtês quoted from that poem (Schol.
ad Apollon. Rhod. ii. 1123): both Hesiod and Pherekydês mentioned the
golden fleece of the ram (Eratosthen.
Catasterism. 19 ; Pherekyd. Fragm. 53,
Didot).
Hekatæus preserved the romance of
the speaking ram (Schol. Apoll. Rhod.
i. 256) ; but Hellanikus dropped the
story of Hellê having fallen into the
sea : according to him she died at
Paktyê in the Chersonesus (Schol.
Apoll. Rhod. ii. 1144).
The poet Asius seems to have given
the genealogy of Athamas by Themistô
much in the same manner as we find it
in Apollodôrus (Pausan. ix. 23, 3).
According to the ingenious refinements of Dionysius and Palæphatus
(Schol. ad Apoll. Rhod. ii. 1144 ; Palæphat. de Incred. c. 81), the ram of
Phryxus was after all a man named
Krios, a faithful attendant who aided
in his escape ; others imagined a ship
with a ram's head at the bow.

[1] Plutarch, Quæst. Græc. c. 38, p.
299. Schol. Apoll. Rhod. ii. 655.

ficed ; others had fled the country for a long time to avoid a similar fate.

The guides who conducted Xerxes and his army through southern Thessaly detailed to him this existing practice, coupled with the local legend, that Athamas, together with Inô, had sought to compass the death of Phryxus, who however had escaped to Kolchis ; that the Achæans had been enjoined by an oracle to offer up Athamas himself as an expiatory sacrifice to release the country from the anger of the gods ; but that Kytissoros, son of Phryxus, coming back from Kolchis, had intercepted the sacrifice of Athamas,[1] whereby the anger of the gods remained still unappeased, and an undying curse rested upon the family.[2]

That such human sacrifices continued to a greater or less extent, even down to a period later than Herodotus, among the family who worshipped Athamas as their heroic ancestor, appears certain : mention is also made of similar customs in parts of Arcadia, and of Thessaly, in honour of Pêleus and Cheirôn.[3] But we may reasonably presume, that in the period of greater humanity which Herodotus witnessed, actual sacrifice had become

[1] Of the Athamas of Sophoklês, turning upon this intended but not consummated sacrifice, little is known, except from a passage of Aristophanês and the Scholia upon it (Nubes, 258)—

ἐπὶ τί στέφανον ; οἴμοι, Σώκρατες, ὥσπερ με τὸν 'Αθάμανθ' ὅπω ; μὴ θύσετε.

Athamas was introduced in this drama with a garland on his head, on the point of being sacrificed as an expiation for the death of his son Phryxus, when Hêraklês interposes and rescues him.

[2] Herodot. vii. 197. Plato, Minôs, p. 315.

[3] Plato, Minôs, c. 5. Καὶ οἱ τοῦ 'Αθάμαντος ἔκγονοι, οἵας θυσίας θύουσιν, Ἕλληνες ὄντες. As a testimony to the fact still existing or believed to exist, this dialogue is quite sufficient, though not the work of Plato.

Μόνιμος δ' ἱστορεῖ, ἐν τῇ τῶν θαυμασίων συναγωγῇ ἐν Πέλλῃ τῆς Θετταλίας 'Αχαιὸν ἄνθρωπον Πηλεῖ καὶ Χείρωνι καταθύεσθαι. (Clemens Alexand. Admon. ad Gent. p. 27, Sylb.) Respecting the sacrifices at the temple of Zeus Lykæus in Arcadia, see Plato, Republ. viii. p. 565. Pausanias (viii. 38, 5) seems to have shrunk, when he was

upon the spot, even from inquiring what they were—a striking proof of the fearful idea which he had conceived of them. Plutarch (De Defectu Oracul. c. 14) speaks of τὰς πάλαι ποιουμένας ἀνθρωποθυσίας. The Schol. ad Lycophr. 229, gives a story of children being sacrificed to Melikertês at Tenedos ; and Apollodôrus (ad Porphyr. de Abstinentiâ, ii. 55, see Apollod. Fragm. 20, ed. Didot) said that the Lacedæmonians had sacrificed a man to Arês—καὶ Λακεδαιμονίους φησὶν ὁ 'Απολλόδωρος τῷ "Αρει θύειν ἄνθρωπον. About Salamis in Cyprus, see Lactantius, De Falsâ Religione, i. c. 21. "Apud Cypri Salaminem, humanam hostiam Jovi Teucrus immolavit, idque sacrificium posteris tradidit : quod est nuper Hadriano imperante sublatum."

Respecting human sacrifices in historical Greece, consult a good section in K. F. Hermann's Gottesdienstliche Alterthümer der Griechen (sect. 27). Such sacrifices had been a portion of primitive Grecian religion, but had gradually become obsolete everywhere —except in one or two solitary cases, which were spoken of with horror. Even in these cases, too, the reality of the fact, in later times, is not beyond suspicion.

very rare. The curse and the legend still remained, but were not called into practical working, except during periods of intense national suffering or apprehension, during which the religious sensibilities were always greatly aggravated. We cannot at all doubt, that during the alarm created by the presence of the Persian king with his immense and ill-disciplined host, the minds of the Thessalians must have been keenly alive to all that was terrific in their national stories, and all that was expiatory in their religious solemnities. Moreover, the mind of Xerxes himself was so awe-struck by the tale, that he reverenced the dwelling-place consecrated to Athamas. The guides who recounted to him the romantic legend gave it as the historical and generating cause of the existing rule and practice: a critical inquirer is forced (as has been remarked before) to reverse the order of precedence, and to treat the practice as having been the suggesting cause of its own explanatory legend.

Traces of ancient human sacrifice.

The family history of Athamas and the worship of Zeus Laphystios are expressly connected by Herodotus with Alos in Achæa Phthiôtis—one of the towns enumerated in the Iliad as under the command of Achilles. But there was also a mountain called Laphystion, and a temple and worship of Zeus Laphystios between Orchomenos and Korôneia, in the northern portion of the territory known in the historical ages as Bœotia. Here too the family story of Athamas is localised, and Athamas is presented to us as king of the districts of Korôneia, Haliartus and Mount Laphystion: he is thus interwoven with the Orchomenian genealogy.[1] Andreus (we are told), son of the river Pêneios, was the first person who settled in the region: from him it received the name Andrêis. Athamas, coming subsequently to Andreus, received from him the territory of Korôneia and Haliartus with Mount Laphystion: he gave in marriage to Andreus Euippê, daughter of his son Leucôn, and the issue of this marriage was Eteoklês, said to be the son of the river Kêphisos. Korônos and Haliartus, grandsons of the Corinthian Sisyphus, were adopted by Athamas, as he had lost all his children. But when his grandson Presbôn, son of Phryxus, returned to him from Kolchis, he divided his territory in such

Athamas in the district near Orchomenos.

_____

1 Pausan. ix. 34, 4.

manner that Korônos and Haliartus became the founders of the
towns which bore their names.   Almôn, the son of Sisyphus, also
received from Eteoklês a portion of territory, where he established
the village Almônes.[1]

With Eteoklês began, according to a statement in one of the
Hesiodic poems, the worship of the Charites or Graces, so long
and so solemnly continued at Orchomenos in the periodical festival of the Charitêsia, to which many neighbouring   Eteoklês—
towns and districts seem to have contributed.[2]   He   festival of
also distributed the inhabitants into two tribes—Eteo-   tbe Chari-
kleia and Kêphisias.   He died childless, and was succeeded by
Almos, who had only two daughters, Chrysê and Chrysogeneia.
The son of Chrysê by the god Arês was Phlegyas, the father and
founder of the warlike and predatory Phlegyæ, who despoiled
every one within their reach, and assaulted not only the pilgrims
on their road to Delphi, but even the treasures of the temple
itself.   The offended god punished them by continued thunder,
by earthquakes, and by pestilence, which extinguished all
this impious race, except a scanty remnant who fled into
Phokis.

Chrysogeneia, the other daughter of Almos, had for issue, by
the god Poseidôn, Minyas : the son of Minyas was Orchomenos.
From these two was derived the name both of Minyæ for the
people, and of Orchomenos for the town.[3]   During the reign of
Orchomenos, Hyêttus came to him from Argos, having become
an exile in consequence of the death of Molyros : Orchomenos
assigned to him a portion of land, where he founded the village
called Hyêttus.[4]   Orchomenos, having no issue, was succeeded
by Klymenos, son of Presbôn, of the house of Athamas : Klymenos was slain by some Thêbans during the festival of Poseidôn
at Onchêstos ; and his eldest son, Erginus, to avenge his death,
attacked the Thêbans with his utmost force ;—an attack in which
he was so successful, that the latter were forced to submit, and to
pay him an annual tribute.

---

[1] Pausan. ix. 34, 5.

[2] Ephorus, Fragm. 68, Marx.

[3] Pausan. ix. 36, 1—3.   See also a
legend, about the three daughters of
Minyas, which was treated by the

Tanagræan poetess Korinna, the contemporary of Pindar (Antonin. Liberalis, Narr. x.).

[4] This exile of Hyêttus was recounted
in the Eoiai.   Hesiod. Fragm. 148,
Markt.

The Orchomenian power was now at its height : both Minyas and Orchomenos had been princes of surpassing wealth, and the former had built a spacious and durable edifice which he had filled with gold and silver. But the success of Erginus against Thêbes was soon terminated and reversed by the hand of the irresistible Hêraklês, who rejected with disdain the claim of tribute, and even mutilated the envoys sent to demand it : he not only emancipated Thêbes, but broke down and impoverished Orchomenos.[1] Erginus in his old age married a young wife, from which match sprang the illustrious heroes, or gods, Trophônius and Agamêdês ; though many (amongst whom is Pausanias himself) believed Trophônius to be the son of Apollo.[2] Trophônius, one of the most memorable persons in Grecian mythology, was worshipped as a god in various places, but with especial sanctity as Zeus Trophônius at Lebadeia : in his temple at this town, the prophetic manifestations outlasted those of Delphi itself.[3] Trophônius and Agamêdês, enjoying matchless renown as architects, built[4] the temple of Delphi, the thalamus of Amphitryôn at Thêbes, and also the inaccessible vault of Hyrieus at Hyria, in which they are said to have left one stone removable at pleasure so as to reserve for themselves a secret entrance. They entered so frequently, and stole so much gold and silver, that Hyrieus, astonished at his losses, at length spread a fine net, in which Agamêdês was inextricably caught : Trophônius cut off his brother's head and carried it away, so that the body, which alone remained, was insufficient to identify the thief. Like Amphiaraos, whom he resembles in more than one respect, Trophônius was swallowed up by the earth near Lebadeia.[5]

Foundation and greatness of Orchomenos.

Overthrown by Hêraklês and the Thêbans.

Trophônius and Agamêdês.

[1] Pausan. ix. 37, 2. Apollod. ii. 4, 11. Diodôr. iv. 10. The two latter tell us that Erginus was slain. Klymenê is among the wives and daughters of the heroes seen by Odysseus in Hadês ; she is termed by the Schol. daughter of Minyas (Odyss. xi. 325).

[2] Pausan. ix. 37, 1—3. Λέγεται δὲ ὁ Τροφώνιος Ἀπόλλωνος εἶναι, καὶ οὐκ Ἐργίνου· καὶ ἐγώ τε πείθομαι, καὶ ὅστις παρὰ Τροφώνιον ἦλθε δὴ μαντευσόμενος.

[3] Plutarch, De Defectu Oracul. c. 5, p. 411. Strabo, ix. p. 414. The mention of the honeyed cakes, both in

Aristophanês (Nub. 508) and Pausanias (ix. 39, 5), indicates that the curious preliminary ceremonies, for those who consulted the oracle of Trophônius, remained the same after a lapse of 550 years. Pausanias consulted it himself. There had been at one time an oracle of Teiresias at Orchomenos : but it had become silent at an early period (Plutarch, Defect. Oracul. c. 44, p. 434).

[4] Homer, Hymn. Apoll. 296. Pausan. ix. 11, 1.

[5] Pausan. ix. 37, 3. A similar story, but far more romantic and amplified,

From Trophônius and Agamêdês the Orchomenian genealogy passes to Askalaphos and Ialmenos, the sons of Arês by Astyochê, who are named in the Catalogue of the Iliad as leaders of the thirty ships from Orchomenos against Troy. Azeus, the grandfather of Astyochê in the Iliad, is introduced as the brother of Erginus[1] by Pausanias, who does not carry the pedigree lower.

Askalaphos and Ialmenos.

The genealogy here given out of Pausanias is deserving of the more attention, because it seems to have been copied from the special history of Orchomenos by the Corinthian Kallippus, who again borrowed from the native Orchomenian poet, Chersias: the works of the latter had never come into the hands of Pausanias. It illustrates forcibly the principle upon which these mythical genealogies were framed, for almost every personage in the series is an Eponymus. Andreus gave his name to the country, Athamas to the Athamantian plain ; Minyas, Orchomenos, Korônus, Haliartus, Almos, and Hyêttos, are each in like manner connected with some name of people, tribe, town, or village ; while Chrysê and Chrysogeneia have their origin in the reputed ancient wealth of Orchomenos. Abundant discrepancies are found, however, in respect to this old genealogy, if we look to other accounts. According to one statement, Orchomenos was the son of Zeus, by Isionê, daughter of Danaus ; Minyas was the son of Orchomenos (or rather Poseidôn) by Hermippê, daughter of Bœôtos ; the sons of Minyas were Presbôn, Orchomenos, Athamas, and Diochthôndas.[2] Others represented Minyas as son of Poseidôn by Kallirrhoê, an Oceanic nymph,[3] while Dionysius called him son of Arês, and Aristodêmus, son of Aleas ; lastly, there were not wanting authors who termed both Minyas and Orchomenos sons of Eteoklês.[4] Nor do we find in any one of these genealogies the name of Amphiôn the son of Iasus, who figures so prominently in the

Discrepancies in the Orchomenian genealogy.

is told by Herodotus (ii. 121), respecting the treasury-vault of Rhampsinitus, king of Egypt. Charax (ap. Schol. Aristoph. Nub. 508) gives the same tale, but places the scene in the treasury-vault of Augeas, king of Elis, which he says was built by Trophônius, to whom he assigns a totally different genealogy. The romantic adventures of the tale rendered it eminently fit to be inter-woven at some point or another of legendary history, in any country.

[1] Pausan. ix. 38, 6 ; 29, 1.

[2] Schol. Apollôn. Rhod. i. 230. Compare Schol. ad Lycophron. 873.

[3] Schol. Pindar, Olymp. xiv. 5.

[4] Schol. Pindar. Isthm. i. 79. Other discrepancies in Schol. Vett. ad Iliad, ii. Catalog. 18.

Odyssey as king of Orchomenos, and whose beautiful daughter Chlôris is married to Nêleus. Pausanias mentions him, but not as king, which is the denomination given to him in Homer.[1]

The discrepancies here cited are hardly necessary in order to prove that these Orchomenian genealogies possess no historical value. Yet some probable inferences appear deducible from the general tenor of the legends, whether the facts and persons of which they are composed be real or fictitious.

Throughout all the historical age, Orchomenos is a member of the
Probable inferences as to the ante-historical Orcho-menos.
Bœôtian confederation. But the Bœôtians are said to have been immigrants into the territory which bore their name from Thessaly ; and prior to the time of their immigration, Orchomenos and the surrounding territory appear as possessed by the Minyæ, who are recognised in that locality both in the Iliad and in the Odyssey,[2] and from whom the constantly recurring Eponymus, king Minyas, is borrowed by the genealogists. Poetical legend connects the Orchomenian Minyæ, on the one side, with Pylos and Triphylia in Peloponnêsus ; on the other side, with Phthiotis and the town of Iôlkos in Thessaly ; also with Corinth,[3] through Sisyphus and his sons. Pherekydês represented Nêleus, king of Pylos, as having also been king of Orchomenos.[4] In the region of Triphylia, near to or coincident with Pylos, a Minyeian river is mentioned by Homer ; and we find traces of residents called Minyæ even in the historical times, though the account given by Herodotus of the way in which they came thither is strange and unsatisfactory.[5]

Before the great changes which took place in the inhabitants of Greece from the immigration of the Thesprôtians into Thessaly,

[1] Odyss. xi. 283. Pausan. ix. 36, 3.
[2] Iliad, ii. 5, 11. Odyss. xi. 283. Hesiod, Fragm. Eoiai, 27, Düntz. Ἴξεν δ' Ὀρχόμενον Μιννήϊον. Pindar, Olymp. xiv. 4. Παλαιγόνων Μινυᾶν ἐπίσκοποι. Herodot. i. 146. Pausanias calls them Minyæ even in their dealings with Sylla (ix. 30, 1). Buttmann, in his Dissertation (über die Minyæ der ältesten Zeit, in the Mythologus, Diss. xxi. p. 218), doubts whether the name Minyæ was ever a real name ; but all the passages make against his opinion.
[3] Schol. Apoll. Rhod. ii. 1186. i. 230. Σκήψιος δὲ Δημήτρος φησὶ τοὺς περὶ τὴν

Ἰωλκὸν οἰκοῦντας Μινύας καλεῖσθαι; and i. 763. Τὴν γὰρ Ἰωλκὸν οἱ Μίνναι ᾤκουν, ὡς φησι Σιμωνίδης ἐν Συμμικτοῖς; also Eustath. ad Iliad. ii. 512. Steph. Byz. v. Μινύα. Orchomenos and Pylos run together in the mind of the poet of the Odyssey, xi. 458.

[4] Pherekyd. Fragm. 56, Didot. We see by the 55th Fragment of the same author, that he extended the genealogy of Phryxos to Pheræ in Thessaly.
[5] Herodot. iv. 145. Strabo, viii. 337 —347. Hom. Iliad, xi. 721. Pausan. v, 1, 7, ποταμὸν Μινυήϊον, near Elis,

of the Bœôtians into Bœôtia, and of the Dôrians and Ætôlians into Peloponnêsus, at a date which we have no means of determining, the Minyæ and tribes fraternally connected with them seem to have occupied a large portion of the surface of Greece, from Iôlkos in Thessaly to Pylos in the Peloponnêsus. The wealth of Orchomenos is renowned even in the Iliad ;[1] and when we study its topography in detail, we are furnished with a probable explanation both of its prosperity and its decay. Orchomenos was situated on the northern bank of the lake Kôpaïs, which receives not only the river Kêphisos from the valleys of Phôkis, but also other rivers from Parnassus and Helicôn. The waters of the lake find more than one subterranean egress—partly through natural rifts and cavities in the limestone mountains, partly through a tunnel pierced artificially more than a mile in length—into the plain on the northeastern side, from whence they flow into the Eubœan sea near Larymna.[2] And it appears that, so long as these channels were diligently watched and kept clear, a large portion of the lake was in the condition of alluvial land, pre-eminently rich and fertile. But when the channels came to be either neglected, or designedly choked up by an enemy, the water accumulated to such a degree as to occupy the soil of more than one ancient town, to endanger the position of Kôpæ, and to occasion the change of the site of Orchomenos itself from the plain to the declivity of Mount Hyphanteion. An engineer, Kratês, began the clearance of the obstructed water-courses in the reign of Alexander the Great, and by his commission—the destroyer of Thêbes being anxious to re-establish the extinct prosperity of Orchomenos. He succeeded so far as partially to drain and diminish the lake, whereby the site of more than one ancient city was rendered visible: but the revival of Thêbes by Kassandar, after the decease of Alexander, arrested the progress of the undertaking,

Its early wealth and industry.

Emissaries of the lake Kôpaïs.

---

[1] Iliad, ix. 381.

[2] See the description of these channels or Katabothra in Colonel Leake's Travels in Northern Greece, vol. ii. c. 15, p. 281—293, and still more elaborately in Fiedler, Reise durch alle Theile des Königreichs Griechenland, Leipzig, 1840. He traced fifteen perpendicular shafts sunk for the purpose of admitting air into the tunnel, the first separated from the last by about 5900 feet; they are now of course overgrown and stopped up (vol. i. p. 115).

Forchhammer states the length of this tunnel as considerably greater than what is here mentioned. He also gives a plan of the Lake Kôpaïs with the surrounding region.

and the lake soon regained its former dimensions, to contract which no further attempt was made.[1]

According to the Thêban legend,[2] Hêraklês, after his defeat of Erginus, had blocked up the exit of the waters, and converted the Orchomenian plain into a lake. The spreading of these waters is thus connected with the humiliation of the Minyæ; and there can be little hesitation in ascribing to these ancient tenants of Orchomenos, before it became bœotised, the enlargement and preservation of the protective channels. Nor could such an object have been accomplished without combined action and acknowledged ascendency on the part of that city over its neighbours, extending even to the sea at Larymna, where the river Kêphisos discharges itself. Of its extended influence, as well as of its maritime activity, we find a remarkable evidence in the ancient and venerated Amphiktyony at Kalauria.

Old Amphiktyony at Kalauria. The little island so named, near the harbour of Trœzên, in Peloponnêsus, was sacred to Poseidôn, and an asylum of inviolable sanctity. At the temple of Poseidôn, in Kalauria, there had existed, from unknown date, a periodical sacrifice, celebrated by seven cities in common—Hermionê, Epidaurus, Ægina, Athens, Prasiæ, Nauplia, and the Minyeian Orchomenos. This ancient religious combination dates from the time when Nauplia was independent of Argos, and Prasiæ of Sparta: Argos and Sparta, according to the usual practice in Greece, continued to fulfil the obligation each on the part of its respective dependent.[3] Six out of the seven states are at once sea-towns, and near enough to Kalauria to account for their participation in this Amphiktyony. But the junction of Orchomenos, from its comparative remoteness, becomes inexplicable, except on the supposition that its territory reached the sea, and that it enjoyed a considerable maritime traffic—a fact which

---

[1] We owe this interesting fact to Strabo, who is however both concise and unsatisfactory, viii. p. 406—407. It was affirmed that there had been two ancient towns, named Eleusis and Athênæ, originally founded by Cecrôps, situated on the lake, and thus overflowed (Steph. Byz. v. 'Aθῆναι. Diogen. Laërt. iv. 23. Pausan. ix. 24, 2). For the plain or marsh near Orchomenos, see Plutarch. Sylla, c. 20—22.

[2] Diodôr. iv. 18. Pausan. ix. 38, 5.

[3] Strabo. viii. p. 374. Ἦν δὲ καὶ 'Αμφικτυονία τις περὶ τὸ ἱερὸν τοῦτο, ἑπτα πόλεων αἳ μετεῖχον τῆς θυσίας· ἦσαν δὲ 'Ερμιῶν, 'Επίδαυρος, Αἴγινα, 'Αθῆναι, Ιλρασιεῖς, Ναυπλιεῖς, 'Ορχόμενος ὁ Μινύειος. 'Υπὲρ μὲν οὖν τῶν Ναυπλιέων 'Αργεῖοι, ὑπὲρ Πρασιέων δὲ Λακεδαιμόνιοι, ξυνετέλουν.

helps to elucidate both its legendary connexion with Iôlkos, and its partnership in what is called the Ionic emigration.[1]

The great power of Orchomenos was broken down and the city reduced to a secondary and half-dependent position by the Bœôtians of Thêbes; at what time and under what circumstances, history has not preserved. The story that the Thêban hero, Hêraklês, rescued his native city from servitude and tribute to Orchomenos, since it comes from a Kadmeian and not from an Orchomenian legend, and since the details of it were favourite subjects of commemoration in the Thêban temples,[2] affords a presumption that Thêbes was really once dependent on Orchomenos. Moreover the savage mutilations inflicted by the hero on the tribute-seeking envoys, so faithfully portrayed in his surname Rhinokoloustês, infuse into the mythe a portion of that bitter feeling which so long prevailed between Thêbes and Orchomenos, and which led the Thêbans, as soon as the battle of Leuktra had placed supremacy in their hands, to destroy and depopulate their rival.[3] The ensuing generation saw the same fate retorted upon Thêbes, combined with the restoration of Orchomenos. The legendary grandeur of this city continued, long after it had ceased to be distinguished for wealth and power, imperishably recorded both in the minds of the nobler citizens and in the compositions of the poets: the emphatic language of Pausanias shows how much he found concerning it in the old epic.[4]

Orchomenos and Thêbes.

Section II.—Daughters of Æolus.

With several of the daughters of Æolus memorable mythical pedigrees and narratives are connected. Alkyonê married Kêyx, the son of Eôsphoros, but both she

Alkyonê and Kêyx.

---

[1] Pausan. ix. 17, 1; 26, 1.
[2] Herod. i. 146. Pausan. vii. 2, 2.
[3] Theocrit. xvi. 104—

'Ω 'Ετεόκλειοι θύγατρες θεαὶ, αἱ Μιν-
    ύειον
'Ορχόμενον φιλέοισαι, ἀπεχθόμενόν ποκα
    Θήβαις.

The Scholiast gives a sense to these words much narrower than they really bear. See Diodôr. xv. 79; Pausan. ix. 15. In the oration which Isokratês places in the mouth of a Platæan, complaining of the oppressions of Thê-bes, the ancient servitude and tribute to Orchomenos are cast in the teeth of the Thêbans (Isokrat. Orat. Plataic, vol. iii. p. 32, Auger).

[4] Pausan. ix. 34, 5. See also the fourteenth Olympic Ode of Pindar, addressed to the Orchomenian Aso-pikus. The learned and instructive work of K. O. Müller, Orchomenos und die Minyer, embodies everything which can be known respecting this once-memorable city; indeed the contents of the work extend much further than its title promises.

and her husband displayed in a high degree the overweening insolence common in the Æolic race. The wife called her husband Zeus, while he addressed her as Hêrê, for which presumptuous act Zeus punished them by changing both into birds.[1]

Canacê had by the god Poseidôn several children, amongst whom were Epôpeus and Alôeus.[2] Alôeus married Iphimêdea, who became enamoured of the god Poseidôn, and boasted of her intimacy with him. She had by him two sons, Otos and Ephialtês, the huge and formidable Aloids,—Titanic beings, nine fathoms in height and nine cubits in breadth, even in their boyhood, before they had attained their full strength. These Alôids defied and insulted the gods in Olympus. They paid their court to Hêrê and Artemis; moreover they even seized and bound Arês, confining him in a brazen chamber for thirteen months. No one knew where he was, and the intolerable chain would have worn him to death, had not Eribœa, the jealous stepmother of the Alôids, revealed the place of his detention to Hermês, who carried him surreptitiously away when at the last extremity. Arês could obtain no atonement for such an indignity. Otos and Ephialtês even prepared to assault the gods in heaven, piling up Ossa on Olympus and Pelion on Ossa, in order to reach them. And this they would have accomplished had they been allowed to grow to their full maturity; but the arrows of Apollo put a timely end to their short-lived career.[3]

Canacê— the Alôids.

---

[1] Apollodôr. i. 7, 4. Kêyx,—king of Trachin,—the friend of Hêraklês and protector of the Hêrakleids to the extent of his power (Hesiod. Scut. Hercul. 355—473; Apollodôr. ii. 7, 5; Hekatæ. Fragm. 353, Didot).

[2] Canacê, daughter of Æolus, is a subject of deep tragical interest both in Euripidês and Ovid. The eleventh Heroic Epistle of the latter, founded mainly on the lost tragedy of the former called Æolus, purports to be from Canacê to Macareus, and contains a pathetic description of the ill-fated passion between a brother and sister: see the Fragments of the Æolus in Dindorf's collection. In the tale of Kaunos and Byblis, both children of Milêtos, the results of an incestuous passion are different, but hardly less melancholy (Parthenios, Narr. xi.). Makar, the son of Æolus, is the

primitive settler of the island of Lesbos (Hom. Hymn. Apoll. 37): moreover, in the Odyssey, Æolus, son of Hippotês, the dispenser of the winds, has six sons and six daughters, and marries the former to the latter (Odyss. x. 7). The two persons called Æolus are brought into connexion genealogically (see Schol. and Odyss. l. c., and Diodôr. iv. 67), but it seems probable that Euripidês was the first to place the name of Macareus and Canacê in that relation which confers upon them their poetical celebrity. Sostratus (ap. Stobæum, t. 614, p. 404) can hardly be considered to have borrowed from any older source than Euripidês. Welcker (Griech. Tragöd. vol. ii. p. 860) puts together all that can be known respecting the structure of the lost drama of Euripidês.

[3] Iliad, v. 386; Odyss. xi. 306; Apollodôr i. 7, 4. So Typhôeus in the

The genealogy assigned to Kalykê, another daughter of Æolus, conducts us from Thessaly to Elis and Ætôlia. She married Aëthlius (the son of Zeus by Prôtogeneia, daughter of Deukaliôn and sister of Hellên), who conducted a colony out of Thessaly, and settled in the territory of Elis. *Kalykê— Elis and Ætôlia— Eleian genealogy.* He had for his son Endymiôn, respecting whom the Hesiodic Catalogue and the Eoiai related several wonderful things. Zeus granted him the privilege of determining the hour of his own death, and even translated him into heaven, which he forfeited by daring to pay court to Hêrê: his vision in this criminal attempt was cheated by a cloud, and he was cast out into the underworld.[1] According to other stories, his great beauty caused the goddess Sêlênê to become enamoured of him, and to visit him by night during his sleep:—the sleep of Endymiôn became a proverbial expression for enviable, undisturbed, and deathless repose.[2]   Endymiôn had for issue (Pausanias gives us three different accounts, and Apollodôrus a fourth, of the name of his wife), Epeios, Ætôlus, Pæôn, and a

Hesiodic Theogony, the last enemy of the gods, is killed before he comes to maturity (Theog. 837). For the different turns given to this ancient Homeric legend, see Heyne, ad Apollodôr. l. c., and Hyginus, f. 28. The Alôids were noticed in the Hesiodic poems (ap. Schol. Apoll. Rhod. i. 482). Odysseus does not see *them* in Hadês, as Heyne by mistake says; he sees their mother Iphimêdea. Virgil (Æn. vi. 582) assigns to them a place among the sufferers of punishment in Tartarus.

Enmêlus, the Corinthian poet, designated Alôeus as son of the god Hêlios and brother of Æêtês, the father of Mêdea (Eumêl. Fragm. 2, Marktscheffel). The scene of their death was subsequently laid in Naxos (Pindar, Pyth. iv. 88): their tombs were seen at Anthêdôn in Bœotia (Pausan. ix. 22, 4). The very curious legend alluded to by Pausanias from Hegisinoos, the author of an Atthis,—to the effect that Otos and Ephialtês were the first to establish the worship of the Muses in Helikôn, and that they founded Askra along with Œôklos, the son of Poseidôn,—is one which we have no means of tracing farther (Pausan. ix. 29, 1).

The story of the Alôids, as Diodôrus gives it (v. 51, 52), diverges on almost every point: it is evidently borrowed

from some Naxian archæologist, and the only information which we collect from it is, that Otos and Ephialtês received heroic honours at Naxos. The views of O. Müller (Orchomenos, p. 387) appear to me unusually vague and fanciful.

Ephialtês takes part in the combat of the giants against the gods (Apollodôr. i. 6, 2), where Heyne remarks, as in so many other cases, "Ephialtes hic non confundendus cum altero Aloei filio". An observation just indeed, if we are supposed to be dealing with personages and adventures historically real—but altogether misleading in regard to these legendary characters. For here the general conception of Ephialtês and his attributes is in both cases the same; but the particular adventures ascribed to him cannot be made to consist, as facts, one with the other.

[1] Hesiod, Akusilaus, and Pherekydês, ap. Schol. Apollon. Rhod. iv. 57. Ἴν δ' αὐτῷ θανάτου ταμίης. The Scholium is very full of matter, and exhibits many of the diversities in the tale of Endymiôn: see also Apollodôr. i. 7, 5; Pausan. v. 1, 2: Conôn, Narr. 14.

[2] Theocrit. iii. 49; xx. 35; where, however, Endymiôn is connected with Latmos in Karia (see Schol. *ad loc.*).

daughter Eurykydê. He caused his three sons to run a race on the stadium at Olympia, and Epeios, being victorious, was rewarded by becoming his successor in the kingdom: it was after him that the people were denominated Epeians.

Epeios had no male issue, and was succeeded by his nephew Eleios, son of Eurykydê by the god Poseidôn: the name of the people was then changed from Epeians to Eleians. Ætôlus, the brother of Epeios, having slain Apis, son of Phorôneus, was compelled to flee from the country: he crossed the Corinthian gulf, and settled in the territory then called Kurêtis, but to which he gave the name of Ætôlia.[1]

The son of Eleios,—or, according to other accounts, of the god Hêlios, of Poseidôn, or of Phorbas,[2]—is Augeas, whom we find mentioned in the Iliad as king of the Epeians or Eleians. Augeas was rich in all sorts of rural wealth, and possessed herds of cattle so numerous, that the dung of the animals accumulated in the stable or cattle-enclosures beyond all power of endurance. Eurystheus, as an insult to Hêraklês, imposed upon him the obligation of cleansing this stable: the hero, disdaining to carry off the dung upon his shoulders, turned the course of the river Alpheios through the building, and 'thus swept the encumbrance away.[3] But Augeas, in spite of so signal a service, refused to Hêraklês the promised reward, though his son Phyleus protested against such treachery, and when he found

Augeas.

---

[1] Pausan. v. 1. 3—6; Apollodôr. i. 7, 6.

[2] Apollodôr. ii. 5, 5; Schol. Apol. Rhod. i. 172. In all probability, the old legend made Augeas the son of the god Hêlios; Hêlios, Augeas, and Agamêdê are a triple series parallel to the Corinthian genealogy, Hêlios, Æêtês, and Mêdea; not to mention that the etymology of Augeas connects him with Hêlios. Theokritus (xx. 55) designates him as the son of the god Hêlios, through whose favour his cattle are made to prosper and multiply with such astonishing success (xx. 117).

[3] Diodor. iv. 13. Ὕβρεως ἕνεκεν Εὐρυσθεὺς προσέταξε καθᾶραι· ὁ δὲ Ἡρακλῆς τὸ μὲν τοῖς ὥμοις ἐξενεγκεῖν αὐτὴν ἀπεδοκίμασεν, ἐκκλίνων τὴν ἐκ τῆς ὕβρεως αἰσχύνην, &c. (Pausan. v. 1, 7; Apollodôr. ii. 5, 5).

It may not be improper to remark that this fable indicates a purely pastoral condition, or at least a singularly rude state of agriculture; and the way in which Pausanias recounts it goes even beyond the genuine story: ὡς καὶ τὰ πολλὰ τῆς χώρας αὐτῷ ἤδη διατελεῖν ἀργὰ ὄντα ὑπὸ τῶν βοσκημάτων τῆς κόπρου. The slaves of Odysseus however know what use to make of the dung heaped before his outer fence (Odyss. xvii. 299); not so the purely carnivorous and pastoral Cyclôps (Odyss. ix. 329). The stabling, into which the cattle go from their pasture, is called κόπρος in Homer,—'Ελθούσας ἐς κόπρον, ἐπὴν βοτανῆς κορέσωνται (Odyss. x. 411): compare Iliad, xviii. 575.—Μυκηθμῷ δ' ἀπὸ κόπρου ἐπεσσεύοντο πέδονδε.

The Augeas of Theocritus has abundance of wheat-land and vineyard, as well as cattle: he ploughs his land three or four times, and digs his vineyard diligently (xx. 20—32).

that he could not induce his father to keep faith, retired in sorrow and wrath to the island of Dulichion.[1] To avenge the deceit practised upon him, Hêraklês invaded Elis ; but Augeas had powerful auxiliaries, especially his nephews, the two Molionids (sons of Poseidôn by Molionê, the wife of Aktôr), Eurytos, and Kteatos. These two mira- culous brothers, of transcendant force, grew together,—having one body, but two heads and four arms.[2] Such was their irresis- tible might, that Hêraklês was defeated and repelled from Elis: but presently the Eleians sent the two Molionid brothers as *Theôri* (sacred envoys) to the Isthmian games, and Hêraklês, placing himself in ambush at Kleônæ, surprised and killed them as they passed through. For this murderous act the Eleians in vain endeavoured to obtain redress both at Corinth and at Argos; which is assigned as the reason for the self-ordained exclusion, prevalent throughout all the historical age, that no Eleian athlête would ever present himself as a competitor at the Isthmian games.[3] The Molionids being thus removed, Hêraklês again invaded Elis, and killed Augeas along with his children,— all except Phyleus, whom he brought over from Dulichion, and put in possession of his father's kingdom. According to the more gentle narrative which Pausanias adopts, Augeas was not killed, but pardoned at the request of Phyleus.[4] He was worshipped as a hero [5] even down to the time of that author.

It was on occasion of this conquest of Elis, according to the old mythe which Pindar has ennobled in a magnificent ode, that Hêraklês first consecrated the ground of Olympia and established the Olympic games. Such at least was one of the many fables respecting the origin of that memorable institution.[6]

The Molionid brothers.

---

[1] The wrath and retirement of Phy- leus is mentioned in the Iliad (ii. 633), but not the cause of it.

[2] These singular properties were as- cribed to them both in the Hesiodic poems and by Pherekydês (Schol. Ven. ad Il. xi. 715—750, et ad Il. xxiii. 638), but not in the Iliad. The poet Ibykus (Fragm. 11, Schneid. ap. Athenæ. ii. 57) calls them ἄλικας ἰσοκεφάλους, ἐνι- γυίους, Ἀμφοτέρους γεγαῶτας ἐν ὠέῳ ἀργυρέῳ.

There were temples and divine honours to Zeus Moliôn (Lactantius, de Falsâ Religione, i. 22).

[3] Pausan. v. 2, 4. The inscription cited by Pausanias proves that this was the reason assigned by the Eleian athlêtes themselves for the exclusion ; but there were several different stories.

[4] Apollodôr. ii. 7, 2. Diodôr. iv. 33. Pausan. v. 2, 2 ; 3, 2. It seems evi- dent from these accounts that the genuine legend represented Hêraklês as having been defeated by the Molio- nids ; the unskilful evasions both of Apollodôrus and Diodôrus betray this. Pindar (Olymp. xi. 25—50) gives the story without any flattery to Hêraklês.

[5] Pausan. v. 4, 1.

[6] The Armenian copy of Eusebius gives a different genealogy respecting

It has already been mentioned that Ætôlus, son of Endymiôn,
Ætolian   quitted Peloponnêsus in consequence of having slain
genealogy.   Apis.[1] The country on the north of the Corinthian
gulf, between the rivers Euênus and Achelôus, received from him
the name of Ætôlia, instead of that of Kurêtis: he acquired possession of it after having slain Dôrus, Laodokus, and Polypœtês,
sons of Apollo and Phthia, by whom he had been well received.
He had by his wife Pronoê (the daughter of Phorbas) two sons,
Pleurôn and Kalydôn, and from them the two chief towns in
Ætôlia were named.[2] Pleuron married Xanthippê, daughter of
Dôrus, and had for his son Agênor, from whom sprang Portheus,
or Porthaôn, and Demonikê: Euênos and Thestius were children
of the latter by the god Arês.[3]

Portheus had three sons, Agrius, Melas, and Œneus: among the
Œneus,   offspring of Thestius were Althæa and Lêda,[4]—names
Meleager,   which bring us to a period of interest in the legendary
Tydeus.   history. Lêda marries Tyndareus and becomes mother
of Helena and the Dioskuri; Althæa marries Œneus, and has,
among other children, Meleager and Deianeira; the latter being
begotten by the god Dionysus, and the former by Arês.[5] Tydeus
also is his son, and the father of Diomêdês: warlike eminence
goes hand in hand with tragic calamity among the members of
this memorable family.

Elis and Pisa: Aëthlius, Epeius, Endymiôn, Alexinus; next Œnomaus and
Pelops, then Hêraklês. Some counted
ten generations, others *three*, between
Hêraklês and Iphitus, who renewed
the discontinued Olympic games (see
Armen. Euseb. copy. c. xxxii. p. 140).
[1] Ephorus said that Ætôlus had
been expelled by Salmôneus king of the
Epeians and Pisatæ (ap. Strab., viii. p.
357): he must have had before him a
different story and different genealogy
from that which is given in the text.
[2] Apollodôr. i. 7, 6. Dôrus, son of
Apollo and Phthia, killed by Ætôlus,
after having hospitably received him,
is here mentioned. Nothing at all is
known of this; but the conjunction of
names is such as to render it probable
that there was some legend connected
with them: possibly the assistance
given by Apollo to the Kurêtes against
the Ætolians, and the death of Meleager by the hand of Apollo, related
both in the Eoiai and the Minyas

(Pausan. x. 31, 2), may have been
grounded upon it. The story connects
itself with what is stated by Apollodôrus about Dôrus son of Hellên.
[3] According to the ancient genealogical poet Asius, Thestius was son of
Agênôr the son of Pleurôn (Asii Fragm.
6, p. 413 ed. Marktsch.). Compare the
genealogy of Ætôlia and the general
remarks upon it, in Brandstäter, Geschichten des Ætol. Landes, &c., Berlin,
1844, p. 23, *seq.*
[4] Respecting Lêda, see the statements of Ibykus, Pherekydês, Hellanikus, &c. (Schol. Apollôn. Rhod. i. 146).
The reference to the Corinthiaca of
Eumêlus is curious: it is a specimen of
the matters upon which these old genealogical poems dwelt.
[5] Apollodôr. i. 8, 1 ; Euripidês, Meleager, Fragm. 1. The three sons of
Portheus are named in the Iliad (xiv.
116) as living at Pleurôn and Kalydôn.
The name Œneus doubtless brings
Dionysus into the legend.

We are fortunate enough to find the legend of Althæa and Meleager set forth at considerable length in the Iliad, in the speech addressed by Phœnix to appease the wrath of Achilles. Œneus, king of Kalydôn, in the vintage sacrifices which he offered to the gods, omitted to include Artemis: the misguided man either forgot her or cared not for her;[1] and the goddess, provoked by such an insult, sent against the vineyards of Œneus a wild boar of vast size and strength, who tore up the trees by the root, and laid prostrate all their fruit. So terrible was this boar, that nothing less than a numerous body of men could venture to attack him: Meleager, the son of Œneus, however, having got together a considerable number of companions, partly from the Kurêtes of Pleurôn, at length slew him. But the anger of Artemis was not yet appeased. She raised a dispute among the combatants respecting the possession of the boar's head and hide—the trophies of victory. In this dispute Meleager slew the brother of his mother Althæa, prince of the Kurêtes of Pleurôn: these Kurêtes attacked the Ætôlians of Kalydôn in order to avenge their chief. So long as Meleager contended in the field the Ætolians had the superiority. But he presently refused to come forth, indignant at the curses imprecated upon him by his mother. For Althæa, wrung with sorrow for the death of her brother, flung herself upon the ground in tears, beat the earth violently with her hands, and implored Hadês and Persephonê to inflict death upon Meleager,—a prayer which the unrelenting Erinnyes in Erebus heard but too well. So keenly did the hero resent this behaviour of his mother, that he kept aloof from the war. Accordingly, the Kurêtes not only drove the Ætolians from the field, but assailed the walls and gates of Kalydon, and were on the point of overwhelming its dismayed inhabitants. There was no hope of safety except in the arm of Meleager; but Meleager lay in his chamber by the side of his beautiful wife Kleopatra, the daughter of Idas, and heeded not the necessity. While the shouts of expected victory were heard from the assailants at the gates, the ancient men of Ætôlia and the priests of the gods earnestly besought Meleager to come

(margin note: Legend of Meleager in Homer.)

---

[1] Ἦ λάθετ', ἢ οὐκ ἐνόησεν· ἀάσσατο δὲ μέγα θυμῷ (Iliad, ix. 533). The destructive influence of Atê is mentioned before, v. 502. The piety of Xenophôn reproduces this ancient circumstance,— Οἰνεως δ' ἐν γήρᾳ ἐπιλαθομένου τῆς θεοῦ, &c. (De Venat. c. 1).

forth,[1] offering him his choice of the fattest land in the plain of Kalydòn. His dearest friends, his father Œneus, his sisters, and even his mother herself, added their supplications—but he remained inflexible. At length the Kurêtes penetrated into the town and began to burn it: at this last moment, Kleopatra his wife addressed to him her pathetic appeal to avert from her and from his family the desperate horrors impending over them all. Meleager could no longer resist : he put on his armour, went forth from his chamber, and repelled the enemy. But when the danger was over, his countrymen withheld from him the splendid presents which they had promised, because he had rejected their prayers, and had come forth only when his own haughty caprice dictated.[2]

Such is the legend of Meleager in the Iliad : a verse in the second book mentions simply the death of Meleager, without farther details, as a reason why Thoas appeared in command of the Ætôlians before Troy.[3]

Later poets both enlarged and altered the fable. The Hesiodic Eoiai, as well as the old poem called the Minyas, represented Meleager as having been slain by Apollo, who aided the Kurêtes in the war ; and the incident of the burning brand, though quite

How altered by poets after Homer. at variance with Homer, is at least as old as the tragic poet Phrynichus, earlier than Æschylus.[4] The Mœræ, or Fates, presenting themselves to Althæa shortly after the birth of Meleager, predicted that the child would die so soon

Althæa and the burning brand. as the brand then burning on the fire near at hand should be consumed. Althæa snatched it from the flames and extinguished it, preserving it with the utmost care, until she became incensed against Meleager for the death of her brother. She then cast it into the fire, and as soon as it was consumed the life of Meleager was brought to a close.

We know from the censure of Pliny, that Sophoklês heightened the pathos of this subject by his account of the mournful death of Meleager's sisters, who perished from excess of grief. They were changed into the birds called Meleagrides, and their never-ceasing tears ran together into amber.[5] But in the hands of Euripidês—

---

[1] These priests formed the Chorus in the Meleager of Sophoklês (Schol. ad Iliad. ix. 575).
[2] Iliad, ix. 525—595.
[3] Iliad, ii. 642.
[4] Pausan. x. 31, 2. The Πλευρώνιαι, a lost tragedy of Phrynichus.
[5] Plin. H. N. xxxvii. 2, 11.

whether originally through him or not,[1] we cannot tell—Atalanta became the prominent figure and motive of the piece, while the party convened to hunt the Kalydônian boar was made to comprise all the distinguished heroes from every quarter of Greece. In fact, as Heyne justly remarks, this event is one of the four aggregate dramas of Grecian heroic life,[2] along with the Argonautic expedition, the siege of Thêbes, and the Trojan war.

To accomplish the destruction of the terrific animal which Artemis in her wrath had sent forth, Meleager assembled not merely the choice youth among the Kurêtes and Ætôlians (as we find in the Iliad), but an illustrious troop, including Kastôr and Pollux, Idas and Lynkeus, Pêleus and Telamôn, Thêseus and Peirithous, Ankæus and Kêpheus, Jasôn, Amphiaraus, Admêtus, Eurytiôn and others. Nestôr and Phœnix, who appear as old men before the walls of Troy, exhibited their early prowess as auxiliaries to the suffering Kalydônians.[3] Conspicuous amidst them all stood the virgin Atalanta, daughter of the Arcadian Schœneus ; beautiful and matchless for swiftness of foot, but living in the forest as a huntress and unacceptable to Aphroditê.[4] Several of the heroes were slain by the boar ; others escaped, by various stratagems : at length Atalanta first shot him in the back, next Amphiaraus in the eye, and, lastly, Meleager killed him. Enamoured of the beauty of Atalanta, Meleager made over to her the chief spoils of the animal, on the plea that she had inflicted the first wound. But his uncles, the brothers of Thestius, took them away from her, asserting their rights as next of kin,[5] if Meleager declined to keep the prize for

(marginal note: Grand Kalydônian boar-hunt—Atalanta.)

---

[1] There was a tragedy of Æschylus called 'Αταλάντη, of which nothing remains (Bothe, Æschyli Fragm. ix. p. 18).
Of the more recent dramatic writers, several selected Atalanta as their subject (see Brandstäter, Geschichten Ætoliens, p. 65).
[2] There was a poem of Stesichorus, Συόθηραι (Stesichor. Fragm. 15, p. 72).
[3] The catalogue of these heroes is in Apollodôr. i. 8, 2; Ovid, Metamorph. viii. 300 ; Hygin. fab. 173. Euripidês, in his play of Meleager, gave an enumeration and description of the heroes (see Fragm. 6 of that play, ed. Matth.). Nestôr, in this picture of Ovid, however, does not appear quite so invincible as in his own speeches in the Iliad.

The mythographers thought it necessary to assign a reason why Hêraklês was *not* present at the Kalydônian adventure : he was just at that time in servitude with Omphalê in Lydia (Apollod. ii. 6, 3). This seems to have been the idea of Ephorus, and it is much in his style of interpretation (see Eph. Fr. 9, ed. Did.).
[4] Eurip. Meleag. Fragm. vi. Matth.—

Κύπριδος δὲ μίσημ', 'Αρκὰς 'Αταλάντη, κύνας
Καὶ τόξ' ἔχουσα, &c.

There was a drama "Meleager" both of Sophoklês and Euripidês : of the former hardly any fragments remain,—a few more of the latter.
[5] Hyginus, fab. 229.

himself : the latter, exasperated at this behaviour, slew them. Althæa, in deep sorrow for her brothers and wrath against her son, is impelled to produce the fatal brand, which she had so long treasured up, and consign it the flames.[1] The tragedy concludes with the voluntary death both of Althæa and Kleopatra.

Interesting as the Arcadian huntress, Atalanta, is in herself, she is an intrusion, and not a very convenient intrusion, into the Homeric story of the Kalydônian boar-hunt, wherein another female, Kleopatra, already occupied the fore-ground. But the more recent version became accredited throughout Greece, and was sustained by evidence which few persons in those days felt any inclination to controvert. For Atalanta carried away with her the spoils and head of the boar into Arcadia ; and there for successive centuries hung the identical hide and the gigantic tusks, of three feet in length, in the temple of Athênê Alea at

Relics of the boar long pre- served at Tegea.

Tegea. Kallimachus mentions them as being there preserved, in the third century before the Christian æra ;[2] but the extraordinary value set upon them is best proved by the fact that the emperor Augustus took away the tusks from Tegea, along with the great statue of Athênê Alea, and conveyed them to Rome, to be there preserved among the public curiosities. Even a century and a half afterwards, when Pausanias visited Greece, the skin worn out with age was shown to him, while the robbery of the tusks had not been forgotten. Nor were these relics of the boar the only memento preserved at Tegea of the heroic enterprise. On the pediment of the temple of Athênê Alea, unparalleled in Peloponnêsus for beauty and grandeur, the illustrious statuary Skopas had executed one of his most finished reliefs, representing the Kalydônian hunt. Atalanta and Meleager were placed in the front rank of the assailants ; while Ankæus, one of the Tegean heroes, to whom the tusks of the boar had proved fatal,[3] was represented as sinking under his

---

[1] Diodôr. iv. 34. Apollodôrus (i. 8, 2—4) gives first the usual narrative, including Atalanta ; next, the Homeric narrative with some additional circum- stances, but not including either Atalanta or the fire-brand on which Meleager's life depended.

[2] Kallimachus, Hymn. ad Dian. 217.—

Οὔ μιν ἐπίκλητοὶ Καλυδώνιοι ἀγρευ-
    τῆρες
Μέμφονται κάπροιο· τὰ γὰρ σημήϊα
    νίκης
'Αρκαδίην εἰσῆλθεν, ἔχει δ' ἔτι θηρὸς
    ὀδόντας.

[3] See Pherekyd. Fragm. 81, ed. Didot.

death-wound into the arms of his brother Epochos. And Pausanias observes that the Tegeans, while they had manifested the same honourable forwardness as other Arcadian communities in the conquest of Troy, the repulse of Xerxês, and the battle of Dipæa against Sparta—might fairly claim to themselves, through Ankæus and Atalanta, that they alone amongst all Arcadians had participated in the glory of the Kalydônian boar-hunt.[1] So entire and unsuspecting is the faith both of the Tegeans and of Pausanias in the past historical reality of this romantic adventure. Strabo indeed tries to transform the romance into something which has the outward semblance of history, by remarking that the quarrel respecting the boar's head and hide cannot have been the real cause of war between the Kurêtes and the Ætôlians ; the true ground of dispute (he contends) was probably the possession of a portion of territory.[2] His remarks on this head are analogous to those of Thucydidês and other critics, when they ascribe the Trojan war, not to the rape of Helen, but to views of conquest or political apprehensions. But he treats the general fact of the battle between the Kurêtes and the Ætôlians, mentioned in the Iliad, as something unquestionably real and historical—recapitulating at the same time a variety of discrepancies on the part of different authors, but not giving any decision of his own respecting their truth or falsehood.

In the same manner as Atalanta was intruded into the Kalydônian hunt, so also she seems to have been introduced into the memorable funeral games celebrated after the decease of Pelias at Iôlkos, in which she had no place at the time when the works on the chest of Kypselus were executed.[3] But her native and

[1] Pausan. viii. 45, 4 ; 46, 1—3 ; 47, 2. Lucian, adv. Indoctum, c. 14, t. iii. p. 111, Reiz.
The officers placed in charge of the public curiosities or wonders at Rome (οἱ ἐπὶ τοῖς θαύμασιν) affirmed that one of the tusks had been accidentally broken in the voyage from Greece : the other was kept in the temple of Bacchus in the Imperial Gardens.
It is numbered among the memorable exploits of Thêseus that he vanquished and killed a formidable and gigantic sow, in the territory of Krommyôn near Corinth. According to some critics, this Krommyônian sow was the mother of the Kalydônian boar (Strabo, viii. p. 380).

[2] Strabo, x. p. 466. Πολέμου δ' ἐμπεσόντος τοῖς Θεστιάδαις πρὸς Οἰνέα καὶ Μελέαγρον, ὁ μὲν Ποιητῆς, ἀμφὶ συὸς κεφαλῇ καὶ δέρματι, κατὰ τὴν περὶ τοῦ κάπρου μυθολογίαν· ὡς δὲ τὸ εἰκὸς, περὶ μέρους τῆς χώρας, &c. This remark is also similar to Mr. Payne Knight's criticism on the true causes of the Trojan war, which were (he tells us) of a political character, independent of Helen and her abduction (Prolegom. ad Homer. c. 53).

[3] Compare Apollodôr. iii. 9, 2, and Pausan. v. 17, 4. She is made to wrestle with Pêleus at these funeral games, which seems foreign to her character.

genuine locality is Arcadia ; where her race-course, near to the town of Methydrion, was shown even in the days of Pausanias.[1] This race-course had been the scene of destruction for more than
Atalanta vanquished in the race by stratagem. one unsuccessful suitor. For Atalanta, averse to marriage, had proclaimed that her hand should only be won by the competitor who would surpass her in running : all who tried and failed were condemned to die, and many were the persons to whom her beauty and swiftness, alike unparalleled, had proved fatal. At length Meilaniôn, who had vainly tried to win her affections by assiduous services in her hunting excursions, ventured to enter the perilous lists. Aware that he could not hope to outrun her except by stratagem, he had obtained, by the kindness of Aphroditê, three golden apples from the garden of the Hesperides, which he successively let fall near to her while engaged in the race. The maiden could not resist the temptation of picking them up, and was thus overcome : she became the wife of Meilaniôn, and the mother of the Arcadian Parthenopæus, one of the seven chiefs who perished in the siege of Thêbes.[2]

---

[1] Pausan. viii. 35, 8.

[2] Respecting the varieties in this interesting story, see Apollod. iii. 9, 2 ; Hygin. f. 185 ; Ovid. Metam. x. 560—700 ; Propert. i. 1, 20 ; Ælian V. H. xiii. i. Μειλανίωνος σωφρονέστερος. Aristophan. Lysistrat. 786 and Schol. In the ancient representation on the chest of Kypselus (Paus. v. 19, 1), Meilaniôn was exhibited standing near Atalanta, who was holding a fawn : no match or competition in running was indicated.

There is great discrepancy in the naming and patronymic description of the parties in the story. Three different persons are announced as fathers of Atalanta, Schœneus, Jasus, and Mænalos ; the successful lover in Ovid (and seemingly in Euripidês also) is called Hippomenês, not Meilaniôn. In the Hesiodic poems Atalanta was daughter of Schœneus ; Hellanikus called her daughter of Jasus. See Apollodôr. l. c. ; Kallimach. Hymn to Dian. 214, with the note of Spanheim ; Schol. Eurip. Phœniss. 150 ; Schol. Theocr. Idyll. iii. 40 ; also the ample commentary of Bachet de Meziriac, sur les Epîtres d'Ovide, vol. i. p. 366. Servius (ad Virg. Eclog. vi. 61 ; Æneid, iii. 113) calls Atalanta a native of Skyros.

Both the ancient scholiasts (see Schol. Apoll. Rhod. i. 769) and the modern commentators, Spanheim and Heyne, seek to escape this difficulty by supposing two Atalantas,—an Arcadian and a Bœôtian : assuming the principle of their conjecture to be admissible, they ought to suppose at least three.

Certainly, if personages of the Grecian mythes are to be treated as historically real, and their adventures as so many exaggerated or miscoloured facts, it will be necessary to repeat the process of multiplying entities to an infinite extent. And this is one among the many reasons for rejecting the fundamental supposition.

But when we consider these personages as purely legendary, so that an historical basis can neither be affirmed nor denied respecting them, we escape the necessity of such inconvenient stratagems. The test of identity is then to be sought in the attributes, not in the legal description,—in the predicates, not in the subject. Atalanta, whether born of one father or another, whether belonging to one place or another, is beautiful, cold, repulsive, daring, swift of foot, and skilful with the bow,—these attributes constitute her identity. The Scholiast on Theo-

We have yet another female in the family of Œneus, whose name the legend has immortalised. His daughter Deianeira was sought in marriage by the river Ache-lôus, who presented himself in various shapes, first as a serpent and afterwards as a bull. From the importunity of this hateful suitor she was rescued by the arrival of Hêraklês, who encountered Achelôus, vanquished him and broke off one of his horns, which Achelôus ransomed by surrendering to him the horn of Amal-theia, endued with the miraculous property of supplying the possessor with abundance of any food and drink which he desired. Hêraklês, being rewarded for his prowess by the possession of Deianeira, made over the horn of Amaltheia as his marriage-present to Œneus.[1] Compelled to leave the residence of Œneus, in consequence of having in a fit of anger struck the youthful attendant Eunomus, and involuntarily killed him,[2] Hêraklês re-tired to Trachin, crossing the river Euênus at the place where the Centaur Nessus was accustomed to carry over passengers for hire. Nessus carried over Deianeira, but when he had arrived on the other side, began to treat her with rudeness, upon which Hêra-klês slew him with an arrow tinged by the poison of the Lernæan hydra. The dying Centaur advised Deianeira to preserve the poisoned blood which flowed from his wound, telling her that it would operate as a philtre to regain for her the affections of Hêraklês, in case she should ever be threatened by a rival. Some time afterwards the hero saw and loved the beautiful Iolê, daughter of Eurytos, king of Œchalia : he stormed the town, killed

Deianeira.

---

critus (iii. 40), in vindicating his sup-position that there were two Atalantas, draws a distinction founded upon this very principle : he says that the Bœô-tian Atalanta was τοξοτίς, and the Arcadian Atalanta δρομαία. But this seems an over-refinement ; both the shooting and the running go to consti-tute an accomplished huntress.

In respect to Parthenopæus, called by Euripidês and by so many others the son of Atalanta, it is of some im-portance to add, that Apollodôrus, Aristarchus, and Antimachus, the author of the Thebaid, assigned to him a pedigree entirely different,—making him an Argeian, the son of Talaos and Lysimachê, and brother of Adrastus. (Apollodôr. i. 9, 13 ; Aristarch. ap. Schol. Soph. Œd. Col. 1320 : Anti-machus ap. Schol. Æschyl. Sept. Theb. 532 ; and Schol. Supplem. ad Eurip. Phœniss. t. viii. p. 461, ed. Matth. Apollodôrus is in fact inconsistent with himself in another passage.)

[1] Sophokl. Trachin. 7. The horn of Amaltheia was described by Phere-kydês (Apollod. ii. 7, 5) : see also Strabo, x. p. 458, and Diodôr. iv. 35, who cites an interpretation of the fables (οἱ εἰκάζοντες ἐξ αὐτῶν τἀληθές) to the effect that it was symbolical of an embankment of the unruly river by Hêraklês, and consequent recovery of very fertile land.

[2] Hellanikus (ap. Athen. ix. p. 410) mentioning this incident, in two diffe-rent works, called the attendant by two different names.

Eurytos, and made Iolê his captive.   The misguided Deianeira now had recourse to her supposed philtre : she sent as a present to Hêraklês a splendid tunic, imbued secretly with the poisoned Death of   blood of the Centaur.   Hêraklês adorned himself with Hêraklês.   the tunic on the occasion of offering a solemn sacrifice to Zeus on the promontory of Kênæon in Eubœa : but the fatal garment, when once put on, clung to him indissolubly, burnt his skin and flesh, and occasioned an agony of pain from which he was only relieved by death.   Deianeira slew herself in despair at this disastrous catastrophe.[1]

We have not yet exhausted the eventful career of Œneus and Tydeus—   his family—ennobled among the Ætôlians especially, old age of   both by religious worship and by poetical eulogy—and Œneus.   favourite themes not merely in some of the Hesiodic poems, but also in other ancient epic productions, the Alkmæônis and the Cyclic Thêbais.[2]   By another marriage, Œneus had for his son Tydeus, whose poetical celebrity is attested by the many different accounts given both of the name and condition of his mother.   Tydeus, having slain his cousins, the sons of Melas, who were conspiring against Œneus, was forced to become an exile, and took refuge at Argos with Adrastus, whose daughter Deipylê

[1] The beautiful drama of the Trachiniæ has rendered this story familiar : compare Apollod. ii. 7, 7. Hygin. f. 36. Diodôr. iv. 36—37.
The capture of Œchalia (Οἰχαλίας ἅλωσις) was celebrated in a very ancient epic poem by Kreophylos, of the Homeric and not of the Hesiodic character ; it passed with many as the work of Homer himself. (See Düntzer, Fragm. Epic. Græcor. p. 8.   Welcker, Der Epische Cyclus, p. 229.)   The same subject was also treated in the Hesiodic Catalogue, or in the Eoiai (see Hesiod, Fragm. 129, ed. Marktsch.): the number of the children of Eurytos was there enumerated.
This exploit seems constantly mentioned as the last performed by Hêraklês, and as immediately preceding his death or apotheosis on Mount Œta : but whether the legend of Deianeira and the poisoned tunic be very old, we cannot tell.
The tale of the death of Iphitos, son of Eurytos, by Hêraklês, is as ancient as the Odyssey (xxi. 19—40): but it is there stated, that Eurytos dying left

his memorable bow to his son Iphitos (the bow is given afterwards by Iphitos to Odysseus, and is the weapon so fatal to the suitors),—a statement not very consistent with the story that Œchalia was taken and Eurytos slain by Hêraklês.   It is plain that these were distinct and contradictory legends.   Compare Soph. Trachin. 260—285 (where Iphitos dies before Eurytos), not only with the passage just cited from the Odyssey, but also with Pherekydês, Fragm. 34, Didot.
Hyginus (f. 33) differs altogether in the parentage of Deianeira : he calls her daughter of Dexamenos ; his account of her marriage with Hêraklês is in every respect at variance with Apollodôrus.   In the latter, Mnêsimachê is the daughter of Dexamenos ; Hêraklês rescues her from the importunities of the Centaur Eurytiôn (ii. 5, 5).

[2] See the references in Apollod. i. 8, 4—5.   Pindar, Isthm. iv. 32.   Μελέταν δὲ σοφισταῖς Διὸς ἕκατι πρόσβαλον σεβιζόμενοι Ἐν μὲν Αἰτωλῶν θυσίαισι φαενναῖς Οἰνεΐδαι κρατεροί, &c.

he married.   The issue of this marriage was Diomêdês, whose brilliant exploits in the siege of Troy were not less celebrated than those of his father at the siege of Thêbes.   After the departure of Tydeus, Œneus was deposed by the sons of Agrios. He fell into extreme poverty and wretchedness, from which he was only rescued by his grandson Diomêdês, after the conquest of Troy.[1]   The sufferings of this ancient warrior, and the final restoration and revenge by Diomêdês, were the subject of a lost tragedy of Euripidês, which even the ridicule of Aristophanês demonstrates to have been eminently pathetic.[2]

Though the genealogy just given of Œneus is in part Homeric, and seems to have been followed generally by the mythographers, yet we find another totally at variance with it in Hekatæus, which he doubtless borrowed from some of the old poets : the simplicity of the story annexed to it seems to attest its antiquity.   Orestheus, son of Deukaliôn, first passed into Ætôlia, and acquired the kingdom : he was father of Phytios, who was father of Œneus.   Ætôlus was son of Œneus.[3]

Discrepant genealogies.

The original migration of Ætôlus from Elis to Ætôlia—and the subsequent establishment in Elis of Oxylus, his descendant in the tenth generation, along with the Dôrian invaders of Peloponnêsus —were commemorated by two inscriptions, one in the Agora of Elis, the other in that of the Ætôlian chief town, Thermum, engraved upon the statues of Ætôlus and Oxylus [4] respectively.

---

[1] Hekat. Fragm. 341, Didot. In this story Œneus is connected with the first discovery of the vine and the making of wine (οἶνος): compare Hygin. f. 129, and Servius ad Virgil. Georgic. i. 9.

[2] See Welcker (Griechisch. Tragöd. ii. p. 583) on the lost tragedy called Œneus.

[3] Timoklês, Comic. ap. Athenæ. vii. p. 223.—

Γερων τις ἀτυχεῖ ; κατέμαθεν τὸν Οἰνέα.

Ovid. Heroid. ix. 153.—

" Heu ! devota domus ! Solio sedet Agrios alto :
Œnea desertum nuda senecta premit."

[4] Ephor. Fragm. 29, Didot, ap. Strab. x.

CHAPTER VII.

THE PELOPIDS.

AMONG the ancient legendary genealogies there was none which
Misfortunes and celebrity of the Pelopids. figured with greater splendour, or which attracted to itself a higher degree of poetical interest and pathos, than that of the Pelopids—Tantalus, Pelops, Atreus and Thyestês, Agamemnon and Menelaus and Ægisthus, Helen and Klytæmnêstra, Orestês and Elektra and Hermionê. Each of these characters is a star of the first magnitude in the Grecian hemisphere : each name suggests the idea of some interesting romance or some harrowing tragedy : the curse, which taints the family from the beginning, inflicts multiplied wounds at every successive generation. So, at least, the story of the Pelopids presents itself, after it had been successively expanded and decorated by epic, lyric, and tragic poets. It will be sufficient to touch briefly upon events with which every reader of Grecian poetry is more or less familiar, and to offer some remarks upon the way in which they were coloured and modified by different Grecian authors.

Pelops is the eponym or name-giver of the Peloponnêsus : to
Pelops— eponym of Peloponnêsus. find an eponym for every conspicuous local name was the invariable turn of Grecian retrospective fancy. The name Peloponnêsus is not to be found either in the Iliad or the Odyssey, nor any other denomination which can be attached distinctly and specially to the entire peninsula. But we meet with the name in one of the most ancient post-Homeric poems of which any fragments have been preserved —the Cyprian Verses—a poem which many (seemingly most persons) even of the contemporaries of Herodotus ascribed to the

author of the Iliad, though Herodotus contradicts the opinion.[1]
The attributes by which the Pelopid Agamemnôn and his house
are marked out and distinguished from the other heroes of the
Iliad, are precisely those which Grecian imagination would naturally seek in an eponymus—superior wealth, power, splendour,
and regality. Not only Agamemnôn himself, but his brother
Menelaus, is " more of a king " even than Nestôr or Diomêdês.
The gods have not given to the king of the "much-golden"
Mykênæ greater courage, or strength, or ability, than to various
other chiefs ; but they have conferred upon him a marked superiority in riches, power, and dignity, and have thus singled him
out as the appropriate leader of the forces.[2] He enjoys this pre-
eminence as belonging to a privileged family and as inheriting
the heaven-descended sceptre of Pelops, the transmission of which
is described by Homer in a very remarkable way. The sceptre
was made " by Hêphæstos, who presented it to Zeus ; Zeus gave
it to Hermês, Hermês to the charioteer Pelops ; Pelops
gave it to Atreus, the ruler of men ; Atreus at his death
left it to Thyestês, the rich cattle-owner ; Thyestês
in his turn left it to his nephew Agamemnôn
to carry, that he might hold dominion over many islands
and over all Argos ".[3]

Deduction of the sceptre of Pelops.

[1] Hesiod. ii. 117. Fragment. Epicc.
Græc. Düntzer, ix. Κύπρια, 8,—

Αἶψα τε Λυγκεὺς
Ταΰγετον προσέβαινε ποσὶν ταχέεσσι
πεποιθώς,
'Ακρότατον δ' ἀναβὰς διεδέρκετο νῆσον
ἅπασαν
Τανταλίδεω Πέλοπος.

Also the Homeric Hymn to Apollo, 419,
430, and Tyrtæus, Fragm. 1 (Εὐνο-
μία).—

Εὐρεῖαν Πέλοπος νῆσον ἀφικόμεθα.

The Schol. ad Iliad. ix. 246, intimates
that the name Πελοπόννησος occurred
in one or more of the Hesiodic epics.
[2] Iliad. ix. 37. Compare ii. 580.
Diomêdês addresses Agamemnôn—

Σοὶ δὲ διάνδιχα δῶκε Κρόνου παῖς
ἀγκυλομήτεω·
Σκήπτρῳ μέν τοι δῶκε τετιμῆσθαι περὶ
πάντων·
'Αλκὴν δ' οὔ τοι δῶκεν, ὅ,τε κράτος
ἐστὶ μέγιστον.

A similar contrast is drawn by Nestôr

(Il. i. 280) between Agamemnôn and
Achilles. Nestôr says to Agamemnôn
(Il. ix. 69)—

'Ατρείδη, σὺ μὲν ἄρχε· σὺ γὰρ
βασιλεύτατός ἐσσι.

And this attribute attaches to Menelaus as well as to his brother. For
when Diomêdês is about to choose his
companion for the night expedition
into the Trojan camp, Agamemnôn
thus addresses him (x. 235)—

Τὸν μὲν δὴ ἕταρόν γ' αἱρήσεαι, ὃν κ'
ἐθέλησθα
Φαινομένων τὸν ἄριστον, ἐπεὶ μεμάασί
γε πολλοί·
Μηδὲ σύ γ', αἰδόμενος σῇσι φρεσί, τὸν
μὲν ἀρείω
Καλλείπειν, σὺ δὲ χείρον' ὀπάσσεαι,
αἰδοῖ εἴκων,
'Ες γενεὴν ὁρόων, εἰ καὶ βασιλεύτερός
ἐστιν.
'Ως ἔφατ', ἔδδεισε δὲ περὶ ξανθῷ Μενε-
λάῳ.

[3] Iliad. ii. 101.

We have here the unrivalled wealth and power of the "king
of men, Agamemnôn," traced up to his descent from Pelops, and
accounted for, in harmony with the recognised epical agencies, by
the present of the special sceptre of Zeus through the hands of
Hermês; the latter being the wealth-giving god, whose blessing is
most efficacious in furthering the process of acquisition, whether
by theft or by accelerated multiplication of flocks and herds.[1] The

Kingly at-
tributes of
the family.

wealth and princely character of the Atreids were proverbial among the ancient epic poets. Paris not
only carries away Helen, but much property along
with her :[2] the house of Menelaus, when Têlemachus visits it in
the Odyssey, is so resplendent with gold and silver and rare ornament,[3] as to strike the beholder with astonishment and admiration. The attributes assigned to Tantalus, the father of Pelops,
are in conformity with the general idea of the family—superhuman abundance and enjoyments, and intimate converse with
the gods, to such a degree that his head is turned, and he commits
inexpiable sin. But though Tantalus himself is mentioned, in
one of the most suspicious passages of the Odyssey (as suffering
punishment in the under-world), he is not announced, nor is any
one else announced, as father of Pelops, unless we are to construe
the lines in the Iliad as implying that the latter was son of
Hermês. In the conception of the author of the Iliad, the
Pelopids are, if not of divine origin, at least a mortal breed
specially favoured and ennobled by the gods—beginning with
Pelops, and localised at Mykênæ. No allusion is made to any
connexion of Pelops either with Pisa or with Lydia.

The legend which connected Tantalus and Pelops with Mount
Sipylus may probably have grown out of the Æolic settlements

Homeric
Pelops.

at Magnêsia and Kymê. Both the Lydian origin and
the Pisatic sovereignty of Pelops are adapted to times
later than the Iliad, when the Olympic games had acquired to
themselves the general reverence of Greece, and had come to

[1] Iliad, xiv. 491. Hesiod, Theog.
444. Homer, Hymn. Mercur. 526—568,
'Ολβου καὶ πλούτου δώσω περικάλλεα
ῥάβδον. Compare Eustath. ad Iliad,
xvi. 182.

[2] Iliad, iii. 72; vii. 363. In the Hesiodic Eoiai was the following couplet
(Fragm. 55, p. 43, Düntzer):—

'Αλκὴν μὲν γὰρ ἔδωκεν 'Ολύμπιος
Αἰακίδησιν,
Νοῦν δ' 'Αμυθαονίδαις, πλοῦτον δ'
ἔπορ' 'Ατρείδησι.
Again, Tyrtæus, Fragm. 9, 4.—
Οὐδ' εἰ Ταρταλίδεω Πέλοπος βασιλεύ-
τερος εἴη, &c.
[3] Odyss. iv. 45—71.

serve as the religious and recreative centre of the Peloponnêsus—
and when the Lydian and Phrygian heroic names, Midas and
Gygês, were the types of wealth and luxury, as well as of chariot-
driving, in the imagination of a Greek.   The inconsiderable
villages of the Pisatid derived their whole importance from the
vicinity of Olympia : they are not deemed worthy of notice in
the Catalogue of Homer.   Nor could the genealogy which connected the eponym of the entire peninsula with Pisa have obtained
currency in Greece unless it had been sustained by pre-established
veneration for the locality of Olympia.   But if the sovereign of
the humble Pisa was to be recognised as forerunner of the thrice-
wealthy princes of Mykênæ, it became necessary to   Lydia, Pisa,
assign some explanatory cause of his riches.   Hence   &c., post-
the supposition of his being an immigrant, son of a   Homeric
wealthy Lydian named Tantalus, who was the offspring   additions.
of Zeus and Ploutô.   Lydian wealth and Lydian chariot-driving
rendered Pelops a fit person to occupy his place in the legend,
both as ruler of Pisa and progenitor of the Mykênæan Atreids.
Even with the admission of these two circumstances there is considerable difficulty, for those who wish to read the legends as
consecutive history, in making the Pelopids pass smoothly and
plausibly from Pisa to Mykênæ.

I shall briefly recount the legends of this great heroic family
as they came to stand in their full and ultimate growth, after the
localisation of Pelops at Pisa had been tacked on as a preface to
Homer's version of the Pelopid genealogy.

Tantalus, residing near Mount Sipylus in Lydia, had two children, Pelops and Niobê.   He was a man of immense possessions
and pre-eminent happiness, above the lot of humanity : the gods
communicated with him freely, received him at their banquets,
and accepted of his hospitality in return.   Intoxicated with such
prosperity, Tantalus became guilty of gross wickedness.   He stole
nectar and ambrosia from the table of the gods, and revealed their
secrets to mankind : he killed and served up to them   Tantalus.
at a feast his own son Pelops.   The gods were horror-
struck when they discovered the meal prepared for them : Zeüs
restored the mangled youth to life, and as Dêmêtêr, then absorbed
in grief for the loss of her daughter Persephonê, had eaten a portion of the shoulder, he supplied an ivory shoulder in place of

1—10

it. Tantalus expiated his guilt by exemplary punishment. He was placed in the under-world, with fruit and water seemingly close to him, yet eluding his touch as often as he tried to grasp them, and leaving his hunger and thirst incessant and unappeased.[1] Pindar, in a very remarkable passage, finds this old legend revolting to his feelings: he rejects the tale of the flesh of Pelops having been served up and eaten, as altogether unworthy of the gods.[2]

Niobê, the daughter of Tantalus, was married to Amphiôn, and had a numerous and flourishing offspring of seven sons and seven daughters. Though accepted as the intimate friend and companion of Lêtô, the mother of Apollo and Artemis,[3] she was presumptuous enough to triumph over that goddess, and to place herself on a footing of higher dignity, on account of the superior number of her children. Apollo and Artemis avenged this insult by killing all the sons and all the daughters : Niobê, thus left a childless and disconsolate mother, wept herself to death, and was turned into a rock, which the later Greeks continued always to identify on Mount Sipylus.[4]

Some authors represented Pelops as not being a Lydian, but a king of Paphlagônia ; by others it was said that Tantalus, having become detested from his impieties, had been expelled from Asia by Ilus the king of Troy,—an incident which served the double purpose of explaining the transit of Pelops to Greece, and of imparting to the siege of Troy by Agamemnôn the character of retribution for wrongs done to his ancestor.[5] When Pelops came over to Greece, he found Œnomaus, son of the god Arês and Harpinna, in possession of the principality of Pisa, immediately bordering on the district of Olympia. Œnomaus, having been apprised by an oracle that death would overtake him if he permitted his daughter Hippodameia to marry, refused to give her in marriage except to some

<table><tr><td>Niobê.</td></tr><tr><td>Pelops and Œnomaus, king of Pisa.</td></tr></table>

[1] Diodôr. iv. 77. Hom. Odyss. xi. 582. Pindar gives a different version of the punishment inflicted on Tantalus : a vast stone was perpetually impending over his head and threatening to fall (Olymp. i. 56 ; Isth. vii. 20).
[2] Pindar, Olymp. i. 45. Compare the sentiment of Iphigeneia in Euripidês, Iph. Taur. 387.
[3] Sapphô (Fragm. 82, Schneidewin), —Λατὼ καὶ Νιόβα μάλα μὲν φίλαι ἦσαν ἑταῖραι. Sapphô assigned to Niobê

eighteen children (Aul. Gell. N. A. iv. V. xx. 7); Hesiod gave twenty ; Homer twelve (Apollod. iii. 5).
The Lydian historian Xanthus gave a totally different version both of the genealogy and of the misfortunes of Niobê (Parthen. Narr. 33).
[4] Ovid, Metam. vi. 164—311. Pausan. i. 21, 5 ; viii. 2, 3.
[5] Apollôn. Rhod. ii. 358, and Schol.; Ister, Fragment. 59, Dindorf; Diodôr. iv. 74.

suitor who should beat him in a chariot-race from Olympia to the Isthmus of Corinth [1] : the ground here selected for the legendary victory of Pelops deserves attention, inasmuch as it is a line drawn from the assumed centre of Peloponnêsus to its extremity, and thus comprises the whole territory with which Pelops is connected as eponym. Any suitor overmatched in the race was doomed to forfeit his life ; and the fleetness of the Pisan horses, combined with the skill of the charioteer Myrtilus, had already caused thirteen unsuccessful competitors to perish by the lance of Œnomaus.[2] Pelops entered the lists as a suitor: his prayers moved the god Poseidôn to supply him with a golden chariot and winged horses; or, according to another story, he captivated the affections of Hippodameia herself, who persuaded the charioteer Myrtilus to loosen the wheels of Œnomaus before he started, so that the latter was overturned and perished in the race.   Having thus won the hand of Hippodameia, Pelops became prince of Pisa.[3] He put to death the charioteer Myrtilus, either from indignation at his treachery to Œnomaus,[4] or from jealousy on the score of Hippodameia ; but Myrtilus was the son of Hermês, and though Pelops erected a temple in the vain attempt to propitiate that god, he left a curse upon his race which future calamities were destined painfully to work out.[5]

Pelops had a numerous issue by Hippodameia : Pittheus, Trœzen and Epidaurus, the eponyms of the two Argolic cities so-called, are said to have been among them : Atreus and Thyestês were also his sons, and his daughter Nikippê married Sthenelus of Mykênæ and became the mother of Eurystheus.[6] We hear nothing of the principality of Pisa afterwards : the Pisatid villages became absorbed into the larger aggregate of Elis, after a vain struggle to maintain

Chariot victory of Pelops—his principality at Pisa.

---

[1] Diodôr. iv. 74.

[2] Pausanias (vi. 21, 7) had read their names in the Hesiodic Eoiai.

[3] Pindar, Olymp. i. 140. The chariot race of Pelops and Œnomaus was represented on the chest of Kypselus at Olympia : the horses of the former were given as having wings (Pausan. v. 17, 4). Pherekydês gave the same story (ap. Schol. ad Soph. Elect. 504).

[4] It is noticed by Herodotus and others as a remarkable fact, that no mules were ever bred in the Eleian territory ; an Eleian who wished to

breed a mule sent his mare for the time out of the region. The Eleians themselves ascribed this phenomenon to a disability brought on the land by a curse from the lips of Œnomaus (Herod. iv. 30 ; Plutarch, Quæst. Græc. p. 303).

[5] Paus. v. 1, 1 ; Sophok. Elektr. 508 ; Eurip. Orest. 985, with Schol. ; Plato, Kratyl. p. 395.

[6] Apollod. ii. 4, 5. Pausan. ii. 30, 8 ; 26, 3 ; v. 8, 1. Hesiod. ap. Schol. ad Iliad. xx. 116.

their separate right of presidency over the Olympic festival. But the legend ran that Pelops left his name to the whole peninsula : according to Thucydidês, he was enabled to do this because of the great wealth which he had brought with him from Lydia into a poor territory. The historian leaves out all the romantic interest of the genuine legends—preserving only this one circumstance, which, without being better attested than the rest, carries with it, from its common-place and prosaic character, a pretended historical plausibility.[1] .

Besides his numerous issue by Hippodameia, Pelops had an illegitimate son named Chrysippus, of singular grace and beauty, towards whom he displayed so much affection as to excite the jealousy of Hippodameia and her sons. Atreus and Thyestês conspired together to put Chrysippus to death, for which they were banished by Pelops and retired to Mykênæ,[2]—an event which brings us into the track of the Homeric legend. For Thucydidês, having found in the death of Chrysippus a suitable ground for the secession of Atreus from Pelops, conducts him at once to Mykênæ, and shows a train of plausible circumstances to account for his having mounted the throne. Eurystheus, king of Mykênæ, was the maternal nephew of Atreus : when he engaged in any foreign expedition, he naturally entrusted the regency to his uncle ; the people of Mykênæ thus became accustomed to be governed by him, and he on his part made efforts to conciliate them, so that when Eurystheus was defeated and slain in Attica, the Mykênæan people, apprehensive of an invasion from the Hêrakleids, chose Atreus as at once the most powerful and most acceptable person for his successor.[3] Such was the tale which Thucydidês derived " from those who had learnt ancient Peloponnêsian matters most clearly from their

Marginal notes: Atreus, Thyestês, Chrysippus.

---

[1] Thucyd. i. 5.

[2] We find two distinct legends respecting Chrysippus : his abduction by Laius king of Thêbes, on which the lost drama of Euripidês called Chrysippus turned (see Welcker, Griech. Tragödien, ii. p. 536), and his death by the hands of his half-brothers. Hyginus (f. 85) blends the two together.

[3] Thucyd. i. 9. λέγουσι δὲ οἱ τὰ Πελοποννησίων σαφέστατα μνήμῃ παρὰ τῶν πρότερον δεδεγμένοι. According to Hellanikus, Atreus the elder son returns to Pisa after the death of Pelops with a great army, and makes himself master of his father's principality (Hellanik. ap. Schol. ad Iliad. ii. 105). Hellanikus does not seem to have been so solicitous as Thucydidês to bring the story into conformity with Homer. The circumstantial genealogy given in Schol. ad Eurip. Orest. 5, makes Atreus and Thyestês reside during their banishment at Makestus in Triphylia: it is given without any special authority, but may perhaps come from Hellanikus.

forefathers". The introduction of so much sober and quasi-political history, unfortunately unauthenticated, contrasts strikingly with the highly poetical legends of Pelops and Atreus, which precede and follow it.

Atreus and Thyestês are known in the Iliad only as successive possessors of the sceptre of Zeus, which Thyestês at his death bequeathes to Agamemnôn. The family dissensions among this fated race commence, in the Odyssey, with Agamemnôn the son of Atreus, and Ægisthus the son of Thyestês. But subsequent poets dwelt upon an implacable quarrel between the two fathers. The cause of the bitterness was differently represented: some alleged that Thyestês had intrigued with the Krêtan Aeropê, the wife of his brother; other narratives mention that Thyestês procured for himself surreptitiously the possession of a lamb with a golden fleece, which had been designedly introduced among the flocks of Atreus by the anger of Hermês, as a cause of enmity and ruin to the whole family.[1] Atreus, after a violent burst of indignation, pretended to be reconciled, and invited Thyestês to a banquet, in which he served up to him the limbs of his own son. The father ignorantly partook of the fatal meal. Even the all-seeing Hêlios is said to have turned back his chariot to the east in order that he might escape the shocking spectacle of this Thyestean banquet: yet the tale of Thyestean revenge—the murder of Atreus perpetrated by Ægisthus, the incestuous offspring of Thyestês by his daughter Pelopia—is no less replete with horrors.[2]

Family horrors among the Pelopids.

Homeric legend is never thus revolting. Agamemnôn and Menelaus are known to us chiefly with their Homeric attributes, which have not been so darkly overlaid by subsequent poets as those of Atreus and Thyestês. Agamemnôn and Menelaus are affectionate brothers; they marry two sisters, the daughters of Tyndareus, king of Sparta, Klytæmnêstra and Helen; for Helen, the real offspring of Zeus, passes as the daughter of Tyndareus.[3] The "king of men" reigns at Mykênæ; Menelaus succeeds Tyndareus at Sparta. Of the rape of Helen, and the siege of Troy consequent upon it, I shall speak

Agamemnôn and Menelaus.

---

[1] Æschyl. Agamem. 1204, 1253, 1608; Hygin. 86; Attii Fragm. 19.
[2] Hygin. fab. 87—88.

[3] So we must say in conformity to the ideas of antiquity: compare Homer, Iliad, xvi. 176; and Herodot. vi. 53.

elsewhere : I now touch only upon the family legends of the Atreids. Menelaus on his return from Troy with the recovered Helen, is driven by storms far away to the distant regions of Phœnicia and Egypt, and is exposed to a thousand dangers and hardships before he again sets foot in Peloponnêsus. But at length he reaches Sparta, resumes his kingdom, and passes the rest of his days in uninterrupted happiness and splendour: being moreover husband of the godlike Helen and son-in-law of Zeus, he is even spared the pangs of death. When the fulness of his days is past, he is transported to the Elysian fields, there to dwell along with "the golden-haired Rhadamanthus" in a delicious climate and in undisturbed repose.[1]

Far different is the fate of the king of men, Agamemnôn. During his absence, the unwarlike Ægisthus, son of Thyestês, had seduced his wife Klytæmnêstra, in spite of the special warning of the gods, who, watchful over this privileged family, had sent their messenger Hermês expressly to deter him from the attempt.[2] A venerable bard had been left by Agamemnôn as the companion and monitor of his wife, and so long as that guardian was at hand, Ægisthus pressed his suit in vain. But he got rid of the bard by sending him to perish in a desert island, and then won without difficulty the undefended Klytæmnêstra. Ignorant of what had passed, Agamemnôn returned from Troy victorious and full of hope to his native country ; but he had scarcely landed when Ægisthus invited him to a banquet, and there, with the aid of the treacherous Klytæmnêstra, in the very hall of festivity and con-gratulation, slaughtered him and his companions "like oxen tied to the manger". His concubine Kassandra, the prophetic daughter of Priam, perished along with him by the hand of Klytæmnêstra herself.[3] The boy Orestês, the only male offspring of Agamem-nôn, was stolen away by his nurse, and placed in safety at the residence of the Phokian Strophius.

For seven years Ægisthus and Klytæmnêstra reigned in tran-quillity at Mykênæ on the throne of the murdered Agamemnôn. But in the eighth year the retribution announced by the gods

---

[1] Hom. Odyss. 280—300 ; iv. 83—560.
[2] Odyss. i. 38 ; iii. 310.—ἀνάλκιδος Αἰγίσθοιο.
[3] Odyss. iii. 260 —275 ; iv. 512—537 ; xi. 405. Deinias, in his Argolica, and

other historians of that territory, fixed the precise day of the murder of Aga-memnôn,—the thirteenth of the month Gamêliôn (Schol. ad Sophocl. Elektr. 275).

overtook them : Orestês, grown to manhood, returned and avenged
his father, by killing Ægisthus, according to Homer ;
subsequent poets add, his mother also.   He recovered Orestês.
the kingdom of Mykênæ, and succeeded Menelaus in that
of Sparta.. Hermionê, the only daughter of Menelaus and
Helen, was sent into the realm of the Myrmidons in Thessaly,
as the bride of Neoptolemus, son of Achilles, according to the
promise made by her father during the siege of Troy.[1]

Here ends the Homeric legend of the Pelopids, the final act of
Orestês being cited as one of unexampled glory.[2]   Later poets
made many additions : they dwelt upon his remorse and hardly-
earned pardon for the murder of his mother, and upon his devoted friendship for Pylades ; they wove many interesting tales,
too, respecting his sisters Iphigeneia and Elektra and his cousin
Hermionê,—names which have become naturalised in every
climate and incorporated with every form of poetry.

These poets did not at all scruple to depart from Homer, and
to give other genealogies of their own, with respect to the chief
persons of the Pelopid family.   In the Iliad and Odyssey, Agamemnôn is son of Atreus.[3]   In Homer he is specially marked
as reigning at Mykênæ ; but Stesichorus, Simonidês, and Pindar [4]
represented him as having both resided and perished at Sparta or
at Amyklæ.   According to the ancient Cyprian Verses, Helen
was represented as the daughter of Zeus and Nemesis : in one of
the Hesiodic poems she was introduced as an Oceanic nymph,
daughter of Oceanus and Têthys.[5]   The genealogical discrepancies,
even as to the persons of the principal heroes and heroines, are far
too numerous to be cited, nor is it necessary to advert to them
except as they bear upon the unavailing attempt to convert

---

[1] Odyss. iii. 306 ; iv. 9.

[2] Odyss. i. 299.

[3] Hesiod. Fragm. 60, p. 44, ed.
Düntzer; Stesichor. Fragm. 44, Kleine.
The Scholiast ad Soph. Elektr. 539, in
reference to another discrepancy between Homer and the Hesiodic poems
about the children of Helen, remarks
that we ought not to divert our attention from that which is moral and salu-
tary to ourselves in the poets (τὰ ἠθικὰ
καὶ χρήσιμα ἡμῖν τοῖς ἐντυγχάνουσι), in
order to cavil at their genealogical
contradictions.

Welcker in vain endeavours to show
that Pleisthenês was originally introduced as the father of Atreus, not as
his son (Griech. Tragöd. p. 678).

[4] Schol. ad Eurip. Orest. 46. Ὅμηρος
ἐν Μυκήναις φησὶ τὰ βασιλεῖα τοῦ Ἀγα-
μέμνονος· Στησίχορος δὲ καὶ Σιμονίδης, ἐν
Λακεδαιμονίᾳ.   Pindar, Pyth. xi. 31 ;
Nem. viii. 21.   Stêsichorus had composed an Ὀρέστεια, copied in many
points from a still more ancient lyric
Oresteia by Xanthus : compare Athen.
xii. p. 513, and Ælian, V. H. iv. 26.

[5] Hesiod. ap. Schol. ad Pindar. Nem.
x. 150.

such legendary parentage into a basis of historical record or chronological calculation.

The Homeric poems probably represent that form of the legend, respecting Agamemnôn and Orestês, which was current and popular among the Æolic colonists. Orestês was the great heroic chief of the Æolic emigration; he, or his sons, or his descendants, are supposed to have conducted the Achæans to seek a new home, when they were no longer able to make head against the invading Dôrians: the great families at Tenedos and other Æolic cities, even during the historical æra, gloried in tracing back their pedigrees to this illustrious source.[1] The legends connected with the heroic worship of these mythical ancestors form the basis of the character and attributes of Agamemnôn and his family, as depicted in Homer, in which Mykênæ appears as the first place in Peloponnêsus, and Sparta only as the second: the former the special residence of "the king of men"; the latter that of his younger and inferior brother, yet still the seat of a member of the princely Pelopids, and moreover the birth-place of the divine Helen. Sparta, Argos, and Mykênæ are all three designated in the Iliad by the goddess Hêrê as her favourite cities;[2] yet the connexion of Mykênæ with Argos, though the two towns were only ten miles distant, is far less intimate than the connexion of Mykênæ with Sparta. When we reflect upon the very peculiar manner in which Homer identifies Hêrê with the Grecian host and its leader,—for she watches over the Greeks with the active solicitude of a mother, and her antipathy against the Trojans is implacable to a degree which Zeus cannot comprehend,[3]—and when we combine this with the ancient and venerated Hêræon, or the temple of Hêrê, near Mykênæ, we may partly explain to ourselves the pre-eminence

The goddess Hêrê and Mykênæ.

---

[1] See the ode of Pindar addressed to Aristagoras of Tenedos (Nem. xi. 35; Strabo, xiii. p. 582). There were Penthilids at Mitylênê, from Penthilus, son of Orestês (Aristot. Polit. v. 8, 13, Schneid.).

[2] Iliad, iv. 52. Compare Euripid. Hêrakleid. 350.

[3] Iliad, iv. 31. Zeus says to Hêrê,—

Δαιμονίη, τί νύ σε Πρίαμος Πριάμοιό τε παῖδες
Τόσσα κακὰ ῥέζουσιν ὅτ᾽ ἀσπερχὲς μενεαίνεις

Ἰλίου ἐξαλαπάξαι ἐϋκτίμενον πτολίεθρον;

Εἰ δὲ σύ γ᾽, εἰσελθοῦσα πύλας καὶ τείχεα μακρὰ,
Ὠμὸν βεβρώθοις Πρίαμον Πριάμοιό τε παῖδας,

Ἄλλους τε Τρῶας, τότε κεν χόλον ἐξακέσαιο.

Again, xviii. 358,—

Ἐξ αὐτῆς ἐγένοντο καρηκομόωντες Ἀχαιοί.

ἦ ῥά νυ σεῖο

conferred upon Mykênæ in the Iliad and Odyssey. The Hêræon was situated between Argos and Mykênæ ; in later times its priestesses were named and its affairs administered by the Argeians : but as it was much nearer to Mykênæ than to Argos, we may with probability conclude that it originally belonged to the former, and that the increasing power of the latter enabled them to usurp to themselves a religious privilege which was always an object of envy and contention among the Grecian communities. The Æolic colonists doubtless took out with them in their emigration the divine and heroic legends, as well as the worship and ceremonial rites, of the Hêræon ; and in those legends the most exalted rank would be assigned to the close-adjoining and administering city.

Mykênæ maintained its independence even down to the Persian invasion. Eighty of its heavy-armed citizens, in the ranks of Leonidas at Thermopylæ, and a number not inferior at Platæa, upheld the splendid heroic celebrity of their city during a season of peril, when the more powerful Argos disgraced itself by a treacherous neutrality. Very shortly afterwards Mykênæ was enslaved and its inhabitants expelled by the Argeians. Though this city so long maintained a separate existence, its importance had latterly sunk to nothing, while that of the Dôrian Argos was augmented very much, and that of the Dôrian Sparta still more.

Legendary importance of Mykênæ.

The name of Mykênæ is imperishably enthroned in the Iliad and Odyssey ; but all the subsequent fluctuations of the legend tend to exalt the glory of other cities at its expense. The recognition of the Olympic games as the grand religious festival of Peloponnêsus gave vogue to that genealogy which connected Pelops with Pisa or Elis and withdrew him from Mykênæ. Moreover, in the poems of the great Athenian tragedians, Mykênæ is constantly confounded and treated as one with Argos. If any one of the citizens of the former, expelled at the time of its final subjugation by the Argeians, had witnessed at Athens a drama of Æschylus, Sophoklês, or Euripidês, or the recital of an ode of Pindar, he would have heard with grief and indignation the city of his oppressors made a partner in the heroic glories of his own.[1] But the great political ascendency acquired by Sparta con-

[1] See the preface of Dissen to the tenth Nem. of Pindar.

tributed still further to degrade Mykênæ, by disposing subsequent
poets to treat the chief of the Grecian armament
against Troy as having been a Spartan. It has been
already mentioned that Stêsichorus, Simonidês, and
Pindar adopted this version of the legend. We know
that Zeus Agamemnôn, as well as the hero Menelaus,
was worshipped at the Dôrian Sparta; [1] and the feeling of intimate identity, as well as of patriotic pride, which had grown up
in the minds of the Spartans connected with the name of Agamemnôn, is forcibly evinced by the reply of the Spartan Syagrus
to Gelôn of Syracuse at the time of the Persian invasion of Greece.
Gelôn was solicited to lend his aid in the imminent danger of
Greece before the battle of Salamis : he offered to furnish an immense auxiliary force, on condition that the supreme command
should be allotted to him. "Loudly indeed would the Pelopid
Agamemnôn cry out (exclaimed Syagrus in rejecting this application), if he were to learn that the Spartans had been deprived
of the headship by Gelôn and the Syracusans." [2] Nearly a century before this event, in obedience to the injunctions of the
Delphian oracle, the Spartans had brought back from Tegea to
Sparta the bones of "the Lacônian Orestês," as Pindar denominates him : [3] the recovery of these bones was announced to them as the means of reversing a course of
ill-fortune, and of procuring victory in their war
against Tegea. [4] The value which they set upon this
acquisition, and the decisive results ascribed to it, exhibit a precise analogy with the recovery of the bones of Thêseus from
Skyros by the Athenian Kimôn shortly after the Persian invasion. [5] The remains sought were those of a hero properly
belonging to their own soil, but who had died in a foreign land,
and of whose protection and assistance they were for that reason
deprived. And the superhuman magnitude of the bones, which
were contained in a coffin seven cubits long, is well suited to the
legendary grandeur of the son of Agamemnôn.

Its decline coincident with the rise of Argos and Sparta.

Agamemnôn and Orestês transferred to Sparta.

[1] Clemens Alexandr. Admonit. ad Gent. p. 24. Ἀγαμέμνονα γοῦν τινα Δία ἐν Σπάρτῃ τιμᾶσθαι Στάφυλος ἱστορεῖ. See also Œnomaus ap. Euseb. Præparat. Evangel. v. 28.
[2] Herodot. vii. 159. Ἦ κε μέγ' οἰμώξειεν ὁ Πελοπίδης Ἀγαμέμνων, πυθόμενος Σπαρτιήτας ἀπαραιρῆσθαι τὴν ἡγεμονίαν ὑπὸ Γέλωνός τε καὶ τῶν Συρακουσίων:
compare Homer, Iliad, vii. 125. See what appears to be an imitation of the same passage in Josephus, De Bello Judaico, iii. 8, 4. Ἡ μεγάλα γ' ἂν στενάξειαν οἱ πάτριοι νόμοι, &c.
[3] Pindar, Pyth. xi. 16.
[4] Herodot. i. 68.
[5] Plutarch, Thêseus, c. 36, Cimôn, c. 8; Pausan. iii. 3, 6.

CHAPTER VIII.

LACÔNIAN AND MESSÊNIAN GENEALOGIES.

THE earliest names in Lacônian genealogy are an indigenous
Lelex and a Naiad nymph Kleochareia. From this
pair sprung a son Eurôtas, and from him a daughter
Sparta, who became the wife of Lacedæmôn, son of
Zeus and Taygetê, daughter of Atlas. Amyklas, son

Lelex—
autoch-
thonous in
Lacônia.

of Lacedæmôn, had two sons, Kynortas and Hyakinthus—the
latter a beautiful youth, the favourite of Apollo, by whose hand
he was accidentally killed while playing at quoits : the festival
of the Hyakinthia, which the Lacedæmônians generally, and the
Amyklæans with special solemnity, celebrated throughout the
historical ages, was traced back to this legend. Kynortas was
succeeded by his son Periêrês, who married Gorgophonê, daughter
of Perseus, and had a numerous issue—Tyndareus, Ikarius,
Aphareus, Leukippus, and Hippokoôn. Some authors gave the
genealogy differently, making Periêrês, son of Æolus, to be the
father of Kynortas, and Œbalus son of Kynortas, from whom
sprung Tyndareus, Ikarius, and Hippokoôn.[1]

Both Tyndareus and Ikarius, expelled by their brother Hippo-
koôn, were forced to seek shelter at the residence of
Thestius, king of Kalydôn, whose daughter, Lêda,
Tyndareus espoused. It is numbered among the exploits of the

Tyndareus
and Lêda.

omnipresent Hêraklês, that he slew Hippokoôn and his sons,
and restored Tyndareus to his kingdom, thus creating for the
subsequent Hêrakleidan kings a mythical title to the throne.
Tyndareus, as well as his brothers, are persons of interest in
legendary narrative : he is the father of Kastôr—of Timandra,
married to Echemus, the hero of Tegea[2]—and of Klytæmnêstra,

---

[1] Compare Apollod. iii. 10, 4. Pausan. iii. 1, 4.

[2] Hesiod, ap. Schol. Pindar. Olymp.
xi. 79.

married to Agamemnôn. Pollux and the ever-memorable Helen
are the offspring of Lêda by Zeus. Ikarius is the father of Pene-

Offspring of
Lêda—
1. Kastôr,
Timandra,
Klytæm-
nêstra.
2. Pollux,
Helen.

lopê, wife of Odysseus : the contrast between her behaviour and that of Klytæmnêstra and Helen became
the more striking in consequence of their being so
nearly related. Aphareus is the father of Idas and
Lynkeus, while Leukippus has for his daughters
Phœbê and Ilaëira. According to one of the Hesiodic
poems, Kastôr and Pollux were both sons of Zeus by Lêda, while
Helen was neither daughter of Zeus nor of Tyndareus, but of
Oceanus and Têthys.[1]

The brothers Kastôr and (Polydeukês or) Pollux are no less
celebrated for their fraternal affection than for their great bodily
accomplishments : Kastôr, the great charioteer and horse-master ;
Pollux, the first of pugilists. They are enrolled both among the
hunters of the Kalydônian boar and among the heroes of the

Kastôr and
Pollux.

Argonautic expedition, in which Pollux represses the
insolence of Amykus, king of the Bebrykes, on the
coast of Asiatic Thrace :—the latter, a gigantic pugilist, from whom
no rival has ever escaped, challenges Pollux, but is vanquished
and killed in the fight.[2]

The two brothers also undertook an expedition into Attica for
the purpose of recovering their sister Helen, who had been
carried off by Thêseus in her early youth, and deposited by him
at Aphidna, while he accompanied Peirithous to the under-world,
in order to assist his friend in carrying off Persephonê. The force
of Kastôr and Pollux was irresistible, and when they re-demanded
their sister, the people of Attica were anxious to restore her : but
no one knew where Thêseus had deposited his prize. The
invaders, not believing in the sincerity of this denial, proceeded
to ravage the country, which would have been utterly ruined,
had not Dekelus, the eponymus of Dekeleia, been able to indicate
Aphidna as the place of concealment. The indigenous Titakus

[1] Hesiod, ap. Schol. Pindar. Nem. x.
150. Fragm. Hesiod. Düntzer, 58, p.
44. Tyndareus was worshipped as a
god at Lacedæmôn (Varro ap. Serv. ad
Virgil. Æneid. viii. 275).

[2] Apollôn. Rhod. ii. 1—96. Apoll. i.
9, 20. Theokrit. xxii. 26—133. In the

account of Apollônius and Apollodôrus,
Amykus is slain in the contest: in that
of Theokritus he is only conquered and
forced to give in, with a promise to
renounce for the future his brutal
conduct : there were several different
narratives. See Schol. Apollôn. Rhod.
ii. 106.

betrayed Aphidna to Kastôr and Pollux, and Helen was recovered: the brothers, in evacuating Attica, carried away into captivity Æthra, the mother of Thêseus. In after-days, when Kastôr and Pollux, under the title of the Dioskuri, had come to be worshipped as powerful gods, and when the Athenians were greatly ashamed of this act of Thêseus—the revelation made by Dekelus was considered as entitling him to the lasting gratitude of his country, as well as to the favourable remembrance of the Lacedæmônians, who maintained the Dekeleians in the constant enjoyment of certain honorary privileges at Sparta,[1] and even spared that dême in all their invasions of Attica. It is not improbable that the existence of this legend had some weight in determining the Lacedæmônians to select Dekeleia as the place of their occupation during the Peloponnêsian war.

Legend of the Attic Dekeleia.

The fatal combat between Kastôr and Polydeukês on the one side, and Idas and Lynkeus on the other, for the possession of the daughters of Leukippus, was celebrated by more than one ancient poet, and forms the subject of one of the yet remaining Idylls of Theokritus. Leukippus had formally betrothed his daughters to Idas and Lynkeus ; but the Tyndarids, becoming enamoured of them, outbid their rivals in the value of the customary nuptial gifts, persuaded the father to violate his promise, and carried of Phœbê and Ilaëira as their brides. Idas and Lynkeus pursued them and remonstrated against the injustice: according to Theokritus, this was the cause of the combat. But there was another tale, which seems the older, and which assigns a different cause to the quarrel. The four had jointly made a predatory incursion into Arcadia, and had driven off some cattle, but did not agree about the partition of the booty—Idas carried off into Messênia a portion of it which the Tyndarids claimed as

Idas and Lynkeus.

---

[1] Diodôr. iv. 63. Herod. ix. 73. Δεκελέων δὲ τῶν τότε ἐργασαμένων ἔργον χρήσιμον ἐς τὸν πάντα χρόνον, ὡς αὐτοὶ Ἀθηναῖοι λέγουσιν. According to other authors, it was Akadêmus who made the revelation, and the spot called Akadêmia, near Athens, which the Lacedæmônians spared in consideration of this service (Plutarch, Thêseus, 31, 32, 33, where he gives several different versions of this tale by Attic writers, framed with the view of exonerating Thêseus). The recovery of Helen and the captivity of Æthra were represented on the ancient chest of Kypselus, with the following curious inscription :—

Τυνδαρίδα 'Ελέναν φέρετον, Αἴθραν δ' Ἀθέναθεν 'Ελκετον.

Pausan. v. 19, 1.

their own. To revenge and reimburse themselves, the Tyndarids invaded Messênia, placing themselves in ambush in the hollow of an ancient oak. But Lynkeus, endued with preternatural powers of vision, mounted to the top of Taygetus, from whence, as he could see over the whole Peloponnêsus, he detected them in their chosen place of concealment. Such was the narrative of the ancient Cyprian Verses. Kastôr perished by the hand of Idas, Lynkeus by that of Pollux. Idas, seizing a stone pillar from the tomb of his father Aphareus, hurled it at Pollux, knocked him down and stunned him ; but Zeus, interposing at the critical moment for the protection of his son, killed Idas with a thunderbolt. Zeus would have conferred upon Pollux the gift of immortality, but the latter could not endure existence without his brother : he entreated permission to share the gift with Kastôr, and both were accordingly permitted to live, but only on every other day.[1]

The Dioskuri, or sons of Zeus,—as the two Spartan heroes, Kastôr and Pollux, were denominated,—were recognised in the historical days of Greece as gods, and received divine honours. This is even noticed in a passage of the Odyssey, which is at any rate a very old interpolation, as well as in one of the Homeric hymns. What is yet more remarkable is, that they were invoked during storms at sea, as the special and all-powerful protectors of the endangered mariner, although their attributes and their celebrity seem to be of a character so dissimilar. They were worshipped throughout most parts of Greece, but with pre-eminent sanctity at Sparta.

Great functions and power of the Dioskuri.

Kastôr and Pollux being removed, the Spartan genealogy passes from Tyndareus to Menelaus, and from him to Orestês.

Originally it appears that Messênê was a name for the western portion of Lacônia, bordering on what is called Pylos : it is so represented in the Odyssey, and Ephorus seems to have included it amongst the possessions of Orestês and his descendants.[2] Throughout the whole duration of the Messênico-Dôrian kingdom,

---

[1] Cypria Carm. Fragm. 8. p. 13, Düntzer. Lykophrôn, 533—566, with Schol. Apollod. iii. 11, 1. Pindar, Nem. x. 55—90. ἑτερήμερον ἀθανασίαν : also Homer, Odyss. xi. 302, with the Commentary of Nitzsch, vol. iii. p. 245.

The combat thus ends more favourably to the Tyndarids ; but probably the account least favourable to them is the oldest, since their dignity went on continually increasing, until at last they became great deities.

[2] Odyss. xxi. 15. Diodôr. xv. 66.

there never was any town called Messênê ; the town was first
founded by Epameinôndas, after the battle of Leuctra.   The
heroic genealogy of Messênia starts from the same Messênian
name as that of Lacônia—from the indigenous Lelex : genealogy.
his younger son Polykaôn marries Messênê, daughter of the Argeian Triopas, and settles in the country.   Pausanias tells us that
the posterity of this pair occupied the country for five generations ; but he in vain searched the ancient genealogical poems to
find the names of their descendants.[1] To them succeeded Periêrês,
son of Æolus ; and Aphareus and Leukippus, acccording to
Pausanias, were sons of Periêrês.

Aphareus, after the death of his sons, founded the town of
Arênê, and made over most part of his dominions to his kinsman,
Nêleus, with whom we pass into the Pylian genealogy.

[1] Pausan. iv. ε, 1

CHAPTER IX.

ARCADIAN GENEALOGY.

THE Arcadian divine or heroic pedigree begins with Pelasgus,
whom both Hesiod and Asius considered as an indige-
Pelasgus. nous man, though Akusilaus the Argeian represented
him as brother of Argos, the son of Zeus by Niobê, daughter of
Phorôneus. Akusilaus wished to establish a community of origin
between the Argeians and the Arcadians.

Lykaôn, son of Pelasgus and king of Arcadia, had, by different
wives, fifty sons, the most savage, impious, and wicked
Lykaôn of mankind : Mænalus was the eldest of them. Zeus,
and his in order that he might himself become a witness of
fifty sons. their misdeeds, presented himself to them in disguise. They
killed a child and served it up to him for a meal : but the god
overturned the table and struck dead with thunder Lykaôn and
all his fifty sons, with the single exception of Nyktimus, the
youngest, whom he spared at the earnest intercession of the
goddess Gæa (the Earth). The town near which the table was
overturned received the name of Trapezus (Tabletown).

This singular legend (framed on the same etymological type
as that of the ants in Ægina, recounted elsewhere)
Legend of seems ancient, and may probably belong to the Hesio-
Lykaôn— dic Catalogue. But Pausanias tells us a story in many
ferocity respects different, which was represented to him in
punished Arcadia as the primitive local account, and which be-
by the gods. comes the more interesting, as he tells us that he himself fully
believes it. Both tales indeed go to illustrate the same point—
the ferocity of Lykaôn's character, as well as the cruel . rites
which he practised. Lykaôn was the first who established the
worship and solemn games of Zeus Lykæus : he offered up a

child to Zeus, and made libations with the blood upon the altar. Immediately after having perpetrated this act, he was changed into a wolf.[1]

"Of the truth of this narrative (observes Pausanias) I feel persuaded : it has been repeated by the Arcadians from old times, and it carries probability along with it. For the men of that day, from their justice and piety, were guests and companions at table with the gods, who manifested towards them approbation when they were good, and anger if they behaved ill in a palpable manner: indeed at that time there were some, who having once been men, became gods, and who yet retain their privileges as such—Aristæus, the Krêtan Britomartis, Hêraklês son of Alkmêna, Amphiaraus the son of Oiklês, and Pollux and Kastôr besides. We may therefore believe that Lykaôn became a wild beast, and that Niobê, the daughter of Tantalus, became a stone. But in my time, wickedness having enormously increased, so as to overrun the whole earth and all the cities in it, there are no farther examples of men exalted into gods, except by mere title and from adulation towards the powerful: moreover the anger of the gods falls tardily upon the wicked, and is reserved for them after their departure from hence."

Deep religious faith of Pausanias.

Pausanias then proceeds to censure those who, by multiplying false miracles in more recent times, tended to rob the old and genuine miracles of their legitimate credit and esteem. The passage illustrates forcibly the views which a religious and instructed pagan took of his past time—how inseparably he blended together in it gods and men,

His view of past and present world.

---

[1] Apollodôr. iii. 8, 1. Hygin. fab. 176. Eratosthen. Catasterism. 8. Pausan. viii. 2, 2—3. A different story respecting the immolation of the child is in Nikolaus Damask. Fragm. p. 41, Orelli. Lykaôn is mentioned as the first founder of the temple of Zeus Lykæus in Schol. Eurip. Orest. 1662; but nothing is there said about the human sacrifice or its consequences. In the historical times, the festival and solemnities of the Lykæa do not seem to have been distinguished materially from the other agônes of Greece (Pindar, Olymp. xiii. 104; Nem. x. 46): Xenias the Arcadian, one of the generals in the army of Cyrus the younger, celebrated the solemnity with great magnificence in the march through Asia Minor (Xen. Anab. i. 2, 10). But the fable of the human sacrifice, and the subsequent transmutation of the person who had eaten human food into a wolf, continued to be told in connexion with them (Plato, de Republic. viii. c. 15, p. 417). Compare Pliny, H. N. viii. 34. This passage of Plato seems to afford distinct indication that the practice of offering human victims at the altar of the Lykæan Zeus was neither prevalent nor recent, but at most only traditional and antiquated; and it therefore limits the sense or invalidates the authority of the Pseudo-Platonic dialogue, Minos, c. 5.

1—11

and how little he either recoguised or expected to find in it the
naked phænomena and historical laws of connexion which belonged to the world before him. He treats the past as the province of legend; the present as that of history ; and in doing this
he is more sceptical than the persons with whom he conversed,
who believed not only in the ancient, but even in the recent, and
falsely reported miracles. It is true that Pausanias does not
always proceed consistently with this position : he often rationalises the stories of the past, as if he expected to find historical
threads of connexion ; and sometimes, though more rarely, accepts
the miracles of the present. But in the present instance he draws
a broad line of distinction between present and past, or rather
between what is recent and what is ancient. His criticism is, in
the main, analogous to that of Arrian in regard to the Amazons
—denying their existence during times of recorded history, but
admitting it during the early and unrecorded ages.

In the narrative of Pausanias, the sons of Lykaôn, instead of
perishing by thunder from Zeus, become the founders of the
various towns in Arcadia. And as that region was subdivided
into a great number of small and independent townships, each
having its own eponym, so the Arcadian heroic genealogy appears
broken up and subdivided. Pallas, Orestheus, Phigalus, Trape-
zeus, Mænalus, Mantineus, and Tegeatês are all numbered
among the sons of Lykaôn, and are all eponyms of various
Arcadian towns.[1]

The legend respecting Kallistô and Arkas, the eponym of
Kallistô
and Arkas.
Arcadia generally, seems to have been originally quite
independent of and distinct from that of Lykaôn.

Eumêlus, indeed, and some other poets made Kallistô
daughter of Lykaôn : but neither Hesiod nor Asius, nor Pherekydês, acknowledged any relationship between them.[2] The
beautiful Kallistô, companion of Artemis in the chase, had bound
herself by a vow of chastity : Zeus, either by persuasion or by
force, obtained a violation of the vow, to the grievous displeasure
both of Hêrê and Artemis. The former changed Kallistô into a
bear ; the latter, when she was in that shape, killed her with an
arrow. Zeus gave to the unfortunate Kallistô a place among the
stars, as the constellation of the Bear : he also preserved the child

---

[1] Paus. viii. 3. Hygin. fab. 177.   [2] Apollod. iii. 8, 2.

Arkas, of which she was pregnant by him, and gave it to the Atlantid nymph Maia to bring up.[1]

Arkas, when he became king, obtained from Triptolemus and communicated to his people the first rudiments of agriculture ; he also taught them to make bread, to spin, and to weave.   He had three sons—Azan, Apheidas, and Elatus : the first was the eponym of Azania, the northern region of Arcadia ; the second was one of the heroes of Tegea ; the third was father of Ischys (rival of Apollo for the affections of Korônis), as well as of Æpytus and Kyllên : the name of Æpytus among the heroes of Arcadia is as old as the Catalogue in the Iliad.[2]

Azan, Apheidas, Elatus.

Aleus, son of Apheidas and king of Tegea, was the founder of the celebrated temple and worship of Athênê Alea in that town.   Lykurgus and Kêpheus were his sons, Augê his daughter, who was seduced by Hêraklês, and secretly bore to him a child : the father, discovering what had happened, sent Augê to Nauplius to be sold into slavery : Teuthras, king of Mysia in Asia Minor, purchased her and made her his wife : her tomb was shown at Pergamus on the river Kaikus even in the time of Pausanias.[3]

Aleus, Augê, Têlephus.

From Lykurgus,[4] the son of Aleus and brother of Augê, we pass to his son Ankæus, numbered among the Argonauts, finally killed in the chase of the Kalydônian boar, and father of Agapenôr, who leads the Arcadian contingent against Troy,—(the adventures of his niece the Tegeatic huntress Atalanta, have

---

[1] Pausan. viii. 3, 2.   Apollod. iii. 8, 2. Hesiod. apud Eratosthen. Catasterism. 1.   Fragm. 182. Marktsch.   Hygin. f. 177.

[2] Homer, Iliad, ii. 604.   Pind. Olymp. vi. 44—63.

The tomb of Æpytus, mentioned in the Iliad, was shown to Pausanias between Pheneus and Stymphalus (Pausan. viii. 16, 2).   Æpytus was a cognomen of Hermês (Pausan. viii. 47, 3).

The hero Arkas was worshipped at Mantineia, under the special injunction of the Delphian oracle (Pausan. viii. 9, 2).

[3] Pausan. viii. 4, 6.   Apollod. iii. 9, 1.   Diodôr. iv. 33.

A separate legend respecting Augê and the birth of Têlephus was current at Tegea, attached to the temple,

statue, and cognomen of Eileithyia in the Tegeatic agora (Pausan. viii. 48, 5).

Hekatæus seems to have narrated in detail the adventures of Augê (Pausan. viii. 4, 4 ; 47, 3.   Hekatæ. Fragm. 345, Didot).

Euripidês followed a different story about Augê and the birth of Têlephus in his lost tragedy called Augê. (See Strabo, xiii. p. 615.)   Respecting the Μυσοί of Æschylus, and the two lost dramas, Ἀλεαδαί and Μυσοί of Sophoklês, little can be made out.   See Welcker, Griechisch. Tragöd. p. 53, 408—414).

[4] There were other local genealogies of Tegea deduced from Lykurgus: Bôtachus, eponym of the dême Bôtachidæ at that place, was his grandson (Nicolaus ap. Steph. Byz. v. Βωταχίδαι).

already been touched upon),—then to Echemus, son of Aëropus and grandson of the brother of Lykurgus, Kêpheus. Echemus is Ankæus— the chief heroic ornament of Tegea. When Hyllus, Echemus. the son of Hêraklês, conducted the Hêrakleids on their first expedition against Peloponnêsus, Echemus commanded the Tegean troops who assembled along with the other Peloponnêsians at the isthmus of Corinth, to repel the invasion : it was agreed that the dispute should be determined by single combat, and Echemus, as the champion of Peloponnêsus, encountered and killed Hyllus. Pursuant to the stipulation by which they had bound themselves, the Hêrakleids retired, and abstained for three generations from pressing their claim upon Peloponnêsus. This valorous exploit of their great martial hero was cited and appealed to by the Tegeates before the battle of Platæa, as the principal evidence of their claim to the second post in the combined army, next in point of honour to that of the Lacedæmônians, and superior to that of the Athenians : the latter replied to them by producing as counter-evidence the splendid heroic deeds of Athens,—the protections of the Hêrakleids against Echemus Eurystheus, the victory over the Kadmeians of Thêbes, kills Hyl- and the complete defeat of the Amazons in Attica.[1] lus—Hê- rakleids re- Nor can there be any doubt that these legendary pelled from glories were both recited by the speakers, and heard Peloponnêsus. by the listeners, with profound and undoubting faith, as well as with heart-stirring admiration.

One other person there is—Ischys, son of Elatus and grandson of Arkas—in the fabulous genealogy of Arcadia whom it would be improper to pass over, inasmuch as his name and adventures are connected with the genesis of the memorable god or hero Korônis Æsculapius, or Asklêpius. Korônis, daughter of and As- Phlegyas, and resident near the lake Bœbëis in klêpius. Thessaly, was beloved by Apollo and became pregnant by him : unfaithful to the god, she listened to the propositions of Ischys, son of Elatus, and consented to wed him : a raven brought to Apollo the fatal news, which so incensed him that he

[1] Herodot. ix. 27. Echemus is described by Pindar (Ol. xi. 69) as gaining the prize of wrestling in the fabulous Olympic games, on their first establishment by Hêraklês. He also found a place in the Hesiodic Catalogue as husband of Timandra, the sister of Helen and Klytæmnêstra (Hesiod, Fragm. 105, p. 318, Marktscheff.).

changed the colour of the bird from white, as it previously had been, into black.[1] Artemis, to avenge the wounded dignity of her brother, put Korônis to death ; but Apollo preserved the male child of which she was about to be delivered, and consigned it to the Centaur Cheirôn to be brought up. The child was named Asklêpius or Æsculapius, and acquired, partly from the teaching of the beneficent leech Cheirôn, partly from inborn and superhuman aptitude, a knowledge of the virtues of herbs and a mastery of medicine and surgery, such as had never before been witnessed. He not only cured the sick, the wounded, and the dying, but even restored the dead to life. Kapaneus, Eriphylê, Hippolytus, Tyndareus, and Glaukus were all affirmed by different poets and logographers to have been endued by him with a new life.[2] But Zeus now found himself under the necessity of taking precautions lest mankind, thus unexpectedly protected against sickness and death, should no longer stand in need of the immortal gods : he smote Asklêpius with thunder and killed him. Apollo was so exasperated by this slaughter of his highly-gifted son that he killed the Cyclôpes who had fabricated the thunder, and Zeus was about to condemn him to Tartarus for doing so ; but on the intercession of Latôna he relented, and was satisfied with imposing upon him a temporary servitude in the house of Admêtus at Pheræ.

[1] Apollodôr. iii. 10, 3 ; Hesiod. Fragment. 141—142, Marktscheff. ; Strab. ix. p. 442 ; Pherekydês, Fr. 8 ; Akusilaus, Fragm. 25, Didot.

Τῷ μὲν ἄρ' ἄγγελος ἦλθε κόραξ, ἱερῆς
   ἀπὸ δαιτὸς
Πυθὼ ἐς ἠγαθέην, καὶ ῥ' ἔφρασεν ἔργ'
   ἀίδηλα
Φοίβῳ ἀκερσεκόμῃ, ὅτι Ἰσχὺς γῆμε
   Κόρωνιν
Εἰλατίδης, Φλεγύαο διογνήτοιο θύ-
   γατρα.
              (Hesiod, Fr.)

The change of the colour of the crow is noticed both in Ovid. Metamorph. ii. 632, in Antonin. Liberal. c. 20, and in Servius ad Virgil. Æneid. vii. 761, though the name " Corvo custode ejus " is there printed with a capital letter, as if it were a man named Corvus.

[2] Schol. Eurip. Alkêst. 1 ; Diodôr. iv. 71 ; Apollodôr. iii. 10, 3 ; Pindar, Pyth. iii. 59 ; Sextus Empiric. adv. Grammatic. i. 12, p. 271. Stêsichorus named Eriphylê—the Naupaktian

verses, Hippolytus—(compare Servius ad Virgil. Æneid. vii. 761) Panyasis, Tyndareus ; a proof of the popularity of this tale among the poets. Pindar says that Æsculapius was "tempted by gold" to raise a man from the dead, and Plato (Legg. iii. p. 408) copies him: this seems intended to afford some colour for the subsequent punishment. "Mercede id captum (observes Boeck ad Pindar. l. c.) Æsculapium fecisse recentior est fictio ; Pindari fortasse ipsius, quem tragici secuti sunt : haud dubie a medicorum avaris moribus profecta, qui Græcorum medicis nostrisque communes sunt." The rapacity of the physicians (granting it to be ever so well-founded, both then and now) appears to me less likely to have operated upon the mind of Pindar, than the disposition to extenuate the cruelty of Zeus, by imputing guilty and sordid views to Asklêpius. Compare the citation from Dikæarchus, infra, p. 177.

Asklêpius was worshipped with very great solemnity at Trikka,
Extended worship of Asklêpius —numerous legends. at Kôs, at Knidus, and in many different parts of Greece, but especially at Epidaurus, so that more than one legend had grown up respecting the details of his birth and adventures : in particular, his mother was by some called Arsinoê. But a formal application had been made on this subject (so the Epidaurians told Pausanias) to the oracle of Delphi, and the god in reply acknowledged that Asklêpius was his son by Korônis.[1] The tale above recounted seems to have been both the oldest and the most current. It is adorned by Pindar in a noble ode, wherein, however, he omits all mention of the raven as messenger—not specifying who or what the spy was from whom Apollo learnt the infidelity of Korônis. By many this was considered as an improvement in respect of poetical effect, but it illustrates the mode in which the characteristic details and simplicity of the old fables[2] came to be exchanged for dignified generalities, adapted to the altered taste of society.

Machaôn and Podaleirius, the two sons of Asklêpius, command
Machaôn and Podaleirius. the contingent from Trikka, in the north-west region of Thessaly, at the siege of Troy by Agamemnôn.[3] They are the leeches of the Grecian army, highly prized and consulted by all the wounded chiefs. Their medical renown was further prolonged in the subsequent poem of Arktinus, the Iliu-Persis, wherein the one was represented as unrivalled in surgical operations, the other as sagacious in detecting and appreciating morbid symptoms. It was Podaleirius who first noticed the glaring eyes and disturbed deportment which preceded the suicide of Ajax.[4]

[1] Pausan. ii. 26, where several distinct stories are mentioned, each springing up at some one or other of the sanctuaries of the god: quite enough to justify the idea of three Æsculapii (Cicero, N. D. iii. 22). Homer. Hymn. ad Æsculap. 2. The tale briefly alluded to in the Homeric Hymn. ad Apollin., 209, is evidently different : Ischys is there the companion of Apollo, and Korônis is an Arcadian damsel. Aristidês, the fervent worshipper of Asklêpius, adopted the story of Korônis, and composed hymns on the γάμον Κορωνίδος καὶ γένεσιν τοῦ θεοῦ (Orat. 23, p. 463, Dind.). [2] See Pindar, Pyth. iii. The Scholiast put a construction upon Pindar's words which is at any rate far-fetched, if indeed it be at all admissible : he supposes that Apollo knew the fact from his own omniscience, without any informant, and he praises Pindar for having thus transformed the old fable. But the words οὐδ' ἔλαθε σκόπον seem certainly to imply some informant : to suppose that σκόπον means the god's own mind is a strained interpretation. [3] Iliad, ii. 730. The Messênians laid claim to the sons of Asklêpius as their heroes, and tried to justify the pretension by a forced construction of Homer (Paus. iii. 4, 2). [4] Arktinus, Epicc. Græc. Fragm. 2. p. 22, Düntzer. The Ilias Minor men-

Galen appears uncertain whether Asklêpius (as well as Dionysus) was originally a god, or whether he was first a man and then became afterwards a god ;[1] but Apollodôrus professed to fix the exact date of his apotheosis.[2] Throughout all the historical ages the descendants of Asklêpius were numerous and widely diffused. The many families or gentes called Asklêpiads, who devoted themselves to the study and practice of medicine, and who principally dwelt near the temples of Asklêpius, whither sick and suffering men came to obtain relief—all recognised the god, not merely as the object of their common worship, but also as their actual progenitor. Like Solôn, who reckoned Nêleus and Poseidôn as his ancestors, or the Milêsian Hekatæus, who traced his origin through fifteen successive links to a god—like the privileged gens at Pêlion in Thessaly,[3] who considered the wise Centaur Cheirôn as their progenitor, and who inherited from him their precious secrets respecting the medicinal herbs of which their neighbourhood was full,—Asklêpiads, even of the later times, numbered and specified all the intermediate links which separated them from their primitive divine parent. One of these genealogies has been preserved to us, and we may be sure that there were many such, as the Asklêpiads were found in many different places.[4] Among them were enrolled highly instructed

Numerous Asklêpiads, or descendants from Asklêpius.

tioned the death of Machaôn by Eurypylus, son of Têlephus (Fragm. 5, p. 19, Düntzer).

[1] Ἀσκληπιός γέ τοι καὶ Διόνυσος, εἴτ' ἄνθρωποι πρότερον ἤστην εἴτε καὶ ἀρχῆθεν θεοί (Galen, Protreptic. 9. t. 1. p. 22, Kühn). Pausanias considers him as θεὸς ἐξ ἀρχῆς (ii. 26, 7). In the important temple at Smyrna he was worshipped as Ζεὺς Ἀσκληπιός (Aristidês, Or. 6, p. 64 ; Or. 23, p. 456, Dind.).

[2] Apollodôr. ap. Clem. Alex. Strom. i. p. 381 ; see Heyne, Fragment. Apollodôr. p. 410. According to Apollodôrus, the apotheosis of Hêraklês and of Æsculapius took place at the same time, thirty-eight years after Hêraklês began to reign at Argos.

[3] About Hekatæus, Her. ii. 143 ; about Solôn, Diog. L., Vit. Plat., init.

A curious fragment, preserved from the lost works of Dikæarchus, tells us of the descendants of the Centaur Cheirôn at the town of Pêlion, or perhaps at the neighbouring town of

Dêmêtrias,—it is not quite certain which, perhaps at both (see Dikæarch. Fragment. ed. Fuhr, p. 408). Ταύτην δὲ τὴν δύναμιν ἐν τῶν πολιτῶν οἶδε γένος, ὁ δὴ λέγεται Χείρωνος ἀπόγονον εἶναι · παραδίδωσι δὲ καὶ δείκνυσι πατὴρ οἵῳ, καὶ οὕτως ἡ δύναμις φυλάσσεται, ὡς οὐδεὶς ἄλλος οἶδε τῶν πολιτῶν · οὐχ ὅσιον δὲ τοὺς ἐπισταμένους τὰ φάρμακα μισθοῦ τοῖς καμνοῦσι βοηθεῖν, ἀλλὰ προῖκα.
Plato, de Republ. iii. 4 (p. 391). Ἀχιλλεὺς ὑπὸ τῷ σοφωτάτῳ Χείρωνι τεθραμμένος. Comp. Xen. De Ven. c. 1.

[4] See the genealogy at length in Le Clerc, Hist. de la Méd. lib. ii. c. 2. p. 78, also p. 287 ; also Littré, Introd. aux Œuvres Complètes d'Hippocrate, t. i. p. 34. Hippokratês was the seventeenth from Æsculapius.

Theopompus the historian went at considerable length into the pedigree of the Asklêpiads of Kôs and Knidus, tracing them up to Podaleirius and his first settlement at Syruus in Karia (see

and accomplished men, such as the great Hippocratês and the historian Ktêsias, who prided themselves on the divine origin of themselves and their gens[1]—so much did the legendary element pervade even the most philosophical and positive minds of his-torical Greece. Nor can there be any doubt that their means of medical observation must have been largely extended by their vicinity to a temple so much fre-quented by the sick, who came in confident hopes of divine relief, and who, whilst they offered up sacrifice and prayer to Æsculapius, and slept in his temple in order to be favoured with healing suggestions in their dreams, might, in case the god withheld his supernatural aid, consult his living descendants.[2] The sick visitors at Kôs, or Trikka, or Epidaurus, were numerous and constant, and the tablets usually hung up to record the particulars of their maladies, the remedies resorted to, and the cures operated by the god, formed both an interesting decoration of the sacred ground and an instructive memorial to the Asklêpiads.[3]

Temples of Asklêpius—sick persons healed there.

Theopomp. Fragm. 111, Didot): Polyan-thus of Kyrênê composed a special treatise περὶ τῆς τῶν Ἀσκληπιαδῶν γενέσεως (Sextus Empiric. adv. Gram-mat. i. 12, p. 271); see Stephan. Byz. v. Κῶς, and especially Aristidês, Orat. vii. *Asclêpiadæ.* The Asklêpiads were even reckoned among the Ἀρχηγέται of Rhodes, jointly with the Hêrakleids (Aristidês, Or. 44, ad Rhod. p. 839, Dind.).

In the extensive sacred enclosure at Epidaurus stood the statues of Asklê-pius and his wife Epionê (Pausan. ii. 29, 1): two daughters are coupled with him by Aristophanês, and he was con-sidered especially εὔπαις (Plutus, 654); Jaso, Panakeia and Hygieia are named by Aristidês.

[1] Plato, Protagór. c. 6. (p. 311). Ἱπποκράτη τὸν Κῶον, τὸν τῶν Ἀσκλη-πιαδῶν; also Phædr. c. 121 (p. 270). About Ktêsias, Galen, Opp. t. v. p. 652, Basil.; and Bahrt, Fragm. Ktêsiæ, p. 20. Aristotle (see Stahr, Aristotelia, i. p. 32) and Xenophon, the physician of the emperor Claudius, were both Asklêpiads (Tacit. Annal. xii. 61). Plato, de Republ. iii. 405, calls them τοὺς κομψοὺς Ἀσκληπιάδας.

Pausanias, a distinguished physician at Gela in Sicily, and contemporary of the philosopher Empedoklês, was also an Asklêpiad: see the verses of Empe-doklês upon him, Diogen. Laërt. viii. 61.

[2] Strabo, viii. p. 374; Aristophan. Vesp. 122; Plutus, 635—750; where the visit to the temple of Æsculapius is described in great detail, though with a broad farcical colouring.

During the last illness of Alexander the Great, several of his principal officers slept in the temple of Serapis, in the hope that remedies would be suggested to them in their dreams (Arrian, vii. 26).

Pausanias, in describing the various temples of Asklêpius which he saw, announces as a fact quite notorious and well understood, "Here cures are wrought by the god" (ii. 36, 1; iii. 26, 7; vii. 27, 4): see Suidas, v. Ἀρίσταρχος. The orations of Aristidês, especially the 6th and 7th, *Asklêpius and the Asklêpiadæ,* are the most striking manifestations of faith and thanks-giving towards Æsculapius, as well as attestations of his extensive working throughout the Grecian world; also Or. 23 and 25, Ἱερῶν Λόγος, 1, 3; and Or. 45 (De Rhet. p. 22, Dind.), αἵ τ᾽ ἐν Ἀσκληπιοῦ τῶν ἀεὶ διατριβόντων ἀγελαί, &c.

[3] Pausan. ii. 27, 3; 36, 1. Ταύταις ἐγγεγραμμένα ἐστὶ καὶ ἀνδρῶν καὶ γυναι-κῶν ὀνόματα ἀκεσθέντων ὑπὸ τοῦ Ἀσκλη-πιοῦ, προσέτι δὲ καὶ νόσημα, ὅ,τι ἕκαστος ἐνόσησε, καὶ ὅπως ἰάθη,—the cures are wrought by the god himself.

The genealogical descent of Hippocratês and the other Asklê-piads from the god Asklêpius is not only analogous to that of Hekatæus and Solôn from their respective ancestral gods, but also to that of the Lacedæmônian kings from Hêraklês, upon the basis of which the whole supposed chronology of the ante-his-torical times has been built, from Eratosthenês and Apollodôrus down to the chronologers of the present century.[1] I shall revert to this hereafter.

[1] "Apollodorus ætatem Herculis pro cardine chronologiæ habuit" (Heyne, ad Apollod. Fr. p. 410).

CHAPTER X.

ÆAKUS AND HIS DESCENDANTS—ÆGINA, SALAMIS, AND PHTHIA.

THE memorable heroic genealogy of the Æakids establishes a fabulous connexion between Ægina, Salamis, and Phthia, which we can only recognise as a fact, without being able to trace its origin.

Æakus was the son of Zeus, born of Ægina, daughter of Asôpus,
Æakus— son of Zeus and Ægina. whom the god had carried off and brought into the island to which he gave her name: she was afterwards married to Aktôr, and had by him Menœtius, father of Patroclus.   As there were two rivers named Asôpus, one between Phlius and Sikyôn, and another between Thêbes and Platæa—so the Æginêtan heroic genealogy was connected both with that of Thêbes and with that of Phlius ; and this belief led to practical consequences in the minds of those who accepted the legends as genuine history.   For when the Thêbans, in the 68th Olympiad, were hard-pressed in war by Athens, they were directed by the Delphian oracle to ask assistance of their next of kin. Recollecting that Thêbê and Ægina had been sisters, common daughters of Asôpus, they were induced to apply to the Æginêtans as their next of kin, and the Æginêtans gave them aid, first by sending to them their common heroes, the Æakids, next by actual armed force.[1]   Pindar dwells emphatically on the heroic brotherhood between Thêbes, his native city, and Ægina.[2]

Æakus was alone in Ægina : to relieve him from this solitude,
Offspring of Æakus— Pêleus, Telamôn, Phôkus. Zeus changed all the ants in the island into men, and thus provided him with a numerous population, who, from their origin, were called Myrmidons.[3]   By his wife Endêis, daughter of Cheirôn, Æakus had for his

[1] Herodot. v. 81.
[1] Nem. iv. 22.   Isth. vii. 16.

[3] This tale, respecting the transformation of the ants into men, is as old

sons Pêleus and Telamôn : by the Nereid Psamathê, he had
Phôkus. A monstrous crime had then recently been committed
by Pelops, in killing the Arcadian prince, Stymphalus, under a
simulation of friendship and hospitality : for this the gods had
smitten all Greece with famine and barrenness. The oracles
affirmed that nothing could relieve Greece from this intolerable
misery except the prayers of Æakus, the most pious of mankind.
Accordingly envoys from all quarters flocked to Ægina, to prevail upon Æakus to put up prayers for them : on his supplications the gods relented, and the suffering immediately ceased.
The grateful Greeks established in Ægina the temple and worship
of Zeus Panhellênius, one of the lasting monuments and institutions of the island, on the spot where Æakus had offered up his
prayer. The statues of the envoys who had come to　Prayers of
solicit him were yet to be seen in the Æakeion, or　Æakus—
sacred edifice of Æakus, in the time of Pausanias :　procure
and the Athenian Isokratês, in his eulogy of Evagoras,　Greece.
the despot of Salamis in Cyprus (who traced his descent through
Teukrus to Æakus), enlarges upon this signal miracle, recounted
and believed by other Greeks as well as by the Æginêtans, as a proof
both of the great qualities and of the divine favour and patronage
displayed in the career of the Æakids.[1] Æakus was also employed
to aid Poseidôn and Apollo in building the walls of Troy.[2]

Pêleus and Telamôn, the sons of Æakus, contracting a jealousy
of their bastard brother, Phôkus, in consequence of　Phôkus
his eminent skill in gymnastic contests, conspired to　killed by
put him to death. Telamôn flung his quoit at him　Telamôn.

---

as the Hesiodic Catalogue of Women.
See Düntzer, Fragm. Epicc. 21, p. 34 ;
evidently an etymological tale from the
name Myrmidones. Pausanias throws
aside both the etymology and the details of the miracle : he says that Zeus
raised men from the earth, at the prayer
of Æakus (ii. 29, 2) : other authors retained the etymology of Myrmidons
from μύρμηκες, but gave a different
explanation (Kallimachus, Fragm. 114,
Düntzer). Μυρμιδόνων ἐσσῆνα (Strabo,
viii. p. 375). Ἐσσῆν, ὁ οἰκιστής (Hygin.
fab. 52).
 According to the Thessalian legend,
Myrmidôn was the son of Zeus by
Eurymedusa, daughter of Kletôr ;
Zeus having assumed the disguise of

an ant (Clemens. Alex. Admon. ad
Gent. p. 25, Sylb.).
 [1] Apollod. iii. 12, 6. Isokrat. Evag.
Encom. vol. ii. p. 278, Auger. Pausan.
i. 44, 13 ; ii. 29, 6. Schol. Aristoph.
Equit. 1253.
 So in the 106th Psalm, respecting
the Israelites and Phinehas, v. 29,
" They provoked the Lord to anger with
their inventions, and the plague brake
in upon them " ; "Then stood up
Phinehas and executed judgment, and
so the plague was stayed " ; "And that
was counted unto him for righteousness,
unto all generations for evermore ".
 [2] Pindar, Olymp. viii. 41, with the
Scholia. Didymus did not find this story
in any other poet older than Pindar.

while they were playing together, and Pêleus despatched him by a blow with his hatchet in the back.   They then concealed the dead body in a wood, but Æakus, having discovered both the act and the agents, banished the brothers from the island.[1]   For both of them eminent destinies were in store.

While we notice the indifference to the moral quality of actions implied in the old Hesiodic legend, when it imputes distinctly and nakedly this proceeding to two of the most admired persons of the heroic world—it is not less instructive to witness the change of feeling which had taken place in the age of Pindar. That warm eulogist of the great Æakid race hangs down his head with shame, and declines to recount, though he is obliged darkly to glance at, the cause which forced the pious Æakus to banish his sons from Ægina.   It appears that Kallimachus, if we may judge by a short fragment, manifested the same repugnance to mention it.[2]

Telamôn retired to Salamis, then ruled by Kychreus, the son of Poseidôn and Salamis, who had recently rescued the island from the plague of a terrible serpent.   This animal, expelled from Salamis, retired to Eleusis in Attica, where it was received and harboured by the goddess Dêmêtêr in her sacred domicile.[3]   Kychreus dying childless left his dominion to Telamôn, who, marrying Periboea, daughter of Alkathoos, and granddaughter of Pelops, had for his son the celebrated Ajax.   Telamôn took part both in the chase of the Kalydônian boar and in the Argonautic expedition : he was also the intimate friend and companion of Hêraklês, whom he accompanied in his enterprise against the Amazons, and in the attack made with only six ships upon Laomedôn, king of Troy.

Telamôn, banished, goes to Salamis.

---

[1] Apollod. iii. 12, 6, who relates the tale somewhat differently ; but the old epic poem Alkmæonis gave the details (ap. Schol. Eurip. Andromach. 685)—

'Ένθα μὲν ἀντίθεος Τελαμὼν τροχοειδεῖ
        δίσκῳ
Πλῆξε κάρη· Πηλεὺς δὲ θοῶς ἀνὰ χεῖρα
        τανύσσας
'Αξίνην εὐχαλκον ἐπεπλήγει μετὰ νῶτα.

[2] Pindar, Nem. v. 15, with Scholia, and Kallimach. Frag. 136.   Apollônius Rhodius represents the fratricide as inadvertent and unintentional (i. 92); one instance amongst many of the tendency to soften down and moralise the ancient tales.

Pindar, however, seems to forget this incident when he speaks in other places of the general character of Pêleus (Olymp. ii. 75-86. Isthm. vii. 40).

[3] Apollod. iii. 12, 7.   Euphoriôn, Fragm. 5, Düntzer, p. 43, Epicc. Græc. There may have been a tutelary serpent in the temple at Eleusis, as there was in that of Athênê Polias at Athens (Herodot. viii. 41, Photius, v. Οἰκοῦρον ὄφιν. Arist. Lysistr. 759, with the Schol.).

This last enterprise having proved completely successful, Telamôn was rewarded by Hêraklês with the possession of the daughter of Laomedôn, Hêsionê, who bore to him Teukros, the most distinguished archer amidst the host of Agamemnôn, and the founder of Salamis in Cyprus.[1]

Pêleus went to Phthia, where he married the daughter of Eurytiôn, son of Aktôr, and received from him the third part of his dominions. Taking part in the Kalydônian boar-hunt, he unintentionally killed his father-in-law Eurytiôn, and was obliged to flee to Iôlkos, where he received purification from Akastus, son of Pelias : the danger to which he became exposed, by the calumnious accusations of the enamoured wife of Akastus, has already been touched upon in a previous section. Pêleus also was among the Argonauts ; the most memorable event in his life, however, was his marriage with the sea-goddess Thetis. Zeus and Poseidôn had both conceived a violent passion for Thetis. But the former, having been forewarned by Promêtheus that Thetis was destined to give birth to a son more powerful than his father, compelled her, much against her own will, to marry Pêleus ; who, instructed by the intimations of the wise Cheirôn, was enabled to seize her on the coast called Sêpias in the southern region of Thessaly. She changed her form several times, but Pêleus held her fast until she resumed her original appearance, and she was then no longer able to resist. All the gods were present, and brought splendid gifts to these memorable nuptials : Apollo sang with his harp, Poseidôn gave to Pêleus the immortal horses Xanthus and Balius, and Cheirôn presented a formidable spear, cut from an ash-tree on Mount Pêlion. We shall have reason hereafter to recognise the value of both these gifts in the exploits of Achillês.[2]

Pêleus goes to Phthia—his marriage with Thetis.

---

[1] Apollod. iii. 12, 7. Hesiod. ap. Strab. ix. p. 393.

The libation and prayer of Hêraklês, prior to the birth of Ajax, and his fixing the name of the yet unborn child, from an eagle (αἰετός) which appeared in response to his words, was detailed in the Hesiodic Eoiai, and is celebrated by Pindar (Isthm. v. 30—54). See also the Scholia.

[2] Apollodôr. iii. 13, 5. Homer, Iliad, xviii. 434; xxiv. 62. Pindar, Nem. iv. 50—68; Isthm. vii. 27—50. Herodot. vii. 192. Catullus, Carm. 64. Epithal. Pel. et Thetidos, with the prefatory remarks of Doering.

The nuptials of Pêleus and Thetis were much celebrated in the Hesiodic Catalogue, or prehaps in the Eoiai (Düntzer, Epic. Græc. Frag. 36, p. 39), and Ægimius—see Schol. ad Apollon. Rhod. iv. 869—where there is a curious attempt of Staphylus to rationalise the marriage of Pêleus and Thetis.

There was a town, seemingly near Pharsalus in Thessaly, called Theti-

The prominent part assigned to Thetis in the Iliad is well known, and the post-Homeric poets of the Legend of Troy introduced her as actively concurring first to promote the glory, finally to bewail the death, of her distinguished son.[1] Pêleus, having survived both his son Achillês and his grandson Neoptolemus, is ultimately directed to place himself on the very spot where he had originally seized Thetis, and thither the goddess comes herself to fetch him away, in order that he may exchange the desertion and decrepitude of age for a life of immortality along with the Nêreids.[2] The spot was indicated to Xerxês when he marched into Greece by the Iônians who accompanied him, and his magi offered solemn sacrifices to her as well as to the other Nêreids as the presiding goddesses and mistresses of the coast.[3]

Neoptolemus or Pyrrhus, the son of Achillês, too young to engage in the commencement of the siege of Troy, comes on the stage after the death of his father as the indispensable and prominent agent in the final capture of the city. He returns victor from Troy,·not to Phthia, but to Epirus, bringing with him the captive Andromachê, widow of Hectôr, by whom Molossus is born to him. He himself perishes in the full vigour of life at Delphi by the machinations of Orestês, son of Agamemnôn. But his son Molossus—like Fleance, the son of Banquo, in Macbeth—becomes the father of the powerful race of Molossian kings, who played so conspicuous a part during the declining vigour of the Grecian cities, and to whom the title and parentage of Æakids was a source of peculiar pride, identifying them by community of heroic origin with genuine and undisputed Hellênes.[4]

Neoptolemus.

The glories of Ajax, the second grandson of Æakus, before Troy, are surpassed only by those of Achillês, He perishes by his own hand, the victim of an insupportable feeling of humiliation, because a less worthy claimant is allowed to carry off from him the arms of

Ajax—his son Philæus the eponymous hero of a dême in Attica.

---

deium. Thetis is said to have been carried by Pêleus to both these places: probably it grew up round a temple and sanctuary of this goddess (Pherekyd. Frag. 16, Didot; Hellanik. ap. Steph. Byz. Θετίδειον).

[1] See the arguments of the lost poems, the Cypria and the Æthiopis, as given by Proclus, in Düntzer, Fragm. Epic. Gr. p. 11—16; also Schol.

ad Iliad. xvi. 140; and the extract from the lost Ψυχοστασία of Æschylus, ap. Plat. de Republic. ii. c. 21 (p. 382, St.).

[2] Eurip. Androm. 1242—1260: Pindar. Olymp. ii. 86.

[3] Herodot. vii. 198.

[4] Plutarch, Pyrrh. 1; Justin. xi. 3; Eurip. Androm. 1253; Arrian, Exp. Alexand. i. 11.

the departed Achillês. His son Philæus receives the citizen-ship of Athens, and the gens or dême called Philaidæ traced up to him its name and its origin : moreover the distinguished Athenians, Miltiadês and Thucydidês, were regarded as members of this heroic progeny.[1]

Teukrus escaped from the perils of the siege of Troy as well as from those of the voyage homeward, and reached Sala-   Teukrus mis in safety. But his father Telamôn, indignant at   banished, settles in his having returned without Ajax, refused to receive   Cyprus. him, and compelled him to expatriate. He conducted his fol-lowers to Cyprus where he founded the city of Salamis : his descendant Evagoras was recognised as a Teukrid and as an Æakid even in the time of Isokrates.[2]

Such was the splendid heroic genealogy of the Æakids,—a family renowned for military excellence. The Æakeion at Ægina, in which prayer and sacrifice were offered to Æakus, remained in undiminished dignity down to the time of Pausa-   Diffusion of nias.[3] This genealogy connects together various emi-   the Æakid nent gentes Achaia Phthiôtis, in Ægina, in Salamis, in   genealogy. Cyprus, and among the Epirotic Molossians. Whether we are entitled to infer from it that the island of Ægina was originally peopled by Myrmidones from Achaia Phthiôtis, as O. Müller imagines,[4] I will not pretend to affirm. These mythical pedigrees seem to unite together special clans or gentes, rather than the

---

[1] Pherekydês and Hellanikus ap. Marcellin. Vit. Thucydid. init. ; Pau-san. ii. 29, 4 ; Plutarch, Solôn, 10. Ac-cording to Apollodôrus, however, Pherekydês said that Telamôn was only the friend of Pêleus, not his brother,—not the son of Æakus (iii. 12, 7): this seems an inconsistency. There was, however, a warm dispute between the Athenians and the Me-garians respecting the title to the hero Ajax, who was claimed by both (see Pausan. i. 42, 4 ; Plutarch, *l. c.*): the Megarians accused Peisistratus of hav-ing interpolated a line into the Cata-logue in the Iliad (Strabo, ix. p. 394).

[2] Herodot. vii. 90 ; Isokrat. Enc. Evag. *ut sup.;* Sophokl. Ajax, 984—395 ; Vellei. Patercul. i. 1 ; Æschyl. Pers. 891, and Schol. The return from Troy of Teukrus, his banishment by Telamôn, and his settlement in Cyprus, formed the subject of the Τεῦκρος of Sophoklês, and of a tragedy under a

similar title by Pacuvius (Cicero de Orat. i. 58 ; ii. 46): Sophokl. Ajax, 892 ; Pacuvii Fragm. Teucr. 15.—

"Te repudio, nec recipio, natum abdico, Facesse."

The legend of Teukrus was connected in Attic archæology with the peculiar functions and formalities of the judi-cature, ἐν Φρεαττοῖ (Pausan. i. 28, 12 ; ii. 29, 7).

[3] Hesiod. Fragm. Düntz. Eoiai, 55, p. 43.—

'Αλκὴν μὲν γὰρ ἔδωκεν 'Ολύμπιος Αἰακίδαισι, Νοῦν δ' 'Αμυθαονίδαις, πλοῦτον δ' ἔπορ' 'Ατρείδῃσι.

Polyb. v. 2.—

Αἰακίδας, πολέμῳ κεχαρηότας ἠΰτε δαιτί.

[4] See his Æginetica, p. 14, his earliest work.

bulk of any community—just as we know that the Athenians generally had no part in the Æakid genealogy, though certain particular Athenian families laid claim to it. The intimate friendship between Achillês and the Opuntian hero Patroklus— and the community of name and frequent conjunction between the Lokrian Ajax, son of Oïleus, and Ajax, son of Telamôn—connect the Æakids with Opus and the Opuntian Lokrians, in a manner which we have no farther means of explaining. Pindar too represents Menœtius, father of Patroklus, as son of Aktôr and Ægina, and therefore maternal brother of Æakus.[1]

[1] Pindar. Olymp. ix. 74. The hero Ajax, son of Oïleus, was especially worshipped at Opus; solemn festivals and games were celebrated in his honour.

CHAPTER XI.

ATTIC LEGENDS AND GENEALOGIES.

THE most ancient name in Attic archæology, as far as our means of information reach, is that of Erechtheus, who is mentioned both in the Catalogue of the Iliad and in a brief allusion of the Odyssey.   Born of the Earth, he is brought up by the goddess Athênê, adopted by her as her ward, and installed in her temple at Athens, where the Athenians offer to him annual sacrifices.   The Athenians are styled in the Iliad, "the people of Erechtheus".[1]   This is the most ancient testimony concerning Erechtheus, exhibiting him as a divine or heroic, certainly a superhuman person, and identifying him with the primitive germination (if I may use a term, the Grecian equivalent of which would have pleased an Athenian ear) of Attic man. And he was recognised in this same character, even at the close of the fourth century before the Christian æra, by the Butadæ, one of the most ancient and important Gentes at Athens, who boasted of him as their original ancestor: the genealogy of the great Athenian orator Lykurgus, a member of this family, drawn up by his son Abrôn, and painted on a public tablet in the Erechtheion, contained as its first and highest name, Erechtheus, son of Hêphæstos and the Earth.   In the Erechtheion, Erechtheus was worshipped conjointly with Athênê: he was identified with the god Poseidôn, and bore the denomination of Poseidôn Erechtheus: one of the family of the Butadæ, chosen among

Erechtheus —auto-chthonous.

---

[1] Iliad, ii. 546. Odyss. vii. 81.—

Οἱ δ᾽ ἄρ᾽ Ἀθήνας εἶχον. . . .
Δῆμον Ἐρεχθῆος μεγαλήτορος, ὅν ποτ᾽
Ἀθήνη
Θρέψε, Διὸς θυγάτηρ, τέκε δὲ ζείδωρος
Ἄρουρα,

Κὰδ δ᾽ ἐν Ἀθήνῃσ᾽ εἶσεν ἑῷ ἐνὶ πίονι νηῷ,
Ἐνθάδε μιν ταύροισι καὶ ἀρνειοῖς ἱλάονται
Κοῦροι Ἀθηναίων, περιτελλομένων ἐνιαυτῶν.

themselves by lot, enjoyed the privilege and performed the functions of hereditary priest.[1] Herodotus also assigns the same earth-born origin to Erechtheus:[2] but Pindar, the old poem called the Danais, Euripidês, and Apollodôrus—all named Erichthonius, son of Hêphæstos and the Earth, as the being who was thus adopted and made the temple-companion of Athênê while Apollodôrus in another place identifies Erichthonius with Poseidôn.[3] The Homeric scholiast treated Erechtheus and Erichthonius as the same person under two names:[4] and since, in regard to such mythical persons, there exists no other test of identity of the subject except perfect similarity of the attributes, this seems the reasonable conclusion.

We may presume, from the testimony of Homer, that the first and oldest conception of Athens and its sacred acropolis places it under the special protection, and represents it as the settlement and favourite abode of Athênê, jointly with Poseidôn; the latter being the inferior, though the chosen companion of the former, and therefore exchanging his divine appellation for the cognomen of Erechtheus. But the country called Attica, which during the historical ages, forms one social and political aggregate with Athens, was originally distributed into many independent dêmes or cantons, and included, besides, various religious clans or hereditary sects (if the expression may be permitted) ; that is, a multitude of persons not necessarily living together in the same locality, but bound together by an hereditary communion of sacred rites, and claiming privileges as well as performing obligations, founded upon the traditional authority of divine persons for whom they

Attic legends—originally from different roots—each dême had its own.

---

[1] See the Life of Lykurgus, in Plutarch's (I call it by that name, as it is always printed with his works) Lives of the Ten Orators, tom. iv. p. 382—384, Wytt. Κατῆγον δὲ τὸ γένος ἀπὸ τούτων καὶ 'Ερεχθέως τοῦ Γῆς καὶ 'Ηφαίστου . . . καὶ ἐστὶν αὐτὴ ἡ καταγωγὴ τοῦ γένους τῶν ἱερασαμένων τοῦ Ποσειδῶνος, &c. Ὃς τὴν ἱερωσύνην Ποσειδῶνος 'Ερεχθέως εἶχε (pp. 882, 383). Erechtheus Πάρεδρος of Athênê—Aristidês, Panathenaic. p. 184, with the Scholia of Frommel.

Butês, the eponymus of the Butadæ, is the first priest of Poseidôn Erichthonius: Apollod. iii. 15, 1. So Kallias (Xenoph. Sympos. viii. 40), ἱερεὺς

θεῶν τῶν ἀπ' 'Ερεχθέως.
[2] Herodot. viii. 55.
[3] Harpokration, v. Αὐτοχθών. Ὁ δὲ Πίνδαρος καὶ ὁ τὴν Δαναΐδα πεποιηκώς φασιν, 'Εριχθόνιον ἐξ 'Ηφαίστου καὶ Γῆς φανῆναι. Εuripidês, Ion, 21. Apollod. iii. 14, 6; 15, 1. Compare Plato, Timæus, c. 6.
[4] Schol. ad Iliad. ii. 546, where he cites also Kallimachus for the story of Erichthonius. Etymologicon Magn. 'Ερεχθεύς. Plato (Kritias, c. 4) employs vague and general language to describe the agency of Hêphæstos and Athênê, which the old fable in Apollodôrus (iii. 14, 6) details in coarser terms. See Ovid Metam. ii. 757.

had a common veneration. Even down to the beginning of the Peloponnêsian war, the demots of the various Attic dêmes, though long since embodied in the larger political union of Attica, and having no wish for separation, still retained the recollection of their original political autonomy. They lived in their own separate localities, resorted habitually to their own temples, and visited Athens only occasionally for private or political business, or for the great public festivals. Each of these aggregates, political as well as religious, had its own eponymous god or hero, with a genealogy more or less extended, and a train of mythical incidents more or less copious, attached to his name, according to the fancy of the local exegetes and poets. The eponymous heroes Marathôn, Dekelus, Kolônus, or Phlyus, had each their own title to worship, and their own position as themes of legendary narrative, independent of Erechtheus, or Poseidôn, or Athênê, the patrons of the acropolis common to all of them.

But neither the archæology of Attica, nor that of its various component fractions, was much dwelt upon by the ancient epic poets of Greece. Thêseus is noticed both in the Iliad and Odyssey as having carried off from Krête Ariadnê, the daughter of Minos—thus commencing that connexion between the Krêtan and Athenian legends which we afterwards find so largely amplified—and the sons of Thêseus take part in the Trojan war.[1] The chief collectors and narrators of the Attic mythes were, the prose logographers, authors of the many compositions called Atthides, or works on Attic archæology. These writers—Hellanikus, the contemporary of Herodotus, is the earliest composer of an Atthis expressly named, though Pherekydês also touched upon the Attic fables—these writers, I say, interwove into one chronological series the legends which either greatly occupied their own fancy, or commanded the most general reverence among their countrymen. In this way the religious and political legends of Eleusis, a town originally independent of Athens, but incorporated with it before the historical age, were worked into one continuous sequence along with those of the Erechtheids. In this way too, Kekrops, the eponymous hero of the portion of Attica called Kekropia, came to be placed in the

Little noticed by the old epic poets.

---

[1] Æthra, mother of Thêseus, is also mentioned (Homer, Iliad, iii. 144).

mythical chronology at a higher point even than the primitive
god or hero Erechtheus.

Ogygês is said to have reigned in Attica[1] 1020 years before the
first Olympiad, or 1796 years B.C.   In his time happened the deluge of Deukaliôn, which destroyed most
of the inhabitants of the country.   After a long interval, Kekrops, an indigenous person, half mán and half serpent, is given
to us by Apollodôrus as the first king of the country ; he bestowed upon the land, which had before been called Aktê, the
name of Kekropia.   In his day there ensued a dispute between
Athênê and Poseidôn respecting the possession of the acropolis at
Athens, which each of them coveted.   First, Poseidôn struck the
rock with his trident, and produced the well of salt water which
existed in it, called the Erechthêis : next came Athênê, who
planted the sacred olive-tree ever afterwards seen and venerated
in the portion of the Erechtheion called the cell of Pandrosus.
The twelve gods decided the dispute ; and Kekrops having testi-
fied before them that Athênê had rendered this inestimable
service, they adjudged the spot to her in preference to Poseidôn.
Both the ancient olive-tree and the well produced by Poseidôn
were seen on the acropolis, in the temple consecrated jointly to
Athênê and Erechtheus, throughout the historical ages.   Poseidôn,
as a mark of his wrath for the preference given to Athênê, inun-
dated the Thriasian plain with water.[2]

During the reign of Kekrops, Attica was laid waste by Karian
pirates on the coast, and by invasions of the Aônian inhabitants
from Bœôtia.   Kekrops distributed the inhabitants of Attica into
twelve local sections—Kekropia, Tetrapolis, Epakria, Dekeleia,
Eleusis, Aphidna, Thorikus, Braurôn, Kythêrus, Sphêttus, Kê-
phisius, Phalêrus.   Wishing to ascertain the number of inhabitants, he commanded each man to cast a single stone into a general
heap : the number of stones was counted, and it was found that
there were twenty thousand.[3]

Kekrops.

[1] Hellanikus, Fragm. 62 ; Philochor.
Fragm. 8, ap. Euseb. Præp. Evang. x.
10, p. 489.   Larcher (Chronologie
d'Hérodote, ch. ix. s. 1, p. 278) treats
both the historical personality and the
date of Ogygès as perfectly well authenticated.
[2] Apollod. iii. 14, 1 ; Herodot. viii.
55 ; Ovid, Metam. vi. 72.   The impression of Poseidôn's trident is still shown
on the rocky floor of the Erechtheum
at Athens.   The story current among
the Athenians represented Kekrops as
the judge of this controversy (Xenoph.
Memor. iii. 5, 10).
[3] Philochor. ap. Strab. ix. p. 397.

CHAP. XI. KEKROPS—PROKNÊ AND PHILOMÊLA. 181

Kekrops married the daughter of Aktæus, who (according to Pausanias's version) had been king of the country before him, and had called it by the name of Aktæa.[1] By her he had three daughters, Aglaurus, Ersê, and Pandrosus, and a son, Erysichthôn.

Erysichthôn died without issue, and Kranaus succeeded him,—another indigenous person and another eponymus,—for the name Kranai was an old denomination of the inhabitants of Attica.[2] Kranaus was dethroned by Amphiktyôn, by some called an indigenous man ; by others, a son of Deuka- lion : Amphiktyôn in his turn was expelled by Erichthonius, son of Hêphæstos and the Earth,—the same person apparently as Erechtheus, but inserted by Apollodôrus at this point of the series. Erichthonius, the pupil and favoured companion of Athênê, placed in the acropolis the original Palladium or wooden statue of that goddess, said to have dropped from heaven : he was moreover the first to celebrate the festival of the Panathenæa. He married the nymph Pasithea, and had for his son and successor Pandiôn.[3] Erichthonius was the first person who taught the art of breaking in horses to the yoke, and who drove a chariot and four.[4]

Kranaus— Pandiôn.

In the time of Pandiôn, who succeeded to Erichthonius, Dionysus and Dêmêtêr both came into Attica ; the latter was received by Keleos at Eleusis.[5] Pandiôn married the nymph Zeuxippê, and had twin sons, Erechtheus and Butês, and two daughters, Proknê and Philomêla. The two latter are the subjects of a memorable and well-known legend. Pandiôn having received aid in repelling the Thêbans from Têreus, king of Thrace, gave him his daughter Proknê in marriage, by whom he had a son, Itys. The beautiful Philomêla, going to visit her sister, inspired the barbarous Thracian with an irresistible passion ; he violated her person, confined her in a distant pastoral hut, and pretended that she was dead, cutting out her tongue to prevent her from revealing the

Daughters of Pandiôn —Proknê, Philomêla. Legend of Têreus.

[1] The Parian chronological marble designates Aktæus as an indigenous person. Marmor Parium, Epoch. 3. Pausan. i. 2, 5.
[2] Herod. viii. 44. Κρανααὶ Ἀθῆναι, Pindar.
[3] Apollod. iii. 14, 6. Pausan. i 6, 27

[4] Virgil, Georgic. iii. 114.
[5] The mythe of the visit of Dêmêtêr to Eleusis, on which occasion she vouchsafed to teach her holy rites to the leading Eleusinians, is more fully touched upon in my first chapter.

truth. After a long interval, Philomêla found means to inform her sister of the cruel deed which had been perpetrated ; she wove into a garment words describing her melancholy condition, and despatched it by a trusty messenger. Proknê, overwhelmed with sorrow and anger, took advantage of the free egress enjoyed by women during the Bacchanalian festival to go and release her sister : the two sisters then revenged themselves upon Têreus by killing the boy Itys, and serving him up for his father to eat ; after the meal had been finished, the horrid truth was revealed to him. Têreus snatched a hatchet to put Proknê to death : she fled, along with Philomêla, and all the three were changed into birds—Proknê became a swallow, Philomêla a nightingale, and Têreus an hoopoe.[1] This tale, so popular with the poets, and so illustrative of the general character of Grecian legend, is not less remarkable in another point of view—that the great historian Thucydidês seems to allude to it as an historical fact,[2] not however directly mentioning the final metamorphosis.

After the death of Pandiôn, Erechtheus succeeded to the kingdom, and his brother, Butês, became priest of Poseidôn Erichthonius ; a function which his descendants ever afterwards exercised, the Butadæ or Eteobutadæ. Erechtheus seems to appear in three characters in the fabulous history of Athens—as a god, Poseidôn Erechtheus [3]—as a hero, Erechtheus, son of the Earth—and now, as a king, son of Pandiôn : so much did the ideas of divine and human rule become confounded and blended together

[1] Apollod. iii. 14, 8; Æsch. Supplic. 51; Soph. Elektr. 107 ; Ovid, Metamorph. vi. 425—670. Hyginus gives the fable with some additional circumstances, fab. 45. Antoninus Liberalis (Nar. 11), or Bœus, from whom he copies, has composed a new narrative by combining together the names of Pandareos Aêdôn, as given in the Odyssey, xix. 523, and the adventures of the old Attic fable. The hoopoe still continued the habit of chasing the nightingale : it was to the Athenians a present fact. See Schol. Aristoph. Aves, 212.

[2] Thucyd. ii. 29. He makes express mention of the nightingale in connexion with the story, though not of the metamorphosis. See below, chap. xvi. So also does Pausanias mention and reason upon it as a real incident: he founds upon it several moral reflections (i. 5, 4 ; x. 4, 5): the author of the

Λόγος Ἐπιτάφιος, ascribed to Demosthenês, treats it in the same manner, as a fact ennobling the tribe Pandionis, of which Pandiôn was the eponymus. The same author, in touching upon Kekrops, the eponymus of the Kekropis tribe, cannot believe literally the story of his being half man and half serpent: he rationalises it, by saying that Kekrops was so called because in wisdom he was like a man, in strength like a serpent (Demosth. p. 1397, 1398, Reiske). Hesiod glances at the fable (Opp. Di. 566). ὀρθρογόη Πανδιονὶς ὦρτο χελιδών : see also Ælian, V. H. xii. 20. The subject was handled by Sophoklês in his lost Têreus.

[3] Poseidôn is sometimes spoken of under the name of Erechtheus simply (Lycophrôn, 158). See Hesychius, v. Ἐρεχθεύς.

in the imagination of the Greeks in reviewing their early times.

The daughters of Erechtheus were not less celebrated in Athenian legend than those of Pandiôn. Prokris, one of them, is among the heroines seen by Odysseus in Hadês : she became the wife of Kephalus, son of Deionês, and lived in the Attic dême of Thorikus.

Daughters of Erechtheus— Prokris.

Kreüsa, another daughter of Erechtheus, seduced by Apollo, becomes the mother of Iôn, whom she exposes immediately after his birth, in the cave north of the acropolis, concealing the fact from every one. Apollo

Kreüsa.— Oreithyia, the wife of Boreas.

prevails upon Hermês to convey the new-born child to Delphi, where he is brought up as a servant of the temple, without knowing his parents. Kreüsa marries Xuthus, son of Æolus, but continuing childless, she goes with Xuthus to the Delphian oracle to inquire for a remedy. The god presents to them Iôn, and desires them to adopt him as their son : their son Achæus is afterwards born to them, and Iôn and Achæus become the eponyms of the Iônians and Achæans.[1]

Oreithyia, the third daughter of Erechtheus, was stolen away by the god Boreas while amusing herself on the banks of the Ilissus, and carried to his residence in Thrace. The two sons of this marriage, Zêtês and Kalais, were born with wings : they took part in the Argonautic expedition, and engaged in the pursuit of the harpies: they were slain at Tênos by Hêraklês. Kleopatra, the daughter of Boreas and Oreithyia, was married to Phineus, and had two sons, Plexippus and Pandiôn ; but Phineus afterwards espoused a second wife, Idæa, the daughter of Dardanus, who, detesting the two sons of the former bed, accused them falsely of attempting her chastity, and persuaded Phineus in his wrath to put out the eyes of both. For this cruel proceeding he was punished by the Argonauts in the course of their voyage.[2]

---

[1] Upon this story of Iôn is founded the tragedy of Euripidês which bears that name. I conceive many of the points of that tragedy to be of the invention of Euripidês himself: but to represent Iôn as a son of Apollo, not of Xuthus, seems a genuine Attic legend. Respecting this drama, see O. Müller, Hist. of Dorians, ii, 2, 13—15. I doubt however the distinction which he draws between the Ionians and the other population of Attica.

[2] Apollodôr. iii. 15, 2 ; Plato, Phædr. c. 3 ; Sophok. Antig. 984 ; also the copious Scholion on Apollôn. Rhod. i. 212.

The tale of Phineus is told very differently in the Argonautic expedition as given by Apollônius Rhodius,

On more than one occasion the Athenians derived, or at least

Prayers of the Athenians to Boreas—his gracious help in their danger.
believed themselves to have derived, important benefits from this marriage of Boreas with the daughter of their primæval hero : one inestimable service, rendered at a juncture highly critical for Grecian independence, deserves to be specified.[1] At the time of the invasion of Greece by Xerxês, the Grecian fleet was assembled at Chalkis and Artemision in Eubœa, awaiting the approach of the Persian force, so overwhelming in its numbers as well by sea as on land. The Persian fleet had reached the coast of Magnêsia and the south-eastern corner of Thessaly without any material damage, when the Athenians were instructed by an oracle " to invoke the aid of their son-in-law ". Understanding the advice to point to Boreas, they supplicated his aid and that of Oreithyia most earnestly, as well by prayer as by sacrifice,[2] and the event corresponded to their wishes. A furious north-easterly wind immediately arose, and continued for three days to afflict the Persian fleet as it lay on an unprotected coast : the number of ships driven ashore, both vessels of war and of provision, was immense, and the injury done to the armament was never thoroughly repaired. Such was the powerful succour which the Athenians derived, at a time of their utmost need, from their son-in-law Boreas ; and their gratitude was shown by consecrating to him a new temple on the banks of the Ilissus.

The three remaining daughters of Erechtheus—he had six in all[3]—were in Athenian legend yet more venerated

Erechtheus and Eumolpus.
than their sisters, on account of having voluntarily devoted themselves to death for the safety of their

---

ii. 180. From Sophoklês we learn that this was the Attic version.

The two winged sons of Boreas and their chase of the Harpies were noticed in the Hesiodic Catalogue (see Schol. Apollôn. Rhod. ii. 296). But whether the Attic legend of Oreithyia was recognised in the Hesiodic poems seems not certain.

Both Æschylus and Sophoklês composed dramas on the subject of Oreithyia (Longin. de Sublimit. c. 3). "Orithyia Atheniensis, filia Terrigenæ, et a Borea in Thraciam rapta" (Servius ad Virg. Æneid. xii. 83). Terrigena is the γηγενὴς Ἐρεχθεύς. Philochorus (Fragm. 30) rationalised

the story, and said that it alluded to the effects of a violent wind.

[1] Herodot. vii. 189. Οἱ δὲ ὧν Ἀθηναῖοί σφι λέγουσι βοηθήσαντα τὸν Βορῆν πρότερον, καὶ τότε ἐκεῖνα κατεργάσασθαι· καὶ ἱρὸν ἀπελθόντες Βορέω ἱδρύσαντο παρὰ ποταμὸν Ἰλισσον.

[2] Herodot. l. c. Ἀθηναῖοι τὸν Βορῆν ἐκ θεοπροπίου ἐπεκαλέσαντο, ἐλθόντος σφι ἄλλου χρηστηρίου, τὸν γαμβρὸν ἐπίκουρον καλέσασθαι. Βορῆς δὲ κατὰ τὸν Ἑλλήνων λόγον ἔχει γυναῖκα Ἀττικήν, Ὠρειθυίην τὴν Ἐρεχθῆος. Κατὰ δὴ τὸ κῆδος τοῦτο, οἱ Ἀθηναῖοι, συμβαλλεόμενοί σφι τὸν Βορῆν γαμβρὸν εἶναι, &c.

[3] Suidas and Photius, v. Παρθένοι: Protogeneia and Pandôra are given as

couutry. Eumolpus of Eleusis was the son of Poseidôn and the eponymous hero of the sacred gens called the Eumolpids, in whom the principal functiona, appertaining to the mysterious rites of Dêmêtêr at Eleusis, were vested by hereditary privilege. He made war upon Erechtheus and the Athenians, with the aid of a body of Thracian allies ; indeed it appears that the legends of Athens, originally foreign and unfriendly to those of Eleusis, represented him as having been himself a Thracian born and an immigrant into Attica.[1] Respecting Eumolpus, however, and his parentage, the discrepancies much exceed even the measure of license usual in the legendary genealogies, and some critics, both ancient and modern, have sought to reconcile these contradictions, by the usual stratagem of supposing two or three different persons of the same name. Even Pausanias, so familiar with this class of unsworn witnesses, complains of the want of native Eleusinian genealogists,[2] and of the extreme license of fiction in which other authors had indulged.

In the Homeric Hymn to Dêmêtêr, the most ancient testimony before us,—composed, to all appearance, earlier than the complete incorporation of Eleusis with Athens,—Eumolpus appears (to repeat briefly what has been stated in a previous chapter) as one of the native chiefs or princes of Eleusis, along with Tripto-

the names of two of them. The sacrifice of Pandôra, in the Iambi of Hippônax (Hippônact. Fragm. xxi. Welck. ap. Athen. ix. p. 370), seems to allude to this daughter of Erechtheus.

[1] Apollodôr. iii. 15, 3 ; Thucyd. ii. 15: Isokratês (Panegyr. t. i. p. 206; Panathenaic. t. ii. p. 560, Auger), Lykurgus, cont. Leocrat. p. 201, Reiske: Pausan. i. 88, 3: Euripid. Erecth. Fr. The Schol. ad Soph. (Ed. Col. 1048, gives valuable citations from Ister, Akestodôrus and Androtiôn: we see that the inquirers of antiquity found it difficult to explain how the Eumolpids could have acquired their ascendant privileges in the management of the Eleusinia, seeing that Eumolpus himself was a foreigner,— Ζητεῖται, τί δήποτε οἱ Εὐμολπίδαι τῶν τελετῶν ἐξάρχουσι, ξένοι ὄντες. Thucydidês does not call Eumolpus a Thracian: Strabo's language is very large and vague (vii. p. 321): Isokratês says that he assailed Athens in order to vindicate the rights of his father Poseidôn

to the sovereign patronage of the city. Hyginus copies this (fab. 46).
[2] Pausan. i. 38, 3. Ἐλευσίνιοί τε ἀρχαῖοι, ἅτε οὐ προσόντων σφίσι γενεαλόγων, ἄλλα τε πλάσασθαι δεδώκασι καὶ μάλιστα ἐς τὰ γένη τῶν ἡρώων. See Heyne ad Apollodôr. iii. 15, 4. "Eumolpi nomen modo communicatum pluribus, modo plurium hominum res et facta cumulata in unum. Is ad quem Hercules venisse dicitur, senior ætate fuit: antiquior est is de quo hoc loco agitur .... antecessisse tamen hunc debet alius, qui cum Triptolemo vixit," &c. See the learned and valuable comments of Lobeck in his Aglaophamus, tom. i. p. 206—213: in regard to the discrepancies of this narrative he observes, I think, with great justice (p. 211), "quo uno exemplo ex innumerabilibus delecto, arguitur eorum temeritas, qui ex variis discordibusque poetarum et mythographorum narratiunculis, antiquæ famæ formam et quasi lineamenta recognosci posse sperant".

lemus, Dioklês, Polyxeinus, and Dolichus ; Keleos is the king, or principal among these chiefs, the son or lineal descendant of the eponymous Eleusis himself.   To these chiefs, and to the three daughters of Keleos, the goddess Dêmêtêr comes in her sorrow for the loss of her daughter Persephonê : being hospitably entertained by Keleos she reveals her true character, commands that a temple shall be built to her at Eleusis, and prescribes to them the rites according to which they are to worship her.[1]   Such seems to have been the ancient story of the Eleusinians respecting their own religious antiquities : Keleos, with Metaneira his wife, and the other chiefs here mentioned, were worshipped at Eleusis, and from thence transferred to Athens as local gods or heroes.[2]   Eleusis became incorporated with Athens, apparently not very long before the time of Solôn ; and the Eleusinian worship of Dêmêtêr was then received into the great religious solemnities of the Athenian state, to which it owes its remarkable subsequent extension and commanding influence.   In the Atticised worship of the Eleusinian Dêmêtêr, the Eumolpids and the Kêrŷkes were the principal hereditary functionaries : Eumolpus, the eponym of this great family, came thus to play the principal part in the Athenian legendary version of the war between Athens and Eleusis.   An oracle had pronounced that Athens

Voluntary self-sacrifice of the three daughters of Erechtheus.

could only be rescued from his attack by the death of the three daughters of Erechtheus ; their generous patriotism consented to the sacrifice, and their father put them to death.   He then went forth confidently to the battle, totally vanquished the enemy, and killed Eumolpus with his own hand.[3]   Erechtheus was worshipped as

---

[1] Homer, Hymn. ad Cerer. 473—475.—

. . . 'Η δὲ κιοῦσα θεμιστοπόλοις βασιλεῦσιν

Δεῖξε, Τριπτολέμῳ τε, Διόκλεί τε πληξίππῳ,

Εὐμόλπου τε βίη, Κελεῷ θ' ἡγήτορι λαῶν,

Δρησμοσύνην ἱερῶν.

Also v. 105.—

Τὴν δὲ ἴδον Κελεοῖο 'Ελευσινίδαο θύγατρες.

The hero Eleusis is mentioned in Pausanias, i. 38, 7; some said that he was the son of Hermês, others that he

was the son of Ogygês.   Compare Hygin. f. 147.

[2] Keleos and Metaneira were worshipped by the Athenians with divine honours (Athenagoras, Legat. p. 53, ed. Oxon.): perhaps he confounds divine and heroic honours, as the Christian controversialists against Paganism were disposed to do.   Triptolemus had a temple at Eleusis (Paus. i. 38, 6).

[3] Apollodôr. iii. 15. 4.   Some said that Immaradus, son of Eumolpus, had been killed by Erechtheus (Pausan. i. 5, 2); others, that both Eumolpus and his son had experienced this fate (Schol. ad Eurip. Phœniss. 854).   But we learn from Pausanias himself

a god, and his daughters as goddesses, at Athens.[1] Their names
and their exalted devotion were cited along with those of the
warriors of Marathôn, in the public assembly of Athens, by
orators who sought to arouse the languid patriot, or to denounce
the cowardly deserter ; and the people listened both to one and
the other with analogous feelings of grateful veneration, as well
as with equally unsuspecting faith in the matter of fact.[2]

Though Erechtheus gained the victory over Eumolpus, yet the
story represents Poseidôn as having put an end to the life and
reign of Erechtheus, who was (it seems) slain in the battle. He
was succeeded by his son Kekrops II., and the latter again by his
son Pandiôn II.,[3]—two names unmarked by any incidents, and
which appear to be mere duplication of the former Kekrops and
Pandiôn, placed there by the genealogisers for the purpose of
filling up what seemed to them a chronological chasm.

Apollodôrus passes at once from Erechtheus to his son Kekrops
II., then to Pandiôn II., next to the four sons of the latter,
Ægeus, Pallas, Nisus, and Lykus. But the tragedians here insert

what the story in the interior of the
Erechtheion was,—that Erechtheus
killed Eumolpus (i. 27, 3).

[1] Cicero, Nat. Deor. iii. 19 ; Philochor. ap. Schol. Œdip. Col. 100. Three
daughters of Erechtheus perished, and
three daughters were worshipped
(Apollodôr. iii. 15, 4 ; Hesychius, Ζεῦγος
τριπάρθενον, Eurip. Erechtheus, Fragm.
3, Dindorf) ; but both Euripidês and
Apollodôrus said that Erechtheus
was only required to sacrifice, and only
did sacrifice, one,—the other two slew
themselves voluntarily, from affection
for their sister. I cannot but think (in
spite of the opinion of Welcker to the
contrary, Griechisch. Tragöd. ii. p.
722) that the genuine legend represented Erechtheus as having sacrificed
all three, as appears in the Iôn of
Euripidês (276) :—

IÔN.　Πατὴρ ’Ερεχθεὺς σὰς ἔθυσε
　　　συγγόνους ;
CREUSA.　’Ετλη πρὸ γαίας σφάγια
　　　παρθένους κτανεῖν.
IÔN.　Σὺ δ’ ἐξεσώθης πῶς κασιγνήτων
　　　μόνη ;
CREUSA.　Βρέφος νέογνον μητρὸς ἦν
　　　ἐν ἀγκάλαις.

Compare with this passage, Demosthen. Λόγος ’Επιτάφ. p. 1397 Reiske.
Just before, the death of the three

daughters of Kekrops, for infringing
the commands of Athênê, had been
mentioned. Euripidês modified this
in his Erechtheus, for he there introduced the mother Praxithea consenting
to the immolation of one daughter, for
the rescue of the country from a foreign
invader : to propose to a mother the
immolation of three daughters at once,
would have been too revolting. In
most instances we find the strongly
marked features, the distinct and
glaring incidents as well as the dark
contrasts, belonging to the Hesiodic
or old post-Homeric legend ; the
changes made afterwards go to soften,
dilute, and to complicate, in proportion as the feelings of the public become milder and more humane ;
sometimes however the later poets
add new horrors.

[2] See the striking evidence contained
in the oration of Lykurgus against
Leocratês (p. 201—204 Reiske ; Demosthen. Λόγ. ’Επιτάφ. l. c. ; and Xenophôn.
Memor. iii. 5, 9) : from the two latter
passages we see that the Athenian
story represented the invasion under
Eumolpus as a combined assault from
the western continent.

[3] Apollodôr. iii. 15, 5 ; Eurip. Iôn,
282 ; Erechth. Fragm. 20, Dindorf.

the story of Xuthus, Kreüsa, and Iôn ; the latter being the son of
Kreüsa and Kreüsa by Apollo, but given by the god to Xuthus,
Iôn. and adopted by the latter as his own. Iôn becomes
the successor of Erechtheus, and his sons (Teleon, Hoplês, Arga-
dês, and Aigikorês) become the eponyms of the four ancient tribes
of Athens, which subsisted until the revolution of Kleisthenês.
Iôn himself is the eponym of the Iônic race both in Asia, in
Europe, and in the Ægean Islands : Dôrus and Achæus are the
sons of Kreüsa by Xuthus, so that Iôn is distinguished from both
of them by being of divine parentage.[1] According to the story given
by Philochorus, Iôn rendered such essential service in rescuing
the Athenians from the attack of the Thracians under Eumolpus,
that he was afterwards made king of the country, and distributed
all the inhabitants into four tribes or castes, corresponding to
different modes of life,—soldiers, husbandmen, goatherds, and
artisans.[2] And it seems that the legend explanatory of the
origin of the festival Boedromia, originally important enough to
furnish a name to one of the Athenian months, was attached to
the aid thus rendered by Iôn.[3]

We pass from Iôn to persons of far greater mythical dignity
and interest,—Ægeus and his son Thêseus.

Pandiôn had four sons, Ægeus, Nisus, Lykus, and Pallas, between whom he divided his dominions. Nisus received
Sons of Pandiôn— the territory of Megaris, which had been under the
Ægeus, &c. sway of Pandiôn, and there founded the seaport of
Nisæa. Lykus was made king of the eastern coast, but a dispute
afterwards ensued, and he quitted the country altogether, to
establish himself on the southern coast of Asia Minor, among the
Termilæ, to whom he gave the name of Lykians.[4] Ægeus, as the
eldest of the four, became king of Athens ; but Pallas received a
portion both of the south-western coast and the interior, and he
as well as his children appear as frequent enemies both to Ægeus
and to Thêseus. Pallas is the eponym of the dême Pallênê,
and the stories respecting him and his sons seem to be connected

[1] Eurip. Iôn, 1570—1595. The
Kreüsa of Sophoklês, a lost tragedy,
seems to have related to the same
subject.
    Pausanias (vii. 1, 2) tell us that
Xuthus was chosen to arbitrate between the contending claims of the
sons of Erechtheus.

[2] Philochor. ap. Harpocrat. v. Βοη-
δρόμια ; Strabo, viii. p. 383.
    [3] Philochor. ap. Harpocrat. v. Βοη-
δρόμια.
    [4] Sophokl. ap. Strab. ix. p. 392;
Herodot. i. 173 ; Strabo, xii. p. 573.

with old and standing feuds among the different dêmes of Attica, originally independent communities. These feuds penetrated into the legend. They explain the story which we find that Ægeus and Thêseus were not genuine Erechtheids, the former being denominated a suppositious child to Pandiôn.[1]

Ægeus[2] has little importance in the mythical history except as the father of Thêseus : it may even be doubted whether his name is anything more than a mere cognomen of the god Poseidôn, who was (as we are told) the real father of this great Attic Hêraklês. As I pretend only to give a very brief outline of the general territory of Grecian legend, I cannot permit myself to recount in detail the chivalrous career of Thêseus, who is found both in the Kalydônian boar-hunt and in the Argonautic expedition—his personal and victorious encounters with the robbers Sinnis, Prokrustês, Periphêtês, Skiron, and others—his valuable service in ridding his country of the Krommyonian sow and the Marathônian bull—his conquest of the Minotaur in Krête, and his escape from the dangers of the labyrinth by the aid of Ariadnê, whom he subsequently carries off and abandons—his many amorous adventures, and his expeditions both against the Amazons and into the under-world along with Peirithous.[3]

Thucydidês delineates the character of Thêseus as a man who combined sagacity with political power, and who conferred upon

----

[1] Plutarch, Thêseus, c. 13. Αἰγεὺς θετὸς γενόμενος Πανδίονι, καὶ μηδὲν τοῖς Ἐρεχθείδαις προσήκων. Apollodôr. iii. 15. 6.

[2] Ægeus had by Mêdea (who took refuge at Athens after her flight from Corinth) a son named Mêdus, who passed into Asia, and was considered as the eponymus and progenitor of the Median people. Datis, the general who commanded the invading Persian army at the battle of Marathôn, sent a formal communication to the Athenians announcing himself as the descendant of Mêdus, and requiring to be admitted as king of Attica: such is the statement of Diodôrus (Exc. Vatic. vii.-x. 48: see also Schol. Aristophan. Pac. 289).

[3] Ovid. Metamorph. vii. 433.—

. . . . . "Te, maxime Theseu,
Mirata est Marathon Cretæi san-
guine Tauri:

Quodque Suis securus arat Cromyona
colonus,
Munus opusque tuum est. Tellus
Epidauria per te
Clavigeram vidit Vulcani occumbere
prolem:
Vidit et immanem Cephisias ora
Procrustem.
Cercyonis letum vidit cerealis Eleu-
sin.
Occidit ille Sinis," &c.

Respecting the amours of Thêseus, Ister especially seems to have entered into great details; but some of them were noticed both in the Hesiodic poems and by Kekrops, not to mention Pherekydês (Athen. xiii. p. 557). Peirithous, the intimate friend and companion of Thêseus, is the eponymous hero of the Attic dême or gens Perithoídæ (Ephorus ap. Photium v. Περιθοῖδαι).

his country the inestimable benefit of uniting all the separate
and self-governing dêmes of Attica into one common political
society.[1] From the well-earned reverence attached to the assertion of Thucydidês, it has been customary to reason upon this
assertion as historically authentic, and to treat the romantic attributes which we find in Plutarch and Diodôrus as if they were
fiction superinduced upon this basis of fact. Such a view of the
case is in my judgment erroneous. The athletic and amorous
knight-errant is the old version of the character—the profound
and long-sighted politician is a subsequent correction, introduced
indeed by men of superior mind, but destitute of historical warranty, and arising out of their desire to find reasons of their own
for concurring in the veneration which the general
public paid more easily and heartily to their national
hero. Thêseus, in the Iliad and Odyssey, fights with
the Lapithæ against the Centaurs : Thêseus, in the Hesiodic
poems, is misguided by his passion for the beautiful Æglê,
daughter of Panopeus :[2] and the Thêseus described in Plutarch's
biography is in great part a continuation and expansion of these
same or similar attributes, mingled with many local legends, explaining, like the Fasti of Ovid, or the lost Aitia of Kallimachus,
the original genesis of prevalent religious and social customs.[3]
Plutarch has doubtless greatly softened down and modified the
adventures which he found in the Attic logographers, as well as
in the poetical epics called Thêsêis. For in his preface to the
life of Thêseus, after having emphatically declared that he is
about to transcend the boundary both of the known and the
knowable, but that the temptation of comparing the founder of
Athens with the founder of Rome is irresistible, he concludes
with the following remarkable words : " I pray that this fabulous
matter may be so far obedient to my endeavours as to receive,
when purified by reason, the aspect of history : in those cases
where it haughtily scorns plausibility and will admit no alliance
with what is probable, I shall beg for indulgent hearers, willing

His legend-ary charac-ter refined.

[1] Thucyd. ii. 15. Ἐπειδὴ δὲ Θησεὺς
ἐβασίλευσε, γενόμενος μετὰ τοῦ ξυνετοῦ
καὶ δυνατὸς, τά τε ἄλλα διεκόσμησε τὴν
χώραν, καὶ καταλύσας τῶν ἄλλων πόλεων
τά τε βουλευτήρια καὶ τὰς ἀρχὰς, ἐς
τὴν νῦν πόλιν οὖσαν . . . ξυνῴκισε
πάντας.

[2] Iliad, i. 265; Odyss. xi. 321. I do
not notice the suspected line, Odyss.
xi. 630.
[3] Diodôrus also, from his disposition
to assimilate Thêseus to Hêraklês, has
given us his chivalrous as well as his
political attributes (iv. 61).

to receive antique narrative in a mild spirit ".[1] We here see that Plutarch sat down, not to recount the old fables as he found them, but to purify them by reason and to impart to them the aspect of history. We have to thank him for having retained, after this purification, so much of what is romantic and marvellous ; but we may be sure that the sources from which he borrowed were more romantic and marvellous still. It was the tendency of the enlightened men of Athens, from the days of Solôn downwards, to refine and politicise the character of Thêseus :[2] even Peisistratus expunged from one of the Hesiodic poems the line which described the violent passion of the hero for the fair Ægle :[3] and the tragic poets found it more congenial to the feelings of their audience to exhibit him as a dignified and liberal sovereign, rather than as an adventurous single-handed fighter. But the logographers and the Alexandrine poets remained more faithful to the old fables. The story of Hekalê, the hospitable old woman who received and blessed Thêseus when he went against the Marathônian bull, and whom he found dead when he came back to recount the news of his success, was treated by Kallimachus :[4] and Virgil must have had his mind full of the unrefined legends, when he numbered this Attic Hêraklês among the unhappy sufferers condemned to endless penance in the under-world.[5]

Plutarch—his way of handling the matter of legend.

Two, however, among the Thêseian fables cannot be dismissed without some special notice,—the war against the Amazons, and the expedition against Krête. The former strikingly illustrates the facility as well as the tenacity of Grecian legendary faith ; the

---

[1] Plutarch, Thêseus, i. Εἴη μὲν οὖν ἡμῖν, ἐκκαθαιρόμενον λόγῳ τὸ μυθῶδες ὑπακοῦσαι καὶ λαβεῖν ἱστορίας ὄψιν· ὅπου δ' ἂν αὐθαδῶς τοῦ πιθανοῦ περιφρονῇ, καὶ μὴ δέχηται τ ὴ ν πρὸς τὸ εἰκὸς μίξιν, εὐγνωμόνων ἀκροατῶν δεησόμεθα, καὶ πρᾴως τὴν ἀρχαιολογίαν προσδεχομένων.
[2] See Isokratês, Panathenaic. (t. ii. p. 510—512, Auger); Xenoph. Memor. iii. 5, 10. In the Helenæ Encomium, Isokratês enlarges more upon the personal exploits of Thêseus in conjunction with his great political merits (t. ii. p. 842—350, Auger).
[3] Plutarch, Thêseus, 20.
[4] See the epigram of Krinagoras, Antholog. Pal. vol. ii. p. 144 ; ep. xv. ed. Brunck. and Kallimach· Frag. 40.

'Αείδει δ' (Kallimachus) 'Εκάλης τε φιλοξείνοιο καλιὴν, Καὶ Θησεῖ Μαραθὼν οὓς ἐπέθηκε πόνους.

Some beautiful lines are preserved by Suidas, v. 'Επαύλια, περὶ 'Εκάλης θανούσης (probably spoken by Thêseus himself, see Plutarch, Thêseus, c. 14).

'Ίθι, πρηεῖα γυναικῶν, Τὴν ὁδὸν, ἣν ἀνίαι θυμαλγέες οὐ περόωσιν· Πολλάκι σεῖ', ὦ μαῖα, φιλοξείνοιο καλιῆς Μνησόμεθα· ξυνὸν γὰρ ἐπαύλιον ἔσκεν ἅπασιν.

[5] Virgil, Æneid, vi. 617. "Sedet æternumque sedebit Infelix Thêseus."

latter embraces the story of Dædalus and Minos, two of the most eminent among Grecian ante-historical personages.

The Amazons, daughters of Arês and Harmonia,[1] are both early creations, and frequent reproductions, of the ancient epic—which was indeed, we may generally remark, largely occupied both with the exploits and sufferings of women, or heroines, the wives and daughters of the Grecian heroes—and which recognised . in Pallas Athênê the finished type of an irresistible female warrior. A nation of courageous, hardy and indefatigable women, dwelling apart from men, permitting only a short temporary intercourse for the purpose of renovating their numbers, and burning out their right breast with a view of enabling themselves to draw the bow freely,— this was at once a general type stimulating to the fancy of the poets, and a theme eminently popular with his hearers. Nor was it at all repugnant to the faith of the latter, who had no recorded facts to guide them, and no other standard of credibility as to the past except such poetical narratives themselves—to conceive communities of Amazons as having actually existed in anterior time. Accordingly, we find these warlike females constantly reappearing in the ancient poems, and universally accepted as past realities. In the Iliad, when Priam wishes to illustrate emphatically the most numerous host in which he ever found himself included, he tells us that it was assembled in Phrygia, on the banks of the Sangarius, for the purpose of resisting the formidable Amazons. When Bellerophôn is to be employed on a deadly and perilous undertaking,[2] by those who indirectly wish to procure his death, he is despatched against the Amazons. In the Æthiopis of Arktinus, describing the post-Homeric war of Troy, Penthesileia, queen of the Amazons, appears as the most effective ally of the besieged city, and as the most formidable enemy of the Greeks, succumbing only to the invincible might of Achilles.[3] The Argonautic heroes find

Legend of the Amazons.

Its antiquity and prevalence.

---

[1] Pherekyd. Fragm. 25, Didot.

[2] Iliad, iii. 186 : vi. 152.

[3] See Proclus's Argument of the lost Æthiopis (Fragm. Epicor. Græcor. ed. Düntzer, p. 16). We are reduced to the first book of Quintus Smyrnæus for some idea of the valour of Penthesileia : it is supposed to be copied more or less closely from the Æthiopis. See Tychsen's Dissertation prefixed to his edition of Quintus, sections 5 and 12. Compare Dio Chrysostom. Or. xi. p. 350, Reisk. Philostratus (Heroica, c. 19. p. 751) gives a strange transformation of this old epical narrative into a descent of Amazons upon the island sacred to Achilles.

the Amazons on the river Thermôdôn, in their expedition along the southern coast of the Euxine. To the same spot Hêraklês goes to attack them, in the performance of the ninth labour imposed upon him by Eurystheus, for the purpose of procuring the girdle of the Amazonian queen Hippolytê;[1] and we are told that they had not yet recovered from the losses sustained in this severe aggression when Thêseus also assaulted and defeated them, carrying off their queen Antiopê.[2] This injury they avenged by invading Attica,—an undertaking (as Plutarch justly observes) "neither trifling nor feminine," especially if, according to the statement of Hellanikus, they crossed the Cimmerian Bosphorus on the winter ice, beginning their march from the Asiatic side of the Palus Mæotis.[3] They overcame all the resistances and difficulties of this prodigious march, and penetrated even into Athens itself; where the final battle, hard-fought and at one time doubtful, by which Thêseus crushed them, was fought—in the very heart of the city. Attic antiquaries confidently pointed out the exact position of the two contending armies: the left wing of the Amazons rested upon the spot occupied by the commemorative monument called the Amazoneion; the right wing touched the Pnyx, the place in which the public assemblies of the Athenian democracy were afterwards held.

(margin note) Glorious achievements of the Amazons.

[1] Apollôn. Rhod. ii. 966, 1004; Apollod. ii. 5—9; Diodôr. ii. 46; iv. 16. The Amazons were supposed to speak the Thracian language (Schol. Apoll. Rhod. ii. 953), though some authors asserted them to be natives of Libya, others of Æthiopia (*ib.* 965). Hellanikus (Fragm. 33, ap. Schol. Pindar. Nem. iii. 65) said that all the Argonauts had assisted Hêraklês in this expedition: the fragment of the old epic poem (perhaps the Ἀμαζόνια) there quoted mentions Telamôn specially.

[2] The many diversities in the story respecting Thêseus and the Amazon Antiopê are well set forth in Bachet de Meziriac (Commentaires sur Ovide, t. i. p. 317). Welcker (Der Epische Cyclus, p. 313) supposes that the ancient epic poem, called by Suidas Ἀμαζόνια, related to the invasion of Attica by the Amazons, and that this poem is the same, under another title, as the Ἀτθίς of Hegesinous cited by Pausanias: I cannot say that he establishes this

conjecture satisfactorily, but the chapter is well worth consulting. The epic Thêsêis seems to have given a version of the Amazonian contest in many respects different from that which Plutarch has put together out of the logographers (see Plut. Thês. 28): it contained a narrative of many unconnected exploits belonging to Thêseus, and Aristotle censures it on that account as ill-constructed (Poetic. c. 17).

The Ἀμαζονίς or Ἀμαζονικά of Onasus can hardly have been (as Heyne supposes, ad Apollod. ii. 5, 9) an epic poem: we may infer from the rationalising tendency of the citation from it (Schol. ad Theocrit. xiii. 46, and Schol. Apollôn. Rhod. i. 1207) that it was a work in prose. There was an Ἀμαζονίς by Possis of Magnêsia (Athenæus, vii. p. 296).

[3] Plutarch, Thêseus, 27. Pindar (Olymp. xiii. 84) represents the Amazons as having come from the extreme north, when Bellerophôn conquers them.

The details and fluctuations of the combat, as well as the final triumph and consequent truce, were recounted by these authors with as complete faith and as much circumstantiality as those of the battle of Platæa by Herodotus. The sepulchral edifice called the Amazoneion, the tomb or pillar of Antiopê near the western gate of the city—the spot called the Horkomosion near the temple of Thêseus—even the hill of Areiopagus itself, and the sacrifices which it was customary to offer to the Amazons at the periodical festival of the Thêseia—were all so many religious mementos of this victory;[1] which was moreover a favourite subject of art both with the sculptor and the painter, at Athens as well as in other parts of Greece.

No portion of the ante-historical epic appears to have been more deeply worked into the national mind of Greece than this invasion and defeat of the Amazons. It was not only a constant theme of the logographers, but was also familiarly appealed to by the popular orators along with Marathôn and Salamis, among those antique exploits of which their fellow-citizens might justly be proud. It formed a part of the retrospective faith of Herodotus, Lysias, Plato and Isokratês,[2] and the exact date of the event was settled by the chronologists.[3] Nor did the Athenians stand alone

<hr>

[1] Plutarch, Thesêus, 27—28; Pausan. i. 2, 4; Plato, Axiochus, c. 2; Harpocratiôn, v. Ἀμαζονεῖον; Aristophan. Lysistrat. 678, with the Scholia. Æschyl. (Eumenid. 685) says that the Amazons assaulted the citadel from the Areiopagus:—

Πάγον δ' Ἄρειον τόνδ', Ἀμαζόνων
  ἕδραν
Σκηνάς θ', ὅτ' ἦλθον Θησέως κατὰ
  φθόνον
Στρατηλατοῦσαι, καὶ πόλιν νεόπτολιν
Τήνδ' ὑψίπυργον ἀντεπύργωσαν πότε.

[2] Herodot. ix. 27. Lysias (Epitaph. c. 3) represents the Amazons as ἄρχουσαι πολλῶν ἐθνῶν: the whole race, according to him, was nearly extinguished in their unsuccessful and calamitous invasion of Attica. Isokratês (Panegyric. t. i. p. 206, Auger) says the same: also Panathênaic. t. iii. p. 560, Anger; Demosth. Epitaph. p. 1391, Reisk. Pausanias quotes Pindar's notice of the invasion, and with the fullest belief of its historical reality (vii. 2, 4). Plato mentions the invasion of Attica by the Amazons in the Menexenus (c. 9), but

the passage in the treatise De Legg. c. ii. p. 804,—ἀκούων γὰρ δὴ μύθους παλαιοὺς πέπεισμαι, &c.—is even a stronger evidence of his own belief. And Xenophôn, in the Anabasis, when he compares the quiver and the hatchet of his barbarous enemies to "those which the Amazons carry," evidently believed himself to be speaking of real persons, though he could have seen only the costumes and armature of those painted by Mikôn and others (Anabas. iv. 4, 10; compare Æschyl. Supplic. 293, and Aristophan. Lysistr. 678; Lucian, Anachars. c. 34, v. iii. p. 318).

How copiously the tale was enlarged upon by the authors of the Atthides, we see in Plutarch, Thêseus, 27-28.

Hekatæus (ap. Steph. Byz. Ἀμαζονεῖον; also Fragm. 350, 351, 352, Didot) and Xanthus (ap. Hesychium, v. Βουλεψίη) both treated of the Amazons: the latter passage ought to be added to the collection of the Fragments of Xanthus by Didot.

[3] Clemens Alexandr. Stromat. i. p. 336; Marmor Parium, Epoch. 21.

in such a belief. Throughout many other regions of Greece, both European and Asiatic, traditions and memorials of the Amazons were found. At Megara, at Trœzen, in Laconia near Cape Tænarus, at Chæroneia in Bœôtia, and in more than one part of Thessaly, sepulchres or monuments of the Amazons were preserved. The warlike women (it was said), on their way to Attica, had not traversed those countries without leaving some evidences of their passage.[1]

Amongst the Asiatic Greeks the supposed traces of the Amazons were yet more numerous. Their proper territory was asserted to be the town and plain of Themiskyra, near the Grecian colony of Amisus, on the river Thermôdôn, a region called after their name by Roman historians and geographers.[2] But they were believed to have conquered and occupied in earlier times a much wider range of territory, extending even to the coast of Iônia and Æolis. Ephesus, Smyrna, Kymê, Myrina, Paphos and Sinôpe were affirmed to have been founded and denominated by them.[3] Some authors placed them in Libya or Ethiopia ; and when the Pontic Greeks on the north-western shore of the Euxine had become acquainted with the hardy and daring character of the Sarmatian maidens,—who were obliged to have slain each an enemy in battle as the condition of obtaining a husband, and who artificially prevented the growth of the right breast during childhood,—they could imagine no more satisfactory mode of accounting for such attributes than by deducing the Sarmatians from a colony of vagrant Amazons, expelled by the Grecian heroes from their territory on the Thermôdôn.[4]

Their ubiquity.

[1] Plutarch, Thês. 27—28. Steph. Byz. v. Ἀμαζονεῖον. Pausan. ii. 32, 8 ; iii. 25, 2.

[2] Pherekydês ap. Schol. Apollon. Rh. ii. 373—992 ; Justin, ii. 4 ; Strabo, xii. p. 547. Θεμίσκυραν, τὸ τῶν Ἀμαζόνων οἰκητήριον : Diodôr. ii. 45—46 ; Sallust ap. Serv. ad Virgil. Æneid. xi. 659 ; Pompon. Mela, i. 19 ; Plin. H. N. vi. 4. The geography of Quintus Curtius (vi. 4) and of Philostratus (Heroic. c. 19) is on this point indefinite, and even inconsistent.

[3] Ephor. Fragm. 87, Didot. Strabo, xi. p. 505 ; xii. p. 573 ; xiii. p. 622. Pausan. iv. 31, 6 ; vii. 2, 4. Tacit. Ann. iii. 61. Schol. Apollon. Rhod. ii. 965.
The derivation of the name Sinopê

from an Amazon was given by Hekatæus (Fragm. 352). Themiskyra also had one of the Amazons for its eponymus (Appian, Bell. Mithridat. 78).
Some of the most venerated religious legends at Sinopê were attached to the expedition of Hêraklês against the Amazons: Autolykus, the oracle-giving hero, worshipped with great solemnity even at the time when the town was besieged by Lucullus, was the companion of Hêraklês (Appian, ib. c. 83). Even a small mountain village in the territory of Ephesus, called Latoreia, derived its name from one of the Amazons (Athenæ. i. p. 31).

[4] Herodot. iv. 108—117, where he gives the long tale imagined by the Pontic Greeks, of the origin of the

Pindar ascribes the first establishment of the memorable temple of Artemis at Ephesus to the Amazons. And Pausanias explains in part the pre-eminence which this temple enjoyed over every other in Greece by the widely diffused renown of its female founders,[1] respecting whom he observes (with perfect truth, if we admit the historical character of the old epic), that women possess an unparalleled force of resolution in resisting adverse events, since the Amazons, after having been first roughly handled by Hêraklês, and then completely defeated by Thêseus, could yet find courage to play so conspicuous a part in the defence of Troy against the Grecian besiegers.[2]

It is thus that in what is called early Grecian history, as the Greeks themselves looked back upon it, the Amazons were among the most prominent and undisputed personages. Nor will the circumstance appear wonderful if we reflect, that the belief in them was first established at a time when the Grecian mind was fed with nothing else but religious legend and epic poetry, and that the incidents of the supposed past, as received from these sources, were addressed to their faith and feelings, without being required to adapt themselves to any canons of credibility drawn from present experience. But the time came when the historians of Alexander the Great audaciously abused this ancient credence. Amongst other tales calculated to exalt the dignity of that monarch, they affirmed that after his conquest and subjugation of the Persian empire, he had been visited in Hyrcania by Thalestris, queen of the Amazons, who, admiring his warlike prowess, was anxious to be enabled to return into her own country in a condition to produce offspring of a breed so invincible.[3] But the Greeks had

Universally received as a portion of the Greek past.

Amazons produced as present by the historians of Alexander.

Sarmatian nation. Compare Hippokratês, De Aëre, Locis et Aquis, c. 17; Ephoris, Fragm. 103; Skymn. Chius, v. 102; Plato, Legg. vii. p. 804; Diodôr. ii. 34.

The testimony of Hippokratês certifies the practice of the Sarmatian women to check the growth of the right breast: Τὸν δέξιον δὲ μαζὸν οὐκ ἔχουσιν. Παιδίοισι γὰρ ἐοῦσιν ἔτι νηπίοισιν αἱ μητέρες χαλκεῖον τετεχνήμενον ἐπ' αὐτέῳ τούτῳ διάπυρον ποιέουσαι, πρὸς τὸν μαζὸν τιθέασι τὸν δέξιον· καὶ ἐπικαίεται, ὥστε τὴν αὔξησιν φθεί

ρεσθαι, ἐς δὲ τὸν δέξιον ὦμον καὶ βραχίονα πᾶσαν τὴν ἰσχὺν καὶ τὸ πλῆθος ἐκδιδόναι.

Ktêsias also compares a warlike Sakian woman to the Amazons (Fragm. Persic. ii. pp. 221, 449, Bähr).

[1] Pausan. iv. 31, 6; vii. 2, 4. Dionys. Periêgêt. 828.

[2] Pausan. i. 15, 2.

[3] Arrian, Exped. Alex. vii. 13; compare iv. 15; Quint. Curt. vi. 4; Justin, xlii. 4. The note of Freinshemius on the above passage of Quintus Curtius is full of valuable references on the subject of the Amazons.

now been accustomed for a century and a half to historical and
philosophical criticism—and that uninquiring faith, which was
readily accorded to the wonders of the past, could no longer be
invoked for them when tendered as present reality. For the
fable of the Amazons was here reproduced in its naked simplicity,
without being rationalised or painted over with historical colours.

Some literary men indeed, among whom were Dêmêtrius of
Skepsis, and the Mitylenæan Theophanês, the companion of
Pompey in his expeditions, still continued their belief both in
Amazons present and Amazons past; and when it became notorious that at least there were none such on the banks of the
Thermôdôn, these authors supposed them to have migrated from
their original locality, and to have settled in the unvisited regions
north of Mount Caucasus.[1] Strabo, on the contrary, feeling that
the grounds of disbelief applied with equal force to the ancient
stories and to the modern, rejected both the one and the other.
But he remarks at the same time, not without some surprise,
that it was usual with most persons to adopt a middle course,—to
retain the Amazons as historical phænomena of the remote past,
but to disallow them as realities of the present, and to maintain
that the breed had died out.[2]　The accomplished intellect of

---

[1] Strabo, xi. p. 503—504; Appian,
Bell. Mithridat. c. 103; Plutarch, Pom-
peius, c. 35; Plin. N. H. vi. 7. Plutarch
still retains the old description of
Amazons from the mountains near the
Thermôdôn : Appian keeps clear of
this geographical error, probably copying more exactly the language of Theophanês, who must have been well
aware that when Lucullus besieged
Themiskyra, he did not find it defended by the Amazons (see Appian,
Bell. Mithridat. c. 78). Ptolemy (v. 9)
places the Amazons in the imperfectly
known regions of Asiatic Sarmatia,
north of the Caspian and near the river
Rha (Volga). "This fabulous community of women (observes Forbiger,
Handbuch der alten Geographie, ii.
77, p. 457) was a phænomenon much
too interesting for the geographers
easily to relinquish."

[2] Strabo. xi. p. 505. Ἴδιον δέ τι συμ-
βέβηκε τῷ λόγῳ περὶ τῶν Ἀμαζόνων. Οἱ
μὲν γὰρ ἄλλοι τὸ μυθῶδες καὶ τὸ ἱστο-
ρικὸν διωρίσμενον ἔχουσι· τὰ γὰρ παλαιὰ
καὶ ψευδῆ καὶ τερατώδη, μῦθοι καλοῦνται·
[Note. Strabo does not always speak

of the μῦθοι in this disrespectful tone;
he is sometimes much displeased with
those who dispute the existence of an
historical kernel in the inside, especially with regard to Homer.] ἡ δ'
ἱστορία βούλεται τἀληθὲς, ἄντε παλαιὸν,
ἄντε νέον· καὶ τὸ τερατῶδες ἢ οὐκ ἔχει,
ἢ σπάνιον. Περὶ δὲ τῶν Ἀμαζόνων τὰ
αὐτὰ λέγεται καὶ νῦν καὶ παλαί, τερατώδη
τ' ὄντα, καὶ πίστεως πόρρω. Τίς γὰρ ἂν
πιστεύσειεν, ὡς γυναικῶν στράτος, ἢ
πόλις, ἢ ἔθνος, συσταίη ἄν ποτε χωρὶς
ἀνδρῶν; καὶ οὐ μόνον συσταίη, ἀλλὰ καὶ
ἐφόδους ποιήσαιτο ἐπὶ τὴν ἀλλοτρίαν, καὶ
κρατήσειεν οὐ τῶν ἐγγὺς μόνον, ὥστε καὶ
μέχρι τῆς νῦν Ἰωνίας προελθεῖν, ἀλλὰ καὶ
διαπόντιον στείλαιτο στρατίαν μέχρι τῆς
Ἀττικῆς; Ἀλλὰ μὴν ταῦτά γε αὐτὰ καὶ
νῦν λέγεται περὶ αὐτῶν· ἐπιτείνει δὲ
τὴν ἰδιότητα καὶ τὸ πιστεύεσθαι
τὰ παλαιὰ μᾶλλον ἢ τὰ νῦν.
There are however other passages in
which he speaks of the Amazons as
realities.

Justin (ii. 4) recognises the great
power and extensive conquests of the
Amazons in very early times, but says
that they gradually declined down to

Julius Cæsar did not scruple to acknowledge them as having once conquered and held in dominion a large portion of Asia.[1] And the compromise between early, traditional, and religious faith on

Conflict of faith and reason in the historical critics.

the one hand, and established habits of critical research on the other, adopted by the historian Arrian, deserves to be transcribed in his own words, as illustrating strikingly the powerful sway of the old legends even over the most positive-minded Greeks:—"Neither Aristobulus nor Ptolemy (he observes), nor any other competent witness, thus recounted this (visit of the Amazons and their queen to Alexander): nor does it seem to me that the race of the Amazons was preserved down to that time, nor have they been noticed either by any one before Alexander, or by Xenophôn, though he mentions both the Phasians and the Kolchians, and the other barbarous nations which the Greeks saw both before and after their arrival at Trapezus, in which marches they must have met with the Amazons, if the latter had been still in existence. Yet *it is incredible to me* that this race of women, celebrated as they have been by authors so many and so commanding, *should never have existed at all.* The story tells of Hêraklês, that he set out from Greece and brought back with him the girdle of their queen Hippolytê; also of Thêseus and the Athenians, that they were the first who defeated in battle and repelled these women in their invasion of Europe; and the combat of the Athenians with the Amazons has been painted by Mikôn, not less than that between the Athenians and the Persians. Moreover Herodotus has spoken in many places of these women, and those Athenian orators who have pronounced panegyrics on the citizens slain in battle, have dwelt upon the victory over the Amazons as among the most memorable of Athenian exploits. If the satrap of Media sent any equestrian women at all to Alexander, I think that they must have come from some of the neighbouring barbarous tribes, prac-

the reign of Alexander, in whose time there were *just a few remaining;* the queen with these few visited Alexander, but shortly afterwards the whole breed became extinct. This hypothesis has the merit of convenience, perhaps of ingenuity.

[1] Suetonius, Jul. Cæsar. c. 22. "In Syriâ quoque regnasse Semiramin (Julius Cæsar said this), magnamque Asiæ partem Amazonas tenuisse quondam."

In the splendid triumph of the emperor Aurelian at Rome after the defeat of Zenobia, a few Gothic women who had been taken in arms were exhibited among the prisoners; the official placard carried along with them announced them as *Amazons* (Vopiscus Aurel. in Histor. August. Scrip. p. 260, ed. Paris).

tised in riding and equipped in the costume generally called Amazonian." [1]

There cannot be a more striking evidence of the indelible force with which these ancient legends were worked into the national faith and feelings of the Greeks, than these remarks of a judicious historian upon the fable of the Amazons. Probably if any plausible mode of rationalising it, and of transforming it into a quasi-political event, had been offered to Arrian, he would have been better pleased to adopt such a middle term, and would have rested comfortably in the supposition that he believed the legend in its true meaning, while his less enquiring countrymen were imposed upon by the exaggerations of poets. But as the story was presented to him plain and unvarnished, either for acceptance or rejection, his feelings as a patriot and a religious man prevented him from applying to the past such tests of credibility as his untrammeled reason acknowledged to be paramount in regard to the present. When we see moreover how much his belief was strengthened, and all tendency to scepticism shut out, by the familiarity of his eye and memory with sculptured or painted Amazons [2]—we may calculate the irresistible force of this sensible demonstration on the convictions of the unlettered public, at once more deeply retentive of passive impressions, and unaccustomed to the countervailing habit of rational investigation into evidence. Had the march of an army of warlike women, from the Thermôdôn or the Tanais into the heart of Attica, been recounted to Arrian as an incident belonging to the time of Alexander the Great, he would have rejected it no less emphatically than Strabo; but cast back as it was into an undefined past, it took rank among the hallowed traditions of divine or heroic antiquity,—gratifying to extol by rhetoric, but repulsive to scrutinise in argument. [3]

---

[1] Arrian, Expedit. Alexand. vii. 13.

[2] Ktêsias described as real animals, existing in wild and distant regions, the heterogeneous and fantastic combinations which he saw sculptured in the East (see this stated and illustrated in Bähr, Preface to the Fragm. of Ktêsias, pp. 58, 59).

[3] Heyne observes (Apollodôr. ii. 5, 9) with respect to the fable of the Amazons, "In his historiarum fidem ant vestigia nemo quæsiverit". Admitting the wisdom of this counsel (and I think it indisputable), why are we required to presume, in the absence of all proof, an historical basis for each of those *other* narratives, such as the Kaledônian boar-hunt, the Argonautic expedition, or the siege of Troy, which go to make up, along with the story of the Amazons, the aggregate matter of Grecian legendary faith? If the tale of the Amazons could gain currency

without any such support, why not other portions of the ancient epic?

An author of easy belief, Dr. F. Nagel, vindicates the historical reality of the Amazons (Geschichte der Amazonen, Stuttgart, 1808). I subjoin here a different explanation of the Amazonian tale, proceeding from another author who rejects the historical basis, and contained in a work of learning and value (*Guhl, Ephesiaca*, Berlin, 1843, p. 132) :—

"Id tantum monendum videtur, Amazonas nequaquam historice accipiendas esse, sed e contrario totas ad mythologiam pertinere. Earum enim fabulas quum ex frequentium hierodularum gregibus in cultibus et sacris Asiaticis ortas esse ingeniose ostenderit Tolken, jam *inter omnes mythologiæ peritos constat*, Amazonibus nihil fere nisi peregrini cujusdam cultûs notionem expressam esse, ejusque cum Græcorum religione certamen frequentibus istis pugnis designatum esse, quas cum Amazonibus tot Græcorum heroes habuisse credebantur, Hercules, Bellerophon, Theseus, Achilles, et vel ipse, quem Ephesi cultum fuisse supra ostendimus, Dionysus. Quæ Amazonum notio primaria, quum paulatim Euemeristicâ (ut ita dicam) ratione ita transformaretur, ut Amazones pro vero feminarum populo haberentur, necesse quoque erat, ut omnibus fere locis, ubi ejusmodi religionum certamina locum habuerunt, Amazones habitasse, vel eo usque processisse, crederentur. Quod cum nusquam manifestius fuerit, quam in Asiâ minore, et potissimum in eâ parte quæ Græciam versus vergit, haud mirandum est omnes fere ejus oræ urbes ab Amazonibus conditas putari."

I do not know the evidence upon which this conjectural interpretation rests, but the statement of it, though it boasts so many supporters among mythological critics, carries no appearance of probability to my mind. Priam fights against the Amazons as well as the Grecian heroes.

CHAPTER XII.

KRÊTAN LEGENDS.—MINÔS AND HIS FAMILY.

To understand the adventures of Thêseus in Krête, it will be necessary to touch briefly upon Minôs and the Krêtan heroic genealogy.

Minôs and Rhadamanthus, according to Homer, are sons of Zeus, by Europê,[1] daughter of the widely-celebrated Phœnix, born in Krête. Minôs is the father of Deukaliôn, whose son Idomeneus, in conjunction with Mêrionês, conducts the Krêtan troops to the host of Agamemnôn before Troy. Minôs is ruler of Knôssus, and familiar companion of the great Zeus. He is spoken of as holding guardianship in Krête—not necessarily meaning the whole of the island : he is farther decorated with a golden sceptre, and constituted judge over the dead in the under-world to settle their disputes, in which function Odysseus finds him—this however by a passage of comparatively late interpolation into the Odyssey. He also had a daughter named Ariadnê, for whom the artist Dædalus fabricated in the town of Knôssus the representation of a complicated dance, and who was ultimately carried off by Thêseus : she died in the island of Dia, deserted by Thêseus and betrayed by Dionysos to the fatal wrath of Artemis. Rhadamanthus seems to approach to Minôs both in judicial functions and posthumous dignity. He is conveyed expressly to Eubœa, by the semi-divine sea-carriers the Phæacians, to inspect the gigantic corpse of the earth-born Tityus—the longest voyage they ever undertook. He

Marginal note: Minôs and Rhadamanthus, sons of Zeus.

---

[1] Europê was worshipped with very peculiar solemnity in the island of Krête (see Dictys Cretensis, De Bello Trojano, i. c. 2).

The venerable plane-tree, under which Zeus and Europê had reposed, was still shown, hard by a fountain at Gortyn in Krête, in the time of Theophrastus : it was said to be the only plane-tree in the neighbourhood which never cast its leaves (Theophrast. Hist. Plant. i. 9).

is moreover after death promoted to an abode of undisturbed bliss in the Elysian plain at the extremity of the earth.[1]

According to poets later than Homer, Europê is brought over by Zeus from Phœnicia to Krête, where she bears to him three sons, Minôs, Rhadamanthus, and Sarpêdôn. The latter leaves Krête and settles in Lykia, the population of which, as well as that of many other portions of Asia Minor, is connected by various mythical genealogies with Krête, though the Sarpêdôn of the Iliad has no connexion with Krête, and is not the son of Europê. Sarpêdôn, having become king of Lykia, was favoured by his father, Zeus, with permission to live for three generations.[2] At the same time the youthful Milêtus, a favourite of Sarpêdôn, quitted Krête, and established the city which bore his name on the coast of Asia Minor. Rhadamanthus became sovereign of and lawgiver among the islands in the Ægean: he subsequently went to Bœôtia, where he married the widowed Alkmênê, mother of Hêraklês.

Europê.

Europê finds in Krête a king Astêrius, who marries her and adopts her children by Zeus; this Astêrius is the son of Krês, the eponym of the island, or (according to another genealogy by which it was attempted to be made out that Minôs was of Dôrian race) he was a son of the daughter of Krês by Tektamus, the son of Dôrus, who had migrated into the island from Greece.

Minôs married Pasiphaê, daughter of the god Hêlios and Perseïs, by whom he had Katreus, Deukaliôn, Glaukus, Androgeos,—names marked in the legendary narrative,—together with several daughters, among whom were Ariadnê and Phædra. He offended Poseidôn by

Pasiphaê and the Minôtaur.

---

[1] Homer, Iliad, xiii. 249, 450; xiv. 321. Odyss. xi. 322—568; xix. 179; iv. 564—vii. 321.

The Homeric Minôs in the underworld is not a judge of the previous lives of the dead, so as to determine whether they deserve reward or punishment for their conduct on earth: such functions are not assigned to him earlier than the time of Plato. He administers justice *among* the dead, who are conceived as a sort of society, requiring some presiding judge : θεμισ-τεύοντα νεκύεσσι, with regard to Minôs, is said very much like (Odyss. xi. 484) νῦν δ' αὖτε μέγα κρατέεις νεκύεσσι with regard to Achilles. See this matter

partially illustrated in Heyne's Excursus xi. to the sixth book of the Æneid of Virgil.

[2] Apollodôr. iii. 1, 2. Καὶ αὐτῷ δίδωσι Ζεὺς ἐπὶ τρεῖς γενεὰς ζῆν. This circumstance is evidently imagined by the logographers to account for the appearance of Sarpêdôn in the Trojan war, fighting against Idomeneus, the grandson of Minôs. Nisus is the eponymus of Nisæa, the port of the town of Megara: his tomb was shown at Athens (Pausan. i. 19, 5). Minôs is the eponym of the island of Minoa (opposite the port of Nisæa), where it was affirmed that the fleet of Minôs was stationed (Pausan. i. 44, 5).

neglecting to fulfil a solemnly-made vow, and the displeased god afflicted his wife Pasiphaê with a monstrous passion for a bull. The great artist Dædalus, son of Eupalamus, a fugitive from Athens, became the confidant of this amour, from which sprang the Minôtaur, a creature half-man and half-bull.[1] This Minô- taur was imprisoned by Minôs in the labyrinth, an inextricable enclosure constructed by Dædalus for that express purpose by order of Minôs.

Minôs acquired great nautical power, and expelled the Karian inhabitants from many of the islands of the Ægean,   Skylla and which he placed under the government of his sons on   Nisus. the footing of tributaries. He undertook several expeditions against various places on the coast—one against Nisus, the son of Pandiôn, king of Megara, who had amongst the hair of his head one peculiar lock of a purple colour : an oracle had pronounced that his life and reign would never be in danger so long as he preserved this precious lock. The city would have remained inexpugnable, if Skylla, the daughter of Nisus, had not con- ceived a violent passion for Minôs. While her father was asleep, she cut off the lock on which his safety hung, so that the Krêtan king soon became victorious. Instead of preforming his promise to carry Skylla away with him to Krête, he cast her from the stern of his vessel into the sea :[2] both Skylla and Nisus were changed into birds.

Androgeos, son of Minôs, having displayed such rare qualities as to vanquish all his competitors at the Panathenaic   Death of festival in Athens, was sent by Ægeus the Athenian   Androgeos, king to contend against the bull of Marathôn,—an   and anger of Minôs enterprise in which he perished, and Minôs made war   against upon Athens to avenge his death. He was for a long   Athens. time unable to take the city : at length he prayed to his father Zeus to aid him in obtaining redress from the Athenians, and Zeus sent upon them pestilence and famine. In vain did they endeavour to avert these calamities by offering up as propitiatory sacrifices the four daughters of Hyakinthus. Their sufferings

---

[1] Apollodôr. iii. 1, 2.

[2] Apollodôr. iii. 15, 8. See the Ciris of Virgil, a juvenile poem on the sub- ject of this fable : also Hyginus, f. 198;

Schol. Eurip. Hippol. 1200. Propertius (iii. 19, 21) gives the features of the story with tolerable fidelity; Ovid takes considerable liberties with it (Metam. viii. 5—150).

still continued and the oracle directed them to submit to any terms which Minôs might exact. He required that they should send to Krête a tribute of seven youths and seven maidens, periodically, to be devoured by the Minôtaur,[1]—offered to him in a labyrinth constructed by Dædalus, including countless different passages, out of which no person could escape.

Every ninth year this offering was to be despatched. The
Athenian
victims for
the Minô-
taur.
more common story was, that the youths and maidens thus destined to destruction were selected by lot—but the logographer Hellanikus said that Minôs came to Athens and chose them himself.[2] The third period for despatching the victims had arrived, and Athens was plunged in the deepest affliction, when Thêseus determined to devote himself as one of them, and either to terminate the sanguinary tribute or to perish. He prayed to Poseidôn for help, while the Delphian god assured him that Aphroditê would sustain and extricate him. On arriving at Knôssus he was fortunate enough
Self-devo-
tion of
Thêseus—
he kills the
Minôtaur.
Ariadnê.
to captivate the affections of Ariadnê, the daughter of Minôs, who supplied him with a sword and a clue of thread. With the former he contrived to kill the Minôtaur, the latter served to guide his footsteps in escaping from the labyrinth. Having accomplished this triumph, he left Krête with his ship and companions unhurt, carrying off Ariadnê, whom however he soon abandoned on the island of Naxos. On his way home to Athens, he stopped at Delos, where he offered a grateful sacrifice to Apollo for his escape, and danced, along with the young men and maidens whom he had rescued from the Minôtaur, a dance called the Geranus, imitated from the twists and convolutions of the Krêtan labyrinth. It had been concerted with his father Ægeus, that if he succeeded in his enterprise against the Minôtaur, he should on his return hoist white sails in his ship in place of the black canvas which she habitually carried when employed on this mournful embassy. But Thêseus forgot to make the change of sails ; so that Ægeus, seeing the ship return with her equipment

---

[1] Apollodôr. iii. 15, 8.

[2] See, on the subject of Thêseus and the Minôtaur, Eckermann, Lehrbuch der Religions-Geschichte und Mytho-logie, vol. ii. ch. xiii. p. 133. He main- tains that the tribute of these human victims paid by Athens to Minôs is an historical fact. Upon what this belief is grounded, I confess I do not see.

of mourning unaltered, was impressed with the sorrowful conviction that his son had perished, and cast himself into the sea.
The ship which made this voyage was preserved by the Athenians
with careful solicitude, being constantly repaired with new
timbers, down to the time of the Phalcrian Dêmêtrius : every
year she was sent from Athens to Delos with a solemn sacrifice
and specially-nominated envoys.   The priest of Apollo decked
her stern with garlands before she quitted the port, Athenian
and during the time which elapsed until her return, commemo-
the city was understood to abstain from all acts monies.
carrying with them public impurity, so that it was unlawful
to put to death any person even under formal sentence by
the dikastery.   This accidental circumstance becomes especially
memorable, from its having postponed for thirty days the death
of the lamented Sokratês.[1]

The legend respecting Thêseus, and his heroic rescue of the
seven noble youths and maidens from the jaws of the Minôtaur,
was thus both commemorated and certified to the Athenian
public, by the annual holy ceremony and by the unquestioned
identity of the vessel employed in it.   There were indeed many
varieties in the mode of narrating the incident ; and some of the
Attic logographers tried to rationalise the fable by transforming
the Minôtaur into a general or a powerful athlete, named Taurus,
whom Thêseus vanquished in Krête.[2]   But this altered version

[1] Plato, Phædon, c. 2, 3 ; Xenoph.
Memor. iv. 8, 2.   Plato especially
noticed τοὺς δὶς ἑπτὰ ἐκείνους, the
seven youths and seven maidens
whom Thêseus convoyed to Krête and
brought back safely : this number
seems an old and constant feature in
the legend, maintained by Sappho and
Bacchylidês, as well as by Euripidês
(Herc. Fur. 1318). See Servius ad Virg.
Æneid. vi. 21.
[2] For the general narrative and its
discrepancies, see Plutarch, Thês. c.
15—19 ; Diodôr. iv. 60—62 ; Pausan. i.
17, 3 ; Ovid, Epist. Ariadn. Thês. 104.
In that other portion of the work of
Diodôrus which relates more especially
to Krête, and is borrowed from Krêtan
logographers and historians (v. 64—80),
he mentions nothing at all respecting
the war of Minôs with Athens.
In the drama of Euripidês called
Thêscus, the genuine story of the
youths and maidens about to be

offered as food to the Minôtaur was
introduced (Schol. ad Aristoph. Vesp.
812).
Ariadnê figures in the Odyssey
along with Thêseus : she is the
daughter of Minôs, carried off by
Thêseus from Krête, and killed by
Artemis in the way home : there is no
allusion to Minôtaur, or tribute, or
self-devotion of Thêseus (Odyss. xi.
324).   This is probably the oldest and
simplest form of the legend—one of
the many amorous (compare Theognis,
1232) adventures of Thêseus : the rest
is added by post-Homeric poets.
The respect of Aristotle for Minôs
induces him to adopt the hypothesis
that the Athenian youths and maidens
were not put to death in Krête, but
grew old in servitude.   (Aristot.
Fragm. Βοττιαίων Πολιτεία, p. 106, ed.
Neumann, of the Fragments of the
treatise Περὶ Πολιτειῶν, Plutarch,
Quæst. Græc. p. 298.)

never overbore the old fanciful character of the tale as maintained
by the poets. A great number of other religious ceremonies and
customs, as well as several chapels or sacred enclosures in honour
of different heroes, were connected with different acts and special
ordinances of Thêseus. To every Athenian who took part in the
festivals of the Oschophoria, the Pyanepsia, or the Kybernesia,
the name of this great hero was familiar ; while the motives for
offering to him solemn worship at his own special festival of the
Thêseia, became evident and impressive.

The same Athenian legends which ennobled and decorated the
character of Thêseus, painted in repulsive colours the attributes
of Minôs ; and the traits of the old Homeric comrade of Zeus
were buried under those of the conqueror and oppressor of Athens.
His history, like that of the other legendary personages of Greece,

Family of consists almost entirely of a string of family romances
Minôs. and tragedies. His son Katreus, father of Aëropê,
wife of Atreus, was apprised by an oracle that he would perish
by the hand of one of his own children : he accordingly sent
them out of the island, and Althæmenês, his son, established
himself in Rhodes. Katreus, having become old, and fancying
that he had outlived the warning of the oracle, went over to
Rhodes to see Althæmenês. In an accidental dispute which arose
between his attendants and the islanders, Althæmenês inadver-
tently took part and slew his father without knowing him.
Glaukus, the youngest son of Minôs, pursuing a mouse, fell into
a reservoir of honey and was drowned. No one knew what had
become of him, and his father was inconsolable ; at length the
Argeian Polyeidus, a prophet wonderfully endowed by the gods,
both discovered the boy and restored him to life, to the exceeding
joy of Minôs.[1]

The latter at last found his death in an eager attempt to over-
Minôs and take and punish Dædalus. This great artist, the
Dædalus— eponymous hero of the Attic gens or dême called the
flight of Dædalidæ, and the descendant of Erechtheus through
the latter
to Sicily. Mêtion, had been tried at the tribunal of Areiopagus
and banished for killing his nephew Talos, whose rapidly improving skill excited his envy.[2] He took refuge in Krête, where

[1] Apollodôr. iii. cap. 2—3.   [2] Pherekyd. Fr. 105 ; Hellanik. Fr.
82 (Didot) ; Pausan. vii. 4, 5.

he acquired the confidence of Minôs, and was employed (as has been already mentioned) in constructing the labyrinth; subsequently however he fell under the displeasure of Minôs, and was confined as a close prisoner in the inextricable windings of his own edifice. His unrivalled skill and resource however did not forsake him. He manufactured wings both for himself and for his son Ikarus, with which they flew over the sea. The father arrived safely in Sicily at Kamikus, the residence of the Sikanian king Kokalus; but the son, disdaining paternal example and admonition, flew so high that his wings were melted by the sun and he fell into the sea, which from him was called the Ikarian sea.[1]

Dædalus remained for some time in Sicily, leaving in various parts of the island many prodigious evidences of mechanical and architectural skill.[2] At length Minôs, bent upon regaining possession of his person, undertook an expedition against Kokalus with a numerous fleet and army. Kokalus, affecting readiness to deliver up the fugitive, and receiving Minôs with apparent friendship, ordered a bath to be prepared for him by his three daughters, who, eager to protect Dædalus at any price, drowned the Krêtan king in the bath with hot water.[3] Many of the Krêtans who had accompanied him remained in Sicily and founded the town of Minoa, which they denominated after him. But not long afterwards Zeus instigated all the inhabitants of Krête (except the towns of Polichna and Præsus) to undertake with one accord an expedition against Kamikus for the purpose of avenging the death of Minôs. They besieged Kamikus in vain for five years, until at last famine compelled them to return. On their way along the coast of Italy, in the Gulf of Tarentum, a terrible storm destroyed their fleet and obliged them to settle permanently in the country : they founded

Marginal notes: Minôs goes to retake him, but is killed. — Semi-Krêtan settlements elsewhere—connected with this voyage of Minôs.

---

[1] Diodôr. iv. 79 ; Ovid, Metamorph. viii. 181. Both Ephorus and Philistus mentioned the coming of Dædalus to Kokalus in Sicily (Ephor. Fr. 99 ; Philist. Fr. 1, Didot); probably Antiochus noticed it also (Diodôr. xii. 71). Kokalus was the point of commencement for the Sicilian historians.

[2] Diodôr. iv. 80.

[3] Pausan. vii. 4, 5 ; Schol. Pindar.

Nem. iv. 95; Hygin. fab. 44 ; Conon, Narr. 25 ; Ovid, Ibis, 291.—
" Vel tua maturet, sicut Minoia fata,
Per caput infusæ fervidus humor
  aquæ."
This story formed the subject of a lost drama of Sophoklês Καμίκιοι or Μίνως; it was also told by Kallimachus, ἐν Αἰτίοις, as well as by Philostepbanus (Schol. Iliad. ii. 145).

Hyria with other cities, and became Messapian Iapỹgians. Other settlers, for the most part Greeks, immigrated into Krête to the spots which this movement had left vacant. In the second generation after Minôs, occurred the Trojan war. The departed Minôs was exceedingly offended with the Krêtans for co-operating in avenging the injury to Menelaus, since the Greeks generally had lent no aid to the Krêtans in their expedition against the town of Kamikus. He sent upon Krête, after the return of Idomeneus from Troy, such terrible visitations of famine and pestilence, that the population again died out or expatriated, and

Sufferings of the Krêtans afterwards from the wrath of Minôs.

was again renovated by fresh immigrations. The intolerable suffering[1] thus brought upon the Krêtans by the anger of Minôs, for having co-operated in the general Grecian aid to Menelaus, was urged by them to the Greeks as the reason why they could take no part in resisting the invasion of Xerxes ; and it is even pretended that they were advised and encouraged to adopt this ground of excuse by the Delphian oracle.[2]

Such is the Minôs of the poets and logographers, with his

Portrait of Minôs— how varied.

legendary and romantic attributes : the familiar comrade of the great Zeus,—the judge among the dead in Hadês,—the husband of Pasiphaê, daughter of the god Hêlios,—the father of the goddess Ariadnê, as well as of Androgeos, who perishes and is worshipped at Athens,[3] and of the boy Glaukus, who is miraculously restored to life by a prophet,—the person beloved by Skylla, and the amorous pursuer of the nymph or goddess Britomartis,[4]—the proprietor of the labyrinth and of

---

[1] This curious and very characteristic narrative is given by Herodot. vii. 169 —171.

[2] Herodot. vii. 169. The answer ascribed to the Delphian oracle, on the question being put by the Krêtan envoys whether it would be better for them to aid the Greeks against Xerxês or not, is highly emphatic and poetical:
Ὦ νήπιοι, ἐπιμέμφεσθε ὅσα ὑμῖν ἐκ τῶν Μενελέῳ τιμωρημάτων Μίνως ἔπεμψε μηνίων δακρύματα, ὅτι οἱ μὲν οὐ ξυνεξεπρήξαντο αὐτῷ τὸν ἐν Καμίκῳ θάνατον γενόμενον, ὑμεῖς δὲ κείνοισι τὴν ἐκ Σπάρτης ἁρπαχθεῖσαν ὑπ' ἀνδρὸς βαρβάρου γυναῖκα.
If such an answer was ever returned at all, I cannot but think that it must

have been from some oracle in Krête itself, not from Delphi. The Delphian oracle could never have so far forgotten its obligations to the general cause of Greece, at that critical moment, which involved moreover the safety of all its own treasures, as to deter the Krêtans from giving assistance.

[3] Hesiod. Theogon. 949 ; Pausan. i. 1, 4.

[4] Kallimach. Hymn. ad Dian. 189. Strabo (x. p. 476) dwells also upon the strange contradiction of the legends concerning Minôs : I agree with Hoeck (Kreta, ii. p. 93) that δασμόλογος in this passage refers to the tribute exacted from Athens for the Minôtaur.

the Minôtaur, and the exactor of a periodical tribute of youths
and maidens from Athens as food for this monster,—lastly, the
follower of the fugitive artist Dædalus to Kamikus, and the victim
of the three ill-disposed daughters of Kokalus, in a bath.   With
this strongly-marked portrait, the Minôs of Thucydidês and
Aristotle has scarcely anything in common except the name.
He is the first to acquire *Thalassokraty*, or command of the Ægean
sea: he expels the Karian inhabitants from the Cyclades islands,
and sends thither fresh colonists under his own sons; he puts
down piracy, in order that he may receive his tribute regularly;
lastly, he attempts to conquer Sicily, but fails in the enterprise
and perishes.[1]   Here we have conjectures, derived from the
analogy of the Athenian maritime empire in the historical times,
substituted in place of the fabulous incidents, and attached to the
name of Minôs.

In the fable a tribute of seven youths and seven maidens is
paid to him periodically by the Athenians; in the historicised
narrative this character of a tribute collector is preserved, but
the tribute is money collected from dependent islands:[2] and
Aristotle points out to us how conveniently Krête is situated to
exercise empire over the Ægean.   The expedition against Kamikus, instead of being directed to the recovery of the fugitive
Dædalus, is an attempt on the part of the great thalassokrat to
conquer Sicily.   Herodotus gives us generally the same view of
the character of Minôs as a great maritime king, but his notice of
the expedition against Kamikus includes the mention of Dædalus

---

[1] Thucyd. i. 4. Μίνως γὰρ, παλαί-
τατος ὧν ἀκοῇ ἴσμεν, ναυτικὸν ἐκτήσατο,
καὶ τῆς νῦν Ἑλληνικῆς θαλάσσης ἐπὶ
πλεῖστον ἐκράτησε, καὶ τῶν Κυκλάδων
νήσων ἦρξέ τε καὶ οἰκιστὴς πρῶτος τῶν
πλείστων ἐγένετο, Κᾶρας ἐξελάσας καὶ
τοὺς ἑαυτοῦ παῖδας ἡγεμόνας ἐγκαταστή-
σας· τό τε λῃστικὸν, ὡς εἰκὸς, καθῄρει ἐκ
τῆς θαλάσσης, ἐφ' ὅσον ἠδύνατο, τοῦ τὰς
προσόδους μᾶλλον ἰέναι αὐτῷ. See also
c. 8.

Aristot. Polit. ii. 7, 2.   Δοκεῖ δ' ἡ
νῆσος καὶ πρὸς τὴν ἀρχὴν τὴν Ἑλληνικὴν
πεφυκέναι καὶ κεῖσθαι καλῶς . . . διὸ
καὶ τὴν τῆς θαλάσσης ἀρχὴν κατέσχεν ὁ
Μίνως, καὶ τὰς νήσους τὰς· μὲν ἐχειρώ-
σατο, τὰς δὲ ᾤκισε· τέλος δ' ἐπιθέμενος
τῇ Σικελίᾳ τὸν βίον ἐτελεύτησεν ἐκεῖ περὶ
Κάμικον.

Ephorus (ap. Skymn. Chi. 542)
repeated the same statement: he
mentioned also the indigenous king
Krês.

[2] It is curious that Herodotus expressly denies this, and in language
which shows that he had made special
inquiries about it: he says that the
Karians or Leleges in the islands (who
were, according to Thucydidês, expelled by Minôs) paid no tribute to
Minôs, but manned his navy, *i.e.*, they
stood to Minôs much in the same relation as Chios and Lesbos stood to
Athens (Herodot. i. 171).   One may
trace here the influence of those discussions which must have been prevalent at that time respecting the
maritime empire of Athens.

as the intended object of it.[1] Ephorus, while he described Minôs
as a commanding and comprehensive lawgiver imposing his commands under the sanction of Zeus, represented him as the imitator
of an earlier lawgiver named Rhadamanthus, and also as an
immigrant into Krête from the Æolic Mount Ida, along with
the priests or sacred companions of Zeus called the Idæi Dactyli.
Aristotle too points him out as the author of the Syssitia, or
public meals common in Krête as well as at Sparta,—other
divergences in a new direction from the spirit of the old
fables.[2]

The contradictory attributes ascribed to Minôs, together with
the perplexities experienced by those who wished to introduce a
regular chronological arrangement into these legendary events,
have led both in ancient and in modern times to the supposition
of two kings named Minôs, one the grandson of the other,—Minôs
I., the son of Zeus, lawgiver and judge,—Minôs II., the thalassokrat,—a gratuitous conjecture, which, without solving the
problem required, only adds one to the numerous artifices employed for imparting the semblance of history to the disparate
matter of legend. The Krêtans were at all times, from Homer
downward, expert and practised seamen. But that they were ever
united under one government, or ever exercised maritime dominion
in the Ægean, is a fact which we are neither able to affirm nor to
deny. The Odyssey, in so far as it justifies any inference at all,
points against such a supposition, since it recognises a great
diversity both of inhabitants and of languages in the island, and
designates Minôs as king specially of Knôssus: it refutes still
more positively the idea that Minôs put down piracy, which the
Homeric Krêtans as well as others continue to practise without
scruple.

Herodotus, though he in some places speaks of Minôs as a
person historically cognisable, yet in one passage severs him
pointedly from the generation of man. The Samian despot

<hr>

[1] Herodot. vii. 170. Λέγεται γὰρ
Μίνω κατὰ ζήτησιν Δαιδάλου ἀπικόμενον
ἐς Σικανίην, τὴν νῦν Σικελίην καλουμένην,
ἀποθανεῖν βιαίῳ θανάτῳ. Ἀνὰ δὲ χρόνον
Κρῆτας, θεοῦ σφὶ ἐποτρύνοντος, &c.
[2] Aristot. Polit. ii. 7, 1; vii. 9, 2.
Ephorus, Fragm. 63, 64, 65. He set
aside altogether the Homeric genealogy
of Minôs, which makes him brother of

Rhadamanthus and born in Krête.
Strabo, in pointing out the many
contradictions respecting Minôs, remarks : Ἔστι δὲ καὶ ἄλλος λόγος οὐχ
ὁμολογούμενος, τῶν μὲν ξένον τῆς νήσου
τὸν Μίνω λεγόντων, τῶν δὲ ἐπιχώριον.
By the former he doubtless means
Ephorus, though he has not here
specified him (x. p. 477).

"Polykratês (he tells us) was the first person who aspired to nautical dominion, excepting Minôs of Knôssus, and others before him (if any such there ever were) who may have ruled the sea ; but Polykratês is the first of that which is called *the generation of man* who aspired with much chance of success to govern Iônia and the islands of the Ægean".[1] Here we find it manifestly intimated that Minôs did not belong to the generation of man, and the tale given by the historian respecting the tremendous calamities which the wrath of the departed Minôs inflicted on Krête confirms the impression. The king of Knôssus is a god or a hero, but not a man ; he belongs to legend, not to history. He is the son as well as the familiar companion of Zeus ; he marries the daughter of Hêlios, and Ariadnê is numbered among his off-spring. To this superhuman person are ascribed the oldest and most revered institutions of the island, religious and political, together with a period of supposed antehistorical dominion. That there is much of Krêtan religious ideas and practice embodied in the fables concerning Minôs can hardly be doubted ; nor is it improbable that the tale of the youths and maidens sent from Athens may be based on some expiatory offerings rendered to a Krêtan divinity. The orgiastic worship of Zeus, solemnized by the armed priests with impassioned motions and violent excite-ment, was of ancient date in that island, as well as the connexion with the worship of Apollo both at Delphi and at Dêlos. To analyse the fables and to elicit from them any trustworthy particular facts, appears to me a fruitless attempt. The religious recollections, the romantic invention, and the items of matter of fact, if any such there be, must for ever remain indissolubly amalgamated as the poet originally blended them, for the amuse-ment or edification of his auditors. Hoeck, in his instructive and learned collections of facts respecting ancient Krête, construes the mythical genealogy of Minôs to denote a combination of the orgiastic worship of Zeus, indigenous among the Eteokrêtes, with the worship of the moon imported from Phœnicia, and signified

---

[1] Herodot. iii. 122. Πολυκράτης γὰρ ἐστὶ πρῶτος τῶν ἡμεῖς ἴδμεν Ἑλλήνων, ὃς θαλασσοκρατέειν ἐπενοήθη, παρὲξ Μίνωός τε τοῦ Κνωσσίου, καὶ εἰ δή τις ἄλλος πρότερος τούτου ἦρξε τῆς θαλάττης· τῆς δὲ ἀνθρωπηίης λεγομένης γενεῆς Πολυκράτης ἐστὶ πρῶτος ἐλπίδας πολλὰς ἔχων Ἰωνίης τε καὶ νήσων ἄρξειν.
The expression exactly corresponds to that of Pausanias, ix. 5, 1, ἐπὶ τῶν καλουμένων Ἡρώων, for the age pre-ceding the ἀνθρωπηίη γενεή ; also viii. 2, 1, ἐς τὰ ἀνωτέρω τοῦ ἀνθρώπων γένους.

by the names Europê, Pasiphaê, and Ariadnê.[1] This is specious
as a conjecture, but I do not venture to speak of it in terms of
greater confidence.

From the connexion of religious worship and legendary tales
Affinity   between Krête and various parts of Asia Minor,—
between   the Troad, the coast of Milêtus and Lykia, especially
Krête and
Asia Minor.   between Mount Ida in Krête, and Mount Ida in Ælois,
—it seems reasonable to infer an ethnographical kindred or
relationship between the inhabitants anterior to the period of
Hellenic occupation. The tales of Krêtan settlement at Minoa
and Engyôn on the south-western coast of Sicily, and in Iapygia
on the Gulf of Tarentum, conduct us to a similar presumption,
though the want of evidence forbids our tracing it farther. In
the time of Herodotus, the Eteokrêtes, or aboriginal inhabitants
of the island, were confined to Polichna and Præsus; but in
earlier times, prior to the encroachments of the Hellênes, they
had occupied the larger portion, if not the whole of the island.
Minôs was originally their hero, subsequently adopted by the
immigrant Hellênes,—at least Herodotus considers him as
barbarian, not Hellenic.[2]

---

[1] Hoeck, Kreta, vol. ii. pp. 56—67. K. O. Müller also (Dorier. ii. 2, 14) puts a religious interpretation upon these Kreto-Attic legends, but he explains them in a manner totally different from Hoeck.

[2] Herodot. 1. 173.

CHAPTER XIII.

ARGONAUTIC EXPEDITION.

THE ship Argô was the theme of many songs during the oldest
periods of the Grecian epic, even earlier than the　Ship Argô
Odyssey.　The king Æêtês, from whom she is depart-　in the
ing, the hero Jasôn, who commands her, and the god-　Odyssey.
dess Hêrê, who watches over him, enabling the Argô to traverse
distances and to escape dangers which no ship had ever before
encountered, are all circumstances briefly glanced at by Odysseus
in his narrative to Alkinous. Moreover Euneus, the son of Jasôn
and Hypsipylê, governs Lêmnos during the siege of Troy by
Agamemnôn, and carries on a friendly traffic with the Grecian
camp, purchasing from them their Trojan prisoners.[1]

The legend of Halus in Achaia Phthiôtis, respecting the
religious solemnities connected with the family of Athamas and
Phryxus (related in a previous chapter) is also interwoven with
the voyage of the Argonauts ; and both the legend and the
solemnities seem evidently of great antiquity. We know further,
that the adventures of the Argô were narrated not only　In Hesiod
by Hesiod and in the Hesiodic poems, but also by　and Eumê-
Eumêlus and the author of the Naupaktian verses—　lus.
by the latter seemingly at considerable length.[2]　But these poems

---

[1] Odyss. xii. 69.—

Οἴη δὴ κείνη γε παρέπλω ποντόπορος
　νηῦς,
'Αργὼ πασιμέλουσα, παρ' Αἰήταο πλέου-
　σα·
Καί νύ κε τὴν ἔνθ' ὦκα βάλεν μεγάλας
　ποτὶ πέτρας,
'Αλλ' Ἥρη παρέπεμψεν, ἐπεὶ φίλος ἦεν
　Ἰήσων.

See also Iliad, vii. 470.

[2] See Hesiod, Fragm. Catalog. Fr. 6,

p. 33, Düntz. ; Eoiai, Fr. 36, p. 39 ;
Frag. 72, p. 47. Compare Schol. ad
Apollôn. Rhod. i. 45 ; ii. 178—297, 1125 ;
iv. 254—284. Other poetical sources—
The old epic poem Ægimius, Frag. 5,
p. 57, Düntz.
Kinæthôn in the Herakléia touched
upon the death of Hylas near Kius in
Mysia (Schol. Apollôn. Rhod. i. 1357).
The epic poem Naupaktia, Frag. 1 to
6, Düntz. p. 61.
Eumêlus, Frag. 2, 3, 5, p. 65, Düntz.

are unfortunately lost, nor have we any means of determining what the original story was ; for the narrative, as we have it, borrowed from later sources, is enlarged by local tales from the subsequent Greek colonies—Kyzikus, Hêrakleia, Sinopê, and others.

Jasôn, commanded by Pelias to depart in quest of the golden fleece belonging to the speaking ram which had car-ried away Phryxus and Hellê, was encouraged by the oracle to invite the noblest youth of Greece to his aid, and fifty of the most distinguished amongst them obeyed the call. Hêraklês, Thêseus, Telamôn and Pêleus, Kastôr and Pollux, Idas and Lynkeus—Zêtês and Kalaïs, the winged sons of Boreas—Meleager, Amphiaraus, Kêpheus, Laertês, Autolykus, Menœtius, Aktor, Erginus, Euphêmus, Ankæus, Pœas, Periklymenus, Augeas, Eurytus, Admêtus, Akastus, Kæneus, Euryalus, Pêne-leôs and Lêitus, Askalaphus, and Ialmenus, were among them. Argus the son of Phryxus, directed by the promptings of Athênê, built the ship, inserting in the prow a piece of timber, from the celebrated oak of Dodona, which was endued with the faculty of speech :[1] Tiphys was the steersman, Idmôn (the son of Apollo) and Mopsus accompanied them as prophets, while Orpheus came to amuse their weariness, and reconcile their quarrels, with his harp.[2]

Marginal note: Jasôn and his heroic companions.

Epimenidês, the Krêtan prophet and poet, composed a poem in 6500 lines, Ἀργοῦς ναυπηγίαν τε καὶ Ἰάσονος εἰς Κόλχους ἀποπλοῦν (Diogen. Laër. i. 10, 5), which is noticed more than once in the Scholia on Apollônius, on subjects connected with the poem (ii. 1125; iii. 42). See Mimnerm. Frag. 10, Schnei-dewin, p. 15.

Antimachus, in his poem *Lydê*, touched upon the Argonautic expedi-tion, and has been partially copied by Apollônius Rhod. (Schol. Ap. Rh. i. 1290; ii. 296; iii. 410; iv. 1153).

The logographers Pherekydês and Hekatæus seem to have related the expedition at considerable length.

The Bibliothek der alten Literatur und Kunst (Göttingen, 1786, 2tes Stück, p. 61) contains an instructive Disserta-tion by Groddeck, Ueber die Argo-nautica, a summary of the various authorities respecting this expedition.

[1] Apollôn. Rhod. i. 525; iv. 580. Apollodôr. i. 9, 16. Valerius Flaccus (i. 300) softens down the speech of the ship Argô into a dream of Jasôn.

Alexander Polyhistor explained what wood was used (Plin. H. N. xiii. 22).

[2] Apollônius Rhodius, Apollodôrus, Valerius Flaccus, the Orphic Argo-nautica, and Hyginus, have all given Catalogues of the Argonautic heroes (there was one also in the lost tragedy called Λήμνιαι of Sophoklês, see Welcker, Gr. Trag. i. 327): the dis-crepancies among them are numerous and irreconcileable. Burmann, in the Catalogus Argonautarum, prefixed to his edition of Valerius Flaccus, has discussed them copiously. I transcribe one or two of the remarks of this conscientious and laborious critic, out of many of a similar tenor, on the impracticability of a fabulous chrono-logy. Immediately before the first article, *Acastus*—" Neque enim in ætatibus Argonantarum ullam ratio-nem temporum constare, neque in stirpe et stemmate deducendâ ordinem ipsum naturæ congruere videbam. Nam et huic militiæ adscribi videbam Heroas, qui per naturæ leges et ordi-nem fati eo usque vitam extrahere non

First they touched at the island of Lêmnos, in which at that time there were no men; for the women, infuriated by jealousy and ill-treatment, had put to death their fathers, husbands, and brothers. The Argonauts, after some difficulty, were received with friendship, and even admitted into the greatest intimacy. They staid some months, and the subsequent population of the island was the fruit of their visit. Hypsipylê, the queen of the island, bore to Jasôn two sons.[1]

Lêmnos.

They then proceeded onward along the coast of Thrace, up the Hellespont, to the southern coast of the Propontis, inhabited by the Doliones and their king Kyzikus. Here they were kindly entertained, but after their departure were driven back to the same spot by a storm; and as they landed in the dark, the inhabitants did not know them. A battle took place, in which the chief, Kyzikus, was killed by Jasôn; whereby much grief was occasioned as soon as the real facts became known. After Kyzikus had been interred with every demonstration of mourning and solemnity, the Argonauts proceeded along the coast of Mysia.[2] In this part of the voyage they left Hêraklês behind. For Hylas, his favourite youthful companion, had been stolen away

Adventures at Kyzikus, in Bithynia, &c. Hêraklês and Hylas. Phineus.

---

potuêre, ut aliis ab hac expeditione remotis Heroum militiis nomina dedisse narrari deberent a Poetis et Mythologis. In idem etiam tempus avos et nepotes conjici, consanguineos ætate longe inferiores prioribus nt æquales adjungi, concoquere vix posse videtur." —Art. *Ancæus:* " Scio objici posse, si seriem illam majorem respiciamus, hunc Ancæum simul cum proavo suo Talao in eandem profectum fuisse expeditionem. Sed similia exempla in aliis occurrent, et in fabulis rationem temporum non semper accuratam licet deducere."—Art. *Jasôn:* "Herculi enim jam provectâ ætate adhæsit Theseus juvenis, et in Amazoniâ expeditione socius fuit, interfuit huic expeditioni, venatui apri Calydonii, et rapuit Helenam, quæ circa Trojanum bellum maxime floruit: quae omnia si Theseus tot temporum intervallis distincta egit, secula duo vel tria vixisse debuit. Certe Jason Hypsipylem neptem Ariadnes, nec videre, nec Lemni cognoscere potuit."—Art. *Meleager:* "Unum

est quod alicui longum ordinem majorum recensenti scrupulum movere possit: nimis longum intervallum inter Æolum et Meleagrum intercedere, ut potuerit interfuisse huic expeditioni: cum nonus fere numeretur ab Æolo, et plurimi ut Jason, Argus, et alii tertiâ tantum ab Æolo generatione distent. Sed sæpe jam notavimus, frustra temporum concordiam in fabulis quæri."

Read also the articles *Castôr and Pollux*, *Nestôr*, *Pêleus*, *Staphylus*, &c.

We may stand excused for keeping clear of a chronology which is fertile only in difficulties, and ends in nothing but illusions.

[1] Apollodôr. i. 9, 17; Apollôn. Rhod. i. 609—915; Herodot. iv. 145. Theokritus (Idyll. xiii. 29) omits all mention of Lêmnos, and represents the Argô as arriving on the third day from Iôlkos at the Hellespont. Diodôrus (iv. 41) also leaves out Lêmnos.

[2] Apollôn. Rhod. 940—1020; Apollodôr. i. 9, 18.

by the nymphs of a fountain, and Hêraklês, wandering about in search of him, neglected to return. At last he sorrowfully retired, exacting hostages from the inhabitants of the neighbouring town of Kius that they would persist in the search.[1]

They next stopped in the country of the Bebrykians, where the boxing contest took place between the king Amykus and the Argonaut Pollux:[2] they then proceeded onward to Bithynia, the residence of the blind prophet Phineus. His blindness had been inflicted by Poseidôn as a punishment for having communicated to Phryxus the way to Kolchis. The choice had been allowed to him between death and blindness, and he had preferred the latter.[3] He was also tormented by the harpies, winged monsters who came down from the clouds whenever his table was set, snatched the food from his lips, and imparted to it a foul and unapproachable odour. In the midst of this misery, he hailed the Argonauts as his deliverers—his prophetic powers having enabled him to foresee their coming. The meal being prepared for him, the harpies approached as usual, but Zêtês and Kalias, the winged sons of Boreas, drove them away and pursued them. They put forth all their speed, and prayed to Zeus to be enabled to overtake the monsters ; when Hermês appeared and directed them to desist, the harpies being forbidden further

---

[1] Apollodôr. i. 9, 19. This was the religious legend, explanatory of a ceremony performed for many centuries by the people of Prusa : they ran round the lake Askanius shouting and clamouring for Hylas—"nt littus Hyla, Hyla omne sonaret". (Virgil, Eclog.) . . . . "in cujus memoriam adhuc solemni cursatione lacum populus circuit et Hylam voce clamat". Solinus, c. 42.

There is endless discrepancy as to the concern of Hêraklês with the Argonautic expedition. A story is alluded to in Aristotle (Politic. iii. 9) that the ship Argô herself refused to take him on board, because he was so much superior in stature and power to all the other heroes—οὐ γὰρ ἐθέλειν αὐτὸν ἄγειν τὴν Ἀργὼ μετὰ τῶν ἄλλων, ὡς ὑπερβάλλοντα πολὺ τῶν πλωτήρων. This was the story of Pherekydês (Fr. 67, Didot) as well as of Antimachus (Schol. Apoll. Rhod. i. 1290).: it is probably a very ancient portion of the legend, inasmuch as it ascribes to the ship sentient powers, in consonance with her other miraculous properties. The etymology of Aphetæ in Thessaly was connected with the tale of Hêraklês having there been put on shore from the Argô (Herodot. vii. 193): Ephorus said that he staid away voluntarily from fondness for Omphalê (Frag. 9, Didot). The old epic poet Kinæthôn said that Hêraklês had placed the Kian hostages at Trachin, and that the Kians ever afterwards maintained a respectful correspondence with that place (Schol. Ap. Rh. i. 1357). This is the explanatory legend connected with some existing custom, which we are unable further to unravel.

[2] See above, chap. viii.

[3] Such was the old narrative of the Hesiodic Catalogue and Eoiai. See Schol. Apollôn. Rhod. ii. 181—296.

to molest Phineus,[1] and retiring again to their native cavern in Krête.[2]

Phineus, grateful for the relief afforded to him by the Argonauts, forewarned them of the dangers of their voyage and of the precautions necessary for their safety; and through his suggestions they were enabled to pass through the terrific rocks called Symplêgades.   These were two rocks which alternately opened and shut, with a swift and violent collision, so that it was difficult even for a bird to fly through during the short interval.   When the Argô arrived at the dangerous spot, Euphêmus let loose a dove, which flew through and just escaped with the loss of a few feathers of her tail.   This was a signal to the Argonauts, according to the prediction of Phineus, that they might attempt the passage with confidence. Accordingly they rowed with all their might, and passed safely through: the closing rocks, held for a moment asunder by the powerful arms of Athênê, just crushed the ornaments at the stern of their vessel.   It had been decreed by the gods that so soon as any ship once got through, the passage should for ever afterwards be safe and easy to all.   The rocks became fixed in their separate places, and never again closed.[3]

Dangers of the Symplêgades.

After again halting on the coast of the Mariandynians, where their steersman Tiphys died, as well as in the country of the Amazons, and after picking up the sons of Phryxus, who had been cast away by Poseidôn, in their attempt to return from Kolchis to Greece, they arrived in safety at the river Phasis and the residence of Æêtês.   In passing by Mount Caucasus, they saw the eagle which gnawed the liver of Promêtheus, nailed to the rock, and heard the groans of the sufferer himself.   The sons of Phryxus were cordially welcomed by their mother Chalkiopê.[4]   Application was made to Æêtês that he would grant to the Argonauts, heroes of divine parentage and

Arrival at Kolchis.

---

[1] This again was the old Hesiodic story (Schol. Apoll. Rhod. ii. 296),—

'Ενθ' οἵγ' εὔχεσθον Αἰνήτῳ ὑψιμέδοντι.

Apollodôrus (i. 9, 21), Apollônius (178—300), and Valerius Flacc. (iv. 428—530) agree in most of the circumstances.

[2] Such was the fate of the harpies as given in the old Naupaktian Verses. (See Fragm. Ep. Græc. Düntzer, Naupakt. Fr. 2, p. 61.)

The adventure of the Argonauts with Phineus is given by Diodôrus in a manner totally different (Diodôr. iv. 44): he seems to follow Dionysius of Mitylênê (see Schol. Apollôn. Rhod. ii. 207).

[3] Apollodôr. i. 9, 22. Apollôn. Rhod. ii. 310—615.

[4] Apollodôr. i. 9, 23. Apollôn. Rhod. ii. 850—1257.

sent forth by the mandate of the gods, possession of the golden
fleece : their aid in return was proffered to him against any or all
of his enemies. But the king was wroth, and peremptorily refused,
except upon conditions which seemed impracticable.[1] Hêphæstos
had given him two ferocious and untamable bulls, with brazen
feet, which breathed fire from their nostrils : Jasôn was invited,
as a proof both of his illustrious descent and of the sanction of
the gods to his voyage, to harness these animals to the yoke, so as
to plough a large field and sow it with dragon's teeth.[2] Perilous
as the condition was, each one of the heroes volunteered to make
the attempt.   Idmôn especially encouraged Jasôn to undertake

Conditions imposed by Æêtês as the price of the golden fleece.

it,[3] and the goddesses Hêrê and Aphroditê made
straight the way for him.[4] Mêdea, the daughter of
Æêtês and Eidyia, having seen the youthful hero in
his interview with her father, had conceived towards
him a passion which disposed her to employ every
means for his salvation and success.   She had received from
Hekatê pre-eminent magical powers, and she prepared for Jasôn
the powerful Prometheian unguent, extracted from a herb which
had grown where the blood of Promêtheus dropped.   The body
of Jasôn, having been thus pre-medicated, became invulnerable[5]
either by fire or by warlike weapons. He undertook the enterprise,
yoked the bulls without suffering injury, and ploughed the field :
when he had sown the dragon's teeth, armed men sprung out of
the furrows.   But he had been forewarned by Mêdea to cast a
vast rock into the midst of them, upon which they began to fight
with each other, so that he was easily enabled to subdue them all.[6]

The task prescribed had thus been triumphantly performed.

Perfidy of Æêtês— flight of the Argonauts and Mêdea with the fleece.

Yet Æêtês not only refused to hand over the golden
fleece, but even took measures for secretly destroying
the Argonauts and burning their vessel.   He designed
to murder them during the night after a festal
banquet ; but Aphroditê, watchful for the safety of

[1] Apollôn. Rhod. iii. 320—385.
[2] Apollôn. Rhod. iii. 410. Apollodôr.
I. 9, 23.
[3] This was the story of the Naupaktian Verses (Schol. Apollôn. Rhod. iii.
515—525): Apollônius and others altered
it. Idmôn, according to them, died in the
voyage before the arrival at Kolchis.
[4] Apollôn. Rhod. iii. 50—200. Valer.

Flacc. vi. 440—480. Hygin. fab. 22.
[5] Apollôn. Rhod. iii. 835. Apollodôr.
i. 9, 23. Valer. Flacc. vii. 356. Ovid.
Epist. xii. 15.
"Isset anhelatos non præmedicatus
          in ignes
Immemor Æsonides, oraque adunca
          boum."
[6] Apollôn. Rhod. iii. 1230—1400.

Jasôn,[1] inspired the Kolchian king at the critical moment with an irresistible inclination for his nuptial bed.   While he slept, the wise Idmôn counselled the Argonauts to make their escape, and Mêdea agreed to accompany them.[2]   She lulled to sleep by a magic potion the dragon who guarded the golden fleece, placed that much-desired prize on board the vessel, and accompanied Jasôn with his companions in their flight, carrying along with her the young Apsyrtus, her brother.[3]

Æêtês, profoundly exasperated at the flight of the Argonauts with his daughter, assembled his forces forthwith, and put to sea in pursuit of them.   So energetic were his efforts that he shortly overtook the retreating vessel, when the Argonauts again owed their safety to the stratagem of Mêdea.   She killed her brother Apsyrtus, cut his body in pieces, and strewed the limbs round about in the sea. Æêtês on reaching the spot found these sorrowful traces of his murdered son ; but while he tarried to collect the scattered fragments, and bestow upon the body an honourable interment, the Argonauts escaped.[4]   The spot on which the unfortunate Apsyrtus was cut up received the name of Tomi.[5]   This fratricide of Mêdea, however, so deeply provoked the indignation of Zeus, that he condemned the Argô and her crew to a trying voyage,

Pursuit of Æêtês—the Argonauts saved by Mêdea.

---

[1] The Naupaktian Verses stated this see the Fragm. 6, ed. Düntzer, p. 61), ap. Schol. Apollôn. Rhod. iv. 59—86.

[2] Such was the story of the Naupaktian Verses. (See Fragm. 6, p. 61, Düntzer ap. Schol. Apollôn. Rhod. iv. 59, 86, 87.)

[3] Apollodôr. i. 9, 23. Apollôn. Rhod. iv. 220.

Pherekydês said that Jasôn killed the dragon (Fr. 74, Did.).

[4] This is the story of Apollodôrus (i. 9, 24), who seems to follow Pherekydês (Fr. 73, Didot). Apollônius (iv. 225—480) and Valerius Flaccus (viii. 262 seq.) give totally different circumstances respecting the death of Apsyrtus : but the narrative of Pherekydês seems the oldest : so revolting a story as that of the cutting up of the little boy cannot have been imagined in later times.

Sophoklês composed two tragedies on the adventures of Jasôn and Mêdea, both lost—the Κολχίδες, and the Σκύθαι. In the former he represented the murder of the child Apsyrtus as having taken place in the house of Æêtês : in the latter he introduced the mitigating circumstance, that Apsyrtus was the son of Æêtês by a different mother from Mêdea (Schol. Apollôn. Rhod. iv. 223).

[5] Apollodôr. i. 9, 24, τὸν τόπον προσηγόρευσε Τόμους.   Ovid. Trist. iii. 9. The story that Apsyrtus was cut in pieces is the etymological legend explanatory of the name Tomi.

There was however a place called Apsarus, on the southern coast of the Euxine, west of Trapezus, where the tomb of Apsyrtus was shown, and where it was affirmed that he had been put to death.   He was the eponymus of the town, which was said to have been once called Apsyrtus, and only corrupted by a barbarian pronunciation. (Arrian. Periplus Euxin. p. 6 ; Geogr. Min. v. 1.)   Compare Procop. Bell. Goth. iv. 2.

Strabo connects the death of Apsyrtus with the Apsyrtides, islands off the coast of Illyria, in the Adriatic (vii. p. 315).

full of hardship and privation, before she was permitted to reach

Return of the Argonauts—circuitous and Perilous.
home. The returning heroes traversed an immeasurable length both of sea and of river: first up the river Phasis into the ocean which flows round the earth—then following the course of that circumfluous stream until its junction with the Nile,[1] they came down the Nile into Egypt, from whence they carried the Argô on their shoulders by a fatiguing land-journey to the lake Tritônis in Libya. Here they were rescued from the extremity of want and exhaustion by the kindness of the local god Tritôn, who treated them hospitably, and even presented to Euphêmus a clod of earth, as a symbolical promise that his descendants should one day found a city on the Libyan shore. The promise was amply redeemed by the flourishing and powerful city of Kyrênê,[2] whose princes, the Battiads, boasted themselves as lineal descendants of Euphêmus.

Refreshed by the hospitality of Tritôn, the Argonauts found themselves again on the waters of the Mediterranean on their way homeward. But before they arrived at Iôlkos they visited Circê, at the island of Ææa, where Mêdea was purified for the murder of Apsyrtus: they also stopped at Korkyra, then called Drepanê, where Alkinous received and protected them. The cave in that island where the marriage of Mêdea with Jasôn was consummated, was still shown in the time of the historian Timæus, as well as the altars to Apollo which she had erected, and the rites and sacrifices which she had first instituted.[3] After leaving Korkyra, the Argô was overtaken by a perilous storm near the

---

[1] The original narrative was, that the Argô returned by navigating the circumfluous ocean. This would be almost certain, even without positive testimony, from the early ideas entertained by the Greeks respecting geography; but we know further that it was the representation of the Hesiodic poems, as well as of Mimnermus, Hekatæus and Pindar, and even of Antimachus. Schol. Parisin. Ap. Rhod. iv. 254. Ἑκαταῖος δὲ ὁ Μιλήσιος διὰ τοῦ Φάσιδος ἀνελθεῖν φησὶν αὐτοὺς εἰς τὸν Ὠκεανόν· διὰ δὲ τοῦ Ὠκεανοῦ κατελθεῖν εἰς τὸν Νεῖλον· ἐκ δὲ τοῦ Νείλου εἰς τὴν καθ᾽ ἡμᾶς θάλασσαν. Ἡσίοδος δὲ καὶ Πίνδαρος ἐν Πυθιονίκαις καὶ Ἀντίμαχος ἐν Λυδῇ διὰ τοῦ Ὠκεανοῦ φασὶν ἐλθεῖν αὐτοὺς εἰς τὴν Λιβύην: εἶτα βαστάσαντας τὴν Ἀργὼ εἰς τὸ ἡμέτερον ἀφικέσθαι πέλαγος.

Compare the Schol. Edit. ad iv. 259.
[2] See the fourth Pythian ode of Pindar, and Apollôn. Rhod. iv. 1551—1756. The tripod of Jasôn was preserved by the Euesperitæ in Libya, Diod. iv. 56 : but the legend connecting the Argonauts with the lake Tritônis in Libya, is given with some considerable differences in Herodotus, iv. 179.
[3] Apollôn. Rhod. iv. 1153—1217. Timæus, Fr. 7—8, Didot. Τίμαιος ἐν Κερκύρᾳ λέγων γενέσθαι τοὺς γάμους, καὶ περὶ τῆς θυσίας ἱστορεῖ, ἔτι καὶ νῦν λέγων ἄγεσθαι αὐτὴν κατ᾽ ἐνιαυτόν, Μηδείας πρῶτον θυσάσης ἐν τῷ τοῦ Ἀπολλῶνος ἱερῷ. Καὶ βωμοὺς δέ φησι μνημεῖα τῶν γάμων ἱδρύσασθαι συνεγγὺς μὲν τῆς θαλάσσης, οὐ μακρὰν δὲ τῆς πόλεως. Ὀνομάζουσι δὲ τὸν μὲν, Νυμφῶν· τὸν δὲ, Νηρηΐδων.

island of Thêra. The heroes were saved from imminent peril by the supernatural aid of Apollo, who, shooting from his golden bow an arrow which pierced the waves like a track of light, caused a new island suddenly to spring up in their track and present to them a port of refuge. The island was called Anaphê; and the grateful Argonauts established upon it an altar and sacrifices in honour of Apollo Æglêtês, which were ever afterwards continued, and traced back by the inhabitants to this originating adventure.[1]

On approaching the coast of Krête, the Argonauts were prevented from landing by Talôs, a man of brass, fabricated by Hêphæstos, and presented by him to Minôs for the protection of the island.[2] This vigilant sentinel hurled against the approaching vessel fragments of rock, and menaced the heroes with destruction. But Mêdea deceived him by a stratagem and killed him ; detecting and assailing the one vulnerable point in his body. The Argonauts were thus enabled to land and refresh themselves. They next proceeded onward to Ægina, where however they again experienced resistance before they could obtain water—then along the coast of Eubœa and Lokris back to Iôlkos in the gulf of Pagasæ, the place from whence they had started. The proceedings of Pelias during their absence, and the signal revenge taken upon him by Mêdea after their return, have already been narrated in a preceding section.[3] The ship Argô herself, in which the chosen heroes of Greece had performed so long a voyage and ·braved so many dangers, was consecrated by Jasôn to Poseidôn at the isthmus of Corinth. According to another account, she was translated to the stars by Athênê, and became a constellation.[4]

Traces of the presence of the Argonauts were found not only in the regions which lay between Iôlkos and Kolchis, but also in the western portion of the Grecian world—distributed more or less over all the spots visited by Grecian mariners or settled by Grecian colonists, and scarcely less numerous than the wanderings of the dispersed Greeks and Trojans after the capture of Troy. The

Numerous and widespread monuments referring to the voyage.

---

[1] Apollodôr. i. 9, 25. Apollôn. Rhod. iv. 1700—1725.

[2] Some called Talôs a remnant of the brazen race of men (Schol. Apoll. Rhod. iv. 1641).

[3] Apollodôr. i. 9, 26. Apollôn. Rhod. vi. 1638.

[4] Diodôr. iv. 53. Eratosth. Catasterism. c. 35.

number of Jasonia, or temples for the heroic worship of Jasôn, was very great, from Abdêra in Thrace,[1] eastward along the coast of the Euxine, to Armenia and Media. The Argonauts had left their anchoring-stone on the coast of Bebrykia, near Kyzikus, and there it was preserved during the historical ages in the temple of the Jasonian Athênê.[2] They had founded the great temple of the Idæan mother on the mountain Dindymon, near Kyzikus, and the Hieron of Zeus Urios on the Asiatic point at the mouth of the Euxine, near which was also the harbour of Phryxus.[3] Idmôn, the prophet of the expedition, who was believed to have died of a wound by a wild boar on the Mariandynian coast, was worshipped by the inhabitants of the Pontic Hêrakleia with great solemnity, as their Heros Poliuchus, and that too by the special direction of the Delphian god. Autolykus, another companion of Jasôn, was worshipped as Œkist by the inhabitants of Sinopê. Moreover, the historians of Hêrakleia pointed out a temple of Hekatê in the neighbouring country of Paphlagonia, first erected by Mêdea ;[4] and the important town of Pantikapæon, on the European side of the Cimmerian Bosporus, ascribed its first settlement to a son of Æêtês.[5] When the returning ten thousand Greeks sailed along the coast, called the Jasonian shore, from Sinopê to Hêrakleia, they were told that the grandson of Æêtês was reigning king of the territory at the mouth of the Phasis, and the anchoring-places where the Argô had stopped were specially pointed out to them.[6] In the lofty regions of the Moschi, near Kolchis, stood the temple of Leukothea, founded by Phryxus, which remained both rich and respected down to the

---

[1] Strabo, xi. p. 526—531.

[2] Apollôn. Rhod. i. 955—960, and the Scholia.
There was in Kyzikus a temple of Apollo under different ἐπικλήσεις; some called it the temple of the Jasonian Apollo.
Another anchor however was preserved in the temple of Rhea on the banks of the Phasis, which was affirmed to be the anchor of the ship Argô. Arrian saw it there, but seems to have doubted its authenticity (Periplus Euxin. Pont. p. 9. Geogr. Min. v. 1).

[3] Neanthês ap. Strab. i. p. 45. Apollôn. Rhod. i. 1125, and Schol. Steph. Byz. v. Φρίξος.

Apollônius mentions the fountain called Jasoneæ, on the hill of Dindymon. Apollôn. Rhod. ii. 532, and the citations from Timosthenês and Herodôrus in the Scholia. See also Appian, Syriac. c. 63.

[4] See the Historians of Hêrakleia, Nymphis, and Promathidas, Fragm. Orelli, pp. 99, 100—104. Schol. ad Apollôn. Rhod. iv. 247. Strabo, xii. p. 546. Autolykus, whom he calls companion of Jasôn, was, according to another legend, comrade of Hêraklês in his expedition against the Amazons.

[5] Stephan. Byz. v. Παντικαπαῖον, Eustath. ad Dionys. Perieget. 311.

[6] Xenophôn. Anabas. vi. 2, 1 ; v. 7, 37.

times of the kings of Pontus, and where it was an inviolable rule not to offer up a ram.[1] The town of Dioskurias, north of the river Phasis, was believed to have been hallowed by the presence of Kastôr and Pollux in the Argô, and to have received from them its appellation.[2] Even the interior of Media and Armenia was full of memorials of Jasôn and Mêdea, and their son Mêdus, or of Armenus the son of Jasôn, from whom the Greeks deduced not only the name and foundation of the Medes and Armenians, but also the great operation of cutting a channel through the mountains for the efflux of the river Araxes, which they compared to that of the Peneius in Thessaly.[3] And the Roman general Pompey, after having completed the conquest and expulsion of Mithridatês, made long marches through Kolchis into the regions of Caucasus, for the express purpose of contemplating the spots which had been ennobled by the exploits of the Argonauts, the Dioskuri, and Hêraklês.[4]

In the west, memorials either of the Argonauts or of the pursuing Kolchians were pointed out in Korkyra, in Krête, in Epirus near the Akrokeraunian mountains, in the islands called Apsyrtides near the Illyrian coast, at the bay of Caieta as well as at Poseidônia on the southern coast of Italy, in the island of Æthalia or Elba, and in Libya.[5]

[1] Strabo, xi. p. 499.

[2] Appian, Mithridatic. c. 101.

[3] Strabo, xi. p. 499, 503, 526, 531; i. p. 45—48. Justin, xlii. 3, whose statements illustrate the way in which men found a present home and application for the old fables,—"Jason, primus humanorum post Herculem et Liberum, qui reges Orientis fuisse traduntur, eam cœli plagam domuisse dicitur. Cum Albanis fœdus percussit, qui Herculem ex Italiâ ab Albano monte, cum, Geryone extincto, armenta ejus per Italiam duceret, secuti dicuntur; quique, memores Italicæ originis, exercitum Cn. Pompeii bello Mithridatico fratres consalutavêre. Itaque Jasoni totus fere Oriens, ut conditori, divinos honores templaque constituit; quæ Parmenio, dux Alexandri Magni, post multos annos dirui jussit, ne cujusquam nomen in Oriente venerabilius quam Alexandri esset."

The Thessalian companions of Alexander the Great, placed by his victories in possession of rich acquisitions in these regions, pleased themselves by vivifying and multiplying all these old fables, proving an ancient kindred between the Medes and Thessalians. See Strabo, xi. p. 530. The temples of Jasôn were τιμώμενα σφόδρα ὑπὸ τῶν βαρβάρων (ib. p. 526).

The able and inquisitive geographer Eratosthenês was among those who fully believed that Jasôn had left his ships in the Phasis, and had undertaken a land expedition into the interior country, in which he had conquered Media and Armenia (Strabo, i. p. 48).

[4] Appian, Mithridatic. 103 : τοὺς Κόλχους ἐπήει, καθ' ἱστορίαν τῆς Ἀργοναυτῶν καὶ Διοσκούρων καὶ Ἡρακλέους ἐπιδημίας, καὶ μάλιστα τὸ πάθος ἰδεῖν ἐθέλων, ὃ Προμηθεῖ φασι γενέσθαι περὶ τὸ Καύκασον ὄρος. The lofty crag of Caucasus called Strobilus, to which Promêtheus had been attached, was pointed out to Arrian himself in his Periplus (p. 12. Geogr. Minor. vol. i.).

[5] Strabo, i. pp. 21, 45, 46 ; v. 224—252. Pompon. Mel. ii. 3. Diodôr. iv.

Such is a brief outline of the Argonautic expedition, one of the
Argonautic
legend
generally. most celebrated and widely-diffused among the ancient
tales of Greece. Since so many able men have treated
it as an undisputed reality, and even made it the pivot
of systematic chronological calculations, I may here repeat the
opinion long ago expressed by Heyne, and even indicated by
Burmann, that the process of dissecting the story in search of a
basis of fact is one altogether fruitless.[1] Not only are we unable
to assign the date, or identify the crew, or decipher the log-book,
of the Argô, but we have no means of settling even the preliminary question, whether the voyage be matter of fact badly
reported or legend from the beginning. The widely-distant
spots in which the monuments of the voyage were shown, no less
than the incidents of the voyage itself, suggest no other parentage
than epical fancy. The supernatural and the romantic not only
constitute an inseparable portion of the narrative, but even
embrace all the prominent and characteristic features ; if they do
not comprise the whole, and if there be intermingled along with
them any sprinkling of historical or geographical fact,—a question
to us indeterminable,—there is at least no solvent by which it
can be disengaged, and no test by which it can be recognised.
Wherever the Grecian mariner sailed, he carried his religious
and patriotic mythes along with him. His fancy and his faith
were alike full of the long wanderings of Jasôn, Odysseus, Perseus,
Hêraklês, Dionysus, Triptolemus or Iô ; it was pleasing to him

56. Apollôn. Rhod. iv. 656. Lycophron,
1273.—

Τύρσιν μακεδνὰς ἀμφὶ Κιρκαίου νάπας
'Αργοῦς τε κλεινὸν ὅρμον Αἰήτην μέγαν.

[1] Heyne, Observ. ad Apollodôr. i. 9,
16. p. 72. "Mirum in modum fallitur,
qui in his commentis certum fundum
historicum vel geographicum aut ex-
quirere studet, aut se reperisse, atque
historicam vel geographicam aliquam
doctrinam, systema nos dicimus, inde
procudi posse, putat," &c.

See also the observations inter-
spersed in Burmann's Catalogus
Argonautarum, prefixed to his edition
of Valerius Flaccus.

The Persian antiquarians whom
Herodotus cites at the beginning of
his history (i. 2—4—it is much to be
regretted that Herodotus did not
inform us who they were, and whether
they were the same as those who said

that Perseus was an Assyrian by birth,
and had become a Greek, vi. 54), joined
together the abductions of Iô and of
Eurôpê, of Mêdea and of Helen, as
pairs of connected proceedings, the
second injury being a retaliation for
the first,—they drew up a debtor and
creditor account of abductions between
Asia and Europe. The Kolchian king
(they said) had sent a herald to Greece
to ask for his satisfaction for the wrong
done to him by Jasôn and to re-demand
his daughter Mêdea ; but he was told
in reply that the Greeks had received
no satisfaction for the previous rape of
Iô.

There was some ingenuity in thus
binding together the old fables, so as
to represent the invasions of Greece by
Darius and Xerxês as retaliations for
the unexpiated destruction wrought by
Agamemnôn.

in success, and consoling to him in difficulty, to believe that their journeys had brought them over the ground which he was himself traversing. There was no tale amidst the wide range of the Grecian epic more calculated to be popular with the seaman than the history of the primæval ship Argô, and her distinguished crew, comprising heroes from all parts of Greece, and especially the Tyndarids Kastôr and Pollux, the heavenly protectors invoked during storm and peril. He localised the legend anew wherever he went, often with some fresh circumstances suggested either by his own adventures or by the scene before him. He took a sort of religious possession of the spot, connecting it by a bond of faith with his native land, and erecting in it a temple or an altar with appropriate commemorative solemnities. The Jasonium thus established, and indeed every visible object called after the name of the hero, not only served to keep alive the legend of the Argô in the minds of future comers or inhabitants, but was accepted as an obvious and satisfactory proof that this marvellous vessel had actually touched there in her voyage.

The epic poets, building both on the general love of fabulous incident and on the easy faith of the people, dealt with distant and unknown space in the same manner as with past and unrecorded time. They created a mythical geography for the former, and a mythical history for the latter. But there was this material difference between the two: that while the unrecorded time was beyond the reach of verification, the unknown space gradually became trodden and examined. In proportion as authentic local knowledge was enlarged, it became necessary to modify the geography, or shift the scene of action, of the old mythes; and this perplexing problem was undertaken by some of the ablest historians and geographers of antiquity,—for it was painful to them to abandon any portion of the old epic, as if it were destitute of an ascertainable basis of truth.

Fabulous geography—gradually modified as real geographical knowledge increased.

Many of these fabulous localities are to be found in Homer and Hesiod, and the other Greek poets and logographers,—Erytheia, the garden of the Hesperides, the garden of Phœbus,[1] to which Boreas transported the Attic maiden Oreithyia, the delicious

---

[1] Sophokl. ap. Strab., vii. p. 295.—
Ὑπέρ τε πόντον πάντ᾽ ἐπ᾽ ἔσχατα χθονὸς,
Νυκτός τε πηγὰς οὐρανοῦ τ᾽ ἀναπτυχὰς,
Φοίβου τε παλαιὸν κῆπον.

1—15

country of the Hyperboreans, the Elysian plain,[1] the floating
island of Æolus, Thrinakia, the country of the Æthiopians, the
Læstrygones, the Kyklôpes, the Lotophagi, the Sirens, the Cim-
merians and the Gorgons,[2] &c.   These are places which (to use
the expression of Pindar respecting the Hyperboreans) you cannot
approach either by sea or by land :[3] the wings of the poet alone
can carry you thither.   They were not introduced into the Greek
mind by incorrect geographical reports, but, on the contrary,
had their origin in the legend, and passed from thence into the
realities of geography,[4] which they contributed much to pervert
and confuse.   For the navigator or emigrant, starting with an
unsuspicious faith in their real existence, looked out for them in
his distant voyages, and constantly fancied that he had seen or
heard of them, so as to be able to identify their exact situation.
The most contradictory accounts indeed, as might be expected,
were often given respecting the latitude and longitude of such
fanciful spots, but this did not put an end to the general belief
in their real existence.

In the present advanced state of geographical knowledge, the
story of that man who after reading Gulliver's Travels went to
look in his map for Lilliput, appears an absurdity.   But those
who fixed the exact locality of the floating island of Æolus or
the rocks of the Sirens did much the same ;[5] and, with their
ignorance of geography and imperfect appreciation of historical

[1] Odyss. iv. 562. The islands of the
blessed, in Hesiod, are near the ocean
(Opp. Di. 169).
[2] Hesiod.Theogon. 275—290. Homer,
Iliad, i. 423. Odyss. i. 23 ; ix. 86—206 ;
x. 4—83 ; xii. 135. Mimnerm. Fragm.
13, Schneidewin.
[3] Pindar, Pyth. x. 29.—

Ναυσὶ δ' οὔτε πεζὸς ἰὼν ἂν εὕροις
Ἐς Ὑπερβορέων ἀγῶνα θαυματὰν ὁδόν.
Παρ' οἷς ποτε Περσεὺς ἐδαίσατο λαγέτας,
        &c.

Hesiod, and the old epic poem called
the Epigoni, both mentioned the
Hyperboreans (Herod. iv. 32—34).
[4] This idea is well stated and
sustained by Völcker (Mythische
Geographie der Griechen und Römer,
cap. i. p. 11), and by Nitzsch in his
Comments on the Odyssey—Introduct.
Remarks to b. ix. p. xii.—xxxiii. The
twelfth and thirteenth chapters of the
History of Orchomenos, by O Müller,

are also full of good remarks on the
geography of the Argonautic voyage
(pp. 274—299).
    The most striking evidence of this
disposition of the Greeks is to be
found in the legendary discoveries of
Alexander and his companions, when
they marched over the untrodden
regions in the east of the Persian
empire (see Arrian, Hist. Al. v. 3:
compare Lucian, Dialog. Mortuor. xiv.
vol. i. p. 212, Tauch.), because these
ideas were first broached at a time
when geographical science was sufficiently advanced to canvass and
criticise them. The early settlers in
Italy, Sicily, and the Euxine, indulged
their fanciful vision without the fear
of any such monitor: there was no
such thing as a map before the days of
Anaximander, the disciple of Thalês.
[5] See Mr. Payne Knight, Prolegg. ad
Homer. c. 49. Compare Spohn—"de
extremâ Odysseæ parte "—p. 97.

evidence, the error was hardly to be avoided. The ancient belief which fixed the Sirens on the islands of Sirenusæ off the coast of Naples—the Kyklôpes, Erytheia, and the Læstrygones in Sicily—the Lotophagi on the island of Mêninx[1] near the Lesser Syrtis—the Phæakians at Korkyra—and the goddess Circê at the promontory of Circeium—took its rise at a time when these regions were first Hellenised and comparatively little visited. Once embodied in the local legends, and attested by visible monuments and ceremonies, it continued for a long time unassailed; and Thucydidês seems to adopt it, in reference to Korkyra and Sicily before the Hellenic colonisation, as matter of fact generally unquestionable,[2] though little avouched as to details. But when geographical knowledge became extended, and the criticism upon the ancient epic was more or less systematised by the literary men of Alexandria and Pergamus, it appeared to many of them impossible that Odysseus could have seen so many wonders or undergone such monstrous dangers, within limits so narrow, and in the familiar track between the Nile and the Tiber.. The scene of his weather-driven course was then shifted farther westward. Many convincing evidences were discovered, especially by Asklepiadês of Myrlea, of his having visited various places in Iberia:[3] several critics imagined that he had wandered about in the

---

[1] Strabo, xvii. p. 834. An altar of Odysseus was shown upon this island, as well as some other evidences (σύμβολα) of his visit to the place.

Apollônius Rhodius copies the Odyssey in speaking of the island of Thrinakia and the cattle of Helios (iv. 965, with Schol.). He conceives Sicily as Thrinakia, a name afterwards exchanged for Trinakria. The Scholiast ad Apoll. (l. c.) speaks of Trinax king of Sicily. Compare iv. 291 with the Scholia.

[2] Thucyd. i. 25—vi. 2. These local legends appear in the eyes of Strabo convincing evidence (i. p. 23—26),—the tomb of the siren Parthenopê at Naples, the stories at Cumæ and Dikæarchia about the νεκυομαντεῖον of Avernus, and the existence of places named after Baius and Misênus, the companions of Odysseus, &c.

[3] Strabo, iii. p. 150—157. Οὐ γὰρ μόνον οἱ κατὰ τὴν Ἰταλίαν καὶ Σικελίαν τόποι καὶ ἄλλοι τινὲς τῶν τοιούτων σημεῖα ὑπογράφουσιν, ἀλλὰ καὶ ἐν τῇ Ἰβηρίᾳ Ὀδύσσεια πόλις δείκνυται, καὶ Ἀθηνᾶς

ἱερὸν, καὶ ἄλλα μύρια ἴχνη τῆς ἐκείνου πλάνης, καὶ ἄλλων τῶν ἐκ τοῦ Τρωϊκοῦ πολέμου περιγενομένων (I adopt Grosskurd's correction of the text from γενομένων to περιγενομένων, in the note to his German translation of Strabo).

Asklepiadês (of Myrlea in Bithynia, about 170 B.C.) resided some time in Turditania, the south-western region of Spain along the Guadalquivir, as a teacher of Greek literature (παιδεύσας τὰ γραμματικὰ), and composed a periegesis of the Iberian tribes, which unfortunately has not been preserved. He made various discoveries in archæology, and successfully connected his old legends with several portions of the territory before him. His discoveries were,—1. In the temple of Athênê, at this Iberian town of Odysseia, there were shields and beaks of ships affixed to the walls, monuments of the visit of Odysseus himself. 2. Among the Kallæki, in the northern part of Portugal, several of the companions of Teukros had settled and left descendants: there

Atlantic Ocean outside of the Strait of Gibraltar,[1] and they
Transposi-
tion of
epical
localities. recognised a section of Lotophagi on the coast of
Mauritania, over and above those who dwelt on the
island of Mêninx.[2] On the other hand, Eratosthenês
and Apollodôrus treated the places visited by Odysseus as
altogether unreal, for which scepticism they incurred much
reproach.[3]

The fabulous island of Erytheia,—the residence of the three-
headed Geryôn with his magnificent herd of oxen, under the
custody of the two-headed dog Orthrus, described by Hesiod, like
the garden of the Hesperides, as extra-terrestrial, on the farther
side of the circumfluous ocean,—this island was supposed, by
the interpreters of Stesichorus the poet, to be named by him off
the south-western region of Spain called Tartêssus, and in the
immediate vicinity of Gadês. But the historian Hekatæus, in
his anxiety to historicise the old fable, took upon himself to
remove Erytheia from Spain nearer home to Epirus. He thought
it incredible that Hêraklês should have traversed Europe from
east to west, for the purpose of bringing the cattle of Geryôn to
Eurystheus at Mykênæ, and he pronounced Geryôn to have been
a king of Epirus, near the Gulf of Ambrakia. The oxen reared

were in that region two Grecian cities,
one called Hellenês, the other called
Amphilochi; for Amphilochus also,
the son of Amphiaraus, had died in
Iberia, and many of his soldiers had
taken up their permanent residence in
the interior. 3. Many new inhabitants
had come into Iberia with the expedition of Hêraklês; some also after
the conquest of Messênê by the
Lacedæmônians. 4. In Cantabria, on
the north coast of Spain, there was a
town and region of Lacedæmonian
colonists. 5. In the same portion of
the country there was the town of
Opsikella, founded by Opsikellas, one
of the companions of Antênôr in his
emigration from Troy (Strabo, iii. p.
157).

This is a specimen of the manner in
which the seeds of Grecian mythus
came to be distributed over so large
a surface. To an ordinary Greek
reader, these legendary discoveries of
Asklepiadês would probably be more
interesting than the positive facts
which he communicated respecting the
Iberian tribes; and his Turditanian

auditors would be delighted to hear—
while he was reciting and explaining
to them the animated passage of the
Iliad, in which Agamemnôn extols
the inestimable value of the bow of
Teukros (viii. 281)—that the heroic
archer and his companions had actually
set foot in the Iberian peninsula.

[1] This was the opinion of Kratês of
Mallus, one of the most distinguished
of the critics on Homer: it was the
subject of an animated controversy
between him and Aristarchus (Aulus
Gellius, N. A. xiv. 6; Strabo, iii. p.
157). See the instructive treatise of
Lehrs, De Aristarchi Studiis, c. v. §. 4.
p. 251. Much controversy also took
place among the critics respecting the
ground which Menelaus went over in
his wanderings (Odyss. iv.). Kratês
affirmed that he had circumnavigated
the southern extremity of Africa and
gone to India: the critic Aristonikus,
Strabo's contemporary, enumerated
all the different opinions (Strabo, i.
p. 38).

[2] Strabo, iii. p. 157.

[3] Strabo, i. p. 22—44; vii. p. 299.

in that neighbourhood were proverbially magnificent, and to get them even from thence and bring them to Mykênæ (he contended) was no inconsiderable task.　Arrian, who cites this passage from Hekatæus, concurs in the same view,—an illustration of the licence with which ancient authors fitted on their fabulous geographical names to the real earth, and brought down the ethereal matter of legend to the lower atmosphere of history.[1]

Both the track and the terminus of the Argonautic voyage appear in the most ancient epic as little within the conditions of reality, as the speaking timbers or the semi-divine crew of the vessel.　In the Odyssey, Æêtês and Circê (Hesiod names Mêdea also) are brother and sister, offspring of Hêlios.　The Ææan island, adjoining the circumfluous ocean, "where the house and dancing-ground of Eôs are situated, and where Hêlios rises," is both the residence of Circê and of Æêtês, inasmuch as How and Odysseus, in returning from the former, follows the when the Argonautic same course as the Argo had previously taken in voyage returning from the latter.[2]　Even in the conception became attachcd to of Mimnermus, about 600 B.C., Æa still retained its Kolchis. fabulous attributes in conjunction with the ocean and Hêlios, without having been yet identified with any known portion of the solid earth ;[3] and it was justly remarked by Dêmêtrius of

[1] Stesichori Fragm. ed. Kleine; Geryonis Fr. 5. p. 60 ; ap. Strab., iii. p. 148 ; Herodot. iv. 8. It seems very doubtful whether Stesichorus meant to indicate any neighbouring island as Erytheia, if we compare Fragm. 10. p. 67 of the Geryonis, and the passages of Athenæus and Eustathius there cited. He seems to have adhered to the old fable, placing Erytheia on the opposite side of the ocean-stream, for Hêraklês crosses the ocean to get to it. Hekatæus, ap. Arrian. Histor. Alex. ii. 16. Skylax places Erytheia, "whither Geryôn is said to have come to feed his oxen," in the Kastid territory near the Greek city of Apollônia on the Ionic Gulf, northward of the Keraunian mountains. There were splendid cattle consecrated to Hêlios near Apollônia, watched by the citizens of the place with great care (Herodot. ix. 93 ; Skylax, c. 26).
About Erytheia, Cellarius observes (Geogr. Ant. ii. 1, 127), "Insula Erytheia, quam veteres adjungunt Gadibus, vel demersa est, vel in scopulis quærenda, vel pars est ipsarum Gadium, neque hodie ejus formæ aliqua, uti descripta est, fertur superesse". To make the disjunctive catalogue complete, he ought to have added, "or it never really existed,"— not the least probable supposition of all.
[2] Hesiod, Theogon. 956—992; Homer, Odyss. xii. 3—69.—

Νῆσον ἐν Αἰαίην, ὅθι τ' Ἠοῦς ἠριγενείης
Οἰκία καὶ χόροι εἰσὶ, καὶ ἀντολαὶ ἠελίοιο.

[3] Mimnerm. Fr. 10—11, Schneidewin; Athenæ. vii. p. 277.—

Οὐδέ κοτ' ἄν μέγα κῶας ἀνήγαγεν αὐτὸς
Ἰήσων
Ἐξ Αἴης τελέσας ἀλγινόεσσαν ὁδὸν,
Ὑβρίστῃ Πελίῃ τελέων χαλεπῆρες ἄεθλον,
Οὐδ' ἄν ἐπ' Ὠκεανοῦ καλὸν ἵκοντο ῥόον.

*　*　*　*　*　*　*

Αἰήταο πόλιν, τόθι τ' ὠκέος Ἡελίοιο
Ἀκτῖνες χρυσέῳ κείαται ἐν θαλάμῳ,
Ὠκεανοῦ παρὰ χείλεσ', ἵν' ᾤχετο θεῖος
Ἰήσων.

Skêpsis in antiquity[1] (though Strabo vainly tries to refute him), that neither Homer nor Mimnermus designates Kolchis either as the residence of Æêtês, or as the terminus of the Argonautic voyage. Hesiod carried the returning Argonauts through the river Phasis into the ocean. But some of the poems ascribed to Eumêlus were the first which mentioned Æêtês and Kolchis, and interwove both of them into the Corinthian mythical genealogy.[2] These poems seem to have been composed subsequent to the foundation of Sinopê, and to the commencement of Grecian settlement on the Borysthenês, between the years 600 and 500 B.C. The Greek mariners who explored and colonised the southern coast of the Euxine, found at the extremity of their voyage the river Phasis and its barbarous inhabitants : it was the easternmost point which Grecian navigation (previous to the time of Alexander the Great) ever attained, and it was within sight of the impassable barrier of Caucasus.[3] They believed, not unnaturally, that they had here found "the house of Eôs (the morning) and the rising-place of the sun," and that the river Phasis, if they could follow it to its unknown beginning, would conduct them to the circum-fluous ocean. They gave to the spot the name of Æa, and the fabulous and real title gradually became associated together into one compound appellation,—the Kolchian Æa, or Æa of Kolchis.[4] While Kolchis was thus entered on the map as a fit representative for the Homeric "house of the morning," the narrow strait of the Thracian Bosphorus attracted to itself the poetical fancy of the Symplêgades, or colliding rocks, through which the heaven-protected Argô had been the first to pass. The powerful Greek cities of Kyzikus, Hêrakleia, and Sinopê, each fertile in local legends, still farther contributed to give this direction to the voyage ; so that in the time of Hekatæus it had become the

---

[1] Strabo, i. p. 45—46. Δημήτριος ὁ Σκήψιος . . . πρὸς Νεάνθη τὸν Κυζικηνὸν φιλοτιμοτέρως ἀντιλέγων, εἰπόντα, ὅτι οἱ Ἀργοναῦται πλέοντες εἰς Φᾶσιν τὸν ὑφ' Ὁμήρου καὶ τῶν ἄλλων ὁμολογούμενον πλοῦν, ἱδρύσαντο τὰ τῆς Ἰδαίας μητρὸς ἱερὰ ἐπὶ Κύζικον . . . ἀρχήν φησι μηδ' εἰδέναι τὴν εἰς Φᾶσιν ἀποδημίαν τοῦ Ἰάσονος Ὅμηρον. Again, p. 46, παραλαβὼν μάρτυρα Μίμνερμον, ὃς ἐν τῷ Ὠκεανῷ ποιήσας οἴκησιν Αἰήτου, &c. The adverb φιλοτιμοτέρως reveals to us the municipal rivalry and contention between the small town Skêpsis and its neighbour Kyzikus, respecting points of comparative archæology.

[2] Eumêlus, Fragm. Εὐρωπία 7, Κορινθιακά 2—5, pp. 63—68, Düntzer.

[3] Arrian, Periplus Pont. Euxin. p. 12; ap. Geogr. Minor. vol. i. He saw the Caucasus from Dioskurias.

[4] Herodot. i. 2; vii. 193—197. Eurip. Med. 2. Valer. Flacc. v. 51.

established belief that the Argô had started from Iôlkos and gone to Kolchis.

Æêtês thus received his home from the legendary faith and fancy of the eastern Greek navigators: his sister Circê, originally his fellow-resident, was localised by the western. **Æêtês and Circê.** The Hesiodic and other poems, giving expression to the imaginative impulses of the inhabitants of Cumæ and other early Grecian settlers in Italy and Sicily,[1] had referred the wanderings of Odysseus to the western or Tyrrhenian sea, and had planted the Kyklôpes, the Læstrygones, the floating island of Æolus, the Lotophagi, the Phæakians, &c., about the coast of Sicily, Italy, Libya, and Korkyra. In this way the Ææan island—the residence of Circê, and the extreme point of the wanderings of Odysseus, from whence he passes only to the ocean and into Hadês—came to be placed in the far west, while the Æa of Æêtês was in the far east—not unlike our East and West Indies. The Homeric brother and sister were separated and sent to opposite extremities of the Grecian terrestrial horizon.[2]

The track from Iôlkis to Kolchis, however, though plausible as far as it went, did not realize all the conditions of the genuine fabulous voyage : it did not explain the evidences of the visit of these maritime heroes which were to be found in Libya, in Krête, in Anaphê, in Korkyra, in the Adriatic Gulf, in Italy, and in Æthalia. It became necessary to devise another route for them in their **Return of the Argonauts— different versions.**

[1] Strabo, i. p. 23. Völcker (Ueber Homerische Geographie, v. 66) is instructive upon this point, as upon the geography of the Greek poets generally. He recognises the purely mythical character of Æa in Homer and Hesiod, but he tries to prove— unsuccessfully in my judgment—that Homer places Æêtês in the east, while Circê is in the west, and that Homer refers the Argonautic voyage to the Euxine Sea.

[2] Strabo (or Polybius, whom he has just been citing) contends that Homer knew the existence of Æêtês in Kolchis, and of Circê at Circeium, as historical persons, as well as the voyage of Jason to Æa as an historical fact. Upon this he (Homer) built a superstructure of fiction (προσμύθευμα): he invented the brotherhood between them, and he placed both the one and the other in the exterior ocean (συγγενείας τε ἔπλασε τῶν οὕτω διῳκισμένων, καὶ ἐξωκεανισμὸν ἀμφοῖν, i. p. 20) ; perhaps also Jasôn might have wandered as far as Italy, as evidences (σημεῖά τινα) are shown that he did (ib.).

But the idea that Homer conceived Æêtês in the extreme east and Circê in the extreme west, is not reconcileable with the Odyssey. The supposition of Strabo is alike violent and unsatisfactory.

Circê was worshipped as a goddess at Circeii (Cicero, Nat. Deor. iii. 19). Hesiod, in the Theogony, represents the two sons of Circê by Odysseus as reigning over all the warlike Tyrrhenians (Theog. 1012), an undefined western sovereignty. The great Mamilian gens at Tusculum traced their descent to Odysseus and Circê (Dionys. Hal. iv. 45).

return, and the Hesiodic narrative was (as I have before observed), that they came back by the circumfluous ocean: first going up the river Phasis into the circumfluous ocean: then following that deep and gentle stream until they entered the Nile, and came down its course to the coast of Libya. This seems also to have been the belief of Hekatæus.[1] But presently several Greeks (and Herodotus amongst them) began to discard the idea of a circumfluous ocean-stream, which had pervaded their old geographical and astronomical fables, and which explained the supposed easy communication between one extremity of the earth and another. Another idea was then started for the returning voyage of the Argonauts. It was supposed that the river Ister, or Danube, flowing from the Rhipæan mountains in the north-west of Europe, divided itself into two branches, one of which fell into the Euxine sea, and the other into the Adriatic.

The Argonauts, fleeing from the pursuit of Æêtês, had been obliged to abandon their regular course homeward, and had gone from the Euxine sea up the Ister; then passing down the other branch of that river, they had entered into the Adriatic, the Kolchian pursuers following them. Such is the story given by Apollônius Rhodius from Timagêtus, and accepted even by so able a geographer as Eratosthenês—who preceded him by one generation, and who, though sceptical in regard to the localities visited by Odysseus, seems to have been a firm believer in the reality of the Argonautic voyage.[2] Other historians again, among

---

[1] There is an opinion cited from Hekatæus in Schol. Apoll. Rhod. iv. 284, contrary to this, which is given by the same scholiast on iv. 259. But, in spite of the remarks of Clausen (ad Fragment. Hekatæi, 187, p. 98), I think that the Schol. ad iv. 284 has made a mistake in citing Hekatæus; the more so, as the scholiast, as printed from the Codex Parisinus, cites the same opinion without mentioning Hekatæus. According to the old Homeric idea, the ocean-stream flowed all round the earth, and was the source of all the principal rivers which flowed into the great internal sea, or Mediterranean (see Hekatæus, Fr. 349; Klausen, ap. Arrian. ii. 16, where he speaks of the Mediterranean as the μεγάλη θάλασσα). Retaining this old idea of the ocean-stream,

Hekatæus would naturally believe that the Phasis joined it: nor can I agree with Klansen (ad Fr. 187) that this implies a degree of ignorance too gross to impute to him.

[2] Apollôn. Rhod. iv. 287; Schol. ad iv. 284; Pindar, Pyth. iv. 447, with Schol.; Strabo, i. p. 46—57; Aristot. Mirabil. Auscult. c. 105. Altars were shown in the Adriatic, which had been erected both by Jason and by Médea (ib.).

Aristotle believed in the forked course of the Ister, with one embouchure in the Euxine and another in the Adriatic: he notices certain fishes called τρίχιαι, who entered the river (like the Argonauts) from the Euxine, went up it as far as the point of bifurcation and descended into the Adriatic (Histor. Animal. viii. 15)

whom was Timæus, though they considered the ocean as an outer sea, and no longer admitted the existence of the old Homeric ocean-stream, yet imagined a story for the return-voyage of the Argonauts somewhat resembling the old tale of Hesiod and Hekatæus. They alleged that the Argô, after entering into the Palus Mæôtis, had followed the upward course of the river Tanais ; that she had then been carried overland and launched in a river which had its mouth in the ocean or great outer sea. When in the ocean, she had coasted along the north and west of Europe until she reached Gadês and the strait of Gibraltar, where she entered into the Mediterranean, and there visited the many places specified in the fable. Of this long voyage, in the outer sea to the north and west of Europe, many traces were affirmed to exist along the coast of the ocean.[1] There was again a third version, according to which the Argonauts came back as they went, through the Thracian Bosporus and the Hellespont. In this way geographical plausibility was indeed maintained, but a large portion of the fabulous matter was thrown overboard.[2]

Such were the various attempts made to reconcile the Argonautic legend with enlarged geographical knowledge and improved historical criticism. The problem remained unsolved, but the faith in the legend did not the less continue. It was a faith originally generated at a time when the unassisted narrative of the inspired poet sufficed for the conviction of his hearers ; it consecrated one among the capital exploits of that heroic and super-human race, whom the Greek was accustomed at once to look back upon as his ancestors and to worship conjointly with his gods : it lay too deep in his mind either to require historical evidence for its support, or to be overthrown by geographical difficulties as they were then appreciated. Supposed traces of the past event, either preserved in the names of places, or embodied

Compare Ukert, Geographie der Griechen und Römer, vol. iii. p. 145—147, about the supposed course of the Ister.

[1] Diodôr. iv. 56 ; Timæus, Fragm. 53, Göller. Skymnus the geographer also adopted this opinion (Schol. Apoll. Rhod. 284—287). The pseudo-Orpheus in the poem called Argonautica seems to give a jumble of all the different stories.

[2] Diodôr. iv. 49. This was the tale both of Sophoklês and of Kallimachus (Schol. Apoll. Rhod. iv. 284).

See the Dissertation of Ukert, Beylage iv. vol. i. part 2, p. 320 of his Geographie der Griechen und Römer, which treats of the Argonautic voyage at some length ; also J. H. Voss, Alte Weltkunde über die Gestalt der Erde, published in the second volume of the Kritische Blätter, pp. 162, 314—326 ; and Forbiger, Handbuch der Alten Geographie, Einleitung, p. 8.

in standing religious customs with their explanatory comments,
Continued   served as sufficient authentication in the eyes of the
faith in the curious inquirer. And even men trained in a more
voyage—
basis of   severe school of criticism contented themselves with
truth deter- eliminating the palpable contradictions and softening
mined by
Strabo.   down the supernatural and romantic events, so as
to produce an Argonautic expedition of their own invention as
the true and accredited history. Strabo, though he can neither
overlook nor explain the geographical impossibilities of the
narrative, supposes himself to have discovered the basis of actual
fact, which the original poets had embellished or exaggerated.
The golden fleece was typical of the great wealth of Kolchis,
arising from gold-dust washed down by the rivers ; and the voyage
of Jasôn was in reality an expedition at the head of a considerable
army, with which he plundered this wealthy country and made
extensive conquests in the interior.[1] Strabo has nowhere laid
down what he supposes to have been the exact measure and
direction of Jasôn's march, but he must have regarded it as very
long, since he classes Jasôn with Dionysus and Hêraklês, and
emphatically characterises all the three as having traversed
wider spaces of ground than any moderns could equal.[2] Such was
the compromise which a mind like that of Strabo made with the
ancient legends. He shaped or cut them down to the level of
his own credence, and in this waste of historical criticism,
without any positive evidence, he took to himself the credit of
greater penetration than the literal believers, while he escaped
the necessity of breaking formally with the bygone heroic world.

[1] Strabo, i. p. 45. He speaks here
of the voyage of Phryxus, as well as
that of Jasôn, as having been a military
undertaking (στρατεία): so again, iii. p.
149, he speaks of the military expedition
of Odysseus—ἡ τοῦ Ὀδυσσέως στρατία,
and ἡ Ἡρακλέους στρατία (ib.). Again,
xi. p. 498. Οἱ μῦθοι, αἰνιττόμενοι τὴν
Ἰάσονος στρατείαν προελθόντος μέχρι
καὶ Μηδίας· ἔτι δὲ πρότερον τὴν Φρίξου.
Compare also Justin, xlii. 2—3 ; Tacit.
Annal. vi. 34.
    Strabo cannot speak of the old fables
with literal fidelity : he unconsciously
transforms them into quasi-historical
incidents of his own imagination.

Diodôrus gives a narrative of the same
kind, with decent substitutes for the
fabulous elements (iv. 40—47—56).
    [2] Strabo, i. p. 48. The far-extending
expeditions undertaken in the eastern
regions by Dionysus and Hêraklês were
constantly present to the mind of
Alexander the Great as subjects of
comparison with himself : he imposed
upon his followers perilous and trying
marches, from anxiety to equal or
surpass the alleged exploits of
Semiramis, Cyrus, Perseus, and
Hêraklês. (Arrian, v. 2, 3 ; vi. 24, 3 ;
vii. 10, 12. Strabo, iii. p. 171 ; xv. p.
686 ; xvii. p. 81.

CHAPTER XIV.

LEGENDS OF THÊBES.

THE Bœotians generally, throughout the historical age, though well endowed with bodily strength and courage,[1] are represented as proverbially deficient in intelligence, taste, and fancy. But the legendary population of Thêbes, the Kadmeians, are rich in mythical antiquities, divine as well as heroic. Both Dionysus and Hêraklês recognise Thêbes as their natal city. Moreover, the two sieges of Thêbes by Adrastus, even taken apart from Kadmus, Antiopê, Amphiôn, and Zêthus, &c., are the most prominent and most characteristic exploits, next to the siege of Troy, of that pre-existing race of heroes who lived in the imagination of the historical Hellênes.

Abundant legends of Thêbes.

It is not Kadmus, but the brothers Amphiôn and Zêthus, who are given to us in the Odyssey as the first founders of Thêbes and the first builders of its celebrated walls. They are the sons of Zeus by Antiopê, daughter of Asôpus. The scholiasts, who desire to reconcile this tale with the more current account of the foundation of Thêbes by Kadmus, tell us that after the death of Amphiôn and Zêthus, Eurymachus, the warlike king of the Phlegyæ, invaded and ruined the newly-settled town,

Amphiôn and Zêthus Homeric founders of Thêbes. Kadmus and Bœôtus —both distinct legends.

---

[1] The eponym Bœôtus is son of Poseidôn and Arnë (Euphorion ap. Eustath. ad Iliad. ii. 507). It was from Arnê in Thessaly that the Bœôtians were said to have come, when they invaded and occupied Bœôtia. Euripidês made him son of Poseidôn and Melanippê. Another legend recited Bœôtus and Hellên as sons of Poseidôn and Antiopê (Hygin. f. 157—186).

The Tanagræan poetess Korinna (the rival of Pindar, whose compositions in the Bœôtian dialect are unfortunately lost) appears to have dwelt upon this native Bœôtian genealogy: she derived the Ogygian gates of Thêbes from Ogygus, son of Bœôtus (Schol. Apollôn. Rhod. iii. 1178), also the Fragments of Korinna in Schneidewin's edition, fr. 2, p. 432.

so that Kadmus on arriving was obliged to re-found it.[1] But Apollodôrus, and seemingly the older logographers before him, placed Kadmus at the top, and inserted the two brothers at a lower point in the series. According to them, Bêlus and Agênôr were the sons of Epaphus (son of the Argeian Iô) by Libya. Agênôr went to Phœnicia and there became king: he had for his offspring Kadmus, Phœnix, Kilix, and a daughter Eurôpa ; though in the Iliad Eurôpa is called daughter of Phœnix.[2] Zeus fell in love with Eurôpa, and assuming the shape of a bull, carried her across the sea upon his back from Egypt to Crête, where she bore to him Minôs, Rhadamanthus, and Sarpêdôn. Two out of the three sons sent out by Agênôr in search of their lost sister, wearied out by a long-protracted as well as fruitless voyage, abandoned the idea of returning home : Kilix settled in Kilikia, and Kadmus in Thrace.[3] Thasus, the brother or nephew of Kadmus, who had accompanied them in the voyage, settled and gave name to the island of Thasus.

Both Herodotus and Euripidês represent Kadmus as an emigrant from Phœnicia, conducting a body of followers in quest of Eurôpa. The account of Apollodôrus describes him as having come originally from Libya or Egypt to Phœnicia : we may presume that this was also the statement of the earlier logographers Pherekydês and Hellanikus. Conôn, who historicises and politicises the whole legend, seems to have found two different accounts : one connecting Kadmus with Egypt, another bringing him from Phœnicia. He tries to melt down the two into one, by representing that the Phœnicians, who sent out Kadmus, had acquired great power in Egypt—that the seat of their kingdom was the Egyptian Thêbes—that Kadmus was despatched, under pretence indeed of finding his lost sister, but really on a project

---

[1] Homer, Odyss. xi. 262, and Eustath. ad loc. Compare Schol. ad Iliad. xii. 301.

[2] Iliad, xiv. 321. Iô is κερόεσσα προμάτωρ of the Thêbans. Eurip. Phœniss. 247—676.

[3] Apollodôr. ii. 1, 8; iii. 1, 8. In the Hesiodic poems (ap. Schol. Apoll. Rhod. ii. 178) Phœnix was recognised as son of Agênôr. Pherekydês also described both Phœnix and Kadmus as sons of Agênôr (Pherekyd. Fragm. 40, Didot).

Compare Servius ad Virgil. Æneid. i. 338. Pherekydês expressly mentioned Kilix (Apollod. ib.). Besides the Εὑρώπεια of Stesichorus (see Stesichor. Fragm. xv. p. 73, ed. Kleine), there were several other ancient poems on the adventures of Eurôpa : one in particular by Eumêlus (Schol. ad Iliad. vi. 138), which, however, can hardly be the same as the τὰ ἔπη τὰ εἰς Εὑρώπην allnded to by Pausanias (ix. 5, 4). See Wüllner de Cyclo Epico, p. 57 (Münster, 1825).

of conquest—and that the name Thêbes, which he gave to his new establishment in Bœotia, was borrowed from Thêbes in Egypt, his ancestorial seat.[1]

Kadmus went from Phœnicia to Thrace, and from Thrace to Delphi to procure information respecting his sister Eurôpa, but the god directed him to take no further trouble about her ; he was to follow the guidance of a cow, and to found a city on the spot where the animal should lie down. The condition was realised on the site of Thêbes. The neighbouring fountain Areia was guarded by a fierce dragon, the offspring of Arês, who destroyed all the persons sent to fetch water. Kadmus killed the dragon, and at the suggestion of Athênê sowed the dragon's teeth in the earth :[2] there sprang up at once the armed men called the Sparti, among whom he flung stones, and they immediately began to assault each other until all were slain except five. Arês, indignant at this slaughter, was about to kill Kadmus ; but Zeus appeased him, condemning Kadmus to an expiatory servitude of eight years, after which he married Harmonia, the daughter of Arês and Aphroditê— presenting to her the splendid necklace fabricated by the hand of Hêphæstos, which had been given by Zeus to Eurôpa.[3] All the gods came to the Kadmeia, the citadel of Thêbes, to present congratulations and gifts at these nuptials, which seem to have been hardly less celebrated in the mythical world than those of Pêleus and Thetis. The issue of the marriage was one son, Polydôrus, and four daughters, Autonoê, Inô, Semelê and Agavê.[4]

How Thêbes was founded by Kadmus.

[1] Conôn, Narrat. 37. Perhaps the most remarkable thing of all is the tone of unbounded self-confidence with which Conôn winds up this tissue of uncertified suppositions—περὶ μὲν Κάδμου καὶ Θηβῶν οἰκίσεως οὗτος ὁ ἀληθὴς λόγος· τὸ δὲ ἄλλο μῦθος καὶ γοητεία ἀκοῆς.

[2] Stesichor. (Fragm. 16, Kleine) ap. Schol. Eurip. Phœniss. 680. The place where the heifer had lain down was still shown in the time of Pausanias (ix. 12, 1).

Lysimachus, a lost author who wrote Thebaïca, mentioned Eurôpa as having come with Kadmus to Thêbes, and told the story in many other respects very differently (Schol. Apoll. Rhod. iii. 1179).

[3] Apollodor. iii. 4, 1—3. Pherekydês

gave this account of the necklace, which seems to imply that Kadmus must have found his sister Eurôpa. The narrative here given is from Hellanikus ; that of Pherekydês differed from it in some respects ; compare Hellanik. Fragm. 8 and 9, and Pherekyd. Frag. 44. The resemblance of this story with that of Jasôn and Æêtês (see above, chap. xiii.) will strike every one. It is curious to observe how the old logographer Pherekydês explained this analogy in his narrative; he said that Athênê had given half the dragon's teeth to Kadmus and half to Æêtês (see Schol. Pindar. Isthm. vi. 13).

[4] Hesiod, Theogon. 976. Leukothea, the sea-goddess, daughter of Kadmus, is mentioned in the Odyssey, v. 334 : Diodôr. iv. 2.

From the five who alone survived of the warriors sprung from
the dragon's teeth, arose five great families or gentes
in Thêbes ; the oldest and noblest of its inhabitants,
coeval with the foundation of the town.   They were
called Sparti, and their name seems to have given rise,
not only to the fable of the sowing of the teeth, but
also to other etymological narratives.[1]

Five primitive families at Thêbes, called Sparti.

All the four daughters of Kadmus are illustrious in fabulous
history.   Inô, wife of Athamas, the son of Æolus, has
already been included among the legends of the Æolids.
Semelê became the mistress of Zeus, and inspired Hêrê
with jealousy.   Misguided by the malicious suggestions of that
goddess, she solicited Zeus to visit her with all the solemnity and
terrors which surrounded him when he approached Hêrê herself.
The god unwillingly consented, and came in his chariot in the
midst of thunder and lightning, under which awful accompaniments the mortal frame of Semelê perished.   Zeus,
taking from her the child of which she was pregnant,
sewed it into his own thigh : after the proper interval the child
was brought out and born, and became the great god Dionysus
or Bacchus.   Hermês took him to Inô and Athamas to receive
their protection.   Afterwards, however, Zeus having transformed
him into a kid to conceal him from the persecution of Hêrê, the
nymphs of the mountain Nysa became his nurses.[2]

The four daughters of Kadmus —1. Inô.

2. Semelê.

Autonoê, the third daughter of Kadmus, married the pastoral
hero or god Aristæus, and was mother of Aktæôn, a
devoted hunter and a favourite companion of the goddess Artêmis.   She however became displeased with
him—either because he looked into a fountain while she was
bathing and saw her naked—or, according to the legend set forth
by the poet Stesichorus, because he loved and courted Semelê —
or, according to Euripidês, because he presumptuously vaunted
himself as her superior in the chase.   She transformed him into a
stag, so that his own dogs set upon and devoured him.   The rock
upon which Aktæôn used to sleep when fatigued with the chase,

3. Autonoê and her son Aktæôn.

---

[1] Eurip. Phœniss. 680, with the
Scholia ;   Pherekydês, Fragm. 44 ;
Andrôtion, ap. Schol. Pindar. Isthm.
vi. 13.   Dionysius (?) called the Sparti
an ἔθνος Βοιωτίας (Schol. Phœniss. l. c.).

Even in the days of Plutarch there
were persons living who traced their
descent to the Sparti of Thebês
(Plutarch, Ser. Num. Vindict. p. 563).
[2] Apollodòr. iii. 4, 2—9 ; Diodòr. iv. 2.

and the spring whose transparent waters had too clearly revealed the form of the goddess, were shown to Pausanias near Platæa, on the road to Megara.[1]

Agavê, the remaining daughter of Kadmus, married Echiôn, one of the Sparti. The issue of these nuptials was Pentheus, who, when Kadmus became old, succeeded him as king of Thêbes. In his reign Dionysus appeared as a god, the author or discoverer of the vine with all its blessings. He had wandered over Asia, India, and Thrace, at the head of an excited troop of female enthusiasts—communicating and inculcating everywhere the Bacchic ceremonies, and rousing in the minds of women that impassioned religious emotion which led them to ramble in solitary mountains at particular seasons, there to give vent to violent fanatical excitement, apart from the men, clothed in fawnskins and armed with the thyrsus. The obtrusion of a male spectator upon these solemnities was esteemed sacrilegious. Though the rites had been rapidly disseminated and

4. Agavê and her son Pentheus.

---

[1] See Apollodôr. iii. 4, 3 ; Stesichor. Fragm. xvii. Kleine ; Pausan. ix. 2, 3 ; Eurip. Bacch. 337 ; Diodôr. iv. 81. The old logographer Akusilaus copied Stesichorus.

Upon this well-known story it is unnecessary to multiply references. I shall however briefly notice the remarks made upon it by Diodôrus and by Pausanias, as an illustration of the manner in which the literary Greeks of a later day dealt with their old national legends.

Both of them appear implicitly to believe the fact that Aktæôn was devoured by his own dogs, but they differ materially in the explanation of it.

Diodôrus accepts and vindicates the miraculous interposition of the displeased goddess to punish Aktæôn, who, according to one story, had boasted of his superiority in the chase to Artemis,—according to another story, had presumed to solicit the goddess in marriage, emboldened by the great numbers of the feet of animals slain in the chase which he had hung up as offerings in her temple. "It is not improbable (observes Diodôrus) that the goddess was angry on both these accounts. For whether Aktæôn abused these hunting presents so far as to make them the means of gratifying his own desires towards one unapproachable in

wedlock, or whether he presumed to call himself an abler hunter than her with whom the gods themselves will not compete in this department,—in either case the wrath of the goddess against him was just and legitimate (ὁμολογουμένην καὶ δικαίαν ὀργὴν ἔσχε πρὸς αὐτὸν ἡ θεός). With perfect propriety therefore (Καθόλου δὲ πιθανῶς) was he transformed into an animal such as those he had hunted, and torn to pieces by the very dogs who had killed them." (Diod. iv 80.)

Pausanias, a man of exemplary piety, and generally less inclined to scepticism than Diodôrus, thinks the occasion unsuitable for a miracle or special interference. Having alluded to the two causes assigned for the displeasure of Artemis (they are the two first-mentioned in my text, and distinct from the two noticed by Diodôrus), he proceeds to say, " But I believe that the dogs of Aktæôn went mad, without the interference of the goddess : in this state of madness they would have torn in pieces without distinction any one whom they met (Paus. ix. 2, 3. ἐγὼ δὲ καὶ ἄνευ θεοῦ πείθομαι νόσον λύσσαν ἐπιβαλεῖν τοῦ ᾿Ακταίωνος τοὺς κύνας)." He retains the truth of the final catastrophe, but rationalises it, excluding the special intervention of Artemis.

fervently welcomed in many parts of Thrace, yet there were some places in which they had been obstinately resisted and their votaries treated with rudeness; especially by Lykurgus, king of the Edonian Thracians, upon whom a sharp and exemplary punishment was inflicted by Dionysus.

Thêbes was the first city of Greece to which Dionysus came, at the head of his Asiatic troop of females, to obtain divine honours, and to establish his peculiar rites in his native city. The venerable Kadmus, together with his daughters and the prophet Teiresias, at once acknowledged the divinity of the new god, and began to offer their worship and praise to him, along with the solemnities which he enjoined. But Pentheus vehemently opposed the new ceremonies, reproving and maltreating the god who introduced them: nor was his unbelief at all softened by the miracles which Dionysus wrought for his own protection and for that of his followers. His mother Agavê, with her sisters and a large body of other women from Thêbes, had gone out from Thêbes to Mount Kithærôn to celebrate their solemnities under the influence of the Bacchic frenzy. Thither Pentheus followed to watch them, and there the punishment due to his impiety overtook him. The avenging touch of the god having robbed him of his senses, he climbed a tall pine for the purpose of overlooking the feminine multitude, who detected him in this position, pulled down the tree, and tore him in pieces. Agavê, mad and bereft of consciousness, made herself the foremost in this assault, and carried back in triumph to Thêbes the head of her slaughtered son. The aged Kadmus, with his wife Harmonia, retired among the Illyrians, and at the end of their lives were changed into serpents, Zeus permitting them to be transferred to the Elysian fields.[1]

> He resists the god Dionysus— his miserable end.

[1] Apollod. iii. 5, 3—4; Theocrit. Idyll. xxvi.; Eurip. Bacch. *passim.* Such is the tragical plot of this memorable drama. It is a striking proof of the deep-seated reverence of the people of Athens for the sanctity of the Bacchic ceremonies, that they could have borne the spectacle of Agavê on the stage with her dead son's head, and the expressions of triumphant sympathy in her action on the part of the Chorus (1168), Μάκαιρ' Ἀγαύη! This drama, written near the close of the life of Euripidês, and exhibited by his son after his death (Schol. Aristoph. Ran. 67), contains passages strongly inculcating the necessity of implicit deference to ancestorial authority in matters of religion, and favourably contrasting the uninquiring faith of the vulgar with the dissenting and inquisitive tendencies of superior minds: see v. 196; compare vv. 389 and 422.—

Οὐδὲν σοφιζόμεσθα τοῖσι δαίμοσιν.
Πατρίους παραδοχάς, ἅς θ' ὁμήλικας
    χρόνῳ

Polydôrus and Labdakus successively became kings of Thêbes : the latter at his death left an infant son, Laius, who was deprived of his throne by Lykus.   And here we approach the legend of Antiopê, Zêthus and Amphiôn, whom the fabulists insert at this point of the Thêban series. Antiopê is here the daughter of Nykteus, the brother of Lykus. She is deflowered by Zeus, and then, while pregnant, flies to Epôpeus, king of Sikyôn : Nykteus dying entreats his brother to avenge the injury, and Lykus accordingly invades Sikyôn, defeats and kills Epôpeus, and brings back Antiopê prisoner to Thêbes. In her way thither, in a cave near Eleutheræ, which was shown to Pausanias,[1] she is delivered of the twin sons of Zeus—Amphiôn and Zêthus—who, exposed to perish, are taken up and nourished by a shepherd, and pass their youth amidst herdsmen, ignorant of their lofty descent.

Antiopê is conveyed to Thêbes, where, after undergoing a long persecution from Lykus and his cruel wife Dirkê, she at length escapes, and takes refuge in the pastoral dwelling of her sons, now grown to manhood.   Dirkê pursues and requires her to be delivered up ; but the sons recognise and protect their mother, taking an ample revenge upon her persecutors.   Lykus is slain, and Dirkê is dragged to death, tied to the horns of a bull.[2]

Labdakus, Antiopê, Amphiôn, and Zêthus.

Κεκτήμεθ᾽, οὐδεὶς αὐτὰ καταβαλεῖ λόγος,
Οὐδ᾽ ἦν δι᾽ ἄκρων τὸ σοφὸν εὕρηται φρένων.

Such reproofs "insanientis sapientiæ" certainly do not fall in with the plot of the drama itself, in which Pentheus appears as a Conservative, resisting the introduction of the new religious rites.   Taken in conjunction with the emphatic and submissive piety which reigns through the drama, they countenance the supposition of Tyrwhitt, that Euripidês was anxious to repel the imputations, so often made against him, of commerce with the philosophers, and participation in sundry heretical opinions.

Pacuvius in his Pentheus seems to have closely copied Euripidês ; see Servius ad Virg. Æneid. iv. 469.

The old Thespis had composed a tragedy on the subject of Pentheus : Suidas, Θέσπις ; also Æschylus ; compare his Eumenidês, 25.

According to Apollodôrus (iii. 5, 5), Labdakus also perished in a similar

way to Pentheus, and from the like impiety,—ἐκείνῳ φρονῶν παραπλήσια.
[1] Pausan. i. 38, 9.
[2] For the adventures of Antiopê and her sons, see Apollodôr. iii. 5 ; Pausan. ii. 6, 2 ; ix. 5, 2.

The narrative given respecting Epôpeus in the ancient Cyprian verses seems to have been very different from this, as far as we can judge from the brief notice in Proclus's argument,—ὡς Ἐπωπεὺς φθείρας τὴν Λυκούργου (Λύκου) γυναῖκα ἐξεπορθήθη : it approaches more nearly to the story given in the seventh fable of Hyginus, and followed by Propertius (iii. 15) ; the eighth fable of Hyginus contains the tale of Antiopê as given by Euripidês and Ennius. The story of Pausanias differs from both.

The Scholiast ad Apollôn. Rhod. i. 735, says that there were two persons named Antiopê ; one, daughter of Asôpus, the other, daughter of Nykteus. Pausanias is content with supposing one only, really the daughter of Nykteus,

Amphiôn and Zêthus, having banished Laius, become kings of Thêbes. The former, taught by Hermês, and possessing exquisite skill on the lyre, employs it in fortifying the city, the stones of the walls arranging themselves spontaneously in obedience to the rhythm of his song.[1]

Zêthus marries Aêdôn, who, in the dark and under a fatal mistake, kills her son Itylus: she is transformed into a nightingale, while Zêthus dies of grief.[2] Amphiôn becomes the husband of Niobê, daughter of Tantalus, and the father of a numerous offspring, the complete extinction of which by the hands of Apollo and Artemis has already been recounted in these pages.

Here ends the legend of the beautiful Antiopê and her twin sons—the rude and unpolished, but energetic, Zêthus—and the refined and amiable, but dreamy, Amphiôn. For so Euripidês, in the drama of Antiopê unfortunately lost, presented the two brothers, in affectionate union as well as in striking contrast.[3] It is evident that the whole story stood originally quite apart from the Kadmeian family, and so the rudiments of it yet stand in the Odyssey ; but the logographers, by their ordinary connecting artifices, have opened a vacant place for it in the descending series of Thêban mythes. And they have here proceeded in a manner

but there was a φήμη that she was daughter of Asôpus (ii. 6, 2). Asius made Antiopê daughter of Asôpus, and mother (both by Zeus and by Epôpeus: such a junction of divine and human paternity is of common occurrence in the Greek legends) of Zêthus and Amphiôn (ap. Paus. l. c.).

The contradictory versions of the story are brought together, though not very perfectly, in Sterk's Essay, De Labdacidarum Historiâ, p. 88—43 (Leyden, 1829).

[1] This story about the lyre of Amphiôn is not noticed in Homer, but it was narrated in the ancient ἔπη ἐς Εὐρώπην which Pausanias had read : the wild beasts as well as the stones were obedient to his strains (Paus. ix. 5, 4). Pherekydês also recounted it (Pherekyd. Fragm. 102, Didot). The tablet of inscription (Ἀναγραφή) at Sikyôn recognised Amphiôn as the first composer of poetry and harp-music (Plutarch, de Musicâ, c. 3, p. 1132).

[2] The tale of the wife and son of Zêthus is as old as the Odyssey (xix. 525). Pausanias adds the statement that Zêthus died of grief (ix. 5, 5; Pherekydês, Fragm. 102, Did.). Pausanias, however, as well as Apollodôrus, tells us that Zêthus married Thêbê, from whom the name Thêbes was given to the city. To reconcile the conflicting pretensions of Zêthus and Amphiôn with those of Kadmus, as founders of Thêbes, Pausanias supposes that the latter was the original settler of the hill of the Kadmeia, while the two former extended the settlement to the lower city (ix. 5, 1—3).

[3] See Valckenaer, Diatribe in Eurip. Reliq. cap. 7, p. 58 ; Welcker, Griechisch. Tragöd. ii. p. 811. There is a striking resemblance between the Antiopê of Euripidês and the Tyrô of Sophoklês in many points.

Plato in his Gorgias has preserved a few fragments, and a tolerably clear general idea of the characters of Zêthus and Amphiôn (Gorg. 90—92); see also Horat. Epist. i. 18, 42.

Both Livius and Pacuvius had tragedies on the scheme of this of Euripidês, the former seemingly a translation.

not usual with them. For whereas they are generally fond of multiplying entities, and supposing different historical personages of the same name, in order to introduce an apparent smoothness in the chronology—they have here blended into one person Amphiôn the son of Antiopê and Amphiôn the father of Chlôris, who seem clearly distinguished from each other in the Odyssey. They have further assigned to the same person all the circumstances of the legend of Niobê, which seems to have been originally framed quite apart from the sons of Antiopê.

Amphiôn and Zêthus being removed, Laius became king of Thêbes. With him commences the ever-celebrated series of adventures of Œdipus and his family. Laius, fore- *Laius— Œdipus— Legendary celebrity of Œdipus and his family.* warned by the oracle that any son whom he might beget would kill him, caused Œdipus as soon as he was born to be exposed on Mount Kithærôn. Here the herdsmen of Polybus king of Corinth accidentally found him and conveyed him to their master, who brought him up as his own child. In spite of the kindest treatment, however, Œdipus when he grew up found himself exposed to taunts on the score of his unknown parentage, and went to Delphi to inquire of the god the name of his real father. He received for answer an admonition not to go back to his country ; if he did so, it was his destiny to kill his father and become the husband of his mother. Knowing no other country but Corinth, he accordingly determined to keep away from that city, and quitted Delphi by the road towards Bœôtia and Phôkis. At the exact spot where the roads leading to these two countries forked, he met Laius in a chariot drawn by mules, when the insolence of one of the attendants brought on an angry quarrel, in which Œdipus killed Laius, not knowing him to be his father.[1]

---

[1] The spot called σχιστὴ ὁδός (the Divided Way) where this event happened was memorable in the eyes of all literary Greeks, and is specially noticed by the traveller Pausanias, who still saw there (x. 5, 2) the tombs of Laius and his attendant. It is moreover in itself a very marked place, where the valley which runs north and south, from Daulis to Ambrysus and Antikyra, is met half way from the westward at right angles, but not crossed, by the ravine, which ascends from the Krissæan plain, passes under Delphi, reaches its highest point at Arakhova, above Delphi, and then descends towards the east. Travellers going eastward from Delphi must always have been stopped at this place by the precipices of Helikon, and must have turned either to the right or to the left. If to the right, they would descend to the Gulf, or they might take their way into Bœôtia by the southern passes, as Kleombrotus did before the battle of

On the death of Laius, Kreôn, the brother of Jokasta, succeeded
to the kingdom of Thêbes. At this time the country was under
the displeasure of the gods, and was vexed by a terrible monster,

The Sphinx. with the face of a woman, the wings of a bird, and the
tail of a lion, called the Sphinx [1]—sent by the wrath
of Hêrê, and occupying the neighbouring mountain of Phikium.
The Sphinx had learned from the Muses a riddle, which she
proposed to the Thêbans to resolve ; on every occasion of failure
she took away one of the citizens and ate him up. Still no person
could solve the riddle ; and so great was the suffering occasioned,
that Kreôn was obliged to offer both the crown and the nuptials
of his sister Jokasta to any one who could achieve the salvation
of the city. At this juncture Œdipus arrived and solved the
riddle : upon which the Sphinx immediately threw herself from
the acropolis and disappeared. As a recompense for this service,
Œdipus was made king of Thêbes, and married Jokasta, not
aware that she was his mother.

These main tragical circumstances—that Œdipus had ignorantly
killed his father and married his mother—belong to the oldest
form of the legend as it stands in the Odyssey. The gods (it is
added in that poem) quickly made the facts known to mankind.
Epikasta (so Jokasta is here called) in an agony of sorrow hanged
herself: Œdipus remained king of the Kadmeians, but underwent many and great miseries, such as the Erinnyes, who avenge
an injured mother, inflict. [2] A passage in the Iliad implies that
he died at Thêbes, since it mentions the funeral games which
were celebrated there in honour of him. His misfortunes were
recounted by Nestôr, in the old Cyprian verses, among the stories

---

Leuktra : if to the left, they would
turn the south-east angle of Parnassus,
and make their way by Daulis to the
valley of Chæroneia and Elateia.
Compare the description in K. O.
Müller, Orchomenos, c. i. p. 37.

[1] Apollodôr. iii. 5, 8. An author
named Lykus, in his work entitled
Thêbaïca, ascribed this visitation to
the anger of Dionysos (Schol. Hesiod,
Theogon. 326). The Sphinx (or Phix,
from the Bœotian Mount Phikium) is
as old as the Hesiodic Theogony.—Φῖκ'
ὀλοὴν τέκε, Καδμείοισιν ὄλεθρον (Theog.
326).

[2] Odyss. xi. 270. Odysseus, describing
what he saw in the under-world, says,—

Μητέρα τ' Οἰδιπόδαο ἴδον, καλὴν Ἐπι-
    κάστην,
Ἡ μέγα ἔργον ἔρεξεν ἀϊδρείῃσι νόοιο,
Γημαμένη ᾧ υἱεῖ· ὁ δ' ὃν πατέρ' ἐξενα-
    ρίξας
Γῆμεν· ἄφαρ δ' ἀνάπυστα θεοὶ θέσαν
    ἀνθρώποισιν.
Ἀλλ' ὁ μὲν ἐν Θήβῃ πολυηράτῳ ἄλγεα
    πάσχων,
Καδμείων ἤνασσε, θεῶν ὀλοὰς διὰ βουλάς·
Ἡ δ' ἔβη εἰς Ἀΐδαο πυλάρταο κρατεροῖο
Ἀψαμένη βρόχον αἰπὺν ἀφ' ὑψηλοῖο
    μελάθρου,
Ὧι ἄχεϊ σχομένη· τῷ δ' ἄλγεα κάλλιπ'
    ὀπίσσω
Πολλὰ μάλ', ὅσσα τε μητρὸς Ἐριννύες
    ἐκτελέουσιν.

of aforetime.[1] A fatal curse hung both upon himself and upon his children, Eteoklês, Polynikês, Antigonê and Ismênê. According to that narrative which the Attic tragedians have rendered universally current, they were his children by Jokasta, the disclosure of her true relationship to him having been very long deferred. But the ancient epic called Œdipodia, treading more closely in the footsteps of Homer, represented him as having after her death married a second wife, Euryganeia, by whom the four children were born to him : and the painter Onatas adopted this story in preference to that of Sophoklês.[2]

The disputes of Eteoklês and Polynikês for the throne of their father gave occasion not only to a series of tragical family incidents, but also to one of the great quasi-historical events of legendary Greece—the two sieges of Thêbes by Adrastus, king of Argos. The two ancient epic poems called the Thêbaïs and the Epigoni (if indeed both were not parts of one very comprehensive poem) detailed these events at great length, and as it appears, with distinguished poetical merit ; for Pausanias pronounces the Cyclic Thêbaïs (so it was called by the subsequent critics to distinguish it from the more modern Thêbaïs of Antimachus) inferior only to the Iliad and Odyssey ; the ancient elegiac poet Kallinus treated it as an Homeric composition.[3] Of this once-valued poem we unfor-

Eteoklês and Polynikês.

---

[1] Iliad, xxiii. 680, with the scholiast who cites Hesiod. Proclus, Argum. ad Cypria, ap. Düntzer. Fragm. Epic. Græc. p. 10. Νέστωρ δὲ ἐν παρεκβάσει διηγεῖται . . . καὶ τὰ περὶ Οἰδίπουν, &c.

[2] Pausan. ix. 5, 6. Compare the narrative from Peïsander in Schol. ad Eurip. Phœniss. 1773; where, however, the blindness of Œdipus seems to be unconsciously interpolated out of the tragedians. In the old narrative of the Cyclic Thêbaïs, Œdipus does not seem to be represented as blind (Leutsch, Thebaidis Cyclici Reliquiæ, Götting. 1830, p. 42).
Pherekydês (ap. Schol. Eurip. Phœniss. 52) tells us that Œdipus had three children by Jokasta, who were all killed by Erginus and the Minyæ (this must refer to incidents in the old poems which we cannot now recover); then the four celebrated children by Euryganeia ; lastly, that he married a third wife, Astymedusa. Apollodôrus

follows the narrative of the tragedians, but alludes to the different version about Euryganeia—εἰσὶ δ᾽ οἵ φασιν, &c. (iii. 5, 8).
Hellanikus (ap. Schol. Eurip. Phœniss. 60) mentioned the self-inflicted blindness of Œdipus ; but it seems doubtful whether this circumstance was included in the narrative of Pherekydês.

[3] Pausan. ix. 9, 3. Ἐποιήθη δὲ ἐς τὸν πόλεμον τοῦτον καὶ ἔπη, Θηβαΐς· τὰ δὲ ἔπη ταῦτα Καλλῖνος, ἀφικόμενος αὐτῶν ἐς μνήμην, ἔφησεν Ὅμηρον τὸν ποιήσαντα εἶναι. Καλλίνῳ δὲ πολλοί τε καὶ ἄξιοι λόγου κατὰ ταῦτα ἔγνωσαν· ἐγὼ δὲ τὴν ποίησιν ταύτην μετά γε Ἰλιάδα καὶ τὰ ἔπη τὰ ἐς Ὀδυσσέα ἐπαινῶ μάλιστα. The name in the text of Pausanias stands Καλαῖνος, an unknown person : most of the critics recognise the propriety of substituting Καλλῖνος, and Leutsch and Welcker have given very sufficient reasons for doing so.
The Ἀμφιάρεω ἐξελασία ἐς Θήβας,

tunately possess nothing but a few scanty fragments. The leading points of the legend are briefly glanced at in the Iliad ; but our knowledge of the details is chiefly derived from the Attic tragedians, who transformed the narratives of their predecessors at pleasure, and whose popularity constantly eclipsed and oblite- rated the ancient version. Antimachus of Kolophôn, contem- porary with Euripidês, in his long epic, probably took no less liberties with the old narrative. His Thêbaïd never became generally popular, but it exhibited marks of study and elaboration which recommended it to the esteem of the Alexandrine critics, and probably contributed to discredit in their eyes the old cyclic poem.

The logographers, who gave a continuous history of this siege
Old epic poems on the sieges of Thébes. of Thêbes, had at least three pre-existing epic poems— the Thêbaïs, the Œdipodia, and the Alkmæônis,— from which they could borrow. The subject was also handled in some of the Hesiodic poems, but we do not know to what extent.[1] The Thêbaïs was composed more in honour of Argos than of Thêbes, as the first line of it, one of the few fragments still preserved, betokens.[2]

SIEGES OF THÉBES.

The legend, about to recount fraternal dissension of the most implacable kind, comprehending in its results not only the immediate relations of the infuriated brothers, but many chosen companions of the heroic race along with them, takes its start from the paternal curse of Œdipus, which overhangs and deter- mines all the gloomy sequel.

Œdipus, though king of Thêbes and father of four children by
Curse pro- nounced by the devoted Œdipus upon his sons. Euryganeia (according to the Œdipodia), has become the devoted victim of the Erinnyes, in consequence of the self-inflicted death of his mother, which he had unconsciously caused, as well as of his unintentional parricide. Though he had long forsworn the use of all the ornaments and luxuries which his father had inherited

alluded to in the pseudo-Herodotean life of Homer, seems to be the description of a special passage in this Thêbaïs.

[1] Hesiod, ap. Schol. Iliad. xxiii. 680, which passage does not seem to

me so much at variance with the incidents stated in other poets as Leutsch imagines.

[2] Ἄργος ἄειδε, θεὰ, πολυδίψιον, ἔνθεν ἄνακτες (see Leutsch, ib. c. 4. p. 29).

from his kingly progenitors, yet when through age he had come
to be dependent upon his two sons, Polynikês one day broke
through this interdict, and set before him the silver table and
the splendid wine-cup of Kadmus, which Laius had always been
accustomed to employ. The old king had no sooner seen these
precious appendages of the regal life of his father, than his mind
was overrun by a calamitous phrenzy, and he imprecated terrible
curses on his sons, predicting that there would be bitter and
endless warfare between them. The goddess Erinnys heard and
heeded him; and he repeated the curse again on another occasion,
when his sons, who had always been accustomed to send to him
the shoulder of the victims sacrificed on the altar, caused the
buttock to be served to him in place of it.[1] He resented this as
an insult, and prayed the gods that they might perish each by the
hand of the other. Throughout the tragedians as well as in the
old epic, the paternal curse, springing immediately from the
misguided Œdipus himself, but remotely from the parricide and
incest with which he has tainted his breed, is seen to domineer
over the course of events—the Erinnys who executes that curse
being the irresistible, though concealed, agent. Æschylus not
only preserves the fatal efficiency of the paternal curse, but even
briefly glances at the causes assigned for it in the Thêbaïs, without
superadding any new motives. In the judgment of Sophoklês,
or of his audience, the conception of a father cursing Novelties
his sons upon such apparently trifling grounds was introduced
odious; and that great poet introduced many aggra- klês.
vating circumstances, describing the old blind father as having

---

[1] Fragm. of the Thêbaïs, ap. Athenæ.
xii. p. 465. ὅτι αὐτῷ παρέθηκαν ἐκπώματα
ἃ ἀπηγορεύκει, λέγων οὕτως ·

Αὐτὰρ ὁ διογένης ἥρως ξανθὸς Πολυνείκης
Πρῶτα μὲν Οἰδίποδι καλὴν παρέθηκε τρά-
πεζαν
᾽Αργυρέην Κάδμοιο θεόφονος · αὐτὰρ
ἔπειτα
Χρύσεον ἔμπλησεν καλὸν δέπας ἥδεος
οἴνου ·
Αὐτὰρ ὅγ᾽ ὡς φράσθη παρακείμενα πατρὸς
ἑοῖο
Τιμήεντα γέρα, μέγα οἱ κακὸν ἔμπεσε
θυμῷ.
Αἶψα δὲ παισὶν ἑοῖσι μετ᾽ ἀμφοτέροισιν
ἐπαρὰς
᾽Αργαλέας ἠρᾶτο · θεὸν δ᾽ οὐ λάνθαν᾽
᾽Ερινννύν ·

Ὡς οὔ οἱ πατρῷα γ᾽ ἐνὶ φιλότητι δάσαιντο,
Εἶεν δ᾽ ἀμφοτέροις αἰεὶ πόλεμοί τε μάχαι
τε.

See Leutsch, Thebaid. Cycl. Reliq.
p. 38.
The other fragment from the same
Thêbaïs is cited by the Schol. ad Soph.
Œdip. Colon. 1378.—

᾽Ισχίον ὡς ἐνόησε, χαμαὶ βάλεν, εἶπέ τε
μῦθον.
*Ω μοι ἐγὼ, παῖδές μοι ὀνειδείοντες
ἔπεμψαν.
Εὔκτο Διὶ βασιλῆϊ καὶ ἄλλοις ἀθανά-
τοισι,
Χερσὶν ὑπ᾽ ἀλλήλων καταβήμεναι ᾽Αΐδος
εἴσω.

Τὰ δὲ παραπλήσια τῷ ἐποποιῷ καὶ

been barbarously turned out of doors by his sons to wander abroad in exile and poverty. Though by this change he rendered his poem more coherent and self-justifying, yet he departed from the spirit of the old legend, according to which Œdipus has contracted by his unconscious misdeeds an incurable taint destined to pass onward to his progeny. His mind is alienated, and he curses them, not because he has suffered seriously by their guilt, but because he is made the blind instrument of an avenging Erinnys for the ruin of the house of Laius.[1]

After the death of Œdipus and the celebration of his funeral games, at which, amongst others, Argeia, daughter of Adrastus (afterwards the wife of Polynikês), was present,[2] his two sons soon quarrelled respecting the succession. The circumstances are differently related; but it appears that, according to the original narrative, the wrong and injustice was on the side of Polynikês; who however, was obliged to leave Thêbes and to seek shelter with Adrastus, king of Argos. Here he met Tydeus, a fugitive, at the same time, from Ætôlia: it was dark when they arrived, and a broil ensued between the two exiles, but Adrastus came out and parted them. He had been enjoined by an oracle to give his two daughters in marriage to a lion and a boar, and he thought that this occasion had now arrived, inasmuch as one of the combatants carried on his shield a lion, the other a boar. He accordingly gave Deipylê in marriage to Tydeus, and Argeia to Polynikês: moreover he resolved to restore by armed assistance both his sons-in-law to their respective countries.[3]

Death of Œdipus—quarrel of Eteoklês and Polynikês for the sceptre.

Polynikês retires to Argos—aid given to him by Adrastus.

Αἰσχύλος ἐν τοῖς Ἑπτα ἐπὶ Θήβας. In spite of the protest of Schütz, in his note, I think that the scholiast has understood the words ἐπίκοτος τροφᾶς (Sept. adv. Theb. 787) in their plain and just meaning.

[1] The curses of Œdipus are very frequently and emphatically dwelt upon both by Æschylus and Sophoklês (Sept. adv. Theb. 70—586, 655—697, &c.; Œdip. Colon. 1293—1378). The former continues the same point of view as the Thêbaïs, when he mentions—
. . . Τὰς περιθύμους
Κατάρας βλαψίφρονος Οἰδιπόδα (727);
or, λόγου τ' ἄνοια καὶ φρενῶν Ἐριννύς
(Soph. Antig. 584).

The Scholiast on Sophoklês (Œd. Col. 1378) treats the cause assigned by the ancient Thêbaïs for the curse vented by Œdipus as trivial and ludicrous.

The Ægeids at Sparta, who traced their descent to Kadmus, suffered from terrible maladies which destroyed the lives of their children; an oracle directed them to appease the Erinnyes of Laius and Œdipus by erecting a temple, upon which the maladies speedily ceased (Herodot. iv.).

[2] Hesiod, ap. Schol. Iliad. xxiii. 680.
[3] Apollodôr. iii. 5, 9; Hygin. f. 69; Æschyl. Sept. adv.Theb. 573. Hyginus says that Polynikês came clothed in

On proposing the expedition to the Argeian chiefs around him, he found most of them willing auxiliaries ; but Amphiaraüs—formerly his bitter opponent, though now reconciled to him, and husband of his sister Eriphylê—strongly opposed him,[1] denouncing the enterprise as unjust and contrary to the will of the gods. Again being of a prophetic stock, descended from Melampus, he foretold the certain death both of himself and of the principal leaders, should they involve themselves as accomplices in the mad violence of Tydeus, or the criminal ambition of Polynikês. Amphiaraüs, already distinguished both in the Kalydônian boar-hunt and in the funeral games of Pelias, was in the Thêban war the most conspicuous of all the heroes, and absolutely indispensable to its success. But his reluctance to engage in it was invincible, nor was it possible to prevail upon him except through the influence of his wife Eriphylê. Polynikês, having brought with him from Thêbes, the splendid robe and necklace given by the gods to Harmonia on her marriage with Kadmus, offered it as a bribe to Eriphylê, on condition that she would influence the determination of Amphiaraüs. The sordid wife, seduced by so matchless a present, betrayed the lurking place of her husband, and involved him in the fatal expedition.[2] Amphiaraüs, reluctantly dragged forth, and foreknowing the disastrous issue of the expedition both to himself and to his associates, addressed his last injunctions, at the moment of mounting his chariot, to his sons Alkmæôn and Amphilochus, commanding Alkmæôn to avenge his approaching death by killing the venal Eriphylê, and by undertaking a second expedition against Thêbes.

The Attic dramatists describe this expedition as having been conducted by seven chiefs, one to each of the seven celebrated

the skin of a lion, and Tydeus in that of a boar ; perhaps after Antimachus, who said that Tydeus had been brought up by swineherds (Antimach. Fragm. 27, ed. Düntzer ; ap. Schol. Iliad. iv. 400). Very probably, however, the old Thêbaïs compared Tydeus and Polynikês to a lion and a boar, on account of their courage and fierceness ; a simile quite in the Homeric character. Menaseas gave the words of

the oracle (ap. Schol. Eurip. Phœniss. 411).

[1] See Pindar, Nem. ix. 30, with the instructive Scholium.

[2] Apollodôr. iii. 6, 2. The treachery of "the hateful Eriphylê" is noticed in the Odyssey, xi. 327 : Odysseus sees her in the under-world along with the many wives and daughters of the heroes.

gates of Thêbes. But the Cyclic Thêbaïs gave to it a much more comprehensive character, mentioning auxiliaries from Arcadia, Messênê, and various parts of Peloponnêsus:[1] and the application of Tydeus and Polynikês at Mykênæ in the course of their circuit made to collect allies, is mentioned in the Iliad. They were well received at Mykênæ; but the warning signals given by the gods were so terrible that no Mykênæan could venture to accompany them.[2] The seven principal chiefs however were Adrastus, Amphiaraüs, Kapaneus, Hippomedôn, Parthenopæus, Tydeus and Polynikês.[3]

Seven chiefs of the army against Thêbes.

The Kadmeians, assisted by their allies the Phôkians and the Phlegyæ, marched out to resist the invaders, and fought a battle near the Ismênian hill, in which they were defeated and forced to retire within the walls. The prophet Teiresias acquainted them that if Menœkeus, son of Kreôn, would offer himself as a victim to Arês, victory would be assured to Thêbes. The generous youth, as soon as he learnt that his life was to be the price of safety to his country, went and slew himself before the gates. The heroes along with Adrastus now commenced a vigorous attack upon the town, each of the seven selecting one of the gates to assault. The contest was long and strenuously maintained; but the devotion of Menœkeus had procured for the Thêbans the protection of the gods. Parthenopæus was killed with a stone by Periklymenus; and when the furious Kapaneus, having planted a scaling ladder, had mounted the walls, he was smitten by a thunderbolt from Zeus, and cast down· dead upon the earth. This event struck terror into the Argeians, and Adrastus called back his troops from the attack. The Thêbans now sallied forth to pursue them, when Eteoklês, arresting the battle, proposed to decide the controversy by single combat with

Defeat of the Thêbans in the field —heroic devotion of Menœkeus.

---

[1] Pausan. ii. 20, 4; ix. 9, 1. His testimony to this, as he had read and admired the Cyclic Thêbaïs, seems quite sufficient, in spite of the opinion of Welcker to the contrary (Æschyleische Trilogie, p. 375).

[2] Iliad, iv. 376.

[3] There are differences in respect to the names of the seven; Æschylus (Sept.adv.Theb.461)leaves out Adrastus as one of the seven, and includes Eteoklus instead of him; others left out Tydeus and Polynikês, and inserted Eteoklus and Mekisteus (Apollodôr. iii. 6, 3). Antimachus, in his poetical *Thêbaïs*, called Parthenopæus an Argeian, not an Arcadian (Schol. ad Æschyl. Sept. adv. Theb. 532).

his brother.   The challenge, eagerly accepted by Polynikês, was
agreed to by Adrastus: a single combat ensued between   Single
the two brothers, in which both were exasperated   combat of
Eteoklês
to fury, and both ultimately slain by each other's   and Polynikês, in
hand.   This equal termination left the result of the   which both
general contest still undetermined, and the bulk of   perish.
the two armies renewed the fight.   In the sanguinary struggle
which ensued, the sons of Astakus on the Thêban side displayed
the most conspicuous and successful valour.   One of
them,[1] Melanippus, mortally wounded Tydeus—while   Repulse and
destruction
two others, Leades and Amphidikus, killed Eteoklus   of the
Argeian
and Hippomedôn.   Amphiaraüs avenged Tydeus by   chiefs—all
killing Melanippus ; but unable to arrest the rout of   except
Adrastus.
the army, he fled with the rest, closely pursued by   Amphiaraüs is
Periklymenus.   The latter was about to pierce him   swallowed
with his spear, when the beneficence of Zeus rescued   up in the
earth.
him from this disgrace—miraculously opening the
earth under him, so that Amphiaraüs with his chariot and
horses was received unscathed into her bosom.[2]   The exact spot
where this memorable incident happened was indicated by a
sepulchral building, and shown by the Thêbans down to the days
of Pausanias—its sanctity being attested by the fact, that no
animal would consent to touch the herbage which grew within
the sacred inclosure.   Amphiaraüs, rendered immortal by Zeus,
was worshipped as a god at Argos, at Thêbes, and at Orôpus—and

---

[1] The story recounted that the head
of Melanippus was brought to Tydeus
as he was about to expire of his wound,
and that he gnawed it with his teeth,
a story touched upon by Sophoklês
(apud Herodian. in Rhetor. Græc. t.
viii. p. 601, Walz.).
   The lyric poet Bacchylidês (ap.
Schol. Aristoph. Aves, 1535) seems to
have handled the story even earlier
than Sophoklês.
   We find the same allegation
embodied in charges against real
historical men : the invective of
Montanus against Aquilius Regulus,
at the beginning of the reign of
Vespasian, affirmed, "datam inter-
fectori Pisonis pecuniam a Regulo,
appetitumque morsu Pisonis caput"
(Tacit. Hist. iv. 42).
   [2] Apollodôr. iii. 6, 8. Pindar, Olymp.

vi. 11 ; Mem. ix. 13—27.   Pausan. ix.
8, 2 ; 18, 2—4.
   Euripidês, in the Phœnissæ (1122
seqq.), describes the battle generally :
see also Æsch. S. Th. 392.   It appears
by Pausanias that the Thêbans had
poems or legends of their own, relative
to this war : they dissented in various
points from the Cyclic Thêbaïs (ix. 18,4).
The Thêbaïs said that Periklymenus
had killed Parthenopæus: the Thêbans
assigned this exploit to Asphodikus, a
warrior not commemorated by any of
the poets known to us.
   The village of Harma, between
Tanagra and Mykalêssus, was affirmed
by some to have been the spot where
Amphiaraüs closed his life (Strabo, ix.
p. 404) ; Sophoklês placed the scene at
the Amphiaræium near Orôpus (ap.
Strabon. ix. p. 399).

for many centuries gave answers at his oracle to the questions of the pious applicant.[1]

Adrastus, thus deprived of the prophet and warrior whom he regarded as "the eye of his army," and having seen the other chiefs killed in the disastrous fight, was forced to take flight singly, and was preserved by the matchless swiftness of his horse Areiôn, the offspring of Poseidôn. He reached Argos on his return, bringing with him nothing except "his garment of woe and his black-maned steed".[2]

Kreôn, father of the heroic youth Menœkeus, succeeding to the administration of Thêbes after the death of the two hostile brothers and the repulse of Adrastus, caused Eteoklês to be buried with distinguished honour, but cast out ignominiously the body of Polynikês as a traitor to his country, forbidding every

Kreôn, king of Thêbes, forbids the burial of Polynikês and the other fallen Argeian chiefs.

one on pain of death to consign it to the tomb. He likewise refused permission to Adrastus to inter the bodies of his fallen comrades. This proceeding, so offensive to Grecian feeling, gave rise to two further tales; one of them at least of the highest pathos and interest. Antigonê, the sister of Polynikês, heard with indignation the revolting edict consigning her brother's body to the dogs and vultures, and depriving it of those rites

---

[1] Pindar, Olymp. vi. 16. Ἑπτα δ᾽ ἔπειτα πυρὰν νέκρων τελεσθέντων Ταλαϊονίδας Εἶπεν ἐν Θήβαισι τοιοῦτόν τι ἔπος· Ποθέω στρατιᾶς ὀφθαλμὸν ἐμᾶς 'Αμφότερον, μάντιν τ᾽ ἀγαθὸν καὶ δουρὶ μάχεσθαι.

The scholiast affirms that these last expressions are borrowed by Pindar from the Cyclic Thêbaïs.

The temple of Amphiaraüs (Pausan. ii. 23, 2), his oracle, seems to have been equal in estimation to every other except that of Delphi (Herodot. i. 52; Pausan. i. 34; Cicero, Divin. i. 40). Crœsus sent a rich present to Amphiaraüs, πυθόμενος αὐτοῦ τήν τε ἀρετὴν καὶ τὴν πάθην (Herod. l. c.); a striking proof how these interesting legends were recounted and believed as genuine historical facts. Other adventures of Amphiaraüs in the expedition against Thêbes were commemorated on the carvings on the Thronus at Amyklæ (Pausan. iii. 18, 4).

Æschylus (Sept. Theb. 611) seems to enter into the Thêban view, doubtless

highly respectful towards Amphiaraüs, when he places in the mouth of the Kadmeian king Eteoklês such high encomiums on Amphiaraüs, and so marked a contrast with the other chiefs from Argos.

[2] Pausan. viii. 25, 5. from the Cyclic Thêbaïs, Εἵματα λυγρὰ φέρων σὺν 'Αρείονι κυανοχαίτῃ; also Apollodôr. iii. 6, 8.

The celebrity of the horse Areiôn was extolled in the Iliad (xxiii. 346), in the Cyclic Thêbaïs, and also in the Thêbaïs of Antimachus (Pausan. l. c.): by the Arcadians of Thelpusia he was said to be the offspring of Dêmêtêr by Poseidôn,—he, and a daughter whose name Pausanias will not communicate, except to the initiated (ἧς τὸ ὄνομα ἐς ἀτελέστους λέγειν οὐ νομίζουσι, l. c.). A different story is in the Schol. Iliad. xxiii. 346; and in Antimachus, who affirmed that "Gæa herself had produced him as a wonder to mortal men" (see Antimach. Frag. 16, p. 102: Epic. Græc. Frag. ed. Düntzer).

which were considered essential to the repose of the dead. Unmoved by the dissuading counsel of an affectionate but timid sister, and unable to procure assistance, she determined to brave the hazard, and to bury the body with her own hands. She was detected in the act ; and Kreôn, though forewarned by Teiresias of the consequences, gave orders that she should be buried alive, as having deliberately set at naught the solemn edict of the city. His son Hæmôn, to whom she was engaged to be married, in vain interceded for her life. In an agony of despair he slew himself in the sepulchre to which the living Antigonê had been consigned ; and his mother Eurydikê, the wife of Kreôn, inconsolable for his death, perished by her own hand. And thus 'the new light which seemed to be springing up over the last remaining scion of the devoted family of Œdipus, is extinguished amidst gloom and horrors—which overshadowed also the house and dynasty of Kreôn.[1]

Devotion and death of Antigonê.

The other tale stands more apart from the original legend, and seems to have had its origin in the patriotic pride of the Athenians. Adrastus, unable to obtain permission from the Thêbans to inter the fallen chieftains, presented himself in suppliant guise, accompanied by their disconsolate mothers, to Thêseus at Eleusis. He implored the Athenian warrior to extort from the perverse Thêbans that last melancholy privilege which no decent or pious Greeks ever thought of withholding, and thus to stand forth as the champion of Grecian public morality in one of its most essential points, not less than of the rights of the subterranean gods. The Thêbans obstinately persisting in their refusal, Thêseus

The Athenians interfere to procure the interment of the fallen chiefs.

undertook an expedition against their city, vanquished them in the field, and compelled them by force of arms to permit the sepulture of their fallen enemies. This chivalrous interposition, celebrated in one of the preserved dramas of Euripidês, formed a subject of glorious recollection to the Athenians throughout the

---

[1] Sophokl. Antigon. 581. Νῦν γὰρ ἐσχάτας ὑπὲρ 'Ρίζας ἐτέτατο φάος ἐν Οἰδίπου δόμοις, &c.

The pathetic tale here briefly recounted forms the subject of this beautiful tragedy of Sophoklês, the argument of which is supposed by Boeckh to have been borrowed in its primary rudiments from the Cyclic Thêbaïs or the Œdipodia (Boeckh, Dissertation appended to his translation of the Antigonê, c. x. p. 146): see Apollodôr. iii. 7, 1.

Æschylus also touches upon the heroism of Antigonê (Sept. Theb. 984).

historical age. Their orators dwelt upon it in terms of animated panegyric; and it seems to have been accepted as a real fact of the past time, with not less implicit conviction than the battle of Marathôn.[1] But the Thêbans, though equally persuaded of the truth of the main story, dissented from the Athenian version of it, maintaining that they had given up the bodies for sepulture voluntarily and of their own accord. The tomb of the chieftains was shown near Eleusis even in the days of Pausanias.[2]

The defeat of the seven chiefs before Thêbes was amply avenged by their sons, again under the guidance of Adrastus :—Ægialeus son of Adrastus, Thersander son of Polynikês, Alkmæôn and

Second siege of Thêbes by Adrastus with the Epigoni, or sons of those slain in the first.

Amphilochus sons of Amphiaraüs, Diomêdês son of Tydeus, Sthenelus son of Kapaneus, Promachus son of Parthenopæus, and Euryalus son of Mekistheus, joined in this expedition. Though all these youthful warriors, called the Epigoni, took part in this expedition, the grand and prominent place appears to have been occupied by Alkmæôn, son of Amphiaraüs. Assistance was given to them from Corinth and Megara, as well as from Messênê and Arcadia; while Zeus manifested his favourable dispositions by signals not to be mistaken.[3] At the river Glisas the Epigoni were met by the Thêbans in arms, and a battle took place in which the latter were completely defeated. Laodamas, son of Eteoklês, killed Ægialeus, son of Adrastus; but he and his army were routed and driven within the walls by the valour and energy of Alkmæôn. The defeated Kadmeians consulted the prophet Teiresias, who informed them that the gods had declared for their enemies, and that there was no longer any hope of successful resistance. By his advice they sent a herald to the assailants offering to surrender the town, while they themselves conveyed away their wives and children, and fled under the command of Laodamas to the Illyrians,[4] upon which the Epigoni

---

[1] Apollodôr. iii. 7, 1 ; Eurip. Supp. passim; Herodot. ix. 27 ; Plato, Menexen. c. 9 ; Lysias, Epitaph. c. 4 ; Isokrat. Orat. Panegyr. p. 196, Auger.

[2] Pausan. i. 39, 2.

[3] Homer, Iliad. iv. 406. Sthenelus, the companion of Diomêdês and one of the Epigoni, says to Agamemnôn,—

Ἡμεῖς τοι πατέρων μέγ' ἀμείνονες εὐχόμεθ' εἶναι.

Ἡμεῖς καὶ Θήβης ἕδος εἵλομεν ἑπταπύλοιο,
Παυρότερον λαὸν ἀγαγόνθ' ὑπὸ τεῖχος
Ἄρειον,
Πειθόμενοι τεράεσσι θεῶν καὶ Ζηνὸς
ἀρωγῇ.
Αὐτοὶ δὲ σφετέρῃσιν ἀτασθαλίῃσιν
ὄλοντο.

[4] Apollodôr. iii. 7, 4. Herodot. v 57—61. Pausan. ix. 5, 7; 9, 2. Diodôr. iv. 65—66.

entered Thêbes, and established Thersander, son of Polynikês, on the throne.

Adrastus, who in the former expedition had been the single survivor amongst so many fallen companions, now found himself the only exception to the general triumph and joy of the conquerors : he had lost his son Ægialeus, and the violent sorrow arising from the event prematurely cut short his life. His soft voice and persuasive eloquence were proverbial in the ancient epic.[1] He was wor-shipped as a hero both at Argos and at Sikyôn, but with especial solemnity in the last-mentioned place, where his Herôum stood in the public agora, and where his exploits as well as his suffer-ings were celebrated periodically in lyric tragedies. Melanippus, son of Astakus, the brave defender of Thêbes, who had slain both Tydeus and Mekistheus, was worshipped with no less solemnity by the Thêbans.[2] The enmity of these two heroes rendered it impossible for both of them to be worshipped close upon the same spot. Accordingly it came to pass during the historical period, shortly after the time of the Solonian legislation at Athens, that Kleisthenês, despot of Sikyôn, wishing to banish the hero Adrastus and abolish the religious solemnities celebrated in honour of the latter by the Sikyonians, first applied to the Delphian oracle for permission to carry this banishment into effect directly and forcibly. That permission being refused, he next sent to Thêbes an intimation that he was anxious to introduce their hero Mela-nippus into Sikyôn. The Thêbans willingly consented, and he assigned to the new hero a consecrated spot in the strongest and most commanding portion of the Sikyonian prytaneium. He did this (says the historian) "knowing that Adrastus would forthwith go away of his own accord ; since Melanippus was of all persons the most odious to him, as having slain both his son-in-law and his brother". Kleisthenês moreover diverted the festivals and sacrifices which had been offered to Adrastus, to the newly-established hero Melanippus ; and the lyric tragedies from

Marginal notes:
Victory of the Epigoni —capture of Thêbes.

Worship of Adrastus at Sikyôn— how abro-gated by Kleisthenês.

Pindar represents Adrastus as concerned in the second expedition against Thêbes (Pyth. viii. 40—58).
[1] Γλῶσσαν τ᾽ Ἀδρήστου μειλιχόγηρυν ἔχοι (Tyrtæus, Eleg. 9, 7, Schneidewin); compare Plato, Phædr. c. 118. "Ad-

rasti pallentis imago" meets the eye of Æneas in the under-world (Æn. vi. 480).
[2] About Melanippus, see Pindar, Nem. x. 36. His sepulchre was shown near the Prœtid gates of Thêbes (Pausan. ix. 18, 1).

the worship of Adrastus to that of Dionysus. But his dynasty did not long continue after his decease, and the Sikyonians then re-established their ancient solemnities.[1]

Near the Prœtid gate of Thêbes were seen the tombs of two combatants who had hated each other during life even more than Adrastus and Melanippus—the two brothers Eteoklês and Polynikês. Even as heroes and objects of worship, they still continued to manifest their inextinguishable hostility : those who offered sacrifices to them observed that the flame and the smoke from the two adjoining altars abhorred all communion, and flew off in directions exactly opposite. The Thêban exegetes assured Pausanias of this fact. And though he did not himself witness it, yet having seen with his own eyes a miracle not very dissimilar at Pioniæ in Mysia, he had no difficulty in crediting their assertion.[2]

Amphiaraüs, when forced into the first attack of Thêbes— against his own foreknowledge and against the warnings of the gods—had enjoined his sons Alkmæôn and Amphilochus not only to avenge his death upon the Thêbans, but also to punish the treachery of their mother, "Eriphylê, the destroyer of her husband".[3] In obedience to this command, and having obtained

---

[1] This very curious and illustrative story is contained in Herodot. v. 67. Ἐπεὶ δὲ ὁ θεὸς τοῦτο οὐ παρεδίδου, ἀπελθὼν ὀπίσω (Kleisthenês, returning from Delphi) ἐφρόντιζε μηχανὴν τῇ αὐτὸς ὁ Ἄδρηστος ἀπαλλάξεται. Ὡς δὲ οἱ ἐξευρῆσθαι ἐδόκεε, πέμψας ἐς Θήβας τὰς Βοιωτίας, ἔφη θέλειν ἐπαγαγέσθαι Μελάνιππον τὸν Ἀστακοῦ· οἱ δὲ Θηβαῖοι ἔδοσαν. Ἐπηγάγετο δὲ τὸν Μελάνιππον ὁ Κλεισθένης, καὶ γὰρ τοῦτο δεῖ ἀπηγήσασθαι, ὡς ἔχθιστον ἐόντα Ἀδρήστῳ· ὅς τόν τε ἀδέλφεον Μηκιστέα ἀπεκτόνεε, καὶ τὸν γαμβρὸν Τυδέα.

The Sikyonians (Herodotus says) τά τε δὴ ἄλλα ἐτίμων τὸν Ἄδρηστον, καὶ πρὸς τὰ πάθεα αὐτοῦ τραγικοῖσι χόροισι ἐγέραιρον· τὸν μὲν Διόνυσον οὐ τιμέωντες, τὸν δὲ Ἄδρηστον.

Adrastus was worshipped as a hero at Megara as well as at Sikyôn : the Megarians affirmed that he had died there on his way back from Thêbes (Pausan. i. 43, 1 ; Dieuchidas, ap. Schol. ad Pindar. Nem. ix. 31). His house at Argos was still shown when Pausanias visited the town (ii. 23, 2).

[2] Pausan. ix. 18, 3. Τὰ ἐπ' αὐτοῖς

δρώμενα οὐ θεασάμενος πιστὰ ὅμως ὑπείληφα εἶναι. Compare Hygin. f. 68.

"Et nova fraterno veniet concordia fumo, Quem vetus accensâ separat ira pyrâ."
(Ovid, Ibis, 35.)

The tale was copied by Ovid from Kallimachus (Trist. v. 5, 38).

[3] Ἀνδροδάμαντ' Ἐριφύλην (Pindar. Nem. ix. 16). A poem Eriphylê was included among the mythical compositions of Stêsichorus : he mentioned in it that Asklêpius had restored Kapaneus to life, and that he was for that reason struck dead by thunder from Zeus (Stêsichor. Fragm. Kleine, 18. p. 74). Two tragedies of Sophoklês once existed, Epigoni and Alkmæôn (Welcker, Griechisch. Tragöd. i. p. 269) : a few fragments also remain of the Latin Epigoni and Alphesibœa of Attius : Ennius and Attius both composed or translated from the Greek a Latin Alkmæôn (Poet. Lat. Scenic. ed. Bothe pp. 33, 164, 198).

the sanction of the Delphian oracle, Alkmæôn slew his mother ;[1] but the awful Erinnys, the avenger of matricide, inflicted on him a long and terrible punishment, depriving him of his reason, and chasing him about from place to place without the possibility of repose or peace of mind. He craved protection and cure from the god at Delphi, who required him to dedicate at the temple, as an offering, the precious necklace of Kadmus, that irresistible bribe which had originally corrupted Eriphylê.[2] He further intimated to the unhappy sufferer, that though the whole earth was tainted with his crime, and had become uninhabitable for him, yet there was a spot of ground which was not under the eye of the sun at the time when the matricide was committed, and where therefore Alkmæôn yet might find a tranquil shelter. The promise was realised at the mouth of the river Achelôus, whose turbid stream was perpetually depositing new earth and forming additional islands. Upon one of these, near Œniadæ, Alkmæôn settled, permanently and in peace ; he became the primitive hero of Akarnania, to which his son Akarnan gave name.[3] The necklace was found among the treasures of Delphi (together with that which had been given by Aphroditê to Helen), by the Phôkian plunderers who stripped the temple in the time of Philip of Macedôn. The Phôkian women quarrelled about these valuable ornaments. We are told that the necklace of Eriphylê was allotted to a woman of gloomy and malignant disposition, who ended by putting her husband to death ; that of Helen to a beautiful but volatile wife, - who abandoned her husband from preference for a young Epirot.[4]

(margin note: Alkmæôn— his matricide and punishment.)

[1] Hyginus gives the fable briefly (f. 73; see also Asklepiadês, ap. Schol. Odyss. xi. 326). In like manner, in the case of the matricide of Orestês, Apollo not only sanctions, but enjoins the deed : but his protection against the avenging Erinnyes is very tardy, not taking effect until after Orestês had been long persecuted and tormented by them (see Æschyl. Eumen. 76, 197, 462).

In the *Alkmæôn* of the latter tragic writer Theodektês, a distinction was drawn : the gods had decreed that Eriphylê should die, but not that Alkmæôn should kill her (Aristot. Rhetoric. ii. 24). Astydamas altered

the story still more in his tragedy, and introduced Alkmæôn as killing his mother ignorantly and without being aware who she was (Aristot. Poetic. c. 27). The murder of Eriphylê by her son was one of the παρειλημμένοι μῦθοι which could not be departed from ; but interpretations and qualifications were resorted to, in order to prevent it from shocking the softened feelings of the spectators : see the criticism of Aristotle on the *Alkmæôn* of Euripidês (Ethic. Nicom. iii. 1, 8).

[2] Ephorus ap. Athenæ. vi. p. 232.

[3] Thucyd. ii. 68—102.

[4] Athenæ. l. c.

There were several other legends respecting the distracted
Alkmæôn, either appropriated or invented by the Attic tragedians. He went to Phêgeus, king of Psôphis in Arcadia,
whose daughter Arsinoê he married, giving as a nuptial present
the necklace of Eriphylê. Being however unable to remain
there, in consequence of the unremitting persecutions of the
maternal Erinnys, he sought shelter at the residence of king
Achelôus, whose daughter Kallirrhoê he made his wife, and on
whose soil he obtained repose.[1] But Kallirrhoê would
not be satisfied without the possession of the necklace
of Eriphylê, and Alkmæôn went back to Psôphis to
fetch it, where Phêgeus and his sons slew him. He had left twin
sons, infants, with Kallirrhoê, who prayed fervently to Zeus that
they might be preternaturally invested with immediate manhood,
in order to revenge the murder of their father. Her prayer was
granted, and her sons Amphoterus and Akarnan, having instan-
taneously sprung up to manhood, proceeded into Arcadia, slew
the murderers of their father, and brought away the necklace of
Eriphylê, which they carried to Delphi.[2]

Fatal neck-
lace of
Eriphylê.

Euripidês deviated still more widely from the ancient epic, by
making Alkmæôn the husband of Mantô, daughter of Teiresias,
and the father of Amphilochus. According to the Cyclic Thêbaïs,
Mantô was consigned by the victorious Epigoni as a special
offering to the Delphian god : and Amphilochus was son of

---

[1] Apollodôr. iii. 7, 5—6; Pausan.
viii. 24, 4. These two authors have
preserved the story of the Akarnanians
and the old form of the legend, representing Alkmæôn as having found
shelter at the abode of the person
or king Achelôus, and married his
daughter : Thucydides omits the *personality* of Achelôus, and merely
announces the wanderer as having
settled on certain new islands deposited
by the river.

I may remark that this is a singularly happy adaptation of a legend to
an existing topographical fact. Generally speaking, before any such adaptation can be rendered plausible, the
legend is of necessity much transformed;
here it is taken exactly as it stands,
and still fits on with great precision.

Ephorus recounted the whole
sequence of events as so much political
history, divesting it altogether of the
legendary character. Alkmæôn and

Diomêdês, after having taken Thêbes
with the other Epigoni, jointly undertook an expedition into Ætôlia and
Akarnania : they first punished the
enemies of the old Œneus, grandfather
of Diomêdês, and established the latter
as king in Kalydôn ; next they conquered Akarnania for Alkmæôn. Alkmæôn, though invited by Agamemnôn
to join in the Trojan war, would not
consent to do so (Ephor. ap. Strab. vii.
p. 326 ; x. p. 462).

[2] Apollodôr. iii. 7, 7 ; Pausan. viii.
24, 3—4. His remarks upon the mischievous longing of Kallirrhoê for the
necklace are curious : he ushers them
in by saying, that "many men, and
still more women, are given to fall into
absurd desires," &c. He recounts it
with all the *bonne foi* which belongs to
the most assured matter of fact.

A short allusion is in Ovid's Metamorphoses (ix. 412).

Amphiaraüs, not son of Alkmæôn.[1] He was the eponymous hero of the town called the Amphilochian Argos, in Akarnania, on the shore of the Gulf of Ambrakia. Thucydidês tells us that he went thither on his return from the Trojan war, being dissatisfied with the state of affairs which he found at the Peloponnêsian Argos.[2] The Akarnanians were remarkable for the numerous prophets which they supplied to the rest of Greece: their heroes were naturally drawn from the great prophetic race of the Melampodids.

Thus ends the legend of the two sieges of Thêbes; the greatest event, except the siege of Troy, in the ancient epic; the greatest enterprise of war, between Greeks and Greeks, during the time of those who are called the Heroes.

---

[1] Thêbaïd, Cycl. Reliqu. p. 70, Leutsch: Schol. Apollôn. Rhod. i. 408. The following lines cited in Athenæus (vii. p. 317) are supposed by Boeckh, with probable reason, to be taken from the Cyclic Thêbaïs; a portion of the advice of Amphiaraüs to his sons at the time of setting out on his last expedition,—

Πουλύποδός μοι, τέκνον, ἔχων νόον, Ἀμ-
    φίλοχ᾽ ἥρως,
Τοῖσιν ἐφαρμόζου, τῶν ἂν κατὰ δῆμον
    ἵκηαι.

There were two tragedies composed by Euripidês, under the title of Ἀλκμαίων, ὁ διὰ Ψωφῖδος, and Ἀλκ-μαίων, ὁ διὰ Κορίνθου (Dindorf. Fragm. Eurip. p. 77).

[2] Apollodôr. iii. 7. 7; Thucyd. ii. 68.

CHAPTER XV.

LEGEND OF TROY.

WE now arrive at the capital and culminating point of the Grecian epic,—the two sieges and captures of Troy, with the destinies of the dispersed heroes, Trojan as well as Grecian, after the second and most celebrated capture and destruction of the city.

It would require a large volume to convey any tolerable idea

Great ex- tent and variety of the tale of Troy. of the vast extent and expansion of this interesting fable, first handled by so many poets, epic, lyric, and tragic, with their endless additions, transformations, and contradictions,—then purged and recast by his- torical inquirers, who, under colour of setting aside the exaggera- tions of the poets, introduced a new vein of prosaic invention,— lastly, moralised and allegorised by philosophers. In the present brief outline of the general field of Grecian legend, or of that which the Greeks believed to be their antiquities, the Trojan war can be regarded as only one among a large number of incidents upon which Hekatæus and Herodotus looked back as constituting their fore-time. Taken as a special legendary event, it is indeed of wider and larger interest than any other, but it is a mistake to single it out from the rest as if it rested upon a different and more trustworthy basis. I must therefore confine myself to an abridged narrative of the current and leading facts ; and amidst the numerous contradictory statements which are to be found respecting every one of them, I know no better ground of preference than comparative antiquity, though even the oldest tales which we possess—those contained in the Iliad—evidently presuppose others of prior date.

The primitive ancestor of the Trojan line of kings is Dardanus, son of Zeus, founder and eponymus of Dardania :[1] Dardanus, in the account of later authors, Dardanus was called son of Zeus. the son of Zeus by Elektra, daughter of Atlas, and was further said to have come from Samothrace, or from Arcadia, or from Italy ;[2] but of this Homer mentions nothing.   The first Dardanian town founded by him was in a lofty position on the descent of Mount Ida ; for he was not yet strong enough to establish himself on the plain.   But his son Erichthonius, by the favour of Zeus, became the wealthiest of mankind.   His flocks and herds having multiplied, he had in his pastures three thousand mares, the offspring of some of whom, by Boreas, produced horses of preternatural swiftness.   Trôs, the son of Erichthonius, and the eponym of the Trojans, had three sons—Ilus, Assaracus, and the beautiful Ganymêdês, whom Zeus stole away to become his cup-bearer in Olympus, giving to his father Trôs, as the price of the youth, a team of immortal horses.[3]

From Ilus and Assaracus the Trojan and Dardanian liner diverge ; the former passing from Ilus to Laomedôn, Ilus, Priam and Hectôr ; the latter from Assaracus to founder of Capys, Anchisês and Æneas.   Ilus founded in the Ilium. plain of Troy the holy city of Ilium ; Assaracus and his descendants remained sovereigns of Dardania.[4]

It was under the proud Laomedôn, son of Ilus, that Poseidôn and Apollo underwent, by command of Zeus, a Walls of temporary servitude ; the former building the walls Ilium built of the town, the latter tending the flocks and herds. dôn. When their task was completed and the penal period had expired, they claimed the stipulated reward ; but Laomedôn angrily repudiated their demand, and even threatened to cut off their ears, to tie them hand and foot, and to sell them in some distant island as slaves.[5]   He was punished for this treachery by a sea-monster, whom Poseidôn sent to ravage his fields and to destroy his subjects.   Laomedôn publicly offered the immortal horses

---

[1] Iliad, xx. 215.
[2] Hellanik. Fragm. 129, Didot ; Dionys. Hal. i. 50—61 ; Apollodôr. iii. 12, 1 ; Schol. Iliad. xviii. 486 ; Varro, ap. Servium ad Virgil. Æneid. iii. 167 ; Kephalon. Gergithius ap. Steph. Byz.

v. 'Αρίσβη.
[3] Iliad, v. 265 ; Hellanik. Fr. 146 : Apollod. ii. 5, 9.
[4] Iliad, xx. 236.
[5] Iliad, vii. 451 ; xxi. 456. Hesiod. ap. Schol. Lycophr. 393.

given by Zeus to his father Trôs, as a reward to any one who would destroy the monster. But an oracle declared that a virgin of noble blood must be surrendered to him, and the lot fell upon Hesionê, daughter of Laomedôn himself. Hêraklês, arriving at this critical moment, killed the monster by the aid of a fort built for him by Athênê and the Trojans,[1] so as to rescue both the exposed maiden and the people ; but Laomedôn, by a second act of perfidy, gave him mortal horses in place of the matchless animals which had been promised. Thus defrauded of his due, Hêraklês equipped six ships, attacked and captured Troy and killed Laomedôn,[2] giving Hesionê to his friend and auxiliary Telamôn, to whom she bore the celebrated archer Teukros.[3] A painful sense of this expedition was preserved among the inhabitants of the historical town of Ilium, who offered no worship to Hêraklês.[4]

Capture of Ilium by Hêraklês.

Among all the sons of Laomedôn, Priam[5] was the only one who had remonstrated against the refusal of the well-earned guerdon of Hêraklês ; for which the hero recompensed him by placing him on the throne. Many and distinguished were his sons and daughters, as well by his wife Hekabê, daughter of Kisseus, as by other women.[6] Among the sons were Hectôr,[7] Paris, Dêiphobus, Helenus, Trôilus, Politês, Polydôrus ; among the daughters Laodikê, Kreüsa, Polyxena, and Kassandra.

Priam and his offspring.

---

[1] Iliad, xx. 145 ; Dionys. i. 52.
[2] Iliad, v. 640. Meneklês (ap. Schol. Venet. ad loc.) affirmed that this expedition of Hêraklês was a fiction ; but Dikæarchus gave, besides, other exploits of the hero in the same neighbourhood, at Thêbê Hypoplakiê (Schol. Iliad. vi. 396).
[3] Diodôr. iv. 32—49. Compare Venet. Schol. ad Iliad. viii. 284.
[4] Strabo, xiii. p. 596.
[5] As Dardanus, Trôs and Ilus are respectively eponyms of Dardania, Troy and Ilium, so Priam is eponym of the acropolis Pergamum. Πρίαμος is in the Æolic dialect Πέρραμος (Hesychius) : upon which Ahrens remarks, "Cæterum ex hac Æolica nominis formâ apparet, Priamum non minus arcis Περγάμων eponymum esse, quam Ilum urbis, Troem populi ; Πέργαμα enim a Περίαμα natum est, ι in γ mutato ". (Ahrens, De Dialecto

Æolicâ, 8, 7, p. 56 ; compare ibid. 28, 8, p. 150, περρ' ἀπάλω.).
[6] Iliad, vi. 248 ; xxiv. 495.
[7] Hectôr was affirmed, both by Stêsichorus and Ibykus, to be the son of Apollo (Stêsichorus, ap. Schol. Ven. ad Iliad. xxiv. 259 ; Ibyci Fragm. xiv. ed. Schneidewin) : both Euphoriôn (Fr. 125, Meineke) and Alexander Ætôlus follow the same idea. Stêsichorus further stated that after the siege Apollo had carried Hekabê away into Lykia to rescue her from captivity (Pausanias, v. 27, 1) : according to Euripidês, Apollo had promised that she should die in Troy (Troad. 427).
By Sapphô, Hectôr was given as a surname of Zeus, Ζεὺς Ἕκτωρ (Hesychius, v. Ἕκτορες) ; a prince belonging to the regal family of Chios, anterior to the Ionic settlement, as mentioned by the Chian poet Iôn (Pausan. vii. 3, 3), was so called.

The birth of Paris was preceded by formidable presage ; for Hekabê dreamt that she was delivered of a firebrand, and Priam, on consulting the soothsayers, was informed that the son about to be born would prove fatal to him. Accordingly he directed the child to be exposed on Mount Ida ; but the inauspicious kindness of the gods preserved him ; and he grew up amidst the flocks and herds, active and beautiful, fair of hair and symmetrical in person, and the special favourite of Aphroditê.[1]

Paris—his judgment on the three goddesses.

It was to this youth, in his solitary shepherd's walk on Mount Ida, that the three goddesses Hêrê, Athênê and Aphroditê were conducted, in order that he might determine the dispute respecting their comparative beauty, which had arisen at the nuptials of Pêleus and Thetis,—a dispute brought about in pursuance of the arrangement, and in accomplishment of the deep-laid designs, of Zeus. For Zeus, remarking with pain the immoderate numbers of the then existing heroic race, pitied the earth for the overwhelming burden which she was compelled to bear, and determined to lighten it by exciting a destructive and long-continued war.[2] Paris awarded the palm of beauty to Aphroditê, who promised him in recompense the possession of Helena, wife of the Spartan Menelaus,—the daughter of Zeus and the fairest of living women. At the instance of Aphroditê, ships were built for him, and he embarked on the enterprise so fraught with eventual disaster to his native city, in spite of the menacing prophecies of his brother Helenus, and the always neglected warnings of Kassandra.[3]

---

[1] Iliad, iii. 45—55; Schol. Iliad. iii. 325; Hygin. fab. 91; Apollodôr. iii. 12, 5.

[2] This was the motive assigned to Zeus by the old epic poem, the Cyprian Verses (Fragm. 1, Düntz. p. 12; ap. Schol. ad Iliad. I. 4):—Ἡ δὲ ἱστορία παρὰ Στασίνῳ τῷ τὰ Κύπρια πεποιηκότι εἰπόντι οὕτως·

Ἦν ὅτε μύρια φῦλα κατὰ χθόνα πλαζό-
μενα
. . . . βαρυστέρνου πλάτος αἴης.
Ζεὺς δὲ ἰδὼν ἐλέησε, καὶ ἐν πυκιναῖς
πραπίδεσσι
Σύνθετο κουφίσαι ἀνθρώπων παμβώτορα
γαῖαν,
Ῥιπίσας πολέμου μεγάλην ἔριν Ἰλιακοῖο,
Ὄφρα κενώσειεν θανάτῳ βάρος· οἱ δ' ἐνὶ
Τροίῃ

Ἥρωες κτείνοντο, Διὸς δ' ἐτελείετο βουλή.

The same motive is touched upon by Eurip. Orest. 1635 ; Helen. 38 ; and seriously maintained, as it seems, by Chrysippus, ap. Plutarch. Stoic. Rep. p. 1049: but the poets do not commonly go back further than the passion of Paris for Helen (Theognis, 1232 ; Simonid. Amorg. Fragm. 6, 118).

The judgment of Paris was one of the scenes represented on the ancient chest of Kypselus at Olympia (Pausan. v. 19, 1).

[3] Argument of the Ἔπη Κύπρια (ap. Düntzer, p. 10). These warnings of Kassandra form the subject of the obscure and affected poem of Lycophrôn.

Paris, on arriving at Sparta, was hospitably entertained by
Carries off
Helen from
Sparta. Menelaus as well as by Kastôr and Pollux, and was enabled to present the rich gifts which he had brought to Helen.[1] Menelaus then departed to Krête, leaving Helen to entertain his Trojan guest—a favourable moment which was employed by Aphroditê to bring about the intrigue and the elopement. Paris carried away with him both Helen and a large sum of money belonging to Menelaus—made a prosperous voyage to Troy—and arrived there safely with his prize on the third day.[2]

Menelaus, informed by Iris in Krête of the perfidious return made by Paris for his hospitality, hastened home in grief and indignation to consult with his brother Agamemnôn, as well as with the venerable Nestôr, on the means of avenging the outrage. They made known the event to the Greek chiefs around them, among whom they found universal sympathy : Nestôr, Palamêdês and others went round to solicit aid in a contemplated attack of Troy, under the command of Agamemnôn, to whom each chief promised both obedience and unwearied exertion until Helen should be recovered.[3] Ten years were spent in
Expedition
of the
Greeks to
recover her equipping the expedition. The goddesses Hêrê and Athêrê, incensed at the preference given by Paris to Aphroditê, and animated by steady attachment to

---

[1] According to the Cyprian Verses, Helena was daughter of Zeus by Nemesis, who had in vain tried to evade the connexion (Athenæ. viii. 334). Hesiod (Schol. Pindar. Nem. x. 150) represented her as daughter of Oceanus and Têthys, an oceanic nymph : Sapphô (Fragm. 17, Schneidewin), Pausanias (i. 33, 7), Apollodôrus (iii. 10, 7), and Isokratês (Encom. Helen. v. ii. p. 366, Auger) reconcile the pretensions of Lêda and Nemesis to a sort of joint maternity (see Heinrichsen, De Carminibus Cypriis, p. 45—46).

[2] Herodot. ii. 117. He gives distinctly the assertion of the Cyprian Verses which contradicts the argument of the poem as it appears in Proclus (Fragm. 1, 1), according to which latter Paris is driven out of his course by a storm and captures the city of Sidôn. Homer (Iliad, vi. 293) seems, however, to countenance the statement in the argument.

That Paris was guilty of robbery, as well as of the abduction of Helen, is several times mentioned in the Iliad (iii. 144 ; vii. 350—363), also in the argument of the Cyprian Verses (see Æschyl. Agam. 534).

[3] The ancient epic (Schol. ad Il. ii. 286—339) does not recognise the story of the numerous suitors of Helen, and the oath by which Tyndareus bound them all before he made the selection among them that each should swear not only to acquiesce, but even to aid in maintaining undisturbed possession to the husband whom she should choose. This story seems to have been first told by Stêsichorus (see Fragm. 20, ed. Kleine ; Apollod. iii. 10, 8). Yet it was evidently one of the prominent features of the current legend in the time of Thucydidês (i. 9; Euripid. Iph. Aul. 51—80 ; Soph. Ajax, 1100).

The exact spot in which Tyndareus exacted this oath from the suitors, near Sparta, was pointed out even in the time of Pausanias (iii. 20, 9).

Argos, Sparta, and Mykênæ, took an active part in the cause ; and the horses of Hêrê were fatigued with her repeated visits to the different parts of Greece.[1]

By such efforts a force was at length assembled at Aulis[2] in Bœôtia, consisting of 1186 ships and more than 100,000 men,—a force outnumbering by more than ten to one anything that the Trojans themselves could oppose, and superior to the defenders of Troy even with all her allies included.[3] It comprised heroes with their followers from the extreme points of Greece—from the north-western portions of Thessaly under Mount Olympus, as well as the western islands of Dulichium and Ithaca, and the eastern islands of Krête and Rhodes. Agamemnôn himself contributed 100 ships manned with the subjects of his kingdom Mykênæ, besides furnishing 60 ships to the Arcadians, who possessed none of their own. Menelaus brought with him 60 ships, Nestôr from Pylus 90, Idomeneus from Krête and Diomêdês from Argos, 80 each. Forty ships were manned by the Eleians, under four different chiefs ; the like number under Megês from Dulichium and the Echinades, and under Thoas from Kalydôn and the other Ætôlian towns. Odysseus from Ithaca, and Ajax from Salamis, brought 12 ships each. The Abantes from Eubœa, under Elephênôr, filled 40 vessels ; the Bœôtians under Peneleôs and Lêitus, 50 ; the inhabitants of Orchomenus and Aspledôn, 30 ; the light-armed Lokrians, under Ajax, son of Oileus,[4] 40 ; the Phôkians as many. The Athenians, under Menestheus, a chief distinguished for his skill in marshalling an army, mustered 50 ships ; the Myrmidons from Phthia and Hellas, under Achilles, assembled in 50 ships ; Protesilaus from Phylakê and Pyrasus, and

Heroes from all parts of Greece combined under Agamemnôn.

[1] Iliad iv. 27—55 ; xxiv. 765 ; Argument. Carm. Cypri. The point is emphatically touched upon by Dio Chrysostom (Orat. xi. p. 335—336) in his assault upon the old legend. Two years' preparation—in Dictys Cret. i.16.

[2] The Spartan king Agesilaus, when about to start from Greece on his expedition into Asia Minor (396 B.C.), went to Aulis personally, in order that he too might sacrifice on the spot where Agamemnôn had sacrificed when he sailed for Troy (Xenoph. Hellen. iii. 4, 4).

Skylax (c. 60) notices the ἱερόν at Aulis, and nothing else : it seems to have been like the adjoining Delium, a temple with a small village grown up around it.

Aulis is recognised as the port from which the expedition started, in the Hesiodic Works and Days (v. 650).

[3] Iliad, ii. 123. Uschold (Geschichte des Trojanischen Kriegs, p. 9, Stuttgart, 1836) makes the total 135,000 men.

[4] The Hesiodic Catalogue notices Oileus, or Ileus, with a singular etymology of his name (Fragm. 136, ed. Marktscheffel).

Eurypylus from Ormenium, each came with 40 ships ; Machaôn and Podaleirius, from Trikka, with 30 ; Eumêlus, from Pheræ and the lake Bœbêis, with 11 ; and Philoktêtês from Melibœa with 7 ; the Lapithæ, under Polypœtês, son of Peirithous, filled 40 vessels ; the Ænianes and Perrhæbians, under Guneus,[1] 22 ; and the Magnêtês, under Prothous, 40 ; these last two were from the northernmost parts of Thessaly, near the mountains Pêlion and Olympus. From Rhodes, under Tlêpolemus, son of Hêraklês, appeared 9 ships ; from Symê, under the comely but effeminate Nireus, 3 ; from Kôs, Krapathus and the neighbouring islands, 30, under the orders of Pheidippus and Antiphus, sons of Thessalus and grandsons of Hêraklês.[2]

Among this band of heroes were included the distinguished

Achilles
and
Odysseus.

warriors Ajax and Diomêdês, and the sagacious Nestôr ; while Agamemnôn himself, scarcely inferior to either of them in prowess, brought with him a high reputation for prudence in command. But the most marked and conspicuous of all were Achilles and Odysseus ; the former a beautiful youth born of a divine mother, swift in the race, of fierce temper and irresistible might ; the latter not less efficient as an ally, from his eloquence, his untiring endurance, his inexhaustible resource under difficulty, and the mixture of daring courage with deep-laid cunning which never deserted him :[3] the blood of the arch-deceiver Sisyphus, through an illicit connexion with his mother Antikleia, was said to flow in his veins,[4] and he was especially patronised and protected by the goddess Athênê. Odysseus, unwilling at first to take part in the expedition, had even simulated insanity ; but Palamêdês,

[1] Γουνεύς is the Heros Eponymus of the town of Gonnus in Thessaly : the duplication of the consonant and shortening of the vowel belong to the Æolic dialect (Ahrens, De Dialect. Æolic. 50, 4, p. 220).

[2] See the Catalogue in the second book of the Iliad. There must probably have been a Catalogue of the Greeks also in the Cyprian Verses ; for a Catalogue of the allies of Troy is specially noticed in the Argument of Proclus (p. 12, Düntzer).

Euripidês (Iphig. Aul. 165—300) devotes one of the songs of the Chorus to a partial Catalogue of the chief heroes.

According to Dictys Cretensis, all the principal heroes engaged in the expedition were kinsmen, all Pelopids (i. 14) : they take an oath not to lay down their arms until Helen shall have been recovered, and they receive from Agamemnôn a large sum of gold.

[3] For the character of Odysseus, Iliad, iii. 202—220 ; x. 247. Odyss. xiii. 295.

The Philoktêtês of Sophoklês carries out very justly the character of the Homeric Odysseus (see v. 1035)—more exactly than the Ajax of the same poet depicts it.

[4] Sophokl. Philoktêt. 417, and Schol. —also Schol. ad Soph. Ajac. 190.

sent to Ithaca to invite him, tested the reality of his madness by placing in the furrow where Odysseus was ploughing his infant son Têlemachus.   Thus detected, Odysseus could not refuse to join the Achæan host, but the prophet Halithersês predicted to him that twenty years would elapse before he revisited his native land.[1]   To Achilles the gods had promised the full effulgence of heroic glory before the walls of Troy ; nor could the place be taken without both his co-operation and that of his son after him.   But they had forewarned him that this brillant career would be rapidly brought to a close ; and that if he desired a long life, he must remain tranquil and inglorious in his native land.   In spite of the reluctance of his mother Thetis, he preferred few years with bright renown, and joined the Achæan host.[2]   When Nestôr and Odysseus came to Phthia to invite him, both he and his intimate friend Patroklus eagerly obeyed the call.[3]

Agamemnôn and his powerful host set sail from Aulis ; but being ignorant of the locality and the direction, they landed by mistake in Teuthrania, a part of Mysia near the river Kaïkus, and began to ravage the country under the persuasion that it was the neighbourhood of Troy.   Têlephus, the king of the country,[4] opposed and repelled them, but was ultimately defeated and severely wounded by Achilles.   The Greeks, now discovering their mistake, retired ; but their fleet was dispersed by a storm and driven back to Greece. Achilles attacked and took Skyrus, and there married Deidamia, the daughter of Lycomêdês.[5]   Têlephus, suffering from his wounds, was directed by the oracle to come to

The Grecian host mistakes Teuthrania for Troy—Têlephus.

---

[1] Homer, Odyss. xxiv. 115 ; Æschyl. Agam. 841 ; Sophokl. Philoktêt. 1011, with the Schol. Argument of the Cypria in Heinrichsen, De Carmin. Cypr. p. 23 (the sentence is left out in Düntzer, p. 11).

A lost tragedy of Sophoklês, 'Οδυσσεὺς Μαινόμενος, handled this subject.

Other Greek chiefs were not less reluctant than Odysseus to take part in the expedition ; see the tale of Pœmandrus, forming a part of the temple legend of the Achilleium at Tanagra in Bœotia (Plutarch. Quæst. Græc. p. 299).

[2] Iliad, i. 352 ; ix. 411.

[3] Iliad, xi. 782.

[4] Têlephus was the son of Augê daughter of king Aleus of Tegea in Arcadia, by Hêraklês : respecting her romantic adventures, see the previous chapter on Arcadian legends—Strabo's faith in the story (xii. p. 572).

The spot called the harbour of the Achæans, near Gryneium, was stated to be the place where Agamemnôn and the chiefs took counsel whether they should attack Têlephus or not (Skylax, c. 97 ; compare Strabo, xiv. p. 622).

[5] Iliad, ix. 664 ; Argum. Cypr. p. 11, Düntzer ; Diktys Cret. ii. 3—4.

Greece and present himself to Achilles to be healed, by applying the scrapings of the spear with which the wound had been given : thus restored, he became the guide of the Greeks when they were prepared to renew their expedition.[1]

The armament was again assembled at Aulis, but the goddess Artemis, displeased with the boastful language of Agamemnôn, prolonged the duration of adverse winds, and the offending chief was compelled to appease her by the well-known sacrifice of his daughter Iphigeneia.[2] They then proceeded to Tenedos, from whence Odysseus and Menelaus were despatched as envoys to Troy, to redemand Helen and the stolen property. In spite of the prudent counsels of Antênôr, who received the two Grecian chiefs with friendly hospitality, the Trojans rejected the demand, and the attack was resolved upon. It was foredoomed by the gods that the Greek who first landed should perish : Protesilaus was generous enough to put himself upon this forlorn hope, and accordingly fell by the hand of Hectôr.

Detention of the Greeks at Aulis— Agamemnôn and Iphigeneia.

Meanwhile the Trojans had assembled a large body of allies from various parts of Asia Minor and Thrace : Dardanians under Æneas, Lykians under Sarpêdôn, Mysians, Karians, Mæonians, Alizonians,[3] Phrygians, Thracians, and Pæonians.[4]

---

[1] Euripid. Têlephus, Fragm. 26, Dindorf; Hygin. f. 101; Diktys, ii. 10. Euripidês had treated the adventure of Têlephus in this lost tragedy : he gave the miraculous cure with the dust of the spear, πρισtoῖσι λογχῆς θέλγεται ῥινήμασι. Diktys softens down the prodigy : "Achilles cum Machaone et Podalirio adhibentes curam vulneri," &c. Pliny (xxxiv. 15) gives to the rust of brass or iron a place in the list of genuine remedies.

"Longe omnino a Tiberi ad Caicum : quo in loco etiam Agamemnon errasset, nisi ducem Telephum invenisset" (Cicero, Pro L. Flacco, c. 29). The portions of the Trojan legend treated in the lost epics and the tragedians, seem to have been just as familiar to Cicero as those noticed in the Iliad.

Strabo pays comparatively little attention to any portion of the Trojan war except what appears in Homer. He even goes so far as to give a reason why the Amazons *did not* come to the aid of Priam : they were at enmity with him, because Priam had aided the Phrygians against them (Iliad, iii. 188 : in Strabo, τοῖς Ἰᾶσιν must be a mistake for τοῖς Φρυξίν). Strabo can hardly have read, and never alludes to, Arktinus, in whose poem the brave and beautiful Penthesileia, at the head of her Amazons, forms a marked epoch and incident of the war (Strabo, xii. 552).

[2] Nothing occurs in Homer respecting the sacrifice of Iphigeneia (see Schol. Ven. ad Il. ix. 145).

[3] No portion of the Homeric Catalogue gave more trouble to Dêmêtrius of Skêpsis and the other expositors than these Alizonians (Strabo, xii. p. 549; xiii. p. 603) : a fictitious place called Alizonium, in the region of Ida, was got up to meet the difficulty (εἶτ' Ἀλιζώνιον, τοῦτ' ἤδη πεπλασμένον πρὸς τὴν τῶν Ἀλιζώνων ὑπόθεσιν, &c., Strabo, l. c.).

[4] See the Catalogue of the Trojans (Iliad, ii. 815—877).

But vain was the attempt to oppose the landing of the Greeks: the Trojans were routed, and even the invulnerable Kyknus,[1] son of Poseidôn, one of the great bulwarks of the defence, was slain by Achilles. Having driven the Trojans within their walls, Achilles attacked and stormed Lyrnêssus, Pêdasus, Lesbos and other places in the neighbourhood, twelve towns on the seacoast, and eleven in the interior : he drove off the oxen of Æneas and pursued the hero himself, who narrowly escaped with his life : he surprised and killed the youthful Trôilus, son of Priam, and captured several of the other sons, whom he sold as prisoners into the islands of the Ægean.[2] He acquired as his captive the fair Brisêis, while Chrysêis was awarded to Agamemnôn : he was moreover eager to see the divine Helen, the prize and stimulus of this memorable struggle ; and Aphroditê and Thetis contrived to bring about an interview between them.[3]

First success of the Greeks on landing near Troy. Brisêis awarded to Achilles.

At this period of the war the Grecian army was deprived of Palamêdês, one of its ablest chiefs. Odysseus had not forgiven the artifice by which Palamêdês had detected his simulated insanity, nor was he without jealousy of a rival clever and cunning in a degree equal, if not superior, to himself ; one who had enriched the Greeks with the invention of letters, of dice for amusement, of night-watches, as well as with other useful suggestions. According to the old Cyprian epic, Palamêdês was drowned while fishing, by the hands of Odysseus and Diomêdês.[4] Neither in the Iliad nor the

Palamêdês —his genius and treacherous death.

---

[1] Kyknus was said by later writers to be king of Kolônæ in the Troad (Strabo, xiii. p. 589—603; Aristotel. Rhetoric. ii. 23). Æschylus introduced upon the Attic stage both Kyknus and Memnôn in terrific equipments (Aristophan. Ran. 957. Οὐδ' ἐξέπληττον αὐτοὺς Κύκνους ἄγων καὶ Μέμνονας κωδωνοφαλαροπώλους). Compare Welcker, Æschyl. Trilogie, p. 433.

[2] Iliad, xxiv. 752; Argument of the Cypria, pp. 11, 12, Düntzer. These desultory exploits of Achilles furnished much interesting romance to the later Greek poets (see Parthênius, Narrat. 21). See the neat summary of the principal events of the war in Quintus Smyrn. xiv. 125—140; Dio Chrysost. Or. xi. p. 338—342.
Trôilus is only once named in the

Iliad (xxiv. 253); he was mentioned also in the Cypria; but his youth, beauty, and untimely end made him an object of great interest with the subsequent poets. Sophoklês had a tragedy called *Trôilus* (Welcker, Griechische Tragöd. i. p. 124); Τὸν ἀνδρόπαιδα δεσπότην ἀπώλεσα, one of the Fragm. Even earlier than Sophoklês, his beauty was celebrated by the tragedian Phrynichus (Athenæ. xiii. p. 564; Virgil, Æneid, i. 474; Lycophrôn, 307).

[3] Argument. Cypr. p. 11, Düntzer. Καὶ μετὰ ταῦτα Ἀχιλλεὺς Ἑλένην ἐπιθυμεῖ θεάσασθαι, καὶ συνήγαγον αὐτοὺς εἰς τὸ αὐτὸ Ἀφροδίτη καὶ Θέτις. A scene which would have been highly interesting in the hands of Homer.

[4] Argum. Cypr. 1, 1; Pausan. x. 31.

Odyssey does the name of Palamêdês occur; the lofty position
which Odysseus occupies in both these poems—noticed with
some degree of displeasure even by Pindar, who described Palamêdês as the wiser man of the two—is sufficient to explain the
omission.[1] But in the more advanced period of the Greek mind,
when intellectual superiority came to acquire a higher place in
the public esteem as compared with military prowess, the character
of Palamêdês, combined with his unhappy fate, rendered him
one of the most interesting personages in the Trojan legend.
Æschylus, Sophoklês and Euripidês each consecrated to him a
special tragedy; but the mode of his death as described in the
old epic was not suitable to Athenian ideas, and accordingly he
was represented as having been falsely accused of treason by
Odysseus, who caused gold to be buried in his tent, and persuaded Agamemnôn and the Grecian chiefs that Palamêdês had
received it from the Trojans.[2] He thus forfeited his life, a
victim to the calumny of Odysseus and to the delusion of the
leading Greeks. The philosopher Sokratês, in the last speech
made to his Athenian judges, alludes with solemnity and fellow-
feeling to the unjust condemnation of Palamêdês, as analogous to
that which he himself was about to suffer; and his companions
seem to have dwelt with satisfaction on the comparison. Palamêdês passed for an instance of the slanderous enmity and
misfortune which so often wait upon superior genius.[3]

The concluding portion of the Cypria
seems to have passed under the title of
Παλαμηδεία (see Fragm. 16 and 18,
p. 15, Düntzer; Welcker, Der Episch.
Cycl. p. 459; Eustath. ad Hom. Odyss.
i. 107).
  The allusion of Quintus Smyrnæus
(v. 197) seems rather to point to the
story in the Cypria, which Strabo (viii.
p. 368) appears not to have read.
  [1] Pindar, Nem. vii. 21; Aristidês,
Orat. 46, p. 260.
  [2] See the Fragments of the three
tragedians Παλαμήδης—Aristeidês, Or.
xlvi. p. 260; Philostrat. Heroic. x.;
Hygin. fab. 95—105. Discourses for
and against Palamêdês, one by Alki-
damas, and one under the name of
Gorgias, are printed in Reiske's Orr.
Græc. t. viii. pp. 64, 102; Virgil,
Æneid, ii. 82, with the ample commentary of Servius—Polyæn. Procœ.
p. 6.

Welcker (Griechisch. Tragöd. vol. i.
p. 130, vol. ii. p. 500) has evolved with
ingenuity the remaining fragments of
the lost tragedies.
  According to Diktys, Odysseus and
Diomêdês prevail upon Palamêdês to
be let down into a deep well, and then
cast stones upon him (ii. 15).
  Xenophon (De Venatione, c. 1)
evidently recognises the story in the
Cypria, that Odysseus and Diomêdês
caused the death of Palamêdês: but
he *cannot* believe that two such exemplary men were really guilty of so
iniquitous an act—κακοὶ δὲ ἔπραξαν τὸ
ἔργον.
  The marked eminence overtopping
Napoli still bears the name of *Pala-
midhi.*
  [3] Plato, Apolog. Socr. c. 32; Xenoph.
Apol. Socr. 26; Memor. iv. 2, 33;
Liban. pro Socr. p. 242, ed. Morell.;
Lucian, Dial. Mort. 20.

In these expeditions the Grecian army consumed nine years,
during which the subdued Trojans dared not give battle without
their walls for fear of Achilles. Ten years was the fixed epical
duration of the siege of Troy, just as five years was the duration
of the siege of Kamikus by the Krêtan armament which came to
avenge the death of Minôs :[1] ten years of preparation, ten years
of siege, and ten years of wandering for Odysseus, were periods
suited to the rough chronological dashes of the ancient epic,
and suggesting no doubts nor difficulties with the
original hearers. But it was otherwise when the same   Epic Chro-
events came to be contemplated by the historicising   nology his-
Greeks, who could not be satisfied without either finding or
inventing satisfactory bonds of coherence between the separate
events. Thucydidês tells us that the Greeks were less numerous
than the poets have represented, and that being moreover very
poor, they were unable to procure adequate and constant provisions : hence they were compelled to disperse their army, and
to employ a part of it in cultivating the Chersonese—a part in
marauding expeditions over the neighbourhood. Could the
whole army have been employed against Troy at once (he says),
the siege would have been much more speedily and easily concluded.[2] If the great historian could permit himself thus to
amend the legend in so many points, we might have imagined
that a simpler course would have been to include the duration
of the siege among the list of poetical exaggerations, and to
affirm that the real siege had lasted only one year instead of
ten. But it seems that the ten years' duration was so capital
a feature in the ancient tale, that no critic ventured to meddle
with it.

A period of comparative intermission however was now at
hand for the Trojans. The gods brought about the memorable
fit of anger of Achilles, under the influence of which he refused
to put on his armour, and kept his Myrmidons in camp.
According to the Cypria, this was the behest of Zeus, who had
compassion on the Trojans : according to the Iliad, Apollo was

[1] Herodot. vii. 170. Ten years is a
proper mythical period for a great war
to last : the war between the Olympic
gods and the Titan gods lasts ten
years (Hesiod, Theogon. 636). Compare δεκάτῳ ἐνιαυτῷ (Hom. Odyss.
xvi. 17).
[2] Thucyd. i. 1.

the originating cause,[1] from anxiety to avenge the injury which
his priest Chrysês had endured from Agamemnôn.
For a considerable time, the combats of the Greeks
against Troy were conducted without their best warrior, and severe indeed was the humiliation which
they underwent in consequence.   How the remaining
Grecian chiefs vainly strove to make amends for his absence—
how Hectôr and the Trojans defeated and drove them to their
ships—how the actual blaze of the destroying flame, applied by
Hectôr to the ship of Protesilaus, roused up the anxious and
sympathizing Patroklus, and extorted a reluctant consent from
Achilles to allow his friend and his followers to go forth and
avert the last extremity of ruin—how Achilles, when Patroklus
had been killed by Hectôr, forgetting his anger in grief for the
death of his friend, re-entered the fight, drove the Trojans
within their walls with immense slaughter, and satiated his
revenge both upon the living and the dead Hectôr—all these
events have been chronicled, together with those divine dispen-
sations on which most of them are made to depend, in the
immortal verse of the Iliad.

(marginal note:) Period of the Homeric Iliad. Hectôr killed by Achilles.

Homer breaks off with the burial of Hectôr, whose body has
just been ransomed by the disconsolate Priam ; while the lost
poem of Arktinus, entitled the Æthiopis, so far as we can judge
from the argument still remaining of it, handled only the subsequent events of the siege.   The poem of Quintus Smyrnæus,
composed about the fourth century of the Christian æra, seems
in its first books to coincide with the Æthiopis, in the subsequent
books partly with the Ilias Minor of Leschês.[2]

The Trojans, dismayed by the death of Hectôr, were again
animated with hope by the appearance of the warlike and
beautiful queen of the Amazons, Penthesileia, daughter of Arês,
hitherto invincible in the field, who came to their assistance from
Thrace at the head of a band of her countrywomen.   She again
led the besieged without the walls to encounter the Greeks in the
open field : and under her auspices the latter were at first driven
back, until she too was slain by the invincible arm of Achilles.

[1] Homer, Iliad, i. 21.
[2] Tychsen, Commentat. de Quinto Smyrnæo, § iii. c. 5—7.   The Ἰλίου Πέρσις was treated both by Arktinus and by Leschês : with the latter it formed a part of the Ilias Minor.

The victor, on taking off the helmet of his fair enemy as she lay on the ground, was profoundly affected and captivated by her charms, for which he was scornfully taunted by Thersitês: exasperated by this rash insult, he killed Thersitês on the spot with a blow of his fist. A violent dispute among the Grecian chiefs was the result, for Diomêdês, the kinsman of Thersitês, warmly resented the proceeding; and Achilles was obliged to go to Lesbos, where he was purified from the act of homicide by Odysseus.[1]

New allies of Troy—Penthesileia.

Next arrived Memnôn, son of Tithônus and Eôs, the most stately of living men, with a powerful band of black Ethiopians, to the assistance of Troy. Sallying forth against the Greeks, he made great havoc among them: the brave and popular Antilochus perished by his hand, a victim to filial devotion in defence of Nestôr.[2] Achilles at length attacked him, and for a long time the combat was doubtful between them: the prowess of Achilles and the supplication of Thetis with Zeus finally prevailed; whilst Eôs obtained for her vanquished son the consoling gift of immortality. His tomb, however,[3] was shown near the Propontis, within a few miles of the mouth of the river Æsêpus, and was visited annually by the birds called Memnonides, who swept it and bedewed it with water from the stream. So the traveller Pausanias was told, even in the second century after the Christian æra, by the Hellespontine Greeks.

Memnôn—killed by Achilles.

[1] Argument of the Æthiopis, p. 16, Düntzer; Quint. Smyrn. lib. i.; Diktys Cret. iv. 2—3.

In the Philoktêtês of Sophoklês, Thersitês survives Achilles (Soph. Phil. 358—445).

[2] Odyss. xi. 522. Κεῖνον δὴ κάλλιστον ἴδον, μετὰ Μέμνονα δῖον: see also Odyss. iv. 187; Pindar, Pyth. vi. 31. Æschylus (ap. Strab. xv. p. 728) conceives Memnôn as a Persian starting from Susa.

Ktesias gave in his history full details respecting the expedition of Memnôn, sent by the king of Assyria to the relief of his dependent, Priam of Troy; all this was said to be recorded in the royal archives. The Egyptians affirmed that Memnôn had come from Egypt (Diodôr. ii. 22; compare iv. 77): the two stories are blended together in Pausanias, x. 31, 2. The Phrygians pointed out the road along which he had marched.

[3] Argum. Æth. ut sup.; Quint. Smyrn. ii. 396—550; Pausan. x. 31, 1. Pindar, in praising Achilles, dwells much on his triumphs over Hectôr, Têlephus, Memnôn, and Kyknus, but never notices Penthesileia (Olymp. ii. 90. Nem. iii. 60; vi. 52. Isthm. v. 43).

Æschylus, in the Ψυχοστασία, introduced Thetis and Eôs, each in an attitude of supplication for her son, and Zeus weighing in his golden scales the souls of Achilles and Memnôn (Schol. Ven. ad Iliad. viii. 70; Pollux, iv. 130; Plutarch, De Audiend. Poet. p. 17). In the combat between Achilles and Memnôn, represented on the chest of Kypselus at Olympia, Thetis and Eôs were given each as aiding her son (Pausan. v. 19, 1).

But the fate of Achilles himself was now at hand. After
Death of   routing the Trojans, and chasing them into the town,
Achilles.   he was slain near the Skæan gate by an arrow from
the quiver of Paris, directed under the unerring auspices of
Apollo.[1] The greatest efforts were made by the Trojans to
possess themselves of the body, which was however rescued and
borne off to the Grecian camp by the valour of Ajax and
Odysseus. Bitter was the grief of Thetis for the loss of her
son; she came into the camp with the Muses and the Nêreids to
mourn over him; and when a magnificent funeral-pile had been
prepared by the Greeks to burn him with every mark of honour, she
stole away the body and conveyed it to a renewed and immortal
life in the island of Leukê in the Euxine Sea. According to
some accounts he was there blest with the nuptials and company
of Helen.[2]

Thetis celebrated splendid funeral games in honour of her son,
Funeral   and offered the unrivalled panoply, which Hêphæstos
games cele-   had forged and wrought for him, as a prize to the
brated in
honour of   most distinguished warrior in the Grecian army.
him—   Odysseus and Ajax became rivals for the distinction,
Quarrel
about his   when Athênê, together with some Trojan prisoners,
panoply—   who were asked from which of the two their country
Odysseus
prevails   had sustained greatest injury, decided in favour of
and Ajax   the former. The gallant Ajax lost his senses with
kills
himself.   grief and humiliation: in a fit of phrenzy he slew
some sheep, mistaking them for the men who had wronged him,
and then fell upon his own sword.[3]

---

[1] Iliad, xxii. 360; Sophokl. Philokt
334; Virgil, Æneid, vi. 56.
[2] Argum. Æthiop. ut sup.; Quint.
Smyrn. 151—583; Homer, Odyss. v.
310; Ovid, Metam. xiii. 284; Eurip.
Androm. 1262; Pausan. iii. 19, 13.
According to Diktys (iv. 11), Paris and
Deiphobus entrap Achilles by the
promise of an interview with Polyxena
and kill him.
A minute and curious description of
the island Leukê, or Ἀχιλλέως νῆσος,
is given in Arrian (Periplus Pont.
Euxin. p. 21; ap. Geogr. Min. t. 1).
The heroic or divine empire of
Achilles in Scythia was recognised
by Alkæus the poet (Alcæi Fragm.
Schneidew. Fr. 46), Ἀχιλλεῦ, ὃς γᾶς

Σκυθικᾶς μέδεις. Eustathius (ad
Dionys. Periègêt. 307) gives the story
of his having followed Iphigeneia
thither: compare Antonin. Liberal.
27.
Ibykus represented Achilles as
having espoused Mêdea in the Elysian
Field (Ibyc. Fragm. 18, Schneidewin).
Simonidês followed this story (ap.
Schol. Apoll. Rhod. iv. 815).
[3] Argument of Æthiopis and Ilias
Minor, and Fragm. 2 of the latter,
pp. 17, 18, Düntz.; Quint. Smyrn. v.
120—482; Hom. Odyss. xi. 550; Pindar,
Nem. vii. 26. The Ajax of Sophoklês,
and the contending speeches between
Ajax and Ulysses in the beginning of
the thirteenth book of Ovid's

Odysseus now learnt from Helenus son of Priam, whom he had captured in an ambuscade,[1] that Troy could not be taken unless both Philoktêtês, and Neoptolemus, son of Achilles, could be prevailed upon to join the besiegers. The former, having been stung in the foot by a serpent, and becoming insupportable to the Greeks from the stench of his wound, had been left at Lemnus in the commencement of the expedition, and had spent ten years,[2] in misery on that desolate island : but he still possessed the peerless bow and arrows of Hêraklês, which were said to be essential to the capture of Troy. Diomêdês fetched Philoktêtês from Lemnus to the Grecian camp, where he was healed by the skill of Machaôn,[3] and took an active part against the Trojans—engaging in single combat with Paris, and killing him with one of the Hêrakleian arrows. The Trojans were allowed to carry away for burial the body of this prince, the fatal cause of all their sufferings ; but not until it had been mangled by the hand of Menelaus.[4] Odysseus went to the island of Skyrus to invite Neoptolemus to the army. The untried but

Philoktêtês and Neoptolemus.

Metamorphoses, are too well known to need special reference.

The suicide of Ajax seems to have been described in detail in the Æthiopis : compare Pindar, Isthm. iii. 51, and the Scholia ad loc., which show the attention paid by Pindar to the minute circumstances of the old epic. See Fragm. 2 of the Ἰλίου Πέρσις of Arktinus, in Düntz. p. 22, which would seem more properly to belong to the Æthiopis. Diktys relates the suicide of Ajax, as a consequence of his unsuccessful competition with Odysseus, not about the arms of Achilles, but about the Palladium, after the taking of the city (v. 14).

There were, however, many different accounts of the manner in which Ajax had died, some of which are enumerated in the argument to the drama of Sophoklês. Ajax is never wounded in the Iliad : Æschylus made him invulnerable except under the armpits (see Schol. ad. Sophoc. Ajac. 833) ; the Trojans pelted him with mud—εἰ πως βαρηθείη ὑπὸ τοῦ πηλοῦ. (Schol. Iliad. xiv. 404.)

[1] Soph. Philokt. 604.
[2] Soph. Philokt. 703. Ὦ μελέα ψυχὰ, Ὃς μηδ' οἰνοχύτου πόματος Ἥσθη δεκετῆ χρόνον, &c.

In the narrative of Diktys (ii. 47),

Philoktêtês returns from Lemnus to Troy much earlier in the war, before the death of Achilles, and without any assigned cause.

[3] According to Sophoklês, Hêraklês sends Asklêpius to Troy to heal Philoktêtês (Soph. Philokt. 1415).

The story of Philoktêtês formed the subject of a tragedy by Æschylus and of another by Euripidês (both lost) as well as by Sophoklês.

[4] Argument. Iliad. Minor. Düntz. l. c. Καὶ τὸν νεκρὸν ὑπὸ Μενελάου κατακισθέντα ἀνελόμενοι θάπτουσιν οἱ Τρῶες. See Quint. Smyrn. x. 240 : he differs here in many respects from the arguments of the old poems as given by Proclus, both as to the incidents and as to their order in time (Diktys, iv. 20). The wounded Paris flees to Œnônê, whom he had deserted in order to follow Helen, and entreats her to cure him by her skill in simples : she refuses, and permits him to die ; she is afterwards stung with remorse, and hangs herself (Quint. Smyrn. x. 285—331 ; Apollodôr. iii. 12, 6 ; Conôn, Narrat. 23 ; see Bachet de Meziriac, Comment. sur. les Epitres d'Ovide, t. i. p. 456). The story of Œnônê is as old as Hellanikus and Kephalôn of Gergis (see Hellan. Fragm 126, Didot'

impetuous youth, gladly obeying the call, received from Odysseus his father's armour ; while on the other hand, Eurypylus, son of Têlephus, came from Mysia, as auxiliary to the Trojans, and rendered to them valuable service—turning the tide of fortune for a time against the Greeks, and killing some of their bravest chiefs, amongst whom were numbered Peneleôs, and the unrivalled leech Machaôn.[1] The exploits of Neoptolemus were numerous, worthy of the glory of his race and the renown of his father. He encountered and slew Eurypylus, together with numbers of the Mysian warriors : he routed the Trojans and drove them within their walls, from whence they never again emerged to give battle : and he was not less distinguished for good sense and persuasive diction than for forward energy in the field.[2]

Troy however was still impregnable so long as the Palladium,
Capture of the Palladium.—The wooden horse.   a statue given by Zeus himself to Dardanus, remained in the citadel ; and great care had been taken by the Trojans not only to conceal this valuable present, but to construct other statues so like it as to mislead any intruding robber. Nevertheless the enterprising Odysseus, having disguised his person with miserable clothing and self-inflicted injuries, found means to penetrate into the city and to convey the Palladium by stealth away. Helen alone recognised him ; but she was now anxious to return to Greece, and even assisted Odysseus in concerting means for the capture of the town.[3]

To accomplish this object, one final stratagem was resorted to. By the hands of Epeius of Panopeus, and at the suggestion of Athênê, a capacious hollow wooden horse was constructed, capable

---

[1] To mark the way in which these legendary events pervaded and became embodied in the local worship, I may mention the received practice in the great temple of Asklêpius (father of Machaôn) at Pergamus, even in the time of Pausanias. Têlephus, father of Eurypylus, was the local hero and mythical king of Euthrania, in which Pergamus was situated. In the hymns there sung, the poem and the invocation were addressed to Têlephus; but nothing was said in them about Eurypylus, nor was it permitted even to mention his name in the temple,—"they knew him to be slayer of Machaôn ": ἄρχονται μὲν ἀπὸ Τηλέφου τῶν ὕμνων,

προσᾴδουσι δὲ οὐδὲν ἐς τὸν Εὐρύπυλον, οὐδὲ ἀρχὴν ἐν τῷ ναῷ θέλουσιν ὀνομάζειν αὐτὸν, οἷα ἐπιστάμενοι φονέα ὄντα Μαχάονος (Pausan. iii. 26, 7).
[2] Argument. Iliad. Minor. p. 18, Düntzer. Homer, Odyss. xi. 510—520. Pausan. iii. 26, 7. Quint. Smyrn. vii. 553 ; viii. 201.
[3] Argument. Iliad. Minor. p. 18, Düntz. ; Arktinus ap. Dionys. Hal. i. 69 ; Homer, Odyss. iv. 246 ; Quint. Smyrn. x. 354 ; Virg., Æn., ii. 164, and the 9th Exc. of Heyne on that book.
Compare, with this legend about the Palladium, the Roman legend respecting the Ancilia (Ovid, Fasti, iii. 381).

of containing one hundred men. In the inside of this horse, the *élite* of the Grecian heroes, Neoptolemus, Odysseus, Menelaus and others, concealed themselves while the entire Grecian army sailed away to Tenedos, burning their tents and pretending to have abandoned the siege. The Trojans, overjoyed to find themselves free, issued from the city and contemplated with astonishment the fabric which their enemies had left behind. They long doubted what should be done with it; and the anxious heroes from within heard the surrounding consultations, as well as the voice of Helen when she pronounced their names and counterfeited the accents of their wives.[1] Many of the Trojans were anxious to dedicate it to the gods in the city as a token of gratitude for their deliverance ; but the more cautious spirits inculcated distrust of an enemy's legacy. Laocoôn, the priest of Poseidôn, manifested his aversion by striking the side of the horse with his spear. The sound revealed that the horse was hollow, but the Trojans heeded not this warning of possible fraud. The unfortunate Laocoôn, a victim to his own sagacity and patriotism, miserably perished before the eyes of his countrymen, together with one of his sons : two serpents being sent expressly by the gods out of the sea to destroy him. By this terrific spectacle, together with the perfidious counsels of Sinon—a traitor whom the Greeks had left behind for the special purpose of giving false information—the Trojans were induced to make a breach in their own walls, and to drag the fatal fabric with triumph and exultation into their city.[2]

---

[1] Odyss. iv. 275; Virgil, Æneid, ii. 14 ; Heyne, Excurs. S. ad Æneid. ii. Stésichorus, in his Ἰλίου Πέρσις, gave the number of heroes in the wooden horse as one hundred (Stesichor. Fragm. 26, ed. Kleine ; compare Athenæ. xiii. p. 610).

[2] Odyss. viii. 492; xi. 522. Argument of the Ἰλίου Πέρσις of Arktinus, p. 21. Düntz. Hygin.f.108—135. Bacchylidês and Euphorion ap. Servium ad Virgil. Æneid. ii. 201.

Both Sinon and Laocoôn came originally from the old epic poem of Arktinus, though Virgil may perhaps have immediately borrowed both them, and other matters in his second book, from a poem passing under the name of Pisander. (See Macrob. Satur. v. 2; Heyne, Excurs. 1. ad Æn. ii.; Welcker,

Der Episch. Cyklus, p. 97.) We cannot give credit either to Arktinus or Pisander for the masterly specimen of oratory which is put into the mouth of Sinon in the Æneid.

In Quintus Smyrnæus (xii. 366), the Trojans torture and mutilate Sinon to extort from him the truth : his endurance, sustained by the inspiration of Hêrê, is proof against the extremity of suffering, and he adheres to his false tale. This is probably an incident of the old epic, though the delicate taste of Virgil, and his sympathy with the Trojans, has induced him to omit it. Euphorion ascribed the proceedings of Sinon to Odysseus: he also gave a different cause for the death of Laocoôn (Fr. 85 —36, p. 55, ed. Düntz., in the Fragments

The destruction of Troy, according to the decree of the gods,
Destruction was now irrevocably sealed. While the Trojans in-
of Troy. dulged in a night of riotous festivity, Sinon kindled
the fire-signal to the Greeks at Tenedos, loosening the bolts of the
wooden horse, from out of which the enclosed heroes descended.
The city, assailed both from within and from without, was
thoroughly sacked and destroyed; with the slaughter or captivity
of the larger portion of its heroes as well as its people. The
venerable Priam perished by the hand of Neoptolemus, having in
vain sought shelter at the domestic altar of Zeus Herkeios. But
his son Deiphobus, who since the death of Paris had become the
husband of Helen, defended his house desperately against Odysseus
and Menelaus, and sold his life dearly. After he was slain, his
body was fearfully mutilated by the latter.[1]

Thus was Troy utterly destroyed—the city, the altars and
temples,[2] and the population. Æneas and Antênôr were permitted to escape, with their families, having been always more
favourably regarded by the Greeks than the remaining Trojans.
According to one version of the story, they had betrayed the city
to the Greeks: a panther's skin had been hung over the door of
Antênôr's house as a signal for the victorious besiegers to spare it
Distribution in general plunder.[3] In the distribution of the prin-
of the cipal captives, Astyanax, the infant son of Hectôr, was
captives
among the cast from the top of the wall and killed, by Odysseus
victors. or Neoptolemus: Polyxena, the daughter of Priam,
was immolated on the tomb of Achilles, in compliance with a

---

of Epic Poets after Alexander the
Great). Sinon is ἑταῖρος Ὀδυσσέως in
Pausan. x. 27, 1.

[1] Odyss. viii. 515; Argument of
Arktinus, ut sup.; Euripid. Hecub.
903; Virg. Æn. vi. 497; Quint. Smyrn.
xiii. 35—229; Leschês ap. Pausan. x.
27, 2; Diktys, v. 12. Ibykus and
Simonidês also represented Deiphobus
as the ἀντεράστης Ἑλένης (Schol. Hom.
Iliad. xiii. 517).
   The night battle in the interior of
Troy was described with all its fearful
details both by Leschês and Arktinus:
the Ἰλίου Πέρσις of the latter seems to
have been a separate poem, that of the
former constituted a portion of the
Ilias Minor (see Welcker, Der Epische
Cyklus, p. 215): the Ἰλίου Πέρσις by

the lyric poets Sakadas and Stêsichorus
probably added many new incidents.
Polygnôtus had painted a succession
of the various calamitous scenes, drawn
from the poem of Leschês, on the walls
of the leschê at Delphi, with the name
written over each figure (Pausan. x.
25—26).
   Hellanikus fixed the precise day of
the month on which the capture took
place (Hellan. Fr. 143—144), the twelfth
day of Thargeliôn.
   [2] Æschyl. Agamemn. 527.—
Βωμοὶ δ' ἄϊστοι καὶ θεῶν ἱδρύματα,
Καὶ σπέρμα πάσης ἐξαπόλλυται χθονός.
   [3] This symbol of treachery also
figured in the picture of Polygnôtus.
A different story appears in Schol.
Iliad. iii. 206.

requisition made by the shade of the deceased hero to his countrymen ;[1] while her sister Kassandra was presented as a prize to
Agamemnôn. She had sought sanctuary at the altar of Athênê,
where Ajax, the son of Oïleus, making a guilty attempt to seize
her, had drawn both upon himself and upon the army the serious
wrath of the goddess, insomuch that the Greeks could hardly be
restrained from stoning him to death.[2] Andromachê and Helenus
were both given to Neoptolemus, who, according to the Ilias
Minor, carried away also Æneas as his captive.[3]

Helen gladly resumed her union with Menelaus : she accompanied him back to Sparta, and lived with him there many years
in comfort and dignity,[4] passing afterwards to a happy immortality in the Elysian fields. She was worshipped as   Helen
a goddess with her brothers the Dioskuri and her   restored to
husband, having her temple, statue and altar at   Menelaus—
Therapnæ and elsewhere. Various examples of her   lives in
miraculous intervention were cited among the Greeks.[5]   dignity at
The lyric poet Stêsichorus had ventured to denounce   Sparta—
her, conjointly with her sister Klytæmnêstra, in a tone of rude   passes to a
happy im-
mortality.
and plain-spoken severity, resembling that of Euripidês and
Lykophrôn afterwards, but strikingly opposite to the delicacy

---

[1] Euripid. Hecub. 38—114, and
Troad. 716 ; Leschês ap. Pausan. x. 25,
9 ; Virgil, Æneid, iii. 322, and Servius
ad loc.
A romantic tale is found in Diktys
respecting the passion of Achilles for
Polyxena (iii. 2).

[2] Odyss. xi. 422. Arktinus, Argum.
p. 21, Düntz. Theognis, 1232. Pausan.
i. 15, 2 ; x. 26, 3 ; 31, 1. As an expiation of this sin of their national hero, the
Lokrians sent to Ilium periodically
some of their maidens, to do menial
service in the temple of Athênê
(Plutarch, Ser. Numin. Vindict. p. 557,
with the citation from Euphorion or
Kallimachus, Düntzer, Epicc. Vet. p.
118)

[3] Leschês, Fr. 7, Düntz. ; ap. Schol.
Lycophr. 1263. Compare Schol. ad
1232, for the respectful recollection of
Andromachê, among the traditions of
the Molossian kings, as their heroic
mother, and Strabo, xiii. p. 594.

[4] Such is the story of the old epic
(see Odyss. iv. 260, and the fourth book
generally ; Argument of Ilias Minor,

p. 20, Düntz.). Polygnôtus, in the
paintings above alluded to, followed
the same tale (Pausan. x. 25, 3).
The anger of the Greeks against
Helen, and the statement that
Menelaus after the capture of Troy
approached her with revengeful
purposes, but was so mollified by her
surpassing beauty as to cast away his
uplifted sword, belongs to the age of
the tragedians (Æschyl. Agamem. 685-
1455 ; Eurip. Androm. 600—629 ; Helen.
75—120 ; Troad. 890—1057 ; compare
also the fine lines in the Æneid, ii.
567—588).

[5] See the description in Herodot. vi.
61, of the prayers offered to her, and
of the miracle which she wrought, to
remove the repulsive ugliness of a little
Spartan girl of high family. Compare
also Pindar, Olymp. iii. 2, and the
Scholia at the beginning of the ode ,
Eurip. Helen. 1662, and Orest. 1652—
1706 ; Isokrat. Encom. Helen. ii. p.
383, Auger ; Dio Chrysost. Or. xi. p.
311. θεὸς ἐνομίσθη παρὰ τοῖς Ἕλλησι :
Theodektês ap. Aristot. Pol. i. 2, 19.
Θείων ἀπ' ἀμφοῖν ἔκγονον ῥιζωμάτων,

and respect with which she is always handled by Homer, who never admits reproaches against her except from her own lips.[1] He was smitten with blindness, and made sensible of his impiety; but having repented and composed a special poem formally retracting the calumny, was permitted to recover his sight. In his poem of recantation (the famous palinode now unfortunately lost) he pointedly contradicted the Homeric narrative, affirming that Helen had never been at Troy at all, and that the Trojans had carried thither nothing but her image or *eidôlon*.[2] It is, probably, to the excited religious feelings of Stêsichorus that we owe the

---

[1] Euripid. Troad. 982 *seq.*; Lycophrôn ap. Steph. Byz. v. Αἰγύς; Stesichorus ap. Schol. Eurip. Orest. 239; Fragm. 9 and 10 of the Ἰλίου Πέρσις, Schneidewin:—

Οὔνεκα Τυνδάρεως ῥέζων ἁπᾶσι θεοῖς μιᾶς
λάθετ' ἠπιοδώρου
Κύπριδος· κείνα δὲ Τυνδάρεω κούραισι
χολωσαμένα
Διγάμους τριγάμους τίθησι
Καὶ λιπεσάνορας . . . .

Further

. . . . Ἑλένη ἐκοῦσ' ἄπηρε, &c.

He had probably contrasted her with other females carried away by force.

Stêsichorus also affirmed that Iphigeneia was the daughter of Helen by Thêseus, born at Argos before her marriage with Menelaus and made over to Klytæmnêstra; this tale was perpetuated by the temple of Eileithyia at Argos, which the Argeians affirmed to have been erected by Helen (Pausan. ii. 22, 7). The ages ascribed by Hellanikus and other logographers (Hellan. Fr. 74) to Theseus and Helen —he fifty years of age and she a child of seven—when he carried her off to Aphidnæ, can never have been the original form of any poetical legend. These ages were probably imagined in order to make the mythical chronology run smoothly; for Thêseus belongs to the generation before the Trojan war. But we ought always to recollect that Helen never grows old (τὴν γὰρ φάτις ἔμμεν' ἀγήρω—Quint. Smyr. x. 312), and that her chronology consists only with an immortal being. Servius observes (ad Æneid. ii. 601)—"Helenam *immortalem* fuisse indicat tempus. Nam constat fratres ejus cum Argonautis fuisse. Argonautarum filii cum Thebanis (Thebano Eteoclis et Polynicis

bello) dimicaverunt. Item illorum filii contra Trojam bella gesserunt. Ergo, si immortalis Helena non fuisset, tot sine dubio seculis durare non posset." So Xenophon, after enumerating many heroes of different ages, all pupils of Cheirôn, says that the life of Cheirôn suffices for all, he being brother of Zeus (De Venatione, c. 1).

The daughters of Tyndareus are Klytæmnêstra, Helen, and Timandra, all open to the charge advanced by Stêsichorus: see about Timandra, wife of the Tegeate Echemus, the new fragment of the Hesiodic Catalogue, recently restored by Geel (Göttling, Pref. Hesiod. p. lxi.).

It is curious to read, in Bayle's article *Hélène*, his critical discussion of the adventures ascribed to her—as if they were genuine matter of history, more or less correctly reported.

[2] Plato, Republic. ix. p. 587, c. 10. ὥσπερ τὸ τῆς Ἑλένης εἴδωλον Στησίχορός φησι περιμάχητον γενέσθαι ἐν Τροίῃ, ἀγνοίᾳ τοῦ ἀληθοῦς.

Isokrat. Encom. Helen. t. ii. p. 370, Auger; Plato, Phædr. c. 44, p. 243—244; Max. Tyr. Diss. xi. p. 320, Davis; Conôn, Narr. 18; Dio Chrysost. Or. xi. p. 323. Τὸν μὲν Στησίχορον ἐν τῇ ὑστέρον ᾠδῇ λέγειν, ὡς τὸ παράπαν οὐδὲ πλεύσειεν ἡ Ἑλένη οὐδάμοσε. Horace, Od. i. 17; Epod. xvii. 42.—

"Infamis Helenæ Castor offensus vicem Fraterque magni Castoris, victi prece, Adempta vati reddidere lumina."

Pausan. iii. 19, 5. Virgil, surveying the war from the point of view of the Trojans, had no motive to look upon Helen with particular tenderness: Deiphobus imputes to her the basest treachery (Æneid. vi. 511, "*scelus exitiale Lacænæ*"; compare ii. 567).

first idea of this glaring deviation from the old legend, which could never have been recommended by any considerations of poetical interest.

Other versions were afterwards started, forming a sort of compromise between Homer and Stêsichorus, admitting that Helen had never really been at Troy, without altogether denying her elopement. Such is the story of her having been detained in Egypt during the whole term of the siege. Paris, on his departure from Sparta, had been driven thither by storms, and the Egyptian king Próteus, hearing of the grievous wrong which he had committed towards Menelaus, had sent him away from the country with severe menaces, detaining Helen until her lawful husband should come to seek her. When the Greeks reclaimed Helen from Troy, the Trojans assured them solemnly, that she neither was, nor ever had been, in the town; but the Greeks, treating this allegation as fraudulent, prosecuted the siege until their ultimate success confirmed the correctness of the statement. Menelaus did not recover Helen until, on his return from Troy, he visited Egypt.[1] Such was the story told by the Egyptian priests to Herodotus, and it appeared satisfactory to his historicising mind. "For if Helen had really been at Troy (he argues) she would certainly have been given up, even had she been mistress of Priam himself instead of Paris : the Trojan king, with all his family and all his subjects, would never knowingly have incurred utter and irretrievable destruction for the purpose of retaining her : their misfortune was, that while they did not possess, and therefore could not restore her, they yet found it impossible to convince the Greeks that such was the fact." Assuming the historical character of the war of Troy, the

Blindness and cure of the poet Stêsichorus—alteration of the legend about Helen.

Egyptian tale about Helen—tendency to historicise.

---

[1] Herodot. ii. 120. οὐ γὰρ δὴ οὕτω γε φρενοβλαβὴς ἦν ὁ Πρίαμος, οὐδ' οἱ ἄλλοι προσήκοντες αὐτῷ, &c. The passage is too long to cite, but is highly curious : not the least remarkable part is the religious colouring which he gives to the new version of the story which he is adopting,—"the Trojans, though they had not got Helen yet could not persuade the Greeks that this was the fact; for it was the divine will that they should be destroyed root and branch, in order to make it plain to mankind that upon great crimes the gods inflict great punishments".

Dio Chrysostom (Or. xi. p. 833) reasons in the same way as Herodotus against the credibility of the received narrative. On the other hand, Isokratês, in extolling Helen, dwells on the calamities of the Trojan war as a test of the peerless value of the prize (Encom. Hel. p. 360, Aug.): in the view of Pindar (Olymp. xiii. 56) as well as in that of Hesiod (Opp. Di. 165), Helen is the one prize contended for.

Euripidês, in his tragedy of Helen,

remark of Herodotus admits of no reply; nor can we greatly wonder that he acquiesced in the tale of Helen's Egyptian detention, as a substitute for the "incredible insanity" which the genuine legend imputes to Priam and the Trojans. Pausanias, upon the same ground and by the same mode of reasoning, pronounced that the Trojan horse must have been in point of fact a battering-engine, because to admit the literal narrative would be to impute utter childishness to the defenders of the city. And Mr. Payne Knight rejects Helen altogether as the real cause of the Trojan war, though she may have been the pretext of it; for he thinks that neither the Greeks nor the Trojans could have been so mad and silly as to endure calamities of such magnitude "for one little woman".[1] Mr. Knight suggests various political causes as substitutes; these might deserve consideration, either if any evidence could be produced to countenance them, or if the subject on which they are brought to bear could be shown to belong to the domain of history.

The return of the Grecian chiefs from Troy furnished matter to the ancient epic hardly less copious than the siege itself, and the more susceptible of indefinite diversity, inasmuch as those who had before acted in concert were now dispersed and isolated. Moreover the stormy voyages and compulsory wanderings of the heroes exactly fell in with the common aspirations after an heroic founder, and enabled even the most remote Hellenic settlers to connect the origin of their town with this prominent event of their ante-historical and semi-divine world. And an absence of ten years afforded room for the supposition of many domestic changes in their native abode, and many family misfortunes and misdeeds during the interval. One of these heroic "Returns," that of Odysseus, has been immortalised by the verse of Homer. The hero, after a series of long-protracted suffering and expatriation, inflicted on him by the anger of Poseidôn, at last reaches his native island, but finds his

Return of the Greeks from Troy.

---

recognises the detention of Helen in Egypt and the presence of her εἴδωλον at Troy, but he follows Stêsichorus in denying her elopement altogether,— Hermês had carried her to Egypt in a cloud (Helen 35—45, 706): compare Von Hoff, De Mytho Helenæ Euripideæ, cap. 2, p. 35 (Leyden, 1843)

[1] Pausan. i. 23, 8; Payne Knight, Prolegg. ad Homer. c. 53. Euphorion construed the wooden horse into a Grecian ship called Ἵππος, "*The Horse*" (Euphorion, Fragm. 34, ap. Düntzer, Fragm. Epicc. Græc. p. 55). See Thucyd. i. 12; vi. 2.

wife beset, his youthful son insulted, and his substance plundered,
by a troop of insolent suitors; he is forced to appear as a wretched
beggar, and to endure in his own person their scornful treatment;
but finally, by the interference of Athênê coming in aid of his
own courage and stratagem, he is enabled to overwhelm his
enemies, to resume his family position, and to recover his property.
The return of several other Grecian chiefs was the subject of an
epic poem by Hagias, which is now lost, but of which a brief
abstract or argument still remains: there were in antiquity various
other poems of similar title and analogous matter.[1]

As usual with the ancient epic, the multiplied sufferings of this
back-voyage are traced to divine wrath, justly provoked by the
sins of the Greeks; who, in the fierce exultation of a victory
purchased by so many hardships, had neither respected nor even[2]
spared the altars of the gods in Troy. Athênê, who had been
their most zealous ally during the siege, was so incensed by their final recklessness, more especially by
the outrage of Ajax, son of Oïleus, that she actively
harassed and embittered their return, in spite of every effort to
appease her. The chiefs began to quarrel among themselves:
their formal assembly became a scene of drunkenness; even
Agamemnôn and Menelaus lost their fraternal harmony, and
each man acted on his own separate resolution.[3] Nevertheless,
according to the Odyssey, Nestôr, Diomêdês, Neoptolemus,
Idomeneus and Philoktêtês, reached home speedily and safely;
Agamemnôn also arrived in Peloponnêsus, to perish by the hand
of a treacherous wife; but Menelaus was condemned to long
wanderings and to the severest privations in Egypt, Cyprus and
elsewhere, before he could set foot in his native land. The
Lokrian Ajax perished on the Gyræan rock.[4] Though exposed
to a terrible storm, he had already reached this place of safety,
when he indulged in the rash boast of having escaped in defiance
of the gods. No sooner did Poseidôn hear this language, than he

Their sufferings —anger of the gods.

[1] Suidas, v. Νόστος. Wüllner, De
Cyclo Epico, p. 93. Also a poem
Ἀτρειδῶν κάθοδος (Athenæ. vii. p. 281).
[2] Upon this the turn of fortune in
Grecian affairs depends (Æschyl.
Agamemn. 338; Odyss. iii. 130;
Euripid. Troad. 69—95).
[3] Odyss. iii. 130—161; Æschyl.
Agamemn. 650—662.

[4] Odyss. iii. 188—196; iv. 5—87.
The Egyptian city of Kanopus, at the
mouth of the Nile, was believed to
have taken its name from the pilot of
Menelaus, who had died and was
buried there (Strabo, xvii. p. 801;
Tacit. Ann. ii. 60). Μενελάϊος νόμος,
so called after Menelaus (Dio Chrysost.
xi. p. 361).

struck with his trident the rock which Ajax was grasping and precipitated both into the sea.[1] Kalchas the soothsayer, together with Leonteus and Polypœtês, proceeded by land from Troy to Kolophon.[2]

In respect however to these and other Grecian heroes, tales *Wanderings* were told different from those in the Odyssey, assign-*of the heroes* ing to them a long expatriation and a distant home. *in all* *directions.* Nestôr went to Italy, where he founded Metapontum, Pisa and Hêrakleia :[3] Philoktêtês[4] also went to Italy, founded Petilia and Krimisa, and sent settlers to Egesta in Sicily. Neoptolemus, under the advice of Thetis, marched by land across Thrace, met with Odysseus, who had come by sea, at Maroneia, and then pursued his journey to Epirus, where he became king of the Molossians.[5] Idomeneus came to Italy, and founded Uria in the Salentine peninsula. Diomêdês, after wandering far and wide, went along the Italian coast into the innermost Adriatic gulf, and finally settled in Daunia, founding the cities of Argyrippa, Beneventum, Atria and Diomêdeia : by the favour of Athênê he became immortal, and was worshipped as a god in many different places.[6] The Lokrian followers of Ajax founded the Epizephyrian Lokri on the southernmost corner of Italy,[7] besides another settlement in Libya. I have spoken in another

---

[1] Odyss. iv. 500. The epic Νόστοι of Hagias placed this adventure of Ajax on the rocks of Kaphareus, a southern promontory of Eubœa (Argum. Νόστοι, p. 23, Düntzer). Deceptive lights were kindled on the dangerous rocks by Nauplius, the father of Palamêdês, in revenge for the death of his son (Sophoklês, Ναύπλιος Πυρκαεύς, a lost tragedy ; Hygin. f. 116; Senec. Agamemn. 567).

[2] Argument. Νόστοι, ut sup. There were monuments of Kalchas near Sipontum in Italy also (Strabo, vi. p. 284), as well as at Selgê in Pisidia (Strabo, xii. p. 570).

[3] Strabo, v. p. 222 ; vi. p. 264. Vellei. Paterc. i. 1 ; Servius ad Æn. x. 179. He had built a temple to Athênê in the island of Keôs (Strabo, x. p. 487).

[4] Strabo, vi. pp. 254, 272 ; Virgil. Æn. iii. 401, and Servius ad loc. : Lycophrôn, 912. Both the tomb of Philoktêtês and the arrows of Hêraklês which he had used against Troy, were for a long time

shown at Thurium (Justin, xx. 1).

[5] Argument. Νόστοι, p. 23, Düntz. ; Pindar, Nem. iv. 51. According to Pindar, however, Neoptolemus comes from Troy by sea, misses the island of Skyrus, and sails round to the Epeirotic Ephyra (Nem. vii. 37).

[6] Pindar, Nem. x. 7, with the Scholia. Strabo, iii. p. 150 ; v. p. 214—215; vi. p. 284. Stephan. Byz. Ἀργύριππα, Διομηδεία. Aristotle recognises him as buried in the Diomedean islands in the Adriatic (Anthol. Gr. Brunck. i. p. 178). The identical tripod which had been gained by Diomêdês, as victor in the chariot-race at the funeral games of Patroklus, was shown at Delphi in the time of Phanias, attested by an inscription, as well as the dagger which had been worn by Helikaôn, son of Antênôr (Athenæ. vi. p. 232).

[7] Virgil, Æneid, iii. 399 ; xi. 265 ; and Servius, ibid. Ajax, the son of Oïleus, was worshipped there as a hero (Conôn, Narr. 18).

place of the compulsory exile of Teukros, who besides founding the city of Salamis in Cyprus, is said to have established some settlements in the Iberian peninsula.[1] Menestheus the Athenian did the like, and also founded both Elæa in Mysia and Skylletium in Italy.[2] The Arcadian chief Agapênôr founded Paphus in Cyprus.[3] Epeius, of Panopeus in Phôkis, the constructor of the Trojan horse with the aid of the goddess Athênê, settled at Lagaria near Sybaris on the coast of Italy; and the very tools which he had employed in that remarkable fabric were shown down to a late date in the temple of Athênê at Metapontum.[4] Temples, altars and towns were also pointed out in Asia Minor, in Samos and in Krête, the foundation of Agamemnôn or of his followers.[5] The inhabitants of the Grecian town of Skionê, in the Thracian peninsula called Pallênê or Pellênê, accounted themselves the offspring of the Pellênians from Achæa in Peloponnêsus, who had served under Agamemnôn before Troy, and who on their return from the siege had been driven on the spot by a storm and there settled.[6] The Pamphylians, on the southern coast of Asia Minor, deduced their origin from the wanderings of Amphilochus and Kalchus after the siege of Troy: the inhabitants of the Amphilochian Argos on the Gulf of Ambrakia revered the same Amphilochus as their founder.[7] The Orchomenians under Ialmenus, on quitting the conquered city, wandered or were driven to the eastern extremity of the Euxine Sea: and the

[1] Strabo, iii. p. 157; Isokratês, Evagor. Encom. p. 192; Justin. xliv. 3. Ajax, the son of Teukros, established a temple of Zeus, and an hereditary priesthood always held by his descendants (who mostly bore the name of Ajax or Teukros), at Olbê in Kilikia (Strabo, xiv. p. 672). Teukros carried with him his Trojan captives to Cyprus (Athenæ. vi. p. 256).

[2] Strabo, iii. p. 140—150; vi. p. 261; xiii. p. 622. See the epitaphs on Teukros and Agapenôr by Aristotle (Antholog. Gr. ed. Brunck. i. p. 179—180).

[3] Strabo, xiv. p. 683; Pausan. viii. 5, 2.

[4] Strabo, vi. p. 263; Justin, xx. 2; Aristot. Mirab. Ausc. c. 108. Also the epigram of the Rhodian Simmias called Πελεκύς (Antholog. Gr. ed. Brunck. i. p. 210).

[5] Vellei. Patercul. i. 1. Stephan. Byz. v. Λάμπη. Strabo, xiii. p. 605; xiv. p. 639. Theopompus (Fragm. 111, Didot) recounted that Agamemnôn and his followers had possessed themselves of the larger portion of Cyprus.

[6] Thucyd. iv. 120.

[7] Herodot. vii. 91; Thucyd. ii. 68. According to the old elegiac poet Kallinos, Kalchas himself had died at Klarus near Kolophôn, after his march from Troy, but Mopsus, his rival in the prophetic function, had conducted his followers into Pamphilia and Kilikia (Strabo, xii. p. 570; xiv. p. 668). The oracle of Amphilochus at Mallus in Kilikia bore the highest character for exactness and truth-telling in the time of Pausanias, μαντεῖον ἀψευδέστατον τῶν ἐπ' ἐμοῦ (Paus. i. 34. 2). Another story recognised Leontius and Polypœtês as the founders of Aspendus in Kilikia (Eustath. ad Iliad. ii. 138).

barbarous Achæans under Mount Caucasus were supposed to have derived their first establishment from this source.[1] Merionês with his Krêtan followers settled at Engyion in Sicily, along with the preceding Krêtans who had remained there after the invasion of Minôs. The Elymians in Sicily also were composed of Trojans and Greeks separately driven to the spot, who, forgetting their previous differences, united in the joint settlements of Eryx and Egesta.[2] We hear of Podaleirius both in Italy and on the coast of Karia ;[3] of Akamas, son of Thêseus, at Amphipolis in Thrace, at Soli in Cyprus, and at Synnada in Phrygia[4]; of Guneus, Prothous and Eurypylus, in Krête as well as in Libya.[5] The obscure poem of Lycophrôn enumerates many of these dispersed and expatriated heroes, whose conquest of Troy was indeed a Kadmeian victory (according to the proverbial phrase of the Greeks), wherein the sufferings of the victor were little inferior to those of the vanquished.[6] It was particularly among the Italian Greeks, where they were worshipped with very special solemnity, that their presence as wanderers from Troy was reported and believed.[7]

Memorials of them throughout the Grecian world.

I pass over the numerous other tales which circulated among the ancients, illustrating the ubiquity of the Grecian and Trojan heroes as well as that of the Argonauts,—one of the most striking features in the Hellenic legendary world.[8] Amongst them all, the most interesting, individually, is Odysseus, whose romantic adventures in fabulous places and among fabulous persons have been made familiarly known by Homer. The goddesses Kalypsô and Circê; the semi-divine

Odysseus— his final adventures and death.

[1] Strabo, ix. p. 416.
[2] Diodôr. iv. 79 ; Thucyd. vi. 2.
[3] Stephan. Byz. v. Σύρνα ; Lycophrôn, 1047.
[4] Æschines, De Falsâ Legat. c. 14 ; Strabo, xiv. p. 683 ; Stephan. Byz. v. Σύνναδα.
[5] Lycophrôn, 877—902, with Scholia; Apollodôr. Fragm. p. 386, Heyne. There is also a long enumeration of these returning wanderers and founders of new settlements in Solinus (Polyhist. c. 2).
[6] Strabo, iii. p. 150.
[7] Aristot. Mirabil. Auscult. 79, 106, 107, 109, 111.
[8] Strabo, i. p. 48. After dwelling emphatically on the long voyages of

Dionysus, Hêraklês, Jasôn, Odysseus, and Menelaus, he says, Αἰνείαν δὲ καὶ Ἀντήνορα καὶ Ἐνετοὺς, καὶ ἁπλῶς τοὺς ἐκ τοῦ Τρωϊκοῦ πολέμου πλανηθέντας εἰς πᾶσαν τὴν οἰκουμένην, ἄξιον μὴ τῶν παλαιῶν ἀνθρώπων νομίσαι ; Συνέβη γὰρ δὴ τοῖς τότε Ἕλλησιν, ὁμοίως καὶ τοῖς βαρβάροις, διὰ τὸν τῆς στρατείας χρόνον, ἀποβαλεῖν τά τε ἐν οἴκῳ καὶ τῇ στρατείᾳ πορισθέντα· ὥστε μετὰ τὴν τοῦ Ἰλίου καταστροφὴν τούς τε νικήσαντας ἐπὶ λῃστείαν τραπέσθαι διὰ τὰς ἀπορίας, καὶ πολλῷ μᾶλλον τοὺς ἡττηθέντας καὶ περιγενομένους ἐκ τοῦ πολέμου. Καὶ δὴ καὶ πόλεις ὑπὸ τούτων κτισθῆναι λέγονται κατὰ πᾶσαν τὴν ἔξω τῆς Ἑλλάδος παραλίαν, ἔστι δ' ὅπου καὶ τὴν μεσόγαιαν.

mariners of Phæacia, whose ships are endowed with consciousness and obey without a steersman ; the one-eyed Cyclôpes, the gigantic Læstrygones, and the wind-ruler Æolos ; the Sirens who ensnare by their song, as the Lotophagi fascinate by their food—all these pictures formed integral and interesting portions of the old epic.   Homer leaves Odysseus re-established in his house and family.   But so marked a personage could never be permitted to remain in the tameness of domestic life : the epic poem called the Telegonia ascribed to him a subsequent series of adventures.   Telegonus, his son by Circê, coming to Ithaka in search of his father, ravaged the island and killed Odysseus without knowing who he was.   Bitter repentance overtook the son for his undesigned parricide : at his prayer and by the intervention of his mother Circê, both Penelopê and Têlemachus were made immortal : Telegonus married Penelopê, and Têlemachus married Circê.[1]

We see by this poem that Odysseus was represented as the mythical ancestor of the Thesprotian kings, just as Neoptolemus was of the Molossian.

It has already been mentioned that Antênôr and Æneas stand distinguished from the other Trojans by a dissatisfaction with Priam and a sympathy with the Greeks, which is by Sophoklês and others construed as treacherous collusion,[2]—a suspicion indirectly glanced at, though emphatically repelled, by the Æneas of Virgil.[3]   In the old epic of Arktinus, next in age to the Iliad and Odyssey, Æneas abandons Troy and retires to Mount Ida, in terror at the miraculous death of Laocoôn, before the entry of the Greeks into the town and the last night battle : yet Leschês, in another of the ancient epic poems, represented him as having been carried away captive by Neoptolemus.[4]   In a remarkable passage of the Iliad,

Æneas and his descendants.

---

[1] The Telegonia, composed by Eugammôn of Kyrênê, is lost, but the Argument of it has been preserved by Proclus (p. 25, Düntzer ; Diktys, vi. 15).

[2] Dionys. Hal. i. 46—48 ; Sophokl. ap. Strab. xiii. p. 608 ; Livy, i. 1 ; Xenophon, Venat. i. 15.

[3] Æn. ii. 433.

[4] Argument of 'Ιλίου Πέρσις ; Fragm. 7, of Leschês, in Düntzer's Collection, p. 19—21.

Hellanikus seems to have adopted this retirement of Æneas to the strongest parts of Mount Ida, but to have reconciled it with the stories of the migration of Æneas, by saying that he only remained in Ida a little time, and then quitted the country altogether by virtue of a convention concluded with the Greeks (Dionys. Hal. i. 47—48).   Among the infinite variety of stories respecting this hero, one was, that after having effected his

Poseidôn describes the family of Priam as having incurred the hatred of Zeus, and predicts that Æneas and his descendants shall reign over the Trojans: the race of Dardanus, beloved by Zeus more than all his other sons, would thus be preserved, since Æneas belonged to it. Accordingly, when Æneas is in imminent peril from the hands of Achilles, Poseidôn specially interferes to rescue him, and even the implacable miso-Trojan goddess Hêrê assents to the proceeding.[1] These passages have been construed by various able critics to refer to a family of philo-Hellenic or semi-Hellenic Æneadæ, known even in the time of the early singers of the Iliad as masters of some territory in or near the Troad, and professing to be descended from, as well as worshipping, Æneas. In the town of Skêpsis, situated in the mountainous range of Ida, about thirty miles eastward of Ilium, there existed two noble and priestly families who professed to be descended, the one from Hectôr, the other from Æneas. The Skêpsian critic

Dêmêtrius (in whose time both these families were still to be found) informs us that Skamandrius son of Hectôr, and Ascanius son of Æneas, were the archegets or heroic founders of his native city, which had been originally situated on one of the highest ranges of Ida, and was subsequently transferred by them to the less lofty spot on which it stood in his time.[2] In Arisbê and Gentinus there seem to have been families professing the same descent, since the same archegets were acknowledged.[3] In

Different stories about Æneas.— Æneadæ at Skêpsis.

---

settlement in Italy, he had returned to Troy and resumed the sceptre, bequeathing it at his death to Ascanius (Dionys. Hal. i. 53): this was a comprehensive scheme for apparently reconciling all the legends.

[1] Iliad, xx. 300. Poseidôn speaks, respecting Æneas—

'Αλλ' ἄγεθ', ἡμεῖς πέρ μιν ὑπ' ἐκ θανάτου ἀγάγωμεν,
Μήπως καὶ Κρονίδης κεχολώσεται, αἴκεν Ἀχιλλεὺς
Τόνδε κατακτείνῃ· μόριμον δέ οἱ ἔστ' ἀλέασθαι,
Ὄφρα μὴ ἄσπερμος γενεὴ καὶ ἄφαντος ὄληται
Δαρδάνου, ὃν Κρονίδης περὶ πάντων φίλατο παίδων,
Οἳ ἕθεν ἐξεγένοντο, γυναικῶν τε θνητάων.
Ἤδη γὰρ Πριάμου γενεὴν ἤχθηρε Κρονίων·
Νῦν δὲ δὴ Αἰνείαο βίη Τρώεσσιν ἀνάξει,

Καὶ παίδων παῖδες, τοί κεν μετόπισθε γένωνται.

Again, v. 339, Poseidôn tells Æneas that he has nothing to dread from any other Greek than Achilles.

[2] See O. Müller, on the causes of the mythe of Æneas, and his voyage to Italy, in Classical Journal, vol. xxvi. p. 308; Klausen, Æneas und die Penaten, vol. i. p. 43—52.
Dêmêtrius Skêps. ap. Strab. xiii. p. 607; Nicolaus ap. Steph. Byz. v. Ἀσκανία. Dêmêtrius conjectured that Skêpsis had been the regal seat of Æneas: there was a village called Æneia near to it (Strabo, xiii. p. 603).

[3] Steph. Byz. v. Ἀρίσβη, Γεντῖνος. Ascanius is king of Ida after the departure of the Greeks (Conôn, Narr. 41; Mela, i. 18). Ascanius portus between Phokæa and Kymê.

Ophrynium, Hectôr had his consecrated edifice, while in Ilium both he and Æneas were worshipped as gods :[1] and it was the remarkable statement of the Lesbian Menekratês, that Æneas, "having been wronged by Paris and stripped of the sacred privileges which belonged to him, avenged himself by betraying the city, and then became one of the Greeks ".[2]

One tale thus among many respecting Æneas, and that too the most ancient of all, preserved among natives of the Troad, who worshipped him as their heroic ancestor, was, that after the capture of Troy he continued in the country as king of the remaining Trojans, on friendly terms with the Greeks. But there were other tales respecting him, alike numerous and irreconcileable: the hand of destiny marked him as a wanderer *(fato profugus)* and his ubiquity is not exceeded even by that of Odysseus. We hear of him at Ænus in Thrace, in Pallênê, at Æneia in the Thermaic Gulf, in Delus, at Orchomenus and Mantineia in Arcadia, in the islands of Kythêra and Zakynthus, in Leukas and Ambrakia, at Buthrotum in Epirus, on the Salentine peninsula and various other places in the southern region of Italy ; at Drepana and Segesta in Sicily, at Carthage, at Cape Palinurus, Cumæ, Misenum, Caieta, and finally in Latium, where he lays the first humble foundation of the mighty Rome and her empire.[3] And the reason why his wanderings were not continued still further was, that the oracles and the pronounced will of the gods directed him to settle in Latium.[4] In each of these numerous places his visit was commemorated and certified by local monuments or special

Ubiquity of Æneas.

---

[1] Strabo, xiii. p. 595 : Lycophrôn, 1208, and Sch. ; Athenagoras, Legat. 1. Inscription in Clarke's Travels, vol. ii. p. 86, Οἱ Ἰλιεῖς τὸν πάτριον θεὸν Αἰνείαν. Lucian. Deor. Concil. c 12. i. 111. p. 534, Hemst.

[2] Menekrat. ap. Dionys. Hal. i. 48. Ἀχαιοὺς δὲ ἀνίη εἶχε (after the burial) καὶ ἐδόκεον τῆς στρατιῆς τὴν κεφαλὴν ἀπηράχθαι. Ὅμως δὲ τάφον αὐτῷ δαίσαντες, ἐπολέμεον γῇ πάσῃ, ἄχρις Ἴλιος ἑάλω, Αἰνείεω ἐνδόντος. Αἰνείης γὰρ ἄτιτος ἐὼν ὑπὸ Ἀλεξάνδρου, καὶ ἀπὸ γερέων ἱερῶν ἐξειργόμενος, ἀνέτρεψε Πρίαμον, ἐργασάμενος δὲ ταῦτα, εἰς Ἀχαιῶν ἐγεγόνει.

[3] Dionys. Halic. A. R. i. 48—54; Heyne, Excurs. 1 ad Æneid. iii. : De Æneæ Erroribus, and Excurs. 1 ad

Æneid. v. ; Conôn, Narr. 46 ; Livy, xl. 4 ; Stephan. Byz. Αἴνεια. The inhabitants of Æneia in the Thermaic Gulf worshipped him with great solemnity as their heroic founder (Pausan. iii. 22, 4 ; viii. 12, 4). The tomb of Anchisês was shown on the confines of the Arcadian Orchomenus and Mantineia (compare Stephan. Byz. v. Κάφυαι), under the mountain called Anchisia, near a temple of Aphroditê : on the discrepancies respecting the death of Anchisês (Heyne, Excurs. 17 ad Æn. iii.) : Segesta in Sicily founded by Æneas (Cicero, Verr. iv. 33).

[4] Τοῦ δὲ μηκέτι προσωτέρω τῆς Εὐρώπης πλεῦσαι τὸν Τρωϊκὸν στόλον, οἵ τε χρησμοὶ ἐγένοντο αἴτιοι, &c. (Dionys. Hal. i. 55.)

legends, particularly by temples and permanent ceremonies in honour of his mother Aphroditê, whose worship accompanied him everywhere: there were also many temples and many different tombs of Æneas himself.[1] The vast ascendency acquired by Rome, the ardour with which all the literary Romans espoused the idea of a Trojan origin, and the fact that the Julian family recognised Æneas as their gentile primary ancestor,—all contributed to give to the Roman version of this legend the preponderance over every other. The various other places, in which monuments of Æneas were found, came thus to be represented as places where he had halted for a time on his way from Troy to Latium. But though the legendary pretensions of these places were thus eclipsed in the eyes of those who constituted the literary public, the local belief was not extinguished ; they claimed the hero as their permanent property, and his tomb was to them a proof that he had lived and died among them.

Antênôr, who shares with Æneas the favourable sympathy of the Greeks, is said by Pindar to have gone from Troy along with Menelaus and Helen into the region of Kyrênê in Libya.[2] But according to the more current narrative, he placed himself at the head of a body of Eneti or Veneti from Paphlagonia, who had come as allies of Troy, and went by sea into the inner part of the Adriatic Gulf, where he conquered the neighbouring barbarians and founded the town of Patavium (the modern Padua); the Veneti in this region were said to owe their origin to his immigration.[3] We learn further from Strabo, that Opsikellas, one of the companions of Antênôr, had continued his wanderings even into Ibêria, and that he had there established a settlement bearing his name.[4]

Antênôr.

Thus endeth the Trojan war, together with its sequel, the dispersion of the heroes, victors as well as vanquished. The account here given of it has been unavoidably brief and imperfect; for in a work intended to follow consecutively the real history of

---

[1] Dionys. Hal. i. 54. Among other places, his tomb was shown at Berecynthia, in Phrygia (Festus v. *Romam*, p. 224, ed. Müller): a curious article, which contains an assemblage of the most contradictory statements respecting both Æneas and Latinus.
[2] Pindar, Pyth. v., and the citation from the Νόστοι of Lysimachus in the Scholia : given still more fully in the Scholia ad Lycophrôn. 875. There was a λόφος 'Αντηνορίδων at Kyrênê.
[3] Livy, i. 1. Servius ad Æneid. i. 242. Strabo, i. 48; v. 212. Ovid, Fasti, iv. 75.
[4] Strabo, iii. p. 157.

the Greeks, no greater space can be allotted even to the most splendid gem of their legendary period. Indeed, although it would be easy to fill a large volume with the separate incidents which have been introduced into the "Trojan cycle," the misfortune is that they are for the most part so contradictory as to exclude all possibility of weaving them into one connected narrative. We are compelled to select one out of the number, generally without any solid ground of preference, and then to note the variations of the rest. No one who has not studied the original documents can imagine the extent to which this discrepancy proceeds: it covers almost every portion and fragment of the tale.[1]

Tale of Troy—its magnitude and discrepancies.

But though much may have been thus omitted of what the reader might expect to find in an account of the Trojan war, its genuine character has been studiously preserved, without either exaggeration or abatement. The real Trojan war is that which was recounted by Homer and the old epic poets, and continued by all the lyric and tragic composers. For the latter, though they took great liberties with the particular incidents, and introduced to some extent a new moral tone, yet worked more or less faithfully on the Homeric scale ; and even Euripidês, who departed the most widely from the feelings of the old legend, never lowered down his matter to the analogy of contemporary life. They preserved its well defined object, at once righteous and romantic, the recovery of the daughter of Zeus and sister of the Dioskuri—its mixed agencies, divine, heroic and human— the colossal force and deeds of its chief actors—its vast magnitude and long duration, as well as the toils which the conquerors underwent, and the Nemesis which followed upon their success. And these were the circumstances which, set forth in the full blaze of epic and tragic poetry, bestowed upon the legend its powerful and imperishable influence over the Hellenic mind. The enterprise was one comprehending all the members of the Hellenic body, of which each individually might be

Trojan war —essentially legendary— its importance as an item in Grecian national faith.

[1] These diversities are well set forth in the useful Dissertation of Fuchs, De Varietate Fabularum Troicarum (Cologne, 1830).
    Of the number of romantic statements put forth respecting Helen and Achilles especially, some idea may be formed from the fourth, fifth and sixth chapters of Ptolemy Héphæstion (apud Westermann, Scriptt. Mythograph. p. 188, &c.).

proud, and in which, nevertheless, those feelings of jealous and
narrow patriotism, so lamentably prevalent in many of the towns,
were as much as possible excluded. It supplied them with a
grand and inexhaustible object of common sympathy, common
faith, and common admiration ; and when occasions arose for
bringing together a Pan-Hellenic force against the barbarians,
the precedent of the Homeric expedition was one upon which
the elevated minds of Greece could dwell with the certainty of
rousing an unanimous impulse, if not always of counterworking
sinister by-motives, among their audience. And the incidents
comprised in the Trojan cycle were familiarised, not only to
the public mind, but also to the public eye, by innumerable
representations both of the sculptor and the painter,—those
which were romantic and chivalrous being better adapted for
this purpose, and therefore more constantly employed, than any
other.

Of such events the genuine Trojan war of the old epic was for
the most part composed. Though literally believed, reverentially

Basis of
history for
it—pos-
sible, and
nothing
more.

cherished, and numbered among the gigantic phænomena of the past, by the Grecian public, it is in the
eyes of modern inquiry essentially a legend and
nothing more. If we are asked whether it be not a
legend embodying portions of historical matter, and
raised upon a basis of truth,—whether there may not really have
occurred at the foot of the hill of Ilium a war purely human and
political, without gods, without heroes, without Helen, without
Amazons, without Ethiopians under the beautiful son of Eôs,
without the wooden horse, without the characteristic and expres-
sive features of the old epical war,—like the mutilated trunk of
Deïphobus in the under world ; if we are asked whether there
was not really some such historical Trojan war as this, our
answer must be, that as the possibility of it cannot be denied, so
neither can the reality of it be affirmed. We possess nothing
but the ancient epic itself without any independent evidence :
had it been an age of records indeed, the Homeric epic in
its exquisite and unsuspecting simplicity would probably never
have come into existence. Whoever therefore ventures to
dissect Homer, Arktinus, and Leschês, and to pick out certain
portions as matters of fact, while he sets aside the rest as fiction,

must do so in full reliance on his own powers of historical divination, without any means either of proving or verifying his conclusions. Among many attempts, ancient as well as modern, to identify real objects in this historical darkness, that of Dio Chrysostom deserves attention for its extraordinary boldness. In his oration addressed to the inhabitants of Ilium, and intended to demonstrate that the Trojans were not only blameless as to the origin of the war, but victorious in its issue—he overthrows all the leading points of the Homeric narrative, and re-writes nearly the whole from beginning to end: Paris is the lawful husband of Helen, Achilles is slain by Hectôr, and the Greeks retire without taking Troy, disgraced as well as baffled. Having shown without difficulty that the Iliad, if it be looked at as a history, is full of gaps, incongruities and absurdities, he proceeds to compose a more plausible narrative of his own, which he tenders as so much authentic matter of fact. The most important point, however, which his Oration brings to view is, the literal and confiding belief with which the Homeric narrative was regarded, as if it were actual history, not only by the inhabitants of Ilium, but also by the general Grecian public.[1]

Historicising innovations—Dio Chrysostom.

The small town of Ilium, inhabited by Æolic Greeks,[2] and raised into importance only by the legendary reverence attached to it, stood upon an elevated ridge forming a spur from Mount Ida, rather more than three miles from the town and promontory of Sigeium, and about twelve stadia, or less than two miles, from the sea at its nearest point. From Sigeium and the neighbouring town of Achilleium (with its monument and temple of Achilles), to the town of Rhœteium on a hill higher up the Hellespont (with its monument and chapel of Ajax called the Aiantcium),[3] was a distance of sixty

Historical Ilium.

---

[1] Dio Chrysost. Or. xi. p. 310—322.

[2] Herodot. v. 122. Pausan. v. 8, 3; viii. 12, 4. Αἰολεὺς ἐκ πόλεως Τρῳάδος, the title proclaimed at the Olympic games: like Αἰολεὺς ἀπὸ Μουρίνας, from Myrina in the more southerly region of Æolis, as we find in the list of victors at the Charitêsia, at Orchomenos in Bœôtia (Corp. Inscrip. Boeckh. No. 1583).

[3] See Pausanias, i. 35, 3, for the legends current at Ilium respecting the vast size of the bones of Ajax in his tomb. The inhabitants affirmed that after the shipwreck of Odysseus, the arms of Achilles, which he was carrying away with him, were washed up by the sea against the tomb of Ajax. Pliny gives the distance at thirty stadia: modern travellers make it something more than Pliny, but considerably less than Strabo.

stadia, or about seven English miles in the straight course by sea: in the intermediate space was a bay and an adjoining plain, comprehending the embouchure of the Skamander, and extending to the base of the ridge on which Ilium stood. This plain was the celebrated plain of Troy, in which the great Homeric battles were believed to have taken place: the portion of the bay near to Sigeium went by the name of the Naustathmon of the Achæans (*i.e.* the spot where they dragged their ships ashore), and was accounted to have been the camp of Agamemnôn and his vast army.[1]

Historical Ilium was founded, according to the questionable statement of Strabo, during the last dynasty of the Lydian kings,[2] that is, at some period later than 720 B.C. Until after the days of Alexander the Great—indeed until the period of Roman preponderance—it always remained a place of inconsiderable power and importance, as we learn not only from the assertion of the geographer, but also from the fact that Achilleium, Sigeium and Rhœteium were all independent of it.[3] But inconsiderable as it might be, it was the only place which ever bore the venerable name immortalised by Homer. Like the Homeric Ilium, it had its temple of Athênê,[4] wherein she was worshipped as the presiding goddess of the town: the inhabitants affirmed that Agamemnôn had not altogether destroyed the town, but that it had been re-occupied after his departure, and had never ceased to exist.[5] Their acropolis was called Pergamum, and in it was

Generally received and visited as the town of Priam.

---

[1] Strabo, xiii. p. 596—598. Strabo distinguishes the Ἀχαιῶν Ναύσταθμον, which was near to Sigeium, from the Ἀχαιῶν λιμήν which was more towards the middle of the bay between Sigeium and Rhœteium; but we gather from his language that this distinction was not universally recognised. Alexander landed at the Ἀχαιῶν λιμήν (Arrian, i. 11).

[2] Strabo, xiii. p. 593.

[3] Herodot. v. 95 (his account of the war between the Athenians and Mitylenæans about Sigeium and Achilleium); Strabo, xiii. p. 593. Τὴν δὲ τῶν Ἰλιέων πόλιν τὴν νῦν τέως μὲν κωμόπολιν εἶναί φασι, τὸ ἱερὸν ἔχουσαν τῆς Ἀθηνᾶς μικρὸν καὶ εὐτελές. Ἀλέξανδρον δὲ ἀναβάντα μετὰ τὴν ἐπὶ Γρανίκῳ

νίκην, ἀναθήμασι τε κοσμῆσαι τὸ ἱερὸν καὶ προσαγορεῦσαι πόλιν, &c.

Again, Καὶ τὸ Ἴλιον, ὃ νῦν ἐστὶ κωμόπολίς τις ἦν ὅτε πρῶτον Ῥωμαῖοι τῆς Ἀσίας ἐπέβησαν.

[4] Besides Athênê, the Inscriptions authenticate Ζεὺς Πολιεύς at Ilium (Corp. Inscrip. Boeckh. No. 3599).

[5] Strabo, xiii. p. 600. Λέγουσι δ' οἱ νῦν Ἰλιεῖς καὶ τοῦτο, ὡς οὐδὲ τέλεως συνέβαινεν ἠφανίσθαι τὴν πόλιν κατὰ τὴν ἅλωσιν ὑπὸ τῶν Ἀχαιῶν, οὐδ' ἐξηλείφθη οὐδέποτε.

The situation of Ilium (or as it is commonly, but erroneously, termed, *New Ilium*) appears to be pretty well ascertained, about two miles from the sea (Rennell, On the Topography of Troy, p. 41-71; Dr. Clarke's Travels, vol. ii. p. 102).

shown the house of Priam and the altar of Zeus Herkeius where that unhappy old man had been slain. Moreover there were exhibited, in the temples, panoplies which had been worn by the Homeric heroes,[1] and doubtless many other relics appreciated by admirers of the Iliad.

These were testimonies which few persons in those ages were inclined to question, when combined with the identity of name and general locality ; nor does it seem that any one did question them until the time of Dêmêtrius of Skêpsis. Hellanikus expressly described this Ilium as being the Ilium of Homer, for which assertion Strabo (or probably Dêmêtrius, from whom the narrative seems to be copied) imputes to him very gratuitously an undue partiality towards the inhabitants of the town.[2] Herodotus relates, that Xerxes in his march into Greece visited the place, went up to the Pergamum of Priam, inquired with much interest into the details of the Homeric siege, made libations to the fallen heroes, and offered to ˙the Athênê of Ilium his magnificent sacrifice of a thousand oxen : he probably represented and believed himself to be attacking Greece as the avenger of the Priamid family. The Lacedæmonian admiral Mindarus, while his fleet lay at Abydus, went personally to Ilium to offer sacrifice to Athênê, and saw from that elevated spot the battle fought between the squadron of Dorieus and the Athenians, off the shore near Rhœteium.[3]   During the interval between the Peloponnesian

---

[1] Xerxes passing by Adramyttium, and leaving the range of Mount Ida on his left hand, ἤιε ἐς τὴν Ἰλιάδα γῆν . . . . Ἀπικομένου δὲ τοῦ στρατοῦ ἐπὶ τὸν Σκάμανδρον . . . ἐς τὸ Πριάμου Πέργαμον ἀνέβη, ἵμερον ἔχων θεήσασθαι. Θεησάμενος δὲ, καὶ πυθόμενος κείνων ἕκαστα, τῇ Ἀθηναίῃ τῇ Ἰλιάδι ἔθυσε βοῦς χιλίας· χοὰς δὲ οἱ μάγοι τοῖσιν ἥρωσιν ἐχέαντο . . . Ἅμα ἡμέρῃ δὲ ἐπορεύετο, ἐν ἀριστερῇ μὲν ἀπέργων Ῥοιτείον πόλιν καὶ Ὀφρυνείον καὶ Δάρδανον, ἤπερ δὴ Ἀβύδῳ ὅμουρός ἐστιν· ἐν δεξιῇ δὲ, Γέργιθας Τευκρούς (Herod. vii. 43).

Respecting Alexander (Arrian, i. 11), Ἀνελθόντα δὲ ἐς Ἴλιον, τῇ Ἀθηνᾷ θῦσαι τῇ Ἰλιάδι, καὶ τὴν πανοπλίαν τὴν αὑτοῦ ἀναθεῖναι εἰς τὸν ναὸν, καὶ καθελεῖν ἀντὶ ταύτης τῶν ἱερῶν τινα ὅπλων ἔτι ἐκ τοῦ Τρωικοῦ ἔργου σωζόμενα· καὶ ταῦτα λέγουσιν ὅτι οἱ ὑπασπισταὶ ἔφερον πρὸ αὐτοῦ ἐς τὰς μάχας. Θῦσαι δὲ αὐτὸν ἐπὶ τοῦ βωμοῦ τοῦ Διὸς τοῦ Ἑρκείου λόγος

κατέχει, μῆνιν Πριάμου παραιτούμενον τῷ Νεοπτολέμου γένει, ὃ δὴ ἐς αὐτὸν καθῆκε.

The inhabitants of Ilium also showed the lyre which had belonged to Paris (Plut. Alex. c. 15).

Chandler, in his History of Ilium, ch. xxii. p. 89, seems to think that the place called by Herodotus the Pergamum of Priam is different from the historical Ilium. But the mention of the Iliean Athênê identifies them as the same.

[2] Strabo, xiii. p. 602. Ἑλλάνικος δὲ χαριζόμενος τοῖς Ἰλιεῦσιν, οἷος ὁ ἐκείνου μῦθος, συνηγορεῖ τῷ τὴν αὐτὴν εἶναι πόλιν τὴν νῦν τῇ τότε. Hellanikus had written a work called Τρωϊκά.

[3] Xenoph. Hellen. i. 1, 10. Skylax places Ilium twenty-five stadia, or about three miles, from the sea (c. 94). But I do not understand how he can call Skêpsis and Kebrên πόλεις ἐπὶ θαλάσσῃ.

war and the Macedonian invasion of Persia, Ilium was always garrisoned as a strong position: but its domain was still narrow, and did not extend even to the sea which was so near to it.[1] Alexander, on crossing the Hellespont, sent his army from Sestus to Abydus, under Parmenio, and sailed personally from Elæeus in the Chersonese, after having solemnly sacrificed at the Elæuntian shrine of Prôtesilaus, to the Harbour of the Achæans between Sigeium and Rhœteium. He then ascended to Ilium, sacrificed to the Iliean Athênê, and consecrated in her temple his own panoply, in exchange for which he took some of the sacred arms there suspended, which were said to have been preserved from the time of the Trojan war. These arms were carried before him when he went to battle by his armour-bearers. It is a fact still more curious, and illustrative of the strong working of the old legend on an impressible and eminently religious mind, that he also sacrificed to Priam himself on the very altar of Zeus Herkeius from which the old king was believed to have been torn by Neoptolemus. As that fierce warrior was his heroic ancestor by the maternal side, he desired to avert from himself the anger of Priam against the Achilleid race.[2]

Respect shown to it by Alexander.

Alexander made to the inhabitants of Ilium many munificent promises, which he probably would have executed, had he not been prevented by untimely death. One of his successors, Antigonus,[3] founded the city of Alexandreia in the Trôad, between Sigeium and the more southerly promontory of Lektum; compressing

Successors of Alexander—foundation of Alexandreia Trôas.

---

[1] See Xenoph. Hellen. iii. i. 16; and the description of the seizure of Ilium, along with Skêpsis and Kebrên, by the chief of mercenaries, Charidêmus, in Demosthen. cont. Aristocrat. c. 38, p. 671: compare Æneas Pol. c. 24, and Polyæn. iii. 14.

[2] Arrian, l. c. Dikæarchus composed a separate work respecting this sacrifice of Alexander, περὶ τῆς ἐν Ἰλίῳ θυσίας (Ath. xiii. p. 603; Dikæarch. Fr. p. 114, ed. Fuhr).

Theophrastus, in noticing old and venerable trees, mentions the φηγοί (*Quercus æsculus*) on the tomb of Ilus at Ilium, without any doubt of the authenticity of the place (De Plant. iv. 14); and his contemporary, the harper Stratonikos, intimates the same feeling, in his jest on the visit of a bad sophist

to Ilium during the festival of the Ilieia (Athenæ. viii. p. 351). The same may be said respecting the author of the tenth epistle ascribed to the orator Æschinês (p. 737), in which his visit of curiosity to Ilium is described—as well as about Apollônius of Tyana, or the writer who describes his life and his visit to the Trôad; it is evident that he did not distrust the ἀρχαιολογία of the Ilieans, who affirmed their town to be the real Troy (Philostr. Vit. Apol. Tyan. iv. 11).

The goddess Athênê of Ilium was reported to have rendered valuable assistance to the inhabitants of Kyzikus, when they were besieged by Mithridatês, commemorated by inscriptions set up in Ilium (Plutarch, Lucull. 10).

[3] Strabo, xiii. p. 603—607.

into it the inhabitants of many of the neighbouring Æolic towns
in the region of Ida,—Skêpsis, Kebrên, Hamaxitus, Kolônæ, and
Neandria, though the inhabitants of Skêpsis were subsequently
permitted by Lysimachus to resume their own city and autonomous
government. Ilium, however, remained without any special mark
of favour until the arrival of the Romans in Asia and their
triumph over Antiochus (about 190 B.C.). Though it retained its
walls and its defensible position, Dêmêtrius of Skêpsis, who
visited it shortly before that event, described it as being then in
a state of neglect and poverty, many of the houses not even having
tiled roofs.[1] In this dilapidated condition, however, it was still

---

[1] Livy xxxv. 43; xxxvii. 9. Polyb.
v. 78—111 (passages which prove
that Ilium was fortified and defensible
about B.C. 218). Strabo, xiii. p. 594.
Καὶ τὸ Ἴλιον δ᾿, ὃ νῦν ἐστι, κωμόπολίς
τις ἦν, ὅτε πρῶτον Ῥωμαῖοι τῆς Ἀσίας
ἐπέβησαν καὶ ἐξέβαλον Ἀντίοχον τὸν
μέγαν ἐκ τῆς ἐντὸς τοῦ Ταύρου. Φησὶ
γοῦν Δημήτριος ὁ Σκήψιος, μειράκιον
ἐπιδήμησαν εἰς τὴν πόλιν κατ᾿ ἐκείνους
τοὺς καιρούς, οὕτως ὠλιγωρημένην ἰδεῖν
τὴν κατοικίαν, ὥστε μηδὲ κεραμωτὰς
ἔχειν τὰς στέγας. Ἡγησιάναξ δὲ, τοὺς
Γαλάτας περαιωθέντας ἐκ τῆς Εὐρώπης,
ἀναβῆναι μὲν εἰς τὴν πόλιν δεομένους
ἐρύματος, παραχρῆμα δ᾿ ἐκλιπεῖν διὰ τὸ
ἀτείχιστον· ὕστερον δ᾿ ἐπανόρθωσιν ἔσχε
πολλήν. Εἶτ᾿ ἐκάκωσαν αὐτὴν πάλιν οἱ
μετὰ Φιμβρίου, &c.
Here is a very clear and precise
statement, attested by an eye-witness.
But it is thoroughly inconsistent with
the statement made by Strabo in the
previous chapter, a dozen lines before,
as the text now stands; for he there
informs us that Lysimachus, after
the death of Alexander, paid great
attention to Ilium, surrounded it with
a wall of forty stadia in circumference,
erected a temple, and aggregated to
Ilium the ancient cities around, which
were in a state of decay. We know
from Livy that the aggregation of
Gergis and Rhœteium to Ilium was
effected, not by Lysimachus, but by
the Romans (Livy, xxxviii. 37); so that
the *first* statement of Strabo is not
only inconsistent with his second, but
is contradicted by an independent
authority.
I cannot but think that this
contradiction arises from a confusion
of the text in Strabo's *first* passage,
and that in that passage Strabo really
meant to speak only of the improve-

ments brought about by Lysimachus
in *Alexandreia Trôas*; that he never
meant to ascribe to Lysimachus any
improvements in *Ilium*, but, on the
contrary, to assign the remarkable
attention paid by Lysimachus to
Alexandreia Trôas, as the reason why
he had neglected to fulfil the promises
held out by Alexander to *Ilium*. The
series of Strabo's allegations runs
thus :—1. Ilium is nothing better than
a κώμη at the landing of Alexander;
2. Alexander promises great additions,
but never returns from Persia to
accomplish them; 3. Lysimachus is
absorbed in Alexandreia Trôas, into
which he aggregates several of the
adjoining old towns, and which
flourishes under his hands; 4. Hence
Ilium remained a κώμη when the
Romans entered Asia, as it had been
when Alexander entered.
This alteration in the text of
Strabo might be effected by the simple
transposition of the words as they now
stand, and by omitting ὅτε καὶ, ἤδη
ἐπεμελήθη, without introducing a
single new or conjectural word, so
that the passage would read thus :—
Μετὰ δὲ τὴν ἐκείνου (Alexander's) τελευ-
τὴν Λυσίμαχος μάλιστα τῆς Ἀλεξανδρείας
ἐπεμελήθη, συνῳκισμένης μὲν ἤδη ὑπ᾿
Ἀντιγόνου, καὶ προσηγορευμένης Ἀντι-
γόνιας, μεταβαλούσης δὲ τοὔνομα· (ἔδοξε
γὰρ εὐσεβὲς εἶναι τοὺς Ἀλεξάνδρου δια-
δεξαμένους ἐκείνου πρότερον κτίζειν
ἐπωνύμους πόλεις, εἶθ᾿ ἑαυτῶν) καὶ νέων
κατεσκεύασε καὶ τεῖχος περιεβάλετο ὅσον
40 σταδίων· συνῴκισε δὲ εἰς αὐτὴν τὰς
κύκλῳ πόλεις ἀρχαίας, ἤδη κεκακωμένας.
Καὶ δὴ καὶ συνέμεινε . . . πόλεων.
If this reading be adopted, the words
beginning that which stands in
Tzschucke's edition as sect. 27, and
which immediately follow the last

mythically recognised both by Antiochus and by the Roman

consul Livius, who went up thither to sacrifice to the Iliean Athênê. The Romans, proud of their origin from Troy and Æneas, treated Ilium with signal munificence ; not only granting to it immunity from tribute, but also adding to its domain the neighbouring territories of Gergis, Rhœteium and Sigeium—and making the Ilieans masters of the whole coast[1] from the Peræa (or continental possessions) of Tenedos (southward of Sigeium) to the boundaries of Dardanus, which had its own title to legendary reverence as the special sovereignty of Æneas. The inhabitants of Sigeium made such resistance to this loss of autonomy, that their city was destroyed by the Ilieans.

The dignity and power of Ilium being thus prodigiously enhanced, we cannot doubt that the inhabitants assumed to themselves exaggerated importance as the recognised parents of all-conquering Rome. Partly, we may naturally suppose, from the jealousies thus aroused on the part of their neighbours at Skêpsis and Alexandreia Trôas—partly from the pronounced tendency of the age (in which Kratês at Pergamus and Aristarchus at Alexandria divided between them the palm of literary celebrity) towards criticism and illustration of the old poets—a blow was

now aimed at the mythical legitimacy of Ilium. Dêmêtrius of Skêpsis, one of the most laborious of the Homeric critics, had composed thirty books of comment upon the Catalogue in the Iliad : Hestiæa, an authoress of Alexandreia Trôas, had written on the same subject : both of them, well acquainted with the locality, remarked that the vast battles described in the Iliad could not be packed into the narrow space between Ilium and the Naustathmon of the Greeks : the more so, as that space, too small even as it then stood, had been considerably enlarged since the date of the Iliad by deposits at the mouth of the Skamander.[2] They

---

word πόλεων, will read quite suitably and coherently—Καὶ τὸ Ἴλιον δ', ὃ νῦν ἐστι, κωμόπολίς τις ἦν, ὅτε πρῶτον 'Ρωμαῖοι τῆς 'Ασίας ἐπέβησαν, &c., whereas with the present reading of the passage they show a contradiction, and the whole passage is entirely confused.

[1] Livy, xxxviii. 39; Strabo, xiii.

p. 600. Κατέσκαπται δὲ καὶ τὸ Σίγειον ὑπὸ τῶν 'Ιλιέων διὰ τὴν ἀπείθειαν· ὑπ' ἐκείνοις γὰρ ἦν ὕστερον ἡ παραλία πᾶσα ἡ μέχρι Δαρδάνου, καὶ νῦν ὑπ' ἐκείνοις ἐστι.

[2] Strabo, xiii. 599. Παρατίθησι δὲ ὁ Δημήτριος καὶ τὴν 'Αλεξανδρίνην 'Εστίαιαν μάρτυρα, τὴν συγγράψασαν περὶ τῆς 'Ομήρου 'Ιλιάδος, πυνθανομένην, εἰ

found no difficulty in pointing out topographical incongruities
and impossibilities as to the incidents in the Iliad, which they
professed to remove by the startling theory that the Homeric
Ilium had not occupied the site of the city so called.   There was
a village, called the village of the Ilieans, situated rather less
than four miles from the city in the direction of Mount Ida,
and further removed from the sea ; here, they affirmed, the
"holy Troy" had stood.

No positive proof was produced to sustain the conclusion, for
Strabo expressly states that not a vestige of the ancient   Supposed
city remained at the Village of the Ilieans.[1] But the   Old Ilium,
or real
fundamental supposition was backed by a second   Troy, dis-
accessory supposition, to explain how it happened that   tinguished
from New
all such vestiges had disappeared.   Nevertheless Strabo   Ilium.
adopts the unsupported hypothesis of Dêmêtrius as if it were an
authenticated fact—distinguishing pointedly between Old and
New Ilium, and even censuring Hellanikus for having maintained
the received local faith.   But I cannot find that Dêmêtrius and
Hestiæa have been followed in this respect by any other writer of
ancient times excepting Strabo.   Ilium still continued to be talked
of and treated by every one as the genuine Homeric Troy: the
cruel jests of the Roman rebel Fimbria, when he sacked the town
and massacred the inhabitants—the compensation made by Sylla,
and the pronounced favour of Julius Cæsar and Augustus,—all
prove this continued recognition of identity.[2]   Arrian, though a
native of Nicomedia, holding a high appointment in Asia Minor,
and remarkable for the exactness of his topographical notices,
describes the visit of Alexander to Ilium, without any suspicion

περὶ τὴν νῦν πόλιν ὁ πόλεμος συνέστη,
καὶ τὸ Τρωϊκὸν πεδίον ποῦ ἔστιν, ὃ μέταξυ
τῆς πόλεως καὶ τῆς θαλάσσης ὁ ποιητὴς
φράζει· τὸ μὲν γὰρ πρὸ τῆς νῦν πόλεως
ὁρώμενον, πρόχωμα εἶναι τῶν ποταμῶν,
ὕστερον γεγονός.

The words ποῦ ἔστιν are introduced
conjecturally by Grosskurd, the excellent German translator of Strabo, but
they seem to me necessary to make the
sense complete.

Hestiæa is cited more than once in
the Homeric Scholia (Schol. Venet. ad
Iliad. iii. 64 ; Eustath. ad Iliad. ii.
538).

[1] Strabo, xiii. p. 599. Οὐδὲν δ᾽ ἴχνος
σώζεται τῆς ἀρχαίας πόλεως—εἰκότως·

ἅτε γὰρ ἐκπεπορθημένων τῶν κύκλῳ
πόλεων, οὐ τελέως δὲ κατεσπασμένων, οἱ
λίθοι πάντες εἰς τὴν ἐκείνων ἀνάληψιν
μετηνέχθησαν.

[2] Appian, Mithridat. c. 53 ; Strabo,
xiii. p. 594 ; Plutarch, Sertorius, c. 1 ;
Velleius Paterc. ii. 23.

The inscriptions attest Panathenaic
games celebrated at Ilium in honour of
Athênê by the Ilieans conjointly with
various other neighbouring cities (see
Corp. Inscr. Boeckh. No. 3601—3602,
with Boeckh's observations).   The
valuable inscription No. 3595 attests
the liberality of Antiochus Soter
towards the Ilian Athênê as early as
278 B.C.

that the place with all its relics was a mere counterfeit : Aristidês, Dio Chrysostom, Pausanias, Appian, and Plutarch hold the same language.[1] But modern writers seem for the most part to have taken up the supposition from Strabo as implicitly as he took it from Dêmêtrius. They call Ilium by the disrespectful appellation of *New* Ilium—while the traveller in the Trôad looks for *Old* Ilium as if it were the unquestionable spot where Priam had lived and moved ; the name is even formally enrolled on the best maps recently prepared of the ancient Trôad.[2]

Strabo alone believes in Old Ilium as the real Troy—other authors continue in the old faith—the moderns follow Strabo.

[1] Arrian, i. 11 ; Appian *ut sup.*; also Aristidês, Or. 43, Rhodiaca, p. 820 (Dindorf, p. 369). The curious Oratio xi. of Dio Chrysostom, in which he writes his new version of the Trojan war, is addressed to the inhabitants of Ilium.

[2] The controversy, now half a century old, respecting Troy and the Trojan war—between Bryant and his various opponents, Morritt, Gilbert Wakefield, the British Critic, &c., seems now nearly forgotten, and I cannot think that the pamphlets on either side would be considered as displaying much ability if published at the present day. The discussion was first raised by the publication of Le Chevalier's account of the plain of Troy, in which the author professed to have discovered the true site of Old Ilium (the supposed Homeric Troy), about twelve miles from the sea near Bounarbashi. Upon this account Bryant published some animadversions followed up by a second Treatise, in which he denied the historical reality of the Trojan war, and advanced the hypothesis that the tale was of Egyptian origin (Dissertation on the War of Troy, and the expedition of the Grecians as described by Homer, showing that no such expedition was ever undertaken, and that no such city of Phrygia existed, by Jacob Bryant ; seemingly 1797, though there is no date in the title-page : Morritt's reply was published in 1798). A reply from Mr. Bryant and a rejoinder from Mr. Morritt, as well as a pamphlet from G. Wakefield, appeared in 1799 and 1800, besides an Expostulation by the former addressed to the British Critic.

Bryant, having dwelt both on the incredibilities and the inconsistencies of the Trojan war, as it is recounted in Grecian legend generally, nevertheless admitted that Homer had a ground-work for his story, and maintained that that groundwork was Egyptian. Homer (he thinks) was an Ithacan, descended from a family originally emigrant from Egypt : the war of Troy was originally an Egyptian war, which explains how Memnôn the Ethiopian came to take part in it : " upon this history, which was originally Egyptian, Homer founded the scheme of his two principal poems, adapting things to Greece and Phrygia by an ingenious transposition " ! he derived information from priests of Memphis or Thêbes (Bryant, pp. 102, 108, 126). The Ἥρως Αἰγύπτιος, mentioned in the second book of the Odyssey (15), is the Egyptian hero, who affords (in his view) an evidence that the population of that island was in part derived from Egypt. No one since Mr. Bryant, I apprehend, has ever construed the passage in the same sense.

Bryant's Egyptian hypothesis is of no value ; but the negative portion of his argument, summing up the particulars of the Trojan legend, and contending against its historical credibility, is not so easily put aside. Few persons will share in the zealous conviction by which Morritt tries to make it appear that the 1100 ships, the ten years of war, the large confederacy of princes from all parts of Greece, &c., have nothing but what is consonant with historical probability ; difficulties being occasionally eliminated by the plea of our ignorance of the time and of the subject (Morritt, p. 7—21). Gilbert Wakefield, who maintains the historical reality of the siege with the utmost intensity, and even compares Bryant to Tom Payne (W. p. 17), is

Strabo has here converted into geographical matter of fact an hypothesis purely gratuitous, with a view of saving the accuracy of the Homeric topography; though in all probability the locality of the pretended Old Ilium would have been found open to difficulties not less serious than those which it was introduced to obviate.[1] It may be true that Dêmêtrius and he were justified in their negative argument, so as to show that the battles described in the Iliad could not possibly have taken place if the city of Priam had stood on the hill inhabited by the Ilieans. But the legendary faith subsisted before, and continued without abatement afterwards, notwithstanding such topographical impossibilities. Hellanikus, Herodotus, Mindarus, the guides of Xerxes, and Alexander, had not been

The mythical faith not shaken by topographical impossibilities.

still more displeased with those who propound doubts, and tells us that "grave disputation in the midst of such darkness and uncertainty is a conflict with chimæras" (W. p. 14).

The most plausible line of argument taken by Morritt and Wakefield is, where they enforce the positions taken by Strabo, and so many other authors, ancient as well as modern, that a superstructure of fiction is to be distinguished from a basis of truth, and that the latter is to be maintained while the former is rejected (Morritt, p. 5; Wake. p. 7—8). To this Bryant replies, that "if we leave out every absurdity, we can make anything plausible : that a fable may be made consistent, and we have many romances that are very regular in the assortment of characters and circumstances : this may be seen in plays, memoirs, and novels. But this regularity and correspondence alone will not ascertain the truth." (Expostulation, pp. 8, 12, 13.) "That there are a great many other fables besides that of Troy, regular and consistent among themselves, believed and chronologised by the Greeks, and even looked up to by them in a religious view (p. 13), which yet no one now thinks of admitting as history."

Morritt, having urged the universal belief of antiquity as evidence that the Trojan war was historically real, is met by Bryant, who reminds him that the same persons believed in centaurs, satyrs, nymphs, augury, aruspicy; Homer maintaining that horses could speak, &c. To which Morritt replies,

"What has religious belief to do with historical facts ? Is not the evidence on which our faith rests in matters of religion totally different in all its parts from that on which we ground our belief in history ?" (Addit. Remarks, p. 47.)

The separation between the grounds of religious and historical belief is by no means so complete as Mr. Morritt supposes, even in regard to modern times; and when we apply his position to the ancient Greeks, it will be found completely the reverse of the truth. The contemporaries of Herodotus and Thucydidês conceived their early history in the most intimate conjunction with their religion.

[1] For example, adopting his own line of argument (not to mention those battles in which the pursuit and the flight reaches from the city to the ships and back again), it might have been urged to him, that by supposing the Homeric Troy to be four miles further off from the sea, he aggravated the difficulty of rolling the Trojan horse into the town ; it was already sufficiently hard to propel this vast wooden animal full of heroes from the Greek Naustathmon to the town of Ilium.

The Trojan horse, with its accompaniments Sinon and Laokoôn, is one of the capital and indispensable events in the epic : Homer, Arktinus, Leschês, Virgil, and Quintus Smyrnæus, all dwell upon it emphatically as the proximate cause of the capture.

The difficulties and inconsistencies of the movements ascribed to Greeks

shocked by them : the case of the latter is the strongest of all, because he had received the best education of his time under Aristotle—he was a passionate admirer and constant reader of the Iliad—he was moreover personally familiar with the movements of armies, and lived at a time when maps, which began with Anaximander, the disciple of Thalês, were at least known to all who sought instruction. Now if, notwithstanding such advantages, Alexander fully believed in the identity of Ilium, unconscious of these many and glaring topographical difficulties, much less would Homer himself, or the Homeric auditors, be likely to pay attention to them, at a period, five centuries earlier, of comparative rudeness and ignorance, when prose records as well as geographical maps were totally unknown.[1] The inspired poet might describe, and his hearers would listen with delight to the tale, how Hectôr, pursued by Achilles, ran thrice round the city of Troy, while the trembling Trojans were all huddled into the city, not one daring to come out even at this last extremity of their beloved prince—and while the Grecian army looked on, restraining unwillingly their uplifted spears at the nod of Achilles, in order that Hectôr might perish by no other hand than his ; nor were they, while absorbed by this impressive recital, disposed to measure distances or calculate topographical possibilities with

and Trojans in the Iliad, when applied to real topography, are well set forth in Spohn, *De Agro Trojano*, Leipsic, 1814 ; and Mr. Maclaren has shown (Dissertation on the Topography of the Trojan War, Edinburgh, 1822) that these difficulties are nowise obviated by removing Ilium a few miles further from the sea.

[1] Major Rennell argues differently from the visit of Alexander, employing it to confute the hypothesis of Chevalier, who had placed the Homeric Troy at Bounarbashi, the site supposed to have been indicated by Dêmêtrius and Strabo :

"Alexander is said to have been a passionate admirer of the Iliad, and he had an opportunity of deciding on the spot how far the topography was consistent with the narrative. Had he been shown the site of Bounarbashi for that of Troy, he would probably have questioned the fidelity either of the historical part of the poem or his guides. It is not within credibility, that a person of so correct a judgment

as Alexander could have admired a poem which contained a long history of military details and other transactions that could not physically have had an existence. What pleasure could he receive, in contemplating as subjects of history, events which could not have happened? Yet he did admire the poem, and *therefore must have found the topography consistent* : that is, Bounarbashi, surely, was not shown to him for Troy." (Rennell, Observations on the Plain of Troy, p. 128.)

Major Rennell here supposes in Alexander a spirit of topographical criticism quite foreign to his real character. We have no reason to believe that the site of Bounarbashi was shown to Alexander as the Homeric Troy, or that *any* site was shown to him *except Ilium*, or what Strabo calls New Ilium. Still less reason have we to believe that any scepticism crossed his mind, or that his deep-seated faith required to be confirmed by measurement of distances.

reference to the site of the real Ilium.[1] The mistake consists in applying to Homer and to the Homeric siege of Troy criticisms which would be perfectly just if brought to bear on the Athenian siege of Syracuse, as described by Thucydidês,[2] in the Peloponnesian war[3]—but which are not more applicable to the epic narrative than they would be to the exploits of Amadis or Orlando.

There is every reason for presuming that the Ilium visited by Xerxês and Alexander was really the "holy Ilium" present to the mind of Homer ; and if so, it must have been inhabited, either by Greeks or by some anterior population, at a period earlier than that which Strabo assigns. History recognises neither Troy the city, nor Trojans, as actually existing ; but the extensive region called Trôas, or the Trôad (more properly Trôïas), is known both to Herodotus and to Thucydidês: it seems to include the territory westward of an imaginary line drawn from the north-east corner of the Adramyttian gulf to the Propontis at Parium, since both Antandrus, Kolônæ, and the district immediately round Ilium, are regarded as belonging to the Trôad.[4] Herodotus further notices the Teukrians of Gergis[5] (a township conterminous with Ilium, and lying to the eastward of the road from Ilium to Abydus), considering them as the remnant of a larger Teukrian population which once resided in the country, and which had in

Historical Trôas and the Teukrians.

---

[1] Strabo, xiii. p. 599.   Οὐδ' ἡ τοῦ Ἔκτορος δὲ περιδρομὴ ἡ περὶ τὴν πόλιν ἔχει τι εὔλογον · οὐ γάρ ἐστι περίδρομος ἡ νῦν, διὰ τὴν συνεχῆ ῥάχιν · ἡ δὲ παλαιὰ ἔχει περιδρομήν.

[2] Mannert (Geographie der Griechen und Römer, Th. 6, Heft 3, b. 8, cap. 8) is confused in his account of Old and New Ilium : he represents that Alexander raised up a new spot to the dignity of having been the Homeric Ilium, which is not the fact: Alexander adhered to the received local belief. Indeed, as far as our evidence goes, no one but Dêmêtrius, Hestiæa, and Strabo appears ever to have departed from it.

[3] There can hardly be a more singular example of this same confusion, than to find elaborate military criticisms from the Emperor Napoleon, upon the description of the taking of Troy in the second book of the Æneid. He shows that gross faults are committed in it, when looked at from the point of view of a general (see an interesting article by Mr. G. C. Lewis, in the Classical Museum, vol. i. p. 205, "Napoleon on the Capture of Troy").

Having cited this criticism from the highest authority on the art of war, we may find a suitable parallel in the works of distinguished publicists. The attack of Odysseus on the Ciconians (described in Homer, Odyss. ix. 39—61) is cited both by Grotius (De Jure Bell. et Pac. iii. 3, 10) and by Vattel (Droit des Gens, iii. 202) as a case in point in international law. Odysseus is considered to have sinned against the rules of international law by attacking them as allies of the Trojans, without a formal declaration of war.

[4] Compare Herodot. 24—122; Thucyd. i. 131.   The Ἰλιὰς γῆ is a part of the Trôad.

[5] Herodot. vii. 43.

very early times undertaken a vast migration from Asia into Europe.[1]　To that Teukrian population he thinks that the Homeric Trojans belonged :[2] and by later writers, especially by Virgil and the other Romans, the names Teukrians and Trojans are employed as equivalents.　As the name *Trojans* is not mentioned in any contemporary historical monument, so the name *Teukrians* never once occurs in the old Epic.　It appears to have been first noticed by the elegiac poet Kallinus, about 660 B.C., who connected it with an alleged immigration of Teukrians from Krête into the region round about Ida.　Others again denied this, asserting that the primitive ancestor, Teukrus, had come into the country from Attica,[3] and that he was of indigenous origin, born from Skamander and the nymph Idæa—all various manifestations of that eager thirst after an eponymous hero which never deserted the Greeks.　Gergithians occur in more than one spot in Æolis, even so far southward as the neighbourhood of Kymê :[4] the name has no place in Homer, but he mentions Gorgythiôn and Kebrionês as illegitimate sons of Priam, thus giving a sort of epical recognition both to Gergis and Kebrên. As Herodotus calls the old epical Trojans by the name Teukrians, so the Attic tragedians call them Phrygians ; though the Homeric hymn to Aphroditê represents Phrygians and Trojans as completely distinct, specially noting the diversity of language ;[5] and in the Iliad the Phrygians are simply numbered among the allies of Troy from the far Ascania, without indication of any more intimate relationship.[6]　Nor do the tales which connect Dardanus with Samothrace and Arcadia find countenance in the Homeric poems, wherein Dardanus is the son of Zeus, having no root anywhere except in Dardania.[7]　The mysterious solemnities of Samothrace, afterwards so highly venerated throughout the Grecian world, date from a period much later than Homer ; and

[1] Herodot. v. 122. εἶλε μὲν Αἰολέας πάντας, ὅσοι τὴν Ἰλιάδα γῆν νέμονται, εἶλε δὲ Γέργιθας, τοὺς ἀπολειφθέντας τῶν ἀρχαίων Τεύκρων.
For the migration of the Teukrians and Mysians into Europe, see Herodot. vii. 20 ; the Pæonians, on the Strymon, called themselves their descendants.
[2] Herodot. ii. 118 ; v. 13.
[3] Strabo, xiii. p. 604 ; Apollodôr. iii. 12, 4.

Kephalôn of Gergis called Teukrus a Krêtan (Stephan. Byz. v. Ἀρίσβη).
[4] Clearchus ap. Athenæ. vi. p. 256 ; Strabo, xiii. p. 589—616.
[5] Homer, Hymn. in Vener. 116.
[6] Iliad. ii. 863. Asius, the brother of Hekabê, lives in Phrygia on the banks of the Sangarius (Iliad. xvi. 717).
[7] See Hellanik. Fragm. 129, 130, ed. Didot ; and Kephalôn Gergithius ap. Steph. Byz. v. Ἀρίσβη.

the religious affinities of that island as well as of Krête with the
territories of Phrygia and Æolis, were certain, according to the
established tendency of the Grecian mind, to beget stories of a
common genealogy.

To pass from this legendary world,—an aggregate of streams
distinct and heterogeneous, which do not willingly come into
confluence, and cannot be forced to intermix,—into the clearer
vision afforded by Herodotus, we learn from him that
in the year 500 B.C. the whole coast-region from
Dardanus southward to the promontory of Lektum
(including the town of Ilium), and from Lektum
eastward to Adramyttium, had been Æolised, or was
occupied by Æolic Greeks—likewise the inland towns of Skêpsis[1]
and Kebrên. So that if we draw a line northward from Adramyttium to Kyzikus on the Propontis—throughout the whole
territory westward from that line, to the Hellespont and the
Ægean Sea, all the considerable towns would be Hellenic.
With the exception of Gergis and the Teukrian population
around it, all the towns worthy of note were either Ionic or
Æolic. A century earlier, the Teukrian population would have
embraced a wider range—perhaps Skêpsis and Kebrên, the latter
of which places was colonised by Greeks from Kymê :[2] a century
afterwards, during the satrapy of Pharnabazus, it appears that
Gergis had become Hellenised as well as the rest. The four
towns, Ilium, Gergis, Kebrên and Skêpsis, all in lofty and strong
positions, were distinguished each by a solemn worship and
temple of Athênê, and by the recognition of that goddess as
their special patroness.[3]

The author of the Iliad conceived the whole of this region as

[marginal note: Æolic Greeks in the Trôad—the whole territory gradually Æolised.]

---

[1] Skêpsis received some colonists
from the Ionic Milêtus (Anaximenês
apud Strabo. xiv. p. 635); but the coins
of the place prove that its dialect was
Æolic. See Klausen, Æneas und die
Penaten, tom. i. note 180.

Arisbê also, near Abydus, seems to
have been settled from Mitylênê
(Eustath. ad Iliad. xii. 97).

The extraordinary fertility and rich
black mould of the plain around Ilium
is noticed by modern travellers (see
Franklin, Remarks and Observations
on the Plain of Troy, London, 1800, p.
44): it is also easily worked : "a couple

of buffaloes or oxen were sufficient to
draw the plough, whereas near Con-
stantinople it takes twelve or fourteen".

[2] Ephorus ap. Harpocrat. v. Κεβρῆνα.

[3] Xenoph. Hellen. i. 1, 10 : iii. 1, 10
—15.

One of the great motives of Dio in
setting aside the Homeric narrative of
the Trojan war, is to vindicate Athênê
from the charge of having unjustly
destroyed her own city of Ilium (Orat.
xi. p. 310: μάλιστα διὰ τὴν Ἀθηνᾶν ὅπως
μὴ δοκῇ ἀδίκως διαφθεῖραι τὴν ἑαυτῆς
πόλιν).

occupied by people not Greek,—Trojans, Dardanians, Lykians, Lelegians, Pelasgians, and Kilikians. He recognises a temple and worship of Athênê in Ilium, though the goddess is bitterly hostile to the Trojans : and Arktinus described the Palladium as the capital protection of the city. But perhaps the most remarkable feature of identity between the Homeric and the historical Æolis is the solemn and diffused worship of the Sminthian Apollo. Chrysê, Killa and Tenedos, and more than one place called Sminthium, maintain the surname and invoke the protection of that god during later times, just as they are emphatically described to do by Homer.[1]

Old date, and long prevalence of the worship of Apollo Sminthius.

When it is said that the Post-Homeric Greeks gradually Hellenised this entire region, we are not to understand that the whole previous population either retired or was destroyed. The Greeks settled in the leading and considerable towns, which enabled them both to protect one another and to gratify their predominant tastes. Partly by force—but greatly also by that superior activity, and power of assimilating foreign ways of thought to their own, which distinguished them from the beginning—they invested all the public features and management of the town with an Hellenic air, distributed all about it their gods, their heroes and their legends, and rendered their language the medium of public administration, religious songs and addresses to the gods, and generally for communications wherein any number of persons were concerned. But two remarks are here to be made : first, in doing this they could not avoid taking to themselves more or less of that which belonged to the parties

---

[1] Strabo, x. p. 473, xiii. p. 604—605. Polemon. Fragm. 31, p. 63, ed. Preller.

Polemon was a native of Ilium, and had written a periegesis of the place (about 200 B.C., therefore earlier than Dêmêtrius of Skêpsis): he may have witnessed the improvement in its condition effected by the Romans. He noticed the identical stone upon which Palamêdês had taught the Greeks to play at dice.

The Sminthian Apollo appears inscribed on the coins of Alexandreia Trôas ; and the temple of the god was memorable even down to the time of the emperor Julian (Ammian. Marcellin. xxii. 8). Compare Menander (the Rhetor) περὶ Ἐπιδεικτικῶν, iv. 14 ; apud Walz. Collect. Rhetor. t. ix. p. 304 ; also περὶ Σμινθιακῶν, iv. 17.

Σμίνθος, both in the Krêtan and the Æolic dialect, meant a field-mouse : the region seems to have been greatly plagued by these little animals.

Polemon could not have accepted the theory of Dêmêtrius, that Ilium was not the genuine Troy: his Periegesis, describing the localities and relics of Ilium, implied the legitimacy of the place as a matter of course.

with whom they fraternised, so that the result was not pure
Hellenism; next, that even this was done only in the towns, without
being fully extended to the territorial domain around, or to those
smaller townships which stood to the town in a dependent
relation. The Æolic and Ionic Greeks borrowed, from the
Asiatics whom they had Hellenised, musical instruments and new
laws of rhythm and melody, which they knew how to turn to
account: they further adopted more or less of those violent and
maddening religious rites, manifested occasionally in self-inflicted
suffering and mutilation, which were indigenous in Asia Minor
in the worship of the Great Mother. The religion of
the Greeks in the region of Ida as well as at Kyzikus
was more orgiastic than the native worship of Greece
Proper, just as that of Lampsacus, Priapus and
Parium was more licentious. From the Teukrian

Asiatic customs and religion—blended with Hellenic.

region of Gergis, and from the Gergithes near Kymê, sprang the
original Sibylline prophecies, and the legendary Sibyll who plays
so important a part in the tale of Æneas. The mythe of the
Sibyll, whose prophecies are supposed to be heard in the hollow
blast bursting out from obscure caverns and apertures in the
rocks,[1] was indigenous among the Gergithian Teukrians, and
passed from the Kymæans in Æolis, along with the other
circumstances of the tale of Æneas, to their brethren
the inhabitants of Cumæ in Italy. The date of the

Sibylline prophecies.

Gergithian Sibyll, or rather of the circulation of her supposed
prophecies, is placed during the reign of Crœsus, a period when
Gergis was thoroughly Teukrian. Her prophecies, though
embodied in Greek verses, had their root in a Teukrian soil and
feelings ; and the promises of future empire which they so
liberally make to the fugitive hero escaping from the flames of
Troy into Italy, become interesting from the remarkable way in
which they were realized by Rome.[2]

---

[1] Virgil, Æneid, vi. 42 :—

Excisum Euboïcæ latus ingens rupis
    in antrum,
Quo lati ducunt aditus centum, ostia
    centum :
Unde ruunt totidem voces, responsa
    Sibyllæ.

[2] Pausanias, x. 12, 8 ; Lactantius, i.
6, 12; Steph. Byz. v. Μέρμησσος ; Schol.

Plat. Phædr. p. 315, Bekker.
    The date of this Gergithian Sibyll,
or of the prophecies passing under her
name, is stated by Hérakleidês of
Pontus, and there seems no reason for
calling it in question.
    Klausen (Æneas und die Penaten,
book ii. p. 205) has worked out copiously
the circulation and legendary import
of the Sibylline prophecies.

At what time Ilium and Dardanus became Æolised we have no
information. We find the Mitylenæans in possession of Sigeium
in the time of the poet Alkæus, about 600 B.C.; and the Athenians,
during the reign of Peisistratus, having wrested it from them and
Settlements   trying to maintain their possession, vindicate the
from   proceeding by saying that they had as much right to
Miletus.
Mitylênê   it as the Mitylenæans, "for the latter had no more
and Athens. claim to it than any of the other Greeks who had
aided Menelaus in avenging the abduction of Helen".[1] This is a
very remarkable incident, as attesting the celebrity of the legend
of Troy, and the value of a mythical title in international
disputes—yet seemingly implying that the establishment of the
Mitylenæans on that spot must have been sufficiently recent.
The country near the junction of the Hellespont and the
Propontis is represented as originally held[2] by Bebrykian
Thracians, while Abydus was first occupied by Milesian colonists
in the reign and by the permission of the Lydian king Gygês[3]—
to whom the whole Trôad and the neighbouring territory
belonged, and upon whom therefore the Teukrians of Ida must
have been dependent. This must have been about 700 B.C., a
period considerably earlier than the Mitylenian occupation of
Sigeium. Lampsacus and Pæsus, on the neighbouring shores of
the Propontis, were also Milesian colonies, though we do not
know their date: Parium was jointly settled from Milêtus,
Erythræ and Parus.

[1] Herodot. v. 94. Σίγειον . . . .
τὸ εἷλε Πεισίστρατος αἰχμῇ παρὰ Μιτυ-
ληναίων . . . . Ἀθηναῖοι, ἀποδεικ-
νύντες λόγῳ οὐδὲν μᾶλλον Αἰολεῦσι
μετεὸν τῆς Ἰλιάδος χώρης, ἢ οὐ καί
σφι καὶ τοῖσι ἄλλοισι, ὅσοι Ἑλλήνων
συνεξεπρήξαντο Μενέλεῳ τὰς Ἑλένης
ἁρπαγάς. In Æschylus (Eumenid.
402) the goddess Athênê claims the
land about the Skamander, as having
been presented to the sons of Thêseus
by the general vote of the Grecian
chiefs :—

Ἀπὸ Σκαμάνδρου γῆν καταφθατουμένη,
Ἦν δή τ᾽ Ἀχαιῶν ἄκτορές τε καὶ πρόμοι
Τῶν αἰχμαλώτων χρημάτων λάχος μέγα,

Ἔνειμαν αὐτόπρεμνον εἰς τὸ πᾶν ἐμοί,
Ἐξαιρετὸν δώρημα Θησέως τόκοις.

In the days of Peisistratus, it
seems, Athens was not bold enough or
powerful enough to advance this vast
pretension.

[2] Charôn of Lampsacus ap. Schol.
Apollôn. Rhod. ii. 2; Bernhardy ad
Dionys. Periêgêt. 805, p. 747.

[3] Such at least is the statement of
Strabo (xii. p. 590); though such an
extent of Lydian rule at that time
seems not easy to reconcile with the
proceedings of the subsequent Lydian
kings.

CHAPTER XVI.

GRECIAN MYTHES, AS UNDERSTOOD, FELT AND INTER-PRETED BY THE GREEKS THEMSELVES.

THE preceding sections have been intended to exhibit a sketch of that narrative matter, so abundant, so characteristic, and so interesting, out of which early Grecian history and chronology have been extracted. Raised originally by hands unseen and from data unassignable, it existed first in the shape of floating talk among the people, from whence a large portion of it passed into the song of the poets, who multiplied, transformed and adorned it in a thousand various ways.

These mythes or current stories, the spontaneous and earliest growth of the Grecian mind, constituted at the same time the entire intellectual stock of the age to which they belonged. They are the common root of all those different ramifications into which the mental activity of the Greeks subsequently diverged; containing, as it were, the preface and germ of the positive history and philosophy, the dogmatic theology and the professed romance, which we shall hereafter trace each in its separate development. They furnished aliment to the curiosity, and solution to the vague doubts and aspirations, of the age; they explained the origin of those customs and standing peculiarities with which men were familiar; they impressed moral lessons, awakened patriotic sympathies, and exhibited in detail the shadowy, but anxious, presentiments of the vulgar as to the agency of the gods: moreover they satisfied that craving for adventure and appetite for the marvellous, which has in modern times become the province of fiction proper.

It is difficult, we may say impossible, for a man of mature age to carry back his mind to his conceptions such as they stood when

[margin note:] The mythes formed the entire mental stock of the early Greeks.

he was a child, growing naturally out of his imagination and feelings, working upon a scanty stock of materials, and borrowing from authorities whom he blindly followed but imperfectly apprehended.   A similar difficulty occurs when we attempt to place ourselves in the historical and quasi-philosophical point of view which the ancient mythes present to us.   We can follow perfectly the imagination and feeling which dictated these tales, and we can admire and sympathise with them as animated, sublime, and affecting poetry ; but we are too much accustomed to matter of fact and philosophy of a positive kind to be able to conceive a time when these beautiful fancies were construed literally and accepted as serious reality.

Nevertheless it is obvious that Grecian mythes cannot be either

State of mind out of which they arose. understood or appreciated except with reference to the system of conceptions and belief of the ages in which they arose.   We must suppose a public not reading and writing, but seeing, hearing and telling—destitute of all records, and careless as well as ignorant of positive history with its indispensable tests, yet at the same time curious and full of eagerness for new or impressive incidents—strangers even to the rudiments of positive philosophy and to the idea of invariable sequences of nature either in the physical or moral world, yet requiring some connecting theory to interpret and regularise the phænomena before them.   Such a theory was supplied by the spontaneous inspirations of an early fancy, which supposed the habitual agency of beings intelligent and voluntary like them-

Tendency to universal personifica-tion. selves but superior in extent of power, and different in peculiarity of attributes.   In the geographical ideas of the Homeric period, the earth was flat and round, with the deep and gentle ocean-stream flowing around and returning into itself: chronology, or means of measuring past time, there existed none.   Nevertheless, unobserved regions might be described, the forgotten past unfolded, and the unknown future predicted—through particular men specially inspired by the gods, or endowed by them with that peculiar vision which detected and interpreted passing signs and omens.

If even the rudiments of scientific geography and physics, now so universally diffused and so invaluable as a security against error and delusion, were wanting in this early stage of society, their place was abundantly supplied by vivacity of imagination and by personifying sympathy.   The unbounded tendency of the Homeric Greeks to multiply fictitious persons, and to construe interesting or formidable phænomena into manifestations of design, is above all things here to be noticed, because the form of personal narrative, universal in their mythes, is one of its many conse-quences.   Their polytheism (comprising some elements of an original fetichism, in which particular objects had themselves been supposed to be endued with life, volition, and design) recog-nised agencies of unseen beings identified and confounded with the different localities and departments of the physical world. Of such beings there were numerous varieties, and many grada-tions both in power and attributes ; there were differences of age, sex, and local residence, relations both conjugal and filial between them, and tendencies sympathetic, as well as repugnant.   The gods formed a sort of political community of their own, which had its hierarchy, its distribution of ranks and duties, its con-tentions for power and occasional revolutions, its public meetings in the agora of Olympus, and its multitudinous banquets or festivals.[1]   The great Olympic gods were in fact only the most exalted amongst an aggregate of quasi-human or ultra-human personages,—dæmons, heroes, nymphs, eponymous (or name giving) genii, identified with each river, mountain,[2] cape, town, village, or known circumscription of territory,—besides horses,

Absence of positive knowledge —supplied by per-sonifying faith.

---

[1] Homer, Iliad, i. 603 ; xx. 7. Hesiod. Theogon. 802.

[2] We read in the Iliad that Astero-pæus was grandson of the beautiful river Axius, and Achilles, after having slain him, admits the dignity of this parentage, but boasts that his own descent from Zeus was much greater, since even the great river Achelôus and Oceanus himself is inferior to Zeus (xxi. 157—191). Skamander fights with Achilles, calling his brother Simoïs to his aid (213—308). Tyrô, the daughter of Salmôneus, falls in love with Enipeus, the most beautiful of rivers (Odyss. xi. 237).   Achelôus appears as a suitor of Deïanira (Sophokl. Trach. 9).

There cannot be a better illustration of this feeling than what is told of the New Zealanders at the present time. The chief Heu-Heu appeals to his ancestor, the great mountain Tonga

Riro : " I am the Heu-Heu, and rule over you all, just as my ancestor, Tonga Riro, the mountain of snow, stands above all this land ".   (E. J. Wakefield, Adventures in New Zealand, vol. i. ch. 17, p. 465.)   Heu-Heu refused permis-sion to any one to ascend the mountain, on the ground that it was his *tipuna,* or ancestor : " he constantly identified himself with the mountain and called it his sacred ancestor " (vol. ii. c. 4, p. 113).   The mountains in New Zealand are accounted by the natives masculine and feminine : Tonga Riro, and Tara-naki, two male mountains, quarrelled about the affections of a small volcanic female mountain in the neighbourhood (*ibid.* ii. c. 4, p. 97).

The religious imagination of the Hindoos also (as described by Colonel Sleeman in his excellent work, Rambles and Recollections of an Indian Official)

bulls, and dogs, of immortal breed and peculiar attributes, and monsters of strange lineaments and combinations, "Gorgons and Harpies and Chimæras dire ". As there were in every *gens* or family special gentile deities and foregone ancestors who watched over its members, forming in each the characteristic symbol and recognised guarantee of their union, so there seem to have been in each guild or trade peculiar beings whose vocation it was to cooperate or to impede in various stages of the business.[1]

Multitude and variety of quasi-human personages.

affords a remarkable parallel to that of the early Greeks. Colonel Sleeman says,—

"I asked some of the Hindoos about us why they called the river Mother Nerbudda, if she was really never married. Her majesty (said they with great respect) would really never consent to be married after the indignity she suffered from her affianced bridegroom the Sohun: and we call her *mother* because she blesses us all, and we are anxious to accost her by the name which we consider to be the most respectful and endearing.

"Any Englishman can easily conceive a poet in his highest calenture of the brain, addressing the Ocean as a steed that knows his rider, and patting the crested billow as his flowing mane. But he must come to India to understand how every individual of a *whole community of many millions can address a fine river as a living being—a sovereign princess who hears and understands all they say, and exercises a kind of local superintendence over their affairs,* without a single temple in which her image is worshipped, or a single priest to profit by the delusion. As in the case of the Ganges, *it is the river itself to whom they address themselves, and not to any deity residing in it, presiding over it*—the stream itself is the deity which fills their imaginations, and receives their homage." (Rambles and Recollections of an Indian Official, ch. iii. p. 20.) Compare also the remarks in the same work on the sanctity of *Mother Nerbudda* (ch. xxvii. p. 261); also of the holy personality of the earth.—" The land is considered as the MOTHER of the prince or chief who holds it, the great parent from whom he derives all that maintains him, his family, and his establishments. If well-treated, she yields this in abundance to her son ; but if he presumes to

look upon her with the eye of *desire,* she ceases to be fruitful ; or the Deity sends down hail or blight to destroy all that she yields. The measuring the surface of the fields, and the frequently inspecting the crops by the chief himself or his immediate agents, were considered by people in this light —either it should not be done at all or the duty should be delegated to inferior agents, whose close inspection of the *great parent* could not be so displeasing to the Deity " (ch. xxii. p. 248).

See also about the Gods who are believed to reside in trees—the Peepul-tree, the cotton-tree, &c. (ch. ix. p. 112), and the description of the annual marriage celebrated between the sacred pebble, or pebble-god, Saligram, and the sacred shrub Toolsea, celebrated at great expense and with a numerous procession (chap. xix. p. 158 ; xxiii. p. 185).

[1] See the song to the potters, in the Homeric Epigrams (14) :—

Εἰ μὲν δώσετε μίσθον, ἀείσω, ὦ κεραμῆες·
Δεῦρ' ἄγ', Ἀθηναίη, καὶ ὑπείρεχε χεῖρα καμίνου.
Εὖ δὲ πεπανθεῖεν κότυλοι, καὶ πάντα κάναστρα
Φρυχθῆναί τε καλῶς, καὶ τιμῆς ὦνον ἀρέσθαι.

. . . .

Ἢν δ' ἐπ' ἀναιδείην τρεφθέντες ψεύδε' ἄρησθε,
Συγκαλέω δὴ 'πειτα καμίνῳ δηλητῆρας·
Σύντριβ' ὅμως, Σμάραγόν τε, καὶ Ἄσβετον, ἠδὲ Σαβάκτην,
Ὠμόδαμόν θ', ὃς τῇδε τέχνῃ κακὰ πολλὰ πορίζοι, &c.

A certain kindred between men and serpents (συγγένειάν τινα πρὸς τοὺς ὄφεις) was recognised in the peculiar gens of the ὀφιογενεῖς near Parion, who possessed the gift of healing by their touches the bite of the serpent·

The extensive and multiform personifications, here faintly sketched, pervaded in every direction the mental system of the Greeks, and were identified intimately both with their conception aud with their description of phænomena, present as well as past. That which to us is interesting as the mere creation of an exuberant fancy, was to the Greek genuine and venerated reality. The earth and the solid heaven (Gæa and Uranos) were both conceived and spoken of by him as endowed with appetite, feeling, sex, and most of the various attributes of humanity. Instead of a sun such as we now see, subject to astronomical laws, and forming the centre of a system the changes of which we can ascertain and foreknow, he saw the great god Hêlios, mounting his chariot in the morning in the east, reaching at mid-day the height of the solid heaven, and arriving in the evening at the western horizon, with horses fatigued and desirous of repose. Hêlios, having favourite spots wherein his beautiful cattle grazed, took pleasure in contemplating them during the course of his journey, and was sorely displeased if any man slew or injured them : he had moreover sons and daughters on earth, and as his all-seeing eye penetrated everywhere, he was sometimes in a situation to reveal secrets even to the gods themselves—while on other occasions he was constrained to turn aside in crder to avoid contemplating scenes of abomination.[1]   To us these now appear

the original hero of this gens was said to have been transformed from a serpent into a man (Strabo, xiii. p. 588).

[1] Odyss. ii. 388; viii. 270; xii. 4, 128, 416; xxiii. 362. Iliad, xiv. 344. The Homeric Hymn to Dêmêtêr expresses it neatly (63)—

'Ηέλιον δ' ἴκοντο, Θεῶν σκόπον ἠδὲ καὶ ἀνδρῶν.

Also the remarkable story of Euênius of Apollônia, his neglect of the sacred cattle of Hêlios, and the awful consequences of it (Herodot. ix. 93 ; compare Theocr. Idyll. xxv. 130).

I know no passage in which this conception of the heavenly bodies as Persons is more strikingly set forth than in the words of the German chief Boiocalus, pleading the cause of himself and his tribe the Ansibarii before the Roman legate Avitus. This tribe, expelled by other tribes from its native possessions, had sat down upon

some of that wide extent of lands on the Lower Rhine which the Roman government reserved for the use of its soldiers, but which remained desert, because the soldiers had neither the means nor the inclination to occupy them. The old chief, pleading his cause before Avitus, who had issued an order to him to evacuate the lands, first dwelt upon his fidelity of fifty years to the Roman cause, and next touched upon the enormity of retaining so large an area in a state of waste (Tacit. Ann. xiii. 55) : "Quotam partem campi jacere, in quam pecora et armenta militum aliquando transmitterentur?   Servarent sano receptos gregibus, inter hominum famam ; modo ne vastitatem et solitudinem mallent, quam amicos populos.   Chamavorum quondam ea arva, mox Tubantum, et post Usipiorum fuisse. Sicuti cœlum Diis, ita terras generi mortalium datas : quæque vacuæ, eas publicas esse. *Solem* deinde respiciens, et *cætera sidera*

puerile, though pleasing fancies, but to an Homeric Greek they seemed perfectly natural and plausible. In his view, the description of the sun, as given in a modern astronomical treatise, would have appeared not merely absurd, but repulsive and impious. Even in later times, when the positive spirit of inquiry had made considerable progress, Anaxagoras and other astronomers incurred the charge of blasphemy for dispersonifying Hêlios, and trying to assign invariable laws to the solar phænomena.[1] Personifying fiction was in this way blended

What we read as poetical fancies were to the Greeks serious realities.

---

vocans, quasi coram interrogabat—*vellentne contueri inane solum? potius mare superfunderent adversus terrarum ereptores.* Commotus his Avitus," &c. The legate refused the request, but privately offered to Boiocalus lands for himself apart from the tribe, which that chief indignantly spurned. He tried to maintain himself in the lands, but was expelled by the Roman arms, and forced to seek a home among the other German tribes, all of whom refused it. After much wandering and privation, the whole tribe of the Ansibarii was annihilated: its warriors were all slain, its women and children sold as slaves.

I notice this afflicting sequel, in order to show that the brave old chief was pleading before Avitus a matter of life and death both to himself and his tribe, and that the occasion was one least of all suited for a mere rhetorical prosopopœia. His appeal is one sincere and heartfelt to the personal feelings and sympathies of Hêlios.

Tacitus, in reporting the speech, accompanies it with the gloss "quasi coram," to mark that the speaker here passes into a different order of ideas from that to which himself or his readers were accustomed. If Boiocalus could have heard, and reported to his tribe, an astronomical lecture, he would have introduced some explanation, in order to facilitate to his tribe the comprehension of Hêlios under a point of view so new to them. While Tacitus finds it necessary to illustrate by a comment the *personification of the sun*, Boiocalus would have had some trouble to make his tribe comprehend the *reification of the god Hêlios.*

[1] Physical astronomy was both new and accounted impious in the time of the Peloponnesian war: see Plutarch, in his reference to that eclipse which proved so fatal to the Athenian army at Syracuse, in consequence of the religious feelings of Nikias : οὐ γὰρ ἠνείχοντο τοὺς φυσικοὺς καὶ μετεωρολέσχας τότε καλουμένους, ὡς εἰς αἰτίας ἀλόγους καὶ δυνάμεις ἀπρονοήτους καὶ κατηναγκασμένα πάθη διατρίβοντας τὸ θεῖον (Plutarch, Nikias, c. 23, and Periklês, c. 32; Diodôr. xii. 39; Dêmêtr. Phaler. ap. Diogen. Laërt. ix. 9, 1).

"You strange man, Melêtus," said Sokratês, on his trial, to his accuser, "are you seriously affirming that I do not think Hêlios and Selênê to be gods, as the rest of mankind think?" "Certainly not, men of the Dikastery; (*this is the reply of Melêtus*), Sokratês says that the sun is a stone, and the moon earth." "Why, my dear Melêtus, you think you are preferring an accusation against Anaxagoras! You account these Dikasts so contemptibly ignorant as not to know that the books of Anaxagoras are full of such doctrines! Is it from me that the youth acquire such teaching, when they may buy the books for a drachma in the theatre, and may thus laugh me to scorn if I pretended to announce such views as my own—*not to mention that they are in themselves so extravagant?*"—(ἄλλως τε καὶ οὕτως ἄτοπα ὄντα, Plato, Apolog. Socrat. c. 14, p. 26).

The divinity of Hêlios and Selênê is emphatically set forth by Plato, Legg. x. p. 886, 889. He permits physical astronomy only under great restrictions and to a limited extent. Compare Xenoph. Memor. iv. 7, 7 ; Diogen. Laërt. ii. 8; Plutarch, De Stoicor. Repugnant. c. 40, p. 1053 ; and Schaubach ad Anaxagoræ Fragmenta, p. 6.

by the Homeric Greeks with their conception of the physical phænomena before them, not simply in the way of poetical ornament, but as a genuine portion of their everyday belief.

The gods and heroes of the land and the tribe belonged, in the conception of a Greek, alike to the present and to the past : he worshipped in their groves and at their festivals ; he invoked their protection, and believed in their superintending guardianship, even in his own day : but their more special, intimate, and sympathising agency was cast back into the unrecorded past.[1] To give suitable utterance to this general sentiment—to furnish body and movement and detail to these divine and heroic pre-existences, which were conceived only in shadowy outline,—to lighten up the dreams of what the past must have been,[2] in the minds of those who knew not what it really had been—such was the spontaneous aim and inspiration of productive genius in the community, and such were the purposes which the Grecian mythes pre-eminently accomplished.

The gods and heroes —their chief agency cast back into the past and embodied in the mythes.

The love of antiquities, which Tacitus notices as so prevalent among the Greeks of his day,[3] was one of the earliest, the most durable, and the most widely diffused of the national propensities.

---

[1] Hesiod, Catalog. Fragm. 76, p. 48, ed. Düntzer :—

Ξυναὶ γὰρ τότε δαῖτες ἔσαν ξυνοί τε
    θόωκοι,
'Αθανάτοις τε θεοῖσι καταθνήτοις τ'
    ἀνθρώποις.

Both the Theogonia and the Works and Days bear testimony to the same general feeling. Even the heroes of Homer suppose a preceding age, the inmates of which were in nearer contact with the gods than they themselves (Odyss. viii. 223 ; Iliad, v. 304 ; xii. 382). Compare Catullus, Carm. 64 ; Epithalam. Peleos et Thetidos, v. 382—408.

Menander the Rhetor (following generally the steps of Dionys. Hal. Art. Rhetor. cap. 1—8) suggests to his fellow-citizens at Alexandreia Trôas, proper and complimentary forms to invite a great man to visit their festival of the Sminthia :—ὥσπερ γὰρ Ἀπόλλωνα πολλάκις ἐδέχετο ἡ πόλις τοῖς Σμινθίοις, ἥνικα ἐξῆν θεοὺς προφανῶς ἐπιδημεῖν τοῖς ἀνθρώποις, οὕτω καὶ σὲ ἡ πόλις νῦν προσδέχεται (περὶ Ἐπιδεικτικ. s. iv. c. 14, ap. Walz. Coll.

Rhetor. t. ix. p. 304). Menander seems to have been a native of Alexandreia Trôas, though Suidas calls him a Laodicean (see Walz. Præf. ad t. ix. p. xv.—xx. ; and περὶ Σμινθιακῶν, sect. iv. c. 17). The festival of the Sminthia lasted down to his time, embracing the whole duration of paganism from Homer downwards.

[2] P. A. Müller observes justly in his *Saga-Bibliothek*, in reference to the Icelandic mythes, "In dem Mythischen wird das Leben der Vorzeit dargestellt, wie es wirklich dem kindlichen Verstande, der jugendlichen Einbildungskraft, und dem vollen Herzen erscheint".

(Lange's Untersuchungen über die Nordische und Deutsche Heldensage, translated from P. A. Müller, Introd. p. 1.)

[3] Titus visited the temple of the Paphian Venus in Cyprus, "spectatâ opulentiâ donisque regum, quæque et *alia lætum* antiquitatibus Græcorum genus *incertæ vetustati adfingit*, de navigatione primum consuluit". (Tacit. Hist. ii. 4—5.)

But the antiquities of every state were divine and heroic, reproducing the lineaments, but disregarding the measure and limits, of ordinary humanity. The gods formed the starting-point, beyond which no man thought of looking, though some gods were more ancient than others : their progeny, the heroes, many of them sprung from human mothers, constitute an intermediate link between god and man. The ancient epic usually recognises the presence of a multitude of nameless men, but they are introduced chiefly for the purpose of filling the scene, and of executing the orders, celebrating the valour, and bringing out the personality of a few divine or heroic characters.[1] It was the glory of bards and story-tellers to be able to satisfy those religious and patriotic predispositions of the public which caused the primary demand for their tales, and which were of a nature eminently inviting and expansive. For Grecian religion was many-sided and many-coloured; it comprised a great multiplicity of persons, together with much diversity in the types of character ; it divinised every vein and attribute of humanity, the lofty as well as the mean—the tender as well as the warlike—the self-devoting and adventurous as well as the laughter-loving and sensual. We shall hereafter reach a time when philosophers protested against such identification of the gods with the more vulgar appetites and enjoyments, believing that nothing except the spiritual attributes of man could properly be transferred to superhuman beings, and drawing their predicates respecting the gods exclusively from what was awful, majestic and terror-striking in human affairs. Such restrictions on the religious fancy were continually on the increase, and the mystic and didactic stamp which marked the last century of paganism in the days of Julian and Libanius, contrasts forcibly with the concrete and vivacious forms, full of vigorous impulse and alive to all the capricious gusts of the human temperament, which people the Homeric Olympus.[2] At

Marked and manifold types of the Homeric gods.

---

[1] Aristotel. Problem. xix. 48. Οἱ δὲ ἡγεμόνες τῶν ἀρχαίων μόνοι ἦσαν ἥρωες· οἱ δὲ λαοὶ ἄνθρωποι. Istros followed this opinion also : but the more common view seems to have considered all who combated at Troy as heroes (see Schol. Iliad. ii. 110; xv. 231), and so Hesiod treats them (Opp. Di. 158).

In reference to the Trojan war, Aristotle says—καθάπερ ἐν τοῖς Ἡρωϊκοῖς περὶ Πριάμου μυθεύεται. (Ethic. Nicom. i. 9; compare vii. 1.)

[2] Generation by a god is treated in the old poems as an act entirely human and physical (ἐμίγη—παρελέξατο); and this was the common opinion in the days of Plato (Plato, Apolog. Socrat.

present, however, we have only to consider the early, or Homeric and Hesiodic paganism, and its operations in the genesis of the mythical narratives.   We cannot doubt that it supplied the most powerful stimulus, and the only one which the times admitted, to the creative faculty of the people ; as well from the sociability, the grada- tions, and the mutual action and reaction of its gods and heroes, as from the amplitude, the variety, and the purely human cast of its fundamental types.

Stimulus which they afforded to the mythopœic faculty.

Though we may thus explain the mythopœic fertility of the Greeks, I am far from pretending that we can render any sufficient account of the supreme beauty of their chief epic and artistical productions.   There is something in the first-rate pro- ductions of individual genius which lies beyond the compass of philosophical theory : the special breath of the Muse (to speak the language of ancient Greece) must be present in order to give them being.   Even among her votaries, many are called, but few

c. 15, p. 15); the hero Astrabakus is father of the Lacedæmonian king Demaratus (Herod. vi. 66). [Herodotus does not believe the story told him at Babylon respecting Belus (i. 182).] Euripidês sometimes expresses dis- approbation of the idea (Ion, 350), but Plato passed among a large portion of his admirers for the actual son of Apollo, and his reputed father Aristo on marrying was admonished in a dream to respect the person of his wife Periktionê, then pregnant by Apollo, until after the birth of the child Plato (Plutarch, Quæst. Sympos. p. 717. viii. 1 ; Diogen. Laërt. iii. 2 ; Origen, cont. Cels. i. p. 29). Plutarch (in Life of Numa, c. 4 ; compare Life of Thêseus, 2) discusses the subject, and is inclined to disallow everything beyond mental sympathy and tenderness in a god ; Pausanias deals timidly with it, and is not always consistent with himself ; while the later rhetors spiritualise it altogether. Menander, περὶ Ἐπιδεικ- τικῶν (towards the end of the third century B.C.), prescribes rules for praising a king : you are to praise him for the gens to which he belongs : perhaps you may be able to make out that he really is the son of some god ; for many who seem to be from men, are really *sent down by God* and are *emanations from the Supreme Potency*— πολλοὶ τὸ μὲν δοκεῖν ἐξ ἀνθρώπων εἰσὶ,

τῇ δ' ἀληθείᾳ παρὰ τοῦ θεοῦ καταπέμ- πονται καί εἰσιν ἀπόρροιαι ὄντως τοῦ κρείττονος· καὶ γὰρ Ἡρακλῆς ἐνομίζετο μὲν Ἀμφιτρύωνος, τῇ δὲ ἀληθείᾳ ἦν Διός. Οὕτω καὶ βασιλεὺς ὁ ἡμέτερος τὸ μὲν δοκεῖν ἐξ ἀνθρώπων, τῇ δὲ ἀληθείᾳ τὴν καταβολὴν οὐρανόθεν ἔχει, &c. (Menander ap. Walz. Collect. Rhetor. t. ix. c. i. p. 218).   Again—περὶ Σμιν- θιακῶν—Ζεὺς γένεσιν παιδῶν δημιουρ- γεῖν ἐνενόησε—Ἀπόλλων τὴν Ἀσκλη- πιοῦ γένεσιν ἐδημιούργησε, p. 322— 327 ; compare Hermogenês, about the story of Apollo and Daphnê, Progym- nasm. c. 4 ; and Julian. Orat. vii. p. 220.

The contrast of the pagan phraseo- logy of this age (Menander had himself composed a hymn of invocation to Apollo—περὶ Ἐγκωμίων, c. 3, t. ix. p. 136, Walz.) with that of Homer is very worthy of notice.   In the Hesiodic Catalogue of Women much was said respecting the marriages and amours of the gods, so as to furnish many suggestions, like the love-songs of Sapphô, to the composers of Epi- thalamic Odes (Menand. *ib.* sect. iv. c. 6, p. 268).

Menander gives a specimen of a prose hymn fit to be addressed to the Sminthian Apollo (p. 320); the spiritual character of which hymn forms the most pointed contrast with the Homeric hymn to the same god.

are chosen ; and the peculiarities of those few remain as yet her own secret.

We shall not however forget that Grecian language was also an indispensable requisite to the growth and beauty of Grecian mythes—its richness, its flexibility and capacity of new combinations, its vocalic abundance and metrical pronunciation ; and many even among its proper names, by their analogy to words really significant, gave direct occasion to explanatory or illustrative stories. Etymological mythes are found in sensible proportion among the whole number.

To understand properly then the Grecian mythes, we must try to identify ourselves with the state of mind of the original mythopœic age ; a process not very easy, since it requires us to adopt a string of poetical fancies not simply as realities, but as the governing realities of the mental system :[1] yet a process

[1] The mental analogy between the early stages of human civilisation and the childhood of the individual is forcibly and frequently set forth in the works of Vico. That eminently original thinker dwells upon the poetic and religious susceptibilities as the first to develop themselves in the human mind, and as furnishing not merely connecting threads for the explanation of sensible phænomena, but also aliment for the hopes and fears, and means of socialising influence to men of genius, at a time when reason was yet asleep. He points out the *personifying instinct* (" istinto d'animazione") as the spontaneous philosophy of man, " to make himself the rule of the universe," and to suppose everywhere a quasi-human agency as the determining cause. He remarks that in an age of fancy and feeling, the conceptions and language of poetry coincide with those of reality and common life, instead of standing apart as a separate vein. These views are repeated frequently (and with some variations of opinion as he grew older) in his Latin work *De Uno Universi Juris Principio*, as well as in the two successive *rédactions* of his great Italian work, *Scienza Nuova* (it must be added that Vico as an expositor is prolix, and does not do justice to his own powers of original thought) : I select the following from the second edition of the latter treatise, published by himself in 1744, *Dela Metafisica Poetica* (see vol. v. p. 189 of Ferrari's edition of his Works, Milan, 1836) : " Adunque la sapienza poetica, che fu la prima sapienza della Gentilità, dovette incominciare de una Metafisica, non *ragionata ed astratta*, qual è questa or degli addottrinati, ma *sentita ed immaginata*, quale dovett' essere di tai primi uomini, siccome quelli che erano di niun raziocinio, e tutti robusti sensi e vigorosissime fantasie, come è stato nelle degnità (the *Axioms*) stabilito. Questa fu la loro propria poesia, la qual in essi fu una faculltà loro connaturale, perchè erano di tali sensi e di sì fatte fantasie naturalmente forniti, nata da *ignoranza di cagioni* la qual fu loro madredi maraviglia di tutte le cose, che quelli ignoranti di tutte le cose fortemente ammiravano. Tal poesia incominciò in essi divina : perchè nello stesso tempo ch' essi immaginavano le cagioni delle cose, che sentivano ed ammiravano, essere Dei, come ora il confermiamo con gli Americani, i quali tutte le cose che superano la loro picciol capacità, dicono esser Dei . . . . nello stesso tempo, diciamo, alle cose ammirate davano l' essere di sostanze dalla propria lor idea : ch' è appunto la natura dei fauciulli, che osserviamo prendere tra mani cose inanimate, e trastullarsi e favellarvi, come fussero quelle persone vive. In cotal guisa i primi uomini delle nazioni gentili, come fanciulli del nascente gener umano, della lor idea creavan essi le

which would only reproduce something analogous to our own childhood. The age was one destitute both of recorded history and of positive science, but full of imagination and sentiment and religious impressibility. From these sources sprung that multitude of supposed persons around whom all combinations of sensible phænomena were grouped, and towards whom curiosity, sympathies and reverence were earnestly directed. The adventures of such persons were the only aliment suited at once both to the appetites and to the comprehension of an early Greek ; and the mythes which detailed them, while powerfully interesting his emotions, furnished to him at the same time a quasi-history and quasi-philosophy. They filled up the vacuum of the unrecorded past, and explained many of the puzzling incognita of the present.[1] Nor need we wonder that the same plausibility which captivated his imagination and his feelings was sufficient to engender spontaneous belief ; or rather that no question, as to truth

Easy faith in popular and plausible stories.

cose . . . . per la loro robusta ignoranza, il facevano in forza d' una corpulentissima fantasia, e perch' era corpolentissima, il facevano con una maravigliosa sublimità, tal e tanta, che perturbava all' eccesso essi medesimi, che fingendo le si creavano . . . . Di questa natura di cose umane restò eterna proprietà spiegata con nobil espressione da Tacito, che vanamente gli uomini spaventati *fingunt simul creduntque.*"

After describing the condition of rude men, terrified with thunder and other vast atmospheric phænomena, Vico proceeds (*ib.* p. 172)—"In tal caso la natura della mente umana porta ch' ella attribuisca all' effetto la sua natura: e la natura loro era in tale stato d' uomini tutti robuste forze di corpo, che urlando, brontolando, spiegavano le loro violentissime passioni, si finsero il cielo esser un gran corpo animato, che per tal aspetto chiamavano Giove, che col fischio dei fulmini e col fragore dei tuoni volesse lor dire qualche cosa . . . . E sì fanno di tutta la natura un vasto corpo animato, che senta passioni ed affetti."

Now the contrast with modern habits of thought :—

" Ma siccome *ora* per la natura delle nostre umane menti troppo ritirata dai sensi nel medesimo volgo—con le tante astrazioni, di quante sono piene le lingue—con tanti vocaboli astratti—e di troppo assottigliata con l' arti dello scrivere, e quasi spiritualezzata con la pratica dei numeri—*ci è naturalmente niegato di poter formare* la vasta imagine di cotal donna che dicono Natura simpatetica, che mentre con la bocca dicono, non hanno nulla in lor mente, perocchè la lor mente è dentro il falso, che è nulla ; nè sono soccorsi dalla fantasia a poterne formare una falsa vastissima imagine. Così *ora ci è naturalmente niè gatodi poter entrare nella vasta immaginativa di quei primi uomini,* le menti dei quali di nulla erano assottigliate, di nulla astratte, di nulla spiritualezzate . . . . . Onde dicemmo sopra che *ora appena intender si può, affatto immaginar non si può,* come pensassero i primi uomini che fondarono la umanità gentilesca."

[1] O. Müller, in his *Prolegomena zu einer wissenschaftlichen Mythologie* (cap. iv. p. 108), has pointed out the mistake of supposing that there existed originally some nucleus of pure reality as the starting-point of the mythes, and that upon this nucleus fiction was superinduced afterwards : he maintains that the real and the ideal were blended together in the primitive conception of the mythes. Respecting the general state of mind out of which the mythes grew, see especially pages 78 and 110

or falsehood of the narrative, suggested itself to his mind. His faith is ready, literal and uninquiring, apart from all thought of discriminating fact from fiction, or of detecting hidden and symbolised meaning; it is enough that what he hears be intrinsically plausible and seductive, and that there be no special cause to provoke doubt. And if indeed there were, the poet overrules such doubts by the holy and all-sufficient authority of the Muse, whose omniscience is the warrant for his recital, as her inspiration is the cause of his success.

The state of mind, and the relation of speaker to hearers, thus depicted, stand clearly marked in the terms and tenor of the ancient epic, if we only put a plain meaning upon what we read. The poet—like the prophet, whom he so much resembles—sings under heavenly guidance, inspired by the goddess to whom he has prayed for her assisting impulse. She puts the word into his mouth and the incidents into his mind: he is a privileged man, chosen as her organ and speaking from her revelations.[1] As the Muse grants the gift of song to whom she will, so she sometimes

Poets—receive their matter from the divine inspiration of the Muse.

---

of that work, which is everywhere full of instruction on the subject of the Grecian mythes, and is eminently suggestive, even where the positions of the author are not completely made out.

The short *Heldensage der Griechen* by Nitzsch (Kiel, 1842, t. v.) contains more of just and original thought on the subject of the Grecian mythes than any work with which I am acquainted. I embrace completely the subjective point of view in which he regards them; and although I have profited much from reading his short tract, I may mention that, before I ever saw it, I had enforced the same reasonings on the subject in an article in the Westminster Review, May, 1843, on the *Heroen-Geschichten* of Niebuhr.

Jacob Grimm, in the preface to his *Deutsche Mythologie* (p. 1, 1st edit. Gött. 1835), pointedly insists on the distinction between "*Sage*" and history, as well as upon the fact that the former has its chief root in religious belief. "Legend and history (he says) are powers each by itself, adjoining indeed on the confines, but having each its own separate and exclusive ground"; also p. xxvii. of the same introduction. A view substantially similar is

adopted by William Grimm, the other of the two distinguished brothers whose labours have so much elucidated Teutonic philology and antiquities. He examines the extent to which either historical matter of fact or historical names can be traced in the *Deutsche Heldensage*; and he comes to the conclusion that the former is next to nothing, the latter not considerable. He draws particular attention to the fact that the audience for whom these poems were intended had not learned to distinguish history from poetry (W. Grimm, *Deutsche Heldensage*, pp. 8, 337, 342, 345, 399, Gött. 1829).

[1] Hesiod, Theogon. 32.—

. . . . ἐνέπνευσαν δέ (the Muses) μοι αὐήδν

Θείην, ὡς κλείοιμι τά τ᾽ ἐσσόμενα, πρό τ᾽ ἐόντα,

Καί με κέλονθ᾽ ὑμνεῖν μακάρων γένος αἰὲν ἐόντων, &c.

Odyss. xxii. 347; viii. 63, 73, 481, 489. Δημόδοκ᾽ . . . . ἦ σέ γε Μοῦσ᾽ ἐδίδαξε, Διὸς παῖς, ἢ σέγ᾽ Ἀπόλλων: that is, Demodokus has either been inspired as a poet by the Muse, or as a prophet by Apollo: for the Homeric Apollo is not the god of song. Kalchas the prophet

in her anger snatches it away, and the most consummate human genius is then left silent and helpless.[1] It is true that these expressions, of the Muse inspiring and the poet singing a tale of past times, have passed from the ancient epic to compositions produced under very different circumstances, and have now degenerated into unmeaning forms of speech ; but they gained currency originally in their genuine and literal acceptation. If poets had from the beginning written or recited, the predicate of singing would never have been ascribed to them ; nor would it ever have become customary to employ the name of the Muse as a die to be stamped on licensed fiction, unless the practice had begun when her agency was invoked and hailed in perfect good faith. Belief, the fruit of deliberate inquiry and a rational scrutiny of evidence, is in such an age unknown. The simple faith of the time slides in unconsciously, when the imagination and feeling are exalted ; and inspired authority is at once understood, easily admitted, and implicitly confided in.

The word mythe (μῦθος, *fabula*, story), in its original meaning, signified simply a statement or current narrative, without any connotative implication either of truth or falsehood. Subsequently the meaning of the word (in Latin and English as well as in Greek) changed, and came to carry with it the idea of an old personal narrative, always uncertified, sometimes untrue or avowedly fictitious.[2]

Meaning of the word mythe—original—altered.

receives his inspiration from Apollo, who confers upon him the same knowledge both of past and future as the Muses give to Hesiod (Iliad, i. 69) :—

Κάλχας Θεστορίδης, οἰωνοπόλων ὄχ᾽
   ἄριστος
῾Ος ᾔδη τά τ᾽ ἐόντα, τά τ᾽ ἐσσόμενα, πρό
   τ᾽ ἐόντα
῾Ην διὰ μαντοσύνην, τήν οἱ πόρε Φοῖβος
   ᾽Απόλλων.

Also Iliad, ii. 485.
Both the μάντις and the ἀοιδός are standing, recognised professions (Odyss. xvii. 383), like the physician and the carpenter, δημιόεργοι.
[1] Iliad, ii. 599.
[2] In this later sense it stands pointedly opposed to ἱστορία, *history*, which seems originally to have designated matter of fact, present and seen by the describer, or the result of his personal inquiries (see Herodot. i. 1; Verrius Flacc. ap. Aul. Gell. v. 18 ;

Eusebius, Hist. Eccles. iii. 12 ; and the observations of Dr. Jortin, Remarks on Ecclesiastical History, vol. i. p. 59).
The original use of the word λόγος was the same as that of μῦθος—a current tale true or false, as the case might be ; and the term designating a person much conversant with the old legends (λόγιος) is derived from it (Herod. i. 1 ; ii. 8). Hekatæus and Herodotus both use λόγος in this sense. Herodotus calls both Æsop and Hekatæus λογοποιοί (ii. 134—143).
Aristotle (Metaphys. i. p. 8, ed. Brandis) seems to use μῦθος in this sense, where he says—διὸ καὶ φιλόμυθος ὁ φιλόσοφός πώς ἐστιν· ὁ γὰρ μῦθος συγκεῖται ἐκ θαυμασίων, &c. In the same treatise (xi. p. 254) he uses it to signify fabulous amplification and transformation of a doctrine true in the main.

And this change was the result of a silent alteration in the mental state of the society,—of a transition on the part of the superior minds (and more or less on the part of all) to a stricter and more elevated canon of credibility, in consequence of familiarity with recorded history and its essential tests, affirmative as well as negative. Among the original hearers of the mythes, all such tests were unknown: they had not yet learned the lesson of critical disbelief: the mythe passed unquestioned from the mere fact of its currency, and from its harmony with existing sentiments and preconceptions. The very circumstances which contributed to rob it of literal belief in after-time, strengthened its hold upon the mind of the Homeric man. He looked for wonders and unusual combinations in the past; he expected to hear of gods, heroes and men, moving and operating together upon earth; he pictured to himself the fore-time as a theatre in which the gods interfered directly, obviously, and frequently, for the protection of their favourites and the punishment of their foes. The rational conception, then only dawning in his mind, of a systematic course of nature, was absorbed by this fervent and lively faith. And if he could have been supplied with as perfect and philosophical a history of his own real past time, as we are now enabled to furnish with regard to the last century of England or France, faithfully recording all the successive events, and accounting for them by known positive laws, but introducing no special interventions of Zeus and Apollo—such a history would have appeared to him not merely unholy and unimpressive, but destitute of all plausibility or title to credence. It would have provoked in him the same feeling of incredulous aversion as a description of the sun (to repeat the previous illustration) in a modern book on scientific astronomy.

Matter of actual history—uninteresting to early Greeks.

To us these mythes are interesting fictions; to the Homeric and Hesiodic audience they were "rerum divinarum et humanarum scientia,"—an aggregate of religious, physical, and historical revelations, rendered more captivating, but not less true and real, by the bright colouring and fantastic shapes in which they were presented. Throughout the whole of "mythe-bearing Hellas"[1]

---

[1] M. Ampère, in his *Histoire Littéraire de la France* (ch. viii. v. i. p. 310), dis- tinguishes the Saga (which corresponds as nearly as possible with the Greek

they formed the staple of the uninstructed Greek mind, upon
which history and philosophy were by so slow degrees superinduced ; and they continued to be the aliment of ordinary
thought and conversation, even after history and philosophy
had partially supplanted the mythical faith among the leading
men, and disturbed it more or less in the ideas of all. The men,
the women, and the children of the remote dêmes and villages of
Greece, to whom Thucydidês, Hippokratês, Aristotle, or Hippar-
chus were unknown, still continued to dwell upon the local fables
which formed their religious and patriotic antiquity. And
Pausanias, even in his time, heard everywhere divine or heroic
legends yet alive, precisely of the type of the old epic ; he found
the conceptions of religious and mythical faith co-existent with
those of positive science, and contending against them at more or
less of odds, according to the temper of the individual. Now it
is the remarkable characteristic of the Homeric age, **Mythical**
that no such co-existence or contention had yet begun. **faith and**
The religious and mythical point of view covers, for **religious point of**
the most part, all the phænomena of nature ; while **view—**
the conception of invariable sequence exists only in **paramount in the Ho-**
the background, itself personified under the name of **meric age.**
the Mœræ, or Fates, and produced generally as an exception to
the omnipotence of Zeus for all ordinary purposes. Voluntary
agents, visible and invisible, impel and govern everything.
Moreover this point of view is universal throughout the com-

μῦθος, λόγος, ἐπιχώριος λόγος), as a
special product of the intellect, not
capable of being correctly designated
either as history, or as fiction, or as
philosophy :—
    " Il est un pays, la Scandinavie, où
la tradition racontée s'est développée
plus complètement qu'ailleurs, où ses
produits ont été plus soigneusement
recueillis et mieux conservés : dans ce
pays, ils ont reçu un nom particulier,
dont l'équivalent exact ne se trouve
pas hors des langues Germaniques :
c'est le mot *Saga, Sage, ce qu'on dit, ce
qu'on raconte*,—la tradition orale. Si
l'on prend ce mot non dans une
acception restreinte, mais dans le sens
général où le prenait Niebuhr quand
il l'appliquoit, par exemple, aux
traditions populaires qui ont pu
fournir à Tite Live une portion de son

histoire, la Saga doit être comptée
parmi les produits spontanés de
l'imagination humaine. La Saga a
son existence propre comme la poësie,
comme l'histoire, comme le roman.
Elle n'est pas la poësie, parce qu'elle
n'est pas chantée, mais parlée ; elle
n'est pas l'histoire, parce qu'elle est
dénuée de critique ; elle n'est pas le
roman, parce qu'elle est sincère, parce
qu'elle a foi à ce qu'elle raconte. Elle
n'invente pas, mais répète : elle peut se
tromper, mais elle ne ment jamais. Ce
récit souvent merveilleux, que personne
ne fabrique sciemment, et que tout
le monde altère et falsifie sans le
vouloir, qui se perpétue à la manière
des chants primitifs et populaires,—ce
récit, quand il se rapporte, non à un
héros, mais à un saint, s'appelle une
légende."

munity,—adopted with equal fervour, and carried out with equal consistency, by the loftiest minds and by the lowest. The great man of that day is he who, penetrated like others with the general faith, and never once imagining any other system of nature than the agency of these voluntary Beings, can clothe them in suitable circumstances and details, and exhibit in living body and action those types which his hearers dimly prefigure.

History, philosophy, &c., properly so called and conforming to our ideas (of which the subsequent Greeks were the first creators), never belonged to more than a comparatively small number of thinking men, though their influence indirectly affected more or less the whole national mind. But when positive science and criticism, and the idea of an invariable sequence of events, came to supplant in the more vigorous intellects the old mythical creed of omni-present personification, an inevitable scission was produced between the instructed few and the remaining community. The opposition between the scientific and the religious point of view was not slow in manifesting itself : in general language, indeed, both might seem to stand together, but in every particular case the admission of one involved the rejection of the other. According to the theory which then became predominant, the course of nature was held to move invariably on, by powers and attributes of its own, unless the gods chose to interfere and reverse it; but they had the power of interfering as often and to as great an extent as they thought fit. Here the question was at once opened, respecting a great variety of particular phænomena, whether they were to be regarded as natural or miraculous. No constant or discernible test could be suggested to discriminate the two : every man was called upon to settle the doubt for himself, and each settled it according to the extent of his knowledge, the force of his logic, the state of his health, his hopes, his fears, and many other considerations affecting his separate conclusion. In a question thus perpetually arising and full of practical consequences, instructed minds, like Periklês, Thucydidês, and Euripidês, tended more and more to the scientific point of

Gradual development of the scientific point of view—its opposition to the religious.

view,[1] in cases where the general public were constantly gravitating towards the religious.

The age immediately prior to this unsettled condition of thought is the really mythopœic age ; in which the creative

[1] See Plutarch, Perikl. capp. 5, 32, 38 ; Cicero, De Republ. i. 15-16 ed. Maii.

The phytologist Theophrastus, in his valuable collection of facts respecting vegetable organisation, is often under the necessity of opposing his scientific interpretation of curious incidents in the vegetable world to the religious interpretation of them which he found current. Anomalous phænomena in the growth or decay of trees were construed as signs from the gods, and submitted to a prophet for explanation (see Histor. Plantar. ii. 3 ; iv. 16 ; v. 3).

We may remark, however, that the old faith had still a certain hold over his mind. In commenting on the story of the willow-tree at Philippi, and the venerable old plane-tree at Antandros (more than sixty feet high, and requiring four men to grasp it round in the girth), having been blown down by a high wind, and afterwards spontaneously resuming their erect posture, he offers some explanation how such a phænomenon might have happened, but he admits, at the end, that there *may* be something extra-natural in the case, Ἀλλὰ ταῦτα μὲν ἴσως ἔξω φυσικῆς αἰτίας ἔστιν, &c. (De Caus. Plant. v. 4) : see a similar miracle in reference to the cedar-tree of Vespasian (Tacit. Hist. ii. 78).

Euripidês, in his lost tragedy called Μελανίππη Σοφή, placed in the mouth of Melanippê a formal discussion and confutation of the whole doctrine of τέρατα, of supernatural indications (Dionys. Halicar. Ars Rhetor. p. 300—356, Reisk.). Compare the Fables of Phædrus, iii. 3 ; Plutarch, Sept. Sap. Conviv. ch. 3, p. 149 ; and the curious philosophical explanation by which the learned men of Alexandria tranquillised the alarms of the vulgar, on occasion of the serpent said to have been entwined round the head of the crucified Kleomenês (Plutarch, Kleomen. c. 39).

It is one part of the duty of an able physician, according to the Hippokratic treatise called Prognosticon (c. 1, t. 2, p. 112, ed. Littré), when he visits his patient, to examine whether there is anything divine in the malady, ἅμα δὲ καὶ εἴ τι θεῖον ἔνεστιν ἐν τῇσι νούσοισι : this, however, does not agree with the memorable doctrine laid down in the treatise, De Aëre, Locis et Aquis (c. 22, p. 78, ed. Littré), and cited hereafter, in this chapter. Nor does Galen seem to have regarded it as harmonising with the general views of Hippocrates. In the excellent Prolegomena of M. Littré to his edition of Hippokratês (t. i. p. 76) will be found an inedited scholium, wherein the opinion of Baccheius and other physicians is given, that the affections of the plague were to be looked upon as divine, inasmuch as the disease came from God; and also the opinion of Xenophôn, the friend of Praxagoras, that the " genus of days of crisis " in fever was divine ; " For (said Xenophôn) just as the Dioskuri, being gods, appear to the mariner in the storm and bring him salvation, so also do the days of crisis, when they arrive, in fever ". Galen, in commenting upon this doctrine of Xenophôn, says that the author " has expressed his own individual feeling, but has no way set forth the opinion of Hippokratês"; Ὁ δὲ τῶν κρισίμων γένος ἡμερῶν εἰπὼν εἶναι θεῖον, ἑαυτοῦ τι πάθος ὡμολόγησεν · οὐ μὴν Ἱπποκράτους γε τὴν γνώμην ἐδειξεν (Galen, Opp. t. v. p. 120, ed. Basil.).

The comparison of the Dioskuri appealed to by Xenophôn is a precise reproduction of their function as described in the Homeric Hymn (Hymn xxxiii. 10) : his personification of the " days of crisis " introduces the old religious agency to fill up a gap in his medical science.

I annex an illustration from the Hindoo vein of thought :—" It is a rule with the Hindoos to bury, and not to burn, the bodies of those who die of the small-pox ; for (say they) the small-pox is not only caused by the goddess Davey, but is, in fact, *Davey herself* ; and to burn the body of a person affected with this disease, is, in reality, neither more nor less than *to burn the goddess*". (Sleeman, Rambles and Recollections, &c., vol. i. ch. xxv. p. 221.)

faculties of the society know no other employment, and the mass

Mythopœic age—anterior to this dissent. of the society no other mental demand. (The perfect expression of such a period, in its full peculiarity and grandeur, is to be found in the Iliad and Odyssey,— poems of which we cannot determine the exact date, but which seem both to have existed prior to the first Olympiad, 776 B.C., our earliest trustworthy mark of Grecian time. For some time after that event, the mythopœic tendencies continued in vigour (Arktinus, Leschês, Eumêlus, and seemingly most of the Hesiodic poems, fall within or shortly after the first century of recorded Olympiads); but from and after this first century, we may trace the operation of causes which gradually enfeebled and narrowed them, altering the point of view from which the mythes were looked at. What these causes were, it will be necessary briefly to intimate.

The foremost and most general of all is, the expansive force of

Expansive force of Grecian intellect. Grecian intellect itself,—a quality in which this remarkable people stand distinguished from all their neighbours and contemporaries. Most, if not all, nations have had mythes, but no nation except the Greeks have imparted to them immortal charm and universal interest; and the same mental capacities, which raised the great men of the poetic age to this exalted level, also pushed forward their successors to outgrow the early faith in which the mythes had been generated and accredited.

One great mark, as well as means, of such intellectual expansion, was the habit of attending to, recording, and combining, positive and present facts, both domestic and foreign. In the genuine Grecian epic, the theme was an unknown and aoristic past ; but even as early as the Works and Days of Hesiod, the present begins to figure. The man who tills the earth appears in his own solitary nakedness, apart from gods and heroes—bound indeed by serious obligations to the gods, but contending against many difficulties which are not to be removed by simple reliance on their help. The poet denounces his age in the strongest terms, as miserable, degraded, and profligate. He looks back with reverential envy to the extinct heroic races who fought at Troy and Thêbes. Yet bad as the present time is, the Muse condescends to look at it along with him, and to prescribe rules for human life—with the assurance that if a man be industrous, frugal, provident, just and friendly in his dealings, the gods will recompense him with affluence and security. Nor does the Muse disdain, while holding out such Transition towards positive and present fact. promise, to cast herself into the most homely details of present existence, and to give advice thoroughly practical and calculating. Men whose minds were full of the heroes of Homer called Hesiod in contempt the poet of the Helots. The contrast between the two is certainly a remarkable proof of the tendency of Greek poetry towards the present and the positive.

Other manifestations of the same tendency become visible in the age of Archilochus (B.C. 680-660). In an age when metrical composition and the living voice are the only means whereby the productive minds of a community make themselves felt, the invention of a new metre, new forms of song and recitation, or diversified accompaniments, constitute an epoch. The iambic, elegiac, choric, and lyric poetry, from Archilochus downwards, all indicate purposes in the poet, and impressibilities of the hearers, very different from those of the ancient epic. In all of them the personal feeling of the poet and the special- The poet becomes the organ of present time instead of past. ties of present time and place, are brought prominently forward ; while in the Homeric hexameter the poet is a mere nameless organ of the historical Muse—the hearers are content to learn, believe, and feel, the incidents of a foregone world—and the tale is hardly less suitable to one time and place than to another. The iambic metre (we are told) was first suggested to Archilochus by the bitterness of his own private antipathies ; and the mortal wounds inflicted by his lampoons, upon the individuals against whom they were directed, still remain attested, though the verses themselves have perished. It was the metre (according to the well-known judgment of Aristotle) most nearly approaching to common speech, and well suited both to the coarse vein of sentiment, and to the smart and emphatic diction of its inventor.[1] Simonidês of

---

[1] Horat. de Art. Poet. 79 :—

" Archilochum proprio rabies armavit Iambo," &c.

Compare Epist. i. 19, 23, and Epod.

vi. 12 ; Aristot. Rhetor. iii. 8, 7, and Poetic. c. 4—also Synesius de Somniis —ὥσπερ Ἀλκαῖος καὶ Ἀρχίλοχος, οἳ δεδαπανήκασι τὴν εὐστομίαν εἰς τὸν οἰκεῖον βίον ἑκάτερος. (Alcæi Frag-

Amorgus, the younger contemporary of Archilochus, employed the same metre, with less bitterness, but with an anti-heroic tendency not less decided. His remaining fragments present a mixture of teaching and sarcasm, having a distinct bearing upon actual life,[1] and carrying out the spirit which partially appears in the Hesiodic Works and Days. Of Alkæus and Sapphô, though unfortunately we are compelled to speak of them upon hearsay only, we know enough to satisfy us that their own personal sentiments and sufferings, their relations private or public with the contemporary world, constituted the soul of those short effusions which gave them so much celebrity.[2] Again in the few remains of the elegiac poets preserved to us—Kallinus, Mimnermus, Tyrtæus—the impulse of some present motive or circumstance is no less conspicuous. The same may also be said of Solôn, Théognis and Phokylidês, who preach, encourage, censure, or complain, but do not recount—and in whom a profound ethical sensibility, unknown to the Homeric poems, manifests itself. The form of poetry (to use the words of Solôn himself) is made the substitute for the public speaking of the agora.[3]

Iambic, elegiac, and lyric poets.

Doubtless all these poets made abundant use of the ancient mythes, but it was by turning them to present account, in the

---

ment. Halle, 1810, p. 205). Quintilian speaks in striking language of the power of expression manifested by Archilochus (x. 1. 60).

[1] Simonidês of Amorgus touches briefly, but in a tone of contempt upon the Trojan war—γυναικὸς οὕνεκ' ἀμφιδηριωμένους (Simonid. Fragm. 8, p. 36, v. 118); he seems to think it absurd that so destructive a struggle should have taken place "pro und mulierculá," to use the phrase of Mr. Payne Knight.

[2] See Quintilian x. 1, 63. Horat. Od. i. 32; ii. 13. Aristot. Polit. iii. 10, 4. Dionys. Halic. observes (Vett. Scriptt. Censur. v. p. 421) respecting Alkæus—πολλαχοῦ γοῦν τὸ μέτρον εἴ τις περιέλοι, ῥητορικὴν ἂν εὕροι πολιτείαν; and Strabo (xiii. p. 617), τὰ στασιωτικὰ καλούμενα τοῦ Ἀλκαίου ποιήματα.

There was a large dash of sarcasm and homely banter aimed at neighbours and contemporaries in the poetry of Sapphô, apart from her impassioned love-songs—ἄλλως σκώπτει τὸν ἄγροικον νύμφιον καὶ τὸν θυρωρὸν τὸν ἐν τοῖς

γάμοις, εὐτελέστατα καὶ ἐν πέζοις ὀνόμασι μᾶλλον ἢ ἐν ποιητικοῖς. Ὥστε αὐτῆς μᾶλλόν ἐστι τὰ ποιήματα ταῦτα διαλέγεσθαι ἢ ᾄδειν· οὐδ' ἂν ἁρμόσαι πρὸς τὸν χόρον ἢ πρὸς τὴν λύραν, εἰ μή τις εἴη χόρος διαλεκτικός (Dēmêtr. Phaler. De Interpret. c. 167).

Compare also Herodot. ii. 135, who mentions the satirical talent of Sapphô, employed against her brother for an extravagance about the courtezan Rhodôpis.

[3] Solôn, Fragm. iv. 1, ed. Schneidewin :—

Αὐτὸς κήρυξ ἦλθον ἀφ' ἱμερτῆς Σαλαμῖνος
Κόσμον ἐπέων ᾠδὴν ἀντ' ἀγορῆς θέμενος, &c.

See *Brandis*, Handbuch der Griechischen Philosophie, sect. xxiv.—xxv. Plato states that Solôn, in his old age, engaged in the composition of an epic poem, which he left unfinished, on the subject of the supposed island of Atlantis and Attica (Plato, Timæus, p. 21, and Kritias, p. 113). Plutarch, Solôn, c. 31.

way of illustration, or flattery, or contrast,—a tendency which we may usually detect even in the compositions of Pindar, in spite of the lofty and heroic strain which they breathe throughout. That narrative or legendary poetry still continued to be composed during the seventh and sixth centuries before the Christian æra, is a fact not to be questioned. But it exhibited the old epical character without the old epical genius ; both the inspiration of the composer and the sympathies of the audience had become more deeply enlisted in the world before them, and disposed to fasten on incidents of their own actual experience. From Solôn and Theognis we pass to the abandonment of all metrical restrictions and to the introduction of prose writing,—a fact the importance of which it is needless to dwell upon,—marking as well the increased familiarity with written records, as the commencement of a separate branch of literature for the intellect, apart from the imagination and emotions wherein the old legends had their exclusive root.

Egypt was first unreservedly opened to the Greeks during the reign of Psammetichus, about B.C. 660 ; gradually it became much frequented by them for military or commercial purposes, or for simple curiosity. It enlarged the range of their thoughts and observations, while it also imparted to them that vein of mysticism, which overgrew the primitive simplicity of the Homeric religion, and of which I have spoken in a former chapter. They *Influence of the opening of Egypt to Grecian commerce. B.C. 660.* found in it a long-established civilization, colossal wonders of architecture, and a certain knowledge of astronomy and geometry, elementary indeed, but in advance of their own. Moreover it was a portion of their present world and it contributed to form in them an interest for noting and describing the actual realities before them. A sensible progress is made in the Greek mind during the two centuries from B.C. 700 to B.C. 500, in the record and arrangement of historical facts ; an *historical* sense arises in the superior intellects, and some idea of evidence as a discriminating test between fact and fiction. And this progressive *Progress— historical, geographical, social, —from that period to B.C. 500.* tendency was further stimulated by increased communication and by more settled and peaceful social relations between the various members of the Hellenic world ; to which may be added material improvements, purchased at the expense of a period of turbulence and revolution, in the internal administration of each separate state. The Olympic, Pythian, Nemean, and Isthmian games became frequented by visitors from the most distant parts of Greece : the great periodical festival in the island of Dêlos brought together the citizens of every Ionic community, with their wives and children, and an ample display of wealth and ornaments.[1] Numerous and flourishing colonies were founded in Sicily, the south of Italy, the coasts of Epirus, and of the Euxine Sea : the Phokæans explored the whole of the Adriatic, established Massalia, and penetrated even as far as the south of Ibéria, with which they carried on a lucrative commerce.[2] The geographical ideas of the Greeks were thus both expanded and rectified : the first preparation of a map, by Anaximander the disciple of Thalês, is an epoch in the history of science.) We may note the ridicule bestowed by Herodotus both upon the supposed people called Hyperboreans and upon the idea of a circumfluous ocean-stream, as demonstrating the progress of the age in this department of inquiry.[3] And even earlier than Herodotus— Xanthus and Xenophanês had noticed the occurrence of fossil marine productions in the interior of Asia Minor and elsewhere, which led them to reflections on the changes of the earth's surface with respect to land and water.[4]

If then we look down the three centuries and a half which

Altered standard of judgment, ethical and intellectual.

elapsed between the commencement of the Olympic æra and the age of Herodotus and Thucydidês, we shall discern a striking advance in the Greeks,— ethical, social, and intellectual. Positive history and chronology has not only been created, but in the case of Thucydidês, the qualities necessary to the historiographer, in their

---

[1] Homer, Hymn. ad Apollin. 155; Thucyd. iii. 104.

[2] Herodot. i. 163.

[3] Herodot. iv. 36. γελῶ δὲ ὁρέων Γῆς περιόδους γράψαντας πολλοὺς ἤδη, καὶ οὐδένα νόον ἔχοντας ἐξηγησάμενον· οἳ Ὠκέανόν τε ῥέοντα γράφουσι πέριξ τὴν γῆν, ἐοῦσαν κυκλοτερέα ὡς ἀπὸ τόρνου, &c., a remark probably directed against Hekatæus.
Respecting the map of Anaximander, Strabo, i. p. 7 ; Diogen.

Laërt. ii. 1; Agathemer. ap. Geograph. Minor. i. 1. πρῶτος ἐτόλμησε τὴν οἰκουμένην ἐν πίνακι γράψαι.
Aristagoras of Milêtus, who visited Sparta to solicit aid for the revolted Ionians against Darius, brought with him a brazen tablet or map, by means of which he exhibited the relative position of places in the Persian empire (Herodot. v. 49).
[4] Xanthus ap. Strab. i. p. 50 ; xii. p. 579. Compare Creuzer, Fragmenta Xanthi, p. 162.

application to recent events, have been developed with a degree
of perfection never since surpassed. Men's minds have assumed
a gentler as well as a juster cast ; and acts come to be criticised
with reference to their bearing on the internal happiness of a
well-regulated community, as well as upon the standing harmony
of fraternal states. While Thucydidês treats the habitual and
licensed piracy, so coolly alluded to in the Homeric poems, as an
obsolete enormity—many of the acts described in the old heroic
and Theogonic legends were found not less repugnant to this
improved tone of feeling. The battles of the gods with the Giants
and Titans,—the castration of Uranus by his son Kronus,—the
cruelty, deceit and licentiousness, often supposed both in the gods
and heroes, provoked strong disapprobation. And the language
of the philosopher Xenophanês, who composed both elegiac and
iambic poems for the express purpose of denouncing such tales,
is as vehement and unsparing as that of the Christian writers,
who, eight centuries afterwards, attacked the whole scheme of
paganism.[1]

It was not merely as an ethical and social critic that Xenophanês
stood distinguished. He was one of a great and eminent
triad—Thalês and Pythagoras being the others—who, Commence-
in the sixth century before the Christian æra, first ment of
opened up those veins of speculative philosophy which physical
occupied afterwards so large a portion of Grecian science—
intellectual energy. Of the material differences between the Thalês, Xenophanês,
Pythagoras.
three I do not here speak ; I regard them only in reference to
the Homeric and Hesiodic philosophy which preceded them, and
from which all three deviated by a step, perhaps the most
remarkable in all the history of philosophy.

They were the first who attempted to disenthral the philosophic
intellect from all-personifying religious faith, and to constitute a
method of interpreting nature distinct from the spon-   Impersonal
taneous inspirations of untaught minds. It is in them nature
that we first find the idea of Person tacitly set aside or conceived as
an object
limited, and an impersonal Nature conceived as the of study.
object of study. The divine husband and wife, Oceanus and
Têthys, parents of many gods and of the Oceanic nymphs, together

---

[1] Xenophan. ap. Sext. Empiric. adv. Græc. ed. Schneidewin, Diogen. Laërt.
Mathemat. ix. 193. Fragm. 1. Poet. ix. 18.

with the avenging goddess Styx, are translated into the material substance *water*, or, as we ought rather to say, the Fluid : and Thalês set himself to prove that water was the primitive element, out of which all the different natural substances had been formed.[1] He, as well as Xenophanês and Pythagoras, started the problem of physical philosophy, with its objective character and invariable laws, to be discoverable by a proper and methodical application of the human intellect.   The Greek word Φύσις, denoting *nature*, and its derivatives *physics* and *physiology*, unknown in that large sense to Homer or Hesiod, as well as the word *Kosmos* to denote the mundane system, first appears with these philosophers.[2] The elemental analysis of Thalês—the one unchangeable cosmic substance, varying only in appearance, but not in reality, as suggested by Xenophanês,—and the geometrical combinations of Pythagoras, —all these were different ways of approaching the explanation of physical phænomena, and each gave rise to a distinct school or succession of philosophers.   But they all agreed in departing from the primitive method, and in recognising determinate properties, a material substratum, and objective truth, in nature—either independent of willing or designing agents, or serving to these latter at once as an indispensable subject-matter and as a limiting condition.   Xenophanês disclaimed openly all knowledge respecting the gods, and pronounced that no man could have any means of ascertaining when he was right and when he was wrong, in affirmations respecting them :[3] while Pythagoras represents in part the scientific tendencies of his age, in part also the spirit of mysticism and of special fraternities for religious and ascetic observance, which became diffused throughout Greece in the sixth century before the Christian æra.   This was another

---

[1] Aristotel. Metaphys. i. 3.

[2] Plutarch, Placit. Philos. ii. 1; also Stobæus, Eclog. Physic. i. 22, where the difference between the Homeric expressions and those of the subsequent philosophers is seen. Damm, Lexic. Homeric. v. Φύσις; Alexander von Humboldt, *Kosmos*, p. 76, the note 9 on page 62 of that admirable work.
The title of the treatises of the early philosophers (Melissus, Dêmokritus, Parmenidês, Empedoklês, Alkmæôn, &c.) was frequently Περὶ Φύσεως (Galen, Opp., tom i p. 56, ed. Basil.).

[3] Xenophan. ap. Sext. Empiric. vii. 50 ; viii. 326.—

Καὶ τὸ μὲν οὖν σαφὲς οὔτις ἀνὴρ ἴδεν,
    οὔτε τίς ἐστιν
Εἰδὼς ἀμφὶ θεῶν τε καὶ ἄσσα λέγω περὶ
    πάντων·
Εἰ γὰρ καὶ τὰ μάλιστα τύχοι τετελεσ-
    μένον εἰπὼν,
Αὐτὸς ὅμως οὐκ οἶδε, δόκος δ' ἐπὶ πᾶσι
    τέτυκται.

Compare Aristotel. De Xenophane, Zenone, et Gorgiâ, capp. 1—2.

point which placed him in antipathy with the simple, unconscious, and demonstrative faith of the old poets, as well as with the current legend.

If these distinguished men, when they ceased to follow the primitive instinct of tracing the phænomena of nature to personal and designing agents, passed over, not at once to induction and observation, but to a misemployment of abstract words, substituting metaphysical *eidôla* in the place of polytheism, and to an exaggerated application of certain narrow physical theories—we must remember that nothing else could be expected from the scanty stock of facts then accessible, and that the most profound study of the human mind points out such transition as an inevitable law of intellectual progress.[1]   At present we have to compare them only with that state of the Greek mind[2] which they partially superseded, and with which they were in decided opposition.   The rudiments of physical science were conceived and developed among superior men ; but the religious feeling of the mass was averse to them ; and the aversion, though gradually mitigated, never wholly died away.   Some of the philosophers were not backward in charging others with irreligion, while the multitude seems to have felt the same sentiment more or less towards all—or towards that postulate of constant sequences, with determinate conditions of occurrence, which scientific study implies, and which they could not reconcile with their belief in the agency of the gods, to whom they were constantly praying for special succour and blessings.

Opposition between scientific method and the religious feeling of the multitude

The discrepancy between the scientific and the religious point of view was dealt with differently by different philosophers.   Thus Sokratês openly admitted it, and assigned to each a distinct and independent province.   He distributed phænomena into two classes ; one

How dealt with by different philosophers.

[1] See the treatise of M. Auguste Comte (*Cours de Philosophie Positive*), and his doctrine of the three successive stages of the human mind in reference to scientific study—the theological, the metaphysical and the positive ;—a doctrine laid down generally in his first lecture (vol. i. p. 4—12), and largely applied and illustrated throughout his instructive work.   It is also re-stated and elucidated by Mr. John Stuart Mill in his System of Logic, Ratiocinative and Inductive, vol. ii. p 610.

[2] " Human wisdom (ἀνθρωπίνη σοφία), as contrasted with the primitive theology (οἱ ἀρχαῖοι καὶ διατρίβοντες περὶ τὰς θεολογίας)," to take the words of Aristotle (Meteorolog. ii. 1, pp. 41—42, ed. Tauchnitz).

wherein the connexion of antecedent and consequent was invariable and ascertainable by human study, and therefore future results accessible to a well-instructed foresight; the other, and those, too, the most comprehensive and important, which the gods had reserved for themselves and their own unconditional agency, wherein there was no invariable or ascertainable sequence, and where the result could only be foreknown by some omen, prophecy, or other special inspired communication from themselves.   Each of these classes was essentially distinct, and required to be looked at and dealt with in a manner radically incompatible with the other.   Sokratês held it wrong to apply the scientific interpretation to the latter, or the theological interpretation to the former.   Physics and astronomy, in his opinion, belonged to the divine class of phænomena, in which human research was insane, fruitless, and impious.[1]

Sokratês.

On the other hand, Hippokratês, the contemporary of Sokratês, denied the discrepancy, and merged into one those two classes of phænomena,—the divine and the scientifically determinable,—which the latter had put asunder.   Hippokratês treated all phænomena as at once both divine and scientifically determinable.   In discussing certain peculiar bodily disorders found among the Scythians, he observes, "The Scythians themselves ascribe the cause of this to God, and reverence and bow down to such sufferers, each man fearing that he may suffer

Hippokratês.

---

[1] Xenoph. Memor. i. 1, 6—9. Τὰ μὲν ἀναγκαῖα (Σωκράτης) συνεβούλευε καὶ πράττειν, ὡς ἐνόμιζεν ἄριστ' ἂν πραχθῆναι· περὶ δὲ τῶν ἀδήλων ὅπως ἀποβήσοιτο, μαντευσομένους ἔπεμπεν, εἰ ποιητέα. Καὶ τοὺς μέλλοντας οἴκους τε καὶ πόλεις καλῶς οἰκήσειν μαντικῆς ἔφη προσδεῖσθαι· τεκτονικὸν μὲν γὰρ ἢ χαλκευτικὸν ἢ γεωργικὸν ἢ ἀνθρώπων ἀρχικὸν, ἢ τῶν τοιούτων ἔργων ἐξεταστικὸν, ἢ λογιστικὸν, ἢ οἰκονομικὸν, ἢ στρατηγικὸν γενέσθαι, πάντα τὰ τοιαῦτα, μαθήματα καὶ ἀνθρώπου γνώμῃ αἱρετέα, ἐνόμιζεν εἶναι· τὰ δὲ μέγιστα τῶν ἐν τούτοις ἔφη τοὺς θεοὺς ἑαυτοῖς καταλείπεσθαι, ὧν οὐδὲν δῆλον εἶναι τοῖς ἀνθρώποις . . . . Τοὺς δὲ μηδὲν τῶν τοιούτων οἰομένους εἶναι δαιμόνιον, ἀλλὰ πάντα τῆς ἀνθρωπίνης γνώμης, δαιμονᾷν ἔφη· δαιμονᾷν δὲ καὶ τοὺς μαντευομένους ἃ τοῖς ἀνθρώποις ἔδωκαν οἱ θεοὶ μαθοῦσι διακρίνειν . . . . Ἔφη δὲ δεῖν, ἃ μὲν μαθόντας ποιεῖν ἔδωκαν οἱ θεοί, μανθάνειν· ἃ δὲ μὴ δῆλα τοῖς ἀνθρώποις ἔστι, πειρᾶσθει διὰ μαντικῆς παρὰ τῶν θεῶν πυνθάνεσθαι· τοὺς θεοὺς γὰρ, οἷς ἂν ὦσιν ἵλεῳ, σημαίνειν. Compare also Memorab. iv. 7, 7 ; and Cyropæd. i. 6, 3, 23—46.

Physical and astronomical phænomena are classified by Sokrates among the divine class, interdicted to human study (Memor. i. 1, 13): τὰ θεῖα or δαιμόνια as opposed to τἀνθρώπεια.   Plato (Phileb. c. 16: Legg. x. p. 886—889; xii. p. 967) held the sun and stars to be gods, each animated with its special soul : he allowed astronomical investigation to the extent necessary for avoiding blasphemy respecting these beings—μέχρι τοῦ μὴ βλασφημεῖν περὶ αὐτά (vii. 821).

the like : and I myself think too that these affections, as well as all others, are divine : no one among them is either more divine or more human than another, but all are on the same footing, and all divine ; nevertheless each of them has its own physical conditions, and not one occurs without such physical conditions".[1]

A third distinguished philosopher of the same day, Anaxagoras, allegorising Zeus and the other personal gods, proclaimed the doctrine of one common pervading Mind, as having first originated movement in the primæval Chaos, the heterogeneous constituents of which were so confused together that none of them could manifest themselves, each was neutralised by the rest, and all remained in rest and nullity. The movement originated by Mind disengaged them from this imprisonment, so that each kind of particle was enabled to manifest its properties with some degree of distinctness. This general doctrine obtained much admiration from Plato and Aristotle ; but they at the same time remarked with surprise, that Anaxagoras never made any use at all of his own general doctrine for the explanation of the phænomena of nature,—that he looked for nothing but physical causes and connecting laws,[2]— so that in fact the spirit of his particular researches was not materially different from those of Demokritus or Leukippus, whatever might be the difference in their general theories. His investigations in meteorology and astronomy, treating the heavenly

(margin note: Anaxagoras.)

---

[1] Hippokratês, De Aëre, Locis et Aquis, c. 22 (p. 78, edit. Littré, sect. 106, ed. Petersen): Ἔτι τε πρὸς τουτέοισι εὐνούχιαι γίγνονται οἱ πλεῖστοι ἐν Σκύθῃσι, καὶ γυναικηΐα ἐργάζονται καὶ ὡς αἱ γυναῖκες διαλέγονταί τε ὁμοίως· καλεῦνταί τε οἱ τοιοῦτοι ἀνανδριεῖς. Οἱ μὲν οὖν ἐπιχώριοι τὴν αἰτίην προστιθέασι θεῷ καὶ σέβονται τουτέους τοὺς ἀνθρώπους καὶ προσκυνέουσι, δεδοικότες περὶ ἑωυτέων ἕκαστοι. Ἐμοὶ δὲ καὶ αὐτέῳ δοκέει ταῦτα τὰ πάθεα θεῖα εἶναι, καὶ τἄλλα πάντα, καὶ οὐδὲν ἕτερον ἑτέρου θειότερον οὐδὲ ἀνθρωπινώτερον, ἀλλὰ πάντα θεῖα· ἕκαστον δὲ ἔχει φύσιν τῶν τοιουτέων, καὶ οὐδὲν ἄνευ φύσιος γίγνεται. Καὶ τοῦτο τὸ πάθος, ὥς μοι δοκέει γίγνεσθαι, φράσω, &c.

Again, sect. 112. Ἀλλὰ γὰρ, ὥσπερ καὶ πρότερον ἔλεξα, θεῖα μὲν καὶ ταῦτά ἐστι ὁμοίως τοῖσι ἄλλοισι, γίγνεται δὲ κατὰ φύσιν ἕκαστα.

Compare the remarkable treatise of Hippokratês, De Morbo Sacro, capp. 1 and 18, vol. vi. p. 352—394, ed. Littré.

See this opinion of Hippokratês illustrated by the doctrines of some physical philosophers stated in Aristotle, Physic. ii. 8. ὥσπερ ὕει ὁ Ζεύς, οὐχ ὅπως τὸν σῖτον αὐξήσῃ, ἀλλ' ἐξ ἀνάγκης, &c. Some valuable observations on the method of Hippokratês are also found in Plato, Phædr. p. 270.

[2] See the graphic picture in Plato, Phædon. p. 97—89 (cap. 46—47) : compare Plato, Legg. xii. p. 967 ; Aristotel. Metaphysic. i. p. 13—14 (ed. Brandis); Plutarch. Defect. Oracul. p. 435.

Simplicius, Commentar. in Aristotel. Physic. p. 38. καὶ ὅπερ δὲ ὁ ἐν Φαίδωνι Σωκράτης ἐγκαλεῖ τῷ Ἀναξαγόρᾳ, τὸ ἐν ταῖς τῶν κατὰ μέρος αἰτιολογίαις μὴ τῷ νῷ κεχρῆσθαι, ἀλλὰ ταῖς ὑλικαῖς ἀποδόσεσιν, οἰκεῖον ἦν τῇ φυσιολογίᾳ. Anaxagoras thought that the superior intelligence of man, compared with other animals, arose from his possession of hands (Aristot. de Part. Animal. iv. 10, p. 687, ed. Bekk.).

bodies as subjects for calculation, have been already noticed as offensive, not only to the general public of Greece, but even to Sokratês himself among them. He was tried at Athens, and seems to have escaped condemnation only by voluntary exile.[1]

The three eminent men just named, all essentially different from each other, may be taken as illustrations of the philosophical mind of Greece during the last half of the fifth century B.C. Scientific pursuits had acquired a powerful hold, and adjusted themselves in various ways with the prevalent religious feelings of the age. Both Hippokratês and Anaxagoras modified their ideas of the divine agency, so as to suit their thirst for scientific research. According to the former, the gods were the really efficient agents in the production of all phænomena,—the mean and indifferent not less than the terrific or tutelary. Being thus alike connected with all phænomena, they were specially associated with none—and the proper task of the inquirer was, to find out those rules and conditions by which (he assumed) their agency was always determined, and according to which it might be foretold. Now such a view of the divine agency could never be reconciled with the religious feelings of the ordinary Grecian believer, even as they stood in the time of Anaxagoras: still less could it have been reconciled with those of the Homeric man, more than three centuries earlier. By him Zeus and Athênê were conceived as definite Persons, objects of special reverence, hopes and fears, and

Contrasted with Grecian religious belief.

---

[1] Xenophôn, Memorab. iv. 7. Sokratês said, καὶ παραφρονῆσαι τὸν ταῦτα μεριμνῶντα οὐδὲν ἧττον ἢ 'Αναξαγόρας παρεφρόνησεν, ὁ μέγιστον φρονήσας ἐπὶ τῷ τὰς τῶν θεῶν μηχανὰς ἐξηγεῖσθαι, &c. Compare Schaubach, Anaxagoræ Fragment. p. 50—141; Plutarch, Nikias, 23, and Periklês, 6—32 ; Diogen. Laërt. ii. 10—14.

The Ionic philosophy, from which Anaxagoras receded more in language than in spirit, seems to have been the least popular of all the schools, though some of the commentators treat it as conformable to vulgar opinion, because it confined itself for the most part to phænomenal explanations, and did not recognise the *noumena* of Plato, or the τὸ ἐν νοητόν of Parmenidês,—"qualis fuit Ionicorum, quæ tum dominabatur, ratio, vulgari opinione et communi sensu comprobata" (Karsten, Parmenidis Fragment., De Parmenidis Philosophiâ, p. 154). This is a mistake : the Ionic philosophers, who constantly searched for and insisted upon physical laws, came more directly into conflict with the sentiment of the multitude than the Eleatic school.

The larger atmospheric phænomena were connected in the most intimate manner with Grecian religious feeling and uneasiness (see Demokritus ap. Sext. Empiric. ix. sect. 19—24, p. 552—554, Fabric.) ; the attempts of Anaxagoras and Demokritus to explain them were more displeasing to the public than the Platonic speculations (Demokritus ap. Aristot. Meteorol. ii. 7 ; Stobæus, Eclog. Physic. p. 594 ; compare Mullach, Democriti Fragmenta, lib. iv. p. 394).

animated with peculiar feelings, sometimes of favour, sometimes of wrath, towards himself or his family or country. They were propitiated by his prayers, and prevailed upon to lend him succour in danger—but offended and disposed to bring evil upon him if he omitted to render thanks or sacrifice. This sense of individual communion with them, and dependence upon them, was the essence of his faith. While he prayed with sincerity for special blessings or protection from the gods, he could not acquiesce in the doctrine of Hippokratês, that their agency was governed by constant laws and physical conditions.

That radical discord between the mental impulses of science and religion, which manifests itself so decisively during the most cultivated ages of Greece, and which harassed more or less so many of the philosophers, produced its most afflicting result in the condemnation
Treatment of Sokratês by the Athenians.
of Sokratês by the Athenians. According to the remarkable passage recently cited from Xenophôn, it will appear that Sokratês agreed with his countrymen in denouncing physical speculations as impious,—that he recognised the religious process of discovery as a peculiar branch, co-ordinate with the scientific,—and that he laid down a theory, of which the basis was, the confessed divergence of these two processes from the beginning—thereby seemingly satisfying the exigences of religious hopes and fears on the one hand, and those of reason, in her ardour for ascertaining the invariable laws of phænomena, on the other. We may remark that the theory of this religious and extra-scientific process of discovery was at that time sufficiently complete; for Sokratês could point out, that those anomalous phænomena which the gods had reserved for themselves, and into which science was forbidden to pry, were yet accessible to the seekings of the pious man, through oracles, omens, and other exceptional means of communication which divine benevolence vouchsafed to keep open.

Now the scission thus produced between the superior minds and the multitude, in consequence of the development of science and the scientific point of view, is a fact of great moment in the history of Greek progress, and forms an important contrast between the age of Homer and Hesiod and that of Thucydidês:

though in point of fact, even the multitude, during this later age,
were partially modified by those very scientific views
which they regarded with disfavour.   And we must
keep in view the primitive religious faith, once
universal and unobstructed, but subsequently disturbed by the intrusions of science; we must follow
the great change, as well in respect to enlarged
intelligence as to refinement of social and ethical
feeling, among the Greeks, from the Hesiodic times downward,
in order to render some account of the altered manner in which
the ancient mythes came to be dealt with.   These mythes, the
spontaneous growth of a creative and personifying interpretation
of nature, had struck root in Grecian associations at a time when
the national faith required no support from what we call evidence.
They were *now* submitted not simply to a feeling, imagining and
believing public, but also to special classes of instructed men,—
philosophers, historians, ethical teachers, and critics,—and to a
public partially modified by their ideas[1] as well as improved by a
wider practical experience.   They were not intended for such an
audience; they had ceased to be in complete harmony even with
the lower strata of intellect and sentiment,—much more so with
the higher.   But they were the cherished inheritance of a past
time; they were interwoven in a thousand ways with the religious
faith, the patriotic retrospect, and the national worship, of every

Scission between the superior men and the multitude—important in reference to the mythes.

---

[1] It is curious to see that some of
the most recondite doctrines of the
Pythagorean philosophy were actually
brought before the general Syracusan
public in the comedies of Epicharmus:
" In comœdiis suis personas sæpe ita
colloqui fecit, ut sententias Pytha-
goricas et in universum sublimia vitæ
præcepta immisceret". (Grysar De
Doriensium Comœdiâ, p. 111, Col. 1828.)
The fragments preserved in Diogen.
Laërt. (iii. 9—17) present both criticisms
upon the Hesiodic doctrine of a primæval chaos, and an exposition of the
archetypal and immutable ideas (as
opposed to the fluctuating phænomena
of sense) which Plato afterwards
adopted and systematised.

Epicharmus seems to have combined
with this abstruse philosophy a strong
vein of comic shrewdness and some
turn to scepticism (Cicero, Epistol. ad
Attic. i. 19): " ut crebro mihi vafer

ille Siculus Epicharmus insusurret
cantilenam suam ".   Clemens Alex.
Strom. v. p. 258.   Νᾶφε καὶ μέμνασ'
ἀπιστεῖν· ἄρθρα ταῦτα τῶν φρενῶν.
Ζῶμεν ἀριθμῷ καὶ λογισμῷ· ταῦτα γὰρ
σώζει βροτούς.   Also his contemptuous
ridicule of the prophetesses of his time
who cheated foolish women out of
their money, pretending to universal
knowledge, καὶ πάντα γιγνώσκοντι τῷ
τηνᾶν λόγῳ (ap. Polluc. ix. 81).   See,
about Epicharmus, O. Müller, Dorians,
iv. 7, 4.

These dramas seem to have been
exhibited at Syracuse between 480—
460 B.C., anterior even to Chionidês
and Magnês at Athens (Aristot. Poet.
c. 3): he says πολλῷ πρότερος, which
can hardly be literally exact.   The
critics of the Horatian age looked
upon Epicharmus as the prototype of
Plautus (Hor. Epistol. ii. 1. 58).

Grecian community; the general type of the mythe was the ancient, familiar and universal form of Grecian thought, which even the most cultivated men had imbibed in their childhood from the poets,[1] and by which they were to a certain degree unconsciously enslaved. Taken as a whole the mythes had acquired prescriptive and ineffaceable possession. To attack, call in question, or repudiate them, was a task painful even to undertake, and far beyond the power of any one to accomplish.

For these reasons, the anti-mythic vein of criticism was of little effect as a destroying force. But nevertheless its dissolving, decomposing and transforming influence was very considerable. To accommodate the ancient mythes to an improved tone of sentiment and a newly created canon of credibility, was a function which even the wisest Greeks did not disdain, and which occupied no small proportion of the whole intellectual activity of the nation. The mythes were looked at from a point of view completely foreign to the reverential curiosity and literal imaginative faith of the Homeric man. They were broken up and recast in order to force them into new moulds such as their authors had never conceived. We may distinguish four distinct classes of minds, in the literary age now under examination, as having taken them in hand—the poets, the logographers, the philosophers, and the historians.

The mythes accommo-dated to a new tone of feeling and judgment.

With the poets and logographers, the mythical persons are real predecessors, and the mythical world an antecedent fact. But it is divine and heroic reality, not human; the present is only half-brother of the past (to borrow[2] an illustration from Pindar in his allusion to gods and men), remotely and generically, but not closely and specifically, ana-logous to it. As a general habit, the old feelings and the old unconscious faith, apart from all proof or evidence, still remain in their minds; but recent feelings have grown up, which compel them to omit, to alter, sometimes even to reject and condemn, particular narratives.

The poets and logo-graphers.

---

[1] The third book of the Republic of Plato is particularly striking in refer-ence to the use of the poets in educa-tion : see also his treatise De Legg. vii. p. 810—811. Some teachers made their pupils learn whole poets by heart (ὅλους ποιητὰς ἐκμανθάνων), others preferred extracts and selections.

[2] Pindar, Nem. vi. 1. Compare Simonidês, Fragm. 1 (Gaisford).

Pindar repudiates some stories and transforms others, because
they are inconsistent with his conceptions of the gods.
Pindar.   Thus he formally protests against the tale that Pelops
had been killed and served up at table by his father, for the
immortal gods to eat.   Pindar shrinks from the idea of imputing
to them so horrid an appetite; he pronounces the tale to have
been originally fabricated by a slanderous neighbour.   Nor can
he bring himself to recount the quarrels between different gods.[1]
The amours of Zeus and Apollo are noway displeasing to him ;
but he occasionally suppresses some of the simple details of the
old mythe, as deficient in dignity.   Thus, according to the
Hesiodic narrative, Apollo was informed by a raven of the
infidelity of the nymph Korônis: but the mention of the raven
did not appear to Pindar consistent with the majesty of the god,
and he therefore wraps up the mode of detection in vague and
mysterious language.[2]   He feels considerable repugnance to the
character of Odysseus, and intimates more than once that Homer
has unduly exalted him, by force of poetical artifice.   With the
character of the Æakid Ajax, on the other hand, he has the
deepest sympathy, as well as with his untimely and inglorious
death, occasioned by the undeserved preference of a less worthy
rival.[3]   He appeals for his authority usually to the Muse, but
sometimes to "ancient sayings of men," accompanied with a
general allusion to story-tellers and bards,—admitting however
that these stories present great discrepancy, and sometimes that
they are false.[4]   Yet the marvellous and the supernatural afford
no ground whatever for rejecting a story : Pindar makes an
express declaration to this effect in reference to the romantic
adventures of Perseus and the Gorgon's head.[5]   He treats even
those mythical characters, which conflict the most palpably with
positive experience, as connected by a real genealogical thread

[1] Pindar, Olymp. i. 30—55 ; ix. 32—
45.
[2] Pyth. iii. 25.   See the allusions to
Semelê, Alkmêna, and Danaê, Pyth.
iii. 98 ;   Nem. x. 10.   Compare also
supra, chap. ix.
[3] Pindar, Nem. vii. 20—30 ; viii. 23—
31.   Isthm. iii. 50—60.
It seems to be sympathy for Ajax,
in odes addressed to noble Æginetan
victors, which induces him thus to

depreciate Odysseus ; for he eulogises
Sisyphus, specially on account of his
cunning and resources (Olymp. xiii.
50), in the ode addressed to Xenophôn
the Corinthian.

[4] Olymp. i. 28 ; Nem. viii. 20 ; Pyth.
i. 93 ; Olymp. vii. 55 ; Nem. vi. 43.
φάντι δ' ἀνθρώπων παλαιαὶ ῥήσιες, &c.

[5] Pyth. x. 49.   Compare Pyth. xii.
11—22

with the world before him.   Not merely the heroes of Troy and
Thêbes, and the demigod seamen of Jasôn in the ship Argô, but
also the Centaur Cheirôn, the hundred-headed Typhôs, the
giant Alkyoneus, Antæus, Bellerophôn and Pegasus, the
Chimæra, the Amazons and the Hyperboreans—all appear
painted on the same canvas, and touched with the same colours,
as the men of the recent and recorded past, Phalaris and Krœsus:
only they are thrown back to a greater distance in the perspective.[1]   The heroic ancestors of those great Æginetan, Thessalian,
Thêban, Argeian, &c., families, whose present members the poet
celebrates for their agonistic victories, sympathise with the exploits
and second the efforts of their descendants : the inestimable value
of a privileged breed, and of the stamp of nature, is powerfully
contrasted with the impotence of unassisted teaching and practice.[2]
The power and skill of the Argeian Theæus and his relatives as
wrestlers, are ascribed partly to the fact that their ancestor
Pamphaês in aforetime had hospitably entertained the Tyndarids
Kastôr and Pollux.[3]   Perhaps however the strongest proof of the
sincerity of Pindar's mythical faith is afforded when he notices a
guilty incident with shame and repugnance, but with an unwilling confession of its truth, as in the case of the fratricide
committed on Phokus by his brothers Pêleus and Telamôn.[4]

Æschylus and Sophoklês exhibit the same spontaneous and
uninquiring faith as Pindar in the legendary anti- Tragic
quities of Greece, taken as a whole ; but they allow poets.
themselves greater licence as to the details.   It was indispensable
to the success of their compositions that they should recast and
group anew the legendary events, preserving the names and
general understood relation of those characters whom they introduced.   The demand for novelty of combination increased with
the multiplication of tragic spectacles at Athens : moreover the
feelings of the Athenians, ethical as well as political, had become
too critical to tolerate the literal reproduction of many among the
ancient stories.

---

[1] Pyth. i. 17 ; iii. 4—7 ; iv. 12 ; viii.
16.   Nem. iv. 27—32 ; v. 89. Isthm. v.
31 ; vi. 44—48.   Olymp. iii. 17 ; viii. 63 ;
xiii. 61—87.

[2] Nem. iii. 39 ; v. 40.   συγγενὴς
εὐδοξία — πότμος συγγενής ; v. 8.
Olymp. ix. 103.   Pindar seems to

introduce φύᾳ in cases where Homer
would have mentioned the divine
assistance.

[3] Nem. x. 37—51.   Compare the
family legend of the Athenian Dêmo-
kratês, in Plato, Lysis. p. 205.

[4] Nem. v. 12—16.

Both of these poets exalted rather than lowered the dignity of
the mythical world, as something divine and heroic
rather than human. The Promêtheus of Æschylus is

Æschylus and Sopho-klês.

a far more exalted conception than his keen-witted
namesake in Hesiod, and the more homely details of the
ancient Thêbaïs and Œdipodia were modified in the like spirit
by Sophoklês.[1] The religious agencies of the old epic are constantly kept prominent by both. The paternal curse,—the wrath
of deceased persons against those from whom they have sustained
wrong,—the judgments of the Erinnys against guilty or foredoomed persons, sometimes inflicted directly, sometimes brought
about through dementation of the sufferer himself (like the
Homeric Atê),—are frequent in their tragedies.[2]

---

[1] See above, chap. xiv. on the Legend of the Siege of Thêbes.

[2] The curse of Œdipus is the deter-mining force in the Sept. ad Theb., Ἀρα τ΄, Ἐρινννὺς πατρὸς ἢ μεγασθενής (v. 70); it reappears several times in the course of the drama, with parti-cular solemnity in the mouth of Eteoklês (695—709, 725, 785, &c.); he yields to it as an irresistible force, as carrying the family to ruin :—

* * * * * *

Ἐπεὶ τὸ πρᾶγμα κάρτ᾽ ἐπισπέρχει θεὸς,
Ἴτω κατ᾽ οὖρον, κῦμα Κωκυτοῦ λαχὸν,
Φοίβῳ στυγηθὲν πᾶν τὸ Λαΐου γένος.

Φίλου γὰρ ἐχθρά μοι πατρὸς τελεῖ᾽ ἄρα
Ξηροῖς ἀκλαύστοις ὄμμασιν προσιζάνει,
&c.

So again at the opening of the Agamemnôn, the μνάμων μῆνις τεκνό-ποινος (v. 155) and the sacrifice of Iphigenia are dwelt upon as leaving behind them an avenging doom upon Agamemnôn, though he took precau-tions for gagging her mouth during the sacrifice and thus preventing her from giving utterance to imprecations —Φθόγγον ἀραῖον οἴκοις Βίᾳ χαλινῶν τ᾽ ἀναύδῳ μένει (κατασχεῖν), v. 246. The Erinnys awaits Agamemnôn even at the moment of his victorious consum-mation at Troy (467; compare 762—990, 1336—1433): she is most to be dreaded after great good fortune : she enforces the curse which ancestral crimes have brought upon the house of Atreus— πρώταρχος ἄτη—παλαιαὶ ἁμαρτίαι δόμων (1187—1197, Choëph. 692)—the curse imprecated by the outraged Thyestês

(1601). In the Choëphoroe, Apollo menaces Orestês with the wrath of his deceased father, and all the direful visitations of the Erinnys, unless he undertakes to revenge the murder (271 —296). Αἶσα and Ἐρινννύς bring on blood for blood (647). But the moment that Orestês, placed between these conflicting obligations (925), has achieved it, he becomes himself the victim of the Erinnyes, who drive him mad even at the end of the Choëphoroe (ἕως δ᾽ ἔτ᾽ ἔμφρων εἰμί, 1026), and who make their appearance bodily, and pursue him throughout the third drama of this fearful trilogy. The Eidôlon of Klytæmnestra impels them to vengeance (Eumenid. 96), and even spurs them on when they appear to relax. Apollo conveys Orestês to Athens, whither the Erinnys pursue him, and prosecute him before the judgment-seat of the goddess Athênê, to whom they submit the award; Apollo appearing as his defender. The debate between "the daughters of Night" and the god, accusing and defending, is eminently curious (576—730): the Erinnyes are deeply morti-fied at the humiliation put upon them when Orestês is acquitted, but Athênê at length reconciles them, and a cove-nant is made whereby they become protectresses of Attica, accepting of a permanent abode and solemn worship (1006): Orestês returns to Argos, and promises that even in his tomb he will watch that none of his descendants shall ever injure the land of Attica (770). The solemn trial and acquittal of Orestês formed the consecrating

Æschylus in two of his remaining pieces brings forward the
gods as the chief personages. Far from sharing the objection of
Pindar to dwell upon dissensions of the gods, he introduces
Promêtheus and Zeus in the one, Apollo and the Eumenides in
the other, in marked opposition. The dialogue, first superinduced by him upon the primitive chorus, gradually became the
most important portion of the drama, and is more elaborated in
Sophoklês than in Æschylus. Even in Sophoklês, however, it
still generally retains its ideal majesty as contrasted with the
rhetorical and forensic tone which afterwards crept in: it grows
out of the piece, and addresses itself to the emotions more than
to the reason of the audience. Nevertheless, the effect of
Athenian political discussion and democratical feeling is visible
in both these dramatists. The idea of rights and legitimate
privileges as opposed to usurping force, is applied by
Æschylus even to. the society of the gods. The
Eumenides accuse Apollo of having, with the insolence of youthful ambition, "ridden down" their old
prerogatives [1]—while the Titan Promêtheus, the
champion of suffering humanity against the unfriendly dispositions of Zeus, ventures to depict the latter as a recent usurper
reigning only by his superior strength, exalted by one successful
revolution, and destined at some future time to be overthrown

Tendencies of Æschylus in regard to the old legends.

legend of the Hill and Judicature of
Areiopagus.
This is the only complete trilogy of
Æschylus which we possess, and the
avenging Erinnyes (416) are the movers
throughout the whole—unseen in the
first two dramas, visible and appalling
in the third. And the appearance of
Kassandra under the actual prophetic
fever in the first, contributes still
farther to impart to it a colouring
different from common humanity.
The general view of the movement
of the Oresteia given in Welcker
(Æschyl. Trilogie, p. 445) appears to
me more conformable to Hellenic ideas
than that of Klausen (Theologumena
Æschyli, pp. 157—169), whose valuable
collection and comparison of passages
is too much affected, both here and
elsewhere, by the desire to bring the
agencies of the Greek mythical world
into harmony with what a religious
mind of the present day would
approve. Moreover he sinks the

personality of Athênê too much in
the supreme authority of Zeus (p.
158—168).
[1] Eumenidês, 150.—

'Ιὼ, παῖ Διὸς, ἐπίκλοπος πέλει,
Νέος δὲ γραίας δαίμονας καθιππάσω, &c.

The same metaphor again, v. 731.
Æschylus seems to delight in contrasting the young and the old gods : compare 70—162, 882.
The Erinnyes tell Apollo that he
assumes functions which do not belong
to him, and will thus desecrate those
which do belong to him (715—754) :—
'Αλλ' αἱματηρὰ πράγματ', οὐ λαχὼν,
σέβεις,
Μαντεῖα δ' οὐκ ἔθ' ἁγνὰ μαντεύσει μένων.

The refusal of the king Pelasgos, in
the Supplices, to undertake what he
feels to be the sacred duty of protecting
the suppliant Danaïdes, without first
submitting the matter to his people
and obtaining their expressed consent,

by another,—a fate which cannot be averted except through warnings communicable only by Promêtheus himself.[1]

Though Æschylus incurred reproaches of impiety from Plato, and seemingly also from the Athenian public, for particular speeches and incidents in his tragedies,[2] and though he does not

and the fear which he expresses of their blame (κατ᾽ ἀρχὰς γὰρ φιλαίτιος λέως), are more forcibly set forth than an old epic poem would probably have thought necessary (see Supplices, 369, 397, 485, 519). The solemn wish to exclude both anarchy and despotism from Athens bears still more the mark of political feeling of the time—μήτ᾽ ἄναρχον μήτε δεσποτούμενον (Eumenid. 527—696).

[1] Promêtheus, 85, 151, 170, 309, 524, 910, 940, 956.

[2] Plato, Republ. ii. 381—383; compare Æschyl. Fragment. 159, ed. Dindorf. He was charged also with having divulged in some of his plays secret matters of the mysteries of Dêmêtêr, but is said to have excused himself by alleging ignorance: he was not aware that what he had said was comprised in the mysteries (Aristot. Ethic. Nicom. iii. 2: Clemens Alex. Strom. ii. p. 387); the story is different again in Ælian, V. H. v. 19.

How little can be made out distinctly respecting this last accusation may be seen in Lobeck, Aglaopham. p. 81.

Cicero (Tusc. Dis. ii. 10) calls Æschylus " almost a Pythagorean": upon what the epithet is founded we do not know.

There is no evidence to prove to us that the Promêtheus Vinctus was considered as impious by the public before whom it was represented; but its obvious meaning has been so regarded by modern critics, who resort to many different explanations of it, in order to prove that when properly construed it is not impious. But if we wish to ascertain what Æschylus really meant, we ought not to consult the religious ideas of modern times; we have no test except what we know of the poet's own time and that which had preceded him. The explanations given by the ablest critics seem generally to exhibit a predetermination to bring out Zeus, as a just, wise, merciful, and all-powerful Being; and all, in one way or another, distort the figures, alter the perspective, and give far-fetched inter-

pretations of the meaning of this striking drama, which conveys an impression directly contrary (see Welcker, Æsch. Trilogie, p. 90—117, with the explanation of Dissen there given; Klausen, Theologum. Æsch. p. 140—154; Schömann, in his recent translation of the play, and the criticism of that translation in the Wiener Jahrbücher, vol. cix. 1845, p. 245, by F. Ritter). On the other hand, Schütz (Excurs. ad Prom. Vinct. p. 149) thinks that Æschylus wished by means of this drama to enforce upon his countrymen the hatred of a despot. Though I do not agree in this interpretation, it appears to me less wide of the truth than the forcible methods employed by others to bring the poet into harmony with their own religious ideas.

Of the Promêtheus Solutus, which formed a sequel to the Promêtheus Vinctus (the entire trilogy is not certainly known), the fragments preserved are very scanty, and the guesses of critics as to its plot have little base to proceed upon. They contend that, in one way or other, the apparent objections which the Prometh. Vinctus presents against the justice of Zeus were in the Promêth. Solutus removed. Hermann, in his *Dissertatio de Æschyli Prometheo Soluto* (Opuscula, vol. iv. p. 256), calls this position in question: I transcribe from his Dissertation one passage, because it contains an important remark in reference to the manner in which the Greek poets handled their religious legends: " while they recounted and believed many enormities respecting individual gods, they always described the Godhead in the abstract as holy and faultless ". . . .

"Immo illud admirari oportet, quod quum de singulis Diis indignissima quæque crederent, tamen ubi sine certo nomine Deum dicebant, immunem ab omni vitio, summâque sanctitate præditum intelligebant. Illam igitur Jovis sævitiam ut excusent defensores Trilogiæ, et jure punitum volunt Prometheum—et in

adhere to the received vein of religious tradition with the same strictness as Sophoklês—yet the ascendency and interference of the gods are never out of sight, and the solemnity with which they are represented, set off by a bold, figurative, and elliptical style of expression (often but imperfectly intelligible to modern readers), reaches its maximum in his tragedies. As he throws round the gods a kind of airy grandeur, so neither do his men or heroes appear like tenants of the common earth. The mythical world from which he borrows his characters, is peopled only with "the immediate seed of the gods, in close contact with Zeus, in whom the divine blood has not yet had time to degenerate" : [1] his individuals are taken, not from the iron race whom Hesiod acknowledges with shame as his contemporaries, but from the extinct heroic race which had fought at Troy and Thêbes. *He maintains undiminished the grandeur of the mythical world.*

It is to them that his conceptions aspire, and he is even chargeable with frequent straining, beyond the limits of poetical taste, to realise his picture. If he does not consistently succeed in it, the reason is because consistency in such a matter is unattainable, since, after all, the analogies of common humanity, the only materials which the most creative imagination has to work upon, obtrude themselves involuntarily, and the lineaments of the man are thus seen even under a dress which promises superhuman proportions.

Sophoklês, the most illustrious ornament of Grecian tragedy, dwells upon the same heroic characters, and maintains their grandeur, on the whole, with little abatement; *Sophoklês.* combining with it a far better dramatic structure, and a wider appeal to human sympathies. Even in Sophoklês, however, we find indications that an altered ethical feeling, and a more predominant sense of artistic perfection, are allowed to modify

---

sequente fabulâ reconciliato Jove, restitutam arbitrantur divinam justitiam. Quo invento, vereor ne non optime dignitati consuluerint supremi Deorum, quem decuerat potius non sævire omnino, quam placari eâ lege, ut alius Promethei vice lueret."

[1] Æschyl. Fragment. 146, Dindorf; ap. Plato, Repub. iii. p. 391; compare Strabo, xii. p. 580.—

. . . . . οἱ θεῶν ἀγχίσποροι

Οἱ Ζηνὸς ἐγγύς, οἷς ἐν Ἰδαίῳ πάγῳ
Διὸς πατρῷου βωμός ἐστ' ἐν αἰθέρι,
Κοὔπω σφιν ἐξίτηλον αἷμα δαιμόνων.

There is one real exception to this statement—the Persæ—which is founded upon an event of recent occurrence; and one apparent exception—the Promêtheus Vinctus. But in that drama no individual mortal is made to appear; we can hardly consider Iô as an ἐφήμερος (253).

the harsher religious agencies of the old epic. Occasional misplaced effusions[1] of rhetoric, as well as of didactic prolixity, may also be detected. It is Æschylus, not Sophoklês, who forms the marked antithesis to Euripidês ; it is Æschylus, not Sophoklês, to whom Aristophanês awards the prize of tragedy, as the poet who assigns most perfectly to the heroes of the past those weighty words, imposing equipments, simplicity of great deeds with little talk, and masculine energy superior to the corruptions of Aphroditê, which beseem the comrades of Agamemnôn and Adrastus.[2]

How deeply this feeling, of the heroic character of the mythical world, possessed the Athenian mind, may be judged by the bitter criticisms made on Euripidês, whose compositions were pervaded, partly by ideas of physical philosophy learnt under Anaxagoras, partly by the altered tone of education and the wide diffusion of practical eloquence forensic as well as political at Athens.[3] While Aristophanês assails Euripidês as the repre-

Euripidês —accused of vulgar- ising the mythical heroes,

[1] For the characteristics of Æschylus see Aristophan. Ran. 755, *ad fin. vassim.* The competition between Æschylus and Euripidês turns upon γνῶμαι ἀγαθαί, 1497 ; the weight and majesty of the words, 1362 ; πρῶτον τῶν Ἑλλήνων πυργώσας ῥήματα σεμνά, 1001, 921, 930 (" sublimis et gravis et grandiloquus sæpe usque ad vitium," Quintil. x. 1) ; the imposing appearance of his heroes, such as Memnôn and Kyknus, 961 ; their reserve in speech, 908 ; his dramas "full of Arês," and his lion-hearted chiefs, inspiring the auditors with fearless spirit in defence of their country,—1014, 1019, 1040 ; his contempt of feminine tenderness, 1042.—

ÆSCH. Οὐδ' οἶδ' οὐδεὶς ἥντιν' ἐρῶσαν
πώποτ' ἐποίησα γυναῖκα.
EURIP. Mὰ Δί', οὐδὲ γὰρ ἦν τῆς Ἀφροδίτης
οὐδέν σοι.
ÆSCH. μηδέ γ' ἐπείη·
'Ἀλλ' ἐπὶ σοί τοι καὶ τοῖς σοῖσιν
πολλὴ πολλοῦ 'πικάθοιτο.

To the same general purpose Nubes (1347—1356), composed so many years earlier. The weight and majesty of the Æschylean heroes (βάρος, τὸ μεγαλοπρεπές) is dwelt upon in the life of Æschylus, and Sophoklês is said to have derided it—"Ὅσπερ γὰρ ὁ Σοφοκλῆς ἔλεγε, τὸν Αἰσχύλου διαπεπαιχὼς ὄγκον, &c. (Plutarch, De Profect. in Virt. Sent. c. 7), unless we are to understand this as a mistake of Plutarch quoting Sophoklês instead of Euripidês as he speaks in the Frogs of Aristophanes, which is the opinion both of Lessing in his Life of Sophoklês and of Welcker (Æschyl. Trilogie, p. 525).

[2] See above. Chapters xiv. and xv. Æschylus seems to have been a greater innovator as to the matter of the mythes than either Sophoklês or Euripidês (Dionys. Halic. Judic. de Vet. Script. p. 422. Reisk.). For the close adherence of Sophoklês to the Homeric epic see Athenæ. vii. p. 277 ; Diogen. Laërt. iv. 20 ; Suidas, v. Πολέμων. Æschylus puts into the mouth of the Eumenidês a serious argument derived from the behaviour of Zeus in chaining his father Kronos (Eumen. 640).

[3] See Valckenaer, Diatribe in Euripid. Fragm. capp. 5 and 6. The fourth and fifth lectures among the *Dramatische Vorlesungen* of August Wilhelm Schlegel depict both justly and eloquently the difference between Æschylus, Sophoklês, and Euripidês, especially on this point of the gradual sinking of the mythical colossus into an ordinary man ; about Euripidês especially in lecture 5, vol. l. p. 206, ed. Heidelberg, 1809,

sentative of this "young Athens," with the utmost keenness of
sarcasm,—other critics also concur in designating him as having
vulgarized the mythical heroes, and transformed them into mere
characters of common life,—loquacious, subtle, and savouring of
the market place.[1] In some of his plays, sceptical expressions
and sentiments were introduced, derived from his philosophical
studies, sometimes confounding two or three distinct gods into
one, sometimes translating the personal Zeus into a substantial
Æthêr with determinate attributes. He put into the mouths
of some of his unprincipled dramatic characters apologetic
speeches, which were denounced as ostentatious sophistry, and as
setting out a triumphant case for the criminal.[2] His thoughts,
his words, and the rhythm of his choric songs, were all accused
of being deficient in dignity and elevation. The mean attire and
miserable attitude in which he exhibited Œneus, Têlephus,
Thyestês, Inô, and other heroic characters, were unmercifully

---

[1] Aristot. Poetic. c. 46. Οἶον καὶ
Σοφοκλῆς ἔφη, αὐτὸς μὲν οἴους δεῖ ποιεῖν,
Εὐριπίδης δὲ, οἷοί εἰσι.
The Ranæ and Acharneis of Aristophanês exhibit fully the reproaches
urged against Euripidês: the language
put into the mouth of Euripidês in the
former play (vv. 935—977) illustrates
specially the point here laid down.
Plutarch (De Gloriâ Atheniens. c. 5)
contrasts ἡ Εὐριπίδου σοφία καὶ ἡ Σοφο-
κλέους λογιότης. Sophoklês either adhered to the old mythes or introduced
alterations into them in a spirit conformable to their original character,
while Euripidês refined upon them.
The comment of Dêmêtrius Phalereus
connects τὸ λόγιον expressly with the
maintenance of the dignity of the tales.
Ἀρξομαι δὲ ἀπὸ τοῦ μεγαλοπρεποῦς, ὅπερ
νῦν λ ό γ ι ο ν ὀνομάζουσιν (c. 38).

[2] Aristophan. Ran. 770, 887, 1066.
Euripidês says to Æschylus, in regard to the language employed by both
of them,—

Ἦν οὖν σὺ λέγῃς Λυκαβήττους
Καὶ Παρνάσσων ἡμῖν μεγέθη, τοῦτ' ἐστὶ
τὸ χρηστὰ διδάσκειν,
Ὃν χρὴ φράζειν ἀνθρωπείως;
Æschylus replies,—

Ἀλλ', ὦ κακόδαιμον, ἀνάγκη
Μεγάλων γνωμῶν καὶ διανοιῶν ἴσα καὶ τὰ
ῥήματα τίκτειν.
Κάλλως εἰκὸς τοὺς ἡ μ ι θ έ ο υ ς τοῖς
ῥήμασι μείζοσι χρῆσθαι·

Καὶ γὰρ τοῖς ἱματίοις ἡμῶν χρῶντας πολὺ
σεμνοτέροισι.
Ἁ 'μοῦ χρηστῶς καταδείξαντος διελυμήνω
σύ.

EURIP.   Τί δράσας;
ÆSCH. Πρῶτον μὲν τοὺς βασιλεύοντας
ῥάκι' ἀμπίσχων, ἵν' ἐλεινοὶ
Τοῖς ἀνθρώποις φαίνοιντ' εἶναι.

For the character of the language
and measures of Euripidês, as represented by Æschylus, see also v. 1297,
and Pac. 527. Philosophical discussion was introduced by Euripidês
(Dionys. Hal. Ars Rhetor. viii. 10—
ix. 11) in the Melanippê, where the
doctrine of prodigies (τέρας) appears
to have been argued. Quintilian (x. 1)
remarks that to young beginners in
judicial pleading,the study of Euripidês
was much more specially profitable
than that of Sophoklês: compare Dio
Chrysostom, Orat. xviii. vol. i. p. 477,
Reiske.

In Euripidês the heroes themselves
sometimes delivered moralising discourses,—εἰσάγων τὸν Βελλεροφόντην
γνωμολογοῦντα (Welcker, Griechische
Tragöd. Eurip. Stheneb. p. 782). Compare the Fragments of his Bellerophôn
(15—25, Matthiæ), and of his Chrysippus (7, ib.). A striking story is found
in Seneca, Epistol. 115; and Plutarch,
de Audiend. Poetis, c. 4, t. i. p. 70,
Wytt.

derided,[1] though it seems that their position and circumstances had always been painfully melancholy; but the effeminate pathos which Euripidês brought so nakedly into the foreground, was accounted unworthy of the majesty of a legendary hero. And he incurred still greater obloquy on another point, on which he is allowed even by his enemies to have only reproduced in substance the pre-existing tales,—the illicit and fatal passion depicted in several of his female characters, such as Phædra and Sthenobœa. His opponents admitted that these stories were true, but contended that they ought to be kept back, and not produced upon the stage,—a proof both of the continued mythical faith and of the more sensitive ethical criticism of his age.[2] The marriage of the six daughters to the six sons of Æolis is of Homeric origin, and stands now, though briefly, stated, in the Odyssey; but the incestuous passion of Makareus and Kanakê, embodied by Euripidês[3] in the lost tragedy called *Æolus*, drew upon him severe censure. Moreover he often disconnected the horrors of the old legends with those religious agencies by which they had been originally forced on, prefacing them by motives of

(marginal note:) and of introducing exaggerated pathos, refinement and rhetoric.

---

[1] Aristophan. Ran. 840.—

ὦ στωμυλιοσυλλεκτάδη
Καὶ πτωχοποιὲ καὶ ῥακιοσυρραπτάδη.

See also Aristophan. Acharn. 385—422. For an unfavourable criticism upon such proceeding, see Aristot. Poet. 27.

[2] Aristophan. Ran. 1050.—

EURIP. Πότερον δ' οὐκ ὄντα λόγον
τοῦτον περὶ τῆς Φαίδρας
ξυνέθηκα;
ÆSCH. Μὰ Δί', ἀλλ' ὄντ'· ἀλλ' ἀπο-
κρύπτειν χρὴ τὸ πονηρὸν τόν
γε ποιητήν,
Καὶ μὴ παράγειν μηδὲ διδάσκειν.

In the Hercules Furens, Euripidês puts in relief and even exaggerates the worst elements of the ancient mythes: the implacable hatred of Hêrê towards Hêraklês is pushed so far as to deprive him of his reason (by sending down Iris and the unwilling Λύσσα), and thus intentionally to drive him to slay his wife and children with his own hands.

[3] Aristoph. Ran. 849, 1041, 1080; Thesmophor. 547; Nubes, 1354. Grauert, De Mediâ Græcorum Comœdiâ in Rheinisch. Museum, 2nd

Jahrg. 1. Heft, p. 51. It suited the plan of the drama of Æolus, as composed by Euripidês, to place in the mouth of Makareus a formal recommendation of incestuous marriages: probably this contributed much to offend the Athenian public. See Dionys. Hal. Rhetor. ix. p. 355.

About the liberty of intermarriage among relatives, indicated in Homer, parents and children being alone excepted, see Terpstra, Antiquitas Homerica, cap. xiii. p. 104.

Ovid, whose poetical tendencies led him chiefly to copy Euripidês, observes (Trist. ii. 1, 380)—

"Omne genus scripti gravitate Tra-
gœdia vincit,
Hæc quoque materiam semper
amoris habet.
Nam quid in Hippolyto nisi cæcæ
flamma novercæ?
Nobilis est Canace fratris amore
sui."

This is the reverse of the truth in regard to Æschylus and Sophoklês, and only very partially true in respect to Euripidês.

a more refined character, such as carried no sense of awful compulsion. Thus the considerations by which the Euripidean Alkmæôn was reduced to the necessity of killing his mother, appeared to Aristotle ridiculous.[1] After the time of this great poet, his successors seem to have followed him in breathing into their characters the spirit of common life. But the names and plot were still borrowed from the stricken mythical families of Tantalus, Kadmus, &c.: and the heroic exultation of all the individual personages introduced, as contrasted with the purely human character of the Chorus, is still numbered by Aristotle among the essential points of the theory of tragedy.[2]

The tendency then of Athenian tragedy—powerfully manifested in Æschylus, and never wholly lost—was to uphold an unquestioning faith and a reverential estimate of the general mythical world and its personages, but to treat the particular narratives rather as matter for the emotions than as recitals of actual fact. The logographers worked along with them to the first of these two ends, but not to the second. Their grand object was, to cast the mythes into a continuous readable series, and they were in consequence compelled to make selection between inconsistent or contradictory narratives; to reject some narratives as false, and to receive others as true. But their preference was determined more by their sentiments as to what was appropriate, than by any pretended historical test. Pherekydês, Akusilaus, and Hellanikus[3] did not seek to banish miraculous or fantastic incidents from the mythical world. They regarded it as peopled with loftier beings, and expected to find in it phænomena not paralleled in their own degenerate days. They reproduced the fables as they found them in the poets, rejecting little except the discrepancies, and producing ultimately what they believed to be not only a continuous, but an exact and trustworthy, history of the past—

The logographers—Pherekydês, &c.

---

[1] Aristot. Ethic. Nicom. iii. 1, 8. καὶ γὰρ τὸν Εὐριπίδου Ἀλκμαίωνα γελοῖα φαίνεται τὰ ἀναγκάσαντα μητροκτονῆσαι. (In the lost tragedy called Ἀλκμαίων ὁ διὰ Ψωφῖδος.)

[2] Aristot. Poetic. 26—27. And in his Problemata also, in giving the reason why the Hypo-Dorian and Hypo-Phrygian musical modes were never assigned to the Chorus, he says—

Ταῦτα δὲ ἄμφω χόρῳ μέν ἀναρμοστά, τοῖς δὲ ἀπὸ σκηνῆς οἰκειότερα. Ἐκεῖνοι μὲν γὰρ ἡρώων μίμηται· οἱ δὲ ἡγεμόνες τῶν ἀρχαίων μόνοι ἦσαν ἥρωες, οἱ δὲ λαοὶ ἄνθρωποι, ὧν ἐστιν ὁ χόρος. Διὸ καὶ ἁρμόζει αὐτῷ τὸ γοερὸν καὶ ἡσύχιον ἦθος καὶ μέλος· ἀνθρωπικὰ γάρ.

[3] See Müller, Prolegom. zu einer wissenschaftlichen Mythologie, c. iii. p. 93.

wherein they carry indeed their precision to such a length, that
Hellanikus gives the year, and even the day, of the capture of Troy.[1]

Hekatæus of Milêtus (500 B.C.), anterior to Pherekydês and
Hellanikus, is the earliest writer in whom we can
detect any disposition to disallow the prerogative and
speciality of the mythes, and to soften down their
characteristic prodigies ; some of which however still find favour
in his eyes, as in the case of the speaking ram who carried
Phryxus over the Hellespont. He pronounced the Grecian
fables to be "many and ridiculous"; whether from their
discrepancies or from their intrinsic improbabilities we do not
know. And we owe to him the first attempt to force them
within the limits of historical credibility ; as where he transforms
the three-headed Cerberus, the dog of Hadês, into a serpent
inhabiting a cavern on Cape Tænarus—and Geryôn of Erytheia
into a king of Epirus rich in herds of oxen.[2] Hekatæus traced
the genealogy of himself and the gens to which he belonged
through a line of fifteen progenitors up to an initial god,[3]—the
clearest proof both of his profound faith in the reality of the
mythical world, and of his religious attachment to it as the point
of junction between the human and the divine personality.

Hekatæus —the mythes rationalised.

We have next to consider the historians, especially Herodotus
and Thucydidês. Like Hekatæus, Thucydidês belonged to a gens which traced its descent from Ajax,
and through Ajax to Æakus and Zeus.[4] Herodotus

The historians— Herodotus.

---

[1] Hellanic. Fragment. 143, ed. Didot.

[2] Hekatæi Fragm. ed. Didot, 332, 346, 349 ; Schol. Apollôn. Rhod. i. 256 ; Athenæ. ii. p. 133 ; Skylax, c. 26. Perhaps Hekatæus was induced to look for Erytheia in Epirus by the brick-red colour of the earth there in many places, noticed by Pouqueville and other travellers (Voyage dans la Grèce, vol. ii. 248; see Klausen, Æneas und die Penaten, vol. i. p. 222). Ἑκαταῖος ὁ Μιλήσιος—λόγον εὗρεν εἰκότα, Pausan. iii. 25, 4. He seems to have written expressly concerning the fabulous Hyperboreans, and to have upheld the common faith against doubts which had begun to rise in his time : the derisory notice of Hyperboreans in Herodotus is probably directed against Hekatæus, iv. 36; Schol. Apollôn. Rhod. ii. 675 ; Diodôr. ii. 47.

It is maintained by Mr. Clinton (Fast. Hell. ii. p. 480) and others (see not. ad Fragment. Hecatæi, p. 30, ed. Didot), that the work on the Hyperboreans was written by Hekatæus of Abdera, a literary Greek of the age of Ptolemy Philadelphus—not by Hekatæus of Milêtus. I do not concur in this opinion. I think it much more probable that the earlier Hekatæus was the author spoken of. The distinguished position held by Hekatæus at Milêtus is marked not only by the notice which Herodotus takes of his opinions on public matters, but also by his negotiation with the Persian satrap Artaphernes on behalf of his countrymen (Diodôr. Excerpt. xlvii. p. 41, ed. Dindorf).

[3] Herodot. ii. 143.

[4] Marcellin. Vit. Thucyd. init.

modestly implies that he himself had no such privilege to boast
of.[1] The curiosity of these two historians respecting the past had
no other materials to work upon except the mythes, which they
found already cast by the logographers into a continuous series,
and presented as an aggregate of antecedent history, chronologically deduced from the times of the gods. In common with
the body of the Greeks, both Herodotus and Thucydidês had
imbibed that complete and unsuspecting belief in the general
reality of mythical antiquity, which was interwoven with the
religion and the patriotism, and all the public demonstrations, of
the Hellenic world. To acquaint themselves with the genuine
details of this foretime, was an enquiry highly interesting to
them. But the increased positive tendencies of their age, as well
as their own habits of personal investigation, had created in them
an *historical sense* in regard to the past as well as to the present.
Having acquired a habit of appreciating the intrinsic tests of
historical credibility and probability, they found the particular
narratives of the poets and logographers, inadmissible as a whole
even in the eyes of Hekatæus, still more at variance with their
stricter canons of criticism. And we thus observe in them the
constant struggle, as well as the resulting compromise, between
these two opposite tendencies ; on one hand a firm belief in the
reality of the mythical world, on the other hand an inability to
accept the details which their only witnesses, the poets and
logographers, told them respecting it.

Each of them however performed the process in his own way.
Herodotus is a man of deep and anxious religious
feeling. He often recognises the special judgments
of the gods as determining historical events : his piety
is also partly tinged with that mystical vein which
the last two centuries had gradually infused into the
religion of the Greeks—for he is apprehensive of giving offence
to the gods by reciting publicly what he has heard respecting
them. He frequently stops short in his narrative, and intimates
that there *is* a sacred legend, but that he will not tell it. In
other cases, where he feels compelled to speak out, he entreats
forgiveness for doing so from the gods and heroes. Sometimes
he will not even mention the name of a god, though he generally

Earnest piety of Herodotus—his mystic reserve.

[1] Herodot. ii. 143.

thinks himself authorised to do so, the names being matter of public notoriety.[1] Such pious reserve, which the open-hearted Herodotus avowedly proclaims as chaining up his tongue, affords a striking contrast with the plain-spoken and unsuspecting tone of the ancient epic, as well as of the popular legends, wherein the gods and their proceedings were the familiar and interesting subjects of common talk as well as of common sympathy, without ceasing to inspire both fear and reverence.

Herodotus expressly distinguishes, in the comparison of Polykratês with Minôs, the human race to which the former belonged, His views from the divine or heroic race which comprised the of the latter.[2] But he has a firm belief in the authentic mythical personality and parentage of all the names in the world. mythes, divine, heroic and human, as well as in the trustworthiness of their chronology computed by generations. He counts back 1600 years from his own day to that of Semelê, mother of Dionysus ; 900 years to Hêraklês, and 800 years to Penelopê, the Trojan war being a little earlier in date.[3] Indeed even the longest of these periods must have seemed to him comparatively short, seeing that he apparently accepts the prodigious series of years which the Egyptians professed to draw from a recorded chronology—17,000 years from their god Hêraklês, and 15,000 years from their god Osiris or Dionysus, down to their king Amasis[4] (550 B.C.). So much was his imagination familiarised with these long chronological computations barren of events, that he treats Homer and Hesiod as "men of yesterday," though separated from his own age by an interval which he reckons as four hundred years.[5]

---

[1] Herodot. ii. 3, 51, 61, 65, 170. He alludes briefly (c. 51) to an ἱρὸς λόγος which was communicated in the Samothracian mysteries, but he does not mention what it was: also about the Thesmophoria, or τελετή of Dêmêtêr (c. 171).

Καὶ περὶ μὲν τούτων τοσαῦτα ἡμῖν εἰποῦσι, καὶ παρὰ τῶν θεῶν καὶ ἡρώων εὐμένεια εἴη (c. 54).

Compare similar scruples on the part of Pausanias (viii. 25 and 37).

The passage of Herodotus (ii. 3) is equivocal, and has been understood in more ways than one (see Lobeck, Aglaopham. p. 1287).

The aversion of Dionysius of Halikarnassus to reveal the divine secrets is not less powerful (see A. R. i. 67, 68).

[2] Herod. iii. 122.

[3] Herod. ii. 145.

[4] Herodot. ii. 43—145. Καὶ ταῦτα Αἰγύπτιοι ἀτρεκέως φασὶ ἐπίστασθαι, ἀεί τε λογιζόμενοι καὶ ἀεὶ ἀπογραφόμενοι τὰ ἔτεα.

[5] Herodot. ii. 53. μέχρι οὖ πρώην τε καὶ χθὲς, ὡς εἰπεῖν λόγῳ. Ἡσίοδον γὰρ καὶ Ὅμηρον ἡλικίην τετρακοσίοισι ἔτεσι δοκέω μευ πρεσβυτέρους γενέσθαι, καὶ οὐ πλέοσι.

Herodotus had been profoundly impressed with what he saw and heard in Egypt. The wonderful monuments, the evident antiquity, and the peculiar civilization of that country, acquired such preponderance in his mind over his own native legends, that he is disposed to *His deference for Egypt and Egyptian statements.* trace even the oldest religious names or institutions of Greece to Egyptian or Phœnician original, setting aside in favour of this hypothesis the Grecian legends of Dionysus and Pan.[1] The oldest Grecian mythical genealogies are thus made ultimately to lose themselves in Egyptian or Phœnician antiquity, and in the full extent of these genealogies Herodotus firmly believes. It does not seem that any doubt had ever crossed his mind as to the real personality of those who were named or described in the popular mythes : all of them have once had reality, either as men, as heroes, or as gods. The eponyms of cities, dêmes and tribes are all comprehended in this affirmative category ; the supposition of fictitious personages being apparently never entertained. Deukaliôn, Hellên, Dôrus,[2]—Iôn, with his four sons, the eponyms of the old Athenian tribes,[3]—the autochthonous Titakus and Dekelus,[4]—Danaus, Lynkeus, Perseus, Amphitryôn, Alkmêna, and Hêraklês,[5]—Talthybius, the heroic progenitor of the privileged heraldic gens at Sparta,—the Tyndarids and Helena,[6] —Agamemnôn, Menelaus, and Orestês,[7]—Nestôr and his son Peisistratus,—Asôpus, Thêbê, and Ægina,—Inachus and Iô, Æêtês and Mêdea,[8]—Melanippus, Adrastus, and Amphiaraüs, as well as Jasôn and the Argô,[9]—all these are occupants of the real past time, and predecessors of himself and his contemporaries. In the veins of the Lacedæmonian kings flowed the blood both of Kadmus and of Danaus, their splendid pedigree being traceable to both of these great mythical names : Herodotus carries the lineage up through Hêraklês first to Perseus and Danaê, then through Danaê to Akrisius and the Egyptian Danaus ; but he drops the paternal lineage when he comes to Perseus (inasmuch as Perseus is the *His general faith in the mythical heroes and eponyms,*

[1] Herodot. ii. 146.
[2] Herod. i. 56.
[3] Herod. v. 66.
[4] Herod. ix. 73.
[5] Herod. ii. 43—44, 91—98, 171—182 (the Egyptians admitted the truth of the Greek legend, that Perseus had come to Libya to fetch the Gorgon's head).
[6] Herod. ii. 113—120 ; iv. 145 ; vii. 134.
[7] Herod. i. 67—68 ; ii. 113 ; vii. 159.
[8] Herod. i. 1, 2, 4 ; v. 81, 65.
[9] Herod. i. 52 ; iv. 145 ; v. 67 ; vii. 193.

son of Zeus by Danaê, without any reputed human father, such as Amphitryôn was to Hêraklês), and then follow the higher members of the series through Danaê alone.[1] He also pursues the same regal genealogy, through the mother of Eurysthenês and Proklês, up to Polynikês, Œdipus, Laius, Labdakus, Polydôrus and Kadmus : and he assigns various ancient inscriptions which he saw in the temple of the Ismenian Apollo at Thêbes, to the ages of Laius and Œdipus.[2]   Moreover the sieges of Thêbes and Troy,—the Argonautic expedition,—the invasion of Attica by the Amazons,—the protection of the Herakleids, and the defeat and death of Eurystheus, by the Athenians,[3]—the death of Mêkisteus and Tydeus before Thêbes by the hands of Melanippus, and the touching calamities of Adrastus and Amphiaraüs connected with the same enterprise,—the sailing of Kastôr and Pollux in the Argô,[4]—the abductions of Iô, Eurôpa, Mêdea and Helena,—the emigration of Kadmus in quest of Eurôpa, and his coming to Bœôtia, as well as the attack of the Greeks upon Troy to recover Helen,[5]—all these events seem to him portions of past history, not less unquestionably certain, though more clouded over by distance and misrepresentation, than the battles of Salamis and Mykalê.

But though Herodotus is thus easy of faith in regard both to the persons and to the general facts of Grecian mythes, yet when

—yet combined with scepticism as to matters of fact.

he comes to discuss particular facts taken separately, we find him applying to them stricter tests of historical credibility, and often disposed to reject as well the miraculous as the extravagant.   Thus even with respect to Hêraklês, he censures the levity of the Greeks in ascribing to him absurd and incredible exploits.   He tries their assertion by the philosophical standard of nature, or of determinate powers and conditions governing the course of events. "How is it consonant to *nature* (he asks), that Hêraklês, being, as he was, according to the statement of the Greeks, *still a man* (*i.e.* having not yet been received among the gods), should kill many thousand persons ?   I pray that indulgence may be shown to me both by gods and heroes for saying so much as this."   The

---

[1] Herod. vi. 52—53.
[2] Herod. iv. 147 ; v. 59—61.
[3] Herod. v. 61 ; ix. 27—28.

[4] Herod. i. 52 ; iv. 145 ; v. 67.
[5] Herod. i. 1—4 ; ii. 49, 113 ; iv. 147 ; v. 94.

religious feelings of Herodotus here told him that he was trenching upon the utmost limits of admissible scepticism.[1]

Another striking instance of the disposition of Herodotus to rationalise the miraculous narratives of the current mythes, is to be found in his account of the oracle of Dôdôna and its alleged Egyptian origin. Here, if in any case, a miracle was not only in full keeping, but apparently indispensable to satisfy the exigences of the religious sentiment; anything less than a miracle would have appeared tame and unimpressive to the visitors of so revered a spot, much more to the residents themselves. Accordingly, Herodotus heard both from the three priestesses and from the Dodonæans generally, that two black doves had started at the same time from Thêbes in Egypt: one of them went to Libya, where it directed the Libyans to establish the oracle of Zeus Ammon; the other came to the grove of Dôdôna, and perched on one of the venerable oaks, proclaiming with a human voice that an oracle of Zeus must be founded on that very spot. The injunction of the speaking dove was respectfully obeyed.[2]

His remarks upon the miraculous foundation of the oracle at Dôdôna.

Such was the tale related and believed at Dôdôna. But Herodotus had also heard, from the priests at Thêbes in Egypt, a different tale, ascribing the origin of all the prophetic establishments, in Greece as well as in Libya, to two sacerdotal women, who had been carried away from Thêbes by some Phœnician merchants and sold, the one in Greece, the other in Libya. The Thêban priests boldly assured Herodotus that much pains had been taken to discover what had become of these women so

---

[1] Herod. ii. 45. Λέγουσι δὲ πολλὰ καὶ ἄλλα ἀνεπισκέπτως οἱ Ἕλληνες· εὐήθης δὲ αὐτέων καὶ ὅδε ὁ μῦθός ἐστι, τὸν περὶ τοῦ Ἡρακλέος λέγουσι . . . Ἔτι δὲ ἕνα ἐόντα τὸν Ἡρακλέα, καὶ ἔτι ἄνθρωπον ὡς δή φασι, κῶς φύσιν ἔχει πολλὰς μυριάδας φονεῦσαι; Καί περὶ μὲν τούτων τοσαῦτα ἡμῖν εἰπούσι, καὶ παρὰ τῶν θεῶν καὶ παρὰ τῶν ἡρώων εὐμένεια εἴη.

We may also notice the manner in which the historian criticises the stratagem whereby Peisistratus established himself as despot at Athens— by dressing up the stately Athenian woman Phyê in the costume of the

goddess Athênê, and passing off her injunctions as the commands of the goddess: the Athenians accepted her with unsuspecting faith, and received Peisistratus at her command. Herodotus treats the whole affair as a piece of extravagant silliness, πρᾶγμα εὐηθέστατον μακρῷ (i. 60).

[2] Herod. ii. 55. Δωδωναίων δὲ αἱ ἱρήιαι . . . ἔλεγον ταῦτα, συνωμολόγεον δέ σφι καὶ οἱ ἄλλοι Δωδωναῖοι οἱ περὶ τὸ ἱρόν.

The miracle sometimes takes another form; the oak at Dôdôna was itself once endued with speech (Dionys. Hal. Ars Rhetoric. i. 6; Strabo.)

exported, and that the fact of their having been taken to Greece and Libya had been accordingly verified.[1]

The historian of Halicarnassus cannot for a moment think of admitting the miracle which harmonised so well with the feelings of the priestesses and the Dodonæans.[2] "How (he asks) could a dove speak with human voice?" But the narrative of the priests at Thêbes, though its prodigious improbability hardly requires to be stated, yet involved no positive departure from the laws of nature and possibility, and therefore Herodotus makes no difficulty in accepting it. The curious circumstance is, that he turns the native Dodonæan legend into a figurative representation, or rather a misrepresentation, of the supposed true story told by the Theban priests. According to his interpretation, the woman who came from Thêbes to Dôdôna was called a dove, and affirmed to utter sounds like a bird, because she was non-Hellenic and spoke a foreign tongue: when she learned to speak the language of the country, it was then said that the dove spoke with a human voice. And the dove was moreover called black, because of the woman's Egyptian colour.

That Herodotus should thus bluntly reject a miracle, recounted to him by the prophetic women themselves as the prime circumstance in the *origines* of this holy place, is a proof of the hold which habits of dealing with historical evidence had acquired over his mind; and the awkwardness of his explanatory mediation between the dove and the woman, marks not less his anxiety, while discarding the legend, to let it softly down into a story quasi-historical and not intrinsically incredible.

We may observe another example of the unconscious tendency of Herodotus to eliminate from the mythes the idea of special aid from the gods, in his remarks upon Melampus. He designates Melampus "as a clever man, who had acquired for himself the art of prophecy"; and had procured through Kadmus much information about the religious rites and customs of Egypt, many of which he

His remarks upon Melampus and his prophetic powers.

---

[1] Herod. ii. 54.
[2] Herod. ii. 57. Ἐπεὶ τέῳ τρόπῳ ἂν πελειάς γε ἀνθρωπηΐη φωνῇ φθέγξαιτο;
According to one statement, the word Πελειάς in the Thessalian dialect meant both a dove and a prophetess

(Scriptor. Rer. Mythicarum, ed. Bode, i. 96). Had there been any truth in this, Herodotus could hardly have failed to notice it, inasmuch as it would exactly have helped him out of the difficulty which he felt.

introduced into Greece[1]—especially the name, the sacrifices, and
the phallic processions of Dionysus: he adds, "that Melampus
himself did not accurately comprehend or bring out the whole
doctrine, but wise men who came after him made the necessary
additions".[2] Though the name of Melampus is here maintained,
the character described[3] is something in the vein of Pythagoras
—totally different from the great seer and leech of the old epic
mythes—the founder of the gifted family of the Amythaonids,
and the grandfather of Amphiaraüs.[4] But that which is most of
all at variance with the genuine legendary spirit, is the opinion
expressed by Herodotus (and delivered with some emphasis as *his
own*), that Melampus "was a clever man who had acquired for
himself prophetic powers". Such a supposition would have
appeared inadmissible to Homer or Hesiod, or indeed to Solôn in
the preceding century, in whose view even inferior arts come
from the gods, while Zeus or Apollo bestows the power of pro-
phesying.[5] The intimation of such an opinion by Herodotus,
himself a thoroughly pious man, marks the sensibly diminished
omnipresence of the gods, and the increasing tendency to look for

[1] Herod. ii. 49. Ἐγὼ μὲν νῦν φημι
Μελάμποδα γενόμενον ἄνδρα σοφόν, μαν-
τικήν τε ἑωυτῷ συστῆσαι, καὶ πυθόμενον
ἀπ' Αἰγύπτου, ἄλλα τε πολλὰ ἐσηγήσασθαι
Ἕλλησι, καὶ τὰ περὶ τὸν Διόνυσον, ὀλίγα
αὐτῶν παραλλάξαντα.
[2] Herod. ii. 49. Ἀτρεκέως μὲν οὐ
πάντα συλλαβὼν τὸν λόγον ἔφηνε (Melampus)· ἀλλ' οἱ ἐπιγενόμενοι τούτῳ
σοφισταὶ μειζόνως ἐξέφηναν.
[3] Compare Herod. iv. 95 ; ii. 81.
Ἑλλήνων οὐ τῷ ἀσθενεστάτῳ σοφιστῇ
Πυθαγόρᾳ.
[4] Homer, Odyss. xi. 290 ; xv. 225.
Apollodôr. i. 9, 11—12. Hesiod, Eoiai,
Fragm. 55, ed. Düntzcr (p. 43).—

Ἀλκὴν μὲν γὰρ ἔδωκεν Ὀλύμπιος Αἰακί-
        δῃσι,
Νοῦν δ' Ἀμυθαονίδαις, πλοῦτον δ'
        ἔπορ' Ἀτρείδῃσι.

Also Frag. 34 (p. 38), and Frag. 65
(p. 45); Schol. Apoll. Rhod. i. 118.
   Herodotus notices the celebrated
mythical narrative of Melampus healing
the deranged Argive women (ix. 34);
according to the original legend, the
daughters of Prœtus. In the Hesiodic
Eoiai (Fr. 16, Düntz., v. Apollod. ii. 2)
the distemper of the Prœtid females
was ascribed to their having repudiated
the rites and worship of Dionysus

(Akusilaus indeed assigned a different
cause), which shows that the old
fable recognised a connexion between
Melampus and these rites.
[5] Homer, Iliad, i. 72—87 ; xv. 412.
Odyss. xv. 245—252 ; iv. 233. Sometimes the gods inspired prophecy for
the special occasion, without conferring
upon the party the permanent gift and
status of a prophet (compare Odyss. i.
202 ; xvii. 383). Solôn, Fragm. xi. 48—
53, Schneidewin :—

Ἄλλον μάντιν ἔθηκεν ἄναξ ἑκάεργος
        Ἀπολλὼν,
Ἔγνω δ' ἀνδρὶ κακὸν τηλόθεν ἐρχό-
        μενον,
Ὧι συνομαρτήσωσι θεοί . . . .

Herodotus himself reproduces the
old belief in the special gift of prophetic power by Zeus and Apollo, in
the story of Euenius of Apollônia (ix.
94).
   See the fine ode of Pindar describing
the birth and inspiration of Jamus,
eponymous father of the great prophetic family in Elis called the Jamids
(Herodot. ix. 33), Pindar, Olymp. vi.
40—75. About Teiresias, Sophoc. Œd.
Tyr. 283—410. Neither Nestôr nor
Odysseus possesses the gift of prophecy.

the explanation of phænomena among more visible and determinate agencies.

We may make a similar remark on the dictum of the historian respecting the narrow defile of Tempê, forming the embouchure of the Pêneus and the efflux of all the waters from the Thessalian basin. The Thessalians alleged that this whole basin of Thessaly had once been a lake, but that Poseidôn had split the chain of mountains and opened the efflux;[1] upon which primitive belief, thoroughly conformable to the genius of Homer and Hesiod, Herodotus comments as follows: "The Thessalian statement is reasonable. For whoever thinks that Poseidôn shakes the earth, and that the rifts of an earthquake are the work of that god, will, on seeing the defile in question, say that Poseidôn has caused it. For the rift of the mountains is, as appeared to me (when I saw it), the work of an earthquake." Herodotus admits the reference to Poseidôn, when pointed out to him, but it stands only in the background : what is present to his mind is, the phænomenon of the earthquake, not as a special act, but as part of a system of habitual operations.[2]

His remarks upon the Thessalian legend of Tempê.

---

[1] More than one tale is found elsewhere, similar to this about the defile of Tempê :—

"A tradition exists that this part of the country was once a lake, and that Salomon commanded two deeves or genii, named Ard and Beel, to turn off the water into the Caspian, which they effected by cutting a passage through the mountains ; and a city, erected in the newly-formed plain, was named after them Ard-u-beel." (Sketches on the shores of the Caspian, by W. R. Holmes.)

Also about the plain of Santa Fe di Bogota, in South America, that it was once under water, until Bochica cleft the mountains and opened a channel of egress (Humboldt, Vues des Cordillères, p. 87—88); and about the plateau of Kashmir (Humboldt, Asie Centrale, vol. i. p. 102), drained in a like miraculous manner by the saint Kâsyapa. The manner in which conjectures, derived from local configuration or peculiarities, are often made to assume the form of *traditions*, is well-remarked by the same illustrious traveller :—

"Ce qui se présente comme une tradition, n'est souvent que le reflet de l'impression que laisse l'aspect des lieux. Des bancs de coquilles à demi-fossiles, répandues dans les isthmes ou sur des plateaux, font naître, même chez les hommes les moins avancés dans la culture intellectuelle, l'idée de grandes inondations, d'anciennes communications entre des bassins limitrophes. Des opinions, que l'on pourroit appeler systématiques, se trouvent dans les forêts de l'Orénoque comme dans les îles de la Mer du Sud. Dans l'une et dans l'autre de ces contrées, elles ont pris la forme des traditions." (A. v. Humboldt, Asie Centrale, vol. ii. p. 147.) Compare a similar remark in the same work and volume, p. 286—294.

[2] Herodot. vii. 129. (Poseidôn was worshipped as Πετραῖος in Thessaly, in commemoration of this geological interference : Schol. Pindar. Pyth. iv. 245.) Τὸ δὲ παλαιὸν λέγεται, οὐκ ἐόντος κω τοῦ αὐλῶνος καὶ διεκρόου τούτου, τοὺς ποταμοὺς τούτους . . . ῥέοντας ποιεῖν τὴν Θεσσαλίην πᾶσαν πέλαγος. Αὐτοὶ μέν νυν Θεσσαλοὶ λέγουσι Ποσειδέωνα ποιῆσαι τὸν αὐλῶνα, δι' οὗ ῥέει ὁ Πηνειὸς, οἰκότα λέγοντες. Ὅστις γὰρ νομίζει Ποσειδέωνα τὴν γῆν σείειν, καὶ τὰ διεστεῶτα ὑπὸ σεισμοῦ τοῦ θεοῦ τούτου ἔργα εἶναι, καὶ ἂν ἐκεῖνο ἰδὼν φαίη Ποσειδέωνα ποιῆσαι. Ἔστι γὰρ σεισμοῦ ἔργον, ὡς ἐμοὶ ἐφαίνετο εἶναι, ἡ διάστασις τῶν

Herodotus adopts the Egyptian version of the legend of Troy, founded on that capital variation which seems to have originated with Stesichorus, and according to which Helen never left Sparta at all—her *eidôlon* had been taken to Troy in her place.   Upon this basis a new story had been framed, midway between Homer and Stesichorus, representing Paris to have really carried off Helen from Sparta, but to have been driven by storms to Egypt, where she remained during the whole siege of Troy, having been detained by Prôteus, the king of the country, until Menelaus came to reclaim her after his

Upon the legend of Troy.

οὐρέων. In another case (viii. 129), Herodotus believes that Poseidôn produced a preternaturally high tide in order to punish the Persians, who had insulted his temple near Potidæa: here was a special motive for the god to exert his power.

This remark of Herodotus illustrates the hostile ridicule cast by Aristophanês (in the Nubes) upon Sokratês, on the score of alleged impiety, because he belonged to a school of philosophers (though in point of fact he discountenanced that line of study) who introduced physical laws and forces in place of the personal agency of the gods. The old man Strepsiades inquires from Sokratês, *Who rains? Who thunders?*   To which Sokratês replies, *Not Zeus*, but the Nephelæ, *i.e. the clouds*: you never saw rain without clouds. Strepsiadês then proceeds to inquire—"But who is it that compels the clouds to move onward? is it not Zeus?"   Sokratês—"Not at all; it is æthereal rotation."   Strepsiadês—"Rotation? that had escaped me: Zeus then no longer exists, and Rotation reigns in his place."

STREPS.   Ὁ δ' ἀναγκάζων ἐστὶ τίς αὐτὰς
        (Νεφέλας), οὐχ ὁ Ζεύς, ὥστε
        φέρεσθαι;
SOKRAT.   Ἥκιστ', ἀλλ' αἰθέριος δῖνος.
STREPS.   Δῖνος; τουτί μ' ἐλελήθει—
        Ὁ Ζεὺς οὐκ ὢν, ἀλλ' ἀντ' αὐτοῦ
        Δῖνος νυνὶ βασιλεύων.

To the same effect v. 1454, Δῖνος βασιλεύει τὸν Δί' ἐξεληλακώς—"Rotation has driven out Zeus, and reigns in his place".

If Aristophanês had had as strong a wish to turn the public antipathies against Herodotus as against Sokratês and Euripidês, the explanation here given would have afforded him a plausible show of truth for doing so; and it is highly probable that the Thessalians would have been sufficiently displeased with the view of Herodotus to sympathise in the poet's attack upon him.   The point would have been made (waiving metrical considerations)—

Σεισμὸς βασιλεύει, τὸν Ποσειδῶν'
ἐξεληλακώς.

The comment of Herodotus upon the Thessalian view seems almost as if it were intended to guard against this very inference.

Other accounts ascribed the cutting of the defile of Tempê to Hêraklês (Diodôr. iv. 18).

Respecting the ancient Grecian faith which recognised the displeasure of Poseidôn as the cause of earthquakes, see Xenoph. Hellen. iii. 3, 2 ; Thucydid. i. 127 ; Strabo, xii. p. 579 ; Diodôr. xv. 48—49.   It ceased to give universal satisfaction even so early as the time of Thalês and Anaximenês (see Aristot. Meteorolog. ii. 7—8 ; Plutarch, Placit. Philos. iii. 15 ; Seneca, Natural. Quæst. vi. 6—23) ; and that philosopher, as well as Anaxagoras, Democritus, and others, suggested different physical explanations of the fact.   Notwithstanding a dissentient minority, however, the old doctrine still continued to be generally received : and Diodôrus, in describing the terrible earthquake in 373 B.C., by which Helikê and Bura were destroyed, while he notices those philosophers (probably Kallisthenês, Senec. Nat. Quæst. vi. 23) who substituted physical causes and laws in place of the divine agency, rejects their views and ranks himself with the religious public who traced this formidable phænomenon to the wrath of Poseidôn (xv. 48—49).

triumph. The Egyptian priests, with their usual boldness of assertion, professed to have heard the whole story from Menelaus himself—the Greeks had besieged Troy, in the full persuasion that Helen and the stolen treasures were within the walls, nor would they ever believe the repeated denials of the Trojans as to the fact of her presence. In intimating his preference for the Egyptian narrative, Herodotus betrays at once his perfect and unsuspecting confidence that he is dealing with genuine matter of history, and his entire distrust of the epic poets, even including Homer, upon whose authority that supposed history rested. His reason for rejecting the Homeric version is, that it teems with historical improbabilities. If Helen had been really in Troy (he says), Priam and the Trojans would never have been so insane as to retain her to their own utter ruin; but it was the divine judgment which drove them into the miserable alternative of neither being able to surrender Helen nor to satisfy the Greeks of the real fact that they never had possession of her—in order that mankind might plainly read, in the utter destruction of Troy, the great punishments with which the gods visit great misdeeds. Homer (Herodotus thinks) had heard this story, but designedly departed from it, because it was not so suitable a subject for epic poetry.[1]

Enough has been said to show how wide is the difference between Herodotus and the logographers with their literal transcript of the ancient legends. Though he agrees with them in admitting the full series of persons and generations, he tries the circumstances narrated by a new standard. Scruples have arisen in his mind respecting violations of the laws of nature: the poets are unworthy of trust, and their narratives must be brought into conformity with historical and ethical conditions, before they can be admitted as truth. To accomplish this conformity, Herodotus is willing to mutilate the old legend in one of its most vital points. He sacrifices the personal presence of Helena in Troy, which ran through every one of the ancient epic

---

[1] Herod. ii. 116. δοκέει δέ μοι καὶ Ὅμηρος τὸν λόγον τοῦτον πυθέσθαι· ἀλλ' οὐ γὰρ ὁμοίως εὐπρεπὴς ἐς τὴν ἐποποιίην ἦν τῷ ἑτέρῳ τῷ περ ἐχρήσατο· ἐς ὃ μετῆκε αὐτόν, δηλώσας ὡς καὶ τοῦτον ἐπισταῖτο τὸν λόγον.

Herodotus then produces a passage from the Iliad, with a view to prove that Homer knew of the voyage of Paris and Helen to Egypt: but the passage proves nothing at all to the point.

Again (c. 120), his slender confidence in the epic poets breaks out—εἰ χρή τι τοῖσι ἐποποιοῖσι χρεώμενον λέγειν.

It is remarkable that Herodotus is disposed to identify Helen with the ξείνη Ἀφροδίτη whose temple he saw at Memphis (c. 112).

poems belonging to the Trojan cycle, and is indeed, under the gods, the great and present moving force throughout.

Thucydidês places himself generally in the same point of view as Herodotus with regard to mythical antiquity; yet with some considerable differences. Though manifesting no belief in present miracles or prodigies,[1] he seems to accept without reserve the preexistent reality of all the persons mentioned in the mythes, and of the long series of generations extending back through so many supposed centuries. In this category, too, are included the eponymous personages, Hellên, Kekrops, Eumolpus, Pandiôn, Amphilochus the son of Amphiaraüs, and Akarnan. But on the other hand, we find no trace of that distinction between a human and an heroic ante-human race, which Herodotus still admitted, —nor any respect for Egyptian legends. Thucydidês, regarding the personages of the mythes as men of the same breed and stature with his own contemporaries, not only tests the acts imputed to them by the same limits of credibility, but presumes in them the same political views and feelings as he was accustomed to trace in the proceedings of Peisistratus or Periklês. He treats the Trojan war as a great political enterprise, undertaken by all Greece; brought into combination through the imposing power of Aga-memnôn, not (according to the legendary narrative) through the influence of the oath exacted by Tyndareus. Then he explains how the predecessors of Agamemnôn arrived at so vast a dominion —beginning with Pelops, who came over (as he says) from Asia with great wealth among the poor Peloponnêsians, and by means of this wealth so aggrandised himself, though a foreigner, as to become the eponym of the peninsula. Next followed his son Atreus, who acquired after the death of Eurystheus the dominion of Mykênæ, which had before been possessed by the descendants

[1] " Ut conquirere fabulosa (says Tacitus, Hist. ii. 50, a worthy parallel of Thucydidês) et fictis oblectare legentium animos, procul gravitate cœpti operis crediderim, ita vulgatis traditisque demere fidem non ausim. Die, quo Bebriaci certabatur, avem inusitatâ specie, apud Regium Lepidum celebri vico consedisse, incolæ memorant; nec deinde cœtu hominum aut circumvolitantium alitum, territam pulsamque, donec Otho se ipse interficcret: tum ablatam ex oculis: et tempora reputantibus, initium finemque miraculi cum Othonis exitu competisse." Suetonius (Vesp. 5) recounts a different miracle, in which three eagles appear.

This passage of Tacitus occurs immediately after his magnificent description of the suicide of the emperor Otho, a deed which he contemplates with the most fervent admiration. His feelings were evidently so wrought up, that he was content to relay the canons of historical credibility.

of Perseus: here the old legendary tale, which described Atreus as having been banished by his father Pelops in consequence of the murder of his elder brother Chrysippus, is invested with a political bearing, as explaining the reason why Atreus retired to Mykênæ. Another legendary tale—the defeat and death of Eurystheus by the fugitive Herakleids in Attica, so celebrated in Attic tragedy as having given occasion to the generous protecting intervention of Athens—is also introduced as furnishing the cause why Atreus succeeded to the deceased Eurystheus: "for Atreus, the maternal uncle of Eurystheus, had been entrusted by the latter with his government during the expedition into Attica, and had effectually courted the people, who were moreover in great fear of being attacked by the Herakleids". Thus the Pelopids acquired the supremacy in Peloponnêsus, and Agamemnôn was enabled to get together his 1200 ships and 100,000 men for the expedition against Troy. Considering that contingents were furnished from every portion of Greece, Thucydidês regards this as a small number, treating the Homeric Catalogue as an authentic muster-roll, perhaps rather exaggerated than otherwise. He then proceeds to tell us why the armament was not larger. Many more men could have been furnished, but there was not sufficient money to purchase provisions for their subsistence: hence they were compelled, after landing and gaining a victory, to fortify their camp, to divide their army, and to send away one portion for the purpose of cultivating the Chersonese, and another portion to sack the adjacent towns. This was the grand reason why the siege lasted so long as ten years. For if it had been possible to keep the whole army together, and to act with an undivided force, Troy would have been taken both earlier and at smaller cost.[1]

Such is the general sketch of the war of Troy, as given by Thucydidês. So different is it from the genuine epical narrative, that we seem hardly to be reading a description of the same event; still less should we imagine that the event was known, to him as well as to us, only through the epic poets themselves. The men, the numbers, and the duration of the siege, do indeed remain the same; but the cast and juncture of events, the determining forces, and the characteristic features, are altogether heterogeneous. But, like Herodotus, and still more than Herodotus, Thucydidês was under the pressure of two conflicting impulses. He shared the general faith in the mythical antiquity, yet at the same time he could not believe in any facts which contradicted the laws of historical credibility or probability. He was thus under the necessity of torturing the matter of the old mythes into conformity with the subjective exigencies of his own mind. He left out, altered, recombined, and supplied new connecting principles and supposed purposes, until the story became such as no one could have any positive reason for calling in question. Though it lost the impressive mixture of religion, romance and individual adventure, which constituted its original charm, it acquired a smoothness and plausibility, and a political *ensemble*, which the critics were satisfied to accept as historical truth. And historical truth it would doubtless have been, if any independent evidence could have been found to sustain it. Had Thucydidês been able to produce such new testimony, we should have been pleased to satisfy ourselves that the war of Troy, as he recounted it, was the real event; of which the war of Troy, as sung by the epic poets, was a misreported, exaggerated, and ornamented recital. But in this case the poets are the only real witnesses, and the narrative of Thucydidês is a mere extract and distillation from their incredibilities.

A few other instances may be mentioned to illustrate the views of Thucydidês respecting various mythical incidents. 1. He treats the residence of the Homeric Phæakians at Korkyra as an undisputed fact, and employs it partly to explain the efficiency of the Korkyrean navy in times preceding the Peloponnesian war.[1] 2. He notices with equal confidence the story of Têreus and Proknê, daughter of Pandiôn, and the murder of the child Itys by Proknê his mother and Philomêla ; and he produces this ancient mythe with especial reference to the alliance between the Athenians and Têrês, king of the Odrysian Thracians, during the time of the Peloponnesian war, intimating that the Odrysian Têrês was neither of the same family nor of the same country as Têreus the husband of Proknê.[2] The conduct of Pandiôn, in

---

[1] Thucyd. i. 25.
[2] Thucyd. ii. 29. Καὶ τὸ ἔργον τὸ ἔπραξαν· πολλοῖς δὲ καὶ τῶν ποιητῶν ἐν   περὶ τὸν Ἴτυν αἱ γυναῖκες ἐν τῇ γῇ ταύτῃ

giving his daughter Proknê in marriage to Têreus, is in his view dictated by political motives and interests. 3. He mentions the Strait of Messina as the place through which Odysseus is said to have sailed.[1] 4. The Cyclôpes and the Læstrygones (he says) were the most ancient reported inhabitants of Sicily; but he cannot tell to what race they belonged, nor whence they came.[2] 5. Italy derived its name from Italus king of the Sikels. 6. Eryx and Egesta in Sicily were founded by fugitive Trojans after the capture of Troy; also Skionê, in the Thracian peninsula of Pallênê, by Greeks from the Achæan town of Pellênê, stopping thither in their return from the siege of Troy: the Amphilochian Argos in the Gulf of Ambrakia, was in like manner founded by Amphilochus son of Amphiaraüs, in his return from the same enterprise. The remorse and mental derangement of the matricidal Alkmæôn, son of Amphiaraüs, is also mentioned by Thucydidês,[3] as well as the settlement of his son Akarnan in the country called after him Akarnania.[4]

ἀηδόνος μνήμη Δαυλιὰς ἡ ὄρνις ἐπωνό-μασται. Εἰκὸς δὲ καὶ τὸ κῆδος Πανδίονα ξυνάψασθαι τῆς θυγατρὸς διὰ τοσούτου, ἐπ' ὠφελείᾳ τῇ πρὸς ἀλλήλους, μᾶλλον ἢ διὰ πολλῶν ἡμερῶν ἐς Ὀδρύσας ὁδοῦ. The first of these sentences would lead us to infer, if it came from any other pen than that of Thucydidês, that the writer believed the metamorphosis of Philoméla into a nightingale: see above, ch. xi.

The observation respecting the convenience of neighbourhood for the marriage is remarkable, and shows how completely Thucydidês regarded the event as historical. What would he have said respecting the marriage of Oreithyia, daughter of Erechtheus, with Boreas, and the prodigious distance which she is reported to have been carried by her husband? Ὑπέρ τε πόντον πάντ', ἐπ' ἔσχατα χθονός, &c. (Sophoklês ap. Strabo. vii. p. 295). From the way in which Thucydidês introduces the mention of this event, we see that he intended to correct the misapprehension of his countrymen, who having just made an alliance with the Odrysian *Têrês*, were led by that circumstance to think of the old mythical *Têreus*, and to regard him as the ancestor of *Têrês*.

[1] Thucyd. iv. 24.
[2] Thucyd. vi. 2.
[3] Thucyd. ii. 68—102; vi. 2. Antio-

chus of Syracuse, the contemporary of Thucydidês, also mentioned Italus as the eponymous king of Italy: he farther named Sikelus, who came to Morges, son of Italus, after having been banished from Rome. He talks about Italus, just as Thucydidês talks about Thêseus, as a wise and powerful king, who first acquired a great dominion (Dionys. H. A. R. i. 12, 35, 73). Aristotle also mentioned Italus in the same general terms (Polit. vii. 9, 2).

[4] We may here notice some particulars respecting Isokratês. He manifests entire confidence in the authenticity of the mythical genealogies and chronology; but while he treats the mythical personages as historically real, he regards them at the same time not as human, but as half-gods, superior to humanity. About Helena, Thêseus, Sarpêdôn, Kyknus, Memnôn, Achilles, &c., see Encom. Helen. Or. x. pp. 282, 292, 295, Bek. Helena was worshipped in his time as a goddess at Therapnæ (*ib.* p. 295). He recites the settlements of Danaus, Kadmus and Pelops in Greece, as undoubted historical facts (p. 297). In his discourse called *Busiris*, he accuses Polykratês the sophist of a gross anachronism in having placed Busiris subsequent in point of date to Orpheus and Æolus (Or. xi. p. 301, Bek.), and he

Such are the special allusions made by this illustrious author in the course of his history to mythical events. From the tenor of his language we may see that he accounted all that could be known about them to be uncertain and unsatisfactory; but he has it much at heart to show, that even the greatest were inferior in magnitude and importance to the Peloponnesian war.[1]   In

adds that the tale of Busiris having been slain by Hêraklês was chronologically impossible (p. 309). Of the long Athenian genealogy from Kekrops to Thêseus, he speaks with perfect historical confidence (Panathenaic. p. 349, Bek.); not less so of the adventures of Hêraklês and his mythical contemporaries, which he places in the mouth of Archidamus as a justification of the Spartan title to Messenia (Or. vi. *Archidamus*, p. 156, Bek.; compare Or. v. *Philippus*, pp. 114, 138), φασιν, οἷς περὶ τῶν παλαιῶν πιστεύομεν, &c. He condemns the poets in strong language for the wicked and dissolute tales which they circulated respecting the gods: many of them (he says) had been punished for such blasphemies by blindness, poverty, exile and other misfortunes (Or. xi. p. 309, Bek.).

In general it may be said, that Isokratês applies no principles of historical criticism to the mythes; he rejects such as appear to him discreditable or unworthy, and believes the rest.

[1] Thucyd. i. 21—22.

The first two volumes of this History have been noticed in an able article of the Quarterly Review for October, 1846; as well as in the Heidelberger Jahrbücher der Literatur (1846, No. 41, pp. 641—655) by Professor Kortüm. While expressing, on several points, approbation of my work, by which I feel much flattered—both my English and my German critic take partial objection to the views respecting Grecian legend. The Quarterly Reviewer contends that the mythopœic faculty of the human mind, though essentially loose and untrustworthy, is never creative, but requires some basis of fact to work upon. Kortüm thinks that I have not done justice to Thucydidês, as regards his way of dealing with legend; that I do not allow sufficient weight to the authority of an historian so circumspect and so cold-blooded (den kaltblütigsten und besonnensten Historiker des Alterthums, p. 653) as a satisfactory voucher

for the early facts of Grecian history in his preface (Herr G. fehlt also, wenn er das anerkannt kritische Prœmium als Gewährsmann verschmäht, p. 654).

No man feels more powerfully than I do the merits of Thucydidês as an historian, or the value of the example which he set in multiplying critical inquiries respecting matters recent and verifiable. But the ablest judge or advocate, in investigating specific facts, can proceed no further than he finds witnesses having the means of knowledge and willing more or less to tell truth. In reference to facts prior to 776 B.C., Thucydidês had nothing before him except the legendary poets, whose credibility is not at all enhanced by the circumstance that he accepted them as witnesses, applying himself only to cut down and modify their allegations. His credibility in regard to the specific facts of these early times depends altogether upon theirs. Now we in our day are in a better position for appreciating their credibility than he was in his, since the foundations of historical evidence are so much more fully understood, and good or bad materials for history are open to comparison in such large extent and variety. Instead of wondering that he shared the general faith in such delusive guides—we ought rather to give him credit for the reserve with which he qualified that faith, and for the sound idea of historical possibility to which he held fast as the limit of his confidence. But it is impossible to consider Thucydidês as a *satisfactory guarantee* (Gewährsmann) for matters of fact which he derives only from such sources.

Professor Kortüm considers that I am inconsistent with myself in refusing to discriminate particular matters of historical fact among the legends—and yet in accepting these legends (in my chap. xx.) as giving a faithful mirror of the general state of early Grecian society (p. 653). It appears to me that this is no inconsistency, but a real and important distinction. Whether

this respect his opinion seems to have been at variance with that which was popular among his contemporaries.

To touch a little upon the later historians by whom these mythes were handled, we find that Anaximenês of Lampsacus composed a consecutive history of events, beginning from the Theogony down to the battle of Mantineia.[1] But Ephorus professed to omit all the mythical narratives which are referred to times anterior to the return of the Herakleids (such restrictions would of course have banished the siege of Troy), and even reproved those who introduced mythes into historical writing; adding, that everywhere truth was the object to be aimed at.[2] Yet in practice he seems often to have departed from his own rule.[3] Theopompus, on the other hand, openly proclaimed that he could narrate fables in his history better than Herodotus, or

---

Hêraklês, Agamemnôn, Odysseus, &c., were real persons, and performed all, or a part, of the possible actions ascribed to them—I profess myself unable to determine. But even assuming both the persons and their exploits to be fictions, these very fictions will have been conceived and put together in conformity to the general social phænomena among which the describer and his hearers lived—and will thus serve as illustrations of the manners then prevalent. In fact the real value of the Preface of Thucydidês, upon which Professor Kortüm bestows such just praise, consists, not in the particular facts which he brings out by altering the legends, but in the rational general views which he sets forth respecting early Grecian society, and respecting the steps as well as the causes whereby it attained its actual position as he saw it.

Professor Kortüm also affirms that the mythes contain "real matter of fact along with mere conceptions": which affirmation is the same as that of the Quarterly Reviewer, when he says that the mythopoeic faculty is not creative. Taking the mythes in a mass, I doubt not that this is true, nor have I anywhere denied it. Taking them one by one, I neither affirm nor deny it. My position is, that whether there be matter of fact or not, we have no test whereby it can be singled out, identified and severed from the accompanying fiction. And it lies upon those, who proclaim the practicability

of such severance, to exhibit some means of verification better than any which has been yet pointed out. If Thucydidês has failed in doing this it is certain that none of the many authors who have made the same attempt after him have been more successful.

It cannot surely be denied that the mythopoeic faculty is *creative*, when we have before us so many divine legends not merely in Greece, but in other countries also. To suppose that these religious legends are mere exaggerations, &c., of some basis of actual fact —that the gods of polytheism were merely divinised men with qualities distorted or feigned — would be to embrace in substance the theory of Euêmerus.

[1] Diodôr. xv. 89. He was a contemporary of Alexander the Great.

[2] Diodôr. iv. 1. Strabo, ix. p. 422, ἐπιτιμήσας τοῖς φιλομυθοῦσιν ἐν τῇ τῆς ἱστορίας γραφῇ.

[3] Ephorus recounted the principal adventures of Hêraklês (Fragm. 8, 9, ed. Marx.), the tales of Kadmus and Harmonia (Fragm. 12), the banishment of Ætôlus from Elis (Fragm. 15; Strabo, viii. p. 357); he drew inferences from the chronology of the Trojan and Theban wars (Fragm. 28); he related the coming of Dædalus to the Sikan king Kokalus, and the expedition of the Amazons (Fragm. 99—103).

He was particularly copious in his information about κτίσεις ἀποικίαι and συγγενείαι (Polyb. ix. ¶

Ktesias, or Hellanicus.[1] The fragments which remain to us
exhibit some proof that this promise was performed as to
quantity;[2] though as to his style of narration, the judgment of
Dionysius is unfavourable. Xenophôn ennobled his favourite
amusement of the chase by numerous examples chosen from the
heroic world, tracing their portraits with all the simplicity of an
undiminished faith. Kallisthenês, like Ephorus, professed to
omit all mythes which referred to a time anterior to the return
of the Herakleids; yet we know that he devoted a separate book
or portion of his history to the Trojan war.[3] Philistus introduced
some mythes in the earlier portions of his Sicilian history; but
Timæus was distinguished above all others by the copious and
indiscriminate way in which he collected and repeated such
legends.[4] Some of these writers employed their ingenuity in
transforming the mythical circumstances into plausible matter of
history: Ephorus in particular converted the serpent Pythô,
slain by Apollo, into a tyrannical king.[5]

But the author who pushed this transmutation of legend into
history to the greatest length, was the Messenian Euêmerus,
contemporary of Kassander of Macedôn. He melted down in
this way the divine persons and legends, as well as the heroic—
representing both gods and heroes as having been mere earthborn
men, though superior to the ordinary level in respect of force
and capacity, and deified or heroified after death as a recompense

<hr>

[1] Strabo, i. p. 74.
[2] Dionys. Halic. de Vett. Scriptt.
Judic. p. 428, Reisk.; Ælian, V. H. iii.
18, Θεόπομπος . . . δεινὸς μυθολόγος.
Theopompus affirmed, that the
bodies of those who went into the
forbidden precinct (τὸ ἄβατον) of Zeus
in Arcadia gave no shadow (Polyb.
xvi. 12). He recounted the story of
Midas and Silênus (Fragm. 74, 75, 76,
ed. Wichers): he said a good deal about
the heroes of Troy; and he seems to
have assigned the misfortunes of the
Νόστοι to an historical cause—the
rottenness of the Grecian ships from
the length of the siege, while the
genuine epic ascribes it to the anger
of Athênê (Fragm. 112, 113, 114; Schol.
Homer. Iliad. ii. 135); he narrated an
alleged expulsion of Kinyras from
Cyprus by Agamemnôn (Fr. 111); he
gave the genealogy of the Macedonian
queen Olympias up to Achilles and
Æakus (Fragm. 232).

[3] Cicero, Epist. ad Familiar. v. 12;
Xenophôn de Venation. c. 1.

[4] Philistus, Fragm. 1 (Göller), Dædalus and Kokalus; about Liber and Juno
(Fragm. 57); about the migration of
the Sikels into Sicily eighty years after
the Trojan war (ap. Dionys. Hal. i. 3).

Timæus (Fragm. 50, 51, 52, 53,
Göller) related many fables respecting
Jasôn, Mêdea, and the Argonauts
generally. The miscarriage of the
Athenian armament under Nikias before Syracuse is imputed to the anger
of Hêraklês against the Athenians
because they came to assist the Eges-
tans, descendants of Troy (Plutarch,
Nikias, 1),—a naked reproduction of
genuine epical agencies by an historian;
also about Diomêdês and the Daunians;
Phaëthôn and the river Eridanus;
the combats of the Gigantes in the
Phlegræan plains (Fragm. 97, 99, 102).

[5] Strabo, ix. p. 422.

for services or striking exploits. In the course of a voyage into the Indian sea, undertaken by command of Kassander, Euêmerus professed to have discovered a fabulous country called Panchaia, in which was a temple of the Triphylian Zeus: he there described a golden column with an inscription purporting to have been put up by Zeus himself, and detailing his exploits while on earth.[1] Some eminent men, among whom may be numbered Polybius, followed the views of Euêmerus, and the Roman poet Ennius [2] translated his Historia Sacra: but on the whole he never acquired favour, and the unblushing inventions which he put into circulation were of themselves sufficient to disgrace both the author and his opinions. The doctrine that all the gods had once existed as mere men offended the religious pagans, and drew upon Euêmerus the imputation of atheism ; but, on the other hand, it came to be warmly espoused by several of the Christian assailants of paganism, —by Minucius Felix, Lactantius, and St. Augustin, who found the ground ready prepared for them in their efforts to strip Zeus and the other pagan gods of the attributes of deity. They believed not only in the main theory, but also in the copious details of Euêmerus ; and the same man whom Strabo casts aside as almost a proverb for mendacity, was extolled by them as an excellent specimen of careful historical inquiry.[3]

But though the pagan world repudiated that "lowering tone

[1] Compare Diodôr. v. 44—46; and Lactantius, De Falsâ Relig. i. 11.

[2] Cicero, De Naturâ Deor. i. 42 ; Varro, De Re Rust. i. 48.

[3] Strabo, ii. p. 102. Οὐ πολὺ οὖν λείπεται ταῦτα τῶν Πύθεω καὶ Εὐημέρου καὶ Ἀντιφάνους ψευσμάτων ; compare also i. p. 47, and ii. p. 104.

St. Augustin, on the contrary, tells us (Civitat. Dei, vi. 7), "Quid de ipso Jove senserunt, qui nutricem ejus in Capitolio posuerunt? Nonne attestati sunt omnes Euemero, qui non fabulosâ garrulitate, sed historicâ diligentiâ, homines fuisse mortalesque conscripsit?" And Minucius Felix (Octav. 20-21), "Euemerus exsequitur Deorum natales : patrias, sepulcra, dinumerat, et per provincias monstrat, Dictæi Jovis, et Apollinis Delphici, et Phariæ Isidis, et Cereris Eleusiniæ". Compare Augustin, Civit. Dei, xviii. 8—14 ; and Clemens Alexand. Cohort. ad Gent. pp. 15—18, Sylb.

Lactantius (De Falsâ Relig. c. 13, 14, 16) gives copious citations from Ennius's translation of the Historia Sacra of Euêmerus.

Εὐήμερος, ὁ ἐπικληθεὶς ἄθεος, Sextus Empiricus, adv. Physicos, ix. § 17—51. Compare Cicero, De Nat. Deor. i. 42 ; Plutarch, De Iside et Osiride, c. 23, tom. ii. p. 475, ed. Wytt.

Nitzsch assumes (Heldensage der Griechen, sect. 7, p. 84) that the voyage of Euêmerus to Panchaia was intended only as an amusing romance, and that Strabo, Polybius, Eratosthenês and Plutarch were mistaken in construing it as a serious recital. Böttiger, in his Kunst-Mythologie der Griechen(Absch. ii. s. 6, p. 190) takes the same view. But not the least reason is given for adopting this opinion, and it seems to me far-fetched and improbable; Lobeck (Aglaopham. p. 989), though Nitzsch alludes to him as holding it, manifests no such tendency, as far as I can observe.

of explanation" which effaced the superhuman personality of
Zeus and the great gods of Olympus—the mythical persons and
narratives generally came to be surveyed more and more from
the point of view of history, and subjected to such alterations
as might make them look more like plausible matter of fact.
Polybius, Strabo, Diodôrus, and Pausanias, cast the mythes into
historical statements—with more or less of transformation, as the
case may require, assuming always that there is a basis of truth,
which may be discovered by removing poetical exaggerations and
allowing for mistakes.   Strabo, in particular, lays down that
principle broadly and unequivocally in his remarks upon Homer.
To give pure fiction, without any foundation of fact, was in his
judgment utterly unworthy of so great a genius ; and he comments with considerable acrimony on the geographer Eratosthenês,
who maintains the opposite opinion.   Again, Polybius tells us
that the Homeric Æolus, the dispenser of the winds by appointment from Zeus, was in reality a man eminently skilled in
navigation, and exact in predicting the weather ; that the
Cyclôpes and Læstrygones were wild and savage real men in
Sicily ; and that Scylla and Charybdis were a figurative representation of dangers arising from pirates in the Strait of Messina.
Strabo speaks of the amazing expeditions of Dionysus and
Hêraklês, and of the long wanderings of Jasôn, Menelaus, and
Odysseus, in the same category with the extended commercial
range of the Phœnician merchant ships.   He explains the report
of Thêseus and Peirithous having descended to Hadês, by their
dangerous earthly pilgrimages,—and the invocation of the Dioskuri
as the protectors of the imperilled mariner, by the celebrity which
they had acquired as real men and navigators.

Diodôrus gave at considerable length versions of the current
fables respecting the most illustrious names in the Grecian
mythical world, compiled confusedly out of distinct and incon-
gruous authors.   Sometimes the mythe is reproduced in its
primitive simplicity, but for the most part it is partially and
sometimes wholly, historicised.   Amidst this jumble of dissentient authorities, we can trace little of a systematic view,
except the general conviction that there was at the bottom of the
mythes a real chronological sequence of persons, and real matter
of fact, historical or ultra-historical.   Nevertheless there are

some few occasions on which Diodôrus brings us back a step
nearer to the point of view of the old logographers. For, in
reference to Hêraklês, he protests against the scheme of cutting
down the mythes to the level of present reality. He contends
that a special standard of ultra-historical credibility ought to be
constituted, so as to include the mythe in its native dimensions,
and do fitting honour to the grand, beneficent, and superhuman
personality of Hêraklês and other heroes or demigods. To apply
to such persons the common measure of humanity (he says), and
to cavil at the glorious picture which grateful man has drawn of
them, is at once ungracious and irrational. All nice criticism
into the truth of the legendary narratives is out of place : we
show our reverence to the god by acquiescing in the incredibilities
of his history, and we must be content with the best guesses
which we can make, amidst the inextricable confusion and
numberless discrepancies which they present.[1] Yet though
Diodôrus here exhibits a preponderance of the religious sentiment over the purely historical point of view, and thus reminds
us of a period earlier than Thucydidês—he in another place
inserts a series of stories which seem to be derived from Euêmerus,
and in which Uranus, Kronus and Zeus appear reduced to the
character of human kings celebrated for their exploits and bene-
factions.[2] Many of the authors, whom Diodôrus copies, have so
entangled together Grecian, Asiatic, Egyptian and Libyan fables,
that it becomes impossible to ascertain how much of this hetero-

---

[1] Diodôr. ix. 1—8. Ἔνιοι γὰρ τῶν
ἀναγινωσκόντων, οὐ δικαίᾳ χρώμενοι
κρίσει, τἀκριβὲς ἐπιζητοῦσιν ἐν ταῖς
ἀρχαίαις μυθολογίαις, ἐπίσης τοῖς πρατ-
τομένοις ἐν τῷ καθ' ἡμᾶς χρόνῳ, καὶ τὰ
διαταζόμενα τῶν ἔργων διὰ τὸ μέγεθος, ἐκ
τοῦ καθ' αὑτοὺς βίου τεκμαιρόμενοι, τὴν
Ἡρακλέους δύναμιν ἐκ τῆς ἀσθενείας τῶν
νῦν ἀνθρώπων θεωροῦσιν, ὥστε διὰ τὴν
ὑπερβολὴν τοῦ μεγέθους τῶν ἔργων ἀπισ-
τεῖσθαι τὴν γραφήν. Καθόλου γὰρ ἐν
ταῖς ἀρχαίαις μυθολογίαις οὐκ ἐκ παντὸς
τρόπου πικρῶς τὴν ἀλήθειαν ἐξε-
ταστέον. Καὶ γὰρ ἐν τοῖς θεάτροις
πεπεισμένοι μήτε Κενταύρους
διφυεῖς ἐξ ἑτερογενῶν σωμάτων ὑπάρξαι,
μήτε Γηρυόνην τρισώματον, ὅμως
προσδεχόμεθα τὰς τοιαύτας
μυθολογίας, καὶ ταῖς ἐπισημα-
σίαις συναύξομεν τὴν τοῦ θεοῦ
τιμήν. Καὶ γὰρ ἄτοπον, Ἡρακλέα μὲν

ἔτι κατ' ἀνθρώπους ὄντα τοῖς ἰδίοις πόνοις
ἐξημερῶσαι τὴν οἰκουμένην, τοὺς δ'
ἀνθρώπους, ἐπιλαθομένους τῆς κοινῆς
εὐεργεσίας, συκοφαντεῖν τὸν ἐπὶ τοῖς
καλλίστοις ἔργοις ἔπαινον, &c.
This is a remarkable passage : first,
inasmuch as it sets forth the total
inapplicability of analogies drawn
from the historical past as narratives
about Hêraklês ; next, inasmuch as it
suspends the employment of critical
and scientific tests, and invokes an
acquiescence interwoven and identified
with the feelings, as the proper mode
of evincing pious reverence for the god
Hêraklês. It aims at reproducing
exactly that state of mind to which
the mythes were addressed, and with
which alone they could ever be in
thorough harmony.
[2] Diodôr. iii. 45—60 ; 41—46

geneous mass can be considered as at all connected with the genuine Hellenic mind.

Pausanias is far more strictly Hellenic in his view of the Grecian mythes than Diodôrus : his sincere piety makes him inclined to faith generally with regard to the mythical narratives, but subject nevertheless to the frequent necessity of historicising or allegorising them.   His belief in the general reality of the mythical history and chronology is complete, in spite of the many discrepancies which he finds in it, and which he is unable to reconcile.

Another author who seem to have conceived clearly, and applied consistently, the semi-historical theory of the Grecian mythes, is Palæphatus, of whose work what appears to be a short abstract has been preserved.[1]   In the short preface of this treatise "con-cerning Incredible Tales," he remarks, that some men, from want of instruction, believe all the current narratives ; while others, more searching and cautious, disbelieve them altogether.   Each of these extremes he is anxious to avoid.   On the one hand, he thinks that no narrative could ever have acquired credence unless it had been founded in truth ; on the other, it is impossible for him to accept so much of the existing narratives as conflicts with the analogies of present natural phænomena.   If such things ever had been, they would still continue to be—but they never have so occurred : and the extra-analogical features of the stories are to be ascribed to the license of the poets.   Palæphatus wishes to adopt a middle course, neither accepting all nor rejecting all ; accordingly, he had taken great pains to separate the true from the false in many of the narratives ; he had visited the localities wherein they had taken place, and made careful inquiries from old men and others.[2]   The results of

---

[1] The work of Palæphatus, probably this original, is alluded to in the *Ciris* of Virgil (88):

   " Docta Palæphatiâ testatur voce papyrus."

The date of Palæphatus is unknown —indeed this passage of the *Ciris* seems the only ground that exists for inference respecting it.   That which we now possess is probably an extract from a larger work—an extract made by an excerptor at some later time :

see Vossius de Historicis Græcis, p. 478, ed. Westermann.

[2] Palæphat. init. ap. Script. Mythogr. ed. Westermann, p. 268. Τῶν ἀνθρώπων οἱ μὲν πείθονται πᾶσι τοῖς λεγομένοις, ὡς ἀνομίλητοι σοφίας καὶ ἐπιστήμης— οἱ δὲ πυκνότεροι τὴν φύσιν καὶ πολυπράγ- μονες ἀπιστοῦσι τὸ παράπαν μηδὲν γενέσθαι τούτων.   Ἐμοὶ δὲ δοκεῖ γενέσθαι πάντα τὰ λεγόμενα· . . . . γενόμενα δέ τινα οἱ ποιηταὶ καὶ λογο- γράφοι παρέτρεψαν εἰς τὸ ἀπιστότερον καὶ θαυμασιώτερον τοῦ θαυμάζειν ἕνεκα τοὺς

his researches are presented in a new version of fifty legends, among the most celebrated and the most fabulous, comprising the Centaurs, Pasiphaê, Aktæôn, Kadmus and the Sparti, the Sphinx, Cycnus, Dædalus, the Trojan horse, Æolus, Scylla, Geryôn, Bellerophôn, &c.

It must be confessed that Palæphatus has performed his promise of transforming the "incredibilia" into narratives in themselves plausible and unobjectionable, and that in doing so he always follows some thread of analogy, real or verbal. The Centaurs (he tells us) were a body of young men from the village of Nephelê in Thessaly, who first trained and mounted horses for the purpose of repelling a herd of bulls belonging to Ixiôn king of the Lapithæ, which had run wild and done great damage : they pursued these wild bulls on horseback, and pierced them with their spears, thus acquiring both the name of *Prickers* (κέντορες) and the imputed attribute of joint body with the horse. Aktæôn was an Arcadian, who neglected the cultivation of his land for the pleasures of hunting, and was thus eaten up by the expense of his hounds. The dragon whom Kadmus killed at Thêbes, was in reality Drako king of Thêbes ; and the dragon's teeth which he was said to have sown, and from whence sprung a crop of armed men, were in point of fact elephants' teeth, which Kadmus as a rich Phœnician had brought over with him: the sons of Drako sold these elephants' teeth and employed the proceeds to levy troops against Kadmus. Dædalus, instead of flying across the sea on wings, had escaped from Krête in a swift sailing-boat under a violent storm: Kottus, Briareus, and Gygês were not persons with one hundred hands, but inhabitants of the village of Hekatoncheiria in Upper Macedonia, who warred with the inhabitants of Mount Olympus against the Titans : Scylla, whom Odysseus so narrowly escaped,

---

ἀνθρώπους. Ἐγὼ δὲ γινώσκω, ὅτι οὐ δύναται τὰ τοιαῦτα εἶναι οἷα καὶ λέγεται · τοῦτο δὲ καὶ διείληφα, ὅτι εἰ μὴ ἐγένετο, οὐκ ἂν ἐλέγετο.

The main assumption of the semi-historical theory is here shortly and clearly stated.

One of the early Christian writers, Minucius Felix, is astonished at the easy belief of his pagan forefathers in miracles. If ever such things had been done in former times (he affirms), they would continue to be done now ; as they cannot be done now, we may be sure that they never were *really* done formerly (Minucius Felix, Octav. c. 20): "Majoribus enim nostris tam facilis in mendaciis fides fuit, ut temerè crediderint etiam alia monstruosa mira miracula, Scyllam multiplicem, Chimæram multiformem, Hydram, et Centauros. Quid illas aniles fabulas —de hominibus aves et feras, immo et de hominibus arbores atque flores ? *Quæ, si essent facta, fierent ; quia fieri non possunt ideo nec facta sunt.*"

was a fast-sailing piratical vessel, as was also Pegasus, the alleged winged horse of Bellerophôn.[1]

By such ingenious conjectures, Palæphatus eliminates all the incredible circumstances, and leaves to us a string of tales perfectly credible and commonplace, which we should readily believe, provided a very moderate amount of testimony could be produced in their favour.   If his treatment not only disenchants the original mythes, but even effaces their generic and essential character, we ought to remember that this is not more than what is done by Thucydidês in his sketch of the Trojan war.   Palæphatus handles the mythes consistently, according to the semi-historical theory, and his results exhibit the maximum which that theory can ever present.[2]   By aid of conjecture we get out of the impossible, and arrive at matters intrinsically plausible, but totally uncertified;

---

[1] Palæphat. Narrat. 1, 3, 6, 13, 20, 21, 29.   Two short treatises on the same subject as this of Palæphatus are printed along with it both in the collection of Gale and of Westermann; the one *Heracliti de Incredibilibus*, the other *Anonymi de Incredibilibus*.   They both profess to interpret some of the extraordinary or miraculous mythes, and proceed in a track not unlike that of Palæphatus.   Scylla was a beautiful courtezan, surrounded with abominable parasites: she ensnared and ruined the companions of Odysseus, though he himself was prudent enough to escape her (Heraclit. c. 2, p. 313, West.).   Atlas was a great astronomer; Pasiphaê fell in love with a youth named Taurus; the monster called the Chimæra was in reality a ferocious queen, who had two brothers called Leo and Drako; the ram which carried Phryxus and Hellê across the Ægean was a boatman named Krius (Heraclit. c. 2, 6, 15, 24).

A great number of similar explanations are scattered throughout the Scholia on Homer and the Commentary of Eustathius, without specification of their authors.

Theôn considers such resolution of fable into plausible history as a proof of surpassing ingenuity (Progymnasmata, cap. 6, ap. Walz. Coll. Rhett. Græc. i. p. 219).   Others among the Rhetors, too, exercised their talents sometimes in vindicating, sometimes in controverting, the probability of the ancient mythes.   See the Progymnasmata of Nicolaus—Κατασκευὴ ὅτι εἰκότα τὰ κατὰ Νιόβην, ᾿Ανασκευὴ ὅτι οὐκ εἰκότα τὰ κατὰ Νιόβην (ap. Walz. Coll. Rhetor. i. p. 284—318), where there are many specimens of this fanciful mode of handling.

Plutarch, however, in one of his treatises, accepts Minotaurs, Sphinxes, Centaurs, &c., as realities; he treats them as products of the monstrous, incestuous, and ungovernable lusts of man, which he contrasts with the simple and moderate passions of animals (Plutarch, Gryllus, p. 990).

[2] The learned Mr. Jacob Bryant regards the explanations of Palæphatus as if they were founded upon real fact.   He admits, for example, the city Nephelê alleged by that author in his exposition of the fable of the Centaurs.   Moreover, he speaks with much commendation of Palæphatus generally: "He (Palæphatus) wrote early, and seems to have been a serious and sensible person; one who saw the absurdity of the fables upon which the theology of his country was founded" (Ancient Mythology, vol. i. p. 411—435).

So also Sir Thomas Browne (Enquiry into Vulgar Errors, Book I. chap. vi. p. 221, ed. 1835) alludes to Palæphatus as having incontestably pointed out the real basis of the fables.   "And surely the fabulous inclination of those days was greater than any since; which swarmed so with fables, and from such slender grounds took hints for fictions, poisoning the world ever after: wherein how far they succeeded, may be exemplified from Palæphatus, in his Book of Fabulous Narrations."

beyond this point we cannot penetrate, without the light of extrinsic evidence, since there is no intrinsic mark to distinguish truth from plausible fiction.

It remains that we should notice the manner in which the ancient mythes were received and dealt with by the philosophers. The earliest expression which we hear, on the part of philosophy, is the severe censure bestowed upon them on ethical grounds by Xenophanês of Kolophôn, and seemingly by some others of his contemporaries.[1] It was apparently in reply to such charges, which did not admit of being directly rebutted, that Theagenês of Rhêgium (about 520 B.C.) first started the idea of a double meaning in the Homeric and Hesiodic narratives,—an interior sense, different from that which the words in their obvious meaning bore, yet to a certain extent analogous, and discoverable by sagacious divination. Upon this principle he allegorised especially the battle of the gods in the Iliad.[2] In the succeeding century, Anaxagoras and Metrodôrus carried out the allegorical explanation more comprehensively and systematically ; the former representing the mythical personages as mere mental conceptions invested with name and gender, and illustrative of ethical precepts,—the latter connecting them with physical principles and phænomena. Metrodôrus resolved not only the persons of Zeus, Hêrê and Athênê, but also those of Agamemnôn, Achilles and Hectôr, into various elemental combinations and physical agencies, and treated the adventures ascribed to them as natural facts concealed under the veil of allegory.[3] Empedoklês, Prodikus,

---

[1] Xenophan. ap. Sext. Empir. adv. Mathemat. ix. 193. He also disapproved of the rites, accompanied by mourning and wailing, with which the Eleates worshipped Leukothea : he told them, εἰ μὲν θεὸν ὑπολαμβάνουσι, μὴ θρηνεῖν· εἰ δὲ ἄνθρωπον, μὴ θύειν (Aristotel. Rhet. ii. 23).

Xenophanês pronounced the battles of the Titans, Gigantes and Centaurs to be "fictions of our predecessors". πλάσματα τῶν προτέρων (Xenophan. Fragm. 1, p. 42, ed. Schneidewin).

See a curious comparison of the Grecian and Roman theology in Dionys. Halicarn. Ant. Rom. ii. 20.

[2] Schol. Iliad. xx. 67 ; Tatian. adv. Græc. c. 48. Hêrakleitus indignantly repelled the impudent atheists who found fault with the divine mythes of the Iliad, ignorant of their true allegorical meaning : ἡ τῶν ἐπιφυομένων τῷ Ὁμήρῳ τόλμα τοὺς Ἥρας δεσμοὺς αἰτιᾶται, καὶ νομίζουσιν ὕλην τινὰ δαψιλῆ τῆς ἀθέου πρὸς Ὅμηρον ἔχειν μανίας ταῦτα—Ἠ οὐ μέμνῃ ὅτι τ᾽ ἐκρέμω ὑψόθεν, &c. λέληθε δ᾽ αὐτοὺς ὅτι τούτοις τοῖς ἔπεσιν ἐκτεθεολόγηται ἡ τοῦ παντὸς γένεσις, καὶ τὰ συνεχῶς ᾀδόμενα τέσσαρα στοιχεῖα τούτων τῶν στίχων ἐστὶ τάξις (Schol. ad Hom. Iliad. xv. 18).

[3] Diogen. Laërt. ii. 11 ; Tatian. adv. Græc. c. 37 ; Hesychius, v. Ἀγαμέμνονα. See the ethical turn given to the stories of Circê, the Syrens and Scylla, in Xenoph. Memorab. i. 3, 7 ; ii. 6, 11—31. Syncellus, Chronic, p. 149. Ἑρμηνεύουσι δὲ οἱ Ἀναξαγόρειοι τοὺς μυθώδεις θεοὺς,

Antisthenês, Parmenides, Hêrakleidês of Pontus, and in a later age, Chrysippus and the Stoic philosophers generally,[1] followed more or less the same principle of treating the popular gods as allegorical personages ; while the expositors of Homer (such as Stesimbrotus, Glaukôn and others, even down to the Alexandrine age), though none of them proceeded to the same extreme length as Metrodôrus, employed allegory amongst other media of explanation for the purpose of solving difficulties, or eluding reproaches against the poet.

In the days of Plato and Xenophôn, this allegorising interpretation was one of the received methods of softening down the obnoxious mythes—though Plato himself treated it as an insufficient defence, seeing that the bulk of youthful hearers could not see through the allegory, but embraced the story literally as it was set forth.[2] Pausanias tells us, that when he first began to write his work, he treated many of the Greek legends

Allegorical interpretation of the mythes—more and more esteemed and applied.

νοῦν μὲν τὸν Δία, τὴν δὲ Ἀθηνᾶν τέχνην, &c.

Uschold and other modern German authors seem to have adopted in its full extent the principle of interpretation proposed by Metrodôrus—treating Odysseus and Penelopê as personifications of the Sun and Moon, &c. See Helbig, Die Sittlichen Zustände des Griechischen Helden-Alters, Einleitung, p. xxix. (Leipzig, 1839).

Corrections of the Homeric text were also resorted to, in order to escape the necessity of imputing falsehood to Zeus (Aristotel. De Sophist. Elench. c. 4).

[1] Sextus Empiric. ix. 18; Diogen. viii. 76; Plutarch, De Placit. Philosoph. i. 3—6 ; De Poesi Homericâ, 92—126 ; De Stoicor. Repugn. p. 1050 ; Menander, De Encomiis, c. 5.

Cicero, de Nat. Deor. i. 14, 15, 16, 11 ; ii. 24—25. "Physica ratio non inelegans inclusa in impias fabulas."

In the *Bacchæ* of Euripidês, Pentheus is made to deride the tale of the motherless infant Dionysus having been sewn into the thigh of Zeus. Teiresias, while reproving him for his impiety, explains the story away in a sort of allegory : the μηρὸς Διός (he says) was a mistaken statement in place of the αἰθὴρ χθόνα ἐγκυκλούμενος (Bacch. 235—290).

Lucretius (iii. 995—1036) allegorises the conspicuous sufferers in Hades,—

Tantalus, Sisyphus, Tityus, and the Danaïds, as well as the ministers of penal infliction, Cerberus and the Furies. The first four are emblematic descriptions of various defective or vicious characters in human nature,—the deisidæmonic, the ambitious, the amorous, or the insatiate and querulous man ; the two last represent the mental terrors of the wicked.

[2] Οἱ νῦν περὶ Ὅμηρον δεινοί—so Plato calls these interpreters (Kratylus, p. 407) ; see also Xenoph. Sympos. iii. 6 ; Plato, Ion, p. 530 ; Plutarch, De Audiend. Poet. p. 19. ὑπόνοια was the original word, afterwards succeeded by ἀλληγορία.

Ἥρας δὲ δεσμοὺς καὶ Ἡφαίστου ῥίψεις ὑπὸ πατρὸς, μέλλοντος τῇ μητρὶ τυπτομένῃ ἀμύνειν, καὶ θεομαχίας ὅσας Ὅμηρος πεποίηκεν, οὐ παραδεκτέον εἰς τὴν πόλιν, οὔτ' ἐν ὑπονοίαις πεποιημένας, οὔτ' ἄνευ ὑπονοιῶν. Ὁ γὰρ νέος οὐχ οἷός τε κρίνειν, ὅ,τι τε ὑπόνοια καὶ ὃ μὴ, ἀλλ' ἃ ἂν τηλικοῦτος ὢν λάβῃ ἐν ταῖς δόξαις, δυσέκνιπτά τε καὶ ἀμετάστατα φιλεῖ γίγνεσθαι (Plato, Republ. ii. 17, p. 378).

The idea of an interior sense and concealed purpose in the ancient poets occurs several times in Plato (Theætet. c. 83, p. 180) : παρὰ μὲν τῶν ἀρχαίων, μετὰ ποιήσεως ἐπικρυπτομένων τοὺς πολλούς, &c. ; also Protagor. c. 20, p. 316.

"Modo Stoicum Homerum faciunt,

as silly and undeserving of serious attention ; but as he proceeded he gradually arrived at the full conviction, that the ancient sages had designedly spoken in enigmatical language, and that there was valuable truth wrapped up in their narratives ; it was the duty of a pious man, therefore, to study and interpret, but not to reject, stories current and accredited respecting the gods.[1] And others,—arguing from the analogy of the religious mysteries, which could not be divulged without impiety to any except such as had been specially admitted and initiated,— maintained that it would be a profanation to reveal directly to the vulgar, the genuine scheme of nature and the divine administration : the ancient poets and philosophers had taken the only proper course, of talking to the many in types and parables, and reserving the naked truth for privileged and qualified intelligences.[2] The allegorical mode of explaining the ancient fables[3] became more and more popular in the third and

---

—modo Epicureum,—modo Peripateticum,—modo Academicum. Apparet nihil horum esse in illo, quia omnia sunt." (Seneca, Ep. 88.) Compare Plutarch, De Defectu Oracul. c. 11—12. t. ii. p. 702, Wytt., and Julian, Orat. vii. p. 216.

[1] Pausan. viii. 8, 2. To the same purpose (Strabo, x. p. 474), allegory is admitted to a certain extent in the fables by Dionys. Halic. Ant. Rom. ii. 20. The fragment of the lost treatise of Plutarch, on the Platæan festival of the Dædala, is very instructive respecting Grecian allegory (Fragm. ix. t. 5, p. 754—763, ed. Wyt. ; ap. Euseb. Præpar. Evang. iii. 1).

[2] This doctrine is set forth in Macrobius (i. 2). He distinguishes between *fabula*, and *fabulosa narratio* : the former is fiction pure, intended either to amuse or to instruct—the latter is founded upon truth, either respecting human or respecting divine agency. The gods did not like to be publicly talked of (according to his view) except under the respectful veil of a fable (the same feeling as that of Herodotus, which led him to refrain from inserting the *ἱεροὶ λόγοι* in his history). The supreme God, the *τἀγαθίν*, the *πρῶτον αἴτιον*, could not be talked of in fables ; but the other gods, the aërial or æthereal powers, and the soul, might be, and ought to be, talked of in that manner alone. Only superior intellects ought to be admitted to a knowledge

of the secret reality. " De Diis cæteris, et de animâ, non frustra se, nec ut oblectent, ad fabulosa convertunt ; sed quia sciunt *inimicam esse naturæ apertam nudamque expositionem sui* : quæ sicut vulgaribus sensibus hominum intellectum sui, vario rerum tegmine operimentoque, subtraxit ; ita à prudentibus arcana sua voluit per fabulosa tractari . . . . Adeo semper ita se et sciri et coli numina maluerunt, qualiter in vulgus antiquitas fabulata est . . . . Secundum hæc Pythagoras ipse atque Empedocles, Parmenides quoque et Heraclides, de Diis fabulati sunt : nec secus Timæus." Compare also Maximus Tyrius, Dissert. x. and xxii. Arnobius exposes the allegorical interpretation as mere evasion, and holds the Pagans to literal historical fact (Adv. Gentes, v. p. 185, ed. Elm.).

Respecting the allegorical interpretation applied to the Greek fables, Böttiger (Die Kunst-Mythologie der Griechen, Abschn. ii. p. 176); Nitzsch (Heldensage der Griech. sect. 6, p. 78); Lobeck (Aglaopham. p. 133—135).

[3] According to the anonymous writer, ap. Westermann (Script. Myth. p. 223), every personal or denominated god may be construed in three different ways : either *πραγματικῶς* (historically as having been a king or a man)—or *ψυχικῶς*, in which theory Hèrè signifies the *soul* ; Athênô, *prudence* ; Aphroditê, *desire* ; Zeus, *mind*, &c.—or *στοιχειακῶς*, in which system Apollo signifies the

fourth centuries after the Christian æra, especially among the new Platonic philosophers; being both congenial to their orientalized turn of thought, and useful as a shield against the attacks of the Christians.

It was from the same strong necessity, of accommodating the old mythes to a new standard both of belief and of appreciation, that both the historical and the allegorical schemes of transforming them arose; the literal narrative being decomposed for the purpose of arriving at a base either of particular matter of fact, or of general physical or moral truth. Instructed men were

Divine legends allegorised. Heroic legends historicised.

sun; Poseidôn, the *sea*; Hêrê, the upper stratum of the air, or *œther*; Athênê, the lower or denser stratum; Zeus, the upper hemisphere; Kronus, the lower, &c. This writer thinks that all the three principles of construction may be resorted to, each on its proper occasion, and that neither of them excludes the others. It will be seen that the first is pure Euemerism; the two latter are modes of allegory.

The allegorical construction of the gods and of the divine mythes is copiously applied in the treatises, both of Phurnutus and Sallustius, in Gale's collection of mythological writers. Sallustius treats the mythes as of divine origin, and the chief poets as inspired (θεόληπτοι): the gods were propitious to those who recounted worthy and creditable mythes respecting them, and Sallustius prays that they will accept with favour his own remarks (cap. 3 and 4, pp. 245—251, Gale). He distributes mythes into five classes: theological, physical, spiritual, material, and mixed. He defends the practice of speaking of the gods under the veil of allegory, much in the same way as Macrobius (in the preceding note): he finds, moreover, a good excuse even for those mythes which imputed to the gods theft, adultery, outrages towards a father, and other enormities: such tales (he says) were eminently suitable, since the mind *must at once see* that the facts as told are *not* to be taken as being themselves the real truth, but simply as a veil disguising some interior truth (p. 247).

Besides the life of Homer ascribed to Plutarch (see Gale, p. 325—332), Hêraclidês (*not* Hêraclidês of Pontus) carries out the process of allegorising the Homeric mythes most earnestly and most systematically. The application of the allegorising theory is, in his view, the only way of rescuing Homer from the charge of scandalous impiety—πάντη γὰρ ἠσέβησεν, εἰ μηδὲν ἠλληγόρησεν (Hêrac. *in init.* p. 407, Gale). He proves at length, that the destructive arrows of Apollo, in the first book of the Iliad, mean nothing at the bottom except a contagious plague, caused by the heat of the summer sun in marshy ground (pp. 416—424). Athênê, who darts down from Olympus at the moment when Achilles is about to draw his sword on Agamemnôn, and seizes him by the hair, is a personification of repentant prudence (p. 435). The conspiracy against Zeus, which Homer (Iliad. i. 400) relates to have been formed by the Olympic gods, and defeated by the timely aid of Thetis and Briareus—the chains and suspension imposed upon Hêrê—the casting of Hêphæstos by Zeus out of Olympus, and his fall in Lêmnus—the destruction of the Grecian wall by Poseidôn, after the departure of the Greeks—the amorous scene between Zeus and Hêrê on mount Gargarus—the distribution of the universe between Zeus, Poseidôn, and Hadês—all these he resolves into peculiar manifestations and conflicts of the elemental substances in nature. To the much-decried battle of the gods he gives a turn partly physical, partly ethical (p. 481). In like manner he transforms and vindicates the adventures of the gods in the Odyssey: the wanderings of Odysseus, together with the Lotophagi, the Cyclôps, Circê, the Sirens, Æolus, Scylla, &c., he resolves into a series of temptations, imposed as a trial upon a man of

commonly disposed to historicise only the heroic legends, and
to allegorise more or less of the divine legends : the attempt
of Euêmerus to historicise the latter was for the most part
denounced as irreligious, while that of Metrodôrus to allegorise
the former met with no success. In allegorising moreover even
the divine legends, it was usual to apply the scheme of allegory
only to the inferior gods, though some of the great Stoic
philosophers carried it farther and allegorised all the separate
personal gods, leaving only an all-pervading cosmic Mind,[1]
essential as a co-efficient along with Matter, yet not separable
from Matter. But many pious pagans seem to have perceived
that allegory pushed to this extent was fatal to all living religious
faith,[2] inasmuch as it divested the gods of their character of
Persons, sympathising with mankind and modifiable in their
dispositions according to the conduct and prayers of
the believer : and hence they permitted themselves
to employ allegorical interpretation only to some of
the obnoxious legends connected with the superior gods, leaving
the personality of the latter unimpeached.

Limits to
this inter-
preting
process.

One novelty, however, introduced seemingly by the philosopher
Empedoklês and afterwards expanded by others, deserves notice,
inasmuch as it modified considerably the old religious creed by
drawing a pointed contrast between gods and dæmons,—a
distinction hardly at all manifested in Homer, but recognised in
the Works and Days of Hesiod.[3] Empedoklês widened the gap
between the two, and founded upon it important consequences.
The gods were good, immortal and powerful agents, having volition and intelligence, but without appetite, passion or infirmity ;

wisdom and virtue, and emblematic
of human life (p. 496). The story of
Arês, Aphroditê, and Hêphæstos, in
the eighth book of the Odyssey, seems
to perplex him more than any other :
he offers two explanations, neither
of which seems satisfactory even to
himself (p. 494).

[1] See Ritter, Geschichte der Philosophie, 2nd edit., part 3, book 11,
chap. 4, p. 592 ; Varro ap. Augustin.
Civitat. Dei, vi. 5, ix. 6 ; Cicero, Nat.
Deor. ii. 24—28.

Chrysippus admitted the most important distinction between Zeus and
the other gods (Plutarch. de Stoicor.

Repugnant. p. 1052).

[2] Plutarch, de Isid. et Osirid. c. 66,
p. 377 ; c. 70, p. 379. Compare on this
subject O. Müller, Prolegom. Mythol.
p. 59 *seq.*, and Eckermann, Lehrbuch
der Religionsgeschichte, vol. i. sect. ii.
p. 46.

[3] Hesiod. Opp. et Di. 122 : to the
same effect Pythagoras and Thalês
(Diogen. Laërt. viii. 32 ; and Plutarch,
Placit. Philos. i. 8).

The Hesiodic dæmons are all good :
Athenagoras (Legat. Chr. p. 8) says
that Thalês admitted a distinction
between good and bad dæmons, which
seems very doubtful.

the dæmons were of a mixed nature between gods and men, ministers and interpreters from the former to the latter, but invested also with an agency and dispositions of their own. Though not immortal, they were still long-lived, and subject to the passions and propensities of men, so that there were among them beneficent and maleficent dæmons with every shade of intermediate difference.[1] It had been the mistake (according to these philosophers) of the old mythes to ascribe to the gods proceedings really belonging to the dæmons, who were always the immediate communicants with mortal nature, inspiring prophetic power to the priestesses of the oracles, sending dreams and omens, and perpetually interfering either for good or for

Distinction between gods and dæmons—altered and widened by Empedoklês.

---

[1] The distinction between Θεοί and Δαίμονες is especially set forth in the treatise of Plutarch, De Defectu Oraculorum, capp. 10, 12, 13, 15, &c. He seems to suppose it traceable to the doctrine of Zoroaster or the Orphic mysteries, and he represents it as relieving the philosopher from great perplexities; for it was difficult to know where to draw the line in admitting or rejecting Providence: errors were committed sometimes in affirming God to be the cause of everything, at other times in snpposing him to be the cause of nothing. Ἐπεὶ τὸ διορίσαι πῶς χρηστέον καὶ μέχρι τινων τῇ προνοίᾳ, χαλεπόν, οἱ μὲν οὐδενὸς ἁπλῶς τὸν θεὸν, οἱ δὲ ὁμοῦ τι πάντων αἴτιον ποιοῦντες, ἀστοχοῦσι τοῦ μετρίου καὶ πρέποντος. Εὖ μὲν οὖν λέγουσιν οἱ λέγοντες, ὅτι Πλάτων τὸ ταῖς γεννωμέναις ποιότησιν ὑποκείμενον στοιχεῖον ἐξευρὼν, ὃ νῦν ὕλην καὶ φύσιν καλοῦσιν, πολλῶν ἀπήλλαξε καὶ μεγάλων ἀποριῶν τοὺς φιλοσόφους· ἐμοὶ δὲ δοκοῦσι πλείονας λῦσαι καὶ μείζονας ἀπορίας οἱ τὸ τῶν δαιμόνων γένος ἐν μέσῳ θεῶν καὶ ἀνθρώπων, καὶ τρόπον τινὰ τὴν κοινωνίαν ἡμῶν σύναγον εἰς ταὐτὸ καὶ σύναπτον, ἐξευρόντες (c. 10). Ἡ δαιμόνων φύσις ἔχουσα καὶ πάθος θνητοῦ καὶ θεοῦ δύναμιν (c. 13). Εἰσὶ γὰρ, ὡς ἐν ἀνθρώποις, καὶ δαίμοσιν ἀρετῆς διαφοραὶ, καὶ τοῦ παθητικοῦ καὶ ἀλόγου τοῖς μὲν ἀσθενὲς καὶ ἀμαυρὸν ἔτι λείψανον, ὥσπερ περίττωμα, τοῖς δὲ πολὺ καὶ δυσκατάσβεστον ἔνεστιν, ὧν ἴχνη καὶ σύμβολα πολλαχοῦ θύσιαι καὶ τελεταί καὶ μυθολογίαι σώζουσι καὶ διαφυλάττουσιν ἐνδιεσπαρμένα (ib.): compare Plutarch. de Isid. et Osir. 25. p. 360.

Καὶ μὴν ὅσας ἔν τε μύθοις καὶ ὕμνοις λέγουσι καὶ ᾅδουσι, τοῦτο μὲν ἁρπαγὰς, τοῦτο δὲ πλάνας θεῶν, κρύψεις τε καὶ φυγὰς καὶ λατρείας, οὐ θεῶν εἰσὶν ἀλλὰ δαιμόνων παθήματα, &c. (c. 15); also c. 23; also de Isid. et Osir. c. 25, p. 366.

Human sacrifices and other objectionable rites are excused, as necessary for the purpose of averting the anger of bad dæmons (c. 14—15).

Empedoklês is represented as the first author of the doctrine which imputed vicious and abominable disposition to many of the dæmons (c. 15, 16, 17, 20), τοὺς εἰσαγομένους ὑπὸ Ἐμπεδοκλέους δαίμονας; expelled from heaven by the gods, θεήλατοι καὶ οὐρανοπετείς (Plutarch, De Vitand. Aër. Alien. p. 830); followed by Plato, Xenokratês and Chrysippus, c. 17: compare Plato (Apolog. Socrat. p. 27; Politic. p. 721; Symposion, c. 28, p. 203), though he seems to treat the δαίμονες as defective and mutable beings, rather than actively maleficent. Xenokratês represents some of them both as wicked and powerful in a high degree:— Ξενοκράτης καὶ τῶν ἡμερῶν τὰς ἀποφράδας, καὶ τῶν ἑορτῶν ὅσαι πληγάς τινας ἢ κοπετοὺς, ἢ νηστείας, ἢ δυσφημίας, ἢ αἰσχρολογίαν ἔχουσιν, οὔτε θεῶν τιμαῖς οὔτε δαιμόνων οἴεται προσήκειν χρηστῶν, ἀλλ' εἶναι φύσεις ἐν τῷ περιέχοντι μεγάλας μὲν καὶ ἰσχυρὰς, δυστρόπους δὲ καὶ σκυθρωπάς, αἳ χαίρουσι τοῖς τοιούτοις, καὶ τυγχάνουσαι πρὸς οὐθὲν ἄλλο χεῖρον τρέπονται (Plutarch, De Isid. et Osir. c. 26, p. 361; Quæstion. Rom. p. 283); compare Stobæus, Eclog. Phys. i. p. 62

evil. The wicked and violent dæmons, having committed many enormities, had thus sometimes incurred punishment from the gods : besides which, their bad dispositions had imposed upon men the necessity of appeasing them by religious ceremonies of a kind acceptable to such beings ;—hence the human sacrifices, the violent, cruel, and obscene exhibitions, the wailings and fastings, the tearing and eating of raw flesh, which it had become customary to practise on various consecrated occasions, and especially in the Dionysiac solemnities. Moreover, the discreditable actions imputed to the gods,—the terrific combats, the Typhonic and Titanic convulsions, the rapes, abductions, flight, servitude, and concealment,—all these were really the doings and sufferings of bad dæmons, placed far below the sovereign agency—equable, undisturbed and unpolluted—of the immortal gods. The action of such dæmons upon mankind was fitful and intermittent : they sometimes perished or changed their local abode, so that oracles which had once been inspired became after a time forsaken and disfranchised.[1]

This distinction between gods and dæmons appeared to save in

Admission of dæmons as partially evil beings —effect of such admission.

a great degree both the truth of the old legends and the dignity of the gods : it obviated the necessity of pronouncing either that the gods were unworthy, or the legends untrue. Yet although devised for the purpose of satisfying a more scrupulous religious sensibility, it was found inconvenient afterwards when assailants arose against paganism generally. For while it abandoned as indefensible a large portion of what had once been genuine faith, it still retained the same word *dæmons* with an entirely altered signification. The Christian writers in their controversies found ample warrant among the *earlier* pagan authors[2] for treating all

---

[1] Plutarch, De Defect. Orac. c. 15. p. 418.   Chrysippus admitted, among the various conceivable causes to account for the existence of evil, the supposition of some negligent and reckless dæmons, δαιμόνια φαυλὰ ἐν οἷς τῷ ὄντι γίνονται καὶ ἐγκλητέαι ἀμέλειαι (Plutarch, De Stoicor. Repugnant. p. 1051). A distinction, which I do not fully understand, between θεοί and δαίμονες, was also adopted among the Lokrians at Opus : δαίμων with them seems to have been equivalent to ἥρως

(Plutarch, Quæstion. Græc. c. 6, p. 292) : see the note above.

[2] Tatian. adv. Græcos, c. 20 ; Clemens Alexandrin. Admonit. ad Gentes, pp. 26—29, Sylb. ; Minuc. Felix, Octav. c. 26.   " Isti igitur impuri spiritus, ut ostensum a Magis, a philosophis, a Platone, sub statuis et imaginibus consecrati delitescunt, et afflatu suo quasi auctoritatem præsentis numinis consequuntur," &c.   This, like so many other of the aggressive arguments of the Christians against paganism, was

the gods as dæmons—and not less ample warrant among the *later* pagans for denouncing the dæmons generally as evil beings.[1]

Such were the different modes in which the ancient mythes were treated, during the literary life of Greece, by the four classes above named—poets, logographers, historians and philosophers.

Literal acceptance, and unconscious, uninquiring faith, such as they had obtained from the original auditors to whom they were addressed, they now found only among the multitude—alike retentive of traditional feeling[2] and fearful of criticising the proceedings of the gods.[3] But with instructed men they became rather subjects of respectful and curious analysis—all agreeing that the Word as tendered to them was inadmissible, yet all equally convinced that it contained important meaning, though hidden yet not undiscoverable. A very large proportion of the

taken from the pagan philosophers themselves.

Lactantius, De Verâ Philosophiâ, iv. 28. "Ergo iidem sunt Dæmones, quos fatentur execrandos esse: iidem Dii, quibus supplicant. Si nobis credendum esse non putant, credant Homero; qui summum illum Jovem Dæmonibus aggregavit," &c.

[1] See above, Chapter II., the remarks on the Hesiodic Theogony.

[2] A destructive inundation took place at Pheneus in Arcadia, seemingly in the time of Plutarch: the subterranean outlet (βάραθρον) of the river had become blocked up, and the inhabitants ascribed the stoppage to the anger of Apollo, who had been provoked by the stealing of the Pythian tripod by Hêraklês: the latter had carried the tripod to Pheneus and deposited it there. Ἄρ᾽ οὖν οὐκ ἀτοπώτερος τούτων ὁ Ἀπόλλων, εἰ Φενεάτας ἀπόλλυσι τοὺς νῦν, ἐμφράξας τὸ βάραθρον, καὶ κυτακλύσας τὴν χώραν ἅπασαν αὐτῶν, ὅτι πρὸ χιλίων ἐτῶν, ὥς φασιν, ὁ Ἡρακλῆς ἀνασπάσας τὸν τρίποδα τὸν μαντικὸν εἰς Φενεὸν ἀπήνεγκε; (Plutarch, de Serâ Numin. Vindictâ, p. 557; compare Pausan. viii. 14, 1). The expression of Plutarch that the abstraction of the tripod by Hêraklês had taken place 1000 years before, is that of the critic, who thinks it needful to historicise and chronologise the genuine legend; which, to an inhabitant of Pheneus at the time of the inundation, was doubtless as little questioned as if the theft of Hêraklês had been laid in the preceding generation.

Agathoclês of Syracuse committed depredations on the coasts of Ithaca and Korkyra: the excuse which he offered was, that Odysseus had come to Sicily and blinded Polyphêmus, and that on his return he had been kindly received by the Phæakians (Plutarch, *ib.*).

This is doubtless a jest, either made by Agathoclês, or more probably invented for him; but it is founded upon a popular belief.

[3] "Sanctiusque et reverentius visum, de actis Deorum credere quam scire." (Tacit. German. c. 34.)

Aristidês however represents the Homeric theology (whether he would have included the Hesiodic we do not know) as believed quite literally among the multitude in his time, the second century after Christianity (Aristid. Orat. iii. p. 25). Ἀπορῶ, ὅπη πότε χρή με διαθέσθαι μεθ᾽ ὑμῶν, πότερα ὡς τοῖς πολλοῖς δοκεῖ καὶ Ὁμήρῳ δὲ συνδοκεῖ, θεῶν παθήματα συμπεισθῆναι καὶ ἡμᾶς, οἷον Ἄρεος δέσμα καὶ Ἀπόλλωνος θητείας καὶ Ἡφαίστου ῥίψεις εἰς θάλασσαν, οὕτω δὲ καὶ Ἰνοῦς ἄχη καὶ φυγάς τινας. Compare Lucian, Ζεὺς Τραγῳδός, c. 20, and De Luctu, c. 2; Dionys. Halicar. A. R. ii. p. 90, Sylb.

Kallimachus (Hymn. ad Jov. 9) distinctly denied the statement of the Kretans that they possessed in Krête the tomb of Zeus, and treated it as an instance of Kretan mendacity; while Celsus did not deny it, but explained it in some figurative manner—αἰνιττόμενος τροπικὰς ὑπονοίας (Origen. cont. Celsum, iii. p. 137).

force of Grecian intellect was engaged in searching after this unknown base, by guesses, in which sometimes the principle of semi-historical interpretation was assumed, sometimes that of allegorical, without any collateral evidence in either case, and without possibility of verification. Out of the one assumption grew a string of allegorised phænomenal truths, out of the other a long series of seeming historical events and chronological persons,—both elicited from the transformed mythes and from nothing else.

The utmost which we accomplish by means of the semi-historical theory even in its most successful applications, is, that after leaving out from the mythical narrative all that is miraculous or high-coloured or extravagant, we arrive at a series of creditable incidents— incidents which *may, perhaps,* have really occurred, and against which no intrinsic presumption can be raised. This is exactly the character of a well-written modern novel (as, for example, several among the compositions of Defoe), the whole story of which is such as may well have occurred in real life : it is plausible fiction and nothing beyond. To raise plausible fiction up to the superior dignity of truth, some positive testimony or positive ground of inference must be shown ; even the highest measure of intrinsic probability is not alone sufficient. A man who tells us that on the day of the battle of Platæa, rain fell on the spot of ground where the city of New York now stands, will neither deserve nor obtain credit, because he can have had no means of positive knowledge ; though the statement is not in the slightest degree improbable. On the other hand, statements in themselves very improbable may well deserve belief, provided they be supported by sufficient positive evidence. Thus the canal dug by order of Xerxes across the promontory of Mount Athos, and the sailing of the Persian fleet through it, is a fact which I believe, because it is well-attested.—notwithstanding its remarkable improbability, which so far misled Juvenal as to induce him to single out the narrative as a glaring example of Grecian mendacity.[1] Again many critics have observed that the

Semi-historical interpretation.

---

[1] Juvenal, Sat. x. 174 :—
  " Creditur olim
Velificatus Athos, et quantum Græcia mendax
Audet in historiâ," &c.

general tale of the Trojan war (apart from the superhuman agencies) is not more improbable than that of the crusades, which every one admits to be an historical fact.   But (even if we grant this position, which is only true to a small extent), it is not sufficient to show an analogy between the two cases in respect to negative presumptions alone ; the analogy ought to be shown to hold between them in respect to positive certificate also.   The crusades are a curious phænomenon in history, but we accept them nevertheless as an unquestionable fact, because the antecedent improbability is surmounted by adequate contemporary testimony.   When the like testimony, both in amount and kind, is produced to establish the historical reality of the Trojan war, we shall not hesitate to deal with the two events on the same footing.

In applying the semi-historical theory to Grecian mythical narrative, it has been often forgotten that a certain strength of testimony, or positive ground of belief, must first be tendered, before we can be called upon to discuss the antecedent probability or improbability of the incidents alleged.   The belief of the Greeks themselves, without the smallest aid of special or contemporary witnesses, has been tacitly assumed as sufficient to support the case, provided only sufficient deduction be made from the mythical narratives to remove all antecedent improbabilities.   It has been taken for granted that the faith of the people must have rested originally upon some particular historical event involving the identical persons, things and places which the original mythes exhibit, or at least the most prominent among them.   But when we examine the psychagogic influences predominant in the society among whom this belief originally grew up, we shall see that their belief is of little or no evidentiary value, and that the growth and diffusion of it may be satisfactorily explained without supposing any special basis of matters of fact.   The popular faith, so far as it counts for anything, testifies in favour of the entire and literal mythes, which are now universally rejected as incredible.[1]   We

Some positive certificate indispensable as a constituent of historical proof— mere popular faith insufficient.

---

[1] Colonel Sleeman observes respecting the Hindoo historical mind— "History to this people is all a fairy tale" (Rambles and Recollections of an Indian Official, vol. i. ch. ix. p. 70). And again, " The popular poem of the Ramaen describes the abduction of the heroine by the monster king of

have thus the very minimum of positive proof, and the maximum of negative presumption: we may diminish the latter by conjectural omissions and interpolations, but we cannot by any artifice increase the former: the narrative ceases to be incredible, but it still remains uncertified,—a mere common-place possibility. Nor is fiction always, or essentially, extravagant and incredible. It is often not only plausible and coherent, but even more like truth (if a paradoxical phrase may be allowed) than truth itself. Nor can we, in the absence of any extrinsic test, reckon upon any intrinsic mark to discriminate the one from the other.[1]

Ceylon, Rawun ; and her recovery by means of the monkey general Hunnooman. Every word of this poem the people assured me was written, if not by the hand of the Deity himself, at least by his inspiration, which was the same thing—and it must consequently be true. Ninety-nine out of a hundred, among the Hindoos, implicitly believe, not only every word of the poem, but every word of every poem that has ever been written in Sanscrit. If you ask a man whether he really believes any very egregious absurdity quoted from these books, he replies, with the greatest *naïveté* in the world : Is it not written in the book, and how should it be there written, if not true? The Hindoo religion reposes upon an entire prostration of mind,—that continual and habitual surrender of the reasoning faculties, which we are accustomed to make occasionally, while engaged at the theatre, or in the perusal of works of fiction. We allow the scenes, characters, and incidents, to pass before our mind's eye, and move our feelings—without stopping a moment to ask whether they are real or true. There is only this difference—that with people of education among us, even in such short intervals of illusion or *abandon*, any extravagance in the acting, or flagrant improbability in the fiction, destroys the charm, breaks the spell by which we have been so mysteriously bound, and restores us to reason and the realities of ordinary life. With the Hindoos, on the contrary, the greater the improbability, the more monstrous and preposterous the fiction—the greater is the charm it has over their minds ; and the greater their learning in the Sanscrit, the more are they under the influence of this charm. Believing all to be written

by the Deity, or under his inspirations, and the men and things of former days to have been very different from men and things of the present day, and the heroes of these fables to have been demigods, or people endowed with powers far superior to those of the ordinary men of their own day—the analogies of nature are never for a moment considered : nor do questions of probability, or possibility, according to those analogies, ever obtrude to dispel the charm with which they are so pleasingly bound. They go on through life reading and talking of these monstrous fictions, which shock the taste and understanding of other nations, without ever questioning the truth of one single incident, or hearing it questioned. There was a time, and that not far distant, when it was the same in England, and in every other European nation ; and there are, I am afraid, some parts of Europe where it is so still. But the Hindoo faith, so far as religious questions are concerned, is not more capacious or absurd than that of the Greeks or Romans in the days of Socrates or Cicero ; the only difference is, that among the Hindoos a greater number of the questions which interest mankind are brought under the head of religion." (Sleeman, Rambles, &c., vol. i. ch. xxvi. p. .227 : compare vol. ii. ch. v. p. 51 ; viii. p. 97).

[1] Lord Littelton, in commenting on the tales of the Irish bards, in his History of Henry II., has the following just remarks (book iv. vol. iii. p. 13, quarto): "One may reasonably suppose that in MSS. written since the Irish received the Roman letters from St. Patrick, *some* traditional truths recorded before by the bards in their unwritten poems may have been

In the semi-historical theory respecting Grecian mythical narrative, the critic unconsciously transports into the Homeric age those habits of classification and distinction, and that standard of acceptance or rejection, which he finds current in his own. Amongst us the distinction between historical fact and fiction is highly valued as well as familiarly understood : we have a long history of the past, deduced from a study of contemporary evidences ; and we have a body of fictitious literature, stamped with its own mark and interesting in its own way. But this *historical sense*, now so deeply rooted in the modern mind that we find a difficulty in conceiving any people to be without it, is the fruit of records and inquiries first applied to the present, and then preserved and studied by subsequent generations ; while in a society which has not yet formed the habit of recording its present, the real facts of the past can never be known ; the difference between attested matter of fact and plausible fiction— between truth and that which is like truth—can neither be discerned nor sought for. Yet it is precisely upon the supposition that this distinction is present to men's habitual thoughts, that the semi-historical theory of the mythes is grounded.

Mistake of ascribing to an unrecording age the historical sense of modern times.

It is perfectly true, as has often been stated, that the Grecian epic contains what are called traditions respecting the past—the larger portion of it indeed consists of nothing else. But what are these traditions ? They are the matter of those songs and stories which have acquired hold on the public mind ; they are the creations of the poets and

Matter of tradition uncertified from the beginning.

preserved to our times. Yet these cannot be so separated from many fabulous stories derived from the same sources, as to obtain a firm credit ; it not being sufficient to establish the authority of suspected traditions, that they can be shown not to be so improbable or absurd as others with which they are mixed—*since there may be specious as well as senseless fictions.* Nor can a poet or bard, who lived in the sixth or seventh century after Christ, if his poem is still extant, be any voucher for facts supposed to have happened before the incarnation ; though his evidence (allowing for poetical licence) may be received on such matters as come within his own time, or the remembrance of old men with whom he conversed. The most judicious historians pay no regard to the Welch or British traditions delivered by Geoffrey of Monmouth, though it is not impossible but that some of these may be true."

One definition of a mythe given by Plutarch coincides exactly with a *specious fiction* : Ὁ μῦθος εἶναι βούλεται λόγος ψευδὴς ἐοικὼς ἀληθινῷ (Plutarch, Bellone an pace clariores fuerunt Athenienses, p. 348).

" Der Grund-Trieb des Mythus (Creuzer justly expresses it) das Gedachte in ein Geschehenes umzusetzen." (Symbolik der Alten Welt, sect. 43, p. 99.)

storytellers themselves, each of whom finds some pre-existing, and adds others of his own, new and previously untold, under the impulse and authority of the inspiring Muse. Homer doubtless found many songs and stories current with respect to the siege of Troy ; he received and transmitted some of these traditions, recast and transformed others, and enlarged the whole mass by new creations of his own. To the subsequent poets, such as Arktinus and Leschês, these Homeric creations formed portions of pre-existing tradition, with which they dealt in the same manner ; so that the whole mass of traditions constituting the tale of Troy became larger and larger with each successive contributor. To assume a generic difference between the older and the newer strata of tradition—to treat the former as morsels of history, and the latter as appendages of fiction—is an hypothesis gratuitous at the least, not to say inadmissible. For the farther we travel back into the past, the more do we recede from the clear day of positive history, and the deeper do we plunge into the unsteady twilight and gorgeous clouds of fancy and feeling. It was one of the agreeable dreams of the Grecian epic, that the man who travelled far enough northward beyond the Rhipæan mountains, would in time reach the delicious country and genial climate of the virtuous Hyperboreans—the votaries and favourites of Apollo, who dwelt in the extreme north beyond the chilling blasts of Boreas. Now the hope that we may, by carrying our researches up the stream of time, exhaust the limits of fiction, and land ultimately upon some points of solid truth, appears to me no less illusory than this northward journey in quest of the Hyperborean elysium.

The general disposition to adopt the semi-historical theory as to the genesis of Grecian mythes, arises in part from reluctance in critics to impute to the mythopœic ages extreme credulity or fraud; together with the usual presumption, that where much is believed some portion of it must be true. There would be some weight in these grounds of reasoning, if the ages under discussion had been supplied with records and accustomed to critical inquiry. But amongst a people unprovided with the former and strangers to the latter, credulity is naturally at its maximum, as well in the narrator himself as in his hearers. The idea of deliberate fraud

Fictitious matter of tradition does not imply fraud or imposture.

is moreover inapplicable,[1] for if the hearers are disposed to accept what is related to them as a revelation from the Muse, the *œstrus* of composition is quite sufficient to impart a similar persuasion to the poet whose mind is penetrated with it. The belief of that day can hardly be said to stand apart by itself as an act of reason. It becomes confounded with vivacious imagination and earnest emotion ; and in every case where these mental excitabilities are powerfully acted upon, faith ensues unconsciously and as a matter of course. How active and prominent such tendencies were among the early Greeks, the extraordinary beauty and originality of their epic poetry may teach us.

It is, besides, a presumption far too largely and indiscriminately applied, even in our own advanced age, that where much is believed, something must necessarily be true—that accredited fiction is always traceable to some basis of historical truth.[2] The influence of imagination and feeling is not confined simply to the process of retouching, transforming, or magnifying narratives originally founded on fact ; it will often create new narratives of its own, without any such preliminary basis. Where there is any general body of sentiment pervading men living in society, whether it be religious or political—love, admiration or antipathy— all incidents tending to illustrate that sentiment are eagerly welcomed, rapidly circulated and (as a general rule) easily accredited. If real incidents are not at hand, impressive fictions will be provided to satisfy the demand. The perfect harmony of such fictions with the prevalent

Plausible fiction often generated and accredited by the mere force of strong and common sentiment, even in times of instruction.

---

[1] In reference to the loose statements of the Highlanders, Dr. Johnson observes—"He that goes into the Highlands with a mind naturally acquiescent, and a credulity eager for wonders, may perhaps come back with an opinion very different from mine ; for the inhabitants, knowing the ignorance of all strangers, in their language and antiquities, are perhaps not very scrupulous adherents to truth : yet I do not say that they deliberately speak studied falsehood, or have a settled purpose to deceive. They have acquired and considered little, and do not always feel their own ignorance. They are not much accustomed to be interrogated by others, and seem never to have thought of interrogating themselves ; *so that if they do not know what they tell to be true, they likewise do not distinctly perceive it to be false.* Mr. Boswell was very diligent in his inquiries, and the result of his investigations was, that the answer to the second question was commonly such as nullified the answer to the first." (Journey to the Western Islands, p. 272, 1st edit. 1775).

[2] I considered this position more at large in an article in the "Westminster Review" for May, 1843, on Niebuhr's Greek Legends, with which article much in the present chapter will be found to coincide.

feeling stands in the place of certifying testimony, and causes men to hear them not merely with credence, but even with delight. To call them in question and require proof is a task which cannot be undertaken without incurring obloquy. Of such tendencies in the human mind abundant evidence is furnished by the innumerable religious legends which have acquired currency in various parts of the world, and of which no country was more fertile than Greece—legends which derived their origin, not from special facts misreported and exaggerated, but from pious feelings pervading the society, and translated into narrative by forward and imaginative minds—legends, in which not merely the incidents, but often even the personages are unreal, yet in which the generating sentiment is conspicuously discернible, providing its own matter as well as its own form. Other sentiments also, as well as the religious, provided they be fervent and widely diffused, will find expression in current narrative, and become portions of the general public belief. Every celebrated and notorious character is the source of a thousand fictions exemplifying his peculiarities. And if it be true, as I think present observation may show us, that such creative agencies are even now visible and effective, when the materials of genuine history are copious and critically studied—much more are we warranted in concluding that in ages destitute of records, strangers to historical testimony, and full of belief in divine inspiration both as to the future and as to the past, narratives purely fictitious will acquire ready and uninquiring credence, provided only they be plausible and in harmony with the preconceptions of the auditors.

The allegorical interpretation of the mythes has been by several learned investigators, especially by Creuzer, connected with the hypothesis of an ancient and highly instructed body of priests, having their origin either in Egypt or in the East, and communicating to the rude and barbarous Greeks religious, physical and historical knowledge under the veil of symbols. At a time (we are told) when language was yet in its infancy, visible symbols were the most vivid means of acting upon the minds of ignorant hearers: the next step was to pass to symbolical language and expressions—for a plain and literal exposition,

Allegorical theory of the mythes —traced by some up to an ancient priestly caste.

even if understood at all, would at least have been listened to with indifference, as not corresponding with any mental demand.   In such allegorising way, then, the early priests set forth their doctrines respecting God, nature and humanity—a refined monotheism and a theological philosophy—and to this purpose the earliest mythes were turned.   But another class of mythes, more popular and more captivating, grew up under the hands of the poets—mythes purely epical, and descriptive of real or supposed past events.   The allegorical mythes, being taken up by the poets, insensibly became confounded in the same category with the purely narrative mythes—the matter symbolised was no longer thought of, while the symbolising words came to be construed in their own literal meaning—and the basis of the early allegory, thus lost among the general public, was only preserved as a secret among various religious fraternities, composed of members allied together by initiation in certain mystical ceremonies, and administered by hereditary families of presiding priests.   In the Orphic and Bacchic sects, in the Eleusinian and Samothracian mysteries, was thus treasured up the secret doctrine of the old theological and philosophical mythes, which had once constituted the primitive legendary stock of Greece, in the hands of the original priesthood and in ages anterior to Homer.   Persons who had gone through the preliminary ceremonies of initiation were permitted at length to hear, though under strict obligation of secrecy, this ancient religious and cosmogonic doctrine, revealing the destination of men and the certainty of posthumous rewards and punishments—all disengaged from the corruptions of poets, as well as from the symbols and allegories under which they still remained buried in the eyes of the vulgar. The mysteries of Greece were thus traced up to the earliest ages, and represented as the only faithful depositary channels of that purer theology and physics which had originally been communicated, though under the unavoidable inconvenience of a symbolical expression, by an enlightened priesthood coming from abroad to the then rude barbarians of the country.[1]

Real import of the mythes supposed to be preserved in the religious mysteries.

[1] For this general character of the Grecian mysteries with their concealed treasure of doctrine, see *Warburton*, Divine Legation of Moses, book ii. sect. 4.
       Payne Knight, On the Symbolical

But this theory, though advocated by several learned men, has been shown to be unsupported and erroneous. It implies a

Language of ancient Art and Mythology, sect. 6, 10, 11, 40, &c.

Saint Croix, Recherches sur les Mystères du Paganisme, sect. 3, p. 103 ; sect. 4, p. 404, &c.

Creuzer, Symbolik und Mythologie der Alten Völker, sect. 2, 3, 23, 39, 42, &c. Meiners and Heeren adopt generally the same view, though there are many divergencies of opinion between these different authors, on a subject essentially obscure. Warburton maintained that the interior doctrine communicated in the mysteries was the existence of one Supreme Divinity, combined with the Euemeristic creed, that the pagan gods had been mere men. See Clemens Alex. Strom. v. p. 592, Sylb.

The view taken by Hermann of the ancient Grecian Mythology is in many points similar to that of Creuzer, though with some considerable difference. He thinks that it is an aggregate of doctrine —philosophical, theological, physical, and moral—expressed under a scheme of systematic personifications, each person being called by a name significant of the function personified : this doctrine was imported from the East into Greece, where the poets, retaining or translating the names, but forgetting their meaning and connexion, distorted the primitive stories, the sense of which came to be retained only in the ancient mysteries. That true sense, however (he thinks), may be recovered by a careful analysis of the significant names : and his two dissertations (De Mythologiâ Græcorum Antiquissimâ, in the Opuscula, vol. ii.) exhibit a specimen of this systematic expansion of etymology into narrative. The dissent from Creuzer is set forth in their published correspondence, especially in his concluding "Brief an Creuzer über das Wesen und die Behandlung der Mythologie," Leipzig, 1819. The following citation from his Latin dissertation sets forth his general doctrine :

Hermann, De Mythologiâ Græcorum Antiquissimâ, p. 4. (Opuscula, vol. ii. p. 171):—"Videmus rerum divinarum humanarumque scientiam ex Asiâ per Lyciam migrantem in Europam : videmus fabulosos poëtas peregrinam doctrinam, monstruoso tumore orientis sive exutam, sive nondum indutam, quasi de integro Græcâ specie pro-

creantes ; videmus poëtas illos, quorum omnium vera nomina nominibus—ab arte, quâ clarebant, petitis—obliterata sunt, diu in Thraciâ hærentes, raroque tandem etiam cum aliis Græciæ partibus commercio junctos : qualis Pamphus, non ipse Atheniensis, Atheniensibus hymnos Deorum fecit. Videmus denique retrusam paulatim in mysteriorum secretam illam sapientum doctrinam, vitiatam religionum perturbatione, corruptam inscitiâ interpretum, obscuratam levitate amœniora sectantium—adeo ut eam ne illi quidem intelligerent, qui hæreditariam a prioribus poësin colentes, quum ingenii præstantiâ omnes præstinguerent, tantâ illos oblivione merserunt, ut ipsi sint primi auctores omnis eruditionis habiti."

Hermann thinks, however, that by pursuing the suggestions of etymology, vestiges may still be discovered, and something like a history compiled, of Grecian belief as it stood anterior to Homer and Hesiod :—"est autem in hac omni ratione judicio maxime opus, quia non testibus res agitur, sed ad interpretandi solertiam omnia revocanda sunt" (p. 172). To the same general purpose the French work of M. Eméric David, Recherches sur le Dieu Jupiter—reviewed by O. Müller : see the Kleine Schriften of the latter, vol. ii. p. 82.

Mr. Bryant has also employed a profusion of learning, and numerous etymological conjectures, to resolve the Greek mythes into mistakes, perversions, and mutilations, of the exploits and doctrines of oriental tribes long-lost and by-gone,—Amonians, Cuthites, Arkites, &c. "It was Noah (he thinks) who was represented under the different names of Thoth, Hermês, Menês, Osiris, Zeuth, Atlas, Phorôneus, Promêtheus, to which list a farther number of great extent might be added: the Νοῦς of Anaxagoras was in reality the patriarch Noah" (Ant. Mythol. vol. ii. p. 253, 272). "The Cuthites or Amonians, descendants of Noah, settled in Greece from the east, celebrated for their skill in building and the arts" (ib. i. p. 502 ; ii. p. 187). "The greatest part of the Grecian theology arose from misconception and blunders, the stories concerning their gods and heroes were founded

mistaken view both of the antiquity and the purport of the mysteries, which cannot be safely carried up even to the age of Hesiod, and which, though imposing and venerable as religious ceremonies, included no recondite or esoteric teaching.[1]

The doctrine supposed to have been originally symbolised and subsequently overclouded, in the Greek mythes, was in reality first intruded into them by the unconscious fancies of later interpreters. It was one of the various roads which instructed men took to escape from the literal admission of the ancient mythes, and to arrive at some new form of belief, more consonant with their ideas of what the attributes and character of the gods ought to be. It was one of the ways of constituting, by help of the mysteries, a philosophical religion apart from the general public, and of connecting that distinction with the earliest periods of Grecian society. Such a distinction was both avowed and justified among the superior men of the later pagan world. Varro and Scævola distributed theology into three distinct departments,—the mythical or fabulous, the civil, and the physical. The first had its place in the theatre, and was left without any interference to the poets ; the second belonged to the city or political community as such,—it comprised the regu-lation of all the public worship and religious rites, and was consigned altogether to the direction of the magistrate ; the third was the privilege of philosophers, but was reserved altogether for

Supposed ancient meaning is really a modern interpreta-tion.

Triple theology of the pagan world.

---

on terms misinterpreted or abused" (*ib.* i. p. 452). "The number of different actions ascribed to the various Grecian gods or heroes all relate to one people or family, and are at bottom one and the same history" (*ib.* ii. p. 57). "The fables of Promê-theus and Tityus were taken from ancient Amonian temples, from hiero-glyphics misunderstood and badly explained" (i. p. 426): see especially vol. ii. p. 160.

[1] The Anti-Symbolik of Voss, and still more the Aglaophamus of Lobeck, are full of instruction on the subject of this supposed interior doctrine, and on the ancient mysteries in general : the latter treatise especially is not less distinguished for its judicious and circumspect criticism than for its copious learning.

Mr. Halhed (Preface to the Gentoo Code of Laws, p. xiii.-xiv.) has good observations on the vanity of all attempts to allegorise the Hindu mythology : he observes, with perfect truth, "The vulgar and illiterate have always understood the mythology of their country in its literal sense : and there was a time to every nation, when the highest rank in it was equally vulgar and illiterate with the lowest . . . . A Hindu esteems the as-tonishing miracles attributed to a Brima, or a Kishen, as facts of the most indubitable authenticity, and the relation of them as most strictly historical."

Compare also Gibbon's remarks on the allegorising tendencies of the later Platonists (Hist. Decl. and Fall, vol. iv. p. 71).

private discussion in the schools apart from the general public.[1]
As a member of the city, the philosopher sympathised with the
audience in the theatre, and took a devout share in the established
ceremonies, nor was he justified in trying what he heard in the
one or saw in the other by his own ethical standard. But in the
private assemblies of instructed or inquisitive men, he enjoyed
the fullest liberty of canvassing every received tenet, and of
broaching his own theories unreservedly, respecting the existence
and nature of the gods. By these discussions the activity of the
philosophical mind was maintained and truth elicited; but it was
such truth as the body of the people ought not to hear, lest their
faith in their own established religious worship should be overthrown. In thus distinguishing the civil theology from the
fabulous, Varro was enabled to cast upon the poets all the blame
of the objectionable points in the popular theology, and to avoid
the necessity of pronouncing censure on the magistrates; who
(he contended) had made as good a compromise with the settled
prejudices of the public as the case permitted.

The same conflicting sentiments which led the philosophers
to decompose the divine mythes into allegory, impelled the
historians to melt down the heroic mythes into something like
continuous political history, with a long series of chronology
calculated upon the heroic pedigrees. The one process as well
as the other was interpretative guesswork, proceeding upon
unauthorised assumptions, and without any verifying test or
evidence. While it frittered away the characteristic beauty of
the mythe into something essentially anti-mythical, it sought to
arrive both at history and philosophy by impracticable roads.
That the superior men of antiquity should have striven hard to

---

[1] Varro, ap. Augustin. De Civ. Dei,
iv. 27; vi. 5—6. "Dicis fabulosos
Deos accommodatos esse ad theatrum,
naturales ad mundum, civiles ad
urbem." "Varro, de religionibus
loquens, multa esse vera dixit, quæ
non modo vulgo scire non sit utile, sed
etiam tametsi falsa sint, aliter existi-
mare populum expediat: et ideo Græcos
teletas et mysteria taciturnitate parie-
tibusque clausisse" (ibid. iv. 31). See
Villoison, De Triplici Theologiâ Com-
mentatio, p. 8; and Lactantius, De
Origin. Error. ii. 3. The doctrine of the
Stoic Chrysippus, ad Etymologicon

Magn. v. Τελεταί—Χρύσιππος δε φησι,
τοὺς περὶ τῶν θείων λόγους εἰκότως
καλεῖσθαι τελετάς, χρῆναι γὰρ τούτους
τελευταίους καὶ ἐπὶ πᾶσι διδάσκεσθαι,
τῆς ψυχῆς ἐχούσης ἕρμα καὶ κεκρατημένης,
καὶ πρὸς τοὺς ἀμνήτους σιωπᾶν δυναμένης·
μέγα γὰρ εἶναι τὸ ἆθλον ὑπὲρ θεῶν ἀκοῦσαί
τε ὀρθ λ, καὶ ἐγκρατεῖς γενέσθαι αὐτῶν.
The triple division of Varro is reproduced in Plutarch, Amatorius, p. 763.
τὰ μὲν μύθῳ, τὰ δὲ νόμῳ, τὰ δὲ λόγῳ,
πίστιν ἐξ ἀρχῆς ἔσχηκε τῆς δ' οὖν περὶ
θεῶν δόξης καὶ παντάπασιν ἡγεμόνες καὶ
διδάσκαλοι γεγόνασιν ἡμῖν οἵ τε ποιηταί,
καὶ οἱ νομοθέται, καὶ τρίτον, οἱ φιλόσοφοι.

save the dignity of legends which constituted the charm of their literature as well as the substance of the popular religion, we cannot be at all surprised ; but it is gratifying to find Plato discussing the subject in a more philosophical spirit. The Platonic Sokratês being asked whether he believes the current Attic fable respecting the abduction of Oreithyia (daughter of Erechtheus) by Boreas, replies, in substance,—" It would not be strange if I disbelieved it, as the clever men do ; I might then show my cleverness by saying that a gust of Boreas blew her down from the rocks above while she was at play, and that having been killed in this manner she was reported to have been carried off by Boreas. Such speculations are amusing enough, but they belong to men ingenious and busy-minded over-much, and not greatly to be envied, if it be only for this reason, *that after having set right one fable, they are under the necessity of applying the same process to a host of others*—Hippocentaurs, Chimæras, Gorgons, Pegasus, and numberless other monsters and incredibilities. A man, who, disbelieving these stories, shall try to find a probable basis for each of them, will display an ill-placed acuteness and take upon himself an endless burden, for which I at least have no leisure: accordingly I forego such researches, and believe in the current version of the stories."[1]

These remarks of Plato are valuable, not simply because they point out the uselessness of digging for a supposed basis of truth in the mythes, but because they at the same time suggest the true reason for mistrusting all such tentatives. The mythes form a class apart, abundant as well as peculiar. To remove any individual mythe from its own class into that of history or philosophy, by simple conjecture and without any collateral evidence, is of no advantage, unless you can perform a similar

[1] Plato, Phædr. c. 7. p. 229.

PHÆDRUS. Εἰπέ μοι, ὦ Σώκρατες, σὺ τοῦτο τὸ μυθολόγημα πείθει ἀληθὲς εἶναι ;

SOKRATÊS. Ἀλλ' εἰ ἀπιστοίην, ὥσπερ οἱ σοφοὶ, οὐκ ἂν ἄτοπος εἴην, εἶτα σοφιζόμενος φαίην αὐτὴν πνεῦμα Βορέου κατὰ τῶν πλησίον πετρῶν σὺν φαρμακείᾳ παίζουσαν ὦσαι, καὶ οὕτω δὴ τελευτήσασαν λεχθῆναι ὑπὸ τοῦ Βορέου ἀναρπαστὸν γεγονέναι . . . . Ἐγὼ δὲ, ὦ Φαῖδρε, ἄλλως μὲν τὰ τοιαῦτα χαρίεντα ἡγοῦμαι, λίαν δὲ δεινοῦ καὶ ἐπιπόνου καὶ οὐ πάνυ εὐτυχοῦς ἀνδρὸς, κατ' ἄλλο μὲν οὐδὲν, ὅτι δ' αὐτῷ ἀνάγκη μετὰ τοῦτο τὸ τῶν Ἱπποκενταύρων εἶδος ἐπανορθοῦσθαι, καὶ αὖθις τὸ τῆς Χιμαίρας. Καὶ ἐπιρρεῖ δὲ ὄχλος τοιούτων Γοργόνων καὶ Πηγάσων, καὶ ἄλλων ἀμηχάνων πλήθη τε καὶ ἀτοπίαι τερατολόγων τινῶν φύσεων· αἷς εἴ τις ἀπιστῶν προσβιβᾷ κατὰ τὸ εἰκὸς ἕκαστον, ἅτε ἀγροίκῳ τινὶ σοφίᾳ χρώμενος, πολλῆς αὐτῷ σχολῆς δεήσει. Ἐμοὶ δὲ πρὸς ταῦτα οὐδαμῶς ἔστι σχολή . . . Ὅθεν δὴ χαίρειν ἐάσας ταῦτα, πειθόμενος δὲ τῷ νομιζομένῳ περὶ αὐτῶν, ὃ νῦν δὴ ἔλεγον, σκοπῶ οὐ ταῦτα ἀλλ' ἐμαυτόν, &c.

process on the remainder. If the process be trustworthy, it ought to be applied to all : and *e converso*, if it be not applicable to all, it is not trustworthy as applied to any one specially ; always assuming no special evidence to be accessible. To detach any individual mythe from the class to which it belongs, is to present it in an erroneous point of view : we have no choice except to admit them as they stand, by putting ourselves approximatively into the frame of mind of those for whom they were destined and to whom they appeared worthy of credit.

If Plato thus discountenances all attempts to transform the mythes by interpretation into history or philosophy, indirectly recognising the generic difference between them—we find sub-

Treatment and use of the mythes according to Plato.

stantially the same view pervading the elaborate precepts in his treatise on the Republic. He there regards the mythes, not as embodying either matter of fact or philosophical principle, but as portions of religious and patriotic faith, and instruments of ethical tuition. Instead of allowing the poets to frame them according to the impulses of their own genius and with a view to immediate popularity, he directs the legislator to provide types of his own for the characters of the gods and heroes, and to suppress all such divine and heroic legends as are not in harmony with these pre-established canons. In the Platonic system, the mythes are not to be matters of history, nor yet of spontaneous or casual fiction, but of prescribed faith : he supposes that the people will believe, as a thing of course, what the poets circulate, and he therefore directs that the latter shall circulate nothing which does not tend to ennoble and improve the feelings. He conceives the mythes as stories composed to illustrate the general sentiments of the poets and the community, respecting the character and attributes of the gods and heroes, or respecting the social relations, and ethical duties as well as motives of mankind : hence the obligation upon the legislator to prescribe beforehand the types of character which shall be illustrated, and to restrain the poets from following out any opposing fancies. "Let us neither believe ourselves (he exclaims), nor permit any one to circulate, that Thêseus son of Poseidôn, and Peirithous son of Zeus, or any other hero or son of a god, could ever have brought themselves to commit abductions or other enormities such as are now falsely

ascribed to them. We must compel the poets to say, either that
such persons were not the sons of gods, or that they were not the
perpetrators of such misdeeds." [1]

Most of the mythes which the youth hear and repeat (according
to Plato) are false, but some of them are true : the
great and prominent mythes which appear in Homer
and Hesiod are no less fictions than the rest. But
fiction constitutes one of the indispensable instruments
of mental training as well as truth ; only the legislator must take
care that the fictions so employed shall be beneficent and not
mischievous.[2] As the mischievous fictions (he says) take their
rise from wrong preconceptions respecting the character of the
gods and heroes, so the way to correct them is to enforce, by
authorised compositions, the adoption of a more correct standard.[3]

The comments which Plato has delivered with so much force
in his Republic, and the enactments which he deduces from
them, are in the main an expansion of that sentiment of condemnation, which he shared with so many other philosophers,
towards a large portion of the Homeric and Hesiodic stories.[4]

His views as to the necessity and use of fiction.

---

[1] Plato, Repub. iii. 5, p. 391. The
perfect ignorance of all men respecting
the gods rendered the task of fiction
easy (Plato, Kritias, p. 107).
[2] Plato, Repub. ii. 16, p. 377. Λόγων
δὲ διττὸν εἶδος, τὸ μὲν ἀληθὲς, ψεῦδος δ᾿
ἕτερον; Ναί. Παιδευτέον δ᾿ ἐν ἀμφοτέροις, πρότερον δ᾿ ἐν τοῖς ψεύδεσιν ·
. . . . Οὐ μανθάνεις, ὅτι πρῶτον τοῖς
παιδίοις μύθους λέγομεν· τοῦτο δέ που
ὡς τὸ ὅλον εἰπεῖν ψεῦδος, ἔνι δὲ καὶ
ἀληθῆ. . . . . Πρῶτον ἡμῖν ἐπιστα-
τητέον τοῖς μυθοποιοῖς, καὶ ὃν μὲν ἂν
καλὸν μῦθον ποιήσωσιν, ἐγκριτέον, ὃν δ᾿
ἃ μὴ, ἀποκριτέον . . . . ὧν δὲ νῦν
λέγουσι, τοὺς πολλοὺς ἐκβλητέον . . .
οὓς Ἡσίοδος καὶ Ὅμηρος ἡμῖν ἐλεγέτην,
καὶ οἱ ἄλλοι ποιηταί. Οὗτοι γάρ που
μύθους τοῖς ἀνθρώποις ψευδεῖς συντιθέντες
ἔλεγόν τε καὶ λέγουσι. Ποίους δὴ, ἦ δ᾿
ὅς, καὶ τί αὐτῶν μεμφόμενος λέγεις;
Ὅπερ, ἦν δ᾿ ἐγὼ, χρὴ καὶ πρῶτον καὶ
μάλιστα μέμφεσθαι, ἄλλως τε καὶ ἐάν τις
μὴ καλῶς ψεύδηται. Τί τοῦτο; Ὅταν
τις εἰκάζῃ κακῶς τῷ λόγῳ περὶ θεῶν τε
καὶ ἡρώων, οἷοί εἰσιν, ὥσπερ γραφεὺς
μηδὲν ἐοικότα γράφων οἷς ἂν ὅμοια βού-
ληται γράψαι.
The same train of thought, and the
precepts founded upon it, are followed
up through chap. 17, 18, and 19 ; compare De Legg. xii. p. 941.

Instead of recognising the popular or
dramatic theology as something distinct from the civil (as Varro did), Plato
suppresses the former as a separate
department and merges it in the latter.
[3] Plato, Repub. ii. c. 21, p. 382.
Τὸ ἐν τοῖς λόγοις ψεῦδος πότε καὶ τί
χρήσιμον, ὥστε μὴ ἄξιον εἶναι μίσους;
Ἆρ᾿ οὐ πρός τε τοὺς πολεμίους καὶ τῶν
καλουμένων φίλων, ὅταν διὰ μανίαν ἤ
τινα ἄνοιαν κακόν τι ἐπιχειρῶσι πράττειν,
τότε ἀποτροπῆς ἕνεκα ὡς φάρμακον χρήσιμον γίγνεται; Καὶ ἐν αἷς νῦν δὴ
ἐλέγομεν ταῖς μυθολογίαις, διὰ
τὸ μὴ εἰδέναι ὅπη τἀληθὲς ἔχει
περὶ τῶν παλαιῶν, ἀφομοιοῦν-
τες τῷ ἀληθεῖ τὸ ψεῦδος, ὅτι
μάλιστα, οὕτω χρήσιμον ποιοῦμεν;
[4] The censure which Xenophanês
pronounced upon the Homeric legends
has already been noticed : Herakleitus
(Diogen. Laërt. ix. 1) and Metrodôrus,
the companion and follower of Epi-
curus, were not less profuse in their
invectives, ἐν γράμμασι τοσούτοις τῷ
ποιητῇ λελοιδόρηται (Plutarch, Non
posse suaviter vivi secundum Epicurum,
p. 1086). He even advised persons not
to be ashamed to confess their utter
ignorance of Homer, to the extent of
not knowing whether Hectôr was a
Greek or a Trojan (Plut. ib. p. 1094).

But the manner in which he has set forth this opinion unfolds
He deals
with the
mythes as
expressions
of feeling
and imagi-
nation—to us more clearly the real character of the mythical
narrative. They are creations of the productive minds
in the community, deduced from the supposed attributes of the gods and heroes : so Plato views them,
and in such character he proposed to amend them.
The legislator would cause to be prepared a better and truer
picture of the foretime, because he would start from truer (that
is to say more creditable) conceptions of the gods and heroes.
For Plato rejects the mythes respecting Zeus and Hêrê, or
Thêseus and Peirithous, not from any want of evidence, but
because they are unworthy of gods and heroes : he proposes to
call forth new mythes, which, though he admits them at the
outset to be fiction, he knows will soon be received as true, and
supply more valuable lessons of conduct.

We may consider then that Plato disapproves of the attempt to
identify the old mythes either with exaggerated history or with
disguised philosophy. He shares in the current faith, without
any suspicion or criticism, as to Orpheus, Palamêdês, Dædalus,
Amphiôn, Thêseus, Achilles, Cheirôn, and other mythical personages ;[1] but what chiefly fills his mind is, the inherited sentiment
of deep reverence for these superhuman characters and for the
age to which they belonged,—a sentiment sufficiently strong to
render him not only an unbeliever in such legends as conflict
with it, but also a deliberate creator of new legends for the
purpose of expanding and gratifying it. The more we examine
this sentiment, both in the mind of Plato as well as in that of the
Greeks generally, the more shall we be convinced that it formed
—sustained
by religious
faith, and
not by any
positive
basis.essentially and inseparably a portion of Hellenic
religious faith. The mythe both presupposes, and
springs out of, a settled basis and a strong expansive
force of religious, social, and patriotic feeling, operating
upon a past which is little better than a blank as to
positive knowledge. It resembles history, in so far as its form is
narrative : it resembles philosophy, in so far as it is occasionally
illustrative ; but in its essence and substance, in the mental
tendencies by which it is created as well as in those by which it

---

[1] Plato, Republic. iii. 4—5, p. 391 ; De Legg. iii. 1, p. 677.

is judged and upheld, it is a popularised expression of the divine and heroic faith of the people.

Grecian antiquity cannot be at all understood except in connection with Grecian religion. It begins with gods and it ends with historical men, the former being recognised not simply as gods, but as primitive ancestors, and connected with the latter by a long mythical genealogy, partly heroic and partly human. Now the whole value of such genealogies arises from their being taken entire: the god or hero at the top is in point of fact the most important member of the whole:[1] for the length and continuity of the series arise from anxiety on the part of historical men to join themselves by a thread of *Grecian antiquity essentially a religious conception.* descent with the being whom they worshipped in their gentile sacrifices. Without the ancestorial god, the whole pedigree would have become not only acephalous, but worthless and uninteresting. The pride of the Herakleids, Asklepiads, Æakids, Neleids, Dædalids, &c. was attached to the primitive eponymous hero and to the god from whom they sprung, not to the line of names, generally long and barren, through which the divine or heroic dignity gradually dwindled down into common manhood. Indeed the length of the genealogy (as I have before remarked) was an evidence of the humility of the historical man, which led him to place himself at a respectful distance from the gods or heroes; for Hekatæus of Milêtus, who ranked himself as the fifteenth descendant of a god, might perhaps have accounted it an overweening impiety in any living man to claim a god for his immediate father.

The whole chronology of Greece, anterior to 776 B.C., consists of calculations founded upon these mythical genea- *Application of chronological calculation divests it of this character.* logies, especially upon that of the Spartan kings and their descent from Hêraklês,—thirty years being commonly taken as the equivalent of a generation, or about three generations to a century. This process of computation was altogether illusory, as applying historical and chronological conditions to a case on which they had no bearing.

---

[1] For a description of similar tendencies in the Asiatic religions, see Movers, Die Phönizier, ch. v. p. 153 (Bonn, 1841): he points out the same phænomena as in the Greek,— coalescence between the ideas of ancestry and worship,—confusion between gods and men in the past,—increasing tendency to Euemerise (p. 156—157).

Though the domain of history was seemingly enlarged, the religious element was tacitly set aside: when the heroes and gods were chronologised, they became insensibly approximated to the limits of humanity, and the process indirectly gave encouragement to the theory of Euêmerus. Personages originally legendary and poetical were erected into definite landmarks for measuring the duration of the foretime, thus gaining in respect to historical distinctness, but not without loss on the score of religious association. Both Euêmerus and the subsequent Christian writers, who denied the ·original and inherent divinity of the pagan gods, had a great advantage in carrying their chronological researches strictly and consistently upwards—for all chronology fails as soon as we suppose a race superior to common humanity.

Moreover it is to be remarked that the pedigree of the Spartan kings, which Apollodôrus and Eratosthenês selected as the basis of their estimate of time, is nowise superior in credibility and trustworthiness to the thousand other gentile and family·pedigrees with which Greece abounded ; it is rather indeed to be numbered among the most incredible of all, seeing that Hêraklês as a progenitor is placed at the head of perhaps more pedigrees than any other Grecian god or hero.[1] The descent of the Spartan king Leonidas from Hêraklês rests upon no better evidence than that of Aristotle or Hippokratês from Asklêpius,[2] —of Evagoras or Thucydidês from Æakus,—of Sokratês from Dædalus,—of the Spartan heraldic family from Talthybius,—of the prophetic Iamid family in Elis from Iamus,—of the rootgatherers in Pêlion from Cheirôn,—and of Hekatæus and his gens from some god in the sixteenth ascending line of the series.

Mythical genealogies all of one class, and all on a level in respect to evidence.

[1] According to that which Aristotle seems to recognise (Histor. Animal. vii. 6), Hêraklês was father of seventy-two sons, but of only one daughter—he was essentially ἀῤῥενόγονος, illustrating one of the physical peculiarities noticed by Aristotle. Euripidês however mentions daughters of Hêraklês in the plural number (Eurip. Herakleid. 45).

[2] Hippokratês was twentieth in descent from Hêraklês, and nineteenth from Asklêpius (Vita Hippocr. by Soranus, ap. Westermann, Scriptor.

Biographic. viii. 1) ; about Aristotle, see Diogen. Laërt. v. 1. Xenophôn, the physician of the emperor Claudius, was also an Asklepiad (Tacit. Ann. xii. 61).

In Rhodes, the neighbouring island to Kôs, was the gens Ἀλιάδαι, or sons of Hêlios, specially distinguished from the Ἀλιασταί of mere associated worshippers of Hêlios, τὸ κοινὸν τῶν Ἀλιαδῶν καὶ τῶν Ἀλιαστῶν (see the Inscription in Boeckh's Collection, No. 2525, with Boeckh's comment).

There is little exaggeration in saying, indeed, that no permanent combination of men in Greece, religious, social or professional, was without a similar pedigree; all arising out of the same exigencies of the feelings and imagination, to personify as well as to sanctify the bond of union among the members. Every one of these *gentes* began with a religious and ended with an historical person. At some point or other in the upward series, entities of history were exchanged for entities of religion; but where that point is to be found we are unable to say, nor had the wisest of the ancient Greeks any means of determining. Thus much however we know, that the series, taken as a whole, though dear and precious to the believing Greek, possesses no value as chronological evidence to the historian.

When Hekatæus visited Thêbes in Egypt, he mentioned to the Egyptian priests, doubtless with a feeling of satisfaction and pride, the imposing pedigree of the gens to which he belonged,— with fifteen ancestors in ascending line, and a god as the initial progenitor. But he found himself immeasurably outdone by the priests "who genealogised against him".[1] They showed to him three hundred and forty-one wooden colossal statues, representing the succession of chief priests in the temple in uninterrupted series from father to son, through a space of 11,300 years. Prior to the commencement of this long period (they said), the gods dwelling along with men, had exercised sway in Egypt; but they repudiated altogether the idea of men begotten by gods or of heroes.[2]

Both these counter-genealogies are, in respect to trustworthiness and evidence, on the same footing. Each represents partly the religious faith, partly the retrospective imagination of the persons from whom it emanated. In each the lower members of the series (to what an extent we cannot tell) are real, the upper members fabulous; but in each also the series derived all its interest and all its imposing effect from being conceived unbroken and entire. Herodotus is much perplexed by the capital discrepancy between the Grecian and

Grecian and Egyptian genealogies.

---

[1] Herodot. ii. 144. Ἑκαταίῳ δὲ γενεη-λογήσαντι ἑωϋτὸν, καὶ ἀναδήσαντι ἐς ἑκκαιδέκατον θεὸν, ἀντεγενεηλόγησαν ἐπὶ τῇ ἀριθμήσει, οὐ δεκόμενοι παρ' αὐτοῦ, ἀπὸ θεοῦ γίνεσθαι ἄνθρωπον· ἀντεγενεη-

λόγησαν δὲ ὧδε, &c.
[2] Herod. ii. 143—145. Καὶ ταῦτα Αἰγύπτιοι ἀτρεκέως φασὶν ἐπίστασθαι, αἰεί τε λογιζόμενοι καὶ αἰεὶ ἀπογραφό-μενοι τὰ ἔτεα.

Egyptian chronologies, and vainly employs his ingenuity in
reconciling them. There is no standard of objective
evidence by which either the one or the other of
them can be tried. Each has its own subjective
value, in conjunction with the faith and feelings of
Egyptian and Greek, and each presupposes in the

Value of
each purely
subjective,
in reference
to the faith
of the
people.

believer certain mental prepossessions which are not to be found
beyond its own local limits. Nor is the greater or less extent of
duration at all important, when we once pass the limits of
evidence and verifiable reality. One century of recorded time,
adequately studded with authentic and orderly events, presents a
greater mass and a greater difficulty of transition to the imagination than a hundred centuries of barren genealogy. Herodotus,
in discussing the age of Homer and Hesiod, treats an anterior
point of 400 years as if it were only yesterday ; the reign of
Henry VI. is separated from us by an equal interval, and the
reader will not require to be reminded how long that interval
now appears.

The mythical age was peopled with a mingled aggregate of
gods, heroes, and men, so confounded together that it
was often impossible to distinguish to which class
any individual name belonged. In regard to the
Thracian god Zalmoxis, the Hellespontic Greeks
interpreted his character and attributes according to

Gods and
men undis-
tinguish-
able in
Grecian
antiquity.

the scheme of Euemerism. They affirmed that he had been a
man, the slave of the philosopher Pythagoras at Samos, and that
he had by abilities and artifice established a religious ascendency
over the minds of the Thracians, and obtained from them divine
honours. Herodotus cannot bring himself to believe this story,
but he frankly avows his inability to determine whether Zalmoxis
was a god or a man,[1] nor can he extricate himself from a similar

---

[1] Herod. iv. 94—96. After having
related the Euemeristic version given
by the Hellespontic Greeks, he concludes, with his characteristic frankness and simplicity—Ἐγὼ δὲ, περὶ μὲν
τούτου καὶ τοῦ καταγαίου οἰκήματος,
οὔτε ἀπιστέω, οὔτε ὦν πιστεύω τι λίην.
δοκέω δὲ πολλοῖσι ἔτεσι πρότερον τὸν
Ζάλμοξιν τοῦτον γενέσθαι Πυθαγόρεω.
Εἴτε δὲ ἐγένετό τις Ζάλμοξις ἄνθρωπος,
εἴτ' ἐστι δαίμων τις Γέτῃσι οὗτος ἐπιχώ-

ριος, χαιρέτω. So Plutarch (Numa, c.
19) will not undertake to determine
whether Janus was a god or a king,
εἴτε δαίμων, εἴτε βασιλεὺς γενόμενος, &c.
Herakleitus the philosopher said
that men were θεοὶ θνητοί, and the
gods were ἄνθρωποι ἀθάνατοι (Lucian,
Vitar. Anctio. c. 13. vol. i. p. 303.
Tauchn. : compare the same author,
Dialog. Mortuor. iii. vol. i. p. 182, ed.
Tauchn.).

embarrassment in respect to Dionysus and Pan. Amidst the
confusion of the Homeric fight, the goddess Athênê confers upon
Diomêdês the miraculous favour of dispelling the mist from his eyes,
so as to enable him to discriminate gods from men ; and nothing
less than a similar miracle could enable a critical reader of the
mythical narratives to draw an ascertained boundary-line between
the two.[1] But the original hearers of the mythes felt neither
surprise nor displeasure from this confusion of the divine with
the human individual. They looked at the past with a film of
faith over their eyes—neither knowing the value, nor desiring the
attainment, of an unclouded vision. The intimate companionship,
and the occasional mistake of identity between gods and men,
were in full harmony with their reverential retrospect. And we
accordingly see the poet Ovid in his Fasti, when he undertakes
the task of unfolding the legendary antiquities of early Rome,
re-acquiring, by the inspiration of Juno, the power of seeing gods
and men in immediate vicinity and conjunct action, such as it
existed before the development of the critical and historical sense.[2]

To resume, in brief, what has been laid down in this and the
preceding chapters respecting the Grecian mythes :— General
1. They are a special product of the imagination recapitu-
and feelings, radically distinct both from history and lation.

---

[1] Iliad, v. 127 :—

'Αχλὺν δ' αὖ τοι ἀπ' ὀφθαλμῶν ἕλον, ἣ
πρὶν ἐπῆεν,
'Οφρ' εὖ γιγνώσκῃς ἠμὲν θεὸν. ἠδὲ καὶ
ἄνδρα.

Of this undistinguishable confusion
between gods and men, striking illustrations are to be found both in the
third book of Cicero de Naturâ Deorum
(16—21), and in the long disquisition of
Strabo (x. pp. 467—474) respecting the
Kabeiri, the Korybantes, the Daktyls
of Ida ; the more so as he cites the
statements of Pherekydês, Akusilaus,
Dêmêtrius of Skêpsis and others.
Under the Roman empire the lands
in Greece belonging to the immortal
gods were exempted from tribute.
The Roman tax-collectors refused to
recognise as immortal gods any persons
who had once been men ; but this rule
could not be clearly applied (Cicero,
Nat. Deor. iii. 20). See the remarks of
Pausanias (ii. 26, 7) about Asklêpius :
Galen, too, is doubtful about Asklêpius

and Dionysus—'Ασκληπιός γέ τοι καὶ
Διόνυσος, εἶτ' ἄνθρωποι πρότερον ἤστην,
εἴτε καὶ ἀρχῆθεν θεοί (Galen in Protreptic. 9. tom. i. p. 22, ed. Kühn). Xenophôn (De Venat. c. i.) considers Cheirôn
as the brother of Zeus.

The ridicule of Lucian (Deorum
Concilium, t. iii. p. 527—538, Hems.)
brings out still more forcibly the confusion here indicated.

[2] Ovid, Fasti, vi. 7—24 :—

" Fas mihi praecipue vultus vidisse
    Deorum,
Vel quia sum vates, vel quia sacra
    cano . . .
Ecce Deas vidi . . .
Horrueram, tacitoque animum pallore
    fatebar :
Cum Dea, quos fecit, sustulit ipsa
    metus.
Namque ait—O vates, Romani conditor
    anni,
Ause per exiguos magna referre modos:
Jus tibi fecisti numen coeleste videndi,
Cum placuit numeris condere festa
    tuis."

1—26

philosophy: they cannot be broken down and decomposed into the one, nor allegorised into the other. There are indeed some particular and even assignable mythes, which raise intrinsic presumption of an allegorising tendency; and there are doubtless some others, though not specially assignable, which contain portions of matter of fact, or names of real persons, embodied in them. But such matter of fact cannot be verified by any intrinsic mark, nor are we entitled to presume its existence in any given case unless some collateral evidence can be produced.

2. We are not warranted in applying to the mythical world the rules either of historical credibility or chronological sequence. Its personages are gods, heroes, and men, in constant juxtaposition and reciprocal sympathy; men, too, of whom we know a large proportion to be fictitious, and of whom we can never ascertain how many may have been real. No series of such personages can serve as materials for chronological calculation.

3. The mythes were originally produced in an age which had no records, no philosophy, no criticism, no canon of belief, and scarcely any tincture either of astronomy or geography,—but which, on the other hand, was full of religious faith, distinguished for quick and susceptible imagination, seeing personal agents where we look only for objects and connecting laws;—an age moreover eager for new narrative, accepting with the unconscious impressibility of children (the question of truth or falsehood being never formally raised) all which ran in harmony with its pre-existing feelings, and penetrable by inspired prophets and poets in the same proportion that it was indifferent to positive evidence. To such hearers did the primitive poet or story-teller address himself. It was the glory of his productive genius to provide suitable narrative expression for the faith and emotions which he shared in common with them, and the rich stock of Grecian mythes attests how admirably he performed his task. As the gods and the heroes formed the conspicuous object of national reverence, so the mythes were partly divine, partly heroic, partly both in one.[1]

[1] The fourth Eclogue of Virgil, under the form of a prophecy, gives a faithful picture of the heroic and divine past, to which the legends of Troy and the Argonauts belonged :—

"Ille Deûm vitam accipiet, Divisque videbit

Permixtos heroas," &c.
" Alter erit tum Tiphys et altera quæ vehat Argo
Delectos heroas: erunt etiam altera bella,
Atque iterum ad Trojam magnus mittetur Achilles."

The adventures of Achilles, Helen, and Diomêdês, of Œdipus and Adrastus, of Meleager and Althæa, of Jasôn and the Argô, were recounted by the same tongues and accepted with the same unsuspecting confidence, as those of Apollo and Artemis, of Arês and Aphroditê, of Poseidôn and Hêraklês.

4. The time however came when this plausibility ceased to be complete. The Grecian mind made an important advance, socially, ethically, and intellectually. Philosophy and history were constituted, prose writing and chronological records became familiar ; a canon of belief more or less critical came to be tacitly recognised. Moreover superior men profited more largely by the stimulus, and contracted habits of judging different from the vulgar: the god Elenchus[1] (to use a personification of Menander), the giver and prover of truth, descended into their minds. Into the new intellectual medium, thus altered in its elements and no longer uniform in its quality, the mythes descended by inheritance ; but they were found, to a certain extent, out of harmony even with the feelings of the people, and altogether dissonant with those of instructed men. Yet the most superior Greek was still a Greek, cherishing the common reverential sentiment towards the foretime of his country. Though he could neither believe nor respect the mythes as they stood, he was under an imperious mental necessity to transform them into a state worthy of his belief and respect. Whilst the literal mythe still continued to float among the poets and the people, critical men interpreted, altered, decomposed and added, until they found something which satisfied their minds as a supposed real basis. They manufactured some dogmas of supposed original philosophy, and a long series of fancied history and chronology, retaining the mythical names and generations, even when they were obliged to discard or recast the mythical events. The interpreted mythe was thus promoted into a reality, while the literal mythe was degraded into a fiction.[2]

---

[1] Lucian, Pseudol. c. 4. Παρακλητέος ἡμῖν τῶν Μενάνδρου προλόγων εἷς, ὁ Ἔλεγχος, φίλος ἀληθείᾳ καὶ παῤῥησίᾳ θεός, οὐχ ὁ ἀσημότατος τῶν ἐπὶ τὴν σκηνὴν ἀναβαινόντων. (See Meineke ad Menandr. p. 284.)

[2] The following passage from Dr. Ferguson's Essay on Civil Society (part. ii. sect. i. p. 126) bears well on the subject before us :—

"If conjectures and opinions formed at a distance have not a sufficient authority in the history of mankind, the domestic antiquities of every nation must for this very reason be received with caution. They are for

The habit of distinguishing the interpreted from the literal mythe has passed from the literary men of antiquity to those of the modern world, who have for the most part construed the divine mythes as allegorised philosophy, and the heroic mythes as exaggerated, adorned, and over-coloured history. The early ages of Greece have thus been peopled with quasi-historical persons and quasi-historical events, all extracted from the mythes after making certain allowances for poetical ornament. But we must not treat this extracted product as if it were the original substance. We cannot properly understand it except by viewing it in connexion with the literal mythes out of which it was obtained, in their primitive age and appropriate medium, before the superior minds had yet outgrown the common faith in an all-personified Nature, and learned to restrict the divine free-agency by the supposition of invariable physical laws. It is in this point of view that the mythes are important for any one who would correctly appreciate the general tone of Grecian thought and feeling ; for they were the universal mental stock of the Hellenic world—common to men and women, rich and poor, instructed and ignorant ; they were in every one's memory and in every one's mouth,[1] while science and history were confined to

the most part the mere conjectures or the fictions of subsequent ages ; and even where at first they contained some resemblance of truth, they still vary with the imagination of those by whom they were transmitted, and in every generation receive a different form. They are made to bear the stamp of the times through which they have passed in the form of tradition, not of the ages to which their pretended descriptions relate . . . When traditionary fables are rehearsed by the vulgar, they bear the marks of a national character, and though mixed with absurdities, often raise the imagination and move the heart : when made the materials of poetry, and adorned by the skill and the eloquence of an ardent and superior mind, they instruct the under-standing as well as engage the passions. It is only in the management of mere antiquaries, or stript of the ornaments which the laws of history forbid them to wear, that *they become unfit even to amuse the fancy or to serve any purpose whatever.*
" It were absurd to quote the fable

of the Iliad or the Odyssey, the legends of Hercules, Theseus, and Œdipus, as authorities in matters of fact relating to the history of mankind ; but they may, with great justice, be cited to ascertain what were the conceptions and sentiments of the age in which they were composed, or to characterise the genius of that people with whose imaginations they were blended, and by whom they were fondly rehearsed and admired. In this manner fiction may be admitted to vouch for the genius of nations, while history has nothing to offer worthy of credit."
To the same purpose M. Paulin Paris (in his Lettre à M. H. de Mon-merqué, prefixed to the Roman de Berte aux Grans Piés, Paris, 1836), respecting the "romans" of the middle Ages :—" Pour bien connaître l'histoire du moyen âge, non pas celle des faits, mais celle des mœurs qui rendent les faits vraisemblables, il faut l'avoir étudiée dans les romans, et voilà pourquoi l'Histoire de France n'est pas encore faite ". (P. xxi.)
[1] A curious evidence of the undi-minished popularity of the Grecian

comparatively few.   We know from Thucydidês how erroneously and carelessly the Athenian public of his day retained the history of Peisistratus, only one century past ;[1] but the adventures of the gods and heroes, the numberless explanatory legends attached to visible objects and periodical ceremonies, were the theme of general talk, and any man unacquainted with them would have found himself partially excluded from the sympathy of his neighbours.   The theatrical representation, exhibited to the entire city population and listened to with enthusiastic interest, both presupposed and perpetuated acquaintance with the great lines of heroic fable.   Indeed in later times even the pantomimic dancers embraced in their representation the whole field of mythical incident, and their immense success proves at once how popular and how well-known such subjects were.   The names and attributes of the heroes were incessantly alluded to in the way of illustration, to point out a consoling, admonitory, or repressive moral: the simple mention of any of them sufficed to call up in every one's mind the principal events of his life, and the poet or rhapsode could thus calculate on touching chords not less familiar than susceptible.[2]

General public of Greece—familiar with their local mythes, careless of recent history.

---

mythes, to the exclusion even of recent history, is preserved by Vopiscus at the beginning of his Life of Aurelian.

The præfect of the city of Rome, Junius Tiberianus, took Vopiscus into his carriage on the festival-day of the Hilaria ; he was connected by the ties of relationship with Aurelian, who had died about a generation before—and as the carriage passed by the splendid temple of the Sun, which Aurelian had consecrated, he asked Vopiscus, what author had written the life of that emperor? To which Vopiscus replied, that he had read some Greek works which touched upon Aurelian, but nothing in Latin. Whereat the venerable præfect was profoundly grieved : " Dolorem gemitûs sui vir sanctus per hæc verba profudit :—Ergo *Thersitem, Sinonem, cœteraque illa prodigia vetustatis, et nos bene scimus, et posteri frequentabunt* : divum Aurelianum, clarissimum principem, severissimum Imperatorem, per quem totus Romano nomini orbis est restitutus, posteri nescient? Deus avertat hanc amentiam ! Et tamen, si bene memini,

ephemeridas illius viri scriptas habemus," &c. (Historiæ August. Scriptt. p. 209, ed. Salmas.)

This impressive remonstrance produced the Life of Aurelian by Vopiscus. The materials seem to have been ample and authentic : it is to be regretted that they did not fall into the hands of an author qualified to turn them to better account.

[1] Thucyd. vi. 56.

[2] Pausan. i. 3, 3.   Λέγεται μὲν δὴ καὶ ἄλλα οὐκ ἀληθῆ παρὰ τοῖς πολλοῖς, οἷα ἱστορίας ἀνηκόοις οὖσι, καὶ ὁπόσα ἤκουον εὐθὺς ἐκ παιδῶν ἔν τε χόροις καὶ τραγῳδίαις πιστὰ ἡγουμένοις, &c. The treatise of Lucian, De Saltatione, is a curious proof how much these mythes wore in every one's memory, and how large the range of knowledge of them was which a good dancer possessed (see particularly c. 76—79, t. ii. p. 308—310, Hemst.).

Antiphanês ap. Athenæ. vi. p. 223 :—

Μακάριόν ἐστιν ἡ τραγῳδία
ποίημα κατὰ πάντ', εἴ γε πρῶτον οἱ λόγοι
ὑπὸ τῶν θεατῶν εἰσιν ἐγνωρίσμενοι

A similar effect was produced by the multiplied religious festivals and processions, as well as by the oracles and prophecies which circulated in every city. The annual departure of the

Religious festivals— their commemorative influence.

Theôric ship from Athens to the sacred island of Dêlos, kept alive in the minds of Athenians generally, the legend of Thêseus and his adventurous enterprise in Krête:[1] and in like manner most of the other public rites and ceremonies were of a commemorative character, deduced from some mythical person or incident

πρὶν καί τιν' εἰπεῖν· ὡς ὑπομνῆσαι μόνον
δεῖ τὸν ποιητήν. Οἰδίπουν γὰρ ἄν γε φῶ,
τὰ δ' ἄλλα πάντ' ἴσασιν· ὁ πατὴρ Λάϊος,
μήτηρ Ἰοκάστη, θυγατέρες, παῖδες τίνες·
τί πείσεθ' οὗτος, τί πεποίηκεν. Ἂν πάλιν
εἴπῃ τις Ἀλκμαίωνα, καὶ τὰ παιδία
πάντ' εὐθὺς εἴρηχ', ὅτι μανεὶς ἀπέκτονε
τὴν μήτερ'· ἀγανακτῶν δ' Ἄδραστος εὐθέως
ἥξει, πάλιν δ' ἄπεισιν, &c.

The first pages of the eleventh Oration of Dio Chrysostom contain some striking passages both as to the universal acquaintance with the mythes, and as to their extreme popularity (Or. xi. p. 307—312, Reisk.). See also the commencement of Heraklidês, De Allegoriâ Homericâ (ap. Scriptt. Myth. ed. Gale, p. 408), about the familiarity with Homer.

The Lydê of the poet Antimachus has composed for his own consolation under sorrow, by enumerating the ἡρωϊκὰς συμφοράς (Plutarch, Consolat. ad Apollôn. c. 9, p. 106: compare Æschines cont. Ctesiph. c. 48). A sepulchral inscription in Thêra, on the untimely death of Admêtus, a youth of the heroic gens Ægidæ, makes a touching allusion to his ancestors Pêleus and Pherês (Boeckh, C. I. t. ii. p. 1087).

A curious passage of Aristotle is preserved by Dêmêtrius Phalereus (Περὶ Ἑρμηνείας, c. 144),—Ὅσῳ γὰρ αὐτίτης καὶ μονώτης εἰμὶ, φιλομυθότερος γέγονα (compare the passage in the Nikomachean ethics, i. 9, μονώτης καὶ ἄτεκνος). Stahr refers this to a letter of Aristotle written in his old age, the mythes being the consolation of his solitude (Aristotelia, i. p. 201).

For the employment of the mythical names and incidents as topics of pleasing and familiar comparison, see Menander, Περὶ Ἐπιδεικτικ. § iv. capp.

9 and 11, ap. Walz. Coll. Rhett. t. ix. p. 283—294. The degree in which they passed into the ordinary songs of women is illustrated by a touching epigram contained among the Chian Inscriptions published in Boeckh's Collection (No. 2236) :—

Βιττὼ καὶ Φαινὶς, φίλη ἡμέρη (?) αἱ συνέριθοι,
Αἱ πενιχραὶ, γραῖαι, τῆδ' ἐκλίθημεν ὁμοῦ.
Ἀμφότεραι Κῷαι, πρῶται γένος—ὦ γλυκὺς ὄρθρος,
Πρὸς λύχνον ᾧ μύθους ᾔδομεν ἡμιθέων.

These two poor women were not afraid to boast of their family descent. They probably belonged to some noble gens which traced its origin to a god or a hero. About the songs of women, see also Agathias, i. 7, 29, ed. Bonn.

In the family of the wealthy Athenian Demokratês was a legend, that his primitive ancestor (son of Zeus by the daughter of the Archêgetês of the dême Aixôneis, to which he belonged) had received Hêraklês at his table : this legend was so rife that the old women sung it,—ἅπερ αἱ γραῖαι ᾄδουσι (Plato, Lysia. p. 205). Compare also a legend of the dême Ἀναγυροῦς, mentioned in Suidas ad voc.

"Who is this maiden?" asks Orestês from Pyladês in the Iphigeneia in Tauris of Euripidês (662), respecting his sister Iphigeneia, whom he does not know as priestess of Artemis in a foreign land :—

Τίς ἐστιν ἡ νεᾶνις; ὡς Ἑλληνικῶς
Ἀνήρεθ' ἡμᾶς τούς τ' ἐν Ἰλίῳ πόνους
Νόστον τ' Ἀχαιῶν, τόν τ' ἐν οἰωνοῖς σοφὸν
Κάλχαντ', Ἀχιλλέως τ' οὔνομ', &c.
. . . . ἐστὶν ἡ ξένη γένος
Ἐκεῖθεν. Ἀργεία τις, &c.

[1] Plato, Phædo, c. 2.

familiarly known to natives, and forming to strangers a portion of the curiosities, of the place.[1]   During the period of Grecian subjection under the Romans, these curiosities, together with their works of arts and their legends, were especially clung to as a set-off against present degradation.   The Theban citizen who found himself restrained from the liberty enjoyed by all other Greeks, of consulting Amphiaraüs as a prophet, though the sanctuary and chapel of the hero stood in his own city—could not be satisfied without a knowledge of the story which explained the origin of such prohibition,[2] and which conducted him back to the originally hostile relations between Amphiaraüs and Thêbes.   Nor can we suppose among the citizens of Sikyôn anything less than a perfect and reverential conception of the legend of Thêbes, when we read the account given by Herodotus of the conduct of the despot Kleisthenês in regard to Adrastus and Melanippus.[3]   The Trœzenian youths and maidens,[4] who universally, when on the eve of marriage, consecrated an offering of their hair at the Herôon of Hippolytus, maintained a lively recollection of the legend of that unhappy recusant whom Aphroditê had so cruelly punished. Abundant relics preserved in many Grecian cities and temples served both as mementos and attestations of other legendary events; and the tombs of the heroes counted among the most powerful stimulants of mythical reminiscence.   The sceptre of Pelops and Agamemnôn, still preserved in the days of Pausanias at Chæroneia in Bœotia, was the work of the god Hêphæstos. While many other alleged productions of the same divine hand were preserved in different cities of Greece, this is the only one which Pausanias himself believed to be genuine: it had been carried by Elektra, daughter of Agamemnôn, to Phôkis, and

---

[1] The Philopseudes of Lucian (t. iii. p. 31, Hemst. cap. 2, 3, 4) shows not only the pride which the general public of Athens and Thêbes took in their old mythes (Triptolemus, Boreas, and Orei-thyia, the Sparti, &c.), but the way in which they treated every man who called the stories in question as a fool or as an atheist.   He remarks that if the guides who showed the antiquities had been restrained to tell nothing but what was true, they would have died of hunger; for the visiting strangers would not care to hear plain truth, even if they could have got it for nothing (μηδὲ ἀμισθὶ τῶν ξένων τἀληθὲς ἀκούειν ἐθελησάντων).

[2] Herodot. viii. 134.

[3] Herodot. v. 67.

[4] Euripid. Hippolyt. 1424 ; Pausan. ii. 32, 1 ; Lucian, De Deâ Syriâ, o. 60, vol. iv. p. 287, Tauch.

It is curious to see in the account of Pausanias how all the petty peculiarities of the objects around became connected with explanatory details growing out of this affecting legend. Compare Pausan. i. 22, 2.

received divine honours from the citizens of Chæroneia.[1] The
spears of Mêrionês and Odysseus were treasured up
at Engyium in Sicily, that of Achilles at Phasêlis;
the sword of Memnôn adorned the temple of
Asklêpius at Nicomêdia; and Pausanias, with unsuspecting confidence, adduces the two latter as proofs that the arms
of the heroes were made of brass.[2] The hide of the Kalydonian
boar was guarded and shown by the Tegeates as a precious
possession; the shield of Euphorbus was in like manner suspended in the temple of Branchidæ near Milêtus, as well as in
the temple of Hêrê in Argos. Visible relics of Epeius and
Philoktêtês were not wanting; moreover Strabo raises his voice
with indignation against the numerous Palladia which were
shown in different cities, each pretending to be the genuine image
from Troy.[3] It would be impossible to specify the number of
chapels, sanctuaries, solemnities, foundations of one sort or
another, said to have been first commenced by heroic or mythical
personages,—by Hêraklês, Jasôn, Mêdea, Alkmæôn, Diomêdês,
Odysseus, Danaus and his daughters,[4] &c. Perhaps in some of
these cases particular critics might raise objections, but the great
bulk of the people entertained a firm and undoubted belief in the
current legend.

Variety and universality of mythical relics.

If we analyse the intellectual acquisitions of a common Grecian
townsman, from the rude communities of Arcadia or Phôkis even
up to the enlightened Athens, we shall find that, over and above
the rules of art or capacities requisite for his daily wants, they
consisted chiefly of the various mythes connected with his gens,
his city, his religious festivals and the mysteries in which he
might have chosen to initiate himself, as well as with the works
of art and the more striking natural objects which he might see
around him—the whole set off and decorated by some knowledge
of the epic and dramatic poets. Such was the intellectual and
imaginative reach of an ordinary Greek, considered apart from
the instructed few: it was an aggregate of religion, of social and

---

[1] Pausan. ix. 40, 6.
[2] Plutarch, Marcell. c. 20; Pausan. iii. 3, 6.
[3] Pausan. viii. 46, 1; Diogen. Laër. viii. 5; Strabo, vi. p. 263; Appian, Bell. Mithridat. c. 77; Æschyl. Eumen. 380.

Wachsmuth has collected the numerous citations out of Pausanias on this
subject (Hellenische Alterthumskunde,
part ii. sect. 115, p. 111).
[4] Herodot. ii. 182; Plutarch, Pyrrh. c. 32; Schol. Apoll. Rhod. iv. 1217; Diodôr. iv. 56.

patriotic retrospect, and of romantic fancy, blended into one indivisible faith.   And thus the subjective value of the mythes, looking at them purely as elements of Grecian thought and feeling, will appear indisputably great, however little there may be of objective reality, either historical or philosophical, discoverable under them.

We must not omit the incalculable importance of the mythes as stimulants to the imagination of the Grecian artist in sculpture, in painting, in carving and in architecture.   From the divine and heroic legends and personages were borrowed those paintings, statues, and reliefs, which rendered the temples, porticos, and public buildings, at Athens and elsewhere, objects of surpassing admiration.   Such visible reproduction contributed again to fix the types of the gods and heroes familiarly and indelibly on the public mind.[1]   The figures delineated on cups and vases as well as on the walls of private houses were chiefly drawn from the same source— the mythes being the great storehouse of artistic scenes and composition.

The mythes in their bearing on Grecian art.

To enlarge on the characteristic excellence of Grecian art would here be out of place : I regard it only in so far as, having originally drawn its materials from the mythes, it reacted upon the mythical faith and imagination—the reaction imparting strength to the former as well as distinctness to the latter.   To one who saw constantly before him representations of the battles of the Centaurs or the Amazons,[2] of the exploits performed by Perseus and Bellerophôn, of the incidents composing the Trojan war or the Kalydonian boar-hunt—the process of belief, even in the more fantastic of these conceptions, became easy in proportion as the conception was familiarised.   And if any person had been slow to believe in the efficacy of the prayers of Æakus, whereby that devout hero once obtained special relief from Zeus, at a moment when Greece was perishing from long-continued sterility—his

Tendency of works of art to intensify the mythical faith.

---

[1] Ἡμιθέων ἀρεταῖς, the subjects of the works of Polygnotus at Athens (Melanthius, ap. Plutarch. Cimôn. c. 4) : compare Theocrit. xv. 138.

[2] The Centauromachia and the Amazonomachia are constantly associated together in the ancient Grecian reliefs (see the Expédition Scientifique de Morée, t. ii. p. 16, in the explanation of the temple of Apollo Epikureíus at Phigaleia).

doubts would probably vanish, when, on visiting the Æakeium at Ægina, there were exhibited to him the statues of the very envoys who had come on behalf of the distressed Greeks to solicit that Æakus would pray for them.[1] A Grecian temple[2] was not simply a place of worship, but the actual dwelling-place of a god, who was believed to be introduced by the solemn dedicatory ceremony, and whom the imagination of the people identified in the most intimate manner with his statue. The presence or removal of the statue was conceived as identical with that of the being represented—and while the statue was solemnly washed, dressed, and tended with all the respectful solicitude which would have been bestowed upon a real person,[3] miraculous tales were often rife respecting the manifestation of real internal feeling in the wood and the marble. At perilous or critical moments, the statue was affirmed to have sweated, to have wept, to have closed its eyes, or brandished the spear in its hands, in token of sympathy or indignation.[4] Such legends, springing up usually in times of suffering and danger, and finding few men

[1] Pausan. ii. 29, 6.

[2] Ernst Curtius, Die Akropolis von Athen, Berlin, 1844, p. 18. Arnobius adv. Gentes, vi. p. 203, ed. Elmenhorst.

[3] See the case of the Æginetans lending the Æakids for a time to the Thebans (Herodot. v 80), who soon however returned them : likewise sending the Æakids to the battle of Salamis (viii. 64—80). The Spartans, when they decreed that only one of their two kings should be out on military service, decreed at the same time that only one of the Tyndarids should go out with them (v. 75): they once lent the Tyndarids as aids to the envoys of Epizephyrian Locri, who prepared for them a couch on board their ship (Diodôr. Excerpt. xvi. p. 15. Dindorf.). The Thebans grant their hero Melanippus to Kleisthenês of Sikyôn (v. 68). What was sent must probably have been a consecrated copy of the genuine statue.
Respecting the solemnities practised towards the statues, see Plutarch, Alkibiad. 34 ; Kallimach. Hymn. ad Lavacr. Palladis, init., with the note of Spanheim ; K. O. Müller, Archæologie der Kunst, § 69 ; compare Plutarch, Quæstion. Romaic. § 61, p. 279 ; and

Tacit. Mor. Germ. c. 40; Diodôr. xvii. 49.
The manner in which the real presence of a hero was identified with his statue (τὸν δίκαιον δεῖ θεὸν Οἴκοι μένειν σώζοντα τοὺς ἱδρυμένους.—Menander, Fragm. Ἡνίοχος, p. 71, Meineke), consecrated ground, and oracle, is nowhere more powerfully attested than in the Heroïca of Philostratus (capp. 2—20, p. 674—692; also De Vit. Apollôn. Tyan. iv. 11), respecting Prôtesilaus at Elæus, Ajax at the Aianteium, and Hectôr at Ilium : Prôtesilaus appeared exactly in the equipment of his statue, —χλαμύδα ἐνῆπται, ξένε, τὸν Θετταλικὸν τρόπον, ὥσπερ καὶ τὸ ἄγαλμα τοῦτο (p. 674). The presence and sympathy of the hero Lykus is essential to the satisfaction of the Athenian dikasts (Aristophan. Vesp. 389—820) : the fragment of Lucilius quoted by Lactantius, De Falsâ Religione (i. 22), is curious.—Τοῖς ἥρωσι τοῖς κατὰ τὴν πόλιν καὶ τὴν χώραν ἱδρυμένοις (Lykurgus cont. Leokrat. c. 1).

[4] Plutarch, Timoleon. c. 12 ; Strabo, vi. p. 264. Theophrastus treats the perspiration as a natural phænomenon in the statues made of cedar-wood (Histor. Plant. v. 10). Plutarch discusses the credibility of this sort of miracles in his Life of Coriolanus, c. 37—38.

bold enough openly to contradict them, ran in complete harmony with the general mythical faith, and tended to strengthen it in all its various ramifications. The renewed activity of the god or hero both brought to mind and accredited the pre-existing mythes connected with his name. When Boreas, during the invasion of Greece by Xerxês and in compliance with the fervent prayer of the Athenians, had sent forth a providential storm to the irreparable damage of the Persian armada,[1] the sceptical minority (alluded to by Plato) who doubted the mythe of Boreas and Oreithyia, and his close connexion thus acquired with Erechtheus and the Erechtheids generally, must for the time have been reduced to absolute silence.

[1] Herodot. vii. 189. Compare the gratitude of the Megalopolitans to Boreas for having preserved them from the attack of the Lacedæmonian king Agis (Pausan. viii. 27, 4—viii. 36, 4). When the Ten Thousand Greeks were on their retreat through the cold mountains of Armenia, Boreas blew in their faces "parching and freezing intolerably". One of the prophets recommended that a sacrifice should be offered to him, which was done, "and the painful effect of the wind appeared to every one forthwith to cease in a marked manner" (καὶ πᾶσι δὴ περιφανῶς ἔδοξε λῆξαι τὸ χαλεπὸν τοῦ πνεύματος.—Xenoph. Anab. iv. 5, 3).

CHAPTER XVII.

THE GRECIAN MYTHICAL VEIN COMPARED WITH THAT OF MODERN EUROPE.

I HAVE already remarked that the existence of that popular
narrative talk, which the Germans express by the
significant word *Sage* or *Volks-Sage*, in a greater or
less degree of perfection or development, is a phænomenon common to almost all stages of society and to
almost all quarters of the globe. It is the natural
effusion of the unlettered, imaginative and believing man, and its
maximum of influence belongs to an early state of the human
mind : for the multiplication of recorded facts, the diffusion of
positive science, and the formation of a critical standard of belief,
tend to discredit its dignity and to repress its easy and abundant
flow. It supplies to the poet both materials to recombine and
adorn, and a basis as well as a stimulus for further inventions of
his own ; and this at a time when the poet is religious teacher,
historian, and philosopher, all in one—not, as he becomes at a
more advanced period, the mere purveyor of avowed, though
interesting, fiction.

*Μῦθος—
Sage—an
universal
manifesta-
tion of the
human
mind.*

Such popular stories, and such historical songs (meaning by
historical simply that which is accepted as history) are found in
most quarters of the globe, and especially among the Teutonic
and Celtic populations of early Europe. The old Gothic songs
were cast into a continuous history by the historian Ablavius ;[1]
and the poems of the Germans respecting Tuisto the earth-born
god, his son Mannus, and his descendants the eponyms of the
various German tribes,[2] as they are briefly described by Tacitus,

[1] Jornandes, De Reb. Geticis, capp.
4—6.

[2] Tacit. Mor. German. c. 2. "Cele-
brant carminibus antiquis. quod unum

remind us of Hesiod, or Eumêlus, or the Homeric Hymns. Jacob Grimm, in his learned and valuable Deutsche Mythologie, has exhibited copious evidence of the great fundamental analogy, along with many special differences, between the German, Scandinavian and Grecian mythical world ; and the Dissertation of Mr. Price (prefixed to his edition of Warton's History of English Poetry) sustains and illustrates Grimm's view. The same personifying imagination—the same ever-present conception of the will, sympathies, and antipathies of the gods as the producing causes of phænomena, and as distinguished from a course of nature with its invariable sequence—the same relations between gods, heroes and men, with the like difficulty of discriminating the one from the other in many individual names—a similar wholesale transfer of human attributes to the gods, with the absence of human limits and liabilities—a like belief in Nymphs, Giants, and other beings neither gods nor men—the same coalescence of the religious with the patriotic feeling and faith—these are positive features common to the early Greeks with the early Germans : and the negative conditions of the two are not less analogous—the absence of prose writing, positive records, and scientific culture. The preliminary basis and encouragements for the mythopœic faculty were thus extremely similar.

Analogy of the Germans and Celts with the Greeks.

But though the prolific forces were the same in kind, the results were very different in degree, and the developing circumstances were more different still.

First, the abundance, the beauty, and the long continuance of early Grecian poetry, in the purely poetical age, is a phænomenon which has no parallel elsewhere.

Secondly, the transition of the Greek mind from its poetical to its comparatively positive state was self-operated, accomplished by its own inherent and expansive force—aided indeed, but by no means either impressed or provoked, from without. From the poetry of Homer to the history of Thucydidês and the philosophy

Differences between them— Grecian poetry matchless— Grecian progress self-operated.

apud eos memoriæ et annalium genus est, Tuistonem Deum terrâ editum, et filium Mannum, originem gentis conditoresque. Quidam licentiâ vetus- tatis, plures Deo ortos, pluresque gentis appellationes, Marsos, Gambrivios, Suevos, Vandaliosque affirmant : eaque vera et antiqua nomina."

of Plato and Aristotle, was a prodigious step, but it was the native growth of the Hellenic youth into an Hellenic man ; and what is of still greater moment, it was brought about without breaking the thread either of religious or patriotic tradition—without any coercive innovation or violent change in the mental feelings. The legendary world, though the ethical judgments and rational criticisms of superior men had outgrown it, still retained its hold upon their feelings as an object of affectionate and reverential retrospect.

Far different from this was the development of the early Germans. We know little about their early poetry, but we shall run no risk of error in affirming that they had nothing to compare with either Iliad or Odyssey. Whether, if left to themselves, they would have possessed sufficient progressive power to make a step similar to that of the Greeks, is a question which we cannot answer. Their condition, mental as well as political, was violently changed by a foreign action from without. The influence of the Roman empire introduced artificially among them new institutions, new opinions, habits and luxuries, and, above all, a new religion ; the Romanised Germans becoming themselves successively the instruments of this revolution with regard to such of their brethren as still remained heathens. It was a revolution often brought about by penal and coercive means : the old gods Thor and Woden were formally deposed and renounced, their images were crumbled into dust, and the sacred oaks of worship and prophecy hewn down. But even where conversion was the fruit of preaching and persuasion, it did not the less break up all the associations of a German with respect to that mythical world which he called his past, and of which the ancient gods constituted both the charm and the sanctity : he had now only the alternative of treating them either as men or as dæmons.[1] That mixed religious and patriotic retrospect, formed by the

German progress brought about by violent influences from without.

[1] On the hostile influence exercised by the change of religion on the old Scandinavian poetry, see an interesting article of Jacob Grimm in the Göttinger Gelehrte Anzeigen, Feb. 1830, p. 268—273 ; a review of Olaf Tryggvson's Saga. The article *Helden* in his Deutsche Mythologie is also full of instruction on the same subject: see also the Einleitung to the book, p. 12, 2nd edition.
A similar observation has been made with respect to the old mythes of the pagan Russians by Eichhoff :—" L'établissement du Christianisme, ce gage du bonheur des nations, fut vivement

coalescence of piety with ancestral feeling, which constituted the appropriate sentiment both of Greeks and of Germans towards their unrecorded antiquity, was among the latter banished by Christianity : and while the root of the old mythes was thus cankered, the commemorative ceremonies and customs with which they were connected, either lost their consecrated character or disappeared altogether. Moreover new influences of great importance were at the same time brought to bear. The Latin language, together with some tinge of Latin literature—the habit of writing and of recording present events—the idea of a systematic law and pacific adjudication of disputes,—all these formed a part of the general working of Roman civilization, even after the decline of the Roman empire, upon the Teutonic and Celtic tribes. A class of specially-educated men was formed upon a Latin basis and upon Christian principles, consisting almost entirely of priests, who were opposed, as well by motives of rivalry as by religious feeling, to the ancient bards and storytellers of the community. The "lettered men"[1] were constituted apart from "the men of story," and Latin literature contributed along with religion to sink the mythes of untaught heathenism. Charlemagne indeed, at the same time that he employed aggressive and violent proceedings to introduce Christianity among the Saxons, also took special care to commit to writing and preserve the old heathen songs. But there can be little doubt that this step was the suggestion of a large and enlightened understanding peculiar to himself. The disposition general among lettered Christians of that age is more accurately represented by his son Louis le Débonnaire, who, having learnt

Operation of the Roman civilization and of Christianity upon the primitive German mythes.

appréció par les Russes, qui dans leur juste reconnaissance, le personnifièrent dans un héros. Vladimir le Grand, ami des arts, protecteur de la religion qu'il protégea, et dont les fruits firent oublier les fautes, devint l'Arthus et le Charlemagne de la Russie, et ses hauts faits furent un mythe national qui domina tous ceux du paganisme. Autour de lui se groupèrent ces guerriers aux formes athlétiques, au cœur généreux, dont la poésie aime à entourer le berceau mystérieux des peuples : et les exploits du vaillant Dobrinia, de Rogdai, d'Ilia, de Curilo, animèrent les ballades nationales, et vivent encore dans de naïfs récits." (Eichhoff, Histoire de la Langue et Littérature des Slaves, Paris, 1839, part iii. ch. 2, p. 190.)

[1] This distinction is curiously brought to view by Saxo Grammaticus, where he says of an Englishman named Lucas, that he was "literis quidem tenuiter instructus, sed historiarum scientiâ apprime eruditis" (p. 330, apud Dahlmann's Historische Forschungen, vol. i. p. 176).

these songs as a boy, came to abhor them when he arrived at
mature years, and could never be induced either to repeat or
tolerate them.[1]

According to the old heathen faith, the pedigree of the Saxon,
Anglian, Danish, Norwegian, and Swedish kings,—probably also
those of the German and Scandinavian kings generally,—was
traced to Odin, or to some of his immediate companions or
heroic sons.[2] I have already observed that the value of these
genealogies consisted not so much in their length, as in the
reverence attached to the name serving as primitive
source. After the worship attached to Odin had been
extinguished, the genealogical line was lengthened up
to Japhet or Noah—and Odin, no longer accounted
worthy to stand at the top, was degraded into one of
the simple human members of it.[3] And we find this
alteration of the original mythical genealogies to have
taken place even among the Scandinavians, although the intro-

*Alteration
in the
mythical
genealogies
—Odin and
the other
gods
degraded
into men.*

---

[1] " Barbara et antiquissima carmina
(says Eginhart in his Life of Charlemagne), quibus veterum regum actus
et bella canebantur, conscripsit."
    Theganus says of Louis le Débon-
naire, " Poetica carmina gentilia, quæ
in juventute didicerat, respuit, nec
legere, nec audire, nec docere, voluit".
(De Gestis Ludovici Imperatoris ap.
Pithœum, p. 304, c. xix.)
    [2] See Grimm's Deutsche Mythologie,
art. *Helden*, p. 356, 2nd edit. Hengist
and Horsa were fourth in descent from
Odin (Venerable Bede, Hist. i. 15).
Thiodolff, the Scald of Harold Haar-
fager king of Norway, traced the
pedigree of his sovereign through
thirty generations to Yngarfrey, the
son of Niord companion of Odin at
Upsal ; the kings of Upsal were called
Ynglinger, and the son of Thiodolff,
Ynglingatal (Dahlmann, Histor. For-
schung. i. p. 379). Eyvind, another
Scald, a century afterwards, deduced
the pedigree of Jarl Hacon from
Saming son of Yngwifrey (p. 381).
Are Frode, the Icelandic historian,
carried up his own genealogy through
thirty-six generations to Yngwe ; a
genealogy which Torfæus accepts as
trustworthy, opposing it to the line of
kings given by Saxo Grammaticus (p.
352). Torfæus makes Harold Haar-
fager a descendant from Odin through
twenty-seven generations ; Alfred of

England through twenty-three generations ; Offa of Mercia through fifteen
(p. 362). See also the translation by
Lange of P. A. Müller's Saga Bibliothek, Introd. p. xxviii. and the genealogical tables prefixed to Snorro Sturleson's Edda.
    Mr. Sharon Turner conceives the
human existence of Odin to be distinctly proved, seemingly upon the
same evidence as Euêmerus believed in
the human existence of Zeus (History
of the Anglo-Saxons, Appendix to b. ii.
ch. 3, p. 219, 5th edit.).
    [3] Dahlmann, Histor. Forschung. t.
i. p. 390. There is a valuable article
on this subject in the Zeitschrift für
Geschichts-Wissenschaft (Berlin, vol.
i. p. 237—282) by Stuhr, " Ueber einige
Hauptfragen des Nordischen Alterthums," wherein the writer illustrates
both the strong motive and the effective tendency, on the part of the
Christian clergy who had to deal
with these newly-converted Teutonic
pagans, to Euemerise the old gods,
and to represent a genealogy, which
they were unable to efface from men's
minds, as if it consisted only of mere
men.
    Mr. John Kemble (Ueber die
Stammtafel der Westsachsen, ap.
Stuhr. p. 254) remarks, that " nobili-
tas" among that people consisted in
descent from Odin and the other gods.

duction of Christianity was in those parts both longer deferred, so as to leave time for a more ample development of the heathen poetical vein—and seems to have created a less decided feeling of antipathy (especially in Iceland) towards the extinct faith.[1] The poems and tales composing the Edda, though first committed to writing after the period of Christianity, do not present the ancient gods in a point of view intentionally odious or degrading.

The transposition above alluded to, of the genealogical root from Odin to Noah, is the more worthy of notice, as it illustrates the genuine character of these genealogies, and shows that they sprung, not from any erroneous historical data, but from the turn of the religious feeling; also that their true value is derived from their being taken entire, as connecting the existing race of men with a divine original. If we could imagine that Grecian paganism had been superseded by Christianity in the year 500 B.C., the great and venerated gentile genealogies of Greece would have undergone the like modification; the Herakleids, Pelopids, Æakids, Asklepiads, &c., would have been merged in some larger aggregate branching out from the archæology of the Old Testament. The old heroic legends connected with these ancestral names would either have been forgotten, or so transformed as to suit the new vein of thought; for the altered worship, ceremonies, and customs would have been altogether at variance with them, and the mythical feeling would have ceased to dwell upon those to whom prayers were no longer offered. If the oak of Dôdôna had been cut down, or the Theôric ship had ceased to be sent from Athens

Colonel Sleeman also deals in the same manner with the religious legends of the Hindoos—so natural is the proceeding of Euêmerus, towards any religion in which a critic does not believe—

"They (the Hindoos) of course think that the incarnations of their three great divinities were beings infinitely superior to prophets, being in all their attributes and prerogatives equal to the divinities themselves. *But we are disposed to think that these incarnations were nothing more than great men whom their flatterers and poets have exalted into gods—this was the way in which men made their gods in ancient Greece and Egypt.*—All that the poets have sung of the actions of these men is now received as revelation from heaven: though nothing can be more monstrous than the actions ascribed to the best incarnation, Krishna, of the best of the gods, Vishnoo." (Sleeman, Rambles and Recollections of an Indian Official, vol. i. ch. viii. p. 61.)

[1] See P. E. Müller, Ueber den Ursprung und Verfall der Isländischen Historiographie, p. 63.

In the Leitfaden zur Nordischen Alterthumskunde, pp. 4—5 (Copenhagen, 1837), is an instructive summary of the different schemes of interpretation applied to the northern mythes : 1. the historical ; 2. the geographical ; 3. the astronomical ; 4. the physical ; 5. the allegorical.

to Delôs, the mythes of Thêseus and of the two black doves

Grecian paganism— what would have been the case, if it had been supplanted by Christianity in 500 B.C.

would have lost their pertinence, and died away. As it was, the change from Homer to Thucydidês and Aristotle took place internally, gradually, and imperceptibly. Philosophy and history were super-induced in the minds of the superior few, but the feelings of the general public continued unshaken— the sacred objects remained the same both to the eye and to the heart—and the worship of the ancient gods was even adorned by new architects and sculptors who greatly strengthened its imposing effect.

While then in Greece the mythopœic stream continued in the same course, only with abated current and influence, in modern Europe its ancient bed was blocked up and it was turned into new and divided channels. The old religion,—though as an ascendant faith, unanimously and publicly manifested, it became extinct,—still continued in detached scraps and fragments, and under various alterations of name and form. The heathen gods and goddesses, deprived as they were of divinity, did not pass out of the recollection and fears of their former worshippers, but were sometimes represented (on principles like those of Euêmerus) as having been eminent and glorious men—sometimes degraded into dæmons, magicians, elfs, fairies and other supernatural agents, of an inferior grade and generally mischievous cast. Christian writers such as Saxo Grammaticus and Snorro Sturleson committed to writing the ancient oral songs of the Scandinavian Scalds, and digested the events contained in them into continuous narrative—performing in this respect a task similar to that of the Grecian logographers Pherekydês and Hellanikus, in reference to Hesiod and the

Saxo Grammaticus and Snorro Sturleson contrasted with Pherekydês and Hellanikus.

Cyclic poets. But while Pherekydês and Hellanikus compiled under the influence of feelings substantially the same as those of the poets on whom they bestowed their care, the Christian logographers felt it their duty to point out the Odin and Thor of the old Scalds as evil dæmons, or cunning enchanters who had fascinated the minds of men into a false belief in their divinity.[1]

[1] "Interea tamen homines Christiani in numina non credant ethnica, nec aliter fidem narrationibus hisce adstruere vel adhibere debent, quam in

In some cases the heathen recitals and ideas were modified so as to suit Christian feeling. But when preserved without such a change, they exhibited themselves palpably, and were designated by their compilers, as at variance with the religious belief of the people, and as associated either with imposture or with evil spirits.

A new vein of sentiment had arisen in Europe, unsuitable indeed to the old mythes, yet leaving still in force the demand for mythical narrative generally. And this demand was satisfied, speaking generally, by two classes of narratives,—the legends of the Catholic Saints and the Romances of Chivalry, corresponding to two types of character, both perfectly accommodated to the feelings of the time,—the saintly ideal and the chivalrous ideal.

Mythopœic tendencies in modern Europe still subsisting, but forced into a new channel. 1. Saintly ideal ; 2. Chivalrous ideal.

Both these two classes of narrative correspond, in character as well as in general purpose, to the Grecian mythes,—being stories accepted as realities, from their full conformity with the predispositions and deep-seated faith of an uncritical audience, and

libri hujus procemio monitum est de causis et occasionibus cur et quomodo genus humanum a verâ fide aberraverit." (Extract from the Proso Edda, p. 75, in the Lexicon Mythologicum ad calcem Eddæ Sæmund. vol. iii. p. 357, Copenhag. edit.)

A similar warning is to be found in another passage cited by P. E. Müller, Ueber den Ursprung und Verfall der Isländischen Historiographie, p. 138, Copenhagen, 1813 : compare the Prologue to the Prose Edda, p. 6, and Mallet, Introduction à l'Histoire de Danemarc, ch. vii. p. 411—132.

Saxo Grammaticus represents Odin sometimes as a magician, sometimes as an evil dæmon, sometimes as a high-priest, or pontiff of heathenism, who imposed so powerfully upon the people around him as to receive divine honours. Thor also is treated as having been an evil dæmon. (See Lexicon Mythologic. ut supra, pp. 567, 915.)

Respecting the function of Snorro as logographer, see Præfat. ad Eddam, ut supra, p. xi. He is much more faithful, and less unfriendly to the old religion, than the other logographers of the ancient Scandinavian Sagas. (Leitfaden der Nordischen Alterthü-

mer, p. 14, by the Antiquarian Society of Copenhagen, 1837.)

By a singular transformation, dependent upon the same tone of mind, the authors of the French Chansons de Geste in the twelfth century turned Apollo into an evil dæmon, patron of the Mussulmans (see the Roman of Garin le Loherain, par M. Paulin Paris, 1833, p. 31) :—" Car mieux vaut Dieux que ne fait Apollis ". M. Paris observes, " Cet ancien Dieu des beaux arts est l'un des démons le plus souvent désignés dans nos poëmes, comme patron des Musulmans ".

The prophet Mahomet, too, anathematised the old Persian epic anterior to his religion. " C'est à l'occasion de Naser Ibn al-Hareth, qui avait apporté de Perse l'Histoire de Rustem et d'Isfendiar, et la faisait réciter par des chanteuses dans les assemblées des Koreischites, que Mahomet prononça le vers suivant (of the Koran) : Il y a des hommes qui achètent des contes frivoles, pour détourner par-la les hommes de la voie de Dieu, d'une manière insensée, et pour la livrer à la risée : mais leur punition les couvrira de honte." (Mohl, Préface au Livre des Rois de Ferdousi, p. xiii.)

prepared beforehand by their authors, not with any reference to the conditions of historical proof, but for the purpose of calling forth sympathy, emotion, or reverence. The type of the saintly character belongs to Christianity, being the history of Jesus Christ as described in the Gospels, and that of the prophets in the Old Testament; whilst the lives of holy men, who acquired a religious reputation from the fourth to the fourteenth century of the Christian æra, were invested with attributes, and illustrated with ample details, tending to assimilate them to this revered model. The numerous miracles, the cure of diseases, the expulsion of dæmons, the temptations and sufferings, the teaching and commands, with which the biography of Catholic saints abounds, grew chiefly out of this pious feeling, common to the writer and to his readers. Many of the other incidents, recounted in the same performances, take their rise from misinterpreted allegories, from ceremonies and customs of which it was pleasing to find a consecrated origin, or from the disposition to convert the etymology of a name into matter of history: many have also been suggested by local peculiarities, and by the desire of stimulating or justifying the devotional emotions of pilgrims who visited some consecrated chapel or image. The dove was connected, in the faith of the age, with the Holy Ghost, the serpent with Satan; lions, wolves, stags, unicorns, &c., were the subjects of other emblematic associations; and such modes of belief found expression for themselves in many narratives which brought the saints into conflict or conjoint action with these various animals. Legends of this kind, indefinitely multiplied and pre-eminently popular and affecting, in the middle ages, are not exaggerations of particular matters of fact, but emanations in detail of some current faith or feeling, which they served to satisfy, and by which they were in turn amply sustained and accredited.[1]

Legends of the saints.

---

[1] The legends of the Saints have been touched upon by M. Guizot (Cours d'Histoire Moderne, leçon xvii.) and by M. Ampère (Histoire Littéraire de la France, t. ii. cap. 14, 15, 16); but a far more copious and elaborate account of them, coupled with much just criticism, is to be found in the valuable Essai sur les Légendes Pieuses du Moyen Age, par L. F. Alfred Maury, Paris, 1843.

M. Guizot scarcely adverts at all to the more or less of matter of fact contained in these biographies: he regards them altogether as they grew out of and answered to the predominant emotions and mental exigencies of the age: "Au milieu d'un déluge de fables

Readers of Pausanias will recognise the great general analogy between the stories recounted to him at the temples which he visited, and these legends of the middle ages. Though the type of character which the latter illustrate is indeed materially different, yet the source as well as the circulation, the generating as well as the sustaining forces, were in both cases the same. Such legends were the natural growth of a religious faith earnest, unexamining, and interwoven with the feelings at a time when the reason does not need to be cheated. The lives of the Saints bring us even back to the simple and ever-operative theology of the Homeric age ; so constantly is the hand of God exhibited even in the minutest details, for the succour of a favoured individual,—so completely is the scientific point of view, respecting the phæno-mena of nature, absorbed into the religious.[1] During the

Their analogy with the Homeric theology.

absurdes, la morale éclate avec un grand empire" (p. 159, ed. 1829). "Les légendes ont été pour les Chrétiens de ce temps (qu'on me permette cette comparaison purement littéraire) ce que sont pour les Orientaux ces longs récits, ces histoires si brillantes et si variées, dont les Mille et une Nuits nous donnent un échantillon. C'était là que l'imagination populaire errait librement dans un monde inconnu, merveilleux, plein de mouvement et de poésie" (p. 175, *ibid.*).

M. Guizot takes his comparison with the tales of the Arabian Nights, as heard by an Oriental with unin-quiring and unsuspicious credence. Viewed with reference to an instructed European, who reads these narratives as pleasing but recognised fiction, the comparison would not be just : for no one in that age dreamt of questioning the truth of the biographies. All the remarks of M. Guizot assume this implicit faith in them as literal his-tories ; perhaps in estimating the feelings to which they owed their extraordinary popularity, he allows too little predominance to the reli-gious feeling, and too much influence to other mental exigencies which then went along with it ; more especially as he remarks in the preceding lecture (p. 116), " Le caractère général de l'époque est la concentration du développement intellectuel dans la sphère religieuse".

How this absorbing religious senti-ment operated in generating and ac-

crediting new matter of narrative, is shown with great fulness of detail in the work of M. Maury:—"Tous les écrits du moyen âge nous apportent la preuve de cette préoccupation exclusive des esprits vers l'Histoire Sainte et les prodiges qui avaient signalé l'avènement du Christianisme. Tous nous montrent la pensée de Dieu et du Ciel, dominant les moindres œuvres de cette époque de naïve et de crédule simplicité. D'ailleurs, n'était-ce pas le moine, le clerc, qui constituaient alors les seuls écrivains ? Qu'y a-t-il d'étonnant que le sujet habituel de leurs méditations, de leurs études, se reflétât sans cesse dans leurs ouvrages? Partout repa-raissait à l'imagination Jésus et ses Saints : cette image, l'esprit l'accueil-lait avec soumission et obéissance : il n'osait pas encore envisager ces célestes pensées avec l'œil de la critique, armé de défiance et de doute ; au contraire, l'intelligence les acceptait toutes indis-tinctement et s'en nourrissait avec avidité. Ainsi s'accréditaient tous les jours de nouvelles fables. *Une foi vive veut sans cesse de nouveaux faits qu'elle puisse croire*, comme la charité veut de nouveaux bienfaits pour s'exercer" (p. 48). The remarks on the History of St. Christopher, whose personality was allegorised by Luther and Melanch-thon, are curious (p. 57).

[1] " Dans les prodiges que l'on ad-mettait avoir dû nécessairement s'opérer au tombeau du saint nouvelle-ment canonisé, l'expression, ' Cæci

intellectual vigour of Greece and Rome, a sense of the invariable course of nature and of the scientific explanation of phænomena had been created among the superior minds, and through them indirectly among the remaining community; thus limiting to a certain extent the ground open to be occupied by a religious legend. With the decline of the pagan literature and philosophy, before the sixth century of the Christian æra, this scientific conception gradually passed out of sight, and left the mind free to a religious interpretation of nature not less simple and *naïf* than that which had prevailed under the Homeric paganism.[1]

---

visum, claudi gressum, muti loquelam, surdi auditum, paralytici debitum membrorum officium, recuperabant,' était devenue plûtot une formule d'usage que la relation littérale du fait." (Maury, Essai sur les Légendes Pieuses du Moyen Age, p. 5.)

To the same purpose M. Ampère, ch. 14, p. 361: "Il y a un certain nombre de faits que l'agiographie reproduit constamment, quelque soit son héros: ordinairement ce personnage a eu dans sa jeunesse une vision qui lui a révélé son avenir: ou bien, une prophétie lui a annoncé ce qu'il serait un jour. Plus tard, il opère un certain nombre de miracles, toujours les mêmes; il exorcise des possédés, ressuscite des morts, il est averti de sa fin par un songe. Puis sur son tombeau s'accomplissent d'autres merveilles à-peu-près semblables."

[1] A few words from M. Ampère to illustrate this: " C'est donc au sixième siècle que la légende se constitue: c'est alors qu'elle prend complètement le caractère naïf qui lui appartient: qu'elle est elle-même, qu'elle se sépare de toute influence étrangère. En même temps, l'ignorance devient de plus en plus grossière, et par suite la crédulité s'accroit: les calamités du temps sont plus lourdes, et l'on a un plus grand besoin de remède et de consolation . . . . Les récits miraculeux se substituent aux argumens de la théologie. Les miracles sont devenus la meilleure démonstration du Christianisme: c'est la seule que puissent comprendre les esprits grossiers des barbares " (c. 15, p. 373).

Again, c. 17, p. 401: " Un des caractères de la légende est de mêler constamment le puéril au grand: il faut l'avouer, elle défigure parfois un peu ces hommes d'une trempe si forte,

en mettant sur leur compte des anecdotes dont le caractère n'est pas toujours sérieux; elle en a usé ainsi pour St. Columban, dont nous verrons tout à l'heure le rôle vis-à-vis de Brunehaut et des chefs Mérovingiens. La légende aurait pu se dispenser de nous apprendre, comment un jour, il se fit rapporter par un corbeau les gants qu'il avait perdus: comment, un autre jour, il empêcha la bière de couler d'un tonneau percé, et diverses merveilles, certainement indignes de sa mémoire."

The miracle by which St. Columban employed the raven to fetch back his lost gloves is exactly in the character of the Homeric and Hesiodic age: the earnest faith, as well as the reverential sympathy, between the Homeric man and Zeus or Athênê, is indicated by the invocation of their aid for his own sufferings of detail and in his own need and danger. The criticism of M. Ampère, on the other hand, is analogous to that of the latter pagans, after the conception of a course of nature had become established in men's minds, so far as that exceptional interference by the gods was understood to be, comparatively speaking, rare, and only supposable upon what were called great emergencies.

In the old Hesiodic legend (see above, ch. ix.), Apollo is apprised by a raven of the infidelity of the nymph Korônis to him—Τῷ μὲν ἄρ' ἄγγελος ἦλθε κόραξ, &c. (the raven appears elsewhere as companion of Apollo, Plutarch. de Isid. et Os. p. 379, Herod. iv. 15). Pindar in his version of the legend eliminated the raven, without specifying *how* Apollo got his knowledge of the circumstance. The Scholiasts praise Pindar much for having rejected the puerile version of the story— ἐπαινεῖ τὸν Πίνδαρον ὁ Ἀρτέμων ὅτι

The great religious movement of the Reformation, and the gradual formation of critical and philosophical habits in the modern mind, have caused these legends of the Saints,—once the charm and cherished creed of a numerous public,[1]—to pass altogether out of credit, without even being regarded, among

παρακρουσάμενος τὴν περὶ τὸν κόρακα ἱστορίαν, αὐτὸν δι᾽ ἑαυτοῦ ἐγνωκέναι φησὶ τὸν Ἀπόλλω . . . χαίρειν οὖν ἐάσας τῷ τοιούτῳ μύθῳ τέλεως ὄντι ληρώδει, &c.—compare also the criticisms of the Schol. ad Soph. Œdip. Col. 1378, on the old epic Thebaïs; and the remarks of Arrian (Exp. Al. iii. 4) on the divine interference by which Alexander and his army were enabled to find their way across the sand of the desert to the temple of Ammon.

In the eyes of M. Ampère, the recital of the biographer of Saint Columban appears puerile (οὔπω ἴδον ὧδε θεοὺς ἀναφανδὰ φιλεῦντας, Odyss. iii. 221): in the eyes of that biographer, the criticism of M. Ampère would have appeared impious. When it is once conceded that phænomena are distributable under two denominations, the natural and the miraculous, it must be left to the feelings of each individual to determine what is and what is not a suitable occasion of a miracle. Diodôrus and Pausanias differed in opinion (as stated in a previous chapter) about the death of Actæon by his own hounds —the former maintaining that the case was one fit for the special intervention of the goddess Artemis; the latter that it was not so. The question is one determinable only by the religious feelings and conscience of the two dissentients: no common standard of judgment can be imposed upon them : for no reasonings derived from science or philosophy are available, inasmuch as in this case the very point in dispute is, whether the scientific point of view be admissible. Those who are disposed to adopt the supernatural belief, will find in every case the language open to them wherewith Dionysius of Halikarnassus (in recounting a miracle wrought by Vesta in the early times of Roman history for the purpose of rescuing an unjustly accused virgin) reproves the sceptics of his time : " It is well worth while (he observes) to recount the special manifestation (ἐπιφάνειαν) which the goddess showed to these unjustly accused virgins. For these circumstances, extraordinary as they

are, have been held worthy of belief by the Romans, and historians have talked much about them. Those persons indeed who adopt the atheistical schemes of philosophy (if indeed we must call them *philosophy*), pulling in pieces as they do *all* the special manifestations (ἀπάσας διασύροντες τὰς ἐπιφανείας τῶν θεῶν) of the gods which have taken place among Greeks or barbarians, will of course turn *these* stories also into ridicule, ascribing them to the vain talk of men, as if none of the gods cared at all for mankind. But those who, having pushed their researches farther, believe the gods not to be indifferent to human affairs, but favourable to good men and hostile to bad—will not treat *these* special manifestations as *more* incredible than others." (Dionys. Halic. ii. 68—69.) Plutarch, after noticing the great number of miraculous statements in circulation, expresses his anxiety to draw a line between the true and the false, but cannot find where : " excess both of credulity and of incredulity (he tells us) in such matters is dangerous ; caution, and nothing too much, is the best course ". (Camillus, c. 6.) Polybius is for granting permission to historians to recount a sufficient number of miracles to keep up a feeling of piety in the multitude, but not more ; to measure out the proper quantity (he observes) is difficult, but not impossible (δυσπαράγραφός ἐστιν ἡ ποσότης, οὐ μὴν ἀπαράγραφός γε, xvi. 12).

[1] The great Bollandist collection of the Lives of the Saints, intended to comprise the whole year, did not extend beyond the nine months from January to October, which occupy fifty-three large volumes. The month of April fills three of those volumes, and exhibits the lives of 1472 saints. Had the collection run over the entire year, the total number of such biographies could hardly have been less than 25,000, and might have been even greater (see Guizot, Cours d'Histoire Moderne leçon xvii. p.157).

Protestants at least, as worthy of a formal scrutiny into the evidence—a proof of the transitory value of public belief, however sincere and fervent, as a certificate of historical truth, if it be blended with religious predispositions.

The same mythopœic vein, and the same susceptibility and facility of belief, which had created both supply and demand for the legends of the Saints, also provided the abundant stock of romantic narrative poetry, in amplification and illustration of Chivalrous ideal— the chivalrous ideal. What the legends of Troy, of Thêbes, of the Kalydonian boar, of Œdipus, Thêseus, Romances of Charle- magne and Arthur. &c., were to an early Greek, the tales of Arthur, of Charlemagne, of the Niebelungen, were to an English- man, or Frenchman, or German, of the twelfth or thirteenth century. They were neither recognised fiction nor authenticated history; they were history, as it is felt and welcomed by minds unaccustomed to investigate evidence and unconscious of the necessity of doing so. That the Chronicle of Turpin, a mere compilation of poetical legends respecting Charlemagne, was accepted as genuine history, and even pro- nounced to be such by papal authority, is well known; and the authors of the Romances announce themselves, not less than those of the old Grecian epic, as being about to recount real matter of fact.[1] It is certain that Charlemagne is a great

---

[1] See Warton's History of English Poetry, vol. i. dissert. i. p. xvii. Again, in sect. iii. p. 140 : "Vincent de Beau- vais, who lived under Louis IX. of France (about 1260), and who, on account of his extraordinary erudition, was appointed preceptor to that king's sons, very gravely classes Archbishop Turpin's Charlemagne among the real histories, and places it on a level with Suetonius and Cæsar. He was himself an historian, and has left a large his- tory of the world, fraught with a variety of reading, and of high repute in the middle ages; but edifying and entertaining as this work might have been to his contemporaries, at present it serves only to record their prejudices and to characterise their credulity." About the full belief in Arthur and the tales of the Round Table during the fourteenth century, and about the strange historical mistakes of the poet Gower in the fifteenth, see the same work, sect. 7, vol. ii. p. 33; sect. 19, vol. ii. p. 239.

"L'auteur de la Chronique de Turpin (says M. Sismondi, Littérature du Midi, vol. i. ch. 7, p. 289) n'avait point l'intention de briller aux yeux du public par une invention heureuse, ni d'amuser les oisifs par des contes merveilleux qu'ils reconnoîtroient pour tels : il présentait aux Français tous ces faits étranges comme de l'histoire, et la lecture des légendes fabuleuses avait accoutumé à croire à de plus grandes merveilles encore; aussi plusieurs de ces fables furent-elles reproduites dans la Chronique de St. Denis."

Again, ib. p. 290 : "Souvent les anciens romanciers, lorsqu'ils entre- prennent un récit de la cour de Charlemagne, prennent un ton plus élevé : ce ne sont point des fables qu'ils vont conter, c'est de l'histoire nationale,—c'est la gloire de leurs

historical name, and it is possible, though not certain, that the name of Arthur may be historical also. But the Charlemagne of history, and the Charlemagne of romance, have little except the name in common ; nor could we ever determine, except by independent evidence (which in this case we happen to possess), whether Charlemagne was a real or a fictitious person.[1] That illustrious name, as well as the more problematical Arthur, is taken up by the romancers, not with a view to celebrate realities previously verified, but for the purpose of setting forth or amplifying an ideal of their own, in such manner as both to rouse the feelings and captivate the faith of their hearers.

To inquire which of the personages of the Carlovingian epic were real and which were fictitious,—to examine whether the expedition ascribed to Charlemagne against Jerusalem had ever taken place or not,—to separate truth from exaggeration in the exploits of the Knights of the Round table,—these were problems which an audience of that day had neither disposition to undertake nor means to resolve. They accepted the narrative as they heard it, without suspicion or reserve : the incidents related, as well as the connecting links between them, were in full harmony with their feelings, and gratifying as well to their sympathies as to their curiosity : nor was anything farther wanting to induce them

ancêtres qu'ils veulent célébrer, et ils ont droit alors à demander qu'on les écoute avec respect ".

The Chronicle of Turpin was inserted, even so late as the year 1566, in the collection printed by Scardius at Frankfort of early German historians (Ginguené, Histoire Littéraire d'Italie, vol. iv. part ii. ch. 3, p. 157).

To the same point—that these romances were listened to as real stories—see Sir Walter Scott's Preface to Sir Tristram, p. lxvii. The authors of the Legends of the Saints are not less explicit in their assertions that everything which they recount is true and well-attested (Ampère, c. 14, p. 358).

[1] The series of articles by M. Fauriel, published in the Revue des deux Mondes, vol. xiii., are full of instruction respecting the origin, tenor, and influence of the Romances of Chivalry. Though the name of Charlemagne appears, the romancers are really unable to distinguish him from Charles Martel or from Charles the Bald (pp. 537—539). They ascribe to him an expedition to the Holy Land, in which he conquered Jerusalem from the Saracens, obtained possession of the relics of the passion of Christ, the crown of thorns, &c. These precious relics he carried to Rome, from whence they were taken to Spain by a Saracen emir named Balan at the head of an army. The expedition of Charlemagne against the Saracens in Spain was undertaken for the purpose of recovering the relics :—" Ces divers romans peuvent être regardés comme la suite, comme le développement, de la fiction de la conquête de Jérusalem par Charlemagne ".

Respecting the Romance of Rinaldo of Montauban (describing the struggles of a feudal lord against the emperor) M. Fauriel observes, "Il n'y a, je crois, aucun fondement historique : c'est, selon toute apparence, la pure expression poétique du fait général," &c. (p. 542).

to believe it, though the historical basis might be ever so slight or even non-existent.[1]

The romances of chivalry represented, to those who heard them, real deeds of the foretime—"glories of the foregone men,"

[1] Among the "formules consacrées" (observes M. Fauriel) of the romancers of the Carlovingian epic, are asseverations of their own veracity, and of the accuracy of what they are about to relate — specification of witnesses whom they have consulted—appeals to pretended chronicles:—"Que ces citations, ces indications, soient parfois sérieuses et sincères, cela peut être ; mais c'est une exception et une exception rare. De telles allégations de la part des romanciers, sont en général un pur et simple mensonge, mais non toutefois un mensonge gratuit. C'est un mensonge qui a sa raison et sa convenance : il tient au désir et au besoin de satisfaire une opinion accoutumée à supposer et à chercher du vrai dans les fictions du genre de celles où l'on allègue ces prétendues autorités. La manière dont les auteurs de ces fictions les qualifient souvent eux-mêmes, est une conséquence naturelle de leur prétention d'y avoir suivi des documens vénérables. Ils les qualifient de chansons de vieille histoire, de haute histoire, de bonne geste, de grande baronnie : et ce n'est pas pour se vanter qu'ils parlent ainsi : la vanité d'auteur n'est rien chez eux, en comparaison du besoin qu'ils ont d'être crus, de passer pour de simples traducteurs, de simples répétiteurs de légendes ou d'histoire consacrée. Ces protestations de véracité, qui, plus ou moins expresses, sont de rigueur dans les romans Carlovingiens, y sont aussi fréquemment accompagnées de protestations accessoires contre les romanciers, qui, ayant déjà traité un sujet donné, sont accusés d'y avoir faussé la vérité." (Fauriel, Orig. de l'Epopée Chevaleresque, in the Revue des Deux Mondes, vol. xiii. p. 554.)

About the Cycle of the Round Table, see the same series of articles (Rev. D. M. t. xiv. p. 170—184). The Chevaliers of the Saint Graal were a sort of idéal of the Knights Templars : "Une race de princes héroïques, originaires de l'Asie, fut prédestinée par le ciel même à la garde du Saint Graal. Perille fut le premier de cette race, qui s'étant converti au Christianisme, passa en Europe sous l'Empereur Vespasien," &c. ; then follows a string of fabulous incidents : the epical agency is similar to that of Homer—Διὸς δ᾽ ἐτελείετο βουλή.

M. Paulin Paris, in his Prefaces to the Romans des Douze Pairs de France, has controverted many of the positions of M. Fauriel, and with success, so far as regards the Provençal origin of the Chansons de Geste, asserted by the latter. In regard to the Romances of the Round Table, he agrees substantially with M. Fauriel ; but he tries to assign a greater historical value to the poems of the Carlovingian epic—very unsuccessfully in my opinion. But his own analysis of the old poem of Garin le Loherain bears out the very opinion which he is confuting : "Nous sommes au règne de Charles Martel, et nous reconnaissons sous d'autres noms les détails exacts de la fameuse défaite d'Attila dans les champs Catalauniques. Saint Loup et Saint Nicaise, glorieux prélats du quatrième siècle, reviennent figurer autour du père de Pépin le Bref : enfin pour compléter la confusion, Charles Martel meurt sur le champ de bataille, à la place du roi des Visigoths, Théodoric .... Toutes les parties de la narration sont vraies : seulement toutes s'y trouvent déplacées. En général, les peuples n'entendent rien à la chronologie : les évènemens restent : les individus, les lieux et les époques, ne laissent aucune trace : c'est, pour ainsi dire, une décoration scénique que l'on applique indifféremment à des récits souvent contraires." (Preface to the Roman de Garin le Loherain, pp. xvi.-xx. : Paris, 1833.) Compare also his Lettre à M. Monmerqué, prefixed to the Roman de Berthe aux Grans Piés, Paris, 1836.

To say that all the parts of the narrative are true, is contrary to M. Paris's own showing : some parts may be true, separately taken, but these fragments of truth are melted down with a large mass of fiction, and cannot be discriminated unless we possess some independent test. The poet who picks out one incident from the fourth century, another from the fifth, and a few more from the eighth, and then blends them all into a continuous tale, along with many additions of his own, shows that he takes the items of fact

to use the Hesiodic expression,[1] at the same time that they embodied and filled up the details of an heroic ideal, such as that age could conceive and admire—a fervent piety, combined with strength, bravery, and the love of adventurous aggression directed sometimes against *Accepted as realities of the foretime.* infidels, sometimes against enchanters or monsters, sometimes in defence of the fair sex.   Such characteristics were naturally popular, in a century of feudal struggles and universal insecurity, when the grand subjects of common respect and interest were the church and the crusades, and when the latter especially were embraced with an enthusiasm truly astonishing.

The long German poem of the Niebelungen Lied, as well as the Volsunga Saga and a portion of the songs of the Edda, relate to a common fund of mythical, superhuman personages, and of fabulous adventure, identified with the earliest antiquity of the Teutonic and Scandinavian race, and representing their primi- *Teutonic and Scandinavian epic—its analogy with the Grecian.* tive sentiment towards ancestors of divine origin.   Sigurd, Brynhilde, Gudrun, and Atle, are mythical characters celebrated as well by the Scandinavian Scalds as by the German epic poets, but with many varieties and separate additions to distinguish the one from the other.   The German epic, later and more elaborated, includes various persons not known to the songs in the Edda, in particular the prominent name of Dieterich of Bern—presenting moreover the principal characters and circumstances as Christian, while in the Edda there is no trace of anything but heathenism.   There is indeed, in this the old and heathen version, a remarkable analogy with many points of Grecian mythical narrative.   As in the case of the short life of Achilles, and of the miserable Labdakids of Thêbes—so in the family of the Volsungs, though sprung from and protected by the gods—a curse of destiny hangs upon them and brings on

because they suit the purposes of his narrative, not because they happen to be attested by historical evidence.   His hearers are not critical : they desire to have their imaginations and feelings affected, and they are content to accept without question whatever accomplishes this end.

[1] Hesiod, Theogon. 100—κλέα προτέρων ἀνθρώπων.   Puttenham talks of

the remnant of bards existing in his time (1589) : " Blind Harpers, or such like Taverne Minstrels, whose matters are for the most part *stories of old time*, as the Tale of Sir Topaze, the Reportes of Bevis of Southampton, Adam Bell, Clymme of the Clough, and such other old Romances or *Historical Rhymes* ". (Arte of English Poesie, book ii cap. 9.)

their ruin, in spite of pre-eminent personal qualities.[1] The more thoroughly this old Teutonic story has been traced and compared, in its various transformations and accompaniments, the less can any well-established connexion be made out for it with authentic historical names or events. We must acquiesce in its personages as distinct in original conception from common humanity, and as belonging to the subjective mythical world of the race by whom they were sung.

Such were the compositions which not only interested the emotions, but also satisfied the undistinguishing historical curiosity, of the ordinary public in the middle ages. The exploits of many of these romantic heroes resemble in several points those of the Grecian : the adventures of Perseus, Achilles, Odysseus, Atalanta, Bellerophôn, Jasôn, and the Trojan war or Argonautic expedition generally, would have fitted in perfectly

[1] Respecting the Volsunga Saga and the Niebelungen Lied, the work of Lange — Untersuchungen über die Geschichte und das Verhältniss der Nordischen und Deutschen Heldensage —is a valuable translation from the Danish Saga-Bibliothek of P. E. Müller.

P. E. Müller maintains indeed the historical basis of the tales respecting the Volsungs (see p. 102—107)—upon arguments very unsatisfactory; though the genuine Scandinavian origin of the tale is perfectly made out. The chapter added by Lange himself at the close (see p. 432, &c.) contains juster views as to the character of the primitive mythology, though he too advances some positions respecting a something "reinsymbolisches" in the background, which I find it difficult to follow (see p. 477, &c.).—There are very ancient epical ballads still sung by the people in the Faro islands, many of them relating to Sigurd and his adventures (p. 412).

Jacob Grimm, in his Deutsche Mythologie, maintains the purely mythical character, as opposed to the historical, of Siegfried and Dieterich (Art. Helden, pp. 344—346).

So, too, in the great Persian epic of Ferdousi, the principal characters are religious and mythical. M. Mohl observes,—" Les caractères des personnages principaux de l'ancienne histoire de Perse se retrouvent dans le livre des Rois (de Ferdousi) tels que les indiquent les parties des livres de Zoroaster que nous possédons encore. Kaioumors, Djemschid, Feridoun, Gushtasp, Isfendiar, &c., jouent dans le poème épique le même rôle que dans les Livres sacrés : à cela près, que dans les derniers ils nous apparaissent à travers une atmosphère mythologique qui grandit tous leurs traits : mais cette différence est précisément celle qu'on devait s'attendre à trouver entre la tradition religieuse et la tradition épique." Mohl, Livre des Rois, par Ferdousi, Préface, p. 1.

The Persian historians subsequent to Ferdousi have all taken his poem as the basis of their histories, and have even copied him faithfully and literally (Mohl, p. 53). Many of his heroes became the subjects of long epical biographies, written and recited without any art or grace, often by writers whose names are unknown (ib. p. 54—70). Mr. Morier tells us that "the Shah Nameh is still believed by the present Persians to contain their ancient history " (Adventures of Hajji Baba, o. 32). As the Christian romancers transformed Apollo into the patron of Mussulmans, so Ferdousi makes Alexander the Great a Christian : "La critique historique (observes M. Mohl) était du temps de Ferdousi chose presqu'inconnue " (ib. p. xlviii.). About the absence not only of all historiography, but also of all idea of it or taste for it, among the early Indians, Persians, Arabians, &c., see the learned book of Nork, Die Götter Syriens, Preface, p. viii. seqq. (Stuttgart, 1842).

to the Carlovingian or other epics of the period.[1] That of the middle ages, like the Grecian, was eminently expansive in its nature.   New stories were successively attached to the names and companions of Charlemagne and Arthur, just as the legend of Troy was enlarged by Arktinus, Leschês, and Stesichorus—that of Thêbes by fresh miseries entailed on the fated head of Œdipus,—and that of the Kalydonian boar by the addition of Atalanta.   Altogether, the state of mind of the hearers seems in both cases to have been much the same—eager for emotion and sympathy, and receiving any narrative attuned to their feeling, not merely with hearty welcome, but also with unsuspecting belief.

Heroic character and self-expanding subject common to both.

Nevertheless there were distinctions deserving of notice, which render the foregoing proposition more absolutely exact with regard to Greece than with regard to the middle ages.   The tales of the epic, and the mythes in their most popular and extended signification, were the only intellectual nourishment with which the Grecian public were supplied, until the sixth century before the Christian æra : there was no prose writing, no history, no philosophy.   But such was not exactly the case at the time when the epic of the middle ages appeared.   At that time, a portion of society possessed the Latin language, the habit of writing, and some

Points of distinction between the two— epic of the middle ages neither stood so completely alone, nor was so closely interwoven with religion, as the Grecian.

---

[1] Several of the heroes of the ancient world were indeed themselves popular subjects with the romancers of the middle ages, Thêseus, Jasòn, &c. ; Alexander the Great more so than any of them.

Dr. Warton observes respecting the Argonautic expedition, "Few stories of antiquity have more the cast of one of the old romances than this of Jasòn. An expedition of a new kind is made into a strange and distant country, attended with infinite dangers and difficulties.   The king's daughter of the new country is an enchantress ; she falls in love with the young prince, who is the chief adventurer.   The prize which he seeks is guarded by brazen-footed bulls, who breathe fire, and by a hideous dragon who never sleeps. The princess lends him the assistance of her charms and incantations to con-

quer these obstacles ; she gives him possession of the prize, leaves her father's court, and follows him into his native country." (Warton, Observations on Spenser, vol. i. p. 178.)

To the same purpose M. Ginguené : "Le premier modèle des Fées n'est-il pas dans Circé, dans Calypso, dans Médée?   Celui des géans, dans Polyphème, dans Cacus, et dans les géans, ou les Titans, cette race ennemie de Jupiter?   Les serpens et les dragons des romans ne sont-ils pas des successeurs du dragon des Hespérides, et de celui de la Toison d'or ? Les Magiciens ! la Thessalie en étoit pleine.   Les armes enchantées et impénétrables ! elles sont de la même trempe, et l'on peut les croire forgées au même fourneau que celles d'Achille et d'Enée." (Ginguené, Histoire Litteraire d'Italie, vol. iv. part ii. ch. 3, p. 151.)

tinge both of history and philosophy : there were a series of
chronicles, scanty indeed and imperfect, but referring to contemporary events and preventing the real history of the past from
passing into oblivion: there were even individual scholars, in the
twelfth century, whose acquaintance with Latin literature was
sufficiently considerable to enlarge their minds and to improve their
judgments. Moreover the epic of the middle ages, though deeply
imbued with religious ideas, was not directly amalgamated with
the religion of the people, and did not always find favour with
the clergy ; while the heroes of the Grecian epic were not only
linked in a thousand ways with existing worship, practices, and
sacred localities, but Homer and Hesiod pass with Herodotus for
the constructors of Grecian theology. We thus see that the
ancient epic was both exempt from certain distracting influences
by which that of the middle ages was surrounded, and more
closely identified with the veins of thought and feeling prevalent
in the Grecian public. Yet these counteracting influences did
not prevent Pope Calixtus II. from declaring the Chronicle of
Turpin to be a genuine history.

If we take the history of our own country as it was conceived
and written from the twelfth to the seventeenth century by
Hardyng, Fabyan, Grafton, Hollinshed, and others, we shall find
that it was supposed to begin with Brute the Trojan, and was
carried down from thence, for many ages and through a long
succession of kings, to the times of Julius Cæsar. A similar
belief of descent from Troy, arising seemingly from a
reverential imitation of the Romans and of their
Trojan origin, was cherished in the fancy of other
European nations. With regard to the English, the
chief circulator of it was Geoffrey of Monmouth. It
passed with little resistance or dispute into the
national faith—the kings from Brute downward
being enrolled in regular chronological series with their respective dates annexed. In a dispute which took place during the
reign of Edward I. (A.D. 1301) between England and Scotland,
the descent of the kings of England from Brute the Trojan was
solemnly embodied in a document put forth to sustain the rights
of the crown of England, as an argument bearing on the case
then in discussion : and it passed without attack from the opposing

(marginal note:) History of England—how con-ceived down to the seventeenth century—began with Brute the Trojan.

party,[1]—an incident which reminds us of the appeal made by
Æschinês, in the contention between the Athenians and Philip
of Macedôn respecting Amphipolis, to the primitive dotal rights
of Akamas son of Thêseus—and also of the defence urged by the
Athenians to sustain their conquest of Sigeium, against the
reclamations of the Mityleneans, wherein the former alleged that
they had as much right to the place as any of the other Greeks
who had formed part of the victorious armament of Agamemnôn.[1]

The tenacity with which this early series of British kings was
defended, is no less remarkable than the facility with
which it was admitted. The chroniclers at the beginning of the seventeenth century warmly protested
against the intrusive scepticism which would cashier so
many venerable sovereigns and efface so many noble
deeds. They appealed to the patriotic feelings of their hearers,
represented the enormity of thus setting up a presumptuous
criticism against the belief of ages, and insisted on the danger of
the precedent as regarded history generally.[3] How this controversy stood, at the time and in the view of the illustrious
author of Paradise Lost, I shall give in his own words as they
appear in the second page of his History of England. After
having briefly touched upon the stories of Samothes son of Japhet,
Albion son of Neptune, &c., he proceeds,—

*Earnest and
tenacious
faith mani-
fested in
the defence
of this early
history.*

---

[1] See Warton's History of English
Poetry, sect. iii. p. 131, note. " No
man before the sixteenth century presumed to doubt that the Francs derived their origin from Francus son of
Hector; that the Spaniards were descended from Japhet, the Britons from
Brutus, and the Scotch from Fergus."
(*Ibid.* p. 140.)

According to the Prologue of the
prose Edda, Odin was the supreme king
of Troy in Asia, "in eâ terrâ quam nos
Turciam appellamus. . . . Hinc omnes
Borealis plagæ magnates vel primores
genealogias suas referunt, atque prin-
cipes illius urbis inter numina locant:
sed in primis ipsum Priamum pro
Odeno ponunt," &c. They also identified *Tros* with *Thor.* (See Lexicon Mythologicum ad calcem Eddæ Sæmund.
p. 552, vol. iii.)

[2] See above, ch. xv. ; also Æschinês,
De Falsâ Legatione, c. 14 ; Herodot. v.
94. The Herakleids pretended a right
to the territory in Sicily near Mount

Eryx, in consequence of the victory
gained by their progenitor Hêraklês
over Eryx, the eponymous hero of the
place (Herodot. v. 43).

[3] The remarks in Speed's Chronicle
(book v. c. 3, sect. 11-12), and the preface to Howes's Continuation of Stow's
Chronicle, published in 1631, are
curious as illustrating this earnest
feeling. The Chancellor Fortescue, in
impressing upon his royal pupil, the
son of Henry VI., the limited character
of English monarchy, deduces it from
Brute, the Trojan :—" Concerning the
different powers which kings claim
over their subjects, I am firmly of
opinion that it arises solely from the
different nature of their original institution. So the kingdom of England
had its original from Brute and
the Trojans, who attended him from
Italy and Greece, and became a mixt
kind of government, compounded of the
regal and the political." (Hallam, Hist.
Mid. Ages, ch. viii. P. 3, page 230.)

"But now of Brutus and his line, with the whole progeny of
kings to the entrance of Julius Cæsar, we cannot so
easily be discharged : descents of ancestry long continued, law and exploits not plainly seeming to be borrowed or
devised, which on the common belief have wrought no small impression : *defended by many, denied utterly by few.* For what though
Brutus and the whole Trojan pretence were yielded up, seeing
they, who first devised to bring us some noble ancestor, were
content at first with Brutus the Consul, till better invention,
though not willing to forego the name, taught them to remove it
higher into a more fabulous age, and by the same remove lighting
on the Trojan tales, in affectation to make the Briton of one
original with the Roman, pitched there : *Yet those old and inborn
kings, never any to have been real persons, or done in their lives at
least some part of what so long hath been remembered, cannot be
thought without too strict incredulity.* For these, and those causes
above-mentioned, that which hath received approbation from so
many, I have chosen not to omit. Certain or uncertain, be that
upon the credit of those whom I must follow : *so far as keeps
aloof from impossible or absurd,* attested by ancient writers from
books more ancient, I refuse not as the due and proper subject of
story." [1]

Judgment of Milton.

Yet in spite of the general belief of so many centuries—in
spite of the concurrent persuasion of historians and poets—in
spite of the declaration of Milton, extorted from his feelings
rather than from his reason, that this long line of quasi-historical
kings and exploits could not be *all* unworthy of belief—in spite
of so large a body of authority and precedent, the historians of
the nineteenth century begin the history of England with Julius
Cæsar. They do not attempt either to settle the date of king
Bladud's accession, or to determine what may be the basis of truth
in the affecting narrative of Lear.[2] The standard of historical

---

[1] "Antiquitas enim recepit fabulas
fictas etiam nonnunquam incondite :
hæc ætas autem jam exculta, præsertim
eludens omne quod fieri non potest
respuit," &c. (Cicero, De Republicâ,
ii. 10, p. 147, ed. Maii.)

[2] Dr. Zachary Grey has the following
observations in his Notes on Shakespeare (London, 1754, vol. i. p. 112).
In commenting on the passage in King

Lear *Nero is an angler in the lake of
darkness,* he says, "This is one of
Shakespeare's most remarkable *ana-
chronisms.* King Lear succeeded his
father Bladud anno mundi 3105 ; and
Nero, anno mundi 4017, was sixteen
years old, when he married Octavia,
Cæsar's daughter. See Funccii Chrono-
logia, p. 94."
Such a supposed chronological dis

credibility, especially with regard to modern events, has indeed been greatly and sensibly raised within the last hundred years.

But in regard to ancient Grecian history, the rules of evidence still continue relaxed. The dictum of Milton, regarding the ante-Cæsarian history of England, still represents pretty exactly the feeling now prevalent respecting the mythical history of Greece:—"Yet those old and inborn kings (Agamemnôn, Achilles, Odysseus, Jasôn, Adrastus, Amphiaraüs, Meleager,

&c.), never any to have been real persons, or done in their lives at least some part of what so long has been remembered, cannot be thought without too strict incredulity". Amidst much fiction (we are still told), there must be some truth : but how is such truth to be singled out? Milton does not even attempt to make the severance : he contents himself with "keeping aloof from the impossible and the absurd," and ends in a narrative which has indeed the merit of being sober-coloured, but which he never for a moment thinks of recommending to his readers as true. So in regard to the legends of Greece,—Troy, Thêbes, the Argonauts, the Boar of Kalydôn, Hêraklês, Thêseus, Œdipus,—the convic-tion still holds in men's minds, that there must be something true at the bottom ; and many readers of this work may be displeased, I fear, not to see conjured up before them the Eidôlon of an authentic history, even though the vital spark of evidence be altogether wanting.[1]

crepancy would hardly be pointed out in any commentary now written.

The introduction prefixed by Mr. Giles to his recent translation of Geof-frey of Monmouth (1842) gives a just view both of the use which our old poets made of his tales, and of the general credence so long and so unsus-pectingly accorded to them. The list of old British kings given by Mr. Giles also deserves attention, as a parallel to the Grecian genealogies anterior to the Olympiads.

[1] The following passage from the Preface of Mr. Price to Warton's His-tory of English Poetry is alike just and forcibly characterised ; the whole Pre-face is indeed full of philosophical reflection on popular fables generally. Mr. Price observes (p. 79) :—

" The great evil with which this long-contested question appears to be threatened at the present day, is an extreme equally dangerous with the incredulity of Mr. Ritson,—a disposi-tion to receive as authentic history, under a slightly fabulous colouring, every incident recorded in the British Chronicle. An allegorical interpreta-tion is now inflicted upon all the mar-vellous circumstances ; a forced con-struction imposed upon the less glaring deviations from probability ; and the usual subterfuge of baffled research,— erroneous readings and etymological sophistry,—is made to reduce every stubborn and intractable text to some-thing like the consistency required. It might have been expected that the notorious failures of Dionysius and

I presume to think that our great poet has proceeded upon
Milton's mistaken views with respect to the old British fables,
way of not less in that which he leaves out than in that
dealing
with the which he retains. To omit the miraculous and the
British fantastic (it is that which he really means by "the
fabulous
history ob- impossible and the absurd "), is to suck the life-blood
jectionable. out of these once popular narratives—to divest them
at once both of their genuine distinguishing mark, and of the
charm by which they acted on the feelings of believers. Still
less ought we to consent to break up and disenchant in a similar
manner the mythes of ancient Greece—partly because they
possess the mythical beauties and characteristics in far higher
perfection, partly because they sank deeper into the mind of a

Plutarch in Roman history would have prevented the repetition of an error which neither learning nor ingennity can render palatable ; and that the havoc and deadly ruin effected by these ancient writers (in other respects so valuable) in one of the most beautiful and interesting monuments of traditional story, would have acted as sufficient corrective on all future aspirants. The favourers of this system might at least have been instructed by the philosophic example of Livy,—if it be lawful to ascribe to philosophy a line of conduct which perhaps was prompted by a powerful sense of poetic beauty,—that traditional record can only gain in the hands of the future historian by one attractive aid,—the grandeur and lofty graces of that incomparable style in which the first decade is written : and that the best duty towards antiquity, and the most agreeable one towards posterity, is to transmit the narrative received as an unsophisticated tradition, in all the plenitude of its marvels and the awful dignity of its supernatural agency. For however largely we may concede that real events have supplied the substance of any traditive story, yet the amount of absolute facts, and the manner of those facts, the period of their occurrence, the names of the agents, and the locality given to the scene, are all combined upon principles so wholly beyond our knowledge, that it becomes impossible to fix with certainty upon any single point better authenticated than its fellow. Probability in such decisions will often prove the most fallacious guide we can follow ; for, independently of the acknowledged historical axiom, that 'le vrai n'est pas toujours le vraisemblable,' innumerable instances might be adduced, where tradition has had recourse to this very probability to confer a plausible sanction upon her most fictitious and romantic incidents. It will be a much more useful labour, wherever it can be effected, to trace the progress of this traditional story in the country where it has become located, by a reference to those natural or artificial monuments which are the unvarying sources of fictitious events ; and, by a strict comparison of its details with the analogous memorials of other nations, to separate those elements which are obviously of a native growth, from the occurrences bearing the impress of a foreign origin. *We shall gain little, perhaps, by such a course for the history of human events;* but it will be an important accession to our stock of knowledge on the *history of the human mind.* It will infallibly display, as in the analysis of every similar record, the operations of that refining principle which is ever obliterating the monotonous deeds of violence, that fill the chronicle of a nation's early career, and exhibit the brightest attribute in the catalogue of man's intellectual endowments—a glowing and vigorous imagination—bestowing upon all the impulses of the mind a splendour and virtuous dignity, which, however fallacious historically considered, are never without a powerfully redeeming good, the ethical tendency of all their lessons."

Greek, and pervaded both the public and private sentiment of the country to a much greater degree than the British fables in England.

Two courses, and two only, are open ; either to pass over the mythes altogether, which is the way in which modern historians treat the old British fables—or else to give an account of them as mythes ; to recognise and respect their specific nature, and to abstain from confounding them with ordinary and certifiable history.   There are good reasons for pursuing this second method in reference to the Grecian mythes ; and when so considered, they constitute an important chapter in the history of the Grecian mind, and indeed in that of the human race generally.   The historical faith of the Greeks, as well as that of other people, in reference to early and unrecorded times, is as much subjective and peculiar to themselves as their religious faith : among the Greeks, especially, the two are confounded with an intimacy which nothing less than great violence can disjoin.   Gods, heroes and men—religion and patriotism—matters divine, heroic and human—were all woven together by the Greeks into one indivisible web, in which the threads of truth and reality, whatever they might originally have been, were neither intended to be, nor were actually, distinguishable.   Composed of such materials, and animated by the electric spark of genius, the mythical antiquities of Greece formed a whole at once trustworthy and captivating to the faith and feelings of the people ; but neither trustworthy nor captivating, when we sever it from these subjective conditions, and expose its naked elements to the scrutiny of an objective criticism.   Moreover the separate portions of Grecian mythical foretime ought to be considered with reference to that aggregate of which they form a part : to detach the divine from the heroic legends, or some one of the heroic legends from the remainder, as if there were an essential and generic difference between them, is to present the whole under an erroneous point of view.   The mythes of Troy and Thêbes are no more to be handled objectively, with a view to detect an historical base, than those of Zeus in Krête, of Apollo and Artemis in Dêlos, of Hermês, or of Promêtheus.   To single

Two ways open of dealing with the Grecian mythes : 1. to omit them : or, 2. to recount them as mythes. Reasons for preferring the latter.

out the siege of Troy from the other mythes, as if it were entitled to pre-eminence as an ascertained historical and chronological event, is a proceeding which destroys the true character and coherence of the mythical world : we only transfer the story (as has been remarked in the preceding chapter) from a class with which it is connected by every tie both of common origin and fraternal affinity, to another with which it has no relationship, except such as violent and gratuitous criticism may enforce.

By drawing this marked distinction between the mythical and the historical world,—between matter appropriate only for subjective history, and matter in which objective evidence is attainable,—we shall only carry out to its proper length the just and well-known position long ago laid down by Varro. That learned man recognised three distinguishable periods in the time preceding his own age : "First, the time from the beginning of mankind down to the first deluge ; a time wholly unknown. Secondly, the period from the first deluge down to the first Olympiad, which is called *the mythical period*, because many fabulous things are recounted in it. Thirdly, the time from the first Olympiad down to ourselves, which is called *the historical period*, because the things done in it are comprised in true histories." [1]

Taking the commencement of true or objective history at the point indicated by Varro, I still consider the mythical and historical periods to be separated by a wider gap than he would have admitted. To select any one year as an absolute point of commencement, is of course not to be understood literally : but in point of fact, this is of every little importance in reference to the present question, seeing that the great mythical events—the sieges of Thêbes and Troy, the Argonautic expedition, the Kalydonian boar-hunt, the return of the Hêrakleids, &c.—are

Triple partition of past time by Varro.

---

[1] Varro ap. Censorin. de Die Natali ; Varronis Fragm. p. 219, ed. Scaliger, 1623. "Varro tria discrimina temporum esse tradit. Primum ab hominum principio usque ad cataclysmum priorem, quod propter ignorantiam vocatur ἄδηλον. Secundum, a cataclysmo priore ad Olympiadem primam, quod, quia in eo multa fabulosa referuntur, *Mythicon*

nominatur. Tertium a primâ Olympiade ad nos ; quod dicitur *Historicon*, quia res in eo gestæ veris historiis continentur."

To the same purpose Africanus, ap. Eusebium, Præp. Ev. xx. p. 487: Μέχρι μὲν Ὀλυμπιάδων, οὐδὲν ἀκριβὲς ἱστόρηται τοῖς Ἕλλησι, πάντων συγκεχυμένων, καὶ κατὰ μηδὲν αὐτοῖς τῶν πρὸ τοῦ συμφωνούντων, &c.

all placed long anterior to the first Olympiad, by those who have applied chronological boundaries to the mythical narratives. The period immediately preceding the first Olympiad is one exceedingly barren of events ; the received chronology recognises 400 years, and Herodotus admitted 500 years, from that date back to the Trojan war

CHAPTER XVIII.

CLOSING EVENTS OF LEGENDARY GREECE.—PERIOD OF
INTERMEDIATE DARKNESS, BEFORE THE DAWN OF
HISTORICAL GREECE.

SECTION I.—RETURN OF THE HERAKLEIDS INTO PELOPONNÊSUS.

IN one of the preceding chapters, we have traced the descending
Exile and
low condi-
tion of the
Herakleids.
series of the two most distinguished mythical families
in Peloponnêsus—the Perseids and the Pelopids. We
have followed the former down to Hêraklês and his
son Hyllus, and the latter down to Orestês son of Agamemnôn,
who is left in possession of that ascendency in the peninsula
which had procured for his father the chief command in the
Trojan war. The Herakleids or sons of Hêraklês, on the other
hand, are expelled fugitives, dependent upon foreign aid or
protection : Hyllus had perished in single combat with Echemus
of Tegea (connected with the Pelopids by marriage with Timandra
sister of Klytæmnêstra[1]), and a solemn compact had been made,
as the preliminary condition of this duel, that no similar attempt
at an invasion of the peninsula should be undertaken by his
family for the space of 100 years. At the end of the stipulated
period the attempt was renewed, and with complete success ; but
its success was owing not so much to the valour of the invaders
as to a powerful body of new allies. The Herakleids reappear
Their reap-
pearance as
a powerful
force along
with the
Dorians.
as leaders and companions of the Dorians,—a northerly
section of the Greek name, who now first come into
importance,—poor indeed in mythical renown, since
they are never noticed in the Iliad, and only once
casually mentioned in the Odyssey, as a fraction
among the many-tongued inhabitants of Krête—but destined to

---

[1] Hesiod, Eoiai, Fragm. 58, p. 43, ed. Düntzer.

form one of the grand and predominant elements throughout all the career of historical Hellas.

The son of Hyllus—Kleodæus—as well as his grandson Aristomachus, were now dead, and the lineage of Hêraklês was represented by the three sons of the latter—Têmenus, Kresphontês, and Aristodêmus. Under their conduct the Dorians penetrated into the peninsula. The mythical account traced back this intimate union between the Herakleids and the Dorians to a prior war, in which Hêraklês himself had rendered inestimable aid to the Dorian king Ægimius, when the latter was hard pressed in a contest with the Lapithæ. Hêraklês defeated the Lapithæ, and slew their king Korônus; in return for which Ægimius assigned to his deliverer one-third part of his whole territory, and adopted Hyllus as his son. Hêraklês desired that the territory thus made over might be held in reserve until a time should come when his descendants might stand in need of it; and that time did come, after the death of Hyllus (see Chap. V.). Some of the Herakleids then found shelter at Trikorythus in Attica, but the remainder, turning their steps towards Ægimius, solicited from him the allotment of land which had been promised to their valiant progenitor. Ægimius received them according to his engagement and assigned to them the stipulated third portion of his territory.[1] From this moment the Herakleids and Dorians became intimately united together into one social communion. Pamphylus and Dymas, sons of Ægimius, accompanied Têmenus and his two brothers in their invasion of Peloponnêsus.

Such is the mythical incident which professes to explain the origin of those three tribes into which all the Dorian communi-

Side note: Mythical account of this alliance, as well as of the three tribes of Dorians.

[1] Diodôr. iv. 37—60; Apollodôr. ii. 7, 7; Ephorus ap. Steph. Byz. v. Δυμᾶν, Fragm. 10, ed. Marx.

The Doric institutions are called by Pindar τεθμοὶ Αἰγιμίου Δωρικοί (Pyth. i. 124).

There existed an ancient epic poem, now lost, but cited on some few occasions by authors still preserved, under the title Αἰγίμιος; the authorship being sometimes ascribed to Hesiod, sometimes to Kerkops (Athenæ. xi. p. 503). The few fragments which remain do not enable us to make out the scheme of it, inasmuch as they embrace different mythical incidents lying very wide of each other,—Iô, the Argonauts, Pêleus and Thetis, &c. But the name which it bears seems to imply that the war of Ægimius against the Lapithæ, and the aid given to him by Hêraklês, was one of its chief topics. Both O. Müller (History of the Dorians, vol. i. bk. l. c. 8) and Welcker (Der Epische Cyklus, p. 263) appear to me to go beyond the very scanty evidence which we possess in their determination of this lost poem; compare Marktscheffel, Præfat. Hesiod. Fragm. cap. 5, p. 159.

ties were usually divided—the Hylléis, the Pamphyli, and the Dymanes—the first of the three including certain particular families, such as that of the kings of Sparta, who bore the special name of Herakleids. Hyllus, Pamphylus, and Dymas are the eponymous heroes of the three Dorian tribes.

Têmenus and his two brothers resolved to attack Peloponnêsus, not by a land-march along the Isthmus, such as that in which

Têmenus, Kresphon- tês, and Aristodê- mus invade Pelopon- nêsus across the Gulf of Corinth. Hyllus had been previously slain, but by sea across the narrow inlet between the promontories of Rhium and Antirrhium with which the Gulf of Corinth commences. According to one story indeed—which however does not seem to have been known to Herodotus—they are said to have selected this line of march by the express direction of the Delphian god, who vouchsafed to expound to them an oracle which had been delivered to Hyllus in the ordinary equivocal phraseology. Both the Ozolian Lokrians, and the Ætolians, inhabitants of the northern coast of the Gulf of Corinth, were favourable to the enterprise, and the former granted to them a port for building their ships, from which memorable circumstance the port ever afterwards bore the name of Naupaktus. Aristodêmus was here struck with lightning and died, leaving twin sons, Eurysthenês and Proklês ; but his remaining brothers continued to press the expedition with alacrity.

At this juncture, an Akarnanian prophet named Karnus pre- sented himself in the camp[1] under the inspiration of Apollo, and uttered various predictions : he was however so much suspected

The prophet Karnus slain by Hippotês. of treacherous collusion with the Peloponnesians, that Hippotês, great grandson of Hêraklês through Phylas and Antiochus, slew him. His death drew upon the army the wrath of Apollo, who destroyed their vessels and

---

[1] Respecting this prophet, compare Œnomaus ap. Eusebium, Præparat. Evangel. v. p. 211. According to that statement, both Kleodæus (here called *Aridæus*), son of Hyllus, and Aristo- machus son of Kleodæus, had made separate and successive attempts at the head of the Herakleids to pene- trate into Peloponnêsus through the Isthmus : both had failed and perished, having misunderstood the admonition of the Delphian oracle. Œnomaus could have known nothing of the pledge given by Hyllus, as the condition of the single combat between Hyllus and Echemus (according to Herodotus), that the Herakleids should make no fresh trial for 100 years : if it had been understood that they had given and then violated such a pledge, such viola- tion would probably have been adduced to account for their failure.

punished them with famine. Têmenus in his distress, again applying to the Delphian god for succour and counsel, was made acquainted with the cause of so much suffering, and was directed to banish Hippotês for ten years, to offer expiatory sacrifice for the death of Karnus, and to seek as the guide of the army a man with three eyes.[1] On coming back to Naupaktus, he met the Ætolian Oxylus son of Andræmôn returning to his country, after a temporary exile in Elis incurred for homicide : Oxylus had lost one eye, but as he was seated on a horse, the man and the horse together made up the three eyes required, and he was adopted as the guide prescribed by the oracle.[2] Conducted by him, they refitted their ships, landed on the opposite coast of Achaia, and marched to attack Tisamenus son of Orestês, then the great potentate of the peninsula. A decisive battle was fought, in which the latter was vanquished and slain, and in which Pamphylus and Dymas also perished. This battle made the Dorians so completely masters of the Peloponnêsus, that they proceeded to distribute the territory among themselves. The fertile land of Elis had been by previous stipulation reserved for Oxylus, as a recompense for his services as conductor : and it was agreed that the three Herakleids— Têmenus, Kresphontês, and the infant sons of Aristodêmus—should draw lots for Argos, Sparta, and Messênê. Argos fell to Têmenus, Sparta to the sons of Aristodêmus, and Messêne to Kresphontês ; the latter having secured for himself this prize, the most fertile territory of the three, by the fraud of putting into the vessel out of which the lots were drawn, a lump of clay instead of a stone, whereby the lots of his brothers were drawn out while his own remained inside. Solemn sacrifices were offered by each upon this partition ; but as they proceeded to the ceremony, a miraculous sign was seen upon the altar of each of the brothers— a toad corresponding to Argos, a serpent to Sparta, and a fox to Messênê. The prophets, on being consulted, delivered the import of these mysterious indications : the toad, as an animal slow and stationary, was an evidence that the possessor of Argos would not

(margin notes: Oxylus chosen as guide. / Division of the lands of Peloponnêsus among the invaders.)

---

[1] Apollodôr. ii. 8, 3 ; Pausan. iii. 13, 3.
[2] Apollodôr. ii. 8, 3. According to the account of Pausanias, the beast upon which Oxylus rode was a mule and had lost one eye (Paus. v. 3, 5).

succeed in enterprises beyond the limits of his own city ; the serpent denoted the aggressive and formidable future reserved to Sparta ; the fox prognosticated a career of wile and deceit to the Messenian.

Such is the brief account given by Apollodôrus of the Return of the Herakleids, at which point we pass, as if touched by the wand of a magician, from mythical to historical Greece. The story bears on the face of it the stamp, not of history, but of legend—abridged from one or more of the genealogical poets,[1] and presenting such an account as they thought satisfactory, of the first formation of the great Dorian establishments in Peloponnêsus, as well as of the semi-Ætolian Elis. Its incidents are so conceived as to have an explanatory bearing on Dorian institutions—upon the triple division of tribes, characteristic of the Dorians—upon the origin of the great festival of the Karneia at Sparta and other Dorian cities, alleged to be celebrated in expiation of the murder of Karnus—upon the different temper and character of the Dorian states among themselves—upon the early alliance of the Dorians with Elis, which contributed to give ascendency and vogue to the Olympic games—upon the reverential dependence of Dorians towards the Delphian oracle—and lastly upon the etymology of the name Naupaktus. If we possessed the narrative more in detail, we should probably find many more examples of colouring of the legendary past suitable to the circumstances of the historical present.

Above all, this legend makes out in favour of the Dorians and their kings a mythical title to their Peloponnesian establishments; Argos, Sparta, and Messênê are presented as rightfully belonging, and restored by just retribution, to the children of Hêraklês. It was to them that Zeus had specially given the territory of Sparta : the Dorians came in as their subjects and auxiliaries.[2]

Explanatory value of these legendary events.

---

[1] Herodotus observes, in reference to the Lacedæmonian account of their first two kings in Peloponnêsus (Eurysthenês and Proklês, the twin sons of Aristodêmus), that the Lacedæmonians gave a *story not in harmony with any of the poets*,—Δακεδαιμόνιοι γὰρ ὁμολογέοντες οὐδενὶ ποιητῇ, λέγουσιν αὐτὸν Ἀριστόδημον . . . . βασιλεύοντα ἀγαγεῖν σφέας ἐς ταύτην τὴν

χώρην τὴν νῦν ἐκτέαται, ἀλλ' οὐ τοὺς Ἀριστοδήμου παῖδας (Herodot. vi. 52).

[2] Tyrtæus, Fragm.—
Αὐτὸς γὰρ Κρονίων, καλλιστεφάνου πόσις Ἥρας,
Ζεὺς Ἡρακλείδαις τήνδε δέδωκε πόλιν ·
Οἷσιν ἅμα, προλιπόντες Ἐρίνεον ἠνεμόεντα,
Εὐρεῖαν Πέλοπος νῆσον ἀφικόμεθα.
In a similar manner Pindar says

Plato gives a very different version of the legend, but we find that he too turns the story in such a manner as to embody a claim of right on the part of the conquerors. According to him, the Achæans who returned from the capture of Troy, found among their fellow-citizens at home—the race which had grown up during their absence—an aversion to re-admit them: after a fruitless endeavour to make good their rights, they were at last expelled, but not without much contest and bloodshed. A leader named Dorieus collected all these exiles into one body, and from him they received the name of Dorians instead of Achæans; then marching back under the conduct of the Herakleids into Peloponnêsus they recovered by force the possessions from which they had been shut out, and constituted the three Dorian establishments under the separate Herakleid brothers, at Argos, Sparta, and Messênê. These three fraternal dynasties were founded upon a scheme of intimate union and sworn alliance one with the other, for the·purpose of resisting any attack which might be made upon them from Asia,[1] either by the remaining Trojans or by their allies. Such is the story as Plato believed it; materially different in the incidents related, yet analogous in mythical feeling, and embodying alike the idea of a rightful reconquest. Moreover the two accounts agree in representing both the entire conquest and the triple division of Dorian Peloponnêsus as begun and completed in one and the same enterprise,—so as to constitute one single event, which Plato would probably have called the Return of the Achæans, but which was commonly known as the Return of the Herakleids. Though this is both inadmissible and inconsistent with other statements which approach close to the historical times, yet it bears every mark of being the primitive view originally presented by the genealogical poets. The broad way in which the incidents are grouped together, was at once easy for the imagination to follow and impressive to the feelings.

Mythical title of the Dorians to Peloponnêsus.

Plato makes out a different title for the same purpose.

that Apollo had planted the sons of Hêraklês, jointly with those of Ægimius, at Sparta, Argos, and Pylus (Pyth. v. 93).

Isokratês (Or. vi. *Archidamus*, p. 120) makes out a good title by a different line of mythical reasoning. There seem to have been also stories, containing mythical reasons why the Herakleids did *not* acquire possession of Arcadia (Polyæn. i. 7).

[1] Plato, Legg. iii. 6—7, pp. 682—686.

The existence of one legendary account must never be understood as excluding the probability of other accounts, current at the same time, but inconsistent with it; and many such there were as to the first establishment of the Peloponnesian Dorians. In the narrative which I have given from Apollodôrus, conceived apparently under the influence of Dorian feeling, Tisamenus is stated to have been slain in the invasion. But according to Other another narrative, which seems to have found favour legends with the historical Achæans on the north coast of Pelorespecting ponnêsus, Tisamenus, though expelled by the invaders the Achæans from his kingdom of Sparta or Argos, was not slain; and he was allowed to retire under agreement, together Tisamenus. with a certain portion of his subjects, and he directed his steps towards the coast of Peloponnêsus south of the Corinthian Gulf, then occupied by the Ionians. As there were relations, not only of friendship, but of kindred origin, between Ionians and Achæans (the eponymous heroes Iôn and Achæus pass for brothers, both sons of Xuthus), Tisamenus solicited from the Ionians admission for himself and his fellow-fugitives into their territory. The leading Ionians declining this request, under the apprehension that Tisamenus might be chosen as sovereign over the whole, the latter accomplished his object by force. After a vehement struggle, the Ionians were vanquished and put to flight, and Tisamenus thus acquired possession of Helikê, as well as of the northern coast of the peninsula, westward from Sikyôn; which coast continued to be occupied by the Achæans, and received its name from them, throughout all the historical times. The Ionians retired to Attica, many of them taking part in what is called the Ionic emigration to the coast of Asia Minor, which followed shortly after. Pausanias indeed tells us that Tisamenus, having gained a decisive victory over the Ionians, fell in the engagement,[1] and did not himself live to occupy the country of which his troops remained masters. But this story of the death of Tisamenus seems to arise from a desire on the part of Pausanias to blend together into one narrative two discrepant legends; at least the historical Achæans in later times continued to regard Tisamenus himself as having lived and

---

[1] Pausan. vii. 1—3.

reigned in their territory, and as having left a regal dynasty which lasted down to Ogygês,[1] after whom it was exchanged for a popular government.[2]

The conquest of Têmenus, the eldest of the three Herakleids, originally comprehended only Argos and its neighbourhood : it was from thence that Trœzen, Epidaurus, Ægina, Sikyôn, and Phlius were successively occupied by Dorians, the sons and son-in-law of Têmenus—Dêiphontês, Phalkês, and Keisus—being the leaders under whom this was accomplished.[3] At Sparta the success of the Dorians was furthered by the treason of a man named Philonomus, who received as recompense the neighbouring town and territory of Amyklæ.[4] Messênia is said to have submitted without resistance to the dominion of the Herakleid Kresphontês, who established his residence at Stenyklarus : the Pylian Melanthus, then ruler of the country and representative of the great mythical lineage of Nêleus and Nestôr, withdrew with his household gods and with a portion of his subjects to Attica.[5]

Occupation of Argos, Sparta, and Messênia by the Dorians.

The only Dorian establishment in the peninsula not directly connected with the triple partition is Corinth, which is said to have been Doricised somewhat later and under another leader, though still a Herakleid. Hippotês—descendant of Hêraklês in the fourth generation, but not through Hyllus—had been guilty (as already mentioned) of the murder of Karnus the prophet at the camp of Naupaktus, for which he had been banished and remained in exile for ten years ; his son deriving the name of Alêtês from the long wanderings endured by the father. At the head of a body of Dorians, Alêtês attacked Corinth : he pitched his camp on the Solygeian eminence near the city, and harassed the inhabitants

Dorians at Corinth— Alêtês.

---

[1] Polyb. ii. 45 ; iv. 1. Strabo, viii. p. 383—384. This Tisamenus derives his name from the memorable act of revenge ascribed to his father Orestês. So in the legend of the Siege of Thêbes, Thersander, as one of the Epigoni, avenged his father Polynikês ; the son of Thersander was also called *Tisamenus* (Herodot. iv. 149). Compare O. Müller, Dorians i. p. 69, note 9, Eng. Trans.

[2] Diodôr. iv. 1. The historian Ephorus embodied in his work a narrative in considerable detail of this grand event of Grecian legend,—the Return of the Herakleids,—with which he professed to commence his consecutive history: from what sources he borrowed we do not know.

[3] Strabo, viii. p. 389. Pausan. ii. 6, 2 ; 12, 1.

[4] Conôn, Narr. 36 ; Strabo, viii. p. 365.

[5] Strabo, viii. p. 359 ; Conôn, Narr. 39.

with constant warfare until he compelled them to surrender. Even in the time of the Peloponnesian war, the Corinthians professed to identify the hill on which the camp of these assailants had been placed. The great mythical dynasty of the Sisyphids was expelled, and Alêtês became ruler and Œkist of the Dorian city; many of the inhabitants however, Æolic or Ionic, departed.[1]

The settlement of Oxylus and his Ætolians in Elis is said by some to have been accomplished with very little opposition; the leader professing himself to be descended from Ætolus, who had been in a previous age banished from Elis into Ætôlia, and the two people, Epeians and Ætolians, acknowledging a kindred origin one with the other.[2] At first indeed, according to Ephorus, the Epeians appeared in arms, determined to repel the intruders, but at length it was agreed on both sides to abide the issue of a single combat. Degmenus, the champion of the Epeians, confided in the long shot of his bow and arrow; but the Ætolian Pyræchmês came provided with his sling,—a weapon then unknown and recently invented by the Ætolians,—the range of which was yet longer than that of the bow of his enemy: he thus killed Degmenus, and secured the victory to Oxylus and his followers. According to one statement the Epeians were expelled; according to another they fraternised amicably with the new-comers. Whatever may be the truth as to this matter, it is certain that their name is from this moment lost, and that they never reappear among the historical elements of Greece :[3] we hear from this time forward only of Eleians, said to be of Ætolian descent.[4]

Oxylus and the Ætolians at Elis.

One most important privilege was connected with the possession of the Eleian territory by Oxylus, coupled with his claim on the gratitude of the Dorian kings. The Eleians acquired the administration of the temple at Olympia, which the Achæans are said to have possessed

Rights of the Eleians to superintend the Olympic games.

---

[1] Thucyd. iv. 42. Schol. Pindar. Olymp. xiii. 17; and Nem. vii. 155. Conôn. Narrat. 26. Ephor. ap. Strab. viii. p. 389.

Thucydidês calls the ante-Dorian inhabitants of Corinth Æolians; Conôn calls them Ionians.

[2] Ephorus ap. Strab. x. p. 463.

[3] Strabo, viii. p. 358; Pausan. v. 4, 1.

One of the six towns in Triphylia mentioned by Herodotus is called Ἐπειον (Herodot. iv. 149).

[4] Herodot. viii. 73; Pausan. v. 1, 2. Hekatæus affirmed that the Epeians were completely alien to the Eleians; Strabo does not seem to have been able to satisfy himself either of the affirmative or negative (Hekatæus, Fr 348, ed. Didot; Strabo, viii. p. 341).

before them ; and in consideration of this sacred function, which subsequently ripened into the celebration of the great Olympic games, their territory was solemnly pronounced to be inviolable. Such was the statement of Ephorus :[1] we find, in this case as in so many others, that the return of the Herakleids is made to supply a legendary basis for the historical state of things in Peloponnêsus.

It was the practice of the great Attic tragedians, with rare exceptions, to select the subjects of their composition from the heroic or legendary world. Euripidês had composed three dramas, now lost, on the adventures of Têmenus with his daughter Hyrnethô and his son-in-law Dêiphontês—on the family misfortunes of Kresphontês and Meropê—and on the successful valour of Archelaus the son of Têmenus in Macedonia, where he was alleged to have first begun the dynasty of the Temenid kings. Of these subjects the first and second were eminently tragical, and the third, relating to Archelaus, appears to have been undertaken by Euripidês in compliment to his contemporary sovereign and patron, Archelaus king of Macedonia : we are even told that those exploits which the usual version of the legend ascribed to Têmenus, were reported in the drama of Euripidês to have been performed by Archelaus his son.[2] Of all the heroes, touched upon by the three Attic tragedians, these Dorian Herakleids stand lowest in the descending genealogical series— one mark amongst others that we are approaching the ground of genuine history.

Family of Têmenus and Kresphontês lowest in the series of subjects for the Heroic drama.

Though the name Achæans, as denoting a people, is henceforward confined to the North-Peloponnesian territory specially called Achaia, and to the inhabitants of Achæa Phthiôtis, north of Mount Œta—and though the great Peloponnesian states always seem to have prided themselves on the title of Dorians—yet we

---

[1] Ephorus ap. Strab. viii. p. 358. The tale of the inhabitants of Pisa, the territory more immediately bordering upon Olympia, was very different from this.

[2] Agatharchides ap. Photium, Sect. 250, p. 1332. Οὐδ' Εὐριπίδου κατηγορῶ, τῷ Ἀρχελάῳ περιτεθεικότος τὰς Τημένου πράξεις.

Compare the Fragments of the Τημενίδαι, Ἀρχέλαος, and Κρεσφόντης, in Dindorf's edition of Euripidês, with the illustrative remarks of Welcker, Griechische Tragödien, pp. 697, 708, 828.

The Prologue of the Archelaus seems to have gone through the whole series of the Herakleidan lineage, from Ægyptus and Danaus downwards.

find the kings of Sparta, even in the historical age, taking pains to appropriate to themselves the mythical glories of the Achæans, and to set themselves forth as the representatives of Agamemnôn

Pretence of the historical Spartan kings to Achæan origin.
and Orestês. The Spartan king Kleomenês even went so far as to disavow formally any Dorian parentage ; for when the priestess at Athens refused to permit him to sacrifice in the temple of Athênê, on the plea that it was peremptorily closed to all Dorians, he replied— "I am no Dorian, but an Achæan".[1] Not only did the Spartan envoy, before Gelôn of Syracuse, connect the indefeasible title of his country to the supreme command of the Grecian military force, with the ancient name and lofty prerogatives of Agamemnôn[2] —but in farther pursuance of the same feeling, the Spartans are said to have carried to Sparta both the bones of Orestês from Tegea, and those of Tisamenus from Helikê,[3] at the injunction of the Delphian oracle. There is also a story that Oxylus in Elis was directed by the same oracle to invite into his country an Achæan, as Œkist, conjointly with himself ; and that he called in Agorius, the great-grandson of Orestês, from Helikê, with a small number of Achæans who joined him.[4] The Dorians themselves, being singularly poor in native legends, endeavoured, not unnaturally, to decorate themselves with those legendary ornaments which the Achæans possessed in abundance.

As a consequence of the Dorian establishments in Peloponnêsus,

Emigrations from Peloponnêsus consequent on the Dorian occupation —Epeians, Pylians, Achæans, Ionians.
several migrations of the pre-existing inhabitants are represented as taking place. 1. The Epeians of Elis are either expelled, or merged in the new-comers under Oxylus, and lose their separate name. 2. The Pylians, together with the great heroic family of Nêleus and his son Nestôr, who preside over them, give place to the Dorian establishment of Messênia, and retire to Athens, where their leader Melanthus becomes king : a large portion of them take part in the subsequent Ionic emigration. 3. A portion of the Achæans, under Penthilus, and other descendants of Orestês, leave Peloponnêsus, and form what is called the Æolic Emigration, to Lesbos, the Trôad, and the Gulf of Adramyttium : the name *Æôlians*, unknown to Homer and

---

[1] Herodot. v. 72.
[2] Herodot. vii. 159.

[3] Herodot. i. 68 ; Pausan. vii. 1, 3.
[4] Pausan. v. 4, 2.

seemingly never applied to any separate tribe at all, being introduced to designate a large section of the Hellenic name, partly in Greece Proper and partly in Asia. 4. Another portion of Achæans expel the Ionians from Achaia properly so called, in the north of Peloponnêsus ; the Ionians retiring to Attica.

The Homeric poems describe Achæans, Pylians, and Epeians, in Peloponnêsus, but take no notice of Ionians in the northern district of Achaia: on the contrary, the Catalogue in the Iliad distinctly included this territory under the dominions of Agamemnôn. Though the Catalogue of Homer is not to be regarded as an historical document, fit to be called as evidence for the actual state of Peloponnêsus at any prior time, it certainly seems a better authority than the statements advanced by Herodotus and others respecting the occupation of northern Peloponnêsus by the Ionians, and their expulsion from it by Tisamenus. In so far as the Catalogue is to be trusted, it negatives the idea of Ionians at Helikê, and countenances what seems in itself a more natural supposition— that the historical Achæans in the north part of Peloponnêsus are a small undisturbed remnant of the powerful Achæan population once distributed throughout the peninsula, until it was broken up and partially expelled by the Dorians.

Ionians in the north of Peloponnêsus—not recognised by Homer.

The Homeric legends, unquestionably the oldest which we possess, are adapted to a population of Achæans, Danaans, and Argeians, seemingly without any special and recognised names, either aggregate or divisional, other than the name of each separate tribe or kingdom. The Post-Homeric legends are adapted to a population classified quite differently—Hellens, distributed into Dorians, Ionians, and Æolians. If we knew more of the time and circumstances in which these different legends grew up, we should probably be able to explain their discrepancy ; but in our present ignorance we can only note the fact.

Whatever difficulty modern criticism may find in regard to the event called "The Return of the Herakleids," no doubt is expressed about it even by the best historians of antiquity. Thucydidês accepts it as a single and literal event, having its assignable date, and carrying at one blow the acquisition of Peloponnêsus. The date of it

Date assigned by Thucydidês to the return of the Herakleids.

he fixes as eighty years after the capture of Troy. Whether he was the original determiner of this epoch, or copied it from some previous author, we do not know. It must have been fixed according to some computation of generations, for there were no other means accessible—probably by means of the lineage of the Herakleids, which, as belonging to the kings of Sparta, constituted the most public and conspicuous thread of connexion between the Grecian real and mythical world, and measured the interval between the Siege of Troy itself and the first recorded Olympiad. Hêraklês himself represents the generation before the siege, and his son Tlêpolemus fights in the besieging army. If we suppose the first generation after Hêraklês to commence with the beginning of the siege, the fourth generation after him will coincide with the ninetieth year after the same epoch ; and therefore, deducting ten years for the duration of the struggle, it will coincide with the eightieth year after the capture of the city ;[1] thirty years being reckoned for a generation. The date assigned by Thucydidês will thus agree with the distance in which Têmenus, Kresphontês, and Aristodêmus stand removed from Hêraklês. The interval of eighty years, between the capture of Troy and the Return of the Herakleids, appears to have been admitted by Apollodôrus and Eratosthenês, and some other professed chronologists of antiquity : but there were different reckonings which also found more or less of support.

SECTION II.—MIGRATION OF THESSALIANS AND BŒOTIANS.

In the same passage in which Thucydidês speaks of the Return of the Herakleids, he also marks out the date of another event a little antecedent, which is alleged to have powerfully affected the condition of Northern Greece. "Sixty years after the capture of Troy (he tells us) the Bœotians were driven by the Thessalians from Arnê, and migrated into the land then called Kadmêïs, but now Bœotia, wherein there had previously dwelt a section of their race, who had contributed the contingent to the Trojan war."

The expulsion here mentioned, of the Bœotians from Arnê "by the Thessalians," has been construed, with probability, to allude

---

[1] The date of Thucydidês is calculated μετὰ 'Ιλίου ἅλωσιν (l. 13).

to the immigration of the Thessalians, properly so called, from the Thesprôtid in Epirus into Thessaly. That the Thessalians had migrated into Thessaly from the Thesprôtid territory, is stated by Herodotus,[1] though he says nothing about time or circumstances. Antiphus and Pheidippus appear in the Homeric Catalogue as commanders of the Grecian contingent from the islands of Kôs and Karpathus, on the south-east coast of Asia Minor: they are sons of Thessalus, who is himself the son of Hêraklês. A legend ran, that these two chiefs, in the dispersion which ensued after the victory, had been driven by storms into the Ionian Gulf, and cast upon the coast of Epirus, where they landed and settled at Ephyrê in the Thesprôtid.[2] It was Thessalus, grandson of Pheidippus, who was reported to have conducted the Thesprotians across the passes of Pindus into Thessaly, to have conquered the fertile central plain of that country, and to have imposed upon it his own name instead of its previous denomination Æolis.[3]

Thessalians move from Thesprôtis into Thessaly.

Whatever we may think of this legend as it stands, the state of Thessaly during the historical ages renders it highly probable that the Thessalians, properly so called, were a body of immigrant conquerors. They appear always as a rude, warlike, violent, and uncivilised race, distinct from their neighbours the Achæans, the Magnêtes, and the Perrhæbians, and holding all the three in tributary dependence. These three tribes stand to them in a relation analogous to that of the Lacedæmonian Periœki towards Sparta, while the Penestæ, who cultivated their lands, are almost an exact parallel of the Helots. Moreover, the low level of taste and intelligence among the Thessalians, as well as certain points of their costume, assimilates them more to Macedonians or Epirots than to Hellens.[4] Their position in Thessaly is in many respects analogous to that

Non-Hellenic character of the Thessalians.

---

[1] Herod. vii. 176.

[2] See the epigram ascribed to Aristotle (Antholog. Græc. t. i. p. 181, ed. Reiske; Velleius Patercul. i. 1). The Scholia on Lycophrôn (912) give a story somewhat different. Ephyrê is given as the old legendary name of the city of Krannon in Thessaly (Kineas, ap. Schol. Pindar. Pyth. x. 85), which creates the confusion with the Thesprotian Ephyrê.

[3] Herodot. vii. 176; Velleius Patercul. i. 2—3; Charax, ap. Stephan. Byz. v. Δώριον; Polyæn. viii. 44.

There were several different statements, however, about the parentage of Thessalus as well as about the name of the country (Strabo, ix. p. 443; Stephan. Byz. v. Αἱμονία).

[4] See K. O. Müller, History of the Dorians, Introduction, sect. 4.

of the Spartan Dorians in Peloponnêsus, and there seems good
reason for concluding that the former, as well as the latter, were
originally victorious invaders, though we cannot pretend to
determine the time at which the invasion took place. The great
family of the Aleuads,[1] and probably other Thessalian families
besides, were descendants of Hêraklês, like the kings of Sparta.

There are no similar historical grounds, in the case of the
alleged migration of the Bœotians from Thessaly to Bœotia, to
justify a belief in the main fact of the legend, nor were the
different legendary stories in harmony one with the other. While
the Homeric epic recognises the Bœotians in Bœotia, but not in
Bœotians— Thessaly, Thucydidês records a statement which he
their migra- had found of their migration from the latter into the
tion from
Thessaly former. But in order to escape the necessity of flatly
into
Bœotia. contradicting Homer, he inserts the parenthesis that
there had been previously an outlying fraction of Bœotians in
Bœotia at the time of the Trojan war,[2] from whom the troops
who served with Agamemnôn were drawn. Nevertheless, the
discrepancy with the Iliad, though less strikingly obvious, is not
removed, inasmuch as the Catalogue is unusually copious in
enumerating the contingents from Thessaly, without once
mentioning Bœotians. Homer distinguishes Orchomenus from
Bœotia, and he does not specially notice Thêbes in the Catalogue :
in other respects his enumeration of the towns coincides pretty
well with the ground historically known afterwards under the
name of Bœotia.

Pausanias gives us a short sketch of the events which he
supposes to have intervened in this section of Greece between the
Siege of Troy and the Return of the Herakleids. Peneleôs, the
leader of the Bœotians at the siege, having been slain by
Eurypylus the son of Têlephus, Tisamenus, son of Thersander
and grandson of Polynikês, acted as their commander both during
the remainder of the siege and after their return. Autesiôn, his
son and successor, became subject to the wrath of the avenging
Erinnyes of Laius and Œdipus : the oracle directed him to
expatriate, and he joined the Dorians. In his place Damasichthôn,

---

[1] Pindar, Pyth. x. 2.
[2] Thucyd. i. 12. ἦν δὲ αὐτῶν καὶ ὧν καὶ ἐς Ἴλιον ἐστράτευσαν.
ἀποδασμὸς πρότερον ἐν τῇ γῇ ταύτῃ ἀφ'

son of Opheltas and grandson of Pêneleôs, became king of the
Bœotians; he was succeeded by Ptolemæus, who was himself
followed by Xanthus.   A war having broken out at that time
between the Athenians and Bœotians, Xanthus engaged in single
combat with Melanthus son of Andropompus, the champion of
Attica, and perished by the cunning of his opponent.   After the
death of Xanthus, the Bœotians passed from kingship to popular
government.[1]   As Melanthus was of the lineage of the Nêleids,
and had migrated from Pylus to Athens in consequence of the
successful establishment of the Dorians in Messênia, the duel with
Xanthus must have been of course subsequent to the Return of
the Herakleids.

Here then we have a summary of alleged Bœotian history
between the siege of Troy and the Return of the   Discrepant
Herakleids, in which no mention is made of the   legends
immigration of the mass of Bœotians from Thessaly,   about the
                                                     Bœotians.
and seemingly no possibility left of fitting in so great and capital
an incident.   The legends followed by Pausanias are at variance
with those adopted by Thucydidês, but they harmonise much
better with Homer.

So deservedly high is the authority of Thucydidês, that the
migration here distinctly announced by him is commonly set
down as an ascertained datum, historically as well as chronologically.   But on this occasion it can be shown that he only
followed one amongst a variety of discrepant legends, none of
which there were any means of verifying.

Pausanias recognised a migration of the Bœotians from Thessaly,
in early times anterior to the Trojan war;[2] and the account of
Ephorus, as given by Strabo, professed to record a series of
changes in the occupants of the country :—first, the non-Hellenic
Aones and Temmikes, Leleges and Hyantes; next, the Kadmeians,
who, after the second siege of Thêbes by the Epigoni, were
expelled by the Thracians and Pelasgians, and retired into
Thessaly, where they joined in communion with the inhabitants
of Arnê,—the whole aggregate being called Bœotians.   After the
Trojan war, and about the time of the Æolic emigration, these
Bœotians returned from Thessaly, and reconquered Bœotia,

---

[1] Pausan. ix. 5, 8.   [2] Pausan. x. 8, 3.

driving out the Thracians and Pelasgians,—the former retiring to Parnassus, the latter to Attica. It was on this occasion (he says) that the Minyæ of Orchomenus were subdued, and forcibly incorporated with the Bœotians. Ephorus seems to have followed in the main the same narrative as Thucydidês, about the movement of the Bœotians out of Thessaly ; coupling it however with several details current as explanatory of proverbs and customs.[1]

The only fact which we make out, independent of these legends,

Affinities between Bœotia and Thessaly. is, that there existed certain homonymies and certain affinities of religious worship, between parts of Bœotia and parts of Thessaly, which appear to indicate a kindred race. A town name Arnê,[2] similar in name to the Thessalian, was enumerated in the Bœotian Catalogue of Homer, and antiquaries identified it sometimes with the historical town Chæroneia,[3] sometimes with Akræphium. Moreover there was near the Bœotian Korôneia a river named Kuarius or Koralius, and a venerable temple dedicated to the Itonian Athênê, in the sacred ground of which the Pambœotia, or public council of the Bœotian name, was held ; there was also a temple and a river of similar denomination in Thessaly, near to a town called Iton or Itônus.[4] We may from these circumstances presume a certain

[1] Ephor. Fragm. 30, ed. Marx.; Strabo, ix. p. 401—402. The story of the Bœotians at Arnê in Polyænus (l. 12) probably comes from Ephorus.

Diodôrus (xix. 53) gives a summary of the legendary history of Thêbes from Deukaliôn downwards: he tells us that the Bœotians were expelled from their country, and obliged to retire into Thessaly during the Trojan war, in consequence of the absence of so many of their brave warriors at Troy ; they did not find their way back into Bœotia until the fourth generation.

[2] Stephan. Byz. v. Ἄρνη, makes the Thessalian Arnê an ἄποικος of the Bœotian.

[3] Homer, Iliad, ii. ; Strabo, ix. p. 413 ; Pausan. ix. 40, 3. Some of the families at Chæroneia, even during the time of the Roman dominion in Greece, traced their origin to Peripoltas the prophet, who was said to have accompanied Opheltas in his invading march out of Thessaly (Plutarch, Kimon, c. 1).

[4] Strabo, ix. 411—435; Homer, Iliad, ii. 696 ; Hekatæus, Fr. 338, Didot. The Fragment from Alkæus (cited by Strabo, but briefly and with a mutilated text) serves only to identify the river and the town.

Itônus was said to be son of Amphiktyôn, and Bœôtus son of Itônus (Pausan. ix. 1, 1. 34, 1: compare Steph. Byz. v. Βοιωτία) by Melanippê. By another legendary genealogy (probably arising after the name Æolic had obtained footing as the class name for a large section of Greeks, but as old as the poet Asius, Olympiad 30) the eponymous hero Bœôtus was fastened on to the great lineage of Æolus, through the paternity of the god Poseidôn either with Melanippê or with Arnê, daughter of Æolus (Asius, Fragm. 8, ed. Düntzer ; Strabo, vi. p. 265 ; Diodôr. v. 67 ; Hellanikus ap. Schol. Iliad. ii. 494). Two lost plays of Euripidês were founded on the misfortunes of Melanippê, and her twin children by Poseidôn—Bœôtus and Æolus (Hygin. Fab. 186 ; see the Fragments of Μελανίππη Σοφή and Μελανίππη Δεσμῶτις in Dindorf's edition, and the instructive comments of Welcker, Griech. Tragöd. vol. ii. p. 840—860).

ancient kindred between the population of these regions, and such a circumstance is sufficient to explain the generation of legends describing migrations backward and forward, whether true or not in point of fact.

What is most important to remark is, that the stories of Thucydidês and Ephorus bring us out of the mythical into the historical Bœotia. Orchomenus is Bœotised, and we hear no more of the once-powerful Minyæ: there are no more Kadmeians at Thêbes, nor Bœotians in Thessaly. The Minyæ and the Kadmeians disappear in the Ionic emigration, which will be presently adverted to. Historical Bœotia is now constituted, apparently in its federative league under the presidency of Thêbes, just as we find it in the time of the Persian and Peloponnesian wars.

Transition from mythical to historical Bœotia.

SECTION III.—EMIGRATIONS FROM GREECE TO ASIA AND THE ISLANDS OF THE ÆGEAN.

1. ÆOLIC.—2. IONIC.—3. DORIC.

To complete the transition of Greece from its mythical to its historical condition, the secession of the races belonging to the former must follow upon the introduction of those belonging to the latter. This is accomplished by means of the Æolic and Ionic migrations.

Secession of the mythical races of Greece.

The presiding chiefs of the Æolic emigration are the representatives of the heroic lineage of the Pelopids: those of the Ionic emigration belong to the Nêleids; and even in what is called the Doric emigration to Thêra, the Œkist Thêras is not a Dorian but a Kadmeian, the legitimate descendant of Œdipus and Kadmus.

The Æolic, Ionic, and Doric colonies were planted along the western coast of Asia Minor, from the coast of the Propontis southward down to Lykia (I shall in a future chapter speak more exactly of their boundaries); the Æolic occupying the northern portion together with the islands of Lesbos and Tenedos; the Doric occupying the southernmost, together with the neighbouring islands of Rhodes and Kôs; and the Ionic being planted between them, comprehending Chios, Samos, and the Cyclades islands.

1. ÆOLIC EMIGRATION.

The Æolic emigration was conducted by the Pelopids: the original story seems to have been that Orestês himself was at the head of the first batch of colonists, and this version of the event is still preserved by Pindar and by Hellanikus.[1] But the more current narratives represented the descendants of Orestês as chiefs of the expeditions to Æolis,— his illegitimate son Penthilus, by Erigonê daughter of Ægisthus,[2] together with Echelatus and Gras, the son and grandson of Penthilus—also Kleuês and Malaus, descendants of Agamemnôn through another lineage. According to the account given by Strabo, Orestês began the emigration, but died on his route in Arcadia; his son Penthilus, taking the guidance of the emigrants, conducted them by the long land-journey through Bœotia and Thessaly to Thrace;[3] from whence Archelaus, son of Penthilus, led them across the Hellespont, and settled at Daskylium on the Propontis. Gras, son of Archelaus, crossed over to Lesbos and possessed himself of the island. Kleuês and Malaus, conducting another body of Achæans, were longer on their journey, and lingered a considerable time near Mount Phrikium in the territory of Lokris; ultimately however they passed over by sea to Asia and took possession of Kymê, south of the Gulf of Adramyttium, the most considerable of all the Æolic cities on the continent.[4] From Lesbos and Kymê, the other less considerable Æolic towns, spreading over the region of Ida as well as the Trôad, and comprehending the island of Tenedos, are said to have derived their origin.

Though there are many differences in the details, the accounts

Æolic migration under the Pelopids.

[1] Pindar, Nem. xi. 43; Hellanic. Fragm. 114, ed. Didot. Compare Stephan. Byz. v. Πέρινθος.

[2] Kinæthon ap. Pausan. ii. 18, 5. Penthilids existed in Lesbos during the historical times (Aristot. Polit. v. 10, 2).

[3] It has sometimes been supposed that the country called Thrace here means the residence of the Thracians near Parnassus; but the length of the journey, and the number of years which it took up, are so specially marked, that I think Thrace in its usual and obvious sense must be intended.

[4] Strabo, xiii. p. 582. Hellanikus seems to have treated of this delay near Mount Phrikium (see Steph. Byz. v. Φρίκιον). In another account (xiii. p. 621), probably copied from the Kynæan Ephorus, Strabo connects the establishments of this colony with the sequel of the Trojan war: the Pelasgians, the occupants of the territory, who had been the allies of Priam, were weakened by the defeat which they had sustained, and unable to resist the immigrants.

agree in representing these Æolic settlements as formed by the Achæans expatriated from Lacônia under the guidance of the dispossessed Pelopids.[1] We are told that in their journey through Bœotia they received considerable reinforcements, and Strabo adds that the emigrants started from Aulis, the port from whence Agamemnôn departed in the expedition against Troy.[2] He also informs us that they missed their course and experienced many losses from nautical ignorance, but we do not know to what particular incidents he alludes.[3]

2. IONIC EMIGRATION.

The Ionic emigration is described as emanating from and directed by the Athenians, and connects itself with the previous legendary history of Athens, which must therefore be here briefly recapitulated.

The great mythical hero Thêseus, of whose military prowess and errant exploits we have spoken in a previous chapter, was still more memorable in the eyes of the Athenians as an internal political reformer. He was supposed to have performed for them the inestimable service of transforming Attica out of many states into one. Each dême, or at least a great many out of the whole number had before his time enjoyed political independence under its own magistrates and assemblies, acknowledging only a federal union with the rest under the presidency of Athens. By a mixture of conciliation and force, Thêseus succeeded in putting down all these separate governments and bringing them to unite in one political system centralised at Athens. He is said to have established a constitutional government, retaining for himself a defined power as king or president, and distributing the people into three classes; Eupatridæ, a sort of sacerdotal noblesse; Geômori and Demiurgi, husbandmen and artisans.[4] Having brought these important changes into efficient working, he commemorated them for his posterity by introducing solemn and appropriate festivals. In confirmation of the dominion of Athens

Ionic emigration —branches off from the legendary history of Athens.

---

1 Velleius Patercul. i. 4; compare Antikleidês ap. Athenæ. xi. c. 3; Pausanias, iii. 2, 1.
2 Strabo, ix. p. 401.
3 Strabo, i. p. 10.
4 Plutarch, Thêseus, c. 24, 25, 26.

over the Megarid territory, he is said farther to have erected a pillar at the extremity of the latter towards the Isthmus, marking the boundary between Peloponnêsus and Iônia.

But a revolution so extensive was not consummated without creating much discontent. Menestheus, the rival of Thêseus,—the first specimen, as we are told, of an artful demagogue,—took advantage of this feeling to assail and undermine him. Thêseus had quitted Attica to accompany and assist his friend Peirithoüs in his journey down to the under world, in order to carry off the goddess Persephonê, —or (as those who were critical in legendary story preferred recounting) in a journey to the residence of Aidôneus, king of the Molossians in Epirus, to carry off his daughter. In this enterprise Peirithoüs perished, while Thêseus was cast into prison, from whence he was only liberated by the intercession of Hêraklês. It was during his temporary absence that the Tyndarids Castôr and Pollux invaded Attica for the purpose of recovering their sister Helen, whom Thêseus had at a former period taken away from Sparta and deposited at Aphidnæ; and the partisans of Menestheus took advantage both of the absence of Thêseus and of the calamity which his licentiousness had brought upon the country, to ruin his popularity with the people. When he returned he found them no longer disposed to endure his dominion, or to continue to him the honours which their previous feelings of gratitude had conferred. Having therefore placed his sons under the protection of Elephênôr in Eubœa, he sought an asylum with Lykomêdês prince of Scyros, from whom however he received nothing but an insidious welcome and a traitorous death.[1]

Thêseus and Menestheus.

Menestheus, succeeding to the honours of the expatriated hero, commanded the Athenian troops at the siege of Troy. But though he survived the capture, he never returned to Athens— different stories being related of the place where he and his companions settled. During this interval the feelings of the Athenians having changed, they restored the sons of Thêseus, who had served at Troy under Elephênôr and had returned unhurt, to the station and functions of their father. The

---

[1] Plutarch, Thêseus, c. 34—35.

Theseids Dêmophoön, Oxyntas, Apheidas, and Thymœtês, had
successively filled this post for the space of about
sixty years,[1] when the Dorian invaders of Peloponnêsus
(as has been before related) compelled Melanthus and
the Nêleid family to abandon their kingdom of Pylus.
The refugees found shelter at Athens, where a fortunate
adventure soon raised Melanthus to the throne.　A war breaking
out between the Athenians and Bœotians respecting the boundary
tract of Œnoê, the Bœotian king Xanthus challenged Thymœtês
to single combat : the latter declining to accept it, Melanthus not
only stood forward in his place, but practised a cunning stratagem
with such success as to kill his adversary.　He was forthwith
chosen king, Thymœtês being constrained to resign.[2]

Restoration
of the sons
of Thêseus
to their
father's
kingdom.

Melanthus and his son Kodrus reigned for nearly sixty years,
during which their large body of fugitives, escaping
from the recent invaders throughout Greece, were
harboured by the Athenians : so that Attica became
populous enough to excite the alarm and jealousy of
the Peloponnesian Dorians.　A powerful Dorian force,
under the command of Alêtês from Corinth and Althæmenês
from Argos, were accordingly despatched to invade the Athenian
territory, in which the Delphian oracle promised them success,
provided they abstained from injuring the person of Kodrus.
Strict orders were given to the Dorian army that Kodrus should
be preserved unhurt ; but the oracle had become known among
the Athenians,[3] and the generous prince determined to bring
death upon himself as a means of salvation to his country.
Assuming the disguise of a peasant, he intentionally provoked a
quarrel with some of the Dorian troops, who slew him without

They are
displaced
by the
Neleids—
Melanthus
and
Kodrus.

---

[1] Eusebius, Chronic. Can. p. 228—
229, ed. Scaliger ; Pausan. ii. 18, 7.

[2] Ephorus ap. Harpocration. v.
Ἀπατούρια :—Ἔφορος ἐν δευτέρῳ, ὡς διὰ
τὴν ὑπὲρ τῶν ὁρίων ἀπάτην γενομένην,
ὅτι πολεμούντων Ἀθηναίων πρὸς Βοιω-
τοὺς ὑπὲρ τῆς τῶν Μελαινῶν χώρας,
Μέλανθος ὁ τῶν Ἀθηναίων βασιλεὺς
Ξάνθον τὸν Θηβαῖον μονομαχῶν ἀπέκ-
τεινεν.　Compare Strabo, ix. p. 393.

　Ephorus derives the term Ἀπατούρια
from the words signifying a trick with
reference to the boundaries, and assumes the name of this great Ionic
festival to have been derived from the
stratagem of Melanthus, described in
Conôn (Narrat. 39) and Polyænus (i.
19).　The whole derivation is fanciful
and erroneous, and the story is a
curious specimen of legend growing
out of etymology.

[3] The orator Lykurgus, in his eulo-
gium on Kodrus, mentions a Delphian
citizen named Kleomantis who secretly
communicated the oracle to the Athenians, and was rewarded by them for
doing so with σίτησις ἐν Πρυτανείῳ
(Lycurg. cont. Leocrat. c. 20).

suspecting his real character. No sooner was this event known, than the Dorian leaders, despairing of success, abandoned their enterprise and evacuated the country.[1] In retiring, however, they retained possession of Megara, where they established permanent settlers, and which became from this moment Dorian, —seemingly at first a dependency of Corinth, though it afterwards acquired its freedom and became an autonomous community. This memorable act of devoted patriotism, analogous to that of the daughters of Erechtheus at Athens, and of Menœkeus at Thêbes, entitled Kodrus to be ranked among the most splendid characters in Grecian legend.

Kodrus is numbered as the last king of Athens : his descen-

Devotion and death of Kodrus —no more kings at Athens. dants wese styled Archons, but they held that dignity for life—a practice which prevailed during a long course of years afterwards. Medon and Neileus, his two sons, having quarrelled about the succession, the Delphian oracle decided in favour of the former ; upon which the latter, affronted at the preference, resolved upon seeking a new home.[3] There were at this moment many dispos-

Quarrel of the sons of Kodrus, and emigration of Neileus. sessed sections of Greeks, and an adventitious popula- tion accumulated in Attica, who were anxious for settlements beyond sea. The expeditions which now set forth to cross the Ægean, chiefly under the conduct of members of the Kodrid family, composed collectively the memorable Ionic emigration, of which the Ionians, recently expelled from Peloponnêsus, formed a part, but, as it would seem, only a small part ; for we hear of many quite distinct races, some renowned in legend, who withdraw from Greece amidst this assemblage of colonists. The Kadmeians, the Minyæ of Orchomenus, the Abantes of Eubœa, the Dryopes ; the Molossi, the Phokians, the Bœotians, the Arcadian Pelasgians, and even the Dorians of Epidaurus—are represented as furnishing each a proportion of the crews of these emigrant vessels.[4] Nor were the

---

[1] Pherekydês, Fragm. 110, ed. Didot ; Vell. Paterc. i. 2 ; Conôn, Narr. 26 ; Polyæn. i. c. 18.
Hellanikus traced the genealogy of Kodrus, through ten generations, up to Deukaliôn (Fragment 10, ed. Didot).
[2] Strabo, xiv. p. 653.
[3] Pausan. vii. 2. 1.

[4] Herodot. i. 146 ; Pausan. vii. 2, 3, 4. Isokratês extols his Athenian an- cestors for having provid-d, by means of this emigration, settlements for so large a number of distressed and poor Greeks, at the expense of Barbarians (Or. xii. Panathenaic. p. 241).

results unworthy of so mighty a confluence of different races.   Not
only the Cyclades islands in the Ægean, but the great
islands of Samos and Chios near the Asiatic coast,
and ten different cities on the coast of Asia Minor,
from Milêtus on the south to Phokæa in the north,
were founded, and all adopted the Ionic name.   Athens
was the metropolis or mother city of all of them : Androklus and
Neileus, the Œkists of Ephesus and Milêtus, and probably other
Œkists also, started from the Prytaneium at Athens,[1] with those
solemnities, religious and political, which usually marked the
departure of a swarm of Grecian colonists.

Different races who furnished the emigrants to Iônia.

Other mythical families, besides the heroic lineage of Nêleus and
Nestôr, as represented by the sons of Kodrus, took a leading part in
the expedition.   Herodotus mentions Lykian chiefs, descendants
from Glaukus son of Hippolochus, and Pausanias tells us of Philôtas
descendant of Peneleôs, who went at the head of a body of Thebans:
both Glaukus and Peneleôs are commemorated in the Iliad.[2]   And
it is a remarkable fact mentioned by Pausanias (though we do not
know on what authority), that the inhabitants of Phokæa—which
was the northernmost city of Iônia on the borders of Æolis, and
one of the last founded—consisting mostly of Phôkian colonists
under the conduct of the Athenians Philogenês and Dæmon, were
not admitted into the Pan-Ionic Amphiktyony until they consented
to choose for themselves chiefs of the Kodrid family.[3]   Proklês,
the chief who conducted the Ionic emigrants from Epidaurus to
Samos, was said to be of the lineage of Iôn son of Xuthus.[4]

Of the twelve Ionic states constituting the Pan-Ionic Amphiktyony—some of them among the greatest cities in Hellas—I shall
say no more at present, as I have to treat of them again when I
came upon historical ground.

3. DORIC EMIGRATIONS.

The Æolic and Ionic emigrations are thus both presented to
us as direct consequences of the event called the
Return of the Herakleids : and in like manner the
formation of the Dorian Hexapolis in the south-

Dorian colonies in Asia.

<hr/>

[1] Herodot. i. 146; vii. 95; viii. 46.
Vellei. Paterc. i. 4.   Pherekydês, Frag.
111, ed. Didot.

[2] Herodot. i. 147 ; Pausan. vii. 2, 7.
[3] Pausan. vii. 2, 2 ; vii. 3, 4.
[4] Pausan. vii. 4, 3.

western corner of Asia Minor : Kôs, Knidus, Halicarnassus and Rhodes, with its three separate cities, as well as the Dorian establishments in Krête, Melos, and Thêra, are all traced more or less directly to the same great revolution.

Thêra, more especially, has its root in the legendary world. Its Œkist was Thêras, a descendant of the heroic lineage of Œdipus and Kadmus, and maternal uncle of the young kings of Sparta, Eurysthenês and Proklês, during whose minority he had exercised the regency. On their coming of age his functions

Thêra. were at an end ; but being unable to endure a private station, he determined to put himself at the head of a body of emigrants. Many came forward to join him, and the expedition was further reinforced by a body of interlopers, belonging to the Minyæ, of whom the Lacdæmonians were anxious to get rid. These Minyæ had arrived in Laconia, not long before, from the island of Lemnos, out of which they had been expelled by the Pelasgian fugitives from Attica. They landed without asking permission, took up their abode and began to "light their fires" on Mount Taygetus. When the Lacedæmonians sent to ask who they were and wherefore they had come, the Minyæ replied that they were sons of the Argonauts who had landed at Lemnos, and that being expelled from their own homes, they thought themselves entitled to solicit an asylum in the territory of their fathers; they asked, withal, to be admitted to share both the lands and the honours of the state. The Lacedæmonians granted the request, chiefly on the ground of a common ancestry—their own great heroes, the Tyndarids, having been enrolled in the crew of the Argô : the Minyæ were then introduced as citizens into the tribes, received lots of land, and began to

Legend of the Minyæ from Lemnos. intermarry with the pre-existing families. It was not long, however, before they became insolent : they demanded a share in the kingdom (which was the venerated privilege of the Herakleids), and so grossly misconducted themselves in other ways, that the Lacedæmonians resolved to put them to death, and began by casting them into prison. While the Minyæ were thus confined, their wives, Spartans by birth and many of them daughters of the principal men, solicited permission to go in and see them : leave being granted, they made use of the interview to change clothes with their husbands, who thus escaped and fled again to Mount Taygetus.   The greater number of them quitted Laconia, and marched to Triphylia in the western regions of Peloponnêsus, from whence they expelled the Paroreatæ and the Kaukones, and founded six towns of their own, of which Lepreum was the chief.   A certain proportion, however, by permission of the Lacedæmonians, joined Thêras and departed with him to the island of Kallistê, then possessed by Phœnician inhabitants who were descended from the kinsmen and companions of Kadmus, and who had been left there by that prince, when he came forth in search of Európa, eight generations preceding.   Arriving thus among men of kindred lineage with himself, Thêras met with a fraternal reception, and the island derived from him the name, under which it is historically known, of Thêra.[1]

Such is the foundation-legend of Thêra, believed both by the Lacedæmonians and by the Theræans, and interesting *Minyæ in* as it brings before us, characteristically as well as *Triphylia.* vividly, the persons and feelings of the mythical world,—the Argonauts with the Tyndarids as their children.   In Lepreum, as in the other towns of Triphylia, the descent from the Minyæ of old seems to have been believed in the historical times, and the mention of the river Minyëius in those regions by Homer tended to confirm it.[2]   But people were not unanimous as to the legend by which that descent should be made out; while some adopted the story just cited from Herodotus, others imagined that Chlôris, who had come from the Minyeian town of Orchomenus as the wife of Nêleus to Pylus, had brought with her a body of her countrymen.[3]

These Minyæ from Lemnos and Imbros appear again as portions

---

[1] Herodot. iv. 145—149; Valer. Maxim. iv. c. 6; Polyæn. vii. 49, who however gives the narrative differently by mentioning "Tyrrhenians from Lemnos aiding Sparta during the Helotic war": another narrative in his collection (viii. 71), though imperfectly preserved, seems to approach more closely to Herodotus.
[2] Homer, Iliad, xi. 721.
[3] Strabo, viii. p. 347. M. Raoul Rochette, who treats the legends for the most part as if they were so much authentic history, is much displeased

with Strabo for admitting this diversity of stories (Histoire des Colonies Grecques, t. iii. ch. 7, p. 54)—"Après des détails si clairs et si positifs, comment est-il possible que ce même Strabon, bouleversant toute la chronologie, fasse arriver les Minyens dans la Triphylie sous la conduite de Chloris, mère de Nestor?"
The story which M. Raoul Rochette thus puts aside is quite equal in point of credibility to that which he accepts: in fact no measure of credibility can be applied.

of another narrative respecting the settlement of the colony of Mêlos. It has already been mentioned, that when the Herakleids and the Dorians invaded Lacônia, Philonomus, an Achæan, treacherously betrayed to them the country, for which he received as his recompense the territory of Amyklæ. He is said to have peopled this territory by introducing detachments of Minyæ from Lemnos and Imbros, who in the third generation after the return of the Herakleids, became so discontented and mutinous, that the Lacedæmonians resolved to send them out of the country as emigrants, under their chiefs Polis and Delphus. Taking the direction of Krête, they stopped in their way to land a portion of their colonists on the island of Melos, which remained throughout the historical times a faithful and attached colony of Lacedæmôn.[1] On arriving in Krête, they are said to have settled at the town of Gortyn. We find, moreover, that other Dorian establishments, either from Lacedæmôn or Argos, were formed in Krête, and Lyktos in particular is noticed, not only as a colony of Sparta, but as distinguished for the analogy of its laws and customs.[2] It is even said that Krête, immediately after the Trojan war, had been visited by the wrath of the gods, and depopulated by famine and pestilence, and that in the third generation afterwards, so great was the influx of immigrants, that the entire population of the island was renewed with the exception of the Eteokrêtes at Polichnæ and Præsus.[3]

Migrations of Dorians to Krête.

There were Dorians in Krête in the time of the Odyssey: Homer mentions different languages and different races of men, Eteokrêtes, Kydônes, Dorians, Achæans, and Pelasgians, as all co-existing in the island, which he describes to be populous, and to contain ninety cities. A legend given by Andrôn, based seemingly upon the statement of Herodotus, that Dôrus the son of Hellen had settled in Histiæôtis, ascribed the first introduction of the three last races to Tektaphus son of Dôrus—who had led forth from that country a colony of

Story of Andrôn.

---

[1] Conôn, Narrat. 36. Compare Plutarch, Quæstion. Græc. c. 21, where Tyrrhenians from Lemnos are mentioned, as in the passage of Polyænus referred to in a preceding note.

[2] Strabo, x. p. 481; Aristot. Polit. ii. 10.

[3] Herodot. vii. 171 (see above, Ch.

xii.). Diodôrus (v. 80), as well as Herodotus, mentions generally large immigrations into Krête from Lacedæmôn and Argos; but even the laborious research of M. Raoul Rochette (Histoire des Colonies Grecques, t. iii. c. 9, p. 60—68) fails in collecting any distinct particulars of them.

Dorians, Achæans, and Pelasgians, and had landed in Krête during the reign of the indigenous king Kres.[1] This story of Andrôn so exactly fits on to the Homeric Catalogue of Kretan inhabitants, that we may reasonably presume it to have been designedly arranged with reference to that Catalogue, so as to afford some plausible account, consistently with the received legendary chronology, how there came to be Dorians in Krête before the Trojan war—the Dorian colonies after the return of the Herakleids being of course long posterior in supposed order of time. To find a leader sufficiently early for his hypothesis, Andrôn ascends to the primitive Eponymus Dôrus, to whose son Tektaphus he ascribes the introduction of a mixed colony of Dorians, Achæans, and Pelasgians into Krête. These are the exact three races enumerated in the Odyssey, and the king Krês, whom Andrôn affirms to have been then reigning in the island, represents the Eteokrêtes and Kydônes in the list of Homer. The story seems to have found favour among native Kretan historians, as it doubtless serves to obviate what would otherwise be a contradiction in the legendary chronology.[2]

Another Dorian emigration from Peloponnêsus to Krête, which extended also to Rhodes and Kôs, is farther said to have been conducted by Althæmenês, who had been one of the chiefs in the expedition against Attica in which Kodrus perished. This prince, a Herakleid and third in descent from Têmenus, was induced to expatriate by a family quarrel, and conducted a body of Dorian colonists from Argos first to Krête, where some of them remained; but the greater

Althæmenês, founder of Rhodes.

---

[1] Steph. Byz. v. Δώριον.—Περὶ ὧν ἱστορεῖ Ἄνδρων, Κρητὸς ἐν τῇ νήσῳ βασιλεύοντος, Τέκταφον τὸν Δώρου τοῦ Ἕλληνος, ὁρμήσαντα ἐκ τῆς ἐν Θετταλίᾳ τότε μὲν Δωρίδος, νῦν δὲ Ἱστιαιώτιδος καλουμένης, ἀφικέσθαι εἰς Κρήτην μετὰ Δωριέων τε καὶ Ἀχαιῶν καὶ Πελασγῶν, τῶν οὐκ ἀπαράντων εἰς Τυρρηνίαν. Compare Strabo, x. p. 475—476, from which it is plain that the story was adduced by Andrôn with a special explanatory reference to the passage in the Odyssey (xv. 175).

The age of Andrôn, one of the authors of Atthídes, is not precisely ascertainable, but he can hardly be put earlier than 300 B.C.; see the preliminary Dissertation of C. Müller to the Fragments Historicorum Græcorum, ed. Didot, p. lxxxii.; and the Prolusio de Atthidum Scriptoribus, prefixed to Lenz's edition of the Fragments of Phanodêmus and Dêmôn, p. xxviii. Lips. 1812.

[2] See Diodôr. iv. 60; v. 80. From Strabo (l. c.), however, we see that others rejected the story of Andrôn.

O. Müller (History of the Dorians, b. i. c. 1. § 9) accepts the story as substantially true, putting aside the name Dôrus, and even regards it as certain that Minos of Knôssus was a Dorian: but the evidence with which he supports this conclusion appears to me loose and fanciful.

number accompanied him to Rhodes, in which island, after expelling the Karian possessors, he founded the three cities of Lindus, Ialysus, and Kamairus.[1]

It is proper here to add, that the legend of the Rhodian archæologists respecting their Œkist Althæmenês, who was worshipped in the island with heroic honours, was something totally different from the preceding. Althæmenês was a Krêtan, son of the king Katreus, and grandson of Minos. An oracle predicted to him that he would one day kill his father: eager to escape so terrible a destiny, he quitted Krête, and conducted a colony to Rhodes, where the famous temple of the Atabyrian Zeus, on the lofty summit of Mount Atabyrum, was ascribed to his foundation, built so as to command a view of Krête. He had been settled on the island for some time, when his father Katreus, anxious again to embrace his only son, followed him from Krête: he landed in Rhodes during the night without being known, and a casual collision took place between his attendants and the islanders. Althæmenês hastened to the shore to assist in repelling the supposed enemies, and in the fray had the misfortune to kill his aged father.[2]

Either the emigrants who accompanied Althæmenês, or some other Dorian colonists afterwards, are reported to have settled at Kôs, Knidus, Karpathus, and Halikarnassus. To the last-mentioned city, however, Anthês of Trœzên is assigned as the œkist; the emigrants who accompanied him were said to have belonged to the Dymanian tribe, one of the three tribes always found in a Doric state: and the city seems to have been characterized as a colony sometimes of Trœzên, sometimes of Argos.[3]

Kôs, Knidus, and Karpathus.

---

[1] Conôn, Narrat. 47; Ephorus, Frag. 62, ed. Marx.

[2] Diodôr. v. 56; Apollodôr. iii. 2, 2. In the chapter next but one preceding this, Diodôrus had made express reference to native Rhodian mythologists,— to one in particular, named Zeno (c. 57). Wesseling supposes two different settlers in Rhodes, both named Althæmenês; this is certainly necessary, if we are to treat the two narratives as historical.

[3] Strabo, xiv. p. 653; Pausan. ii. 39,

8; Kallimachus apud Stephan. Byz. v. Ἁλικάρνασσος.

Herodotus (vii. 99) calls Halikarnassus a colony of Trœzên; Pomponius Mela (i. 16), of Argos. Vitruvius names both Argos and Trœzên (ii. 8, 12); but the two œkists whom he mentions, Melas and Arevanius, were not so well known as Anthês; the inhabitants of Halikarnassus being called *Antheadæ* (see Stephan. Byz. v. Ἀθῆναι; and a curious inscription in Boeckh's Corpus Inscriptionum, No. 2655).

We thus have the Æolic, the Ionic, and the Doric colonial establishments in Asia, all springing out of the legendary age, and all set forth as consequences, direct or indirect, of what is called the Return of the Herakleids, or the Dorian conquest of Peloponnêsus.   According to the received chronology, they are succeeded by a period, supposed to comprise nearly three centuries, which is almost an entire blank, before we reach authentic chronology and the first recorded Olympiad —and they thus form the concluding events of the mythical world, out of which we now pass into historical Greece, such as it stands at the last-mentioned epoch. *Intervening blank between legend and history.*

It is by these migrations that the parts of the Hellenic aggregate are distributed into the places which they occupy at the dawn of historical daylight—Dorians, Arcadians, Ætolo-Eleians, and Achæans, sharing Peloponnêsus unequally among them—Æolians, Ionians, and Dorians, settled both in the islands of the Ægean and the coast of Asia-Minor.   The Return of the Herakleids, as well as the three emigrations, Æolic, Ionic, and Doric, present the legendary explanation, suitable to the feelings and belief of the people, showing how Greece passed from the heroic races who besieged Troy and Thêbes, piloted the adventurous Argô, and slew the monstrous boar of Kalydôn—to the historical races, differently named and classified, who furnished victors to the Olympic and Pythian games.

A patient and learned French writer, M. Raoul Rochette—who construes all the events of the heroic age, generally speaking, as so much real history, only making allowance for the mistakes and exaggerations of poets,—is greatly perplexed by the blank and interruption which this supposed continuous series of history presents, from *Difficulty of explaining that blank, on the hypothesis of continuous tradition.* the Return of the Herakleids down to the beginning of the Olympiads.   He cannot explain to himself so long a period of absolute quiescence, after the important incidents and striking adventures of the heroic age.   If there happened nothing worthy of record during this long period—as he presumes from the fact that nothing has been transmitted—he concludes that this must have arisen from the state of suffering and exhaustion in which previous wars and revolution had left the Greeks ; a long interval of complete inaction being required to heal such wounds.[1]

Assuming M. Rochette's view of the heroic ages to be correct, Such an interval essentially connected with the genesis of legend. and reasoning upon the supposition that the adventures ascribed to the Grecian heroes are matters of historical reality, transmitted by tradition from a period of time four centuries before the recorded Olympiads, and only embellished by describing poets—the blank which he here dwells upon is, to say the least of it, embarrassing and unaccountable. It is strange that the stream of tradition, if it had once begun to flow, should (like several of the rivers in Greece) be submerged for two or three centuries and then re-appear. But when we make what appears to me the proper distinction between legend and history, it will be seen that a period of blank time between the two is perfectly conformable to the conditions under which the former is generated. It is not the immediate past, but a supposed remote past, which forms the suitable atmosphere of mythical narrative,—a past originally quite undetermined in respect to distance from the present, as we see in the Iliad and Odyssey. And even when we come down to the genealogical poets, who affect to give a certain measure of bygone time, and a succession of persons as well as of events, still the names whom they most delight to honour and upon whose

---

[1] "La période qui me semble la plus obscure et la plus remplie de difficultés, n'est pas celle que je viens de parcourir : c'est celle qui sépare l'époque des Héraclides de l'institution des Olympiades. La perte des ouvrages d'Éphore et de Théopompe est sans doute la cause en grande partie du vide immense que nous offre dans cet intervalle l'histoire de la Grèce. Mais si l'on en excepte l'établissement des colonies Éoliennes, Doriennes, et Ioniennes, de l'Asie Mineure, et quelques évènemens, très rapprochés de la première de ces époques, l'espace de plus de quatre siècles qui les sépare est couvert d'une obscurité presque impénétrable, et l'on aura toujours lieu de s'étonner que les ouvrages des anciens n'offrent aucun secours pour remplir une lacune aussi considérable. Une pareille absence doit aussi nous faire soupçonner qu'il se passa dans la Grèce peu de ces grands évènemens qui se gravent fortement dans la mémoire des hommes : puisque, si les traces ne s'en étaient point conservées dans les écrits des contemporains, au moins le souvenir s'en serait-il perpétué par des monumens : or les monumens et l'histoire se taisent également. Il faut donc croire que la Grèce, agitée depuis si long temps par des révolutions de toute espèce, épuisée par ses dernières émigrations, se tourna toute entière vers des occupations paisibles, et ne chercha, pendant ce long intervalle, qu'à guérir, au sein du repos et de l'abondance qui en est la suite, les plaies profondes que sa population avait souffertes." (Raoul Rochette, Histoire des Colonies Grecques, t. ii. c. 16, p. 455.)

To the same purpose Gillies (History of Greece, ch. iii. p. 67, quarto): "The obscure transactions of Greece, during the four following centuries, ill correspond with the splendour of the Trojan, or even of the Argonautic expedition," &c.

exploits they chiefly expatiate, are those of the ancestral gods and heroes of the tribe and their supposed contemporaries ; ancestors separated by a long lineage from the present hearer.   The gods and heroes were conceived as removed from him by several generations, and the legendary matter which was grouped around them appeared only the more imposing when exhibited at a respectful distance, beyond the days of father and grandfather and of all known predecessors.   The Odes of Pindar strikingly illustrate this tendency.   We thus see how it happened that between the times assigned to heroic adventure and those of historical record, there existed an intermediate blank, filled with inglorious names ; and how amongst the same society, which cared not to remember proceedings of fathers and grandfathers, there circulated much popular and accredited narrative respecting real or supposed ancestors long past and gone.   The obscure and barren centuries which immediately precede the first recorded Olympiad, form the natural separation between the legendary return of the Herakleids and the historical wars of Sparta against Messêné ;—between the province of legend wherein matter of fact (if any there be) is so intimately combined with its accompaniments of fiction, as to be undistinguishable without the aid of extrinsic evidence—and that of history, where some matters of fact can be ascertained, and where a sagacious criticism may be usefully employed in trying to add to their number

CHAPTER XIX.

APPLICATION OF CHRONOLOGY TO GRECIAN LEGEND.

I NEED not repeat, what has already been sufficiently set forth in the preceding pages, that the mass of Grecian incident anterior to 776 B.C. appears to me not reducible either to history or to chronology, and that any chronological systems which may be applied to it must be essentially uncertified and illusory. It was however chronologised in ancient times, and has continued to be so in modern; and the various schemes employed for this purpose may be found stated and compared in the first volume (the last published) of Mr. Fynes Clinton's Fasti Hellenici. There were among the Greeks, and there still are among modern scholars, important differences as to the dates of the principal events: Eratosthenês dissented both from Herodotus and from Phanias and Kallimachus, while Larcher and Raoul Rochette (who follow Herodotus) stand opposed to O. Müller and to Mr. Clinton.[1]

Different schemes of chronology proposed for the mythical events.

---

[1] Larcher and Raoul Rochette, adopting the chronological date of Herodotus, fix the taking of Troy at 1270 B.C., and the Return of the Herakleids at 1190 B.C. According to the scheme of Eratosthenês, these two events stand at 1184 and 1104 B.C.

O. Müller, in his Chronological Tables (Appendix vi. to History of Dorians, vol. ii. p. 441, Engl. transl.), gives no dates or computation of years anterior to the Capture of Troy and the Return of the Herakleids, which he places with Eratosthenês in 1184 and 1104 B.C.

O. Müller thinks (in his Annotatio ad Marmor Parium, appended to the Fragmenta Historicorum Græcorum, ed. Didot, pp. 556, 568, 572; compare his Prefatory Notice of the Fragments of Hellanikus, p. xxviii. of the same volume) that the ancient chronologists in their arrangement of the mythical events as antecedent and consequent, were guided by certain numerical attachments, especially by a reverence for the cycle of 63 years, product of the sacred numbers $7 \times 9 = 63$. I cannot think that he makes out his hypothesis satisfactorily, as to the particular cycle followed, though it is not improbable that some preconceived numerical theories *did* guide these early calculators. He calls attention to the fact that the Alexandrine computation of dates was only one among a number of others discrepant, and that modern inquirers are too apt to treat it as if it stood alone, or carried some superior authority (pp. 568—572; compare

That the reader may have a general conception of the order in
which these legendary events were disposed, I transcribe from
the Fasti Hellenici a double chronological table, contained in p.
139, in which the dates are placed in series, from Phorôneus
to the Olympiad of Corœbus in B.C. 776—in the first column,
according to the system of Eratosthenês, in the second according
to that of Kallimachus.

"The following table (says Mr. Clinton) offers a summary view
of the leading periods from Phorôneus to the Olympiad of
Corœbus, and exhibits a double series of dates; the one proceeding from the date of Eratosthenês, the other from a date
founded on the reduced calculations of Phanias and Kallimachus,
which strike out fifty-six years from the amount of Eratosthenês.
Phanias, as we have seen, omitted fifty-five years between the
Return and the registered Olympiads; for so we may understand the account: Kallimachus, fifty-six years between the
Olympiad in which Corœbus won.[1] The first column of this
table exhibits the *current* years before and after the fall of
Troy: in the second column of dates the *complete* intervals are
expressed."

Wherever chronology is possible, researches such as those of
Mr. Clinton, which have conduced so much to the
better understanding of the later times of Greece,
deserve respectful attention. But the ablest chronologist can accomplish nothing, unless he is supplied
with a certain basis of matters of fact, pure and
distinguishable from fiction, and authenticated by witnesses,
both knowing the truth and willing to declare it. Possessing
this preliminary stock, he may reason from it to refute distinct
falsehoods and to correct partial mistakes: but if all the original
statements submitted to him contained truth (at least wherever
there *is* truth), in a sort of chemical combination with fiction,
which he has no means of decomposing,—he is in the condition
of one who tries to solve a problem without data: he is first

The data, essential to chronological determination, are here wanting.

Clemen. Alex. Stromat. i. p. 145,
Sylb.). For example, O. Müller observes (Appendix to Hist. of Dorians,
p. 442), that "Larcher's criticism and
rejection of the Alexandrine chronologists may perhaps be found as ground-
less as they are presumptuous," an

observation which, to say the least of
it, ascribes to Eratosthenês a far higher
authority than he is entitled to.
[1] The date of Kallimachus for *Iphitus*
is approved by Clavier (Prem. Temps,
tom. ii. p. 203), who considers it as not
far from the truth.

Years before the Fall of Troy.		Years intervening between the different events.	B.C. Eratosth.	B.C. Kallimach.
(570)[1]	*Phoroneus*, p. 19	287	(1753)	(1697)
(283) {	*Danaus*, p. 73 .. *Pelasgus V.*, p. 13, 88 ..	} 33	(1466)	(1410)
(250)	*Deukalion*, p. 42	50	(1433)	(1377)
(200) {	*Erechtheus* .. *Dardanus*, p. 88	} 50	(1383)	(1327)
(150)	*Asan, Aphidas, Elatus*	20	(1333)	(1277)
130	*Kadmus*, p. 85 ..	30	1313	1257
(100)	*Pelops* ..	22	(1283)	(1227)
78	Birth of *Hercules*	36	1261	1205
(42)	Argonauts	12	(1225)	(1169)
30	First Theban war, p. 51, h. ..	4	1213	1157
26	Death of *Hercules*	2	1209	1153
24	Death of *Eurystheus*, p. 106, x.	4	1207	1151
20	Death of *Hyllus*	2y 9m	1203	1147
18	Accession of *Agamemnon*	2	1200	1144
16	Second Theban war, p. 87, l	6	1198	1142
10	Trojan expedition (9y 1m) ..	9	1192	1186
Years after the Fall of Troy.				
	Troy taken	7	1183	1127
8	*Orestes* reigns at Argos in the 8th year ..	52	1176	1120
60 {	The *Thessali* occupy Thessaly .. The *Bœoti* return to Bœotia in the 60th year .. Æolic migration under *Penthilus* ..	} 20	1124	1068
80	Return of the *Heraclidæ* in the 80th year ..	29	1104	1048
109	*Aletes* reigns at Corinth, p. 130, m.	1	1075	1019
110	Migration of *Theras* ..	29	1074	1018
131	Lesbos occupied 130 years after the æra ..	8	1053	997
139	Death of *Codrus* ..	1	1045	989
140	Ionic migration 60 years after the Return	11	1044	988
151	Cymê founded 150 years after the æra ..	18	1033	977
169	Smyrna, 168 years after the æra, p. 105, t. ..	131	1015	959
300	Olympiad of *Iphitus* ..	{ 229 108 52	} 884	828
408 352 }	Olympiad of *Corœbus* ..	..	776	776

[1] These dates, distinguished from the rest by brackets, are proposed as mere conjectures, founded upon the probable length of generations.

obliged to construct his own data, and from them to extract his conclusions.　The statements of the epic poets, our only original witnesses in this case, correspond to the description here given. Whether the proportion of truth contained in them be smaller or greater, it is at all events unassignable,—and the constant and intimate admixture of fiction is both indisputable in itself, and indeed essential to the purpose and profession of those from whom the tales proceed.　Of such a character are all the deposing witnesses, even where their tales agree ; and it is out of a heap of such tales, not agreeing, but discrepant in a thousand ways, and without a morsel of pure authenticated truth,—that the critic is called upon to draw out a methodical series of historical events adorned with chronological dates.

If we could imagine a modern critical scholar transported into Greece at the time of the Persian war—endued with his present habits of appreciating historical evidence, without sharing in the religious or patriotic feelings of the country—and invited to prepare, out of the great body of Grecian epic which then existed, a History and Chronology of Greece anterior to 776 B.C., assigning reasons as well for what he admitted as for what he rejected—I feel persuaded that he would have judged the undertaking to be little better than a process of guess-work. But the modern critic finds that not only Pherekydês and Hellanikus, but also Herodotus and Thucydidês have either attempted the task or sanctioned the belief that it was practicable,—a matter not at all surprising, when we consider both their narrow experience of historical evidence and the powerful ascendency of

Modern chronologists take up the same problem as ancient, but with a different canon of belief.

religion and patriotism in predisposing them to antiquarian belief,—and he therefore accepts the problem as they have bequeathed it, adding his own efforts to bring it to a satisfactory solution.　Nevertheless, he not only follows them with some degree of reserve and uneasiness, but even admits important distinctions quite foreign to their habits of thought.　Thucydidês talks of the deeds of Hellên and his sons with as much confidence as we now speak of William the Conqueror ; Mr. Clinton recognises Hellên with his sons Dôrus, Æolus and Xuthus, as fictitious persons.　Herodotus recites the great heroic genealogies down from Kadmus and Danaus with a belief not less complete in the higher members of the series than in the lower : but Mr. Clinton admits a radical distinction in the evidence of events before and after the first recorded Olympiad, or 776 B.C.—" the first date in Grecian chronology (he remarks, p. 123) which can be fixed upon *authentic evidence*"—the highest point to which Grecian chronology, *reckoning upward*, can be carried. Of this important epoch in Grecian development,—the commencement of authentic chronological life,—Herodotus and Thucydidês had no knowledge or took no account : the later chronologists, from Timæus downwards, noted it, and made it serve as the basis of their chronological comparisons, so far as it went : but neither Eratosthenês nor Apollodôrus seems to have recognised (though Varro and Africanus did recognise) a marked difference in respect of certainty or authenticity between the period before and the period after.

In further illustration of Mr. Clinton's opinion that the first recorded Olympiad is the earliest date which can be fixed upon

Mr. Clinton's opinion on the computation of the date of the Trojan war.

authentic evidence, we have in p. 138 the following just remarks in reference to the dissentient views of Eratosthenês, Phanias and Kallimachus, about the date of the Trojan war :—" The chronology of Eratosthenês (he says), founded on a careful comparison of circumstances, and approved by those to whom the same stores of information were open, is entitled to our respect. But we must remember that a conjectural date can never rise to the authority of evidence ; that what is accepted as a substitute for testimony, is not an equivalent ; witnesses only can prove a date, and in the want of these, the knowledge of it is plainly beyond our reach. If, in the absence of a better light, we seek for what is probable, we are not to forget the distinction between conjecture and proof; between what is probable and what is certain. The computation then of Eratosthenês for the war of Troy is open to inquiry ; and if we find it adverse to the opinions of many preceding writers, who fixed a lower date, and adverse to the acknowledged length of generation in the most authentic dynasties, we are allowed to follow other guides, who give us a lower epoch."

Here Mr. Clinton again plainly acknowledges the want of evidence and the irremediable uncertainty of Grecian chronology before the Olympiads. Now the reasonable conclusion from his argument is, not simply that "the computation of Eratosthenês was open to inquiry" (which few would be found to deny), but that both Eratosthenês and Phanias had delivered positive opinions upon a point on which no sufficient evidence was accessible, and therefore that neither the one nor the other was a guide to be followed.[1]   Mr. Clinton does indeed speak of authentic dynasties prior to the first recorded Olympiad, but if there be any such, reaching up from that period to a supposed point coeval with or anterior to the war of Troy—I see no good reason for the marked distinction which he draws between chronology before and chronology after the Olympiad of Korœbus, or for the necessity which he feels of suspending his upward reckoning at the last-mentioned epoch, and beginning a different process, called "a downward reckoning," from the higher epoch (supposed to be somehow ascertained without any upward reckoning) of the first patriarch from whom such authentic dynasty emanates.[2]

[1] Karl Müller observes (in the Dissertation above referred to, appended to the Fragmenta Historicorum Græcorum, p. 568)—"Quod attinet æram Trojanam, tot obruimur et tam diversis veterum scriptorum computationibus, ut singulas enumerare negotium sit tædii plenum, eas vel probare vel improbare res vana nec vacua ab arrogantiâ.   Nam nemo hodie nescit quænam fides his habenda sit omnibus."

[2] The distinction which Mr. Clinton draws between an upward and a downward chronology is one to which I cannot assent.   His doctrine is, that upward chronology is trustworthy and practicable up to the first recorded Olympiad: downward chronology is trustworthy and practicable from Phoroneus down to the Ionic migration: what is uncertain is the length of the intermediate line which joins the Ionic migration to the first recorded Olympiad,—the downward and the upward terminus. (See Fasti Hellenici, vol. i. Introduct. p. ix. second edit. and p. 123, ch. vi.)

All chronology must begin by reckoning upwards; when by this process we have arrived at a certain determined æra in earlier time, we may from that date reckon downwards, if we please.   We must be able to reckon upwards from the present time to the Christian æra, before we can employ that event as a fixed point for chronological determinations generally.   But if Eratosthenês could perform correctly the upward reckoning from his own time to the fall of Troy, so he could also perform the upward reckoning up to the nearer point of the Ionic migration.   It is true that Eratosthenês gives all his statements of time from an older point to a newer (so far at least as we can judge from Clemens Alex. Strom. l. p. 326); he says, "From the capture of Troy to the return of the Herakleids is 80 years; from thence to the Ionic migration, 60 years; then further on, to the guardianship of Lykurgus, 159 years; then to the first year of the first Olympiad, 108 years; from which Olympiad to the invasion of Xerxês, 297 years; from whence to the beginning of the Peloponnesian war, 48 years," &c.   But here is no difference between upward reckoning as high as the first Olympiad, and then downward reckoning for the intervals of time above it.   Eratosthenês first found or made some upward reckoning to the Trojan capture, either from his own time or from some time at a known distance from his own: he then assumes the capture of Troy as an æra, and gives statements of intervals going downwards to the Peloponnesian war: amongst other statements, he assigns clearly that interval which Mr. Clinton pronounces to be undiscoverable, viz. the space of

Herodotus and Thucydidês might well, upon this supposition, ask of Mr. Clinton, why he called upon them to alter their method of proceeding at the year 776 B.C., and why they might not be allowed to pursue their "upward chronological reckoning" without interruption from Leonidas up to Danaus, or from Peisistratus up to Hellên and Deukaliôn, without any alteration in the point of view. Authentic dynasties from the Olympiads, up to an epoch above the Trojan war, would enable us to obtain chronological proof of the latter date, instead of being reduced (as Mr. Clinton affirms that we are) to "conjecture" instead of proof.

The whole question, as to the value of the reckoning from the Olympiads up to Phorôneus, does in truth turn upon this one point :—Are those genealogies which profess to cover the space between the two authentic and trustworthy or not? Mr. Clinton appears to feel that they are not so, when he admits the essential

Value of the chronological computations depends on the trustworthiness of the genealogies.
difference in the character of the evidence, and the necessity of altering the method · of computation before and after the first recorded Olympiad : yet in his Preface he labours to prove that they possess historical worth and are in the main correctly set forth : moreover, that the fictitious persons, wherever any such are intermingled, may be detected and

eliminated. The evidences upon which he relies, are—1. Inscriptions ; 2. The early poets.

1. An inscription, being nothing but a piece of writing on

Mr. Clinton's vindication of the genealogies— his proofs.
marble, carries evidentiary value under the same conditions as a published writing on paper. If the inscriber reports a contemporary fact which he had the means of knowing, and if there be no reason to suspect misrepresentation, we believe this assertion :

if, on the other hand, he records facts belonging to a long period before his own time, his authority counts for little,

time between the Ionic emigration and the first Olympiad, interposing one epoch between them. I reject the computation of Eratosthenês, or any other computation, to determine the supposed date of the Trojan war ; but if I admitted it, I could have no hesitation in admitting also the space which

he defines between the Ionic migration and the first Olympiad. Eusebius (Præp. Ev. x. 9, p. 485) reckons upwards from the birth of Christ, making various halts but never breaking off, to the initial phænomena of Grecian antiquity —the deluge of Deukaliôn and the conflagration of Phaëthôn.

except in so far as we can verify and appreciate his means of knowledge.

In estimating therefore the probative force of any inscription, the first and most indispensable point is to assure ourselves of its date. Amongst all the public registers and inscriptions alluded to by Mr. Clinton, there is not one which can be positively referred to a date anterior to 776 B.C. The quoit of Iphitus—the public registers at Sparta, Corinth, and Elis—the list of the priestesses of Juno at Argos—are all of a date completely uncertified. O. Müller does indeed agree with Mr. Clinton (though in my opinion without any sufficient proof) in assigning the quoit of Iphitus to the age ascribed to that prince : and if we even grant thus much, we shall have an inscription as old (adopting Mr. Clinton's determination of the age of Iphitus) as 828 B.C. But when Mr. Clinton quotes O. Müller as admitting the registers of Sparta, Corinth, and Elis, it is right to add that the latter does not profess to guarantee the authenticity of these documents, or the age at which such registers began· to be kept. It is not to be doubted that there were registers of the kings of Sparta carrying them up to Hêraklês, and of the kings of Elis from Oxylus to Iphitus : but the question is, at what time did these lists begin to be kept continuously ? This is a point which we have no means of deciding, nor can we accept Mr. Clinton's unsupported conjecture, when he tell us—"*Perhaps* these were begun to be written as early as B.C. 1048, the probable time of the Dorian conquest". Again he tells us—"At Argos a register was preserved of the priestesses of Juno, which *might be* more ancient than the catalogues of the kings of Sparta or Corinth. That register, from which Hellanikus composed his work, contained the priestesses from the earliest times down to the age of Hellanikus himself. . . . But this catalogue *might have* been commenced as early as the Trojan war itself, and even at a still earlier date" (pp. x. xi.). Again, respecting the inscriptions quoted by Herodotus from the temple of the Ismenian Apollo at Thêbes, in which Amphitryo and Laodamas are named, Mr. Clinton says—"They were ancient in the time of Herodotus, which *may* perhaps carry them back 400 years before his time : and in that case they *might* approach within 300 years of

1. Inscriptions—none of proved antiquity.

Laodamas and within 400 years of the probable time of Kadmus himself."—"It is granted (he adds in a note) that these inscriptions were *not genuine*, that is, not of the date to which they were assigned by Herodotus himself. But that they were ancient cannot be doubted," &c.

The time when Herodotus saw the temple of the Ismenian Apollo at Thêbes can hardly have been earlier than 450 B.C.: reckoning upwards from hence to 776 B.C., we have an interval of 326 years : the inscriptions which Herodotus saw may well therefore have been *ancient*, without being earlier than the first recorded Olympiad. Mr. Clinton does indeed tell us that *ancient* "may perhaps" be construed as 400 years earlier than Herodotus. But no careful reader can permit himself to convert such bare possibility into a ground of inference, and to make it available, in conjunction with other similar possibilities before enumerated, for the purpose of showing that there really existed inscriptions in Greece of a date anterior to 776 B.C. Unless Mr. Clinton can make out this, he can derive no benefit from inscriptions, in his attempt to substantiate the reality of the mythical persons or of the mythical events.

The truth is that the Herakleid pedigree of the Spartan kings (as has been observed in a former chapter) is only one out of the numerous divine and heroic genealogies with which the Hellenic world abounded, —a class of documents which become historical evidence only so high in the descending series as the names composing them are authenticated by contemporary, or

Genealogies numerous, and of unascertainable date.

[1] See the string of fabulous names placed at the head of the Halicarnassian Inscription, professing to enumerate the series of priests of Poseidôn from the foundation of the city (Inscript. No. 2655, Boeckh), with the commentary of the learned editor : compare also what he pronounces to be an inscription of a genealogy partially fabulous at Hierapytna in Krête (No. 2563).

The memorable Parian marble is itself an inscription, in which legend and history,—gods, heroes, and men—are blended together in the various successive epochs without any consciousness of transition in the mind of the inscriber.

That the Catalogue of priestesses of Hêrê at Argos went back to the extreme of fabulous times, we may discern by the Fragments of Hellanikus (Frag. 45-53). So also did the registers at Sikyôn : they professed to record Amphion, son of Zeus and Antiopê, as the inventor of harp-music (Plutarch, De Musicâ, c. 3, p. 1132).

I remarked in a preceding page that Mr. Clinton erroneously cites K. O. Müller as a believer in the chronological *authenticity* in the lists of the early Spartan kings: he says (vol. iii. App. vi. p. 330), " Mr. Müller is of opinion that an *authentic* account of the years of each Lacedæmonian reign from the return of the Heraclidæ to the Olympiad

nearly contemporary, enrolment.   At what period this enrolment
began, we have no information.   Two remarks however may be
made, in reference to any approximate guess as to the time when
actual registration commenced :—First, that the number of names
in the pedigree, or the length of past time which it professes to
embrace, affords no presumption of any superior antiquity in the
time of registration :—Secondly, that looking to the acknowledged
paucity and rudeness of Grecian writing even down to the 60th
Olympiad (540 B.C.), and to the absence of the habit of writing,
as well as the low estimate of its value, which such a state of
things argues, the presumption is, that written enrolment of
family genealogies did not commence until a long time after 776
B.C., and the obligation of proof falls upon him who maintains
that it commenced earlier.   And this second remark is farther
borne out when we observe, that there is no registered list, except
that of the Olympic victors, which goes up even so high as 776
B.C.   The next list which O. Müller and Mr. Clinton produce, is
that of the Karneonikæ or victors at the Karneian festival, which
reaches only up to 676 B.C.

of Korœbus had been preserved to the
time of Eratosthenês and Apollodôrus".
But this is a mistake: for Müller
expressly disavows any belief in the
authenticity of the lists (Dorians, i. p.
146): he says, "I do not contend that
the chronological accounts in the
Spartan lists form *an authentic document*, more than those in the catalogue
of the priestesses of Hêrê and in the
list of Halicarnassian priests.   The
chronological statements in the Spartan
lists may have been formed from imperfect memorials : but the Alexandrine
chronologists must have found such
tables in existence," &c.

The discrepancies noticed in Herodotus (vi. 52) are alone sufficient to
prove that continuous registers of the
names of the Lacedæmonian kings did
not begin to be kept until very long
after the date here assigned by Mr.
Clinton.

Xenophôn (Agesilaus, viii. 7) agrees
with what Herodotus mentions to have
been the native Lacedæmonian story—
that Aristodêmus (and not his sons) was
the king who conducted the Dorian
invaders to Sparta.   What is farther
remarkable is that Xenophôn calls him
—Ἀριστόδημος ὁ Ἡρακλέους.   The
reasonable inference here is, that

Xenophôn believed Aristodemus to be
the *son* of Hêraklês. and that this was
one of the various genealogical stories
current.   But here the critics interpose :
"ὁ Ἡρακλέους (observes Schneider), non
παῖς, sed ἀπόγονος, ut ex Herodoto viii.
131 admonuit Weiske".   Surely if
Xenophôn had meant this, he would
have said ὁ ἀφ' Ἡρακλέους.

Perhaps particular exceptional cases
might be quoted, wherein the very
common phrase of ὁ followed by a
genitive means *descendant*, and not *son*.
But if any doubt be allowed upon this
point, chronological computations,
founded on genealogies, will be exposed
to a serious additional suspicion.   Why
are we to assume that Xenophôn *must*
give the same story as Herodotus,
unless his words naturally tell us
so?

M. John Brandis, in an instructive
Dissertation (De Temporum Græcorum
Antiquissimorum Rationibus, Bonn,
1857) insists forcibly on the point that
Herodotus knew nothing of these
registers of Spartan kings, and that
they did not exist at Sparta when his
history was composed (p. 6).   M.
Brandis conceives Hellanikus to be the
first arranger and methodiser of these
early genealogies (p. 8—37).

If Mr. Clinton then makes little out of inscriptions to sustain
2. Early poets. his view of Grecian history and chronology anterior
to the recorded Olympiads, let us examine the infer-
ences which he draws from his other source of evidence—the
early poets. And here it will be found, First, that in order to
maintain the credibility of these witnesses, he lays down positions
respecting historical evidence both indefensible in themselves,
and especially inapplicable to the early times of Greece: Secondly,
that his reasoning is at the same time inconsistent—inasmuch as
it includes admissions, which if properly understood and followed
out, exhibit these very witnesses, as habitually, indiscriminately,
and unconsciously, mingling truth and fiction, and therefore little
fit to be believed upon their solitary and unsupported testimony.

To take the second point first, he says (Introduction, p. ii.-iii.)—
"The authority even of the genealogies has been called in question
by many able and learned persons, who reject Danaus, Kadmus,
Hercules, Thêseus, and many others, as fictitious persons. It is
evident that any fact would come from the hands of the poets
embellished with many fabulous additions: and fictitious genealogies were undoubtedly composed. Because, however, some
genealogies were fictitious, we are not justified in concluding that
all were fabulous. . . . In estimating then the historical value
of the genealogies transmitted by the early poets, we may take
a middle course ; not rejecting them as wholly false, nor yet
implicitly receiving all as true. The genealogies *contain many
real persons*, but these are *incorporated with many fictitious names*.
The fictions however will have a basis of truth : the genealogical
expression may be false, but the connexion which it describes is
real. Even to those who reject the whole as fabulous, the exhi-
bition of the early times which is presented in this volume may
still be not unacceptable : because it is necessary to the right
understanding of antiquity that the opinions of the Greeks concerning their own origin should be set before us, even if these are
erroneous opinions, and that their story should be told as they
have told it themselves. The names preserved by the ancient
genealogies may be considered of three kinds ; either they were
the name of a race or clan converted into the name of an individual, or they were altogether fictitious, or lastly, they were real
historical names. An attempt is made in the four genealogical

tables inserted below to distinguish these three classes of names. . . . Of those who are left in the third class (*i.e.* the real) all are not entitled to remain there. But I have only placed in the third class those names concerning which there seemed to be little doubt. The rest are left to the judgment of the reader."

Pursuant to this principle of division, Mr. Clinton furnishes four genealogical tables,[1] in which the names of persons representing races are printed in capital letters, and those of purely fictitious persons in italics. And these tables exhibit a curious sample of the intimate com- mixture of fiction with that which he calls truth : real son and mythical father, real husband and mythical wife, or *vice versâ.*

Mr. Clin-
ton's separa-
tion of the
genealogical
persons into
real and
fabulous :
principles
on which it
is founded.

Upon Mr. Clinton's tables we may remark—

1. The names singled out as fictitious are distinguished by no common character, nor any mark either assignable or defensible, from those which are left as real. To take an example (p. 40), why is Itônus the 1st pointed out as a fiction, while Itônus the 2nd, together with Physcus, Cynus, Salmôneus, Ormenus, &c., in the same page, are preserved as real, all of them being eponyms of towns just as much as Itônus?

Remarks on
his opinion.

2. If we are to discard Hellên, Dôrus, Æolus, Iôn, &c., as not being real individual persons, but expressions for personified races, why are we to retain Kadmus, Danaus, Hyllus, and several others, who are just as much eponyms of races and tribes as the four above mentioned? Hyllus, Pamphylus and Dymas are the eponyms of the three Dorian tribes,[2] just as Hoplês and the other three sons of Iôn were of the four Attic tribes : Kadmus and Danaus stand in the same relation to the Kadmeians and Danaans, as Argus and Achæus to the Argeians and Achæans. Besides, there are many other names really eponymous, which we cannot now recognise to be so, in consequence of our imperfect acquaint- ance with the subdivisions of the Hellenic population, each of which, speaking generally, had its god or hero, to whom the original of the name was referred. If, then, eponymous names are to be excluded from the category of reality, we shall find that

---

[1] See Mr. Clinton's work, pp. 32, 40, 100.

[2] " From these three" (Hyllus, Pamphylus and Dymas), says Mr. Clinton, vol. i. ch. 5, p. 109, " the three Dorian tribes derived their names ".

the ranks of the real men will be thinned to a far greater extent
than is indicated by Mr. Clinton's tables.

3. Though Mr. Clinton does not carry out consistently either
of his disfranchising qualifications among the names and persons
of the old mythes, he nevertheless presses them far enough to
strike out a sensible proportion of the whole. By conceding thus
much to modern scepticism, he has departed from the point of
view of Hellanikus and Herodotus, and the ancient historians
generally ; and it is singular that the names, which he has been
the most forward to sacrifice, are exactly those to which they
were most attached and which it would have been most painful to
their faith to part with—I mean the eponymous heroes. Neither
Herodotus, nor Hellanikus, nor Eratosthenês, nor any one of the
chronological reckoners of antiquity, would have admitted the
distinction which Mr. Clinton draws between persons real and
persons fictitious in the old mythical world, though they might
perhaps occasionally, on special grounds, call in question the
existence of some individual characters amongst the mythical

His conces-
sions are
partial and
inconsis-
tent, yet
sufficient to
render the
genealogies
inapplicable
for chrono-
logy.

ancestry of Greece ; but they never dreamt of that
general severance into real and fictitious persons
which forms the principle of Mr. Clinton's "middle
course". Their chronological computations for Grecian
antiquity assumed that the mythical characters in
their full and entire sequence were all real persons.
Setting up the entire list as real, they calculated so
many generations to a century, and thus determined
the number of centuries which separated themselves from the
gods, the heroes, and the autochthonous men, who formed in
their view the historical starting-point. But as soon as it is
admitted that the personages in the mythical world are divisible
into two classes, partly real and partly fictitious, the integrity of
the series is broken up, and it can be no longer employed as a
basis for chronological calculation. In the estimate of the ancient
chronologers, three succeeding persons of the same lineage--
grandfather, father and son—counted for a century ; and this
may pass in a rough way, so long as you are thoroughly satisfied
that they are all real persons : but if in the succession of persons
A, B, C, you strike out B as a fiction, the continuity of data
necessary for chronological computation disappears. Now Mr.

Clinton is inconsistent with himself in this—that while he abandons the unsuspecting historical faith of the Grecian chronologers, he nevertheless continues his chronological computations upon the data of that ancient faith,—upon the assumed reality of all the persons constituting his ante-historical generations.   What becomes, for example, of the Herakleid genealogy of the Spartan kings, when it is admitted that eponymous persons are to be cancelled as fictions; seeing that Hyllus, through whom those kings traced their origin to Hêraklês, comes in the most distinct manner under that category, as much so as Hoplês the son of Iôn?   It will be found that when we once cease to believe in the mythical world as an uninterrupted and unalloyed succession of real individuals, it becomes unfit to serve as a basis for chronological computations, and that Mr. Clinton, when he mutilated the data of the ancient chronologists, ought at the same time to have abandoned their problems as insoluble.   Genealogies of real persons, such as Herodotus and Eratosthenês believed in, afford a tolerable basis for calculations of time, within certain limits of error: "genealogies containing many real persons, but incorporated with many fictitious names" (to use the language just cited from Mr. Clinton), are essentially unavailable for such a purpose.

It is right here to add, that I agree in Mr. Clinton's view of these eponymous persons: I admit with him that "the genealogical expression may often be false, when the connexion which it describes is real".   Thus, for example, the adoption of Hyllus by Ægimius, the father of Pamphylus and Dymas, to the privileges of a son and to a third fraction of his territories, may reasonably be construed as a mythical expression of the fraternal union of the three Dorian tribes, Hylleis, Pamphyli, and Dymanes: so about the relationship of Iôn and Achæus, of Dôrus and Æolus. But if we put this construction on the name of Hyllus, or Iôn, or Achæus, we cannot at the same time employ either of these persons as units in chronological reckoning; nor is it consistent to recognise them in the lump as members of a distinct class, and yet to enlist them as real individuals in measuring the duration of past time.

4. Mr. Clinton, while professing a wish to tell the story of the Greeks as they have told it themselves, seems unconscious how capitally his point of view differs from theirs.   The distinction

which he draws between real and fictitious persons would have appeared unreasonable, not to say offensive, to Herodotus or Eratosthenês. It is undoubtedly right that the early history (if so it is to be called) of the Greeks should be told as they have told it themselves, and with that view I have endeavoured in the previous narrative, as far as I could, to present the primitive legends in their original colour and character—pointing out at the same time the manner in which they were transformed and distilled into history by passing through the retort of later annalists. It is the legend as thus transformed which Mr. Clinton seems to understand as the story told by the Greeks themselves—which cannot be admitted to be true, unless the meaning of the expression be specially explained. In his general distinction, however, between the real and fictitious persons of the mythical world, he departs essentially from the point of view even of the later Greeks. And if he had consistently followed out that distinction in his particular criticisms, he would have found the ground slipping under his feet in his upward march even to Troy—not to mention the series of eighteen generations farther up to Phorôneus; but he does *not* consistently follow it out, and therefore in practice he deviates little from the footsteps of the ancients.

Enough has been said to show that the witnesses upon whom Mr. Clinton relies blend truth and fiction habitually, indiscriminately and unconsciously, even upon his own admission. Let us now consider the positions which he lays down respecting historical evidence. He says (Introduct. p. vi. vii.):—

Mr. Clinton's position respecting historical evidence.

"We may acknowledge as real persons all those whom there is no reason for rejecting. The presumption is in favour of the early tradition, if no argument can be brought to overthrow it. The persons may be considered real, when the description of them is consonant with the state of the country at that time : when no national prejudice or vanity could be concerned in inventing them : when the tradition is consistent and general : when rival or hostile tribes concur in the leading facts: when the acts ascribed to the person (divested of their poetical ornament) enter into the political system of the age, or form the basis of other transactions which fall within known historical times. Kadmus and Danaus appear to be real persons; for it is conformable to

the state of mankind, and perfectly credible, that Phœnician and
Egyptian adventurers, in the ages to which these persons are
ascribed, should have found their way to the coasts of Greece :
and the Greeks (as already observed) had no motive from any
national vanity to feign these settlements. Hercules was a real
person. His acts were recorded by those who were not friendly
to the Dorians ; by Achæans and Æolians and Ionians, who had
no vanity to gratify in celebrating the hero of a hostile and rival
people. His descendants in many branches remained in many
states down to the historical times. His son Tlepolemus and his
grandson and great-grandson Cleodæus and Aristomachus are
acknowledged (*i.e.* by O. Müller) to be real persons : and there
is no reason that can be assigned for receiving these, which will
not be equally valid for establishing the reality both of Hercules
and Hyllus. Above all, Hercules is authenticated by the testimonies both of the Iliad and Odyssey."

These positions appear to me inconsistent with sound views of
the conditions of historical testimony. According to what is here
laid down, we are bound to accept as real all the persons mentioned
by Homer, Arktinus, Leschês, the Hesiodic poets, Eumêlus, Asius,
&c., unless we can adduce some positive ground in each particular
case to prove the contrary. If this position be a true one, the
greater part of the history of England, from Brute the Trojan
down to Julius Cæsar, ought at once to be admitted as valid and
worthy of credence. What Mr. Clinton here calls the *early
tradition,* is in point of fact the narrative of these early poets. The
word *tradition* is an equivocal word, and begs the whole question ;
for while in its obvious and literal meaning it implies only something handed down, whether truth or fiction—it is tacitly
understood to imply a tale descriptive of some real matter of fact,
taking its rise at the time when that fact happened, and originally
accurate, but corrupted by subsequent oral transmission. Understanding therefore by Mr. Clinton's words *early tradition,* the
tales of the old poets, we shall find his position totally inadmissible
—that we are bound to admit the persons or statements of Homer
and Hesiod as real, unless where we can produce reasons to the
contrary. To allow this, would be to put them upon a par with
good contemporary witnesses ; for no greater privilege can be
claimed in favour even of Thucydidês, than the title of his

testimony to be believed unless where it can be contradicted on special grounds. The presumption in favour of an asserting witness is either strong, or weak, or positively nothing, according to the compound ratio of his means of knowledge, his moral and

To what extent presumption may stand in favour of the early poets.

intellectual habits, and his motive to speak the truth. Thus, for instance, when Hesiod tells us that his father quitted the Æolic Kymê and came to Askra in Bœôtia, we may fully believe him; but when he describes to us the battles between the Olympic gods and the Titans, or between Hêraklês and Kyknus—or when Homer depicts the efforts of Hectôr, aided by Apollo, for the defence of Troy, and the struggles of Achilles and Odysseus, with the assistance of Hêrê and Poseidôn, for the destruction of that city, events professedly long past and gone—we cannot presume either of them to be in any way worthy of belief. It cannot be shown that they possessed any means of knowledge, while it is certain that they could have no motive to consider historical truth: their object was to satisfy an uncritical appetite for narrative, and to interest the emotions of their hearers. Mr. Clinton says, that "the persons may be considered real when the description of them is consistent with the state of the country at that time". But he has forgotten, first, that we know nothing of the state of the country except what these very poets tell us; next, that fictitious persons may be just as consonant to the state of the country as real persons. While therefore, on the one hand, we have no independent evidence either to affirm or to deny that Achilles or Agamemnôn are consistent with the state of Greece or Asia Minor at a certain supposed date 1183 B.C.,—so, on the other hand, even assuming such consistency to be made out, this of itself would not prove them to be real persons.

Mr. Clinton's reasoning altogether overlooks the existence of

Plausible fiction satisfies the conditions laid down by Mr. Clinton—not distinguishable from truth without the aid of evidence.

plausible fiction—fictitious stories which harmonise perfectly well with the general course of facts, and which are distinguished from matters of fact not by any internal character, but by the circumstance that matter of fact has some competent and well-informed witness to authenticate it, either directly or through legitimate inference. Fiction may be, and often is, extravagant and incredible; but it may also be plausible and specious, and in that case there is nothing but the want of an attesting certificate to distinguish it from truth. Now all the tests, which Mr. Clinton proposes as guarantees of the reality of the Homeric persons, will be just as well satisfied by plausible fiction as by actual matter of fact; the plausibility of the fiction consists in its satisfying those and other similar conditions. In most cases, the tales of the poets *did* fall in with the existing current of feelings in their audience: "prejudice and vanity" are not the only feelings, but doubtless prejudice and vanity were often appealed to, and it was from such harmony of sentiment that they acquired their hold on men's belief. Without any doubt the Iliad appealed most powerfully to the reverence for ancestral gods and heroes among the Asiatic colonists who first heard it: the temptation of putting forth an interesting tale is quite a sufficient stimulus to the invention of the poet, and the plausibility of the tale a sufficient passport to the belief of the hearers. Mr. Clinton talks of "consistent and general tradition". But that the tale of a poet, when once told with effect and beauty, acquired general belief—is no proof that it was founded on fact: otherwise, what are we to say to the divine legends, and to the large portion of the Homeric narrative which Mr. Clinton himself sets aside as untrue under the designation of "poetical ornament"? When a mythical incident is recorded as "forming the basis" of some known historical fact or institution—as for instance the successful stratagem by which Melanthus killed Xanthus in the battle on the boundary, as recounted in my last chapter,—we may adopt one of two views: we may either treat the incident as real, and as having actually given occasion to what is described as its effect—or we may treat the incident as a legend imagined in order to assign some plausible origin of the reality,—"Aut ex re nomen, aut ex vocabulo fabula".[1] In cases where the legendary incident is referred to a time long anterior to any records—as it commonly is—the second mode of proceeding appears to me far more consonant to reason and probability than the first. It is to be recollected that all the persons and facts, here defended as matter of real history by Mr. Clinton, are referred to an age long preceding the first beginning of records.

[1] Pomponius Mela, iii. 7.

I have already remarked that Mr. Clinton shrinks from his
own rule in treating Kadmus and Danaus as real
persons, since they are as much eponyms of tribes or
races as Dôrus and Hellên. And if he can admit
Hêraklês to be a real man, I do not see upon what
reason he can consistently disallow any one of the
mythical personages, for there is not one whose exploits
are more strikingly at variance with the standard of
historical probability. Mr. Clinton reasons upon the supposition
that "Hercules was a *Dorian* hero": but he was Achæan and
Kadmeian as well as Dorian, though the legends respecting him
are different in all the three characters. Whether his son
Tlepolemus and his grandson Kleodæus belong to the category of
historical men, I will not take upon me to say, though O. Müller
(in my opinion without any warranty) appears to admit it; but
Hyllus certainly is not a real man, if the canon of Mr. Clinton
himself respecting the eponyms is to be trusted. "The descendants
of Hercules (observes Mr. Clinton) remained in many states down
to the historical times." So did those of Zeus and Apollo, and of
that god whom the historian Hekatæus recognised as his progenitor
in the sixteenth generation : the titular kings of Ephesus, in the
historical times, as well as Peisistratus, the despot of Athens, traced
their origin up to Æolus and Hellên, yet Mr. Clinton does not hesitate to reject Æolus and Hellên as fictitious persons. I dispute
the propriety of quoting the Iliad and Odyssey (as Mr. Clinton does)
in evidence of the historic personality of Hercules. For even with
regard to the ordinary men who figure in those poems, we have no
means of discriminating the real from the fictitious ; while the
Homeric Hêraklês is unquestionably more than an ordinary man,
—he is the favourite son of Zeus, from his birth predestined to a
life of labour and servitude, as preparation for a glorious immortality. Without doubt the poet himself believed in the reality of
Hercules, but it was a reality clothed with superhuman attributes.

Mr. Clinton observes (Introd. p. ii.), that "because some
genealogies were fictitious, we are not justified in concluding that all were fabulous". It is no way necessary
that we should maintain so extensive a position : it is
sufficient that all are fabulous so far as concerns gods
and heroes,—*some* fabulous throughout,—and none

Marginal notes:
Kadmus, Danaus, Hyllus, &., all eponyms, and falling under Mr. Clinton's definition of fictitious persons.

What is real in the genealogies cannot be distinguished from what is fictitious.

ascertainably true, for the period anterior to the recorded Olympiads. How much, or what particular portions, may be true, no one can pronounce. The gods and heroes are, from our point of view, essentially fictitious ; but from the Grecian point of view they were the most real (if the expression may be permitted, *i.e.* clung to with the strongest faith) of all the members of the series. They not only formed parts of the genealogy as originally conceived, but were in themselves the grand reason why it was conceived,—as a golden chain to connect the living man with a divine ancestor. The genealogy therefore taken as a whole (and its value consists in its being taken as a whole) was from the beginning a fiction ; but the names of the father and grandfather of the living man, in whose day it first came forth, were doubtless those of real men. Wherever therefore we can verify the date of a genealogy, as applied to some living person, we may reasonably presume the two lowest members of it to be also those of real persons : but this has no application to the time anterior to the Olympiads—still less to the pretended times of the Trojan war, the Kalydonian boar-hunt, or the deluge of Deukaliôn. To reason (as Mr. Clinton does, Introd. p. vi.),— "Because Aristomachus was a real man, therefore his father Cleodæus, his grandfather Hyllus, and so farther upwards, &c., must have been real men,"—is an inadmissible conclusion. The historian Hekatæus was a real man, and doubtless his father Hegesander also—but it would be unsafe to march up his genealogical ladder fifteen steps to the presence of the ancestorial god of whom he boasted : the upper steps of the ladder will be found broken and unreal. Not to mention that the inference, from real son to real father, is inconsistent with the admissions in Mr. Clinton's own genealogical tables ; for he there inserts the names of several mythical fathers as having begotten real historical sons.

The general authority of Mr. Clinton's book, and the sincere respect which I entertain for his elucidations of the later chronology, have imposed upon me the duty of assigning those grounds on which I dissent from his conclusions prior to the first recorded Olympiad. The reader who desires to see the numerous and contradictory guesses (they deserve no better name) of the Greeks themselves in the attempt to chronologise their mythical narratives,

will find them in the copious notes annexed to the first half of his
first volume. As I consider all such researches not merely as
fruitless in regard to any trustworthy result, but as serving to
divert attention from the genuine form and really illustrative
character of Grecian legend, I have not thought it right to go
over the same ground in the present work. Differing as I do,
however, from Mr. Clinton's views on this subject, I concur with
him in deprecating the application of etymology (Introd. p.
xi.-xii.) as a general scheme of explanation to the characters and
events of Greek legend. Amongst the many causes which operated
as suggestives and stimulants to Greek fancy in the creation of
these interesting tales, doubtless Etymology has had its share;
but it cannot be applied (as Hermann, above all others, has
sought to apply it) for the purpose of imparting supposed sense
and system to the general body of mythical narrative. I have
already remarked on this topic in a former chapter.

It would be curious to ascertain at what time, or by whom, the
earliest continuous genealogies, connecting existing persons with

At what
time did
the poets
begin to
produce
continuous
genealogies,
from the
mythical to
the real
world?

the supposed antecedent age of legend, were formed
and preserved. Neither Homer nor Hesiod mentioned
any verifiable *present* persons or circumstances: had
they done so, the age of one or other of them could
have been determined upon good evidence, which we
may fairly presume to have been impossible, from the
endless controversies upon this topic among ancient
writers. In the Hesiodic Works and Days, the
heroes of Troy and Thêbes are even presented as an extinct race,[1]
radically different from the poet's own contemporaries, who are a
new race, far too depraved to be conceived as sprung from the
loins of the heroes; so that we can hardly suppose Hesiod (though
his father was a native of the Æolic Kymê) to have admitted
the pedigree of the Æolic chiefs, as reputed descendants of
Agamemnôn. Certain it is that the earliest poets did not
attempt to measure or bridge over the supposed interval, between
their own age and the war of Troy, by any definite series of
fathers and sons: whether Eumêlus or Asius made any such
attempt, we cannot tell, but the earliest continuous backward

---

[1] See above, Chap. ii.

genealogies which we find mentioned are those of Pherekydês, Hellanikus, and Herodotus.   It is well known that Herodotus, in his manner of computing the upward genealogy of the Spartan kings, assigns the date of the Trojan war to a period 800 years earlier than himself, equivalent about to B.C. 1270-1250 ; while the subsequent Alexandrine chronologists, Eratosthenês and Apollodôrus, place that event in 1184 and 1183 B.C. ; and the Parian marble refers it to an intermediate date, different from either—1209 B.C.   Ephorus, Phanias, Timæus, Kleitarchus, and Duris, had each his own conjectural date ; but the compntation of the Alexandrine chronologists was the most generally followed by those who succeeded them, and seems to have passed to modern times as the received date of this great legendary event—though some distinguished inquirers have adopted the epoch of Herodotus, which Larcher has attempted to vindicate in an elaborate, but feeble, dissertation.[1]   It is unnecessary to state that in my view the inquiry has no other value except to illustrate the ideas which

---

[1] Larcher, Chronologie d'Hérodote, chap. xiv. p. 352—401.

From the capture of Troy down to the passage of Alexander with his invading army into Asia, the latter a known date of 334 B.C., the following different reckonings were made :—

Phanias	gave	715	years.
Ephorus	„	735	„
Eratosthenês	„	774	„
Timæus	} „	820	„
Kleitarchus			
Duris	„	1000	„

(Clemens. Alexand. Strom. i. p. 337.)

Democritus estimated a space of 730 years between his composition of the Μικρὸς Διάκοσμος and the capture of Troy (Diogen. Laërt. ix. 41). Isokratês believed the Lacedæmonians to have been established in Peloponnêsus 700 years, and he repeats this in three different passages (Archidam. p. 118; Panathen. p. 275; De Pace, p. 178). The dates of these three orations themselves differ by twenty-four years, the Archidamus being older than the Panathenaïc by that interval ; yet he employs the same number of years for each in calculating backwards to the Trojan war, (see Clinton, vol. i. Introd. p. 5).   In round numbers, his calculation coincides pretty nearly with the 800 years given by Herodotus in the preceding century.

The remarks of Boeckh on the Parian marble generally, in his Corpus Inscriptionum Græc. t. ii. p. 322—336, are extremely valuable, but especially his criticism on the epoch of the Trojan war, which stands the twenty-fourth in the Marble.   The ancient chronologists, from Damastês and Hellanikus downwards, professed to fix not only the exact year, but the exact month, day and hour in which this celebrated capture took place. [Mr. Clinton pretends to no more than the possibility of determining the event within fifty years, Introduct. p. vi.]   Boeckh illustrates the manner of their argumentation.

O. Müller observes (History of the Dorians, t. ii. p. 442, Eng. Tr.), "In reckoning from the migration of the Heraklidæ downward, we follow the Alexandrine chronology, of which it should be observed, that our materials only enable us to restore it to its original state, *not to examine its correctness*".

But I do not see upon what evidence even so much as this can be done.   Mr. Clinton, admitting that Eratosthenês fixed his date by conjecture, supposes him to have chosen "a middle point between the longer and shorter computations of his predecessors".   Boeckh thinks this explanation unsatisfactory (*l. c.* p 828.).

guided the Greek mind, and to exhibit its progress from the
days of Homer to those of Herodotus. For it argues
a considerable mental progress when men begin to
methodise the past, even though they do so on fictitious
principles, being as yet unprovided with those records
which alone could put them on a better course. The
Homeric man was satisfied with feeling, imagining,
and believing, particular incidents of a supposed past, without
any attempt to graduate the line of connexion between them and
himself: to introduce fictitious hypotheses and media of connexion is the business of a succeeding age, when the stimulus of
rational curiosity is first felt, without any authentic materials to
supply it. We have then the form of history operating upon
the matter of legend—the transition-state between legend and
history; less interesting indeed than either separately, yet
necessary as a step between the two.

Evidence of mental progress when men methodise the past, even on fictitious principles.

END OF VOL. I.

PRINTED AT THE EDINBURGH PRESS, 9 AND 11 YOUNG STREET.

Lightning Source UK Ltd.
Milton Keynes UK
UKOW04f0246050814

236365UK00007B/105/P